CW00957392

4 - 99.

WINDOWS™ COMPLETE 3.1

A practical user's guide to learning, installing, customizing and optimizing Microsoft's new Windows 3.1

Juergen Baer,
Irene Bauder,
Harald Frater,
Markus Schueller,
Helmut Tornsdorf,
Manfred Tornsdorf

Abacus
A Data Becker Book

First Printing 1992

Library of Congress Cataloging-in-Publication Data

Windows 3.1 complete / Jurgen Baer ... [et al.].
p. cm.
Includes index.
ISBN 1-55755-153-7 : $34.95
1. Microsoft Windows (Computer program) I. Baer, Jurgen, 1961-.
QA76.76.W56W533 1992
005.4'3--dc20 92-12774
CIP

Contents

Preface

Windows is considered the standard in graphical user interfaces. GUI (Graphical User Interface) and SAA (Standard Application Architecture) are important in the PC world today. The object of these standards is to make using and exchanging data between applications, and even programming your own applications, more uniform and, therefore, easier.

Windows also has multitasking capabilities—the ability to run more than one program simultaneously. This often saves time and increases computing capacity. Windows also implements multimedia, using the computer as an innovative source of visual and audio output.

Windows is easy to use

It's important to remember that Windows helps beginners become more familiar with the mysterious world of PCs. With Windows, users no longer need to memorize commands. Instead, they can use the mouse to select the functions and programs that appear in the form of icons.

The topics of this book

We organized this book according to specific subject areas. Besides an introduction to the Windows concept, the first chapters also provide the information beginners need to learn Windows. We'll explain both the mouse and keyboard operation.

The later chapters concentrate on some of the more technical aspects of Windows (i.e., optimizing Windows and your computer). We'll describe the Windows applications and provide a detailed explanation of linking applications and exchanging data.

We also included chapters on multimedia and on using Windows within a network environment. This book also provides a comprehensive view of programming Windows applications. The companion diskette for the book contains numerous useful applications.

March 1992

An Explanation of the Icons

We use several icons, which should help you locate information quickly:

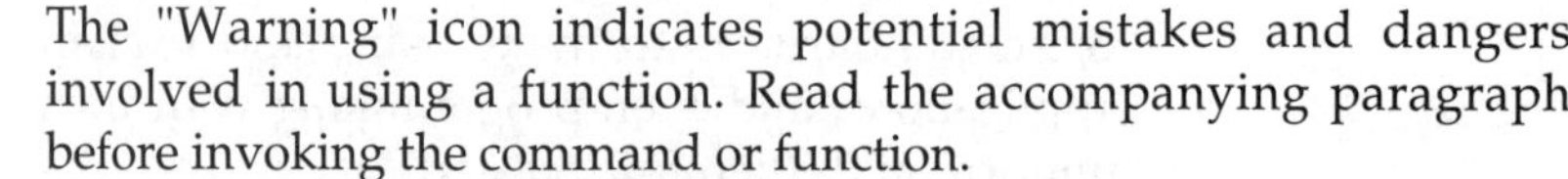

The "Warning" icon indicates potential mistakes and dangers involved in using a function. Read the accompanying paragraph before invoking the command or function.

The "Error" icon indicates typical errors that may occur. So, you can avoid these errors before they occur. If you get a software error message, look up the solution here.

The "Note" icon provides information about the current topic or refers you to other chapters. This helps you find information about a topic quickly and gives you an overview of the relationships between individual topic groups.

The "Example" icon identifies passages with concrete examples of topics that have already been explained. If you don't immediately understand a topic and you're looking for a pertinent example, this icon shows you where to find the example.

The "Hint" icon indicates tips and tricks for using the corresponding command or function.

The "Practical" icon provides practical information about using a function or command in your everyday work.

1. What Is Windows?

The user interface

The user interface of a program or operating system refers to the direct link between the computer and the user. The interface is basically what you see on the computer screen.

The Windows concept

Windows acts as a mediator between the operating system and applications. While other programs require specific files for screen, mouse, and printer management, Windows supplies these needs to Windows applications without additional drivers.

The components of Windows

This section discusses the components that comprise Windows. The terms introduced will be used throughout the book. If you're a beginner, use this section to familiarize yourself with the basics of the Windows world. Once you know how the individual components work together, you'll understand how Windows operates.

New features in Version 3.1

Windows 3.1 introduces several changes from Version 3.0. This section also discusses the new characteristics of Windows 3.1. You'll find more detailed information about these developments in the chapters dealing specifically with those topics. We'll also discuss the fundamental changes that modify the basic operation of Windows. The two most important developments are TrueType fonts and OLE (more on these later).

1.1 User Interfaces

The user interface of a program or operating system refers to the direct interaction between the computer and the user. So, the interface is actually what you see on the computer screen.

Text-oriented interfaces

Since computers were first introduced, both beginners and experienced users have had trouble understanding the operating system. For example, the DOS system prompt (C> or C:\>) is the only indication that the operating system is running. So, to master using the operating system, you must learn numerous DOS commands.

Parameter handling

However, for each of these DOS commands, you must also learn several parameters that control the command's execution. These commands, along with their parameters, control how your computer operates.

Programs designed for specific applications, such as editing text or graphics, usually provide more information than the operating system. Many of these programs display their commands on the screen or offer menu control.

Programs that have clearly named and arranged commands are considered "user-friendly". However, when compared to the operating system, almost any program is user-friendly.

The operating system interface

A new user interface for the operating system, called the MS-DOS Shell, was introduced in DOS Versions 4.0 and 5.0. You can execute commands from this Shell without referring to the DOS manual.

The MS-DOS Shell is one example of a *text-oriented interface*, in which programs and system commands are represented as text. Microsoft Word 5.5, the Norton Commander, and dBASE IV also use text-oriented interfaces.

Graphic-oriented interfaces

Years before the development of the MS-DOS Shell, Apple Computer introduced a family of computers based on a *graphic-oriented interface*. This type of interface uses icons and other graphic elements to represent commands and functions.

This pictorial method of display allowed most beginners to learn the computer's operation in a much more intuitive, almost playful manner, while allowing experienced users to operate completely unfamiliar programs based on their experience with other programs.

Using the mouse

Accessing these icons and graphic elements required an input device other than the keyboard. The *mouse* was first developed in the 1960s, but didn't become popular until the 1980s. Using the mouse instead of the keyboard, you can move a small arrow-shaped pointer around the screen, and select or execute elements, over which the pointer is located, by *clicking* (pressing) a mouse button.

At first, text-oriented user interfaces were written specifically to accept mouse input. Although Word 5.0 or PC Tools can be used with a mouse, the quality of the Apple graphic-oriented interface was much better.

A breakthrough

The mouse became a popular device on the PC because of the GEM and Windows GUIs (Graphical User Interfaces). Graphic-oriented applications became more user-friendly because they could offer mouse driven user interfaces. Windows evolved and set new standards; now many users consider Windows the primary GUI for the PC.

1.2 The Windows Concept

The development of these new user interfaces resulted in another problem for users. Although many programs were more user-friendly, the user interfaces changed from program to program.

Differing operating concepts

Some programs supported a mouse, while others used multiple command levels (e.g., Lotus 1-2-3), in which you might have to move through seven menu levels to perform a single command.

Methods of command selection

The various ways commands can be selected confuse even the most experienced users. Selecting commands from the keyboard using key combinations or the cursor keys is a fairly easy way to access commands. However, to use several different programs, you must learn the appropriate command selection methods for each program.

Manufacturer-based concepts

Eventually software companies developed standards for their own products. So, all the programs from a specific software company work the same way. For example, many of the same key combinations used in a word processor also apply to similar commands in a spreadsheet program from the same software company. The screen layout may also be very similar. In this way, software companies can integrate logical and practical concepts into their programs and user interfaces.

Windows as an industry-wide standard

Microsoft Corporation has taken this concept a step further: All programs must follow the same general guidelines for user interfaces. You'll find that Word for Windows, Excel, PageMaker, and other programs use the same graphic elements, characteristics, and commands as Windows, regardless of their purpose. This wide-reaching concept is called System Application Architecture (SAA), and describes the common and unifying structure of all Windows applications. However, SAA includes text-oriented systems such as Word 5.5 or the MS-DOS Shell of DOS Version 5.0.

Windows acts as a mediator between the operating system and the Windows applications. When you work with a Windows application, such as Excel, this program uses the Windows screen manager for its own output. Since Windows applications don't have their own screen managers, the output is adapted to match the Windows standard.

Programming under SAA

The SAA concept starts at the programming level. Since the technical characteristics of the user interface are already determined, the programmer can access a large library of existing routines to develop Windows applications. This simplifies developing custom Windows applications.

Data exchange as an essential characteristic

Various manufacturers use different file formats. This is another drawback of conventional programs. A standardized data organization and structure is essential to exchanging data between programs or applications. For example, if you want to add graphics to a word processor file, the word processor must be able to decipher the graphic information. The Windows SAA dictates a standard file format, so that data can even be exchanged between extremely different applications. By adding programs that don't use the Windows user interface, it's also possible to exchange data between these programs, even if this information is stored in different file formats.

Windows presents an environment under which all other Windows applications operate. Windows mediates between applications, the operating system, and the individual hardware components. In addition, Windows presents a graphical interface that provides a standardized format for these applications. The term "Windows" refers to two basic functions: The management of all system resources, and the graphic display of all functions to the user.

1.3 The Components of Windows

In this section we'll discuss the components that make up Windows. The terms introduced here will be used throughout the book. If you're a beginner, use this section to familiarize yourself with the basics of the Windows world. Once you know how the individual components work together, you'll understand how Windows operates.

The mouse pointer

By moving the mouse on a flat surface, you can move a small arrow-shaped pointer across your screen. If you position this mouse pointer on an icon or a command button and *click* (press and release the mouse button), the appropriate function or program is selected. By *double-clicking* (pressing and releasing the mouse button twice in rapid succession), you can start programs, copy files, or create directories.

Icons

Windows uses icons extensively. Icons are graphic symbols that represent specific programs and functions. For example, to start a program, simply double-click its icon. Icons are identified by their appearance as well as an accompanying label. Often, specific functions are also displayed in icon form.

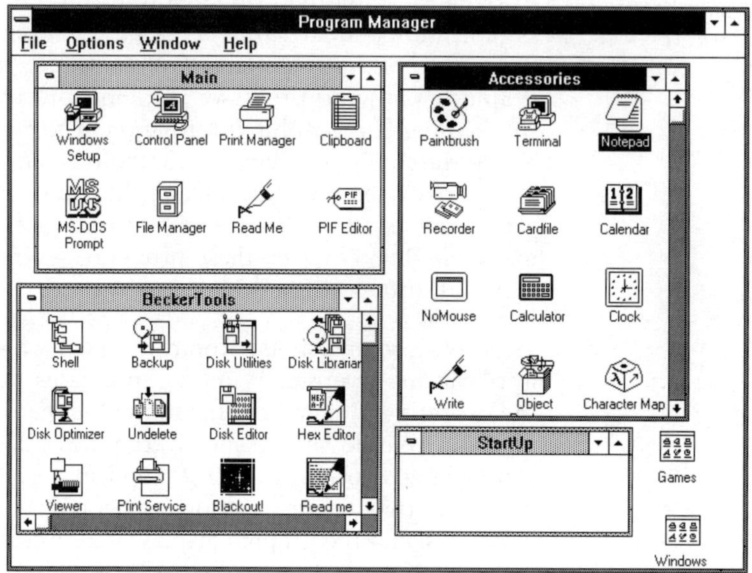

Icons representing individual programs

Windows

As the name implies, Windows' user interface consists of windows. A window is a defined area of the screen whose shape, size, and position can be changed. Several of these windows can appear on your screen simultaneously, and they may overlap and completely cover one another.

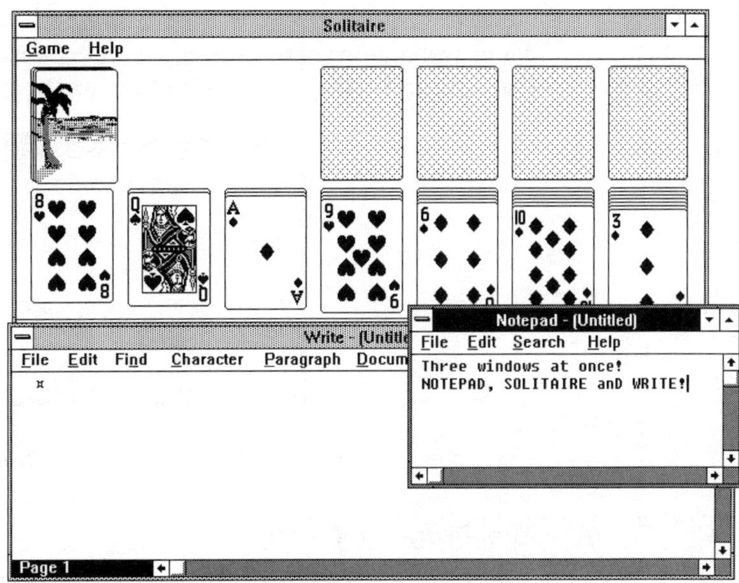

Each program runs in its own window

Dialog boxes

Often a command needs additional information before execution. In these instances, a *dialog box* appears when the command is selected. In this dialog box you can set or enter the information needed by the command. This is done by using command buttons, option buttons, text boxes, or list boxes.

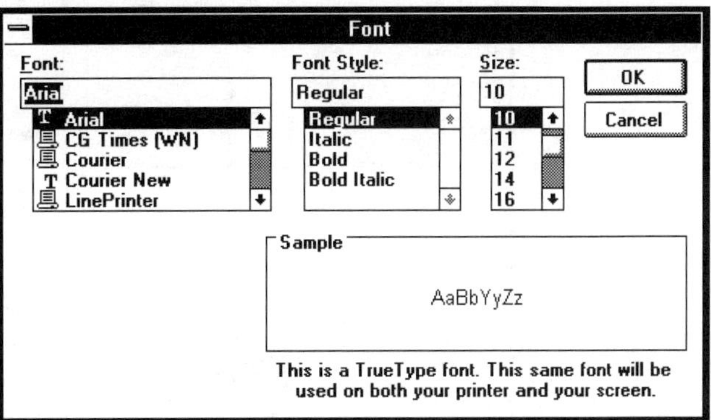

A typical dialog box

Command buttons

Command buttons (buttons for short) are frequently used in dialog boxes. These buttons appear as 3D representations of push buttons and perform specific functions. Command buttons usually verify entries in dialog boxes and activate or cancel a command. Some command buttons open additional dialog boxes. The text or graphic that appears on the command button describes its function.

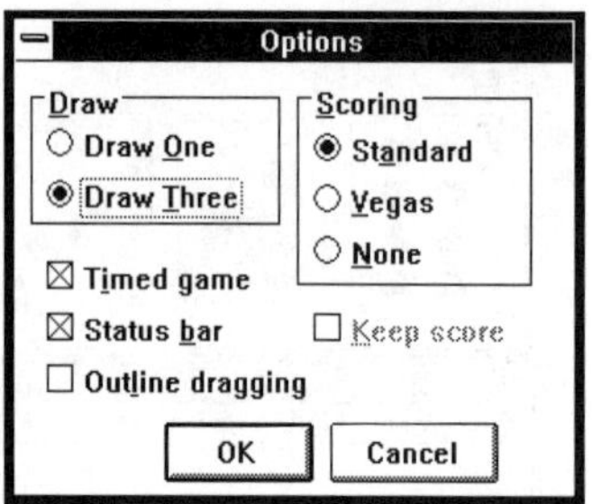

Command buttons with different functions

The Program Manager

The Program Manager manages all Windows programs or applications, such as word processors, databases, and graphics programs. You can activate these applications by clicking on their icons. It's also possible to organize these icons into program groups; the Program Manager allows you to add new applications to these groups. Existing icons can be deleted, moved, or copied to another group.

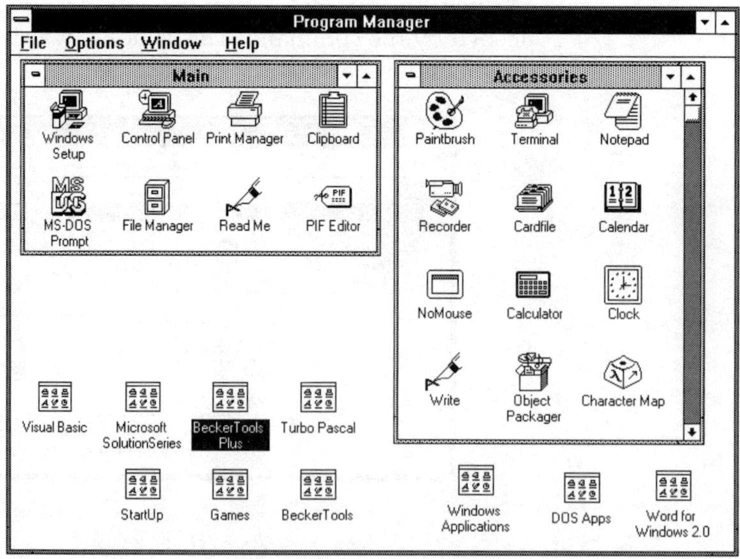

The Program Manager

The Task Manager

The Task Manager manages all running applications. If an application is started from Windows, the Task Manager controls its execution. The Task Manager also allows you to switch between running applications.

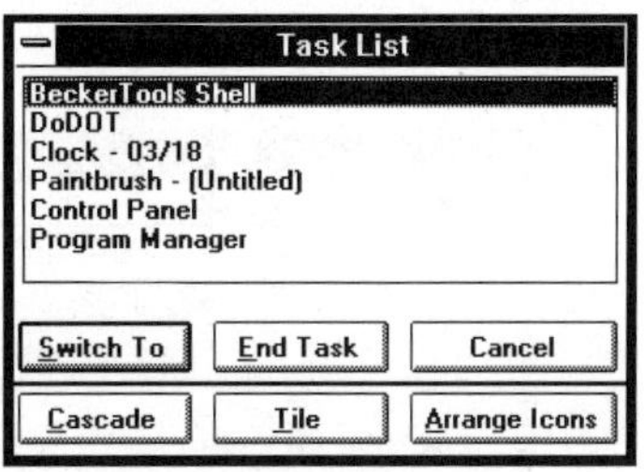

The Task Manager

The File Manager

The File Manager performs tasks such as copying, deleting, and renaming files. So, the File Manager is entirely responsible for managing diskettes and the hard drive(s), and can replace the DOS interface and the MS-DOS Shell. The File Manager is started from the Program Manager and is controlled by the Task Manager.

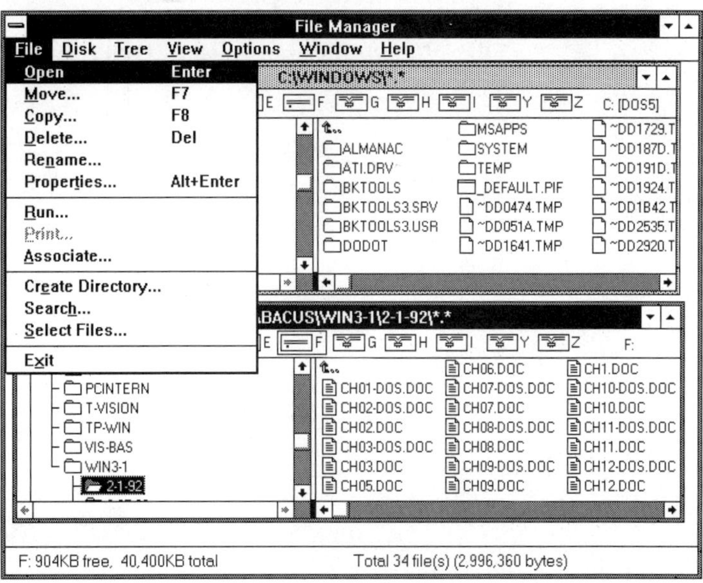

The File Manager

The Print Manager

The Print Manager controls the operation of printers used under Windows. This manager also acts as a spooler (memory buffer), so that you can continue working with your application while printing the document. If the Print Manager is active, each print command executed from an application immediately accesses the Print Manager.

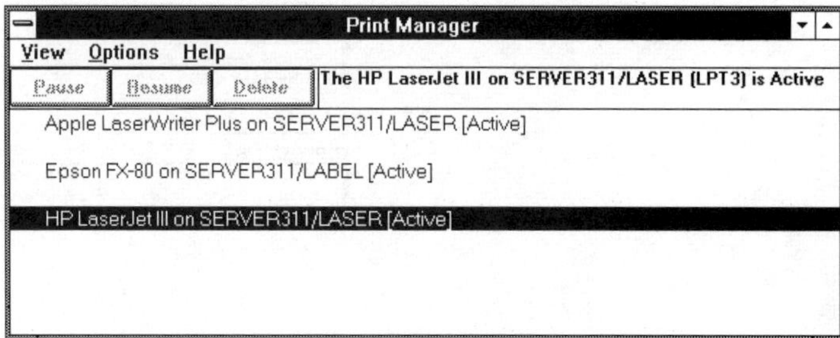

The Print Manager

Windows applications

The term "Windows applications" refers to various types of programs that use the Windows user interface. Some applications are included in the Windows package (Write, Paintbrush, Calendar, and Terminal). Other applications, such as Excel, Word for Windows, Superbase, or PageMaker, are provided by numerous software companies, and are designed specifically for use under Windows.

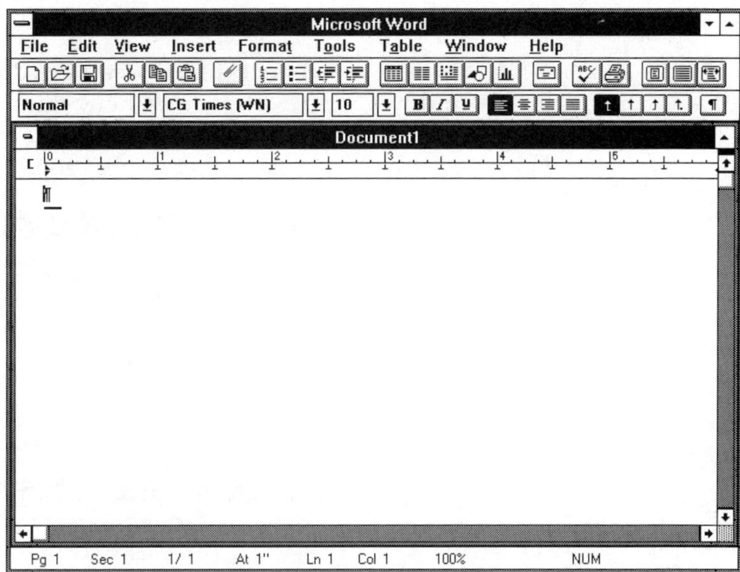

Word for Windows is a full Windows application

Non-Windows applications

Non-Windows applications include all programs that utilize a text-oriented user interface, such as Word 5.5 or dBASE IV. However, these applications can operate under Windows and can be added to, and started from, the Program Manager. The Task Manager then controls their execution. You'll be able to start almost any program from the Program Manager and, if you're using a 386 computer or higher, these programs may even be displayed in a Windows window.

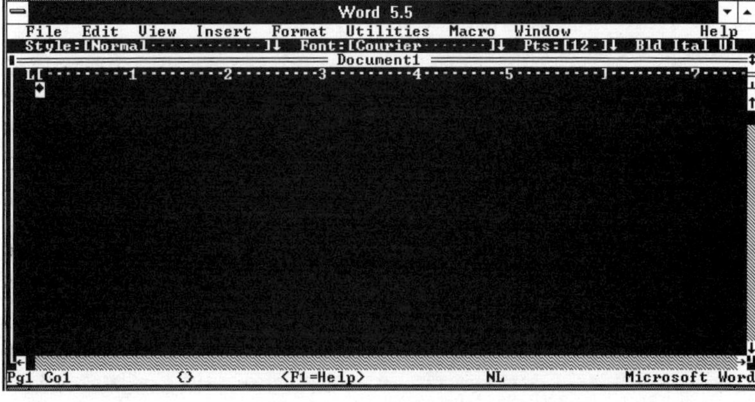

A non-Windows application using a text-oriented user interface displayed in a window

The Clipboard

The Clipboard is a connection between Windows applications and non-Windows applications. When data is placed in the Clipboard, its format is standardized. The data can then be copied or moved into almost any other application.

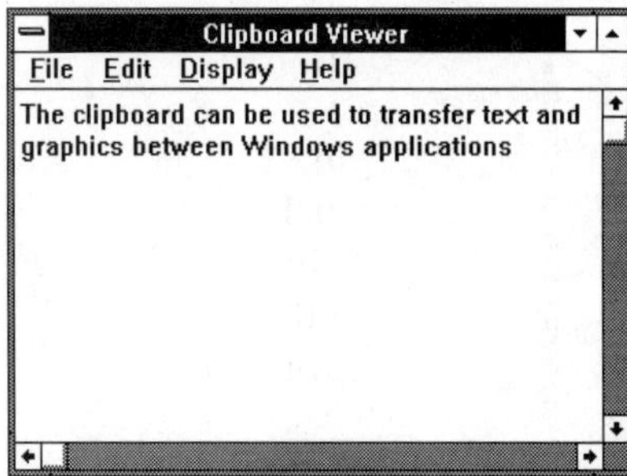

The Clipboard

1.4 New Features in Version 3.1

Windows 3.1 introduces several changes from Version 3.0. However, you'll notice most of these changes only after you've worked with Version 3.1 for awhile. In this section we'll discuss the new characteristics of Windows Version 3.1. You'll find more detailed information about these developments in the chapters dealing specifically with those topics.

We'll also discuss the basic changes that modify the basic operation of Windows. The two most important developments are TrueType fonts and OLE (more on these later).

System organization

Windows 3.1 has been completely reorganized. Its increased speed allows Windows to operate at an adequate speed, even on 80286 based machines. Its revamped memory allocation ensures fewer system crashes and fewer "Unrecoverable Application Error" messages. Also, both Windows and non-Windows applications are executed more smoothly.

Warm starts are "intercepted"

When an application crashes, simply press Ctrl + Alt + Del to activate a warm start. Version 3.1 of Windows also offers other alternatives. You can use Esc to return to Windows without performing a warm start or you can try to close your application by using Enter. If both of these attempts are unsuccessful, then you must perform the warm start.

Object Linking and Embedding (OLE)

The dynamic link technique used by Windows applications increases the level of information exchange between individual Windows applications. You may have already encountered this technique in Excel. OLE refers to the linking of objects from one application to another, and creating a dynamic link between the two applications.

For example, you can dynamically link an object created in Paintbrush or Excel to a Microsoft Windows Write file. The link is simply a pointer to the application, which created the object, instead of to the object itself. Now if you change the linked object, the change appears in the Write file.

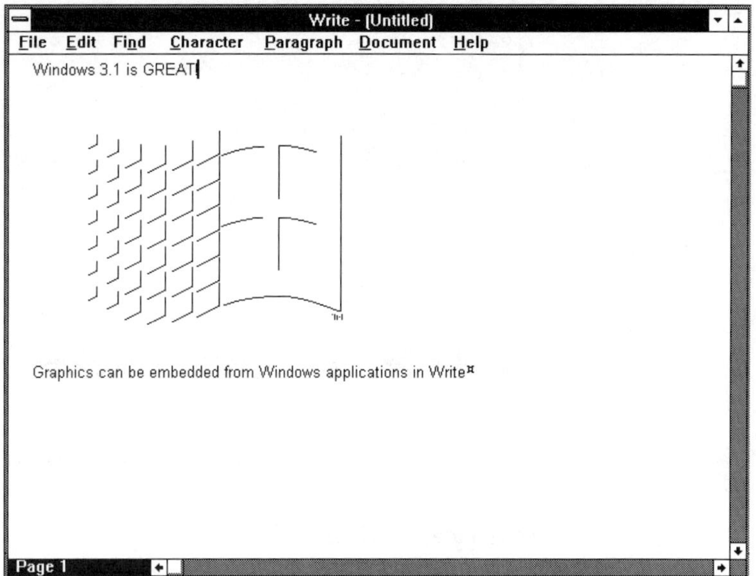

Embedded objects in Write

When an object is embedded, it's linked separately with each individual application. So, if an Excel object is embedded in Write and Paintbrush, it can be changed in Write without this change automatically affecting the object embedded in Paintbrush.

Making changes with a double-click

If you want to change an embedded object, double-click the object to open its source application. There you can change the object and return to the previous application by closing the source application. You'll return to Write (or the appropriate application in which the object is embedded) and you'll see that the embedded object has accepted the new changes.

Creating Icons

By using the Object Packager you can create icons to graphically represent these dynamic links. The link can be attached to the icon and copied to any desired Windows application. By clicking the icon, the object's source application, in which you can modify the object, is automatically opened. One advantage of this system is that the information concerning the object is visible only when it's actually needed.

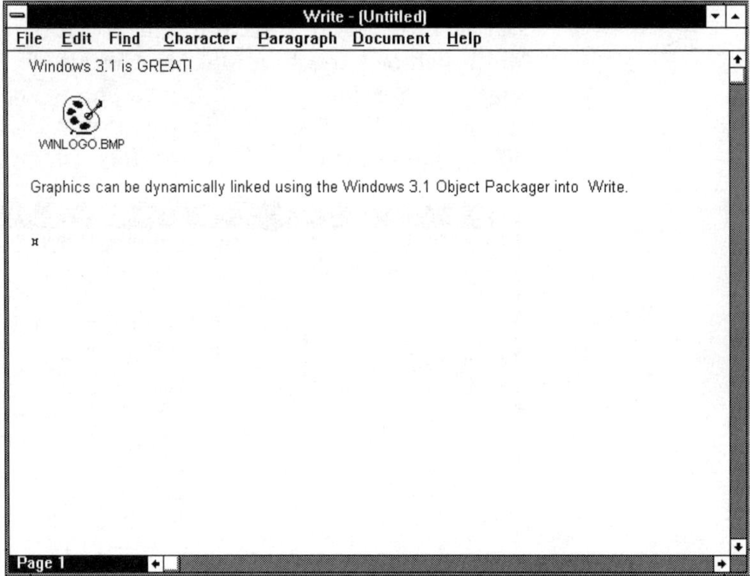

Dynamically linked icon from the Object Packager

TrueType fonts

In previous versions of Windows, many users complained about the font display. Windows supplied predefined screen fonts that barely resembled their names or their actual printed typefaces. However, in Version 3.1, Windows provides TrueType fonts. The sizes of these fonts can easily be modified and font programs are needed only for special fonts.

Sizeable fonts

Windows now offers the Arial, Times New Roman, Courier, and Symbol TrueType fonts, which can be displayed in bold, italic, and bold italic. The fonts are selected through the Windows Control Panel. You can use either the TrueType fonts or your own custom fonts with other applications.

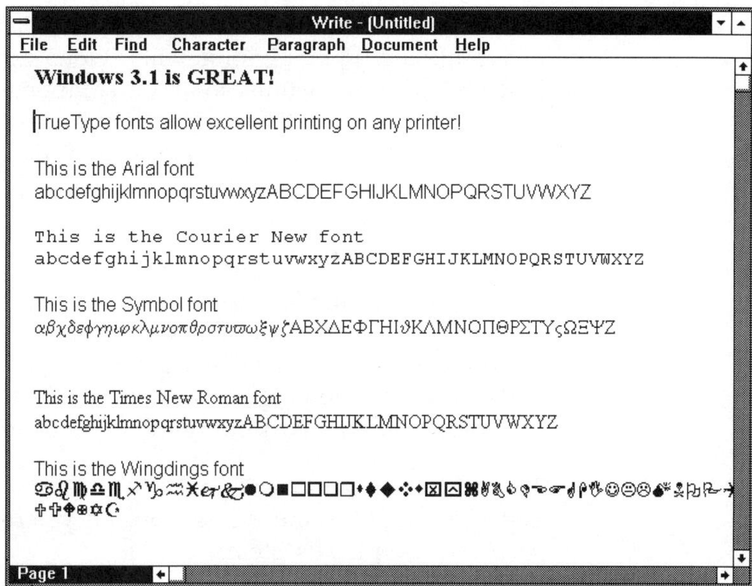

TrueType fonts

These fonts look great in both the screen display and printed output. The *jaggies* (rough edges) are minimal, unlike fonts in previous versions of Windows. One way to use the TrueType fonts is within the File Manager. You can increase the font size so that it's easier to view files and directories. To do this, use the *Font...* command in the File Manager's *Options* menu.

File selection

Within the Windows applications you'll find a new file selector dialog box. Drives and directories are now handled separately. Directories are represented by icons in the File Manager. A separate list box has been installed for the available drives.

You can determine what type of files are displayed through a file type selection provided by this dialog box. The available file types depend on the application, to which the dialog box belongs.

Standard installation

Windows can be installed in several ways. Basically you can choose between the standard installation and the custom (user-defined) installation. Windows checks whether an older version of Windows is located in the system and can update the existing version. If a previous version of Windows isn't present, Version 3.1 is installed as a completely new unit.

The standard installation automatically checks your system to determine the type of components (video card, keyboard, etc.) it has. The standard values for each component are automatically passed to the installation procedure, and are stored in the SYSTEM.INI file, under the [Boot Description] segment. This type of installation is quick and convenient for the inexperienced user.

Custom installation

The custom installation lists the component types that are found by the automatic system check. You can then either change the standard entries for these component types or insert your own drivers. In previous Windows versions, this installation was considered the standard installation procedure.

The hardware components and driver selections can be saved to a file. This simplifies the system setup if you're installing Windows on several identical systems.

Learning to use the mouse

Before the text screen changes to a graphics screen, you can start a tutorial program that introduces you to the mouse.

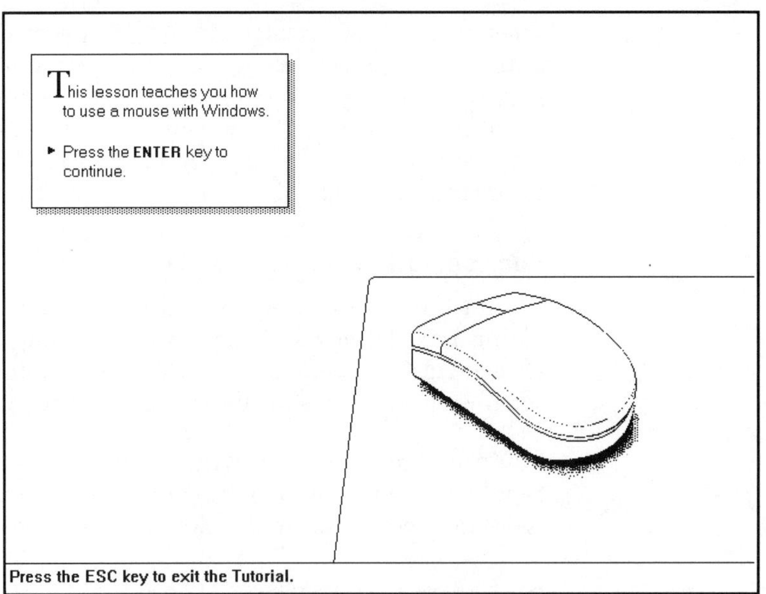
This lesson teaches you how to use a mouse with Windows.
▸ Press the ENTER key to continue.
Press the ESC key to exit the Tutorial.

The Mouse Tutorial

Expanded printer list

While setting up your printer, you may notice that the list of printer drivers has significantly increased. You'll even find an option that enables you to access PostScript emulation for the HP Laserjet printer. Various video card drivers, including TIGA and VIDEO7 cards, are also available.

Program Manager

You've probably already noticed the colorful icons, which have been improved since the last Windows version. Two new icons, which you can access through the *Properties...* item of the *File* menu, have been added. You'll also notice that icon labels can now occupy multiple lines of text. Icons can be spaced more closely without their labels overlapping. However, it's also possible to display icon labels on only one line.

The StartUp group

In addition to the usual program groups, the Program Manager now contains a new group, called the StartUp group. Icons placed in this group are automatically loaded by Windows upon startup. However, they aren't added to the WIN.INI file [LOAD=].

Program organization

The arrangement of programs into groups is more organized than in previous versions. The PIF Editor is now located in the Main group. The groups don't distinguish between Windows applications and non-Windows applications, and usually only one group is available for these applications.

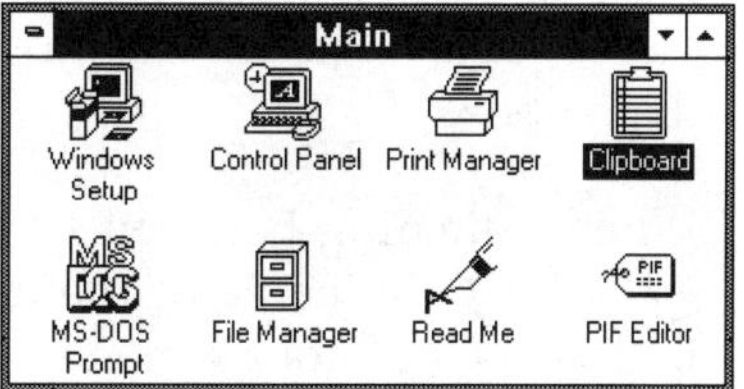

The Main program group of the Program Manager

Program properties

You can equip each application with a working directory and a key combination, with which the application can be opened. The working directory is extremely useful. In earlier versions of Windows, you had to search the directory tree in order to find a specific file.

Windows and non-Windows applications

Those non-Windows applications, which operate in graphics mode, can operate within a window. For example, this is possible with Word 5.5 or Lotus 3.1. This means that most applications can be displayed in a window. The biggest advantage of this capability is how easily data can be exchanged through the Windows Clipboard.

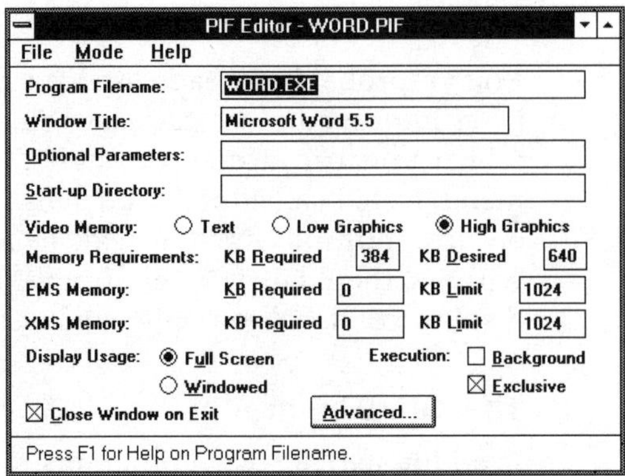

Program Information File properties for Word 5.5

When you select *Run...* from the *File* menu of your Program Manager, a dialog box, from which you can select the file to be executed, opens. The list in this dialog box displays all COM, EXE, PIF, and BAT files so that only executable files are visible.

The *Options* menu now contains an item named *Save Settings on Exit*, and its status is indicated by a checkmark. This replaces the old *Save Changes* check box that was in Windows 3.0's closing dialog box.

When switching between several applications using Alt + Tab or Alt + Esc, the name of the next application is displayed in a box in the center of your screen.

File Manager

The File Manager has been completely revised. The most important change is that the directory contents have been linked to the directory tree.

The contents of the current directory are displayed within the File Manager. If you switch to another directory, the directory contents change accordingly. Since it's now possible to save the contents of directory and file boxes at any time, the new File Manager can be configured similar to PC Tools 6.0, for example.

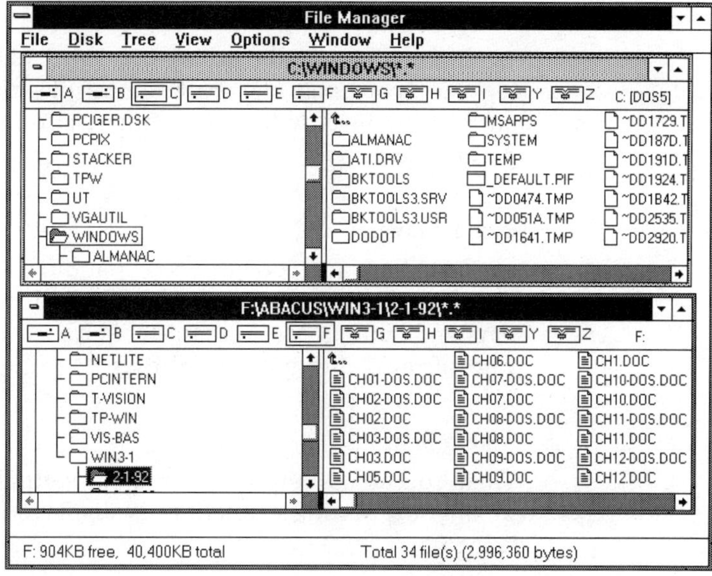

The new File Manager

A File Manager similar to PC Tools

It is now also possible to open more than one directory box at a time. For example, if you have a hard drive C: and a hard drive D:, you can open a directory box for each drive and arrange these on your screen.

Windows applications

The Windows applications were changed only slightly. The following is a list of the most important modifications:

PIF Editor

Several settings within the PIF Editor have been regrouped. You'll now find the dialog boxes for the EMS and XMS memory manager in the main dialog box. The expanded options are reserved for functions that are rarely needed.

Setup

The *Options* menu of Windows Setup provides a new menu item called *Add/Remove Windows Components....* This item lets you add or remove individual Windows components. You're already familiar with its dialog box from the initial setup. If you didn't install components initially but want to add these components in the future, use this menu item.

Sound Recorder

Together with a sound card and a microphone, the Sound Recorder lets you record and play back sound files. Individual sound files can be combined with one another, edited, and equipped with special effects.

Media Player

Using Media Player, you can access audio sources such as a normal CD player. This process is controlled with the appropriate command buttons. More complex equipment, such as MIDI sources, are controlled through special files.

System Settings

When you access any of the system settings, a help text, which explains the setting's function, is displayed at the bottom of the dialog box.

Changing the colors of individual controls

Expanded options in desktop colors now allow you to determine the colors of individual controls. This allows you to color almost every Windows element according to your own needs.

Activating the Screen Saver

It's also possible to activate a Windows Screen Saver from the *Desktop...* menu item of the Control Panel. You can choose from four different savers, and you can set the desired time delay in the corresponding box. By clicking the appropriate button, you can view the selected screen saver.

In addition to controlling the interaction with a sound card, the system settings also allow you to install special drivers (such as MIDI sequencers), which can be addressed by the Windows applications Media Player and Sound Recorder.

MS-DOS Prompt

If you access the DOS interface by clicking the appropriate icon, Windows displays a message informing you of the various control options. This message explains how to exit to Windows by typing EXIT Enter, and how the Alt + Tab and Alt + Esc key combinations work.

Clock

The clock displays the time and the date. The analog version displays the date in the window's title bar, while the digital version displays the date below the time. The date display can also be controlled separately, and a special function allows you to keep the clock in the foreground of the Windows screen at all times.

Minesweeper

Minesweeper replaces the old Reversi game that was provided with Windows 3.0. In this game, you must locate mines based on the information the game provides.

Minesweeper

Character Map

The Accessories group contains a complete character set listing of the ANSI character set. All available characters are displayed for each font. Clicking a specific character reveals its character code. You can use this tool to copy characters, which aren't on your keyboard, to the Clipboard so that other applications can use them.

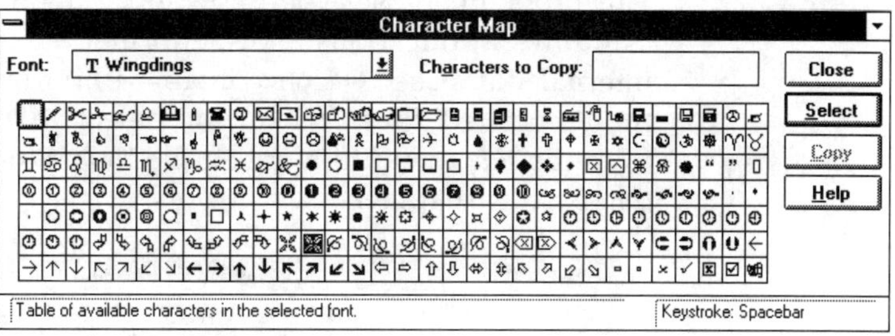

The character set table

Help

Windows Help is now context-sensitive. This means that help information is displayed for any current problem or selected item. If you want Help information for a specific command, simply select the command and open the Help window.

Help is always accessible

You can now access the Help function from almost any dialog box by clicking the corresponding button. This displays the Help text for that dialog box.

Tutorial

The tutorial is located, as an icon, in the Main program group. It introduces the mouse to Windows beginners. Several short examples are used to demonstrate mouse movement, clicking, double-clicking, and dragging.

"Read Me" Texts

You can open the *Read Me* icon from the Main group. These files contain information that was released after the Windows manual was printed. You should read these files if you plan to work more closely with Windows. These files mainly contain information about the compatibility of Windows with other applications or with specific hardware. This information isn't very useful to the Windows beginner and to those who plan to run only user-oriented applications.

The Windows 3.1 package includes several applications and files, which are briefly discussed later in this book. These utility programs and informational text files are very useful for more advanced work with Windows. Several of these programs appeared in previous versions of Windows, but weren't documented until now.

REGEDIT.EXE

This program enables you to see registration information related to Windows applications. This information is stored in a type of internal database, which contains important information about the associated files. When you select *Merge Registration File...* from the *File* menu to merge a file to a Windows application, this database is displayed.

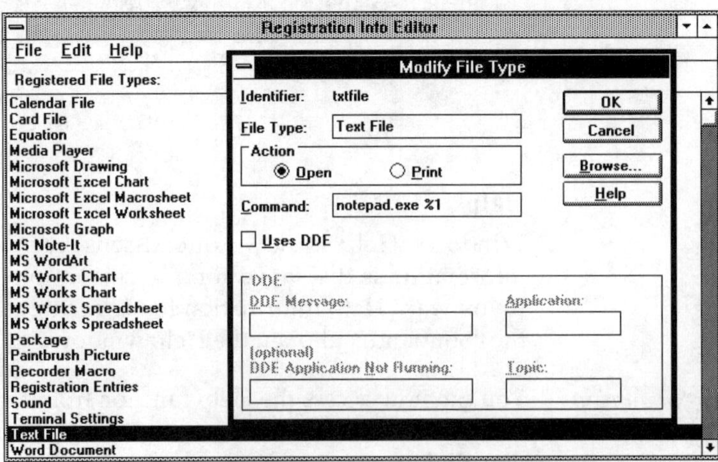

File Registration

You can also install links for dynamic data exchange (DDE) between individual applications or files. Several settings can already be found in the SETUP.REG file.

WINVER.EXE

This simple Windows application displays the current version number of Windows. It also indicates the mode under which Windows is currently operating.

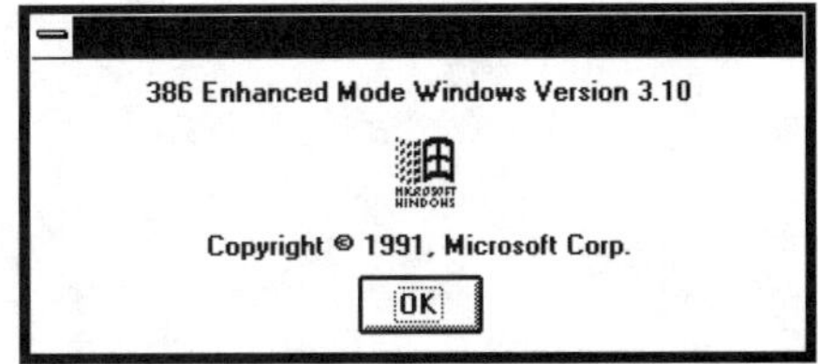

Version and mode

SYSEDIT.EXE

The System Configuration Editor is a text editor that's designed specifically for modifying the AUTOEXEC.BAT, CONFIG.SYS, WIN.INI, and SYSTEM.INI files.

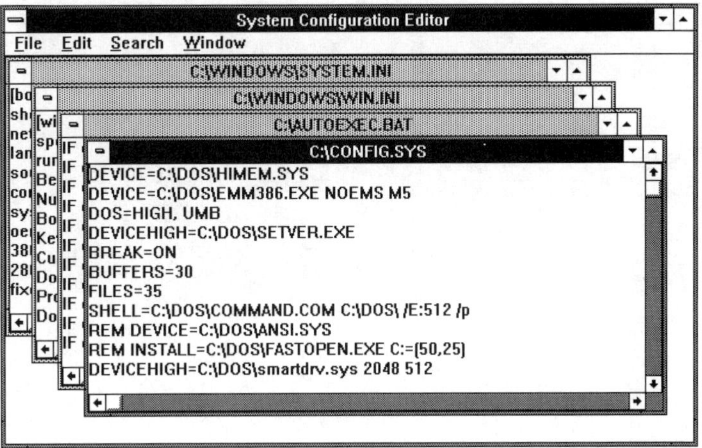

The System Editor for special modifications

Each file appears in a separate window, and can be edited in the usual way. This function is particularly useful for the more experienced user who wants to tailor Windows and the entire system to his/her specific needs.

2. Starting And Exiting Windows

Simplified startup

Windows can be started in different modes. The optimum mode depends on the type of computer and its configuration.

Starting in Standard mode

On an AT or AT compatible (80286 processor) computer equipped with at least 256K of extended memory and 640K of conventional memory, Windows starts in Standard mode. In this mode, Windows surpasses the memory limit set by DOS and can access a larger memory area for your Windows applications.

Starting in 386 Enhanced mode

On a 386 or 486 (has a 80386 or 80486 processor) computer with at least 1024K of extended memory, Windows will automatically start in 386 Enhanced mode. Besides permitting optimal memory use, this mode also allows Windows to use virtual memory. Windows can address this memory range in the same way as the computer's conventional and extended memory.

Optional parameters

Several other parameters can be used when starting Windows. These allow specific functions to be executed at startup. These are used to start Windows in a specific mode or to automatically start a Windows application.

Displaying the mode

You can easily determine which mode Windows is running. This is the only way you can ensure that Windows is fully utilizing your computer and its memory.

Starting Windows with applications

In Windows, you can start applications in several ways. This section shows the different methods for starting Windows applications.

Exiting Windows

When working with Windows it is important to exit Windows correctly.

2.1 Simplified Start

Windows can be started several ways. If you believe that Windows is installed correctly and optimally for your system, switch on your computer and wait until the DOS prompt (C:\>) appears on your screen. Now type the following:

```
win
```

Since DOS isn't case sensitive, you can enter either uppercase or lowercase letters. To activate this command and tell your computer to process it, press the following key:

Enter

This tells your computer to load all the data, needed by Windows, from disk into your computer's memory. Then the Program Manager will appear on your screen.

If your computer responds as follows:

```
Bad command or filename
```

one of the following probably occurred:

- Windows isn't installed on your computer.
- A search path isn't set for Windows.

In the first case, you should look at your hard drive directory using the following DOS command:

```
dir /p [Enter]
```

Look for a directory called WINDOWS, or something similar. If you cannot find this directory, you must install Windows (see Chapter 5 for information on installing Windows correctly).

In the second case, Windows is installed but there isn't a search path to direct DOS to the correct directory. The search path is important because when you enter a command and press [Enter], DOS searches the hard drive for a file of the same name. However, it doesn't automatically search all the subdirectories that may be located on your drive. So, first you must switch to the directory that contains Windows. This directory is usually called WINDOWS. You can verify the directory by typing the following to display the contents of your hard drive:

```
dir /p [Enter]
```

To start Windows, you must type the following DOS commands:

```
cd windows [Enter]
win [Enter]
```

You should edit the PATH command in your AUTOEXEC.BAT file (see Section 5.8 for more information). It's also possible to start Windows automatically when you switch on your computer.

The modes of Windows operation

Windows can operate in one of several modes, depending on your computer's processor and the amount of memory on the system.

Your hardware determines the operating mode

If don't select a specific mode, Windows automatically selects the appropriate operating mode upon startup. Windows considers the following criteria when selecting the mode:

1. If you're working with an 80386 processor with at least 2 Meg of memory, Windows automatically runs in 386 Enhanced mode. However, the memory allocation must specify at least 640K as conventional memory and 1024K as extended memory.

2. If you start Windows on an 80286 system and at least 1 Meg of memory, where 640K are allocated as conventional memory and 256K as extended memory, Windows selects the Standard mode.

In the following sections we'll demonstrate how to select a specific mode manually.

Windows Version 3.1 no longer supports Real mode. You can only choose from Standard and 386 Enhanced modes. This means that older applications that were designed for Windows 2.x versions may now be incompatible. A few of these applications still might start, but they will probably crash or return errors during operation.

2.2 Starting in Standard Mode

If you're working with an 80286 system equipped with at least 256K of extended memory and 640K of conventional memory, Windows starts in Standard mode. In this mode, Windows surpasses the memory limit set by DOS and can access a larger linear memory area for your Windows applications. So more memory is available for your applications and their data.

You'll find more information about Windows memory management in Chapter 6.

Standard mode on 386 computers

On 386/486 computers, Windows will start in Standard mode only if the amount of extended memory available plus 640K of conventional memory is between 256—1024K in size. If the amount of extended memory exceeds 1024K, Windows will start in 386 Enhanced mode.

If the above conditions are fulfilled, Windows can be started in Standard mode by typing:

```
win [Enter]
```

Even if you have a 386/486 computer capable of running Windows in 386 mode, it's still possible to operate Windows in Standard mode. If your 386/486 is equipped with a sufficient amount of extended memory (over 2 Meg) and you'll run only a few Windows applications, it's more effective to run Windows in Standard mode. This is because Standard mode requires Windows to perform less work. You can force Windows to start in Standard mode by using the following command:

```
win /s [Enter]
```

You can use either the /S switch or the number 2.

2.3 Starting in 386 Enhanced Mode

If your computer is a 386 or 486 (has a 80386 or 80486 processor) and has at least 1024K of extended memory, Windows will automatically start in 386 Enhanced mode. Windows reveals all its capabilities in this mode. Besides permitting optimal memory use, this mode also allows Windows to use virtual memory. In this instance, virtual memory is an area of your hard drive that acts as computer memory. Windows can address this memory range in the same way as the computer's conventional and extended memory.

Windows in multitasking operation

Because of the way it uses the microprocessor, Windows is capable of multitasking (performing several tasks simultaneously). You'll find more information about multitasking in Chapter 12. We'll discuss virtual memory in Chapters 6 and 7.

If you're working with non-Windows applications, you can run these applications within windows. This allows you to determine the size and shape of these individual windows and facilitates easy data exchange between Windows and non-Windows applications.

As long as your hardware meets the above conditions, the following command will automatically start Windows in 386 Enhanced mode:

`win` Enter

If you're working with a computer that has less than 1024K of extended memory, you can force Windows to start in 386 Enhanced mode by using the following command:

`win /3` Enter

This enables you to use all the enhanced Windows capabilities. However, this reduces your system's speed. So, you should determine whether your tasks can also be performed in Standard mode.

2.4 Optional Parameters

Several other parameters can be used when starting Windows. These allow specific functions to be executed at startup. To display the parameters that can be used at Windows startup, type the following command:

`win /?` Enter

This command displays the following list of optional parameters without starting Windows:

```
Starts Windows.

WIN [/3] [/S] [/B] [/D:[F][S][V][X]]

/3    Starts Windows in 386 enhanced mode.
/S    Starts Windows in standard mode.
/B    Creates a file, BOOTLOG.TXT, that records system messages generated
      during system startup (boot).
/D    Used for troubleshooting when Windows does not start correctly.
  :F  Turns off 32-bit disk access.
      Equivalent to SYSTEM.INI file setting: 32BitDiskAccess=FALSE.
  :S  Specifies that Windows should not use ROM address space between
      F000:0000 and 1 MB for a break point.
      Equivalent to SYSTEM.INI file setting: SystemROMBreakPoint=FALSE.
  :V  Specifies that the ROM routine will handle interrupts from the hard
      disk controller.
      Equivalent to SYSTEM.INI file setting: VirtualHDIRQ=FALSE.
  :X  Excludes all of the adapter area from the range of memory that Windows
      scans to find unused space.
      Equivalent to SYSTEM.INI file setting: EMMExclude=A000-FFFF.

In this configuration, WIN without any switches will launch standard mode.
```

Boot log tracing

At startup, the drivers that control the hardware (mouse, keyboard, screen, etc.) are loaded. However some Windows startups may end in a system crash because of incompatibilities between drivers and their corresponding hardware. This is usually caused by a defective piece of hardware. The startup process can be traced and documented with diagnostic messages. To do this, start Windows with a special parameter.

To activate the boot log tracing, start Windows with the following parameter:

win /b Enter

This creates the BOOTLOG.TXT file, which contains all important diagnostic messages. The file is created the first time you call Windows with this parameter; subsequent calls with this parameter will append further boot messages to the file. The number preceding [boot] indicates the startup to which the set of messages pertains. BOOTLOG.TXT has the following structure:

```
1. [boot]
LoadStart = SYSTEM.DRV
LoadSuccess = SYSTEM.DRV
LoadStart = keyboard.drv
LoadSuccess = keyboard.drv
LoadStart = MOUSE.DRV
LoadSuccess = MOUSE.DRV
LoadStart = VGA.DRV
LoadSuccess = VGA.DRV
LoadStart = MMSOUND.DRV
LoadSuccess = MMSOUND.DRV
LoadStart = COMM.DRV
LoadSuccess = COMM.DRV
LoadStart = VGASYS.FON
```

```
LoadSuccess = VGASYS.FON
LoadStart = VGAOEM.FON
LoadSuccess = VGAOEM.FON
LoadStart = GDI.EXE
LoadStart = FONTS.FON
LoadSuccess = FONTS.FON
LoadStart = VGAFIX.FON
LoadSuccess = VGAFIX.FON
LoadStart = OEMFONTS.FON
LoadSuccess = OEMFONTS.FON
LoadSuccess = GDI.EXE
LoadStart = USER.EXE
INIT=Keyboard
INITDONE=Keyboard
INIT=Mouse
STATUS=Mouse driver installed
INITDONE=Mouse
INIT=Display
LoadStart = DISPLAY.drv
LoadSuccess = DISPLAY.drv
INITDONE=Display
INIT=Display Resources
INITDONE=Display Resources
LoadStart = KBDGR.DLL
LoadSuccess = KBDGR.DLL
INIT=Fonts
INITDONE=Fonts
INIT=Lang Driver
LoadStart = LANGGER.DLL
LoadSuccess = LANGGER.DLL
INITDONE=Lang Driver
LoadSuccess = USER.EXE
LoadStart = setup.exe
LoadStart = LZEXPAND.DLL
LoadSuccess = LZEXPAND.DLL
LoadStart = VER.DLL
LoadSuccess = VER.DLL
LoadSuccess = setup.exe
INIT=Final USER
INITDONE=Final USER
INIT=Installable Drivers
INITDONE=Installable Drivers
```

.INI entries as parameters

Hardware problems that arise during Windows startups can usually be solved by placing special entries in the Windows system file SYSTEM.INI. However, continually modifying this file can be inconvenient. So, it's possible to specify several INI entries directly as parameters with the Windows startup command.

```
SystemROMBreakPoint
VirtualHDIRQ
EMMExclude
```

Refer to Chapter 10 for more information on INI functions.

2.5 Displaying the Mode

If you've started Windows in a specific mode by using one of the mode parameters, you'll definitely know which mode Windows is using. However, if you've started Windows by simply entering "win", you should determine whether the mode corresponding to your computer's hardware capabilities has been selected. This is the only way you can ensure that Windows is fully utilizing your computer and its memory.

From the Program Manager, open the *Help* menu and select the *About Program Manager...* menu item.

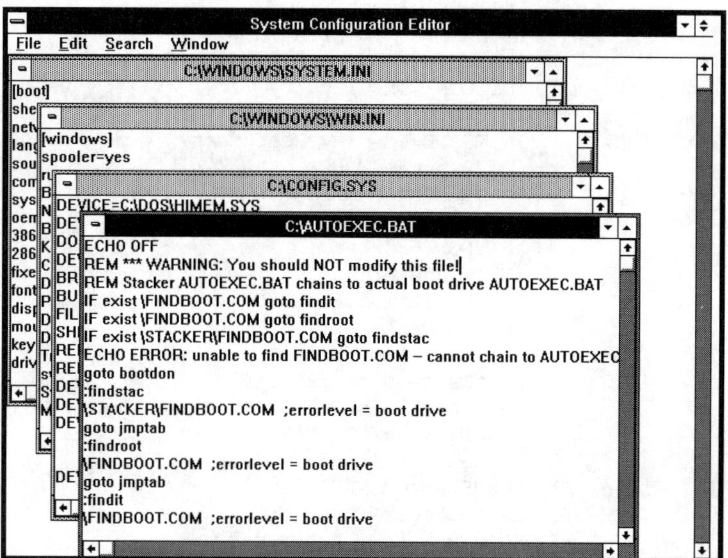

Information about the Windows mode

Along with copyright and license information, this dialog box displays the current mode in which Windows is operating. Here you can determine whether Windows is operating in the mode that's best for your system.

The dialog box also displays the amount of available memory. If an application is started, this value decreases by the amount of memory required by that application. You'll also see a value indicating the percentage of all available system resources currently being utilized. However, since Windows also uses some of these resources, this figure will never reach 100%.

When Windows operates in 386 Enhanced mode, these values may indicate that more memory is available than your computer actually has. This occurs when Windows uses virtual memory. This type of memory is included as part of the system resources.

2.6 Starting Windows with Applications

In Windows, you can start applications in several ways. Usually, you open an application from within Windows by double-clicking the icon in the Program Manager.

You can also select the filename and the *File/Run...* command from within the File Manager.

However, you usually know which application you'll be using first. There are several ways this application can be loaded automatically when Windows starts.

Which method is ideal for you depends on how often you use the application.

Executing applications in the StartUp group

If you'll be using the application only in the near future or only during the current computing session instead of permanently, copy its icon to a special StartUp group of the Program Manager.

The applications in this group are automatically loaded when Windows starts.

Copying application icons to the StartUp group

To copy an icon to the StartUp group, select the icon by clicking it and choose *Copy...* from the *File* menu. Then, in the dialog box that appears, select the StartUp group as the destination for this icon. The next time you start Windows, the application will open automatically.

Removing icons from the group

Copying an application icon into the StartUp group won't modify the WIN.INI file, as was the case in Windows 3.0, so this isn't a permanent operation. If you don't want this application to load automatically at your next startup, simply remove it from the StartUp group.

Before doing this, determine whether the icon was originally copied or moved into the group. If it was copied into the group, you can delete the icon by selecting it and pressing Del or by selecting *Delete* from the *File* menu.

However, if the icon was moved to the StartUp group, then you should move it back to its original source group. This prevents the application from being completely removed from your Program

Manager. To move the icon, you can either drag it to its original location with your mouse (by pressing and holding the mouse button and moving your mouse) or by marking the icon and selecting *Move...* from the *File* menu.

Starting applications together with Windows

An application can also be started directly by adding its name to the Windows startup command. For example, to start Write together with Windows, use the following command:

```
win write Enter
```

The space between the two commands is very important. Both program calls don't require a filename extension. Windows will look for the specified application in the WINDOWS directory. If you want to start an application that's located in a different directory, you must specify its path:

```
win c:\programs\word5\word Enter
```

It's also possible to load a specific file that belongs to the specified application at the same time. Simply enter the path, if necessary, and the filename after the Windows and application calls. For instance, to call a Word file named "Letter1", you could use the following command:

```
win c:\programs\word5\word c:\files\wordfiles\Letter1 Enter
```

In this example, the text file is located in a different directory than its application. This helps keep the disk organized.

Loading/starting applications at Windows startup

If you always work with the same applications, you can specify these application names in the WIN.INI file. Windows can either load these applications as icons or start them immediately. To modify the WIN.INI file, either use the SYSEDIT.EXE application or simply open the file (this will automatically place the file in the Notepad).

In the first section of WIN.INI you'll see the line "load=". Immediately after this line enter the names of the applications or files that should be loaded as icons. For example, if you want to load the Clock, Calendar, and Paintbrush, type the following:

```
load=clock calendar pbrush
```

Since these files are located in the Windows directory, you don't have to include the paths. Filename extensions are also unnecessary because all loadable or executable files must contain .COM, .EXE, .BAT, or .PIF filename extensions. If applications located in other directories must be loaded, you must specify their paths.

If specific applications must be started immediately upon loading Windows, you must enter their filenames in the Run line. Use the same conventions here as mentioned in conjunction with load.

Once you've completed the changes to WIN.INI, save the file and restart Windows. Your changes will be effective and you can observe the results of the modified INI file.

Remember, the procedure we just described is a permanent change that will remain in effect until WIN.INI is changed again.

2.7 Exiting Windows

Open the *File* menu of your Program Manager and select the *Exit Windows...* menu item. Before quitting, Windows displays a dialog box, in which you can confirm your actions or cancel the exit command. Click the OK button in this dialog box to exit Windows.

You can also select *Close* from the Control menu of your Program Manager to exit Windows. This command closes a window. Since the Program Manager is the window that represents the Windows interface, when this window closes, you'll leave Windows. To access the *Close* command more quickly, press Alt + F4.

Closing Windows together with applications

If an application is running when you press this key combination (e.g., if you've started Excel), this open application window (Excel) closes. This applies to all applications that are still open within your Program Manager. If you've started several Windows applications and want to exit Windows, you should switch from your Task Manager to the Program Manager (press Alt + Esc) and then close Windows. By doing this, you don't have to close each application window. Instead, Windows checks whether any changes have been made with each application and suggests saving any such changes before quitting.

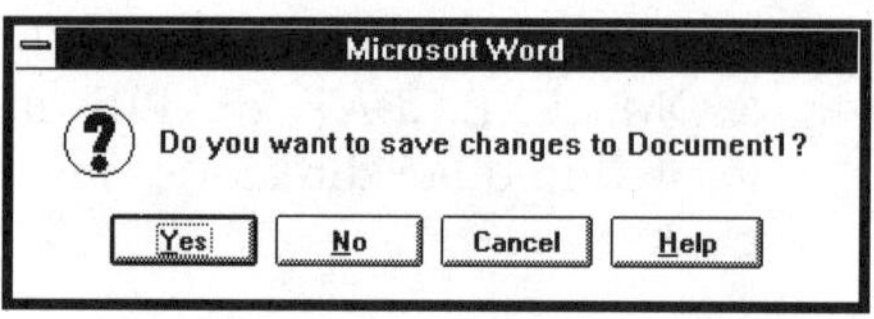

Confirmation to save any changed files

If you've been working with non-Windows applications, you won't be able to use the above procedure because the Program Manager cannot close these applications. In these instances, you must activate the non-Windows applications and close them using the appropriate commands. Only then can you exit Windows from the Program Manager.

You can also close non-Windows applications by using the *Settings...* item in the Control menu of the application icon or window. The Terminate... command button is located there. This is identical to using the End Task button in your Task Manager. However, be extremely careful when using these methods. Since these functions simply halt the running applications, any open files aren't properly saved and closed. This may result in data loss. So, you should always close non-Windows applications properly.

Saving the Program Manager settings

Once you've rearranged your Program Manager interface according to your own needs, you can save this arrangement so that it will remain intact for future Windows sessions. To save these current settings, select *Save Settings on Exit* from the *Options* menu of the Program Manager. A checkmark next to this option indicates that it's active. The next time you start Windows, the current user interface settings will be used.

However, if you want to retain your current settings indefinitely, you should start Windows again after quitting it, and remove the checkmark from the *Save Settings on Exit* option. Otherwise, any changes you make in your next and future sessions will be saved when you exit Windows. This could alter the current settings, which you want to retain.

3. Using Windows

Using the mouse and keyboard

Although you can access all Windows functions through the keyboard, only by using the mouse can you fully use Windows' user-friendliness.

Window controls

Windows contain control elements that are used to manipulate the Windows. They are use to move, size, minimize, maximize, and close windows.

Selecting a menu

Menus can be selected using the mouse or with the keyboard. Menus are used to access the commands of Windows.

Selecting a command

Commands can be selected using the mouse or with the keyboard. Commands are used when working with Windows.

The dialog box

Dialog boxes are used to inform the users of what Windows is doing. They form a type of dialog between Windows and the user.

Components of a dialog box

Dialog boxes contain control elements that are used to interact with Windows. Using these control elements you can inform Windows of your choices for commands.

Activating a window

A Window must be made active before you can work with it. You can activate a Window with the keyboard or the mouse.

Minimizing a window

A Window can be minimized and displayed as an icon. This is useful when you are not currently working in a Window.

Moving a window

A Window can be moved so the other open Windows can be displayed.

Sizing a window

A Window can be sized so the other open Windows can be displayed.

Maximizing a window

A Window can be maximized to use the entire display screen of Windows. This is useful when you are currently working in the Window.

Closing applications through the Control menu

The Control menu of a window allows you to close the application at any time.

3.1 Using the Mouse and Keyboard

As we mentioned, both the mouse and the keyboard can be used to operate Windows. In this section we'll discuss both of these methods. Although using shortcut keys on the keyboard can noticeably speed up operations, mouse access is the most efficient way to use Windows. Once you've worked with both the mouse and the keyboard, you can determine when the mouse should be used and when the keyboard should be used.

Positioning

Using the mouse

The term *positioning* your mouse refers to placing the mouse pointer over a specific object on the Windows screen. The arrow shaped *mouse pointer* follows the movement of the mouse on your desk or tabletop. So, to position the mouse pointer on a particular object, move the mouse in the appropriate direction until the mouse pointer is located on the desired object.

Using the keyboard

Using the keyboard for positioning is more complicated because Windows has several *object levels*. If you're within a specific window, you can use the cursor keys for positioning. However, a mouse pointer isn't visible. Instead, the currently selected object is usually identified by a highlight. This highlighted object is considered *selected* or *marked*. Since a window represents one object level, you cannot access any object outside this window with your cursor keys. To exit this object level you must use the Ctrl + F6 key combination. This moves you to another object level, in which you can use your cursor keys to *select* an object. You can also use Tab to move among object levels. For a complete listing of all key combinations, refer to the Appendices.

Clicking

Using the mouse

The mouse is one of the easiest and frequently-used devices. Clicking your mouse involves positioning the mouse pointer on a specific object and pressing one of the mouse buttons. Most PC mice have two buttons; occasionally a mouse will have three. The left mouse button is usually the one that must be clicked. Clicking the right mouse button is rarely required but we'll indicate when this is necessary. Clicking enables you to *select* objects or *execute* commands.

Using the keyboard

Clicking an object with your mouse is equivalent to *selecting* it, with the cursor keys, as previously described. So, when you use your cursor keys for *positioning*, you automatically *select* or *mark* the object so the next function will apply to it.

Double-clicking

Using the mouse

To *activate* or *execute* an object, move the mouse pointer to the object and quickly press the mouse button twice (without moving the mouse between clicks). For example, if you position your mouse pointer on an application icon and double-click the mouse button, the application will start. It may take you awhile to become familiar with double-clicking. Try holding the mouse absolutely still and quickly press the mouse button twice.

Using the keyboard

The keyboard equivalent of *double-clicking* is pressing the Enter key. As you know from DOS, this key tells your PC to process or execute the commands you've entered. To activate a certain function or to start a specific application, use the cursor keys to select the appropriate object and press Enter.

Dragging

Using the mouse

You can *drag* an object across your screen to change its position. Simply position the mouse pointer on the desired object and hold down the mouse button. Then, while depressing the mouse button, move the mouse until the object is in the desired location on the screen.

Using the keyboard

Unfortunately, there isn't a direct keyboard equivalent for dragging objects with your mouse. However, Windows does provide functions that allow you to move objects. We'll discuss these functions later.

Marking (selecting)

Using the mouse

Marking or *selecting* involves designating the objects and areas that will be affected by the next function that's activated. This process saves time when the same task must be performed for various items. For example, you can use your mouse to *mark* several different files that must be deleted or copied.

Objects and areas are selected or marked in the same way they are dragged. The current object level determines which action (marking/selecting or dragging) is performed. For example, within a text, you can drag the mouse pointer or cursor over any desired area of text, which will then appear highlighted. The selected text can then be modified with any command. So, depending on the current object level, this action will either *drag* or *mark* objects or areas.

Using the keyboard

When using the keyboard, use the cursor keys to make selections. If you want to mark a text, place the cursor at the beginning of the desired area, hold down Shift, and move the cursor over the area using the cursor keys. Similar to areas selected with the mouse, this text will then appear highlighted.

Key combinations

You've already encountered several *key combinations,* such as Ctrl + F6 for moving from one object level to another. In a key combination, two or more keys must be used together in order to perform a task. For example, for the Ctrl + F6 key combination, hold down the Ctrl key while pressing the F6 key. The first key must be depressed before you press the second key; otherwise the desired function won't be executed.

3.2 Window Controls

During a simple startup of Windows (no application included in the program call), the *Program Manager* window appears on the screen. We'll use this window as an example to demonstrate how a window operates in Windows.

The Windows *surface* contains a series of objects and symbols. The term *control* is often used in conjunction with these objects and symbols. This term refers to an object or Windows element that's linked to a specific function.

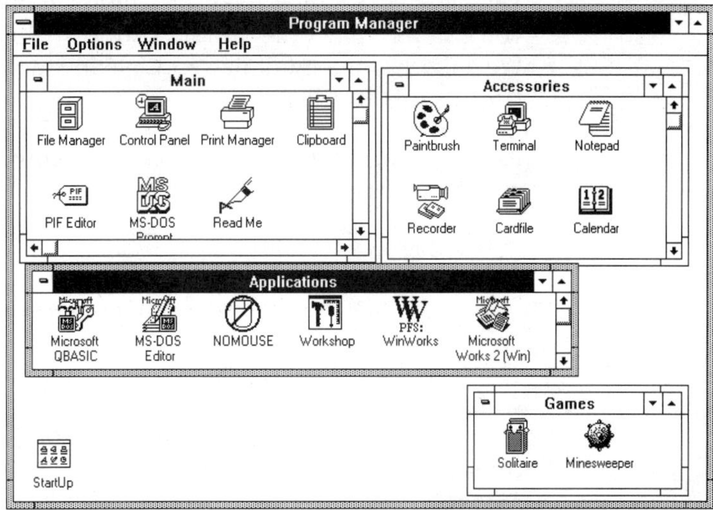

The Program Manager window

The Program Manager title bar

The window has several different controls. The first control is the *title bar*, which displays the window's title. Usually the name of the application, to which the window belongs, appears in the title bar. However, sometimes the name of a particular file that's being displayed in the window may also be used. In the case of the analog display Clock, for example, the title bar displays the date.

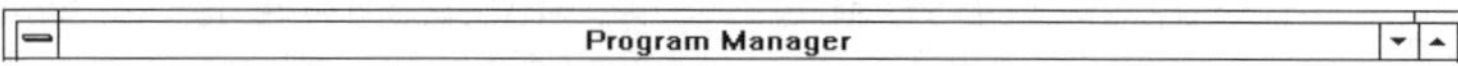

The Program Manager title bar

One important control is the Control menu box, which is located to the left of the title bar. When you click on this control, the Control menu opens. This menu contains commands that enable you to control the execution and display of an application. Which items are included in this menu depends on the application.

Group name

Most of the title bar is used to display the application's name. So, in this case, you'll see *Program Manager* displayed in the title bar. The title bars of the group windows contained in the Program Manager display their corresponding names.

To the right of the title bar, you'll see two other controls. One control is an Up arrow symbol and the other is a Down arrow symbol. The Up arrow is called the Maximize button. This button allows you to *maximize* the window so it occupies the entire screen. The Down arrow is called the Minimize button. With this button you can *minimize* the window so it's displayed only as an *icon*. We'll discuss the minimize and maximize functions in more detail later in this chapter.

Another horizontal bar is located below the title bar. This is called the *menu bar*.

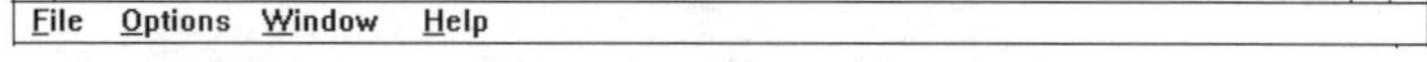

The Program Manager menu bar

Menu bar commands

The menu bar displays the names of the individual menus, from which you can select commands. The *File*, *Options*, *Window*, and *Help* menus are included in the Program Manager. These menus contain all the commands that are needed to operate the *Program Manager*.

Scroll bars

If a window is too small to display its entire contents at one time, *scroll bars* appear to the right (vertical) and at the bottom (horizontal) of the window. Depending on the proportions of the window contents, only one of the scroll bars may appear. For example, if the window contents are too wide, the horizontal scroll bar is displayed. If the window contents are too long, the vertical scroll bar is displayed. To display a scroll bar in a window that doesn't have one, decrease the window's size until part of its contents are no longer visible.

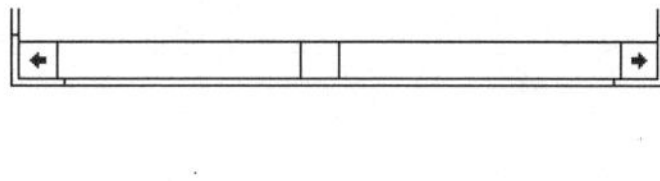

A scroll bar

You can use scroll bars to move the window contents within the window's workspace. Practice using these controls in your Program Manager window. Clicking an arrow button on the horizontal scroll bar moves the window contents to the left or right, depending on the button you've clicked. Also, clicking a button on the vertical scroll bar moves the window contents up or down.

Scrolling window contents

So, by pressing the correct arrow button on a scroll bar, you can move the window contents horizontally or vertically in character or line increments. To scroll more quickly, use the *scroll box*, which is located within the scroll bar. Use the mouse to drag this box to any location on the scroll bar. Moving the scroll box within the scroll bar moves the window contents proportionally.

Scrolling faster

Another way to scroll the contents of a window is by clicking on the scroll bar between one of the arrow buttons and the scroll box. This is a quick way to scroll the contents of a window because it uses larger increments than the arrow buttons.

3.3 Selecting a Menu

The commands that are available in any given Windows application are located under the menu titles listed in the menu bar. These are called pull-down menus. This means that in order to view the commands contained in one of the menus, you must *pull down* that menu. There are several ways to do this. The easiest way is to click on the menu title. For example, click *File*, to open the menu of that name. Notice how the list of menu items is "pulled down" as the menu is opened.

Closing a menu

To close a menu, either click its title again or click the mouse on any other location within the window. If you want to open another menu, the menu that's already opened doesn't have to be closed. Simply open the new menu by clicking its title in the menu bar.

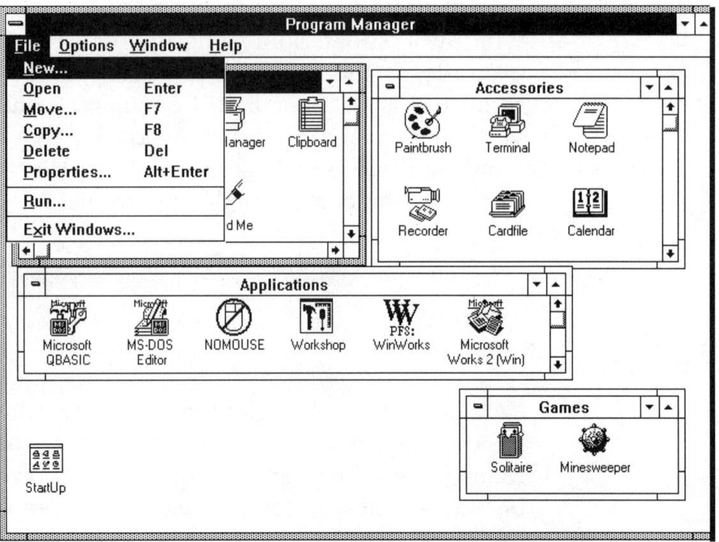

Program Manager with opened File menu

Using the keyboard

To open a menu using the keyboard, simply hold down Alt and press the first letter or the underlined letter of the menu title. So, to open the *File* menu of the Program Manager, press Alt + F.

As you can see, each menu title's first letter is underlined. In applications that have more than one menu title beginning with the same letter, another letter of the menu title is underlined. So, each menu has its own access letter. These letters are also used in combination with Alt. However, unlike in key combinations, Alt doesn't have to be pressed simultaneously with the access letter. Instead, it activates the menu bar. When activated, a highlight appears behind the menu bar. To deactivate the menu bar, press Alt again.

To close a menu, simply press Esc. To switch to another menu without closing the one you've already opened, use the cursor keys to move to the desired menu. You can also press the menu's key combination (Alt + <access letter>).

The Control menu

The Control menu is accessed by the Control menu control box, which is located to the left of the title bar. To open this menu with your mouse, simply click this box. To open this menu with the keyboard, press Alt + Spacebar. We'll describe the various Control menu functions later.

Document window Control menu

The Control menu of a document window is opened using a different key combination than the Control menu of an application window. For example, if you're working with an application, such as Excel, you can access its Control menu by pressing Alt + Spacebar, as previously described. However, within the Excel application window you can open several document windows that also have Control menus. These menus are accessed by pressing Alt + -.

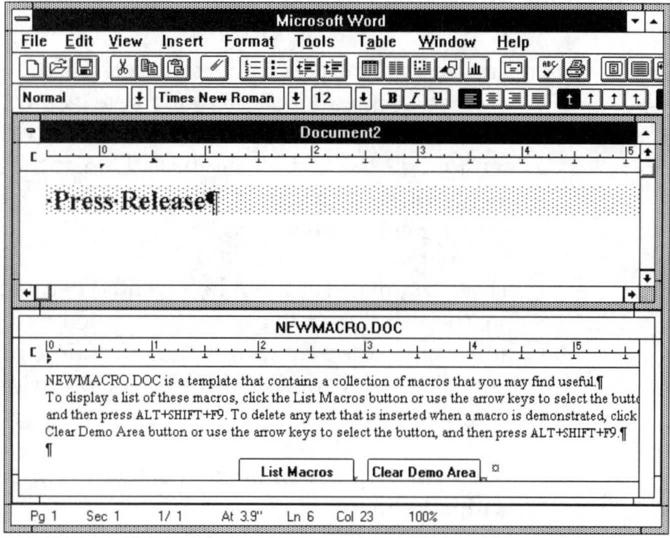

Word 2.0 application window and document window(s)

3.4 Selecting a Command

Using the mouse

To select a command from an open menu, simply click the correct command name. If you've just opened the menu and are still holding down the mouse button, you can move the mouse pointer to the desired command, which will appear in inverse video, and release the mouse button.

Using the keyboard

To select a command with the keyboard, use the cursor keys to move the highlight to the appropriate command. Once the highlight is located on the proper command name, press Enter to execute that command.

However, you can also select a command from an open menu by simply typing its first or underlined letter. For example, to execute *Open* from the active *File* menu, simply type the letter "O." The command is immediately executed.

Using hotkeys

The fastest way to access a command is to use its *hotkey* combination. To determine whether a specific command has a *hotkey*, simply open the menu containing that command. If a command has a hotkey, its key combination is displayed to the right of the command name. For example, the hotkey for *Close*, which is located in the Control menu of any application, is Alt + F4.

With hotkey combinations, you can execute commands without having to open the menu containing the command. Simply press the key combination that executes the desired command.

Inactive commands are shown grayed

You've probably noticed that certain requirements must be met before a command can actually be executed. For example, the *Copy* and *Move* commands in the *File* menu of the Program Manager cannot be executed all the time. Unlike the other commands in the menu, these commands are displayed in gray type. Commands in gray type are called ghosted.

These commands cannot be executed because no objects are selected. So, these commands cannot be applied to anything. *Copy* and *Move* allow you to copy or move files and directories. However, currently only the icons for the different application groups are visible in your window.

So, a command can be executed only if it appears in black type within its menu.

3.5 The Dialog Box

After some commands are selected, a dialog box appears before the command is actually executed. Windows uses these dialog boxes either to receive more information about how the command should be executed or to confirm that the command should be executed.

Commands that use dialog boxes are identified by three periods (...), which follow the command's name in the corresponding menu. A similar dialog box appears when you exit Windows, for instance, after selecting *Close* from the Control menu of your Program Manager.

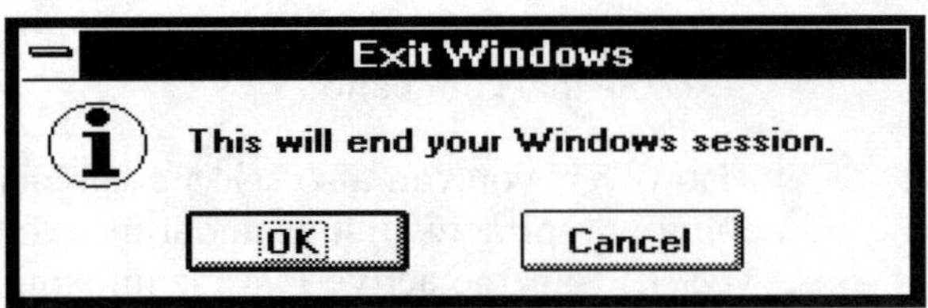

The Exit Windows dialog box before leaving Windows

This dialog box is similar to an application window; it contains a title bar as well as Control menu box, which represents the dialog box's Control menu. This menu contains two commands, of which only one is active. This Control menu and its commands operate the same way as any normal Control menu.

The *Exit Windows* dialog box provides only a limited range of options. It's only purpose is to verify an action. In this case, it verifies whether you really intend to exit Windows.

Diverse dialog boxes

Some commands need additional information or specific parameters from the user in order to execute. These commands usually have more complicated dialog boxes. This type of dialog box appears, for example, when you select *Print* from the *File* menu in the Write application.

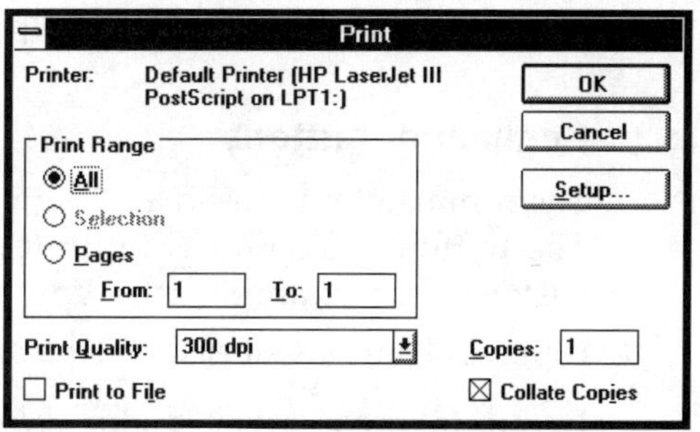

A more diverse dialog box requesting further information

Message boxes

In addition to the normal dialog boxes, Windows uses *message boxes*, which inform the user of a certain status or display an error message. Their structure is identical to normal dialog boxes. Message boxes generally contain one control, which allow you to verify that you've read the message and to continue with your work.

3.6 Components of a Dialog Box

A dialog box can have various types of controls. Some controls are included in all dialog boxes, while others appear only in a few dialog boxes. The most common control is the command button. The following illustration shows the individual controls that are used in dialog boxes:

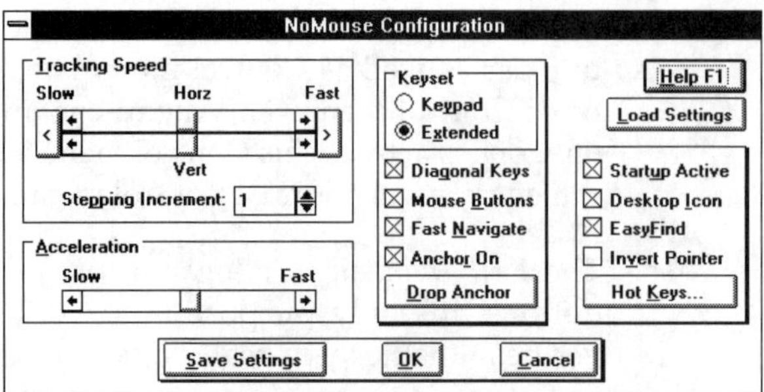

Controls used in dialog boxes

Using the Tab key

To move from one control to another, simply press Tab. The highlight will move from one control to the next, in a predetermined order called the *tab order*. By pressing Shift + Tab, you can move backwards through the tab order.

Command buttons

The command buttons in a dialog box are used for various functions. The button's function is indicated by the name displayed on its surface. For example, the *Exit Windows* dialog box has two command buttons labeled OK and Cancel These buttons are also found in most other dialog boxes. When the OK button is activated, the command is executed with the settings that were last specified in the dialog box. By activating the Cancel button, you can abort the command entirely. The dialog box closes and any changes that were made will be disregarded.

Using the mouse

The easiest way to activate a command button is by using the mouse. Simply click on the button's surface. The button will actually look like it's being pressed. This is why the term *push button* is commonly used.

Using the keyboard

Before using the keyboard to activate a command button, carefully look at the controls in the dialog box. In the Exit Windows dialog box, you'll see the OK button is outlined and its label is surrounded by a dotted line. This indicates the OK button has the *focus*. When you press Enter, the control that has the focus is activated.

If you want to activate the button that doesn't have the focus, you must first switch the focus to that button. So, in the Exit Windows dialog box, you must switch the focus to the Cancel button before you can activate it. To move the focus, simply press Tab to move to the next control in the tab order. You'll see that the Cancel button is now surrounded by a border and its label is surrounded by a dotted line. Now when you press Enter, this command button is activated.

The labels of some command buttons have an underlined letter. Just as you can open a menu by typing Alt along with the underlined letter in its menu title, you can activate this type of command button by pressing Alt and its underlined letter.

Check boxes

In the *Print* dialog box of the *Write* application, you'll see a control that consists of a small box, which may contain an "x." These controls are known as *check boxes*. When an option's check box contains an "x", the option is active. If the check box doesn't contain an "x", the option is deactivated. In the *Print* dialog box you'll see a check box that enables you to direct the output to a file. If this check box is activated, Write will ask you for the filename to which the data will be written. However, this check box usually isn't activated so output can be directed to the printer.

To activate a check box, click on it with your mouse. You can also press its underlined letter along with Alt. However, since this only moves the focus to the check box, you must then press Spacebar to activate the box. The check box can be deactivated in exactly the same way.

Option buttons

Option buttons are always used in groups. These buttons always refer to a specific function or action that can be executed in various ways. By setting a specific option button within this group, you can determine in which way a function should be executed. In a group of option buttons, only one button may be active at any given time.

The *Print* dialog box contains an option button group that allows you to specify the print range. You can select either *All*, *Selection*, or *Pages*. If text hasn't been selected, then the *Selection* option is invalid and is displayed in gray type. The *Pages* option also contains two text boxes, in which you can enter the range of pages to be printed.

Text boxes

Text boxes enable you to enter information in a dialog box. Various functions require additional information from the user. Text boxes, which are also called entry fields, may be used to specify filenames or to enter information, such as the page range for a print job. These boxes are miniature text editors and their entries can be edited at any time. Text boxes usually appear either completely empty or with a default text already entered.

Making entries in empty text boxes

To enter text in a text box, either click the box with the mouse or select the text box by pressing Tab until the box has the focus. A blinking cursor will then appear in the box. Now you can enter text. Several keys are used for editing your text. Use Backspace to delete characters to the left of the cursor. Use your cursor keys to move within the text box. To delete a block of text, first select the text with the mouse. Then press Del to remove the selected text.

Text boxes with proposed text

Some text boxes contain a default text. When a dialog box, which contains this type of a text box, is opened, the default text in the box is automatically selected. So, if you want to edit the text, it doesn't have to be deleted first. The selected text is deleted as soon as you type your entry. If you want to modify the proposed text, simply click on the character(s) or want to edit. You can also use the cursor keys to move to this character.

List boxes

The list box is another control that's included in most dialog boxes. List boxes contain a list of items that can be selected. To select an item from a list box, click on it with the mouse and then select the appropriate command button, or simply double-click the item. With the keyboard, use the cursor keys to move the highlight to the desired item or type the first letter of the item, and then press Enter.

Some list boxes contain a text box, with a proposed entry, in addition to a list of items. These boxes are called drop-down list boxes. In these boxes, you can either enter text in the text box or select the appropriate item from the list. Which type of list box is used depends on the particular function.

To make an entry in the text box of a drop-down list box, simply click the mouse pointer within the text box. The current entry will appear in inverse video. This indicates that the text is currently selected. So, if you type a new text, it will automatically replace the selected entry. Pressing Backspace will delete the selected text and the blinking cursor will appear in the text box. You can then type a new entry.

However, it's much easier to select an item from the list. To display the list, simply click the Down arrow button to the right of the text box.

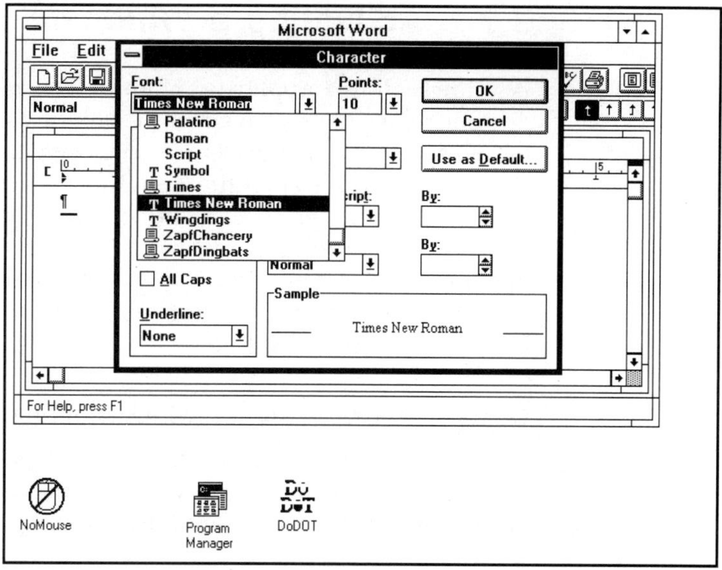

An open list box in a dialog box

Click on the appropriate item to place it in the text box as the current entry. If all of the items cannot fit in the list box, a scroll bar is displayed. Click the up or down arrow button on this scroll bar to locate the desired item.

This process is more complicated with the keyboard. First you must set the focus on the list box. Press Tab until the current item appears in inverse video in the text box, which indicates that the list box is active.

Editing the active item

Now you can edit the entry as previously described. However, you can also use the keyboard to select an item from the list. The Down arrow button to the right of the text box is underlined. This indicates that you can use the keyboard to activate the button by pressing it along with the Alt key. So, simply press Alt + ↓ to open the list box. Now you can move through the list with the cursor keys until you find the desired item.

You can also scroll through the items in the list without actually opening the list. Instead of pressing Alt + ↓, as previously described, simply press ↓. The item located below the current item in the list appears in the text box. You can use ↑ in the same way; the item above the current entry appears in the text box.

Once you've selected the proper item, you can move to another control, such as an option group, by pressing either Tab or the key combination that activates the other control.

3.7 Activating a Window

Windows allows applications and files, usually referred to as documents, to be displayed in their own windows. This is useful because several windows can be displayed on your screen simultaneously. Depending on their sizes and shapes, these windows may overlap each other partially or even completely. Therefore, Windows allows you to alter the size, shape, and position of each individual window. In the following sections we'll describe how to use these windows. We'll start by discussing the basic structure of a window.

General information on window management

There are two types of windows: Windows in which individual applications are running and windows in which files or documents belonging to these applications are opened.

Application and document windows

The Program Manager is actually an application. Its window can be moved to any location on the screen, and its size can be increased to fill the entire screen. However, once its window size is *maximized,* it can no longer be repositioned.

The program groups can also be displayed in a separate window. However, the group window cannot be moved outside of the Program Manager window. Even when the group window is maximized, it doesn't extend beyond the edges of the Program Manager window.

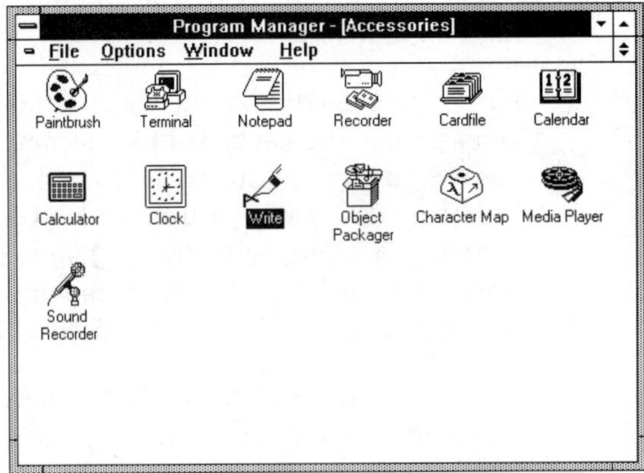

Document windows never lie outside their application windows

If you call an application from within a group window, this application can be moved across the entire screen. So, document windows are always limited in size by the application window to which they belong.

Using the mouse

To switch between windows using the mouse, move the pointer within the window's boundaries and press the mouse button. The active window is indicated by its title bar, which is displayed in a different color than all the inactive windows.

If application windows are completely covered by other windows so they cannot be clicked, you'll need to use the Task Manager to place the window into the foreground again. The Task Manager is called with the *Switch To* command or by pressing Ctrl + Esc. Using the mouse, you can simply double-click the desktop to open the Task Manager.

Using the keyboard

When switching between windows using your keyboard, Windows distinguishes between application windows and document windows. Application windows can be activated from the Task Manager, which is opened by pressing Ctrl + Esc. A faster way to do this is to press Tab while holding down the Alt key. If Tab is pressed repeatedly, all open applications are accessed consecutively. If these keys are released at any time, the currently accessed application is placed in the foreground.

To switch between the document windows of a particular application, use the Ctrl + F6 key combination as previously described. This key combination accesses all document windows consecutively.

3.8 Minimizing a Window

If you aren't currently using an application window, you should minimize the window so it's displayed as an icon. This provides more system resources for the active applications.

The *Maximize* command in the Control menu changes applications, which are currently displayed as icons, to full screen size. To reduce open application windows to icons, use the *Minimize* command. These icons are displayed in the background, at the bottom of your screen. Instead of being closed, the application remains open in the background. A good example of this is the Windows Clock, which displays the current time even as an icon.

Minimizing

Press Alt + Spacebar to open the Control menu in the upper-left corner of your screen. If you're using the mouse, simply click the Control menu box, which is located to the left of the title bar.

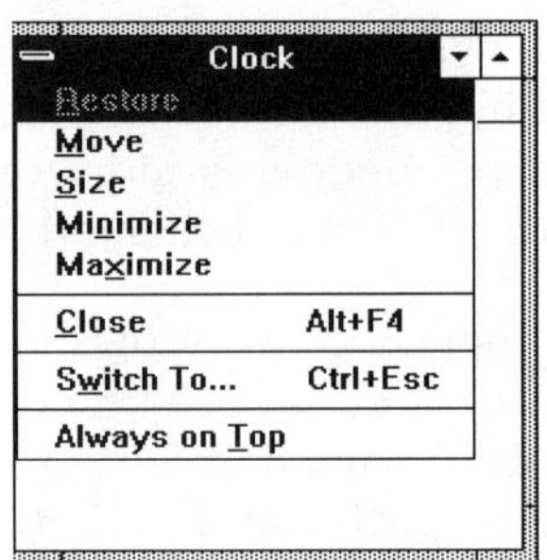

Control menu of the Clock

The icon bar

Select *Icon* and press Enter. In the icon bar, in the lower portion of your screen, a small clock icon should appear. This represents the Clock application. You can see that this application is still in memory and is running in the background.

The Clock window

The Minimize button

It's much easier to minimize a window by using the mouse. There are two arrow buttons located to the right of a window's title bar. The left button (the Down arrow) represents the *Minimize* function. If you click this button, the window is displayed as an icon on your desktop.

Icons in 386 Enhanced mode

In 386 Enhanced mode, a DOS application can be executed in the background while another application runs in the foreground. The *Settings* command in the Control menu allows you to access the dialog box that controls the amount of processing time allotted to the application in the background.

Restore

Use the *Restore* command from the Control menu to return a window, which has been minimized, to its original size. If the window was originally displayed as full size, it will be returned to this size. The *Maximize* command could also be used here.

3.9 Moving a Window

Windows can be moved around the screen. Application windows can be placed at any location on the screen, but document windows can never be moved outside their application window. If you've opened several windows, you may want to reposition and resize them in order to maintain a complete overview.

Using the keyboard

To move a window using your keyboard, open the Control menu of the window you want to move. After selecting *Move*, you'll see that the mouse pointer changes to a four-headed arrow, pointing up, down, left, and right.

Now you can use the cursor keys to move the window in any of the four directions, without affecting its size or shape. When you first press the cursor keys, you'll see that a frame, representing the window, moves in the specified direction. Once you've positioned this frame where you want the window, press [Enter] to move the window to this location.

Using the mouse

To move a window with your mouse, grab the window's title bar by positioning the mouse pointer on the bar and pressing the mouse button. Don't release the button until you've finished moving the window. Now when you move the mouse, a frame, which has the same size and shape as the window, is dragged in the same direction. Once you release the mouse button, the window appears at the new location of the frame.

Whenever you move a window, that window will be active. Because of this, the window may cover other, inactive windows when you move it.

3.10 Sizing a Window

Each window can be individually enlarged. However, the size of a window is determined by its type.

Application windows (e.g., Program Manager, Write, Excel, etc.) can cover the entire screen. But windows within applications, such as the group window within the Program Manager, can only be enlarged up to the boundaries of their parent window.

Using the keyboard

Select *Size* from the window's Control menu. The mouse pointer again appears as a four-headed arrow and is located in the center of the window. Using the cursor keys, you can determine in which direction you want to increase or decrease the window size.

Pressing a cursor key moves the mouse pointer to one of the window borders. For example, [↓] moves the pointer to the lower edge of your window and [↑] moves the pointer to the upper edge. If you press the same cursor key again, a frame representing the window's border is moved. You can continue to press this key until you reach the desired size.

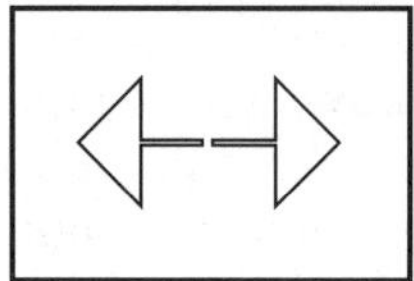

Double arrow indicates the direction

Each window border can always be moved in either direction. Depending on the cursor key you press, the window size will either increase or decrease.

It's also possible to resize a horizontal and vertical side proportionally. For example, if you want to resize the lower and left sides of a window, select *Size* and press [↓]. A double arrow now appears at the lower edge of the window. Now press [←], and the double arrow will appear in the lower-left corner of the window. Then you can use the cursor keys to change both of these sides proportionally.

Using the mouse

However, it's easier and faster to size a window using a mouse. Simply position the mouse pointer on a side or corner of the window border. A double arrow will appear. By holding down the mouse button, you can move the window border in the desired direction. Releasing the mouse button will resize the window accordingly.

3.11 Maximizing a Window

By using *Maximize*, you can enlarge an active window or icon to full screen size. This is particularly useful if you want to work with only one application. Remember that document windows are limited by the size of their application windows, which they cannot exceed. For example, if you maximize the group window within the Program Manager, it will still lie inside the borders of the Program Manager.

Activate a window that you want to maximize. Then select *Maximize* from the window's Control menu.

It's easier to maximize a window by using the mouse. Simply click the Maximize button. This button is located to the right of a window's title bar and is identified by the Up arrow.

To return a window to its original size, simply select *Restore* from its Control menu.

The Restore button

If you're using a mouse, you can restore the window to its original size by clicking the Restore button. This button is located where the Maximize button was before the window was maximized.

However, now it's identified by two arrows instead of one. By clicking this button, you'll restore the window to its normal size.

The Restore button is located only in windows that have been maximized. If a window is currently displayed as an icon in the lower portion of the screen, you can access its Control menu by clicking on it.

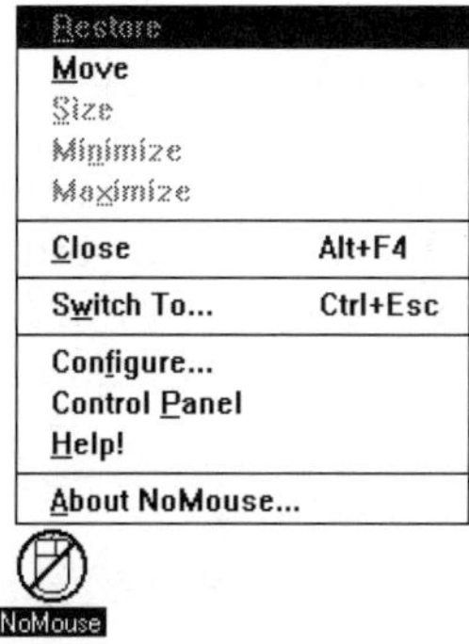

Control menu of an icon

You can also use *Restore* to return the window to its original size.

3.12 Closing Applications through the Control Menu

Every Windows application runs in its own window. Some of these applications, such as Word and Excel, are able to work with several documents simultaneously. To make it easier to manage these documents, each one is located in a separate window.

If a window is closed, its application or document is also closed. An application that has been closed isn't minimized as an icon and must be restarted if you want to work with it again. This also applies to document windows.

Closing applications

To close an application, activate its window and open the Control menu either with your mouse or by pressing Alt + Spacebar. When you select *Close* the application ends and the window closes.

Closing documents

If you want to close a document window, for instance in Word for Windows, activate the document window and open its Control menu or press Alt + -. Selecting *Close* will close the document window. If you press Alt + Spacebar, the Control menu of the actual application, in this case Word, would open.

Using shortcut keys

Windows provides two key combinations for closing application and document windows. By using these key combinations, you don't have to access the Control menu. To close a particular window, simply activate the window and press one of the following key combinations (a menu cannot be opened at this time):

Alt + F4 for closing an application window

Ctrl + F4 for closing a document window

Exiting Windows

If you close a window while the Program Manager is active, you'll exit Windows. So, the Program Manager represents Window's main window or *shell*. If this window is closed, Windows will first ask for verification and then return you to the DOS surface.

Verifications

Once you've selected the command or entered the appropriate key combination for closing a window, Windows checks the application's files to determine whether any changes were made since the last save. For example, if you entered something in the Notepad, but didn't save this change before closing the window, Windows displays a warning message.

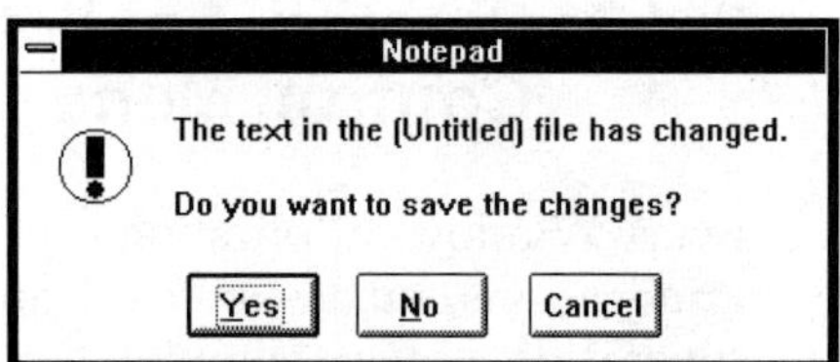

Forget to save? No problem!

Then you must specify whether the changes should be saved. If you haven't specified a filename for the document but select *Yes*, Windows will ask you to enter a filename for the document.

These safety checks are performed only for Windows applications. If you answer *No* when you're asked whether the changes should be saved, the application simply closes without saving any changes. So, before answering "No" to this verification, you should determine whether these changes are important.

Closing non-Windows applications

If you're operating Windows in Enhanced 386 mode and running a non-Windows application, such as dBASE IV or Word 5, within a window, you cannot use the previous method to close the application. In these instances the window only presents an environment, in which the application can operate, and has only limited influence on how this application operates. If you open the Control menu of a window containing a non-Windows application, you'll notice that *Close* is displayed as grayed, which indicates that this command isn't active.

So, you must close non-Windows applications through their own appropriate commands or functions. This is the only way their windows will be cleared from the screen.

☞ You can also close non-Windows applications by using the *Settings* command in the Control menu of the application's window. Under this function you'll find the *Quit* button, which is equivalent to the *End Task* button in the Task Manager. However, you should use these methods very carefully. Since these functions interrupt the application without warning, its files cannot be closed properly and data can easily be lost. So, you should close non-Windows applications with their own commands whenever possible.

Closing with PIF option

Usually you cannot close Windows, or the Program Manager, if a non-Windows application is still open. First you must activate the non-Windows application and close it using its own command before Windows can be exited. This rule applies in all cases except when the *Close window at end* option is marked in a PIF file belonging to the application. However, you should use this option very carefully because it prevents Windows from making any type of verification before the application is closed, even if changes have been made.

4. The Windows Help System

Using the help system

By using the Windows Help system, you can easily obtain online help texts about an application. For example, a Help text can contain explanations on operating the program, important information, tips for insiders, or responses to error messages.

Since the user-friendliness of programs is becoming more important, most Windows applications contain a Help system that provides special information.

The window in which the Help texts are displayed is provided by the Windows system and is called WINHELP.EXE.

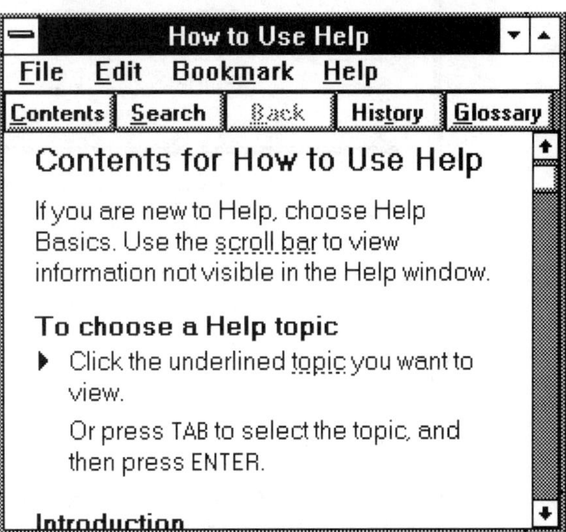

The Help function

In this chapter we'll explain how to operate the Help system, its buttons, and its menus.

Later, we'll discuss how you can create your own custom Help system using Microsoft QuickC for Windows (see Chapter 33).

4.1 Using the Help System

Starting Help

There are several options for starting the Windows Help system. Which option you use depends on the particular program from which you want to start Help.

Most Windows programs, such as the Program Manager, have a *Help* menu that contains several menu items. *Help* is the last menu in the menu bar. Only the last item, *About...*, displays its own descriptive dialog box, instead of branching to the Help system.

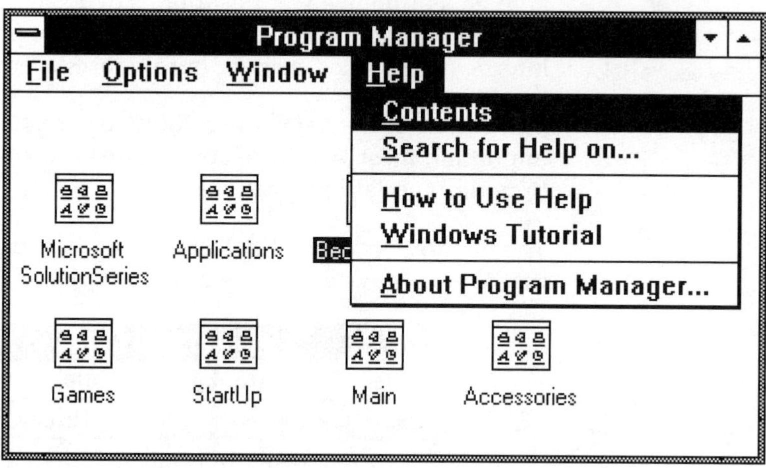

Starting the Help system from the Program Manager

When you select any other menu item from the Help menu, the Help window opens and displays the corresponding Help text. This window looks the same in all applications but its contents change. Selecting the *Contents* menu item takes you to the current Help system's index. This index lists all the Help topics that are available on the current application.

The *Windows Tutorial* menu item in the Program Manager doesn't enable the normal Help system. Instead, it loads a special maximized window, which contains a brief mouse tutorial for Windows. You can exit this tutorial at any time by pressing Esc.

The F1 key

You can also enable the Help system by pressing F1. If you haven't made any selections in the current application, pressing F1 returns you to the Contents. In many applications, pressing F1 when a menu item is selected displays Help system information that applies to that menu item. This method of accessing the Help system is called context-sensitive help.

If you've used a programming language, such as Visual Basic, Microsoft QuickC for Windows, or Turbo Pascal for Windows, then you've probably used their respective Help systems. Each of these languages has a comprehensive Help system that provides information about Windows and language-specific information.

The Turbo Pascal editor and QuickC editor react differently. For example, if you need information on the MessageBox parameters in Turbo Pascal, select the word "MessageBox" and click the right mouse button. Turbo Pascal searches the Help system, then displays a description of MessageBox. If you need information about MessageBox from within the QuickC Editor, select MessageBox and press F1.

You can close the Help window at any time from the Control menu. Be sure to close Help no later than the end of the program from which you called Help. This doesn't occur automatically; it must be programmed accordingly.

Additional information

Many terms in the Help texts are underlined with dotted lines. This indicates that you can obtain additional information about this term in a special pop-up or secondary window. Simply click the word to display the information. The explanation disappears as soon as you press any key. The pointer changes to a hand when it overlaps an underlined word.

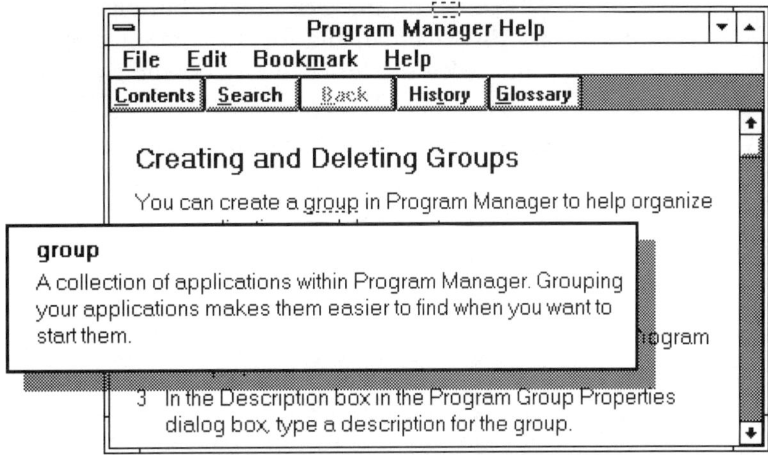

Additional information about the underlined terms

The Help buttons

The tasks of the buttons

After you start Help, the Help topic that loads determines which buttons are visible and can be selected or which buttons are inactive.

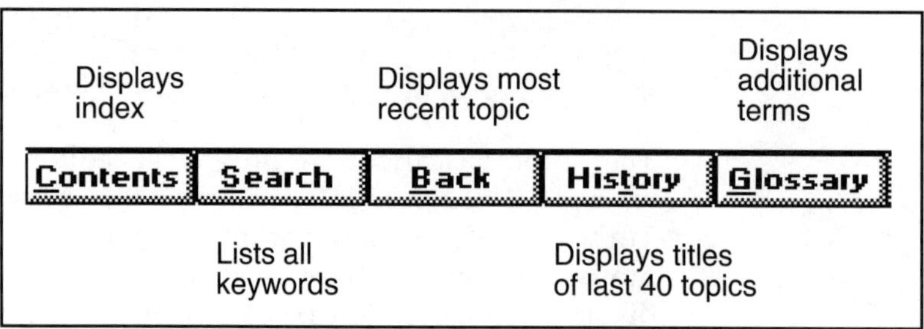

The Help buttons

The Contents button

Contents

When you're in the Help system, you can always move to the top level by clicking the Contents button. Each Help system has a Contents topic that lists other topics that are underlined. When you move the pointer to a topic, it turns into a hand. This indicates that you can click this term to move to this topic.

The Search button

Search

When you select the Search button, a dialog box, containing two list boxes and three command buttons, appears. All the keywords are displayed in the top list box in alphabetical order. You can either type the term you're looking for in the text box above this list box or scroll through the list using the scroll bar until you find the desired term. Then either click the Show Topics button or press Enter to display all the topics available on this keyword in the bottom list box.

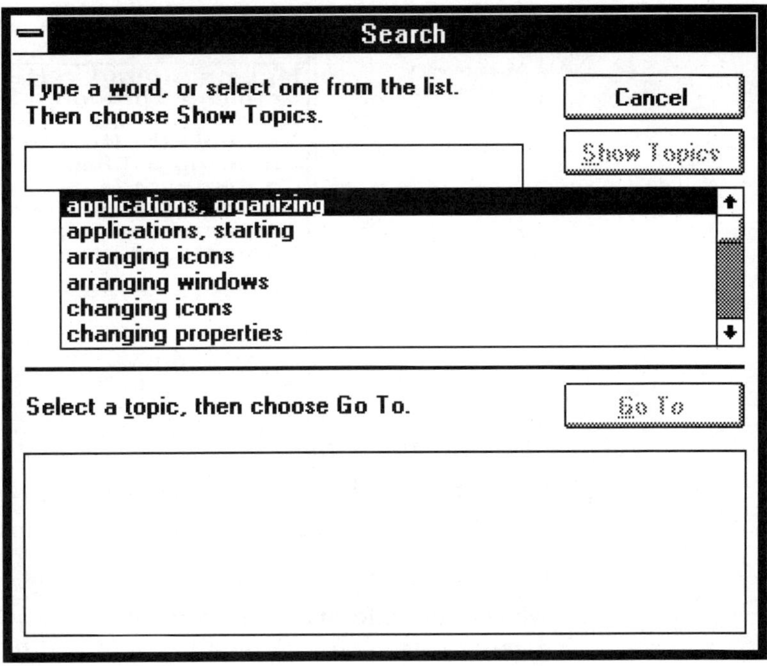

Looking for information in the Search dialog box

You can either press Enter or click the Go To button to display information about the topic you've selected. To cancel the search at any time, click Close. This removes the *Search* dialog box from the screen. The next time you enable *Search*, the last keyword you searched for is displayed.

Ideal Help systems include enough keywords to address each topic. This makes the Help system extremely user-friendly.

The Back button

Back

The Help system stores the sequence in which you moved through Help topics. Click the Back button to reconstruct the path you took through the different topics.

The History button

History

When you click the History button, a small window appears listing the previously selected topics. You can trace up to 40 topics. To return to a particular topic, simply double-click its title.

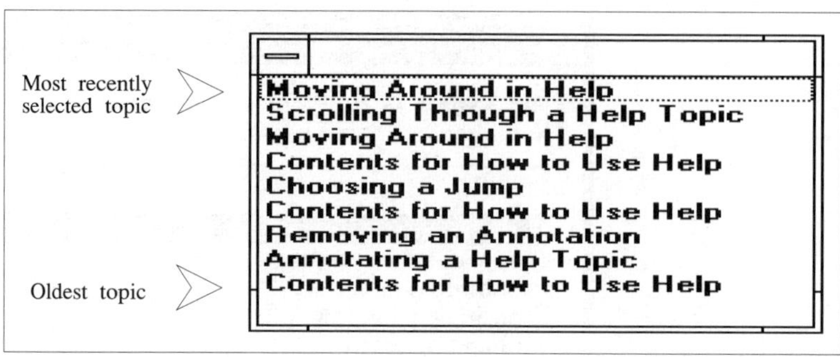

History

The Glossary button

Glossary

If you enable Help from the Program Manager or the File Manager, there is an extra button in Help called Glossary. Clicking the Glossary button displays a small window containing terms for which more information is available. An explanation of the term appears when you click on a keyword and then disappears when you press any key.

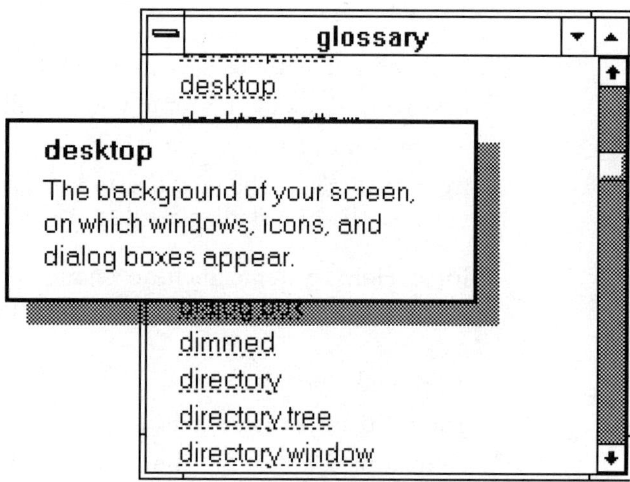

Glossary

Additional buttons: The << and >> buttons

Browsing with << and >>

These two buttons let you browse through a sequence of interrelated keywords so that you can access the previous or subsequent term. When you reach the first or last keyword in the sequence, the corresponding button is displayed in gray, indicating that you are at the beginning or the end of the sequence.

Along with these buttons, the Help window also has a menu with four menu titles: *File*, *Edit*, *Bookmark*, and *Help*. These titles and their menu items are explained in the next section.

The Help menus

The File menu

File

This menu consists of four menu items. Two of these menu items allow you to print information and one lets you close the Help window.

The *Open...* item loads Help files from other Windows applications. This allows you to read Help texts from other programs without loading the applications themselves. You can select the desired Help file from a dialog box.

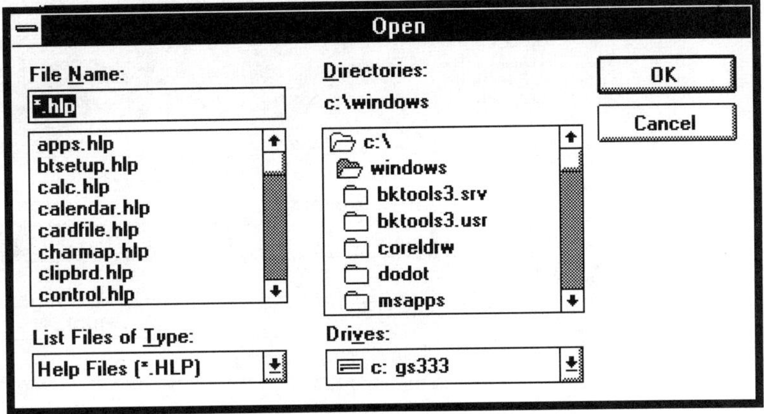

Open dialog box

The Edit menu

Edit

Select *Copy* to place the current text in the Help window in the Clipboard. When you select *Copy*, another window, which contains the entire text of the current topic, is activated. You can either copy everything to the Clipboard by clicking the Copy button or select only a specific part of the text and then click the Copy button. Then only the selected text is copied.

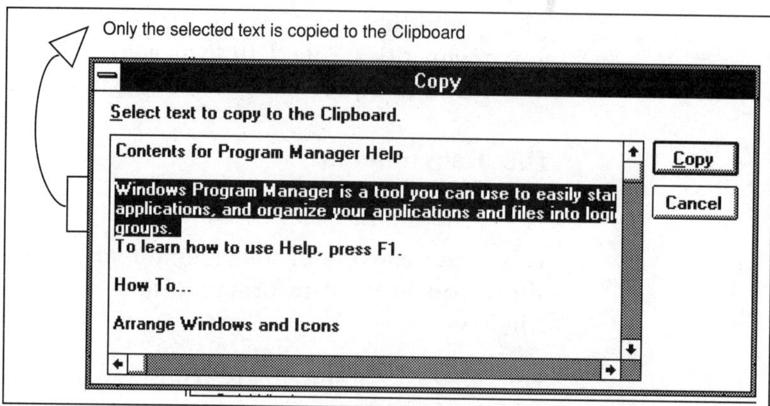

Copying the text of the Help system

If you want to supplement the existing Help text with notes of your own, use the *Annotate...* menu item. When you select *Annotate...*, a dialog box appears with a text box, in which you can type in your own text or paste text from the Clipboard.

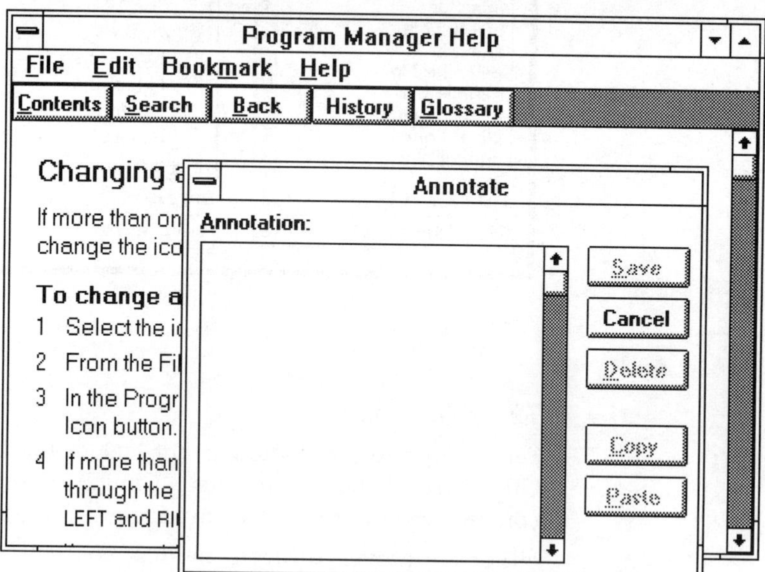

Annotate dialog box

The dialog box disappears when you click the Save button. Help places a paper clip icon to the left of the current Help topic's title. This indicates an annotation. You can read the annotation by double-clicking the paper clip icon.

The Bookmark menu

Bookmark

You can add a bookmark to any topic and then use it to jump directly to that topic. You can specify your own name or use a predefined title for each bookmark. When you select *Bookmark*, all the existing bookmarks are displayed. When the user selects a name, Help jumps to the appropriate topic.

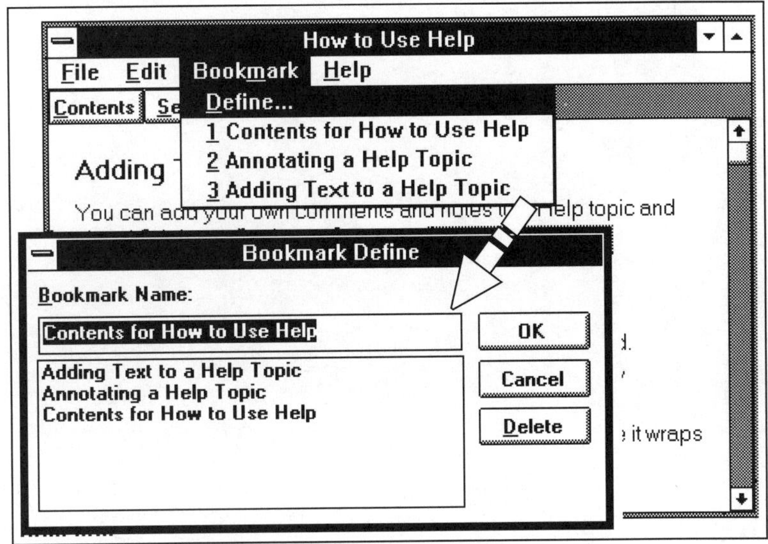

The Bookmark menu

The Help menu

Help

The WINHELP.EXE Help function also has its own help file. It provides basic explanations about how to use Help. When you enable the *Help/How to Use Help* command, you see *Contents for How to Use Help* in the Help window. Then you can jump to one of the following topics.

- Help Basics
- Help Buttons
- Help Menu Commands
- Various HOW TOs

For information on creating your own Help system, see Chapter 33.

5. Installing Windows Correctly

Making backup copies

Make copies of the original Windows diskettes, use the copies to install Windows. Store the original Windows diskette in a safe place.

Starting the installation program

Windows must be installed properly before it can run effectively on your computer. In this chapter we'll discuss the options and running the SETUP program.

Installing unsupported drivers

Most computer and monitor types, graphics cards, etc. are currently supported by Windows. If you have components that aren't listed, you'll have to try the options listed in this section to install the correct driver.

The Windows phase of SETUP

The Windows phase of the Setup program allows you to customize Windows to your machine. This phase setups your printers and the applications on your hard drive.

5.1 Making Backup Copies

Windows includes an easy-to-use installation program that helps you copy the necessary data from diskette to the hard drive. Before starting the installation procedure, you should create backup copies of the Windows system diskettes. You should use only diskettes that have the same disk capacity. Windows is distributed in two different disk formats:

Format	Capacity	Requires
3.5"	720K	7 diskettes
5.25"	1.2 Meg	5 diskettes

Making backup copies

To make backup copies with only one disk drive, use the DOS command:

```
DISKCOPY A: A:
```

You'll be prompted to insert the original diskettes in the disk drive. When you press Enter the copy process begins. As the copying process continues, you'll be prompted to place a new diskette in the disk drive. Unformatted diskettes can also be used.

This procedure must be repeated several times until a diskette is completely copied. Perform the same procedure with the remaining diskettes. After all diskettes are copied, store the original diskettes in a safe place. Then continue working with the backup copies.

5.2 Starting the Installation Program

You can start the Windows installation program in various ways by using switches. Each switch specifies a different type of execution. The following gives a brief description of all SETUP switches:

SETUP /?

This switch lists all the switches and their meanings.

SETUP /A

With the Administrative switch, all data on the Windows diskettes will be uncompressed and copied to the hard drive. The data will also be write-protected. This switch is needed to install Windows on a network.

SETUP /N

With the network server switch, a windows installation is performed on a network. This network usually contains only the drivers for special hardware components and the data groups for the corresponding workstation. However, first all the Windows files must be copied to the server with the /A switch.

SETUP /I

Windows performs an automatic test so the corresponding drivers for the selected components will be included in the installation process. Use this switch to avoid this hardware test. With many network cards and controllers, Windows may lock up during this test. If this occurs, start SETUP without the test and manually configure the components during installation.

SETUP /B

This switch specifies monochrome mode.

SETUP /P

This switch specifies standard mode.

SETUP /O:filespec

This switch specifies the location of the SETUP.INF file (if it isn't located on the current drive).

SETUP /S:filepath

If the Windows setup files aren't located on the current drive, use this switch to specify their location.

SETUP /H :filespec

This switch specifies batch mode setup. The files specified in this switch contain the user's configuration settings. So, only limited user input is necessary during the installation. This switch is helpful when Windows will be installed on similar computers because the hardware components must be installed only once.

The SETUP program

Place the first diskette in the A: drive and log to it by typing:

`A:` Enter

To call the installation program, type the following command:

`SETUP` Enter

The program loads after a few seconds. Then several messages, which provide information about the installation procedure, appear. The installation is divided between a DOS and a Windows procedure. In the DOS portion the selected hardware is tested, the Windows path is placed on the hard drive, and the files from the Windows diskettes, which are needed for starting Windows and running the Windows procedure, are copied to the hard drive.

The Setup can be performed in two ways:

1. Express Setup Press Enter
   If you're completely unfamiliar with your computer, you should choose *Express Setup*. User input isn't required with this option. Windows will be installed as well as possible on your computer with help from standard setup.

   It's always possible that, depending on the type of computer, this option won't select optimum settings. However, this usually applies to only non-standard computers.

2. Custom Setup Press C
   Custom Setup requires user input several times during the installation procedure. These requests allow you to alter the standard configuration and adapt it to your own needs.

   So, you can, for example, determine the directory in which Windows should be installed. Also, it's only possible to install special drivers (e.g., monitor drivers) by using *Custom Setup*.

The following setup options can be performed only with *Custom Setup*:

Update from a previous version

After a selection has been made, SETUP looks on the hard drive for a previous version of Windows. If a previous version is found, the special files can be updated.

So, the files that have been changed since the last version are simply copied. However, if you want to install Windows anew, then you must change the default of the standard directory for Windows. The name *C:\WINDOWS* is given as the default.

When you press Enter, the names are overwritten and the directory path is automatically created on your hard drive.

However, if you want to install Windows on a second hard drive (if available) and under another directory path, press the Backspace key and enter the desired command.

Selection of hardware components

The following is a display of the selected hardware:

```
Windows Setup
=============

    Setup has determined that your system includes the following hardware
    and software components. If your computer or network appears on the
    Hardware Compatibility List with an asterisk, press F1 for Help

       Computer:          MS-DOS System
       Display:           VGA
       Mouse:             Microsoft, or IBM PS/2
       Keyboard:          Enhanced 101 or 102 key US and Non US keyboards
       Keyboard Layout:   US
       Language:          English (American)
       Network:           No Network Installed

       No Changes:        The above list matches my computer.

    If all the items in the list are correct, press ENTER to indicate
    "No Changes." If you want to change any item in the list, press the
    UP or DOWN ARROW key to move the highlight to the item you want to
    change. Then press ENTER to see alternatives for that item.

 ENTER=Continue  F1=Help  F3=Exit
```

The hardware selection for Windows 3.1.

Configuration of the computer

The installation program automatically determines your computer's configuration. However, you should carefully check the list of hardware settings because a computer error can occur. To activate a setting, select it using the cursor keys. The active setting appears in inverse video. Press the Enter key.

A menu appears which offers several options. From this list you can select the corresponding monitor, keyboard driver, etc. The following settings must be made:

Computer and peripherals

- Computer (MS-DOS, Hewlett Packard, Olivetti)
- Display (CGA, EGA, VGA, Hercules...)
- Mouse (Microsoft, Logitech...)
- Keyboard (Standard or extended...)
- Keyboard Layout (German, Finnish dialect...)
- Network (Novell, LAN Manager, none...)

When all input is complete, select the *No Changes* option to install the corresponding drivers.

5.3 Installing Unsupported Drivers

Most computer and monitor types, graphics cards, etc. are currently supported. If you encounter components that aren't listed, you'll have to try a few options.

Using high-performance graphics cards

You can obtain professional results by using high resolution graphics cards. This is especially true if you have the Video Seven 1024i graphics card, for which Windows provides a compatible driver. Many other high performance VGA cards also support a configuration of 800x600 pixels with 256 colors or even 1024x786 pixels with 256 colors. The resulting display has an almost photographic quality.

If you have a high-performance graphics card, simply try the driver for the Video Seven (1024i) or the IBM high-resolution (8514/a). Perhaps your graphics card is compatible with one of these standards. If it isn't, you must obtain a driver from the graphics card manufacturer.

If you cannot obtain a driver from your manufacturer, you should ask them if other graphics cards are compatible with their card. You may be able to obtain a suitable driver in this way. If you cannot find a driver, the standard VGA driver will provide the best results.

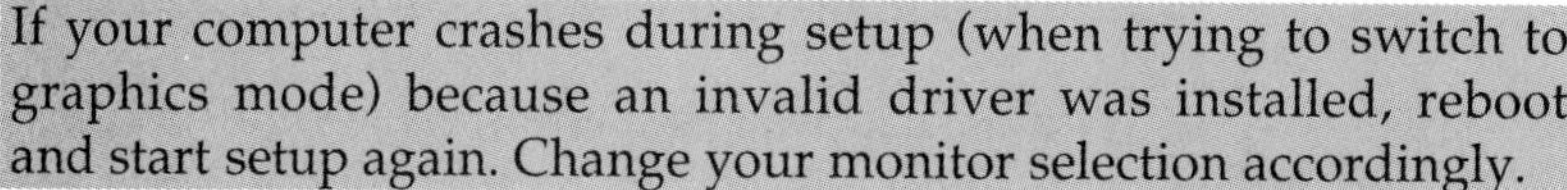

If your computer crashes during setup (when trying to switch to graphics mode) because an invalid driver was installed, reboot and start setup again. Change your monitor selection accordingly.

You'll be surprised by the high resolution and variety of colors that Windows provides. Using 256 colors with a resolution of 800x600 pixels is a configuration designed for graphics programs, such as Designer or Microsoft Powerpoint.

High resolution is extremely interesting when used with Excel or Word for Windows. Under Excel, a resolution of 800x600 pixels with a 14-inch monitor displays 27 rows simultaneously. This is almost 7 rows more than with the previous VGA standard. More rows can also be displayed in Word for Windows.

When installing unsupported drivers (this also includes printer or mouse drivers), the *Others* option appears under several sub-options. If this option is selected, the program expects you to insert the disks corresponding to the respective manufacturer in drive A: and specify the subdirectory, in which the driver files for Windows are located. The setup program will search the diskette for the matching drivers.

For more information, refer to your user manual. If you don't find the information there, you must cancel the installation procedure at this point. Next look at the driver diskettes to determine whether there is a documentation file (README.DOC, INFO.TXT etc.). This file may contain the instructions. Finally, you could search the diskettes to determine whether they contain a directory that has a name corresponding to Windows (WIN, WINDOWS, etc.).

Many graphics cards are automatically installed

Many graphics card manufactures include a program which installs the correct drivers in the Windows directory. It is usually distributed on the driver diskette. Then the desired configuration can be set by the Windows setup.

After the directory has been given, the corresponding driver name appears on the screen. After a driver is selected, the corresponding files will be copied onto the hard drive. Then insert the first Windows diskette in the drive again.

When all settings have been made (the printer settings are specified later), the installation portion is complete. The required files will now be copied to the designated subdirectory on the hard drive and installed.

Slow display refresh

By using the appropriate driver, a resolution of up to 1024x786 pixels can be obtained with a high-performance graphics card. However, such a high resolution may slow down display output when processing large amounts of data that must be transferred to the card. If this occurs, you should use a lower resolution, which requires less memory. It's important to find a compromise between display resolution and display speed (output).

5.4 The Windows Phase of SETUP

As soon as the driver files for the display output have been copied to the hard drive, SETUP appears in Windows mode. This is shown by a corresponding display indicator in the selected graphics mode. You can already see that the new version of Windows has advantages that aren't found in previous versions of Windows. If you have a VGA or EGA graphics card and a color monitor, you'll quickly realize how important they are for screen resolution and displaying colors.

If you eventually upgrade your hardware, you can run the setup program from Windows again. This enables you to change the setup without having to install Windows again.

The SETUP selection screen

Windows consists of several individual components, all of which aren't required in order for Windows to function properly. So, individual components can be excluded from the installation procedure to save space on the hard drive.

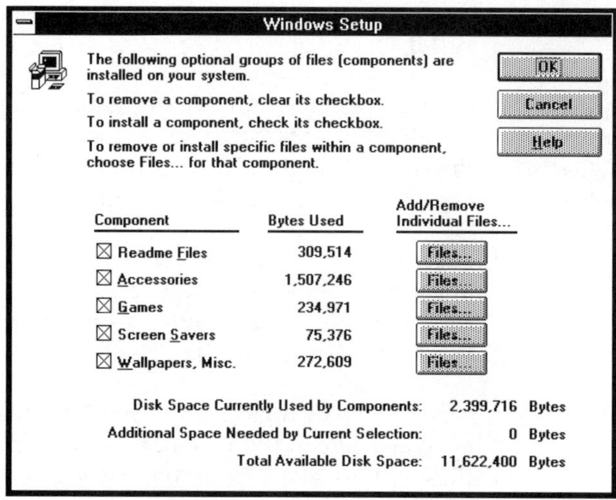

Marking individual Windows components

Select all the components that should be transferred from the Windows diskettes to the hard drive. If you remove a selection, this component won't be copied onto the hard drive. More detailed information is available by clicking the Help button.

However, once Windows is installed you can copy individual components onto the hard drive or remove installed components from the hard drive later using the Windows SETUP program.

Installing subroutines

After the Windows components to be installed are selected, three options are available:

1. Printer installations
2. Applications
3. ReadMe files

The check boxes for these are enabled when they contain Xs. This indicates that all of these functions should be performed. If you want to skip one of the functions, remove the corresponding cross by clicking on it with the mouse or by pressing the key that's underlined in the option name. This can save you some time.

When you press Enter or click the OK button with the mouse, the second part of the installation procedure begins.

At this point, you'll be prompted to insert the next diskette. The Windows programs Paintbrush, Write, Calendar, etc. will now be copied onto the hard drive. A progress bar, which indicates what percentage of the installation is complete, is displayed.

Building program groups

During the installation (when you'll be prompted several times to change diskettes), the file groups are created. At this time, individual programs will be sorted and linked together in groups. Each group represents a window, which contains the individual programs in compiled form. Various groups are created:

- Main group
- Accessories
- Applications
- Games
- Startup

These groups can be modified once Windows is installed.

Modifying system files

The Windows SETUP program can automatically make the necessary additions to the CONFIG.SYS and AUTOEXEC.BAT system files. The drivers inserted into these files are given standard parameters. Although these aren't the most ideal settings, they're the best alternative for the beginner.

If the automatic modification is selected, the original file contents are saved under the names CONFIG.OLD and AUTOEXEC.OLD. In the AUTOEXEC.BAT file, the path command will be expanded to include the Windows directory. The environment variable SET TEMP will also be set to the Windows directory so temporary files will be saved in this directory. Windows provides the configuration file CONFIG.SYS with the driver HIMEM.SYS for use with extended memory and the driver SMARTDRV.SYS for use with Windows disk cache.

To change these files before the automatic modification, select the corresponding option. Each of the files can be checked and modified with a text editor. The contents will appear in two overlapping windows, which are displayed before and after the changes. You can manually make changes in this window.

If the modifications won't be activated until a later time, Windows saves the proposed changes under the file names CONFIG.WIN and AUTOEXEC.WIN. These files can be renamed later if necessary.

To make changes yourself, prevent the changes on the control panel with break and modify the AUTOEXEC.BAT and CONFIG.SYS files outside of Windows.

Installing the printer

If all the files have been copied to the hard drive, then the first Windows program of the main group is started. This is the Control Panel. This program is used to install the desired printer driver(s). For the moment, however, this applies only to the installation.

Configuring programs

The last installation process involves configuring the programs that you just installed on the hard drive. Obviously this procedure is necessary only if there are programs on the disk. A message, asking which disks should be searched, is displayed. After you specify the disks to be searched, the following window appears:

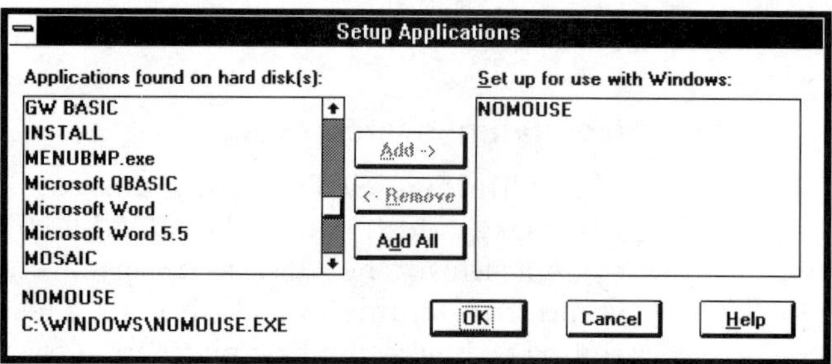

Searching for programs

In the left window, Windows lists the programs that it found on your disk. By selecting the Add button, the marked program is transferred from the left window to the right window. If you select All, the displayed programs will be marked and transferred to the right window. After you've confirmed your actions by pressing the OK button, the program group Applications is created.

All programs in this group are represented by a corresponding icon. Windows applications have their own icons. The non-Windows applications, however, are represented by a very plain icon, which indicates the DOS version of a program. As you'll see later, Windows doesn't always find all the non-Windows applications by searching the directories. Instead, it usually finds only the known ones, such as Word, Lotus, Ventura Publisher, etc. Windows knows these programs because of a special setup file. Under certain conditions, several small utility programs aren't indicated.

In Chapter 12 we'll discuss configuring applications under Windows. You'll learn how to configure all installed programs in an existing group, as well as how to configure those in a new group.

ReadMe files

After Windows has been completely installed, the SETUP program allows you to view the ReadMe information files. These files contain information about any changes that have occurred since the Windows manual was published. These files can also be viewed later, by clicking on the respective file icon with the mouse. This automatically places them in the Notepad. All the files in the windows directory should have the extension .TXT.

Rebooting the system

The configurations and modifications in the CONFIG.SYS and AUTOEXEC.BAT system files are activated only after the computer is restarted. So, activate the reboot icon. Once this is done, the installation procedure for Windows is complete.

Windows is installed in two directories. This is where the Start directory, which calls WIN, is accessed. If you chose another directory during installation, then this directory is your Start directory. All Windows programs, such as SETUP, Calculator and Paintbrush are usually placed in this directory. These files have the extension .EXE.

All additional help files, which are indicated by the extension .HLP, are also found in this directory. Files with the names of the program groups, with the corresponding extension .GRP, are also located here. The names of the programs that are linked to the corresponding groups are found in these files.

A directory with the name \SYSTEM is found under the Start directory. All driver files are found here, for example. Those are the files that Windows requires to work together with the peripheral devices of your computer, such as the monitor, printer, and mouse. These files are indicated by the extension .DRV.

6. Windows Memory Management

Extended memory

Because the MS-DOS operating system has problems addressing more than 640K of main memory, developers have found ways to access extended memory beyond 640K. This chapter explains how extended memory works.

Windows versus DOS

Windows uses extended memory differently than DOS. By using the protected mode of the processor, a connected addressing of complete memory is possible.

Virtual memory

Windows can address additional main memory on an area of the hard drive in 386 Enhanced mode. By swapping between program blocks and data blocks, several applications can run simultaneously, even with small amounts of main memory.

Computer configuration

Besides knowing the fundamentals of memory management, you must also know how additional memory is made available to Windows and which configuration is used. Otherwise, incorrect parameters may be used, causing Windows to slow down.

6.1 Memory Basics

Memory is one of the most important parts of a computer. There are two types of memory. One type is mass memory, such as hard drives and diskettes. With this type of memory, data can be permanently stored. The other type is main memory, which is used to process information. Main memory is considered volatile (temporary), because the data contained in it is lost when the user switches off the computer. Main memory, also called RAM (Random Access Memory), is loaded by the operating system when the computer is switched on. If you enter a command from the keyboard (e.g., if you start Windows), then the Windows portion of your hard drive loads into main memory. This is needed to display and operate the Windows environment.

Measuring the amount of memory

Like diskettes and hard drives, main memory size is measured in kilobytes (K) or megabytes (Meg). One kilobyte equals 1024 bytes (2^{10} bytes). One thousand kilobytes (2^{20} bytes, or 1,048,576 bytes) equals one megabyte.

Main memory is divided into several sectors, each possessing fixed addresses. These addresses locate data that's stored in memory. The addresses are given as physical locations. With main memory addressing, the physical memory is also designated. The operating system or an application accesses physical memory, whose addresses can store information.

Under DOS there have always been limitations to a computer's main memory. The maximum amount of main memory that can be directly addressed by DOS is 640K. As today's programs become more memory-intensive, this limit becomes more of a problem. However, new processors are more efficient than their predecessors. Another problem is that after the computer is switched on, the operating system is loaded into main memory, which leaves less than 640K available for other applications.

Actually, the newer processors must manage more memory, as is the case with DOS.

More than 640K are available

There is a way to avoid these memory limitations and access additional memory so that larger applications can run. This is done by tricking DOS into believing that more memory actually exists. However, before you can do this, you must examine the processor and the computer's memory management system.

Windows as a memory genius

As you know, Windows is a simple interface that enables you to open applications easily. Windows also provides multitasking, so that several applications can run simultaneously. So, it's possible to run several memory-intensive programs, such as Word for Windows and Excel, at the same time. These tasks usually require more than 640K of main memory.

Unlike the tricks that must be used to access additional memory under DOS, Windows can address the entire installed main memory continuously and make it available to almost every application.

After installation

Extended memory is recognized during the Windows installation. Installing the HIMEM.SYS driver in the CONFIG.SYS file enables Windows to use this memory. This is usually performed by a standard installation, which can be changed later. If you add additional memory, you must configure it for Windows. Also, additional expanded memory can be used with certain prerequisites, but must be configured accordingly.

6.2 Memory Management Under DOS

In this section we'll discuss how a PC manages its memory. You'll learn how to install expanded memory under Windows and understand how this memory operates.

The basis of memory management: the 8086/8088

Since all PCs are based on the architecture of the 8086/8088 processor, we'll discuss the memory management of this processor group.

8086/8088 processor memory limits

Each memory location of the PC is addressed over an address bus. For example, if the 8086 processor communicates with the memory location over 20 address lines, a 20-bit address bus is used. So, the processor must, with 220 = 1,048,576 memory cells, manage one megabyte of memory. This means that an XT processor can address one Meg of memory.

Dividing addressable memory locations

The directly addressable memory locations are accessed because DOS is loaded in another area. Under DOS, the processor can access a maximum of 640K for applications. The remaining 384K above the 640K limit are reserved for video RAM, the system BIOS, and other extensions, such as additional ROM.

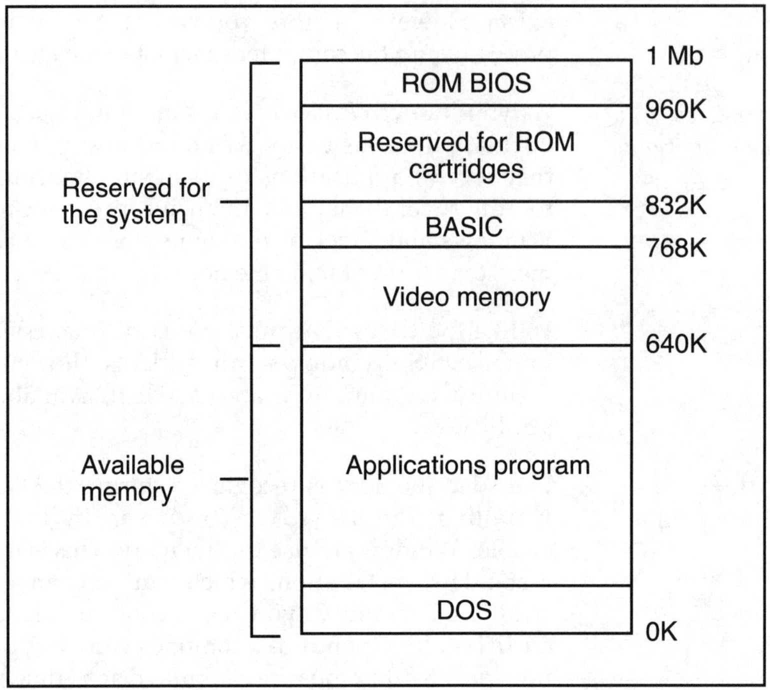

Memory management of the 8086 is designated as "real time"

Main memory, which is also called conventional memory, isn't used only for processing applications. When the computer is switched on, this is where the processor command file COMMAND.COM is located. The file contains the internal DOS commands, such as DIR and COPY, as well as other drivers that are loaded into main memory. The MEM command indicates that several resources in main memory are busy after the computer starts. Actually, less than 600K of memory are available after booting the computer.

Video RAM is located in the address locations behind main memory. The ROM BASIC of the first PCs was located in the address area between 768K and 832K. The area between 832K and 960K was reserved for ROM cartridges, which makes it possible to keep resident programs in the computer. ROM cartridges are still used today in laptop computers to avoid overloading the disk and working memory. However, programs that are located in ROM can be modified only by the manufacturer. Write access to this area isn't possible. The computer's ROM BIOS lies in the last section under the one Meg limit. This area specifies how the operating system interacts with the hardware.

The 80286 and 80386 processors

By using the 80286, 80386SX, etc. processors, an advanced system can access more memory. With the expanded 24-bit memory bus, it's capable of directly addressing 224 (16,777,216) physical memory locations, which is equivalent to 16 Meg. The address area above 1 Meg is designated as extended memory (additional memory). This is the memory area that's addressable by adding four data lines.

Protected mode performs better

The essential difference with the 8086 is that the 80286 can work in Real mode and Protected mode. However, the 80286 is compatible with the 8086 only in Real mode. Because of this, Real mode is automatically activated during system startup. You cannot change to Protected mode under DOS. This is because the 80286 usually imitates the 8086; it emulates its processing.

So, although the 80286 is able to address the 15 Meg of additional memory because of its architecture, DOS prevents it from using this memory. So, under normal conditions, this large memory area cannot be used as processing memory. The 80286's performance significantly improves on operating systems (e.g., UNIX, OS/2) that support Protected mode.

32-bit is also compatible

This also applies to the 80386 and 80486 processors. These processors support a 32-bit address bus and can theoretically address four gigabytes (2^{32}) of memory. Also, since they are supported only in Real mode, they are affected by the DOS limitations.

So, under DOS, the 80286 and 80386 processors operate like very fast 8086 processors. Under DOS, 286 and 386 systems are simply faster versions of their predecessors.

However, there are ways to better use the processor. Windows, which is also considered an "operating system extension", has revolutionized memory management because it can continuously address normal main memory and extended memory. However, this doesn't apply to XTs because they cannot address extended memory.

6.3 Extended and Expanded Memory

So far we've discussed only processing memory and extended memory. As we've mentioned, the XT cannot use extended memory. Although ATs and 386 systems can address this memory area, they cannot use it for applications under DOS because DOS doesn't support this type of memory.

Memory is extended

Besides the processing memory, which is usually too small, there is also expanded memory. Among these areas is a memory window (see following figure), whose address lies within the 384K system memory area between 640 and 1024K. All processors, including the 8086, can access this area.

Memory pages, which are controlled by a special driver, can be placed in this area. Applications, which are designed to use expanded memory, can store data files or program sections in the memory pages. Doing this increases the amount of processing memory that's available to applications.

Remember that video RAM, the BIOS, and the ROM routines are assigned to memory locations above the 640K limit. However, these programs don't use the entire available area. Since an overlaid window that's only 64K is produced as expanded memory, space is already found there in the area between 768K and 832K. So, an area of 64K, which can be addressed by the processing memory of DOS, can be used for applications.

Memory is managed by a driver

Expanded memory can be addressed only with software drivers. The LIM/EMS (Expanded Memory Specification) Standard drivers, which were developed by Lotus, Intel, and Microsoft, represent the basis for using expanded memory.

The LIM/EMS standard

The answer to the memory problems encountered under DOS came from three leading hardware and software developers: Lotus, Intel, and Microsoft. They developed a standard that finally made it possible to expand processing memory.

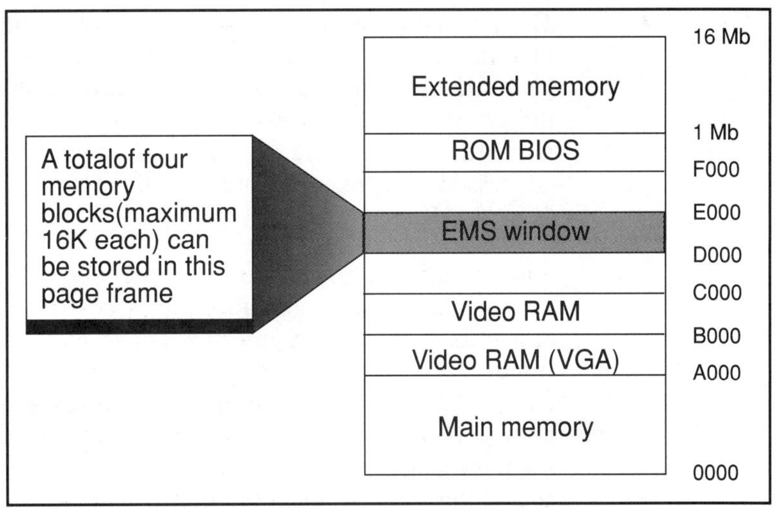

The Expanded Memory "Window"

The operative word is bank-switching

EMS uses a well-known technique, called bank-switching. By using this technique, 64K of unused space is defined within the 20-bit address area (under 1 Meg) to overlay additional RAM capacity. A maximum of four memory blocks of up to 16K each can be stored in this "window" (page frame). A special device driver, called the Expanded Memory Manager (EMM.SYS), manages the window. This device driver is part of the installation software that's included with the EMS-compatible memory expansion cards (e.g., Intel's Above Board). A standard driver is also included on your DOS diskettes.

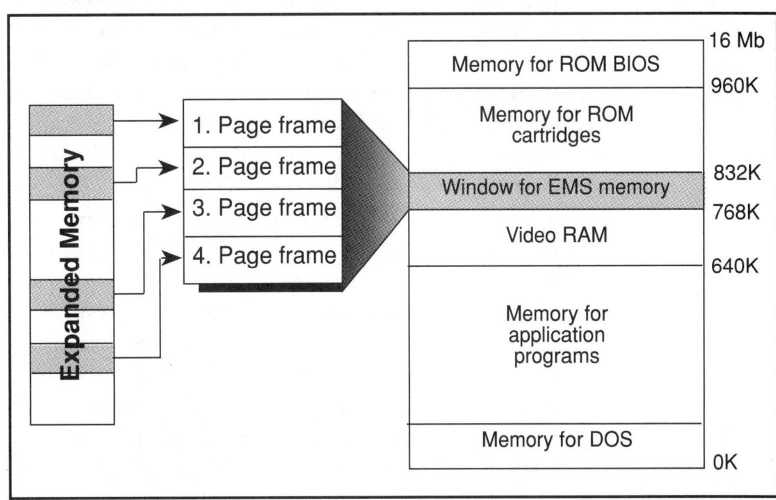

The individual memory pages of expanded memory in the memory window

The previous figure shows the normal "memory shell column". Like this 1 Meg of memory, additional memory exists, which can be located on a memory expansion card or on the motherboard of the computer. Now, however, only a 64K expanded *memory window* is available within the memory shell that can be addressed. The memory found on the memory card is divided into several 16K areas (memory pages).

Since barely any space is used in the memory window of 64K, the manager takes all the memory pages (4*16=64) of the memory card and adds them to the memory window. Now memory pages can be filled with data from a program. If the memory window is completely filled, the memory windows are passed by the manager to the memory card and stored there. Four new, empty memory pages will then be added to the memory window. Of course the manager must remember what kind of files are contained on which memory pages. If the program looks for files that have been processed in memory in this way, the manager searches the memory card and moves the required memory pages back into the memory window.

Memory definition on the motherboard

Since EMS was introduced, numerous motherboards (called NEAT boards) have been developed. These motherboards are adapted for the LIM standard. This means that specific areas of the RAM banks can be defined as expanded memory. You can also choose between extended and expanded memory with memory expansion cards. Jumpers or DIP switches usually specify this memory division.

Beginning with EMS Version 4.0, expanded memory can also be used as program memory. In this case, memory pages are placed in main memory. With this *large page frame* method, only memory pages with a maximum size of 64K can be used. However, because of the expanded memory window, a total of only 32 Meg of expanded memory can be managed. If the memory window is located between 768K and 1024K in the system memory, it's called a *small page frame*. Small page frame mode is generally used in LIM Version 3.2.

Memory overlay only works in the expanded memory window if the corresponding memory space exists physically. Usually additional memory must be available either on the motherboard or on the memory expansion card. 286 or 386 computers often have more than 640K of memory available on the motherboard. With EMS-compatible boards, the area above 640K can be either completely or partially defined as expanded memory. Any remaining area is automatically addressed as extended memory. Many of the available 16-bit to 32-bit RAM expansion cards for these computers also allow a flexible partition for expanded and extended memory.

The XMS standard

As we mentioned earlier, the 80286, 80386, and 80486 processors can address more than 1 Meg of memory. With the 80286 and 80386SX, it's possible to address a total of 16 Meg, depending on the address bus. With the 80386 and 80486, up to 4 gigabytes can be addressed.

The memory above 1 Meg is designated as extended memory. This memory can be addressed only if the processor is working in protected mode. Since some programs, such as Lotus 1-2-3 Version 3 and Windows 3, work in the Protected mode of the processor, they can fully utilize extended memory. Main memory and extended memory can be continuously addressed in Standard mode and in Enhanced mode.

This made it possible to set a standard for accessing extended memory. This standard, called "eXtended Memory Specification" (XMS), was developed by Microsoft, Intel, Lotus and Ast. The HIMEM.SYS driver fulfills all the requirements of the XMS standard.

6.4 Memory Management of Windows

An operating system's performance mainly depends on how it manages its limited resources. Unfortunately, even with megabit chips, main memory can still be a limited resource. This occurs because the memory requirements for today's programs have increased along with the memory capacity of modules.

The Microsoft developers have concentrated on solving this problem. The result is a Windows version for PC processors from the 80286 to the 80486.

Windows automatically adjusts to the hardware environment it encounters when it's started. Internally, there are two types of drivers that simultaneously try to use the special performance features of the processor (the most efficient memory management and addressing). We'll describe the performance range of the different driver types, Standard and Enhanced mode, in more detail later. However, since the processors are compatible to the 8088 processor, the fundamentals of memory management in DOS should be explained in the description of the Real mode. (If the "higher" processors emulate the 8088, they are in Real mode.)

Real mode

The memory management used in Real mode is identical to the segmented addressing methods used in DOS. We'll explain this in more detail later. For the moment, remember that the maximum address space in Real mode is 1 Meg, from which 640K are available to the MS-DOS user. This address space is partitioned in Real mode as the following shows:

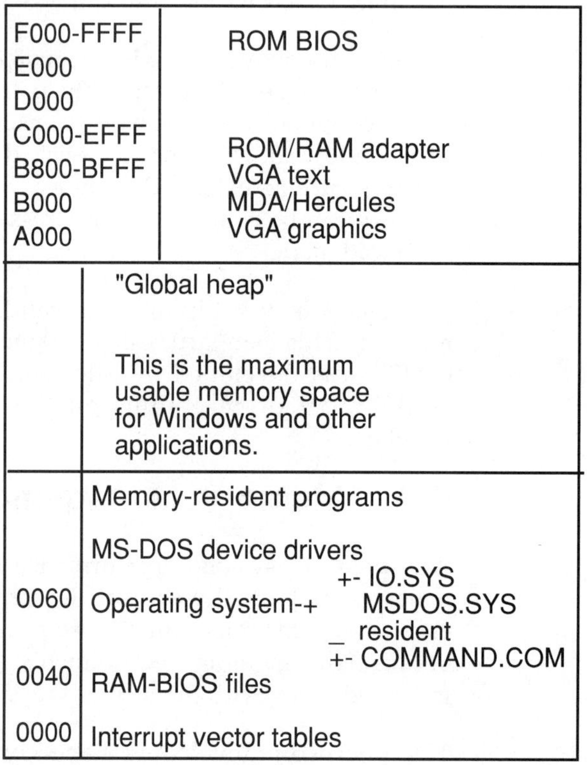

```
F000-FFFF   ROM BIOS
E000
D000
C000-EFFF   ROM/RAM adapter
B800-BFFF   VGA text
B000        MDA/Hercules
A000        VGA graphics

            "Global heap"

            This is the maximum
            usable memory space
            for Windows and other
            applications.

            Memory-resident programs

            MS-DOS device drivers
                                 +- IO.SYS
0060        Operating system-+     MSDOS.SYS
                                 _ resident
                                 +- COMMAND.COM
0040        RAM-BIOS files

0000        Interrupt vector tables
```

Memory partitioning in Real mode

As the previous figure shows, the global heap is represented in the basic configuration as a dependent area, whose maximum size is 640K, which is available to DOS.

The memory manager

When discussing driver modes, we must determine how the memory manager manages the global heap. As we mentioned earlier, the heap is divided into segments. These segments contain either instructions (code) or files. It's possible to assign attributes to the segments so that you can influence how the memory manager handles segments.

Since attributes are a complicated topic, we'll discuss them in more detail later. Remember that the memory distinguishes between non-moveable (fixed), moveable, and discardable segments. In Real mode, these segments are arranged in the global heap as follows:

0x9FFF	Upper limit of the global heap in physical memory
	↓ Discardable code segments ↓ ↑ Moveable code and file segments as well as discardable file segments ↑
	↑ Fixed code and file segments ↑
	Lower limit of the global heap in physical memory

Partitioning of the global heap in Real mode

Windows Version 3.1 doesn't support Real mode. If you still have Windows applications that were developed for Versions 2.X, there is generally no support for running them under Windows 3.1.

Standard mode

An alternative to Real mode is Standard mode. Windows automatically switches to this driver type if the following hardware requirements are specified:

- Processor type: Minimum 80286 processor
- Main memory: Minimum 1 Meg of main memory

The difference from Real mode

The basic difference between Standard mode and Real mode is that Windows switches the processor to Protected mode. We'll provide information about the effects of this when we discuss hardware-related memory addressing methods of the processor types. Remember that programs, including Windows itself, no longer work directly with physical memory addresses in Protected mode. Instead, these programs address memory by using logical addresses.

Block partitioning

In Standard mode, the global heap is partitioned into a maximum of three different blocks. The first block corresponds to the essential type of partitioning found in Real mode. The two other blocks are located in different memory areas. These areas are located in extended memory.

With extended memory, the main memory area is designated as the area located above the 1 Meg limit. This area can usually be accessed if the CPU is operating in Protected mode. With this block configuration, Windows uses a special device driver, called the extended memory driver (XMS).

The memory manager handles all subsequent accesses by directly bypassing the XMS driver. The exact location and size of these blocks depends on what was originally located there when Windows was started.

High memory area

The last block is an area that belongs to the high memory area (HMA). This is the first 64K-sized segment in extended memory, directly under the 1 Meg limit, between 0x10000 and 0x11000.

This block is configured with the help of a special device driver called HIMEM.SYS.

If Windows won't switch to Standard or Enhanced mode even though your PC fulfills all of the hardware-related requirements, check the CONFIG.SYS file. HIMEM.SYS, which is located on the Windows diskettes, must be accessed from CONFIG.SYS. However, you can also use a Windows-compatible XMS driver, such as QEMM. The next chapter provides more information on memory configuration.

In Standard mode, these three non-contiguous memory blocks form the global heap.

The illustration on the following page shows how the global heap is used by the memory manager.

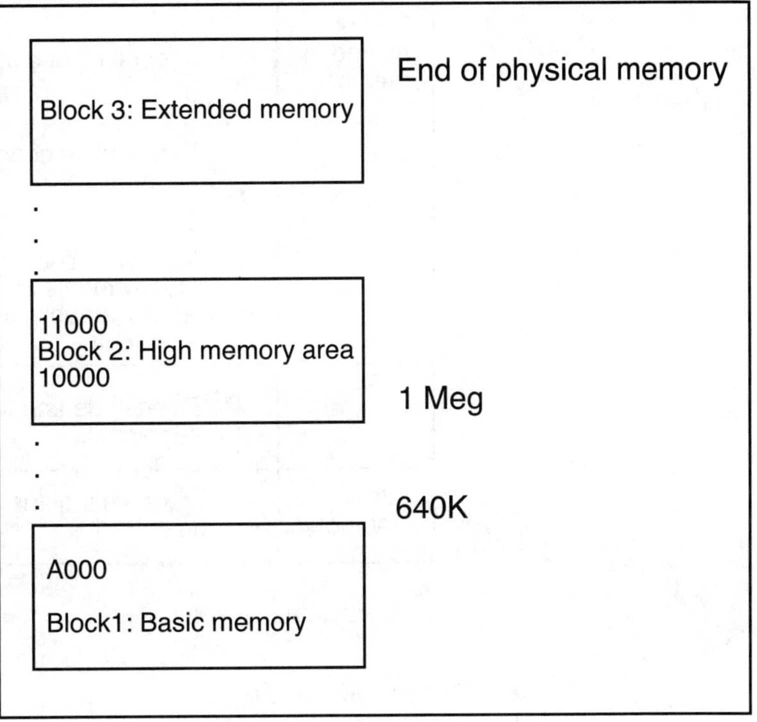

The composition of the global heap in Standard mode

Similarities to Real mode

The previous figure shows that the principal heap partition is comparable to the one used in Real mode. However, unlike the configuration in Real mode, this configuration doesn't handle one contiguous memory area.

End of extended memory	Upper limit of global heap
	↓ Discardable code segments ↓ ↑ Moveable code and file segments as well as discardable file segments ↑
	↑ Fixed code and file segments ↑
Basic memory	Lower limit of the global heap

Partition of global heap in Standard mode

386 Enhanced mode

Another alternative to Real mode is provided by 386 Enhanced mode. However, this mode places the greatest demands on the hardware:

- Processor type: Minimum 80386SX
- Main memory: Minimum 2 Meg

386 Enhanced mode

Windows works most effectively in 386 Enhanced mode. So, this mode is considered a serious alternative to OS/2.

The working environment

The following is a brief overview of the working environment of Windows in this mode:

Demand paging and virtual memory addressing

This mode of memory management even makes it possible to run programs that are larger than the system's available memory.

Virtual MS-DOS machines

A multitasking mechanism has been implemented using timeslicing. This method uses the capabilities of the 386 processor, that's switched to virtual 8086 mode, and starts a separate virtual 8086 CPU for each MS-DOS application.

So, you can run up to 16 standard MS-DOS applications, more or less in parallel, according to the timeslicing method. Each application exists in a separate address space, which can be a maximum of 600K. This is often larger than the space that's allocated to a single application running directly under MS-DOS.

You can also run the MS-DOS application as a full screen or inside a window.

Windows and OS/2

A discussion of the differences between Windows 3.1 and OS/2 would require a book in itself. However, we'll briefly comment on these differences.

Since OS/2 Version 2 will provide a Windows environment so that old Windows applications can be used under OS/2, IBM is trying to get its product on the market. The OS/2 Presentation Manager has taken a unique course of development with the break between IBM and Microsoft. Given the very high RAM (you should have at least 8 Meg) and hard drive requirement, this operating system isn't suitable for the home computer.

Unfortunately, Windows development has encountered problems. One problem that hasn't been solved is the break-up of the individual MS-DOS applications. So, if an MS-DOS application crashes, the entire system will crash.

Another problem is that multitasking by the timeslice method hasn't been completely implemented. All Windows applications continue to run, as under Windows/386, on a virtual 8086 processor. So, as the application continues to work, the CPU must be freed as soon as it is no longer needed. So the type of multitasking used in earlier Windows versions, which was based on the message polling principle, has been retained. The multitasking features of OS/2 and Presentation Manager are definitely more efficient because the operating system, instead of only the application, controls access to the processor.

Virtual memory management and demand paging

Because of how memory requests work, the memory manager tries to place one of the memory requests in the corresponding area of the heap of the application to be used. This process is repeated until the entire physical memory resources have been shared. Only then does the memory manager introduce demand paging. As the name suggests, this paging occurs on an "as needed" basis.

To do this, the entire main memory is divided into 4K pages. By using the "least recently used" (LRU) algorithm, Windows selects the pages that haven't been accessed for the longest period of time. The memory manager places these pages in a swap file on the hard drive. The size of this file can be defined from within the Windows installation. A permanent swap file ensures that a secure area on the hard drive is reserved for memory swapping.

With a temporary swap file, swapping occurs according to need and space. The latter method is clearly slower.

If an application tries to access code or file pages that have been placed in the swap file by the memory manager, the 80386 processor activates a "page-fault" interrupt. This causes the memory manager to swap other memory pages, and place the code or file pages requested by the application in the newly-created free space. If LONG or FAR pointers exist on these kinds of pages, they lose their attributes in the swapping process, which isn't securely placed so that main memory can be stored in the same location.

In 386 Enhanced mode, Windows allocates a maximum memory size of 4 gigabytes, which is actually determined by the size of physical main memory and the swap file. The global heap in extended 80386 mode is comparable to the basic configuration in Real mode, as with the global heap separated into three different blocks in Standard mode. If the global heap in the basic configuration represents a corresponding area in physical main memory, then it is a larger, more homogenous, virtual address space in 386 Enhanced mode.

End of extended memory	Upper limit of the global heap in virtual address space
	↓ Discardable code segments ↓ ↑ Moveable code and file segments as well as discardable file segments ↑
	↑ Fixed code and file segments ↑
	Lower limit of the global heap in virtual address space

Partitioning of the global heap in Enhanced mode

This can also be explicitly assumed when Windows is started. One of the following switches described is applied for this. It's obvious that Windows can only work in the mode specified by the switch setting, if it's available for the necessary hardware.

Switch for Windows operating modes:

Switch	Operating mode	System minimum
/s /2	Standard	80x86/1 Meg
/3	386 Enhanced	80386SX/2 Meg

6.5 Your Computer's Configuration

Additional memory can be installed in several ways. The type of memory expansion depends on the programs you'll use. Windows works as well with extended memory as it does with expanded memory.

If you work with only true Windows applications, such as Word for Windows and Excel, you should install additional memory as extended memory, so that Windows can fully utilize the system memory.

If you install non-Windows applications that work with expanded memory, you can configure one part of memory as expanded memory and another part as extended memory, provided this is possible with your memory card.

If your entire additional memory is configured as expanded memory, you can run Windows in either Standard or 386 Enhanced mode. So, this depends on the applications that you want to install under Windows, and the size of the existing additional memory that can be used.

The following section contains guidelines you can use to determine your own configuration.

Conditions for the Windows operating mode

Before the Windows operating mode can place special demands on the computer hardware, certain conditions must be met.

Windows in Standard mode:

Hardware:	286, 386SX, 386, i486
Memory:	Conventional memory:640K
	Extended memory:Minimum 192K
Remarks:	Performance limits for 286 complete memory addressing

Windows in 386 Enhanced mode:

Hardware:	386SX, 386, i486
Memory:	Conventional memory:640K
	Extended memory:Minimum 1024K
Remarks:	Multitasking through virtual addressing

Configuring additional memory

If you want to configure existing additional memory according to your own needs, the following configurations are possible:

1. Your computer runs above only the 640K memory limit. In this case, you cannot operate Windows. You must reserve at least 1 Meg of your main memory.

2. Your computer has extended memory, which cannot be changed to expanded memory. Activate the driver HIMEM.SYS and start Windows in Standard mode or 386 Enhanced mode (depending on the processor type). This also applies when you can work only with Windows applications even though your additional memory can emulate expanded memory.

3. You can use expanded memory and should work with non-Windows applications in this memory.

4. If you want to work with Windows in Standard or 386 Enhanced mode, expanded memory is needed for a non-Windows application. In this case, you must install extended memory in addition to expanded memory.

The configuration of your computer

A computer's configuration depends on the type of application (as previously described). For a standard 286 with 1 Meg of memory, the driver HIMEM.SYS must be activated so that extended memory is applied and Windows can run in Standard mode.

SMARTDRIVE should be installed in extended memory so that you don't have to wait for hard drive access under Windows.

Beginning with a memory capacity of 2 Meg, you can define a RAM disk with RAMDRIVE to accelerate screen refresh. In the configuration of an application that works with expanded memory, you must install additional memory as expanded memory with a special driver (the Expanded Memory Manager).

Using all resources

You should always try to use all of Windows' capabilities. Depending on your configuration and your application, you can install your memory using the combinations previously presented. We'll explain how to use these individual configurations in the following chapters.

Information for device driver files

Windows requires device drivers (system files), which are located in the CONFIG.SYS file, in order to configure additional memory or peripherals, such as a mouse driver. The following section provides information on which device drivers you'll need. In many cases, you must copy one or more device driver files with the extension *.SYS from the Windows diskettes to your hard drive.

Compressed files

To save space, these files are stored in compressed format. The files needed for the Windows installation are automatically uncompressed. However, if you manually copy such a file, you must first uncompress the file. Windows provides the EXPAND.EXE program for this purpose. Compressed device driver files are identified on the diskettes by the extension *.SY_. In order to uncompress and simultaneously place the file on the hard drive, use the following command:

```
expand a:\mouse.sy$ c:\windows\mouse.sys
```

With this command, first the file is expanded and then copied to the correct target directory.

6.6 Building Extended Memory

Extended memory exists in two formats. This memory can reside on the main chip by using special modules, or special memory cards can accept the corresponding memory modules.

An additional memory card can be easily installed in a free slot in the computer. The "normal" main memory up to 640K must be installed. Many additional memory cards offer the option of filling an existing empty area up to 640K and then designating the remaining memory for use as additional memory.

Some memory cards can be used only as extended memory and others can be used as extended or expanded memory (e.g., Intel's Above Board). Closely examine the manufacturer's information when buying a memory expansion kit. Usually extended memory is more useful. However, some applications run the same even with expanded memory. Therefore, your additional memory should be able to support both types of memory.

On-board memory

In addition to the memory card, which is inserted into a free slot in the computer, "on-board" memory is often found on the 286 and 386 models. This enables you to install and uninstall processing memory easily. With older computers, the memory chips (often only a portion) are directly connected to the processor. So, in order to exchange chips, you must be able to use a soldering iron. In this case, you should use a RAM card.

The organization of the new 286 models makes it possible to have a RAM capacity of 4 Meg on the main processor. However, high-performance chips with a capacity of 1 Meg are also useful.

386 systems are the memory giants

386 systems offer a memory capacity of up to 8 Meg on the motherboard. To save space, these motherboards are equipped with SIMM or SIP modules. This configuration has a small plug-in board, which has a capacity of 1 Meg (comparable to the new "normal" megabit chips), that can be inserted into the assigned slot. With the combination of RAM banks and SIMM or SIP banks, the corresponding memory capacity is achieved. This method is being used more frequently on 286 systems.

This type of memory module enables you to configure memory on the board more easily. A RAM bank can be completely extended and added manually. If you use SIMMs, the pins may bend or break off. SIMM and SIP elements have a capacity from 256 to 2048K. A disadvantage to these modern memory modules is that defective chips can no longer be individually exchanged. So, if there is a defect, the complete SIMM or SIP element must be replaced.

Memory configuration in Setup

If you want to expand the memory, you must use the Setup program included with your system (not to be confused with the Windows Setup). Most new computers include the Setup program in the BIOS, and can be activated through a combination of keystrokes during the system check after the computer is switched on. Setup still be started from diskettes only if you're using an old 286. If you have an IBM PS/2 computer, you must run the IBM configuration diskette after installing the memory expansion.

Entering changes with the system Setup

With the Setup program, all the components of your computer, such as the hard drive, diskette drives, memory, system clock, and data are stored in CMOS, so that the computer can control these components. The information in CMOS remains after the computer is switched off because it's battery-powered.

With the NEAT boards and with 386 system boards, Setup partitions memory. This means that a formal partitioning in extended or expanded memory can be performed. However, this determines only how memory should be used. In the following sections you'll see how Windows can use extended or expanded memory.

Memory expansion in the PS/2

If you configure memory in IBM PS/2 computers through a memory module expansion, then you must start with the accompanying reference diskette. The automatic configuration of new memory can be initiated with the help of this diskette.

6.7 Configuring Expanded Memory

To configure expanded memory for Windows, you'll need the corresponding driver for your memory expansion card. For example, if you're using the Intel Above Board, you'll need the REMM.SYS file for the AST RAMpage and the PS2EMM.SYS file for the IBM PS/2 Expanded Memory Option. These files are distributed with Windows. If you have a 386 or 486 system, refer to the next section.

Intel Above Board

For the Intel Above Board, configuration occurs following a special installation program, which is on the driver diskette distributed by Intel. However, first you must copy the file EMM.SYS onto this diskette.

Place this diskette in drive A: and start the Setboard program. The card will be automatically configured.

The driver file for the Expanded Memory Manager must be entered as a device statement in the CONFIG.SYS file. With Above Board, this is done automatically. In this case, the following statement is shown:

```
device=emm.sys at d000 208 nd
```

Parameter

The file name of the Expanded Memory Manager (EMM.SYS) appears directly after the device statement. The parameter "AT" represents PC/AT and compatible computers. The parameter PC (for IBM PC/XT and compatibles) or MOD30 (for IBM PS/2 Model 30) can correspondingly be applied.

The second parameter designates the start address for the memory window. A standard value is assigned here. This value was originally planned for additional ROM under DOS and is now almost useless.

The third parameter designates the input/output address of the memory expansion card. In this case, it's address is 208. If you're using more than one memory card, each one has its own address. This is automatically assigned.

After restarting the computer, the initialization of the memory card is shown by a corresponding message. This message indicates the available main memory and the installed expanded or extended memory. Later the controlled memory size will be shown by the Expanded Memory Manager. A message, similar to the following, indicates the amount of memory the computer has available:

```
Expanded Memory Manager Version 4.0 Revision A
Copyright 1985, 1986, 1988 Intel Corporation
Testing Page 56
Conventional Memory   640 KB
Expanded Memory       896 KB
Extension Memory      3072 KB
EMM length            9536 KB
```

Some memory cards, which can be configured for expanded memory, have their own driver. The parameter can also be slightly different. If a configuration program isn't included with your memory expansion kit, try it manually with a minimal input. If an individual driver still isn't available, try one of the drivers that's included with Windows. The standard input in the CONFIG.SYS file is:

```
device=emm.sys
```

Pay attention to the messages on the display during the restart, after which expanded memory has been configured. After this prompt, the memory size is usually indicated, as previously shown.

Ensure that this entry in the CONFIG.SYS file precedes all other device statements.

Expanded memory for 386 and 486 computers

If you want to run Windows on a computer that is based on a 386 or 486 processor, you can configure expanded memory with the help of an EMM file that's included with Windows. However, you should consider whether this is actually necessary. Usually you'll need the installation only if you're working with programs that access expanded memory. In this case, EMM386.EXE emulates expanded memory for such applications in additional memory. The simulation usually appears automatically if you let Windows run in 386 Enhanced mode. The driver must then only be installed if you're running Windows in Real mode and Standard mode and expanded memory should be simulated when necessary. Ensure that you're not using any other emulation programs, such as CEMM.SYS (Compaq), because this can only be run under Windows in Real mode.

Entering Memory Manager in the CONFIG.SYS file

Enter the emulation program to be configured under the current line in the CONFIG.SYS file. This program will then first be activated after a warm-start of your computer.

```
device=c:\windows\emm386.sys [size]
```

The configured area is also defined with the size parameter. Define only as much memory capacity as your application actually needs; otherwise the rest of the memory space will be given up.

6.8 Configuring Extended Memory

Extended memory is continuously addressed by Windows in Standard and 386 Enhanced mode. For controlled memory access, Microsoft uses an "Extended Memory Manager" called HIMEM.SYS. QEMM from Quarterdeck can also use HIMEM.SYS.

HIMEM.SYS is a device driver that accesses extended memory and makes a portion of it available for normal main memory. This driver reserves the first 64K of extended memory (high memory area) for DOS. Main memory is thus increased by about 50K, of which the driver itself requires several bytes. This is very useful if you have many drivers assigned in the CONFIG.SYS file that remain resident in main memory.

Assigning drivers in the CONFIG.SYS file

The XMS driver is assigned in the CONFIG.SYS file as follows:

```
device=c:\windows\himem.sys
```

Include the drive letter and path in which the file is found. First copy the driver from the diskette to the Windows directory.

Be sure that an old version of HIMEM.SYS isn't being used under Windows 3.1. In any case, the correct version must be used.

Setting HIMEM parameters

If you start Windows in Standard mode and use extended memory, the HIMEM driver must be loaded so that extended memory will be addressed under Windows. Depending on the hardware being used, you may have to set parameters so that extended memory will be correctly addressed under Windows. If you modify the settings of the HIMEM driver in the CONFIG.SYS file, you must reboot your computer so that the changes will be activated.

Depending on the type of computer and applications, corresponding parameters can be included in the entry. If the standard settings cause problems, you should try the corresponding parameters. The available parameters can be specified either by name or number. The effect is the same.

IBM AT and compatible	at	1
IBM PS/2	ps2	2
Phoenix Bios	pt1cascade	3
HP Vectra	hpvectra	4
AT&T 6300 Plus	att6300plus	5
Acer 1100	acer1100	6
Tosch 1200/1600XE	toshiba	7
Wyse 12.5 Mhz 286	wyse	8

For example, if you're working on a HP Vectra and extended memory cannot be properly addressed under Windows, enter the following parameters in the DEVICE statement of the CONFIG.SYS file:

```
device=c:\windows\himem.sys /m:hpvectra
```

or

```
device=c:\windows\himem.sys /m:4
```

Configuring Shadow RAM

Another parameter must be specified when using Shadow RAM. In this case, the ROM data is copied into RAM, which is usually much faster. However, not all models can use Shadow RAM. The configuration is useful in computers that have more than 384K of extended memory available. In this case, Shadow RAM is loaded into extended memory and this area is no longer accessible for other applications. Try to determine whether the performance of your computer improves. To activate the Shadow RAM, the following parameters must be set:

```
device=c:\windows\himem.sys /shadow:on
```

To deactivate Shadow RAM, simply set the parameter to "off."

How HIMEM.SYS works

The HIMEM.SYS settings speed up Windows because of the Code Pagings. Since Windows programs are sometimes larger than the available processing memory, they are divided into several segments. These segments are then loaded into memory as needed.

The advantage is that only those segments that are needed for the execution of a command can be loaded. The remaining segments are located on the hard drive.

There are two types of segments. Some segments can be placed in memory and others can be overwritten by new segments. If a new segment is loaded into memory from the hard drive, unused segments located in memory will be swapped again.

Originally, the memory-swapping succeeded again on the hard drive. However, under HIMEM.SYS, the segments are essentially swapped onto fast extended memory, which saves a significant amount of time.

7. Optimizing Your Hard Drive

Buffers

The number of buffers allocated in your CONFIG.SYS file determines Windows' access to the hard drive. In this chapter we'll discuss the tasks the buffers perform and which values should be set.

Using a hard drive cache with SMARTDRV

Since Windows programs are read into RAM and written back to the hard drive block by block, your processing speed ultimately depends on the machine's access speed to the hard drive. SMARTDRV creates an additional memory area, in which it places program blocks in temporary storage. Disk access is noticeably faster using a cache than when using only the hard drive.

Using a RAM disk

Setting up a RAM disk in extended memory or expanded memory increases processing speed during operations that temporarily store data. Accessing a RAM disk instead of the disk drive significantly speeds up your system's performance.

Hard drives and controllers

By installing and properly using your hard drive, you can run applications more quickly under Windows. Since Windows accesses the disk often, it's important to defragment your files frequently and to ensure that optimal interleave factors are set for the reading speed of the hard drive, controller, and bus interfaces.

7.1 Why Optimize the Hard Drive?

Windows is loaded into your computer's RAM while it runs. The complete program isn't loaded. Instead, only the currently necessary program segments, or blocks, are read into memory.

When a new program block is called, it's loaded from the hard drive. Simultaneously, another program block, which has been located in RAM but hasn't been used, is re-written to the hard drive. Also, Windows uses the hard drive as an expanded memory area in 386 Enhanced mode. If RAM is too small, a portion of it is copied to the hard drive and if it's needed again, it's re-read. This process, which is called *swapping*, uses the hard drive to create virtual memory areas. The hard drive is also used to store data files. During operations with larger files (e.g., databases), the data is usually loaded from the hard drive to RAM.

Advantages during processing

So, the hard drive is important to the operation of Windows. You must look not only at the processor for speed but also at the entire machine as a group of components. The type of hard drive and its settings are especially important. You can obtain optimal processing speed from an apparently slow hard drive by using the proper settings and specific software tools.

Optimization options

Optimization options for the hard drive are based on physical settings of the drive and specific DOS and Windows programs that are used to enhance access speed. If the wrong optimization options are made, then reading data from the hard drive into RAM takes longer. This will slow down the processing speed of your computer.

Access to highly fragmented data is also time-consuming. When data is written to a hard drive it can become fragmented, which means that the data is not written as a contiguous block on the hard drive. The read/write head of the hard drive must "jump" from one sector to another to access the data. To avoid this problem, there are programs which will defragment the data on the hard drive. This process is referred to as file compression.

There's also another advantage to file compression. You can create a large swapfile for use in 386 Enhanced mode. If you use a permanent swapfile in 386 Enhanced mode, by compressing the disk first, a larger swapfile can be set up before the compression because a swapfile requires a contiguous surface area on the hard drive.

7.2 Using a Cache Program

The DOS operating system includes several utility programs that optimize the hard drive input and output. Unfortunately, sometimes these files don't operate correctly with the optimization programs included with Windows and the way Windows operates. You should know the DOS and Windows optimization program parameters. You can often avoid conflicting situations and adverse effects.

Depending on the nature of disk access and using incorrect parameters, access to the hard drive can actually become slower if the options aren't set up properly. Optimization effects can sometimes cancel each other out.

What's a disk cache?

The most important optimization programs are cache programs. A cache program minimizes the input and output operations to the hard drive. Many Windows applications work with overlays (sections of programs). During this process, the complete program is not in RAM, only the sections needed are loaded from the hard drive. This procedure is also used by programs that read individual data blocks and also write the data blocks, which aren't being used, back to the hard drive.

Blocks stored in the temporary storage cache

During the constant storage and retrieval operations, many disk access operations are needed. This is where a cache program can help. Data, or program blocks, are temporarily stored in the cache, rather than loaded directly from the hard drive. The cache is an area in RAM reserved by the cache program. Depending on the size of the cache programs, several blocks of the hard drive can be loaded into a temporary storage cache.

Instead of directly accessing the hard drive, the program obtains the necessary data from the cache. Since access to RAM is much faster than access to the hard drive, using a cache results in a noticeable advantage in speed.

Using a cache in expanded memory

New information is read into the cache following a specific algorithm; older data is re-written to the hard drive or discarded as the new data arrives. All cache programs use a different procedure to do this. This also applies to the portion of the storage area that can be reserved with the cache. If the cache is set up in conventional memory, it occupies space for applications.

These applications must begin to set aside program segments in the temporary storage areas. This loop can be broken by using a cache program that accesses the expanded memory areas, as does SMARTDRV. The DOS-cache BUFFERS only works in conventional memory areas.

Using BUFFERS

The configuration file CONFIG.SYS manages BUFFERS with an entry such as:

```
BUFFERS=x
```

"x" represents the number of buffers that should be set. BUFFERS accepts values ranging from 1 to 99. This line determines the number of buffers that are reserved for the DOS cache. Each buffer reserves 512 bytes in the temporary storage area.

A simple calculation: the maximum number of buffers multiplied by the unit number results in a maximum cache size of 99 x 512 bytes = 49.5K.

The cache size must be larger than 49.5K to maximize Windows' effectiveness. Also, BUFFERS can only reserve space in conventional memory (with DOS Versions 5.0 and below). This is a disadvantage for non-Windows applications that use conventional memory areas.

Therefore, you should use the SMARTDRV cache program supplied with Windows. It provides significant advantages over BUFFERS.

☞ If you use SMARTDRV in addition to BUFFERS, Windows looks for the BUFFERS memory area first to determine the location of each block. Then it searches the SMARTDRV storage area. If a high value is entered in BUFFER, it takes a moment for Windows (or the program) to find the block. To avoid this, the smallest possible value must entered for BUFFERS.

The following entry is considered an optimal setting for BUFFERS:

```
BUFFERS=10
```

7.3 Using Temporary Directories

While working under Windows, data must be temporarily stored on the hard drive. For example, when switching between several applications, data from the background programs are stored to the hard drive in a temporary file, which can be re-read if necessary. This is what happens in the pause between several applications when toggling with the combination Alt + Tab. The screen change takes several seconds and there is activity on the hard drive.

Deleting temporary files when problems occur

The following procedure applies to programs that load large quantities of data into RAM temporarily. The "temporary" files are stored (usually with the file extension .TMP) in a specific directory on the hard drive. This is usually the application directory or main directory.

If, instead of being exited properly, an application ends with a warm boot, for example, the files in this directory aren't automatically closed and temporary files aren't deleted. In this case, under some circumstances, numerous temporary files can remain on a hard drive, which wastes storage space.

It also makes sense to define a place on the hard drive where temporary files should be stored. This saves time when you want to delete unnecessary files. If a program doesn't run normally after a system crash, this is usually caused by an undeleted temporary file.

Deleting these files is very useful when you want to ensure consistent execution of applications. The directory you create can be on the hard drive or, for example, on a RAM disk (in which case access would be faster than when using the hard drive).

Using several directories

To define a place for temporary files, you must differentiate between Windows applications and non-Windows applications. Two different areas should be made available to the processor to avoid conflicts when creating temporary files. Usually these directories will be different. Create two directories, named TEMPWIN and TEMPDOS, on your hard drive. If you separate them now, you'll be able to differentiate the origin of the temporary files later. If you want to use a RAM disk for temporary storage, add the two directories to the RAM disk in AUTOEXEC.BAT. This requires even less time and ensures that temporary files don't collide.

Setting up temporary storage areas

The WIN.INI file manages the location of temporary files in DOS applications that are started from Windows. The following entry in the [windows] section of the WIN.INI file determines the location of the DOS temporary files.

```
swapdisk=[drive][directory]
```

Enter the disk drive or directory you want to reserve for temporary files here. For Windows applications and general DOS applications, which aren't started under Windows, the same setting is made in an environment variable:

```
set temp=[drive][directory]
```

This should be added to the AUTOEXEC.BAT file so that the definition is always available.

7.4 Using SMARTDRV

The cache program included in Windows is automatically set up during Windows installation when you choose to have your system files modified during the installation procedure. SMARTDRV can also be installed after Windows is set up, and you can change its parameters at any time.

The SMARTDRV cache program uses areas in expanded memory that can be reserved for data storage. The algorithm it uses to exchange the blocks is much more efficient than the one used in BUFFERS.

During Windows installation, SMARTDRV is automatically set up and the necessary line:

```
LOADHIGH C:\WINDOWS\SMARTDRV.EXE [max] [min]
```

is written into the AUTOEXEC.BAT file.

The range of extended memory that Windows automatically designates to SMARTDRV depends on the amount of extended memory you have installed.

Program parameters

The max and min parameters determine the "size" of the cache storage area to be installed. If a size isn't entered, SMARTDRV automatically installs a 256K storage area. If you do define the size, use a kilobyte value that is a multiple of 64. Increase the value if you work with programs that frequently access the hard drive, such as database programs, drawing programs, or PageMaker.

If you don't enter a value for the size, Windows reduces the cache to a minimum size of 256K in both Standard and 386 Enhanced modes. This is useful because Windows needs the additional memory itself. This also applies if you use SMARTDRV under Real mode in expanded memory. In this case, Windows doesn't reduce SMARTDRV to its smallest size until it accesses expanded memory. For example, suppose that you rarely use programs that frequently access the hard drive. Also, you've installed SMARTDRV in an area of 1 Meg in the additional memory area. In this instance, you should set the size parameter to the lowest possible value, which is 256K. This would free other areas for other Windows applications.

The size value in this case would be as follows:

```
C:\WINDOWS\SMARTDRV.EXE 1024 256
```

Optimum parameters

Since Windows doesn't always use the entire memory area defined as a cache, the 2048K that could (maximally) be saved with this set up are available for SMARTDRV and shouldn't be considered lost. The smallest cache size is the size of the area reserved for SMARTDRV. This area is no longer available for other applications including Windows itself.

Extremely large buffers affect Windows

Use the size setting carefully. Don't be too generous with available storage capacity. An upper limit should be a maximum of 1024K. This ensures that Windows will still be able to manage memory areas. The lowest value that should be used is 256K. The maximum available storage capacity for SMARTDRV is also limited in specific ways. An increase in disk buffer areas from 256K to 512K is much more noticeable than an increase from 1024K to 1280K. According to Microsoft, a 20% increase in speed occurs in the first case, while only a 2% increase is possible in the second case.

7.5 Virtual Disk Drives Using a RAM Disk

Theoretically, creating a RAM disk involves setting up an area (e.g., in expanded memory) that can be used instead of a normal disk drive. Accessing RAM is much faster than accessing a hardware disk drive. To do this, specify a drive designation in CONFIG.SYS while creating the RAM disk.

Once this is done, all commands that control hard drive operations can be used on that drive. This produces a significant increase in speed. Access is directed to a RAM drive instead of to an actual disk drive. By using this procedure, you can quickly perform many operations, such as creating directories to receive temporary files in AUTOEXEC.BAT.

Disadvantages of a RAM disk

Unfortunately, a RAM disk has several disadvantages. Since the RAM disk is located in RAM, its contents are resident only if the computer is switched on. When you switch off the computer, all the information that's on the RAM disk is lost, unless you've copied it elsewhere. So, you must ensure that only temporary data is stored on the RAM disk. However, using a RAM disk for temporary storage is very useful when you frequently switch between several programs.

Match the program versions

You must use the same version of SMARTDRV as RAMDRIVE. The programs included in the same version of Windows are the only ones that work together properly.

Setting up a RAM disk

To set up a RAM disk, enter the following in the CONFIG.SYS file:

```
DEVICE=C:\DOS\RAMDRIVE.SYS (size)
```

Again, ensure that the driver file is in the correct directory. "Size" determines the portion of expanded memory that must be reserved for the RAM disk. If an entry isn't made, the default value is 64K. Theoretically, only as much memory area as is necessary can be reserved for certain applications. A maximum value of 4096K can be set up as a RAM disk.

Calculating your memory needs

Suppose that you constantly toggle between two non-Windows applications. Determine the storage capacity of the largest program and add 75K, which Windows needs for specific information such as the screen change, to this value. Multiply the result by the number of non-Windows applications you want to use.

Then multiply this result by 1.02. This value is a constant (according to Microsoft), that routinely adds 2 percent to the required storage capacity. The result of this calculation is rounded up to the next whole number. The final result should be the size parameter of the RAMDRIVE command line.

You don't have to determine the storage required by each program you use. Instead, you can simply triple the storage needs required by your largest program and use this as the size parameter value.

However, if you reserve too much memory by using this method, Windows won't have enough memory.

Setting up a RAM disk in expanded memory

To set up a RAM disk in expanded memory, add a space and the /A switch after the size value. If you're using extended memory, use the /E switch instead of the /A switch.

After the next warm boot, the RAM drive reports its presence with the following (this is an example taken from a machine with a 2 Meg RAM disk):

Screen display

```
Microsoft RAMDrive Version 3.06  virtual disk D:
 Disk size: 2048K
 Sector size: 512 bytes
Allocation unit: 1 sectors
Directory entries: 64
```

When you're using RAMDRIVE, additional parameters can also be set. Since these parameters apply only to specialized applications, we'll only briefly discuss them.

```
RAMDRIVE (size) (sectors) (entries) /(letter)
```

Parameter change in sectors

The values 128, 256, and 512 are accepted for RAMDRIVE sectors. All other values are rounded. If there isn't an entry, the default value is 128. DOS accepts a maximum of 512 bytes for each sector.

The larger the sectors, the higher the execution speed. Unfortunately, space can be wasted if too much space is reserved at the end of files.

Parameter change in entries

The more memory available, the more file entries can be managed via the directory for the virtual disk. Set this number only if you need more than 64 file entries. If you do, change the parameter entries to multiples of 16 (128, 144, 256, 304, etc.).

If you change the "entries" value, you must also make an entry for "sectors," because the values may be read incorrectly if one is omitted.

An entry for a 1 Meg memory expansion board would look as follows:

```
DEVICE=RAMDRIVE.SYS 1024 128 144 /e
```

7.6 Optimizing Free Disk Space

Another way to effectively use the storage space on a hard drive is to frequently reorganize the disk surface. This involves removing the file fragmentation that occurs when working with files.

Why fragmentation occurs

When files are created, the available storage space on the surface of the disk is used in units, called blocks. In DOS Versions 4.01 and below, a block consists of a contiguous area of 4096 bytes. So, if a file is smaller than 4096 bytes, a disk space of 4096 bytes is still reserved for the file.

If a file is larger than 4096 bytes (larger than a block), then the number of blocks that are needed to store the file are reserved. As a result, an area on the disk, whose size is a multiple of 4096 bytes, is reserved on the disk.

Faster access without track changes

Blocks are contiguous segments of 4096 bytes, which are sent from the read head to the controller. If a file is stored in several blocks, it's best if they are located sequentially on the disk. In this case, the entire file is read with no or few track changes on the disk. These optimal conditions are possible only when the entire file is stored at once, instead of gradually increasing in size. If a file's size gradually increases, DOS must search for the next free block to continue writing the file. Then it stores the new data in this block. However, the next free block isn't necessarily located near the preceding block. Instead, this block could be located several clusters away.

If other files have been created between saving the original file and continuing to write it, or if the free space is already fragmented, the file is split up.

Free use of blocks

When you work with the hard drive, new files are constantly created, expanded, reduced, or deleted. So, if you start from a clean disk surface, an unmanageable arrangement of free and used blocks is quickly created.

Fragmentation occurs when files are stored in different physical areas. If a disk surface is extremely fragmented, it takes longer to access and process data. This occurs because the tracks must be frequently changed.

Seeing the fragmentation

Programs such as the BeckerTools Disk Optimizer for Windows, or PC Tools Compress for DOS, allow you to check the fragmentation of the disk surface.

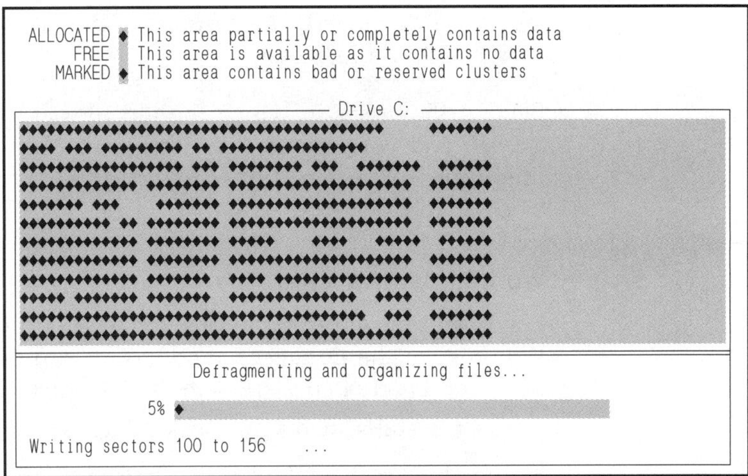

BeckerTools for Windows Disk Optimizer optimization program (at the start of optimization)

Compressing free disk space

The above utilities remove disk fragmentation. BeckerTools Disk Optimizer does this by moving all reserved file blocks and files to contiguous areas. Free blocks are moved to the area behind the "reserved" area.

Defragmenting increases speed

As a result, the physical fragmentation on the disk surface is eliminated.

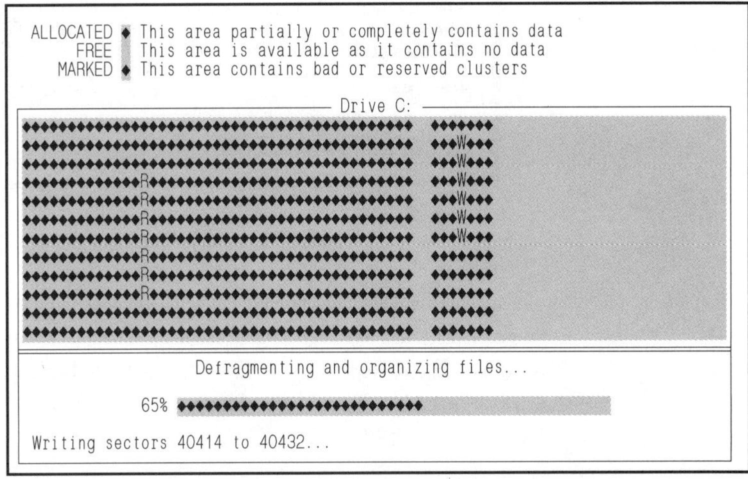

BeckerTools Disk Optimizer optimization program (during optimization)

The blocks are reorganized according to the criterion "free" or "allocated" and by file which means that the files are no longer logically fragmented. Hard drives compressed in this way provide very effective file access.

Beyond the areas, in which the old files are re-allocated, there is a large and contiguous free area available for new files. This is important for applications that require several contiguous free blocks to run.

Working with a swap file

For example, a permanent swap file, which will be used by Windows in the Enhanced mode as an additional virtual memory area, can be created. The Windows Control Panel 386 Enhanced program installs such a swap file. Click on the Virtual Memory... button, then on the Change> > button to see the options.

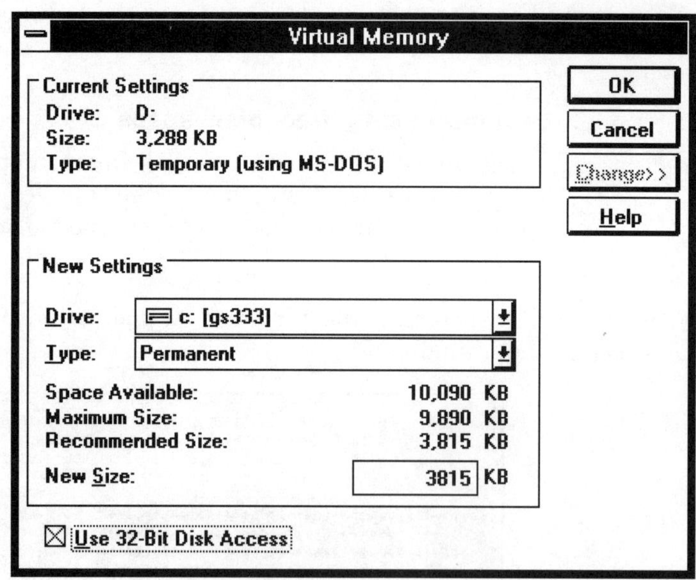

Swap files require contiguous disk space

To work with a swap file, first determine how large your permanent swap file should be. However, this must be available as a contiguous area on the disk. This isn't the same as free disk capacity, because free disk capacity can be quite large on a fragmented disk.

Swap file requires contiguous disk space

Depending on the condition of your disk surface, you should optimize the disk surface before creating a swap file. Doing this can create a large enough area for this file. This only applies to configuring a permanent swap file.

If you need a temporary swap file, Windows doesn't need contiguous disk space. Temporary storage files are written in single blocks of 1024 bytes. When Windows works with this temporary file, it increases beyond the limit defined within SETUP.

Essentially, this is the same as file expansion. So, a large, contiguous block isn't immediately necessary. However, the more these temporary storage files access the disk, the slower the access speed, depending on the amount of file fragmentation on the hard drive's surface.

The hard drive access speed determines the processing speed, especially while accessing auxiliary virtual memory areas. If you work with Windows in the 386 Enhanced mode, you must sacrifice speed if you omit the frequent compression of its hard drives from your routines.

Hidden swap files

Remember that when you've configured a size for the permanent swap files, you cannot use that space as long as the setting is maintained. Free space on your hard drive depends on what size storage space you've set. You cannot display the swap file with the DOS DIR command because it's configured as a hidden file. You can view the file by using the /A:S switch of the MS-DOS 5.0 DIR command.

```
C:\>DIR /A:S


 Volume in drive C is 105MEG
 Volume Serial Number is 454A-1CD0
 Directory of C:\

IO       SYS     33430 04-09-91   5:00a
MSDOS    SYS     37394 04-09-91   5:00a
D_D_VOL  000  52549632 03-19-92   9:31a
386SPART PAR   3891200 03-30-92   3:00p <-Windows swap file
        4 file(s)   56511656 bytes
                     6434816 bytes free
```

Swap file 386spart.par in Norton Commander

7.7 Optimizing the Interleave Factors

You can also optimize the hard drive by fine tuning the mass storage media. Tuning data access for the disk drives can improve the processing speed of the entire system. This can improve the data transfer rate between the hard drive and the controller. This is usually only necessary on older 80286 computers.

The data access and data transfer rate to the controller are extremely important when you're working with Windows and using swap files in Standard mode (and in 386 Enhanced mode using virtual RAM). This is because a virtual disk is actually created in either a temporary or permanent swap file on the hard drive.

Optimizing access

Besides Windows, the procedures we've described in this chapter aren't equally important for all applications. Obviously, if a program doesn't access the disk, the disk access speed and the data transfer rate aren't important.

Processing many data sets in a database requires constant reading and writing to a disk. So the time factor gained depends on the type of data sets used. Optimizing storage media access refers to faster access to the hard drive and increased data transfer flow to the controller. These features can be divided into two categories, depending on where they are implemented: Optimizing software with cache programs like SMARTDRV, or exchanging hardware for more productive components.

Matching system components

Your system's speed depends on the interaction between different components. Data access to the hard drive almost always begins and ends in a temporary storage area. An application needs data and the processor requests it. The processor then instructs the controller to obtain the information. The disk sends the data it finds to the controller, which decodes the information and makes it available to the processor. The processor ensures that the data reaches the proper application, or rather, that the data is sent to the correct temporary storage area.

You can see that many components of the system are involved in the process. So, to increase the hard drive access speed, all the components must work together.

Interleave factors and the data transfer rate

Before discussing settings and interleave factor correction, we'll define the term interleave factor. Well also discuss why an incorrectly configured interleave factor can negatively effect data access and, consequently, make Windows operation less efficient.

Interleave factor defined

The interleave factor is the number of sectors that the read/write head can skip between two consecutively numbered sectors. Interleave factors influence the processing speed or performance of a hard drive and controller. If the interleave factor is too small or too large, the processing speed in the hard drive control unit is decreased.

Hard drives are divided into tracks and sectors. During the MFM format process, each track on the hard drive is physically divided into 17 equal sectors.

An example of interleave factors

We'll use an example to explain interleave factors. Think of a disk as a dart board. The outer track is divided into 17 equal fields (sectors). The disk spins at a constant speed. Your task is to throw darts at the disk until you hit all 17 sectors, when each consecutively numbered field reaches the top. Since you're extremely accurate, you always immediately hit the correct sector (the top sector). The darts are passed to you at a constant speed. When the entire track is filled (i.e., when all 17 sectors contain darts), you've accomplished your task.

This example helps illustrate a problem. If the darts are passed quickly enough, you can complete the task in one rotation of the target disk. However, if the next dart is delayed, you'll need several rotations. The time it takes for you to receive the dart determines the number of sectors that are omitted while you wait. If we translate this example into interleave factors, the disk with the sectors is the hard drive and you're the read/write head that accesses the disk. The darts are the data and the person handing you the darts is the controller. The controller also has a helper, called the computer system data bus.

A faster controller and higher interleave factors

The number of sectors that pass under the read/write head before receiving the next command from the controller corresponds to the number of disk revolutions needed to finish reading or writing the track. A fast controller mounted on a fast data bus (e.g., an 80386 machine) passes the data so quickly that each sector can be read in physical sequence. After a single revolution of the hard drive in a sixtieth of a second, the track is read and the data are already on the way to the processor.

With a slower controller, the logical order of sectors is arranged differently than the physical order when the hard drive is formatted. This is done by setting the interleave factors. With an interleave factor of 3, for example, 2 sectors would be omitted from each pass. Only each third sector would be accessed. Three disk revolutions would be needed until the entire track is read and transferred. Here the controller and the disk work with an interleave factor of 1:3, which means that three disk revolutions (three sixtieths of a second) complete a read/write operation to a single track.

Various factors

Generally a PC/XT controller works with an interleave factor of 1:5 or 1:6 (i.e., five or six disk revolutions are needed to read each track). The hard drive controller on a standard 80286 works at 6

MHz with an interleave factor of 1:3. Many 80386 machines and controllers operate with an interleave factor of 1:1.

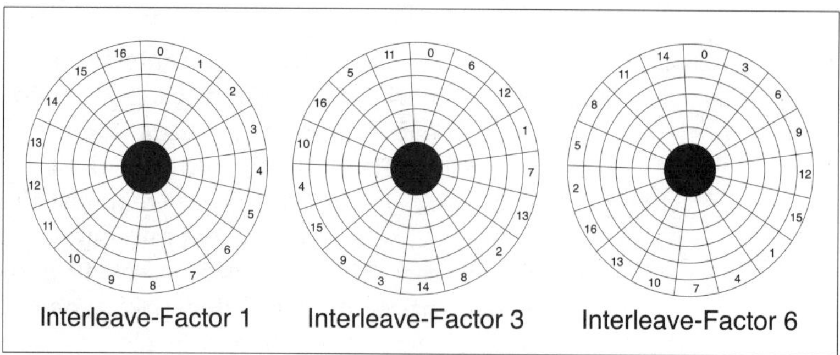

Interleave factors of 1, 3, and 6 for tracks with 17 sectors

A high speed controller with an interleave factor of 1:1 doesn't help a slow computer. The opposite is true if a controller is fast, but the data bus is slow in receiving the data. The controller would be hampered and may be forced to wait a full rotation until it can read the next sector. This is an interleave factor of 1:17. In this case, you can achieve better results by using an interleave of 1:5.

The fastest 80386 with a fast hard drive doesn't perform much better if the controller is too slow. This can slow down the other system components. It works much slower than matched components.

Optimal component combinations

A computer system is more than clock rates, access times, data transfer rates, and interleave factors. Each computer works with the software that's assembled to perform a certain procedure, such as manipulating data. If the components are adjusted to work with one another, the task will be performed more efficiently. Finding an optimal configuration is more important than gathering the most advanced components.

This advice also applies to Windows. As an operating system expansion, Windows provides numerous features which must be attuned to the hardware on which they're installed. There will always be higher demands on processing rates and access times.

Determining interleave factors

As we mentioned earlier, optimizing interleave factors is a relatively easy way to speed up data access.

Before making any changes to the interleave factor, check the results (quantity of data per unit of time) of the present setting between the controller and the hard drive during data transfer.

Special software is needed to do this. Similarly, resetting the interleave factors is also only possible with appropriate utility programs.

Interleave factor effects

As you now know, the interleave factor sets the number of disk revolutions that are needed to read or write a track on the hard drive. An interleave factor of 1:1 means that the logical sequence of sector numbering is the same as the physical sequence. This setting is only used for very fast systems. If the computer (e.g., an original IBM AT with 6 MHz system speed) is too slow for this setting, the data transfer rate decreases. In this instance, a factor of 1:3 should be used. An interleave factor set to 1:3 indicates that the logical sequence of sectors is different than the physical sequence. So, the physical fourth sector would logically receive the number two, the physical seventh the number three, etc. Two sectors are always omitted; three full disk revolutions are needed in order to access all the sectors of a specific track.

We'll use an example to explain the effect of incorrect interleave factor settings. These settings affect both the data transfer rate and the processing speed as a whole. We recommend using a utility program that determines the present interleave factor and data transfer rate. This utility program can change these rates without any data loss.

Changing the interleave factors

A program called Calibrate, part of the Norton utilities, performs this task. A common hard drive with a capacity of 20 Meg and a medium access speed of 65 ms (e.g., the Seagate ST-225) built into an 80386 (25 MHz system speed) with an MFM controller was used for this example. It was prepared for data reception with a program called SPEEDSTOR. Like low-level format processes, Calibrate prompts for the interleave factor that's installed and offers a default setting of 3 for the IBM AT (80286). We accepted this setting.

Using Calibrate to measure the data output from the hard drive, the data transfer rate was 182K per second. Calibrate also calculates the data flow rate for each possible interleave factor.

The hard drive was divided into 17 sectors and 17 possible settings.

In this instance, the optimal setting would be a factor of 1:1. However, the data transfer rate is 297K per second. By correcting the interleave factor, 40% more data could be transferred in the same amount of time.

The worst setting would reduce the data flow to 33K per second. The same hard drive on a 10-MHz AT-286, at the same interleave setting, yields a data flow of 33K per second. A correction to the factor 1:3 increases the data transfer rate to 182K per second. This example illustrates two connections. First, the same hard drive can produce a higher transfer rate in a system that is faster overall and second, the correct setting of the interleave factor determines whether the hard drive speed slows down the processing speed of the entire system.

Setting and correcting the interleave factors

It's very easy to use the Calibrate program to analyze and correct the interleave factors. The program works with DOS and is menu driven. You can follow the program's progress. Although your data isn't affected, you should back up the data on your hard drive before making any changes.

Using SPEEDSTOR

Other hard drive installation utility programs also set the interleave factor. SPEEDSTOR enables you to choose from an "Initialization Menu" with an option called "Re-Initialize." This re-sets the interleave factor of a hard drive that's already formatted (and contains data) without affecting your data.

Changing the setting with the DEBUG.COM program forces a new initialization of the hard drive with a changed interleave factor. All data on the hard drive is lost in this process.

These programs don't contain a test routine that specifies how the changed interleave factors affect the data transfer rate. If you don't have a program that tests the results of different settings, you must test each setting until you find the best one.

7.8 Installing a Faster Hard Drive

If the interleave factors are set properly, data flow between the hard drive and the processor is increased. Further increases are possible by reducing access time to the hard drive. Access time is the amount of time the heads need to access the data (i.e., to move to the place on the disk where the data is stored). Access times vary depending on where the data is stored on the disk. However, the differences cannot be perceived by the human eye. The access speed of a hard drive is usually indicated by the manufacturer, with a median unit of milliseconds.

Performance loss through frequent access

The more often an application accesses the hard drive, the more important the access speed is to the processing speed of the entire system. In these instances, "performance" can be increased by exchanging a comparatively slow hard drive for a "faster" one. Hard drives with access times of less than 28 milliseconds are common. However, faster drives are more expensive than slower ones.

Choosing according to your needs

For most applications and especially for word processing, an access speed of 40 to 50 milliseconds is entirely acceptable. A faster hard drive is barely noticeable.

Remember that the processor of the new (faster) hard drive must be compatible with the method the old disk used (MFM, RLL, IDE); otherwise you'll have to purchase another hard drive controller.

Installing a faster controller

Even hard drive controllers have differences that can affect the processing speed of the entire system. A slower controller in an otherwise fast system acts as a brake. It's useless to obtain data quickly from the bus and place it in the controller if the controller slows down the flow because it cannot keep up the pace. So, a perfectly configured interleave factor for the hard drive is almost useless if the controller can't handle the flow.

Use matching components

The degree of interaction between the internal components involved in data transfer is the determining factor of total processing speed for the entire system.

If a controller is slowing down the other components in the system, you may have to exchange it for a faster version or a controller card that allows a higher data flow rate. The determining factors are device class, bus width, and the application you're using.

8. Setting Your Windows Environment

Changing colors and patterns

The colors that appear after a successful installation can be adjusted to fit your preferences from the Control Panel. All elements of the Windows screen can be changed, or the whole look can be changed by picking a finished combination of colors and patterns.

Screen savers

Using a screen saver program increases the life of your screen by projecting a moving picture, if no user input occurs within a certain length of time. You can also set the icon label spacing and the distance between icons.

Fonts

To look at the same fonts on the screen as would be printed on your printer, a number of typefaces are available as default fonts and TrueType fonts. Delete the fonts you are not using to save hard drive space.

Country settings

The exchange of data from different country settings occurs often in some programs. Difficulties are encountered when parameters such as commas, decimal spaces and the time and date settings do not coincide. Under Windows these parameters can be adjusted; all of these can be changed in one pass by altering the country choice.

8.1 Using the Control Panel

Windows allows you to change the Control Panel settings according to your own needs. The Control Panel sets the correct time and date, the screen colors, fonts, and many other Windows settings.

Select the Program Manager in the main window. Then click on the Control Panel icon to change the settings used by Windows and Windows applications.

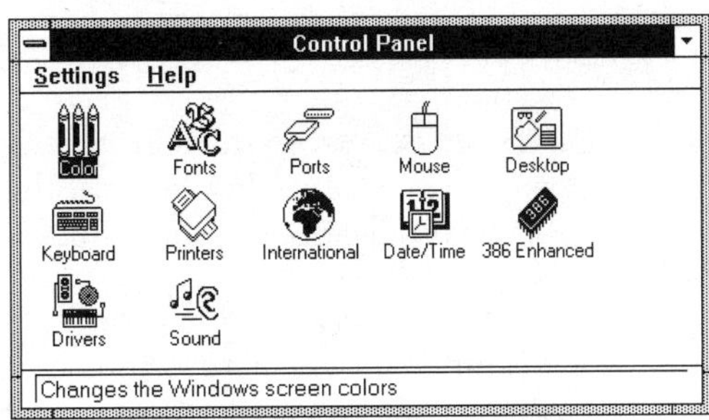

The Control Panel

Settings

You can adjust the following settings: the colors of windows on your screen, the fonts used by the printer, serial interface configuration from COM1: to COM4:, mouse movement on the screen, the double-click interval, background pattern display, the printers that are installed, country-specific settings (e.g., currency and date format), your keyboard, the time, the date, and whether you want to hear a beep if an error occurs. The control panel also installs multimedia MIDI interface drivers and sound cards.

Installing multitasking options by selecting the 386 Enhanced icon is discussed in Chapter 12.

8.2 Date and Time

To set the system date or to change the time, select the command *Date/Time...* from the *Settings* menu or click on the corresponding icon in the Control Panel.

Changing the system date and time

A dialog box appears displaying the current system values. To change the month, day, or year, simply select the appropriate setting and type the new setting. If you're using the mouse, select the appropriate setting and click on the Up or Down arrow. Each mouse click increases or decreases the setting by one.

To save any changes and exit the dialog box, click the OK button. To exit the *Date & Time* dialog box without saving any changes, click Cancel or select *Close* from the Control menu.

8.3 Changing Mouse Settings

Select *Mouse...* from the *Settings* menu or click on the Mouse icon to open the *Mouse* dialog box. In this dialog box you can determine how the mouse operates in Windows.

The *Mouse Tracking Speed* option determines the speed at which the pointer moves across the screen. This can be set from *Slow* to *Fast*. To change this setting, drag the scroll box to the left or right or click on the appropriate arrow. You can also use the ← or → cursor key to move the scroll box.

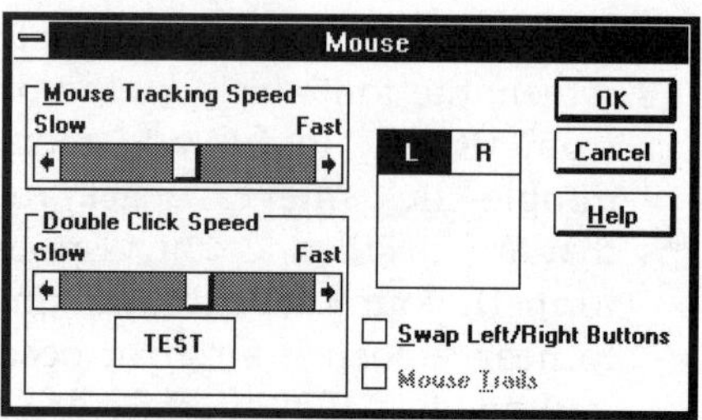

Individual mouse settings

How fast is your double-click?

Another mouse setting is the *Double Click Speed* option. This determines the amount of time Windows takes to register a double-click.

To change this setting, drag the scroll box or click the appropriate arrow. You can also use the ← or → cursor key to change this setting. Then use the Test button to test your setting.

Switching the right and left mouse buttons

Another mouse setting involves switching the functions of the right and left mouse buttons. This is helpful for left-handed users. To switch these functions, select the *Swap Left/Right Buttons* check box.

When you've made the necessary settings, either click the OK or Cancel button. You can also select *Close* from the *Control* menu.

Mouse with LCD display

If you're using Windows on a monochrome LCD display, sometimes it's difficult to see the mouse pointer.

Moving the mouse pointer on this type of display creates a delay that cannot be properly represented on the screen. It takes so long to display the mouse pointer that, if the mouse is moved quickly, the pointer disappears before it can be displayed. You can follow the pointer on the screen only if you move the mouse pointer very slowly.

To solve this problem, select the *Mouse Trails* option. When this option is selected, a trail of mouse pointers appears on the screen as you move the mouse. So, it's much easier to see the mouse pointer on the screen. This option is activated as soon as you select the *Mouse Trails* check box.

When you've completed your mouse settings, click the OK button or the Cancel button, or select *Close* from the Control menu.

8.4 Adding Fonts

Select the *Fonts...* command from the *Settings* menu or click on the Fonts icon in the Control Panel. The *Fonts* dialog box displays the installed fonts. When you select a font from this list, it's displayed in all available sizes in the lower portion of the dialog box.

This enables you to see how the fonts will look on the screen and how they'll appear when printed. The fonts are divided into TrueType Fonts and defined screen fonts (e.g., VGA resolution). TrueType fonts are scalable and are printed on a printer exactly as they appear on the screen.

Defined screen fonts are usually only available in certain sizes and the characters aren't always printed as they appear on the screen.

For example, suppose that you want to use an 11 point printer font in Word for Windows. This size won't be available in the list of defined screen fonts because these fonts are usually only available in even sizes, such as 10 or 12 points.

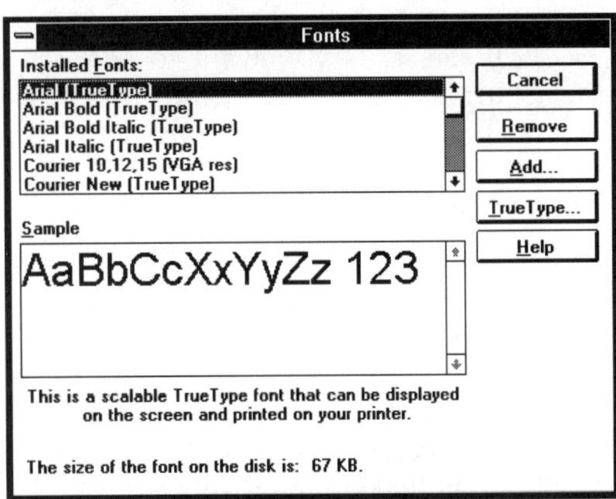

Selecting fonts

TrueType options

Unfortunately, TrueType fonts occupy a lot of memory. Each font occupies about 60 to 70 kilobytes on the hard drive. The exact size for each font appears at the bottom of the Fonts dialog box. Activate the TrueType button to set the options for TrueType fonts.

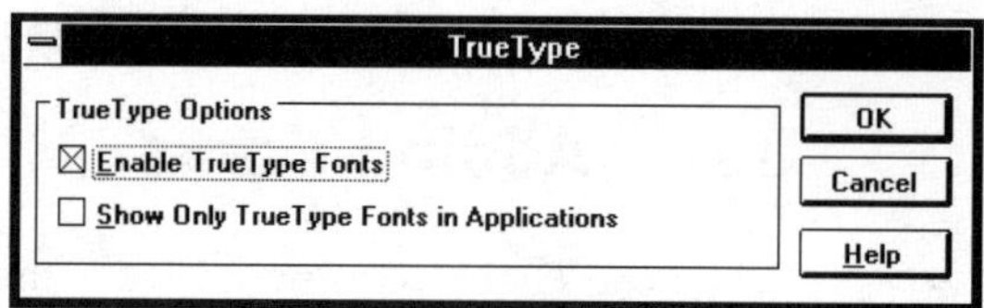

TrueType options

Windows can use the installed TrueType fonts only when the *Enable TrueType Fonts* option is selected. If this option isn't selected, only defined screen fonts can be used, which can lead to display problems.

If the *Show Only TrueType Fonts in Application* option is selected, applications use TrueType fonts exclusively. The defined screen fonts are then removed from memory and are no longer displayed in the font list.

Adding additional fonts

To install additional fonts, select the Add button. Windows opens a dialog box, in which you must select the directory or drive designator that contains the font files.

If the fonts you want to add are located on a diskette, type the drive designation and insert the diskette in the drive. The command is then executed.

A list displays all the files on the diskette that have the .FON extension. Select the fonts you want to install, then select the OK button. Windows copies these files from the diskette into the Windows directory.

If you install fonts that cannot be output to your printer or to your screen, Windows replaces these fonts (if possible) with similar fonts that can be displayed.

Removing fonts

To remove fonts that cannot be printed or displayed, first select the font(s) you want to remove. Then select the Remove button. When you press OK, the font is removed from memory and from the Installed Fonts list.

8.5 Configuring Serial Ports

To install an output device (printer, plotter, modem, etc.) with a serial connection, you must specify how information is transferred from the computer to the device. To do this, select the *Ports...* command from the *Settings* menu or click on the Ports icon in the Control Panel. Then select the Settings... button.

Baud rate

In the dialog box that appears, you can set a baud rate (110, 300, 600, 1200, 2400, 4800, 9600, or 19200). This is the speed with which data is transferred between the devices.

Data bits

The *Data Bits* drop-down list box specifies the number of data bits the processor sends.

Parity

Parity sets the method of error testing for the serial interface.

Stop bits

In the *Stop Bits* drop-down list box you can set the time between transmitted characters.

Flow control

Use the *Flow Control* option to determine how the flow of data is controlled. Your selection determines which flow control method is used after each byte is transferred from one computer.

With the Advanced... button you can select additional settings or the selected port.

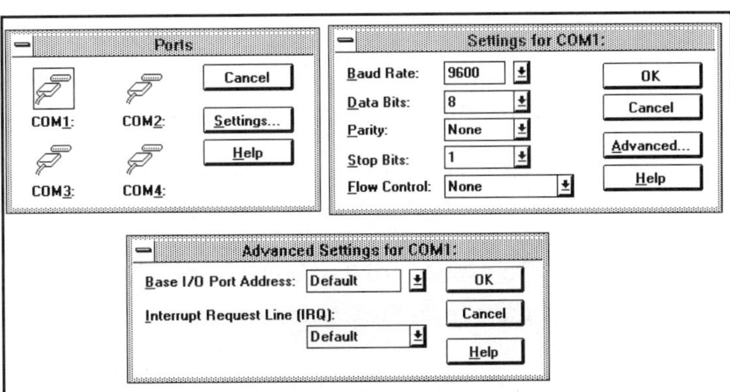

Serial data transfer

For more information about the settings for a particular device, such as a modem or plotter, refer to its manual.

When you're finished, confirm your settings by selecting the OK button. You'll return to the *Ports* dialog box. If you want to configure another interface, repeat the process. Select Cancel to exit this dialog box.

8.6 Keyboard Settings

By selecting the *Keyboard* icon, you can change the keystroke repetition rate (*Repeat Rate*). The keystroke repetition rate controls how many characters appear on the screen when you continue to press a key for a period of time. It also sets the time that elapses before the repetition starts. The *Delay Before First Repeat* check box must be active for any delay to take place.

To change the keyboard settings, select *Keyboard* from the *Settings* menu or click on the Keyboard icon. In the dialog box that appears you can change the keystroke *Repeat Rate*. This rate specifies how fast a key repeats when you press and hold it down. You can also set the time that elapses before the computer repeats a key after you press it and hold it down.

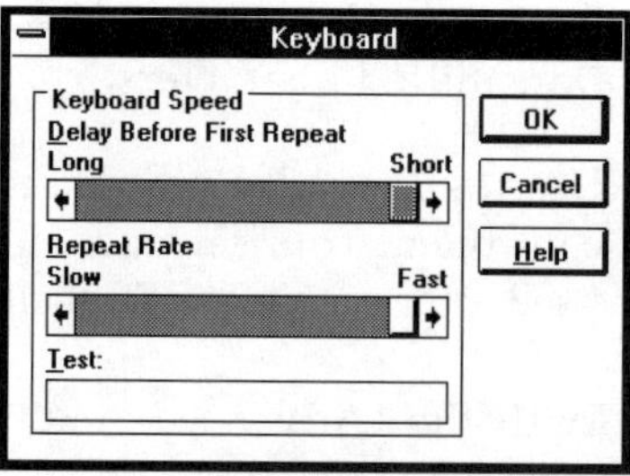

Keystroke speed setting

With a high repeat rate more characters appear in the same amount of time than with a slow rate.

Use the scroll bars in the dialog box to set these options. Use the test option to test the settings.

To exit this dialog box, click OK or Cancel. You can also select *Close* from the Control menu.

8.7 Sound

Activating and suppressing sounds

Under the default settings, if a user error occurs while selecting a command in a dialog box, a tone indicates an error.

To switch off this tone, select *Sound...* from the *Settings* menu or click on the Sound icon in the Control Panel. Then activate the *Enable System Sounds* option and select the OK button.

Using a sound card

A sound card with an attached speaker can emit many different sounds for many different events.

On the left side of the *Sound* dialog box, select an event for which a sound can be defined. The *Sound Recorder* application can modify or mix existing sounds according to your needs.

You'll find more information about sound in Section 8.12 of this chapter, and in Chapter 28 of this book.

8.8 Country Settings

The *International* setting specifies country-specific time, date, currency, and number formats. Select *International* from the *Settings* menu or click the International icon from the Control Panel.

In the dialog box that appears, you can specify certain settings for country, keyboard layout, language, and a unit of measurement. You can also change the country-specific default settings.

The *Country:* option allows you to select from 28 countries. When you select a country, the other format settings for the country are automatically activated (date, time, currency, number etc.). For example, if you select France, all the country-specific settings are changed accordingly.

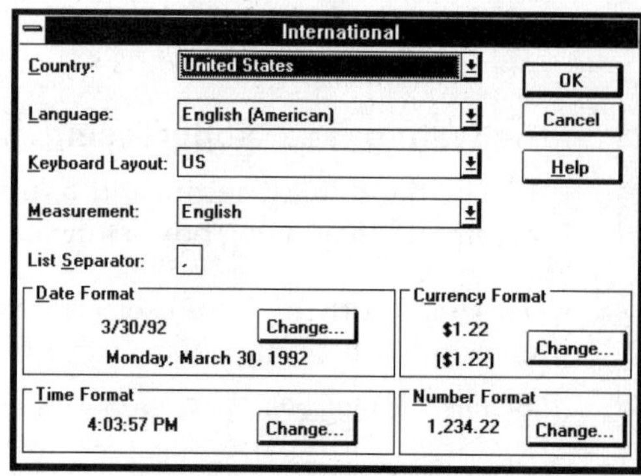

A country-specific setting

Specifying country settings

Language settings

The *Language* option adjusts settings for language-specific tasks, such as sorting. If you choose a language other than the one used to install Windows and press the OK button, you'll be prompted to insert a Windows installation disk that contains the translation file for the new language.

Keyboard layout

The *Keyboard Layout* option enables you to set up a keyboard layout for the language you're using. Your keyboard layout should match the country and language you've selected. This ensures that you can use the special characters and symbols of the selected language.

Metric or English measurement units

Use the *Measurement* option to select the unit of measurement that will be used. You can select either the Metric system, which is used in European countries or the English system, which is based on inches.

The list separator

The List Separator option specifies the character that should be used to separate elements in a list.

Changing country-specific formats

You can change some country-specific formats according to your needs. To do this, select the Change... button for the appropriate format and change the values appropriately.

For example, to change the Date format, click its Change... button. The *International - Date Format* dialog box appears.

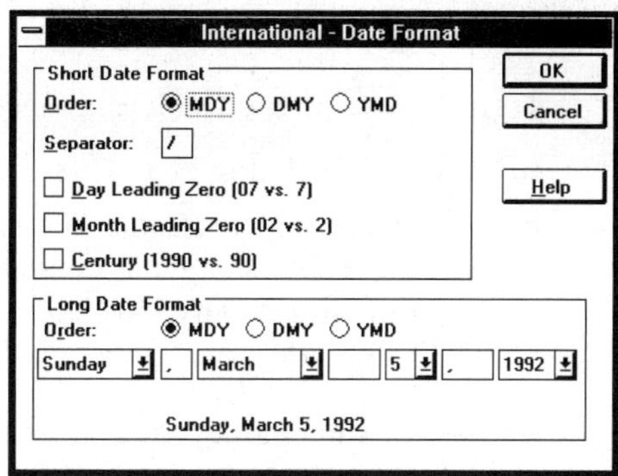

Setting the date format

In this dialog box you can specify the various date formats that should be used in all Windows applications. Excel, for example, displays a currency symbol in a numeric format that's based on the setting you've chosen for *Country*.

8.9 Setting Screen Colors

To set the Windows screen colors, select *Color...* in the *Settings* menu or click on the Color icon in the Control Panel.

The *Color* dialog box is used to select a color for each element of the Windows screen. Select different color schemes from the drop-down list box or design your own. If you want to design a color scheme, you can use any combination. The Color Palette > > button displays preset options (46 colors), to which you can assign different elements of the screen.

By using the Define Custom Colors... button you can mix the 16 colors together. To color a screen element with a specific hue, first indicate which element you want to change. To do this, either click on the appropriate element in the sample screen or select the element from the *Screen Element* drop-down list box.

Saving a scheme

By clicking the Save Scheme button a user-defined color scheme can be saved. The scheme will be added to the list of complete schemes.

Removing a scheme

To remove a color scheme, select the Remove Scheme button.

If you have a Hercules graphics adapter, Windows will only display in gray scales. Windows cannot display colors without running an EGA adapter with an EGA screen.

Defining your own colors

To define your own colors, select the Color Palette > > button from the *Color* dialog box. Then select the Define Custom Colors... button. The *Custom Color Selector* dialog box will appear. To create your color, drag the cursor in the color refiner box and the arrow in the luminosity bar. You can also create a color by entering values in the *Hue:*, *Sat:*, *Lum:*, *Red:*, *Green:*, and *Blue:* boxes.

Values for the colors red, green, and blue represent the amount of basic color in the mixed color. The shade being mixed is shown on the left half of the *Color/Solid* box. The right half of this box shows the solid color your custom color most closely resembles. To use the solid color or to start by using it as the basis for another color, press the key combination Alt + O.

Solid colors are displayed directly on the screen and mixed colors are simulated by using differently dense colored pixel grids on the screen.

To use a user-defined color in a color scheme, you must add the color to the definable part of the color palette. Click on the Add Color button to do this.

If you're using the mouse, select the color values by clicking on the Up or Down arrows. To choose solid colors, double-click on the *Solid* field.

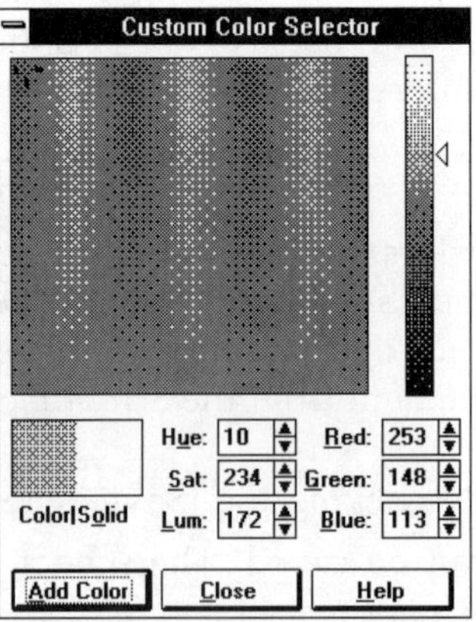

Defining individual colors

Once the color settings are complete, click on the Close button. You'll return to the original *Color* dialog box. The settings you choose are purely a matter of taste; you don't have to make any changes. Usually the default values are good enough.

8.10 Desktop Settings

With the Desktop setting you can specify the appearance of your desktop. Some of the settings include icon controls, cursor control, screen saver options, and background patterns. Select *Desktop...* from the *Settings* menu or click the Settings icon in the Control Panel.

Choosing a background pattern

The *Desktop* dialog box will appear. You can select a pattern, which is a design that appears across the desktop.

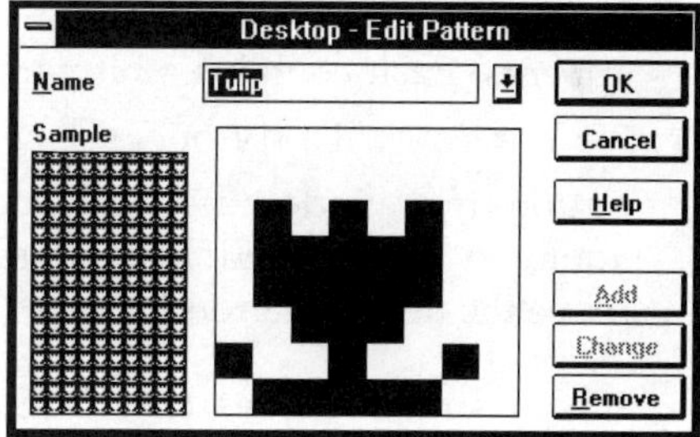

Working with the Tulip pattern

Choosing a pattern

The default installation values for Windows display the background pattern as a gray screen with a blue-gray background for the icon labels. If you want to use other colors for these elements, select a pattern from the *Pattern Name:* drop-down list box.

If you want to change an existing pattern, select the Edit Pattern... button. The *Desktop - Edit Pattern* dialog box appears. Select the pattern you want to change from the *Name* drop-down list box.

If you select this button, the pattern of pixels that composes the picture appears in the *Sample* box, as previously shown in the illustration of the Tulip pattern. To change the pattern, click the mouse in the cell that appears to the right of the *Sample* box. Doing this reverses the colors in the pattern. The *Sample* box will display your changes. When you've finished changing the pattern, select the Change button and then the OK button.

Adding a pattern

To add a new pattern, repeat the procedure previously explained but type a new name for the selected pattern in the *Name* text box.

Then, when you're finished changing the pattern, select the Add button and then the OK button.

Choosing a background picture

The Windows default settings don't display a background picture on your desktop. The background is usually gray or contains the pattern you've selected. However, it's possible to select a bitmap image that can be used as your background. To do this, use the *Wallpaper* option from the Desktop dialog box.

To display the available bitmap images, open the *File:* drop-down list box. A list of file names with the .BMP extension appears. Each contains a bitmap that can be used as a background for Windows. To try one, select the file name and press the OK button. If a window is at full screen size, you won't be able to see your new background. In this case, return the window to normal size to see the new background.

If you still don't see the image, the *Center* option is probably selected. This option displays the chosen background image in the center on the screen. If the image is relatively small, such as ARCADE.BMP, the new background can be entirely covered by a normal size window.

Select *Desktop...* again and then select the *Tile* option in the *Wallpaper* option. This option repeats the image until the entire screen is filled.

Using your own background images

If you don't want to use any of the existing bitmap files, you can create your own. For example, you may want to use your own initials or a company logo. To create a bitmap, use a graphics program, such as Paintbrush.

Paintbrush, which is a graphics program that creates bitmap files, is included in the Windows package. Store the bitmap in the directory where Windows is located.

Then, the file will be displayed in the *File:* drop-down list box in the *Wallpaper* setting.

Changing a background picture

You can also change the available background bitmap images. Load an existing file into a graphics program and make any changes. Then save the file in the appropriate directory again.

The other settings in the *Desktop* dialog box are a matter of personal preference. These settings include the blinking speed of the cursor, the distance between icons, and the screen orientation.

Selecting and using a screen saver

A screen saver program can help protect your monitor from "screen burn." This occurs when the same screen display remains on the monitor for an extended time period. The text or image displayed can "burn" into the monitor. So, you can still see the text or image, even when the monitor is switched off.

You can eliminate this problem by using the *Screen Saver* option. The screen saver switches to a moving picture when no actions are performed for a certain amount of time. A moving image appears at one screen location for a few seconds and then moves to a different location. Windows provides four screen savers.

To display a screen saver, select its name from the *Name* drop-down list box and select the Test button.

In the *Delay:* box, enter a time in minutes. After this time has elapsed, the screen saver will be activated if the computer isn't used.

Using a screen saver

When you select a screen saver, the Setup... button becomes available. Depending on the screen saver, different setup options can be used.

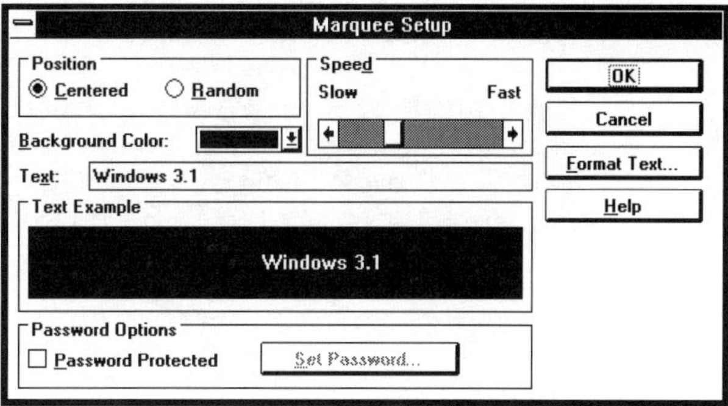

Settings for the screen saver

One screen saver is Marquee. This screen saver displays a line of text, which moves across the screen. Any text, such as a company motto, can be displayed. In the *Marquee Setup* dialog box, you can specify certain settings for this screen saver.

To change the text that's displayed, type the desired text in the *Text:* text box. To format this text, select the [Format Text...] button. The *Format Text* dialog box appears. Specify the font and style for the screen saver text in this dialog box. Then click [OK] to confirm your changes.

The speed at which the text moves across the screen is set by moving the scroll box in the *Speed* setting. Select the background color in the *Background Color:* drop-down list box. The available colors depend on your graphics card and driver. To specify the position of the text on the screen, use the *Position* setting. To center the text, select the *Centered* option button. If you want the text to appear in different locations, select *Random*.

If you frequently leave your desk but don't want to switch off your computer each time, protect yourself against unauthorized access by using the password option for the screen saver. If you set up a password, an activated screen saver can be deactivated only if the correct password is entered.

Select the *Password Protected* check box to switch on password protection. Then select the [Set Password...] button. In the dialog box that appears, type the password in the *New Password:* text box. As you type, the letters (or numbers) are displayed as asterisks. So, to confirm your password, type it in the *Retype New Password:* text box.

If a password is installed and the screen saver is activated, the password must be entered in order to return to Windows.

Unfortunately, the password protection feature isn't foolproof. It can be bypassed by performing a warm boot. Although the password protection isn't deleted, it can be deactivated by switching off the *Password Protected* check box. Password protection can also be avoided by deleting the entry in *Control.ini* file.

Deleting the password

To delete a password, select the [Set Password...] button. Enter the old password in the *Old Password:* text box. If a new password isn't specified in the second and third text boxes, the old password is deleted when you select the [OK] button.

Setting cursor blinking speed

To change the blinking speed of the text cursor, use the *Cursor Blink Rate* option. This setting affects only applications, in which text must be entered. In these instances the text cursor appears as a blinking vertical line.

To set the cursor blink rate, drag the scroll box to either Fast or Slow. You can also use the right and left cursor keys to move the scroll box. Your setting is indicated by the text cursor that appears next to the scroll bar.

Setting icon spacing

To set the spacing between icons, use the *Icon* option. A value between 0 and 512 pixels can be specified. The default setting is 75 pixels. To change this setting, in the Spacing box either type a new number or click on the arrows to increase or decrease the number.

Multi-line icon titles

If you switch on the *Wrap Title* option, icon descriptions are continued on the next line. This is useful for longer icon titles, which may overlap if there isn't enough space.

Setting the sizing grid

With the *Sizing Grid* option you can specify how the windows should be displayed on the screen. This involves determining window borders and setting the spacing of the invisible grid, on which windows and icons in the desktop are aligned.

The *Granularity* option specifies the spacing of the grid. The default value for this option is zero pixels, which means that a no grid orients the windows and icons on the screen. If you enter a value other than zero, all movements or enlargements, whether they are performed with the mouse or the keyboard, can only occur in the indicated increment. The highest value that can be specified is 49 pixels.

Setting border width

The *Border Width:* option specifies the widths of the borders around a window. The default value for this option is three pixels. However, you can specify a value between 1 and 50.

Applications

The *Applications* option enables you to switch on fast application switching. This option is helpful when you're working with several applications simultaneously. You can switch between the applications with the key combination Alt + Tab. If you use the *Fast "Alt"+"Tab" Switching* option, you can press Alt and Tab to display the name of the next active application.

The application that will be activated when you release the Alt key is displayed in a field in the middle of the screen. If you decide not to activate the application and to your original application, continue to hold the Alt key and press Esc. Your original application will be displayed in the foreground.

8.11 Defining Multitasking Options

If you're running Windows in the 386 Enhanced mode, several applications can run simultaneously. Occasionally these applications simultaneously demand access to the same peripheral device. The *386 Enhanced* options allow you to specify how the applications will use the peripheral devices and how much of the computer's resources should be allocated to Windows and non-Windows applications.

These options apply to only non-Windows applications. If several Windows applications are running simultaneously, Windows handles this task without using these options.

Device conflict control options

When you select the 386 Enhanced icon, a dialog box appears. This dialog box displays all peripheral device interface attachments that could be simultaneously accessed by several applications.

You must select the port that's connected to the device you want to control. There are three *Device Contention* option buttons that control simultaneous device access.

Competing I/O operations are reported

If the *Always Warn* option is selected, a message is displayed every time more than one application demands access to the same peripheral device. You must answer this message by indicating which application should have control.

The *Never Warn* option suppresses all warnings of access conflict. Under this setting, it's possible for two programs to try to send output to the printer simultaneously. You should use this option only if you're sure that simultaneous I/O access to a peripheral device won't occur.

With the *Idle (in sec.)* option you can determine the length of time between two requests to a peripheral device; you can use a value between 1 and 999 seconds. This can prevent many problems when a device can switch between two applications. For example, if you're working with a transparent communications program, you can use an external modem to establish connection to a host, then later switch to terminal emulation in the session without losing the connection.

Multitasking options

With the *Scheduling* options, you can establish a hierarchy of applications in 386 Enhanced mode. Non-Windows applications can run in 386 Enhanced mode, but they aren't automatically prioritized.

The calculation basics

The *Minimum Timeslice* box allows you to set a value of time in milliseconds. This is the length of time a program can run before Windows gives control to another application.

All Windows applications share one timeslice, while each non-Windows application has its own slice.

The *Windows in Foreground* option is a value of time between 1 and 10,000. This setting specifies the amount of processor time that must be given to the Windows application that's running in the foreground. In order to calculate this setting, you must refer to the entries made to the timeslice under *Windows in Background* or the background settings made for other applications with the PIF Editor.

The *Windows in Background* option is the amount of processor time given to Windows applications running in the background; again the range 1 and 10,000 is used.

We'll use an example to explain these calculations. Suppose that you've specified 100 for both the foreground and background applications. This indicates that the foreground application and all other applications running in the background have equal amounts of processor time.

If you specified 150 for the foreground application and 100 for the background, the foreground application would receive 60% of the processor time and the background applications would divide the remaining 40%.

The relative values you enter serve as the basis for comparison.

100% for Windows

By selecting the *Exclusive in Foreground* check box, you give the Windows application in the foreground 100% of the processor time. This means that all active Windows applications split 100% of the processor time and that during that period, all other (non-Windows) applications are idle.

Creating a swap file

Select the Virtual Memory... button to define or change a swap file to hold program blocks. For more information, refer to the section on adding and removing Windows components.

8.12 Installing a Multimedia Driver

To install a multimedia card, such as a sound card (Ad Lib or Sound Blaster) or a CD-ROM drive, the appropriate drivers must be installed under Windows. A driver must be installed before you can access the *Media Player* and *Sound Recorder* applications.

Select *Drivers...* from the *Settings* menu or click on the Drivers icon in the Control Panel. A dialog box appears containing a list of installed drivers.

Installing a Sound Blaster card

If another multimedia device must be installed, the corresponding driver must be added to this list. If you don't have a card installed, exit Windows, switch off the computer, remove the case and install the device in the computer.

A Sound Blaster card would be inserted in a vacant expansion slot in the computer. You would also add a speaker or microphone. Replace the case, switch on the computer and start Windows. Run the *Drivers* application.

Select the driver, and click on the Add button in the *Drivers* dialog box to add a driver.

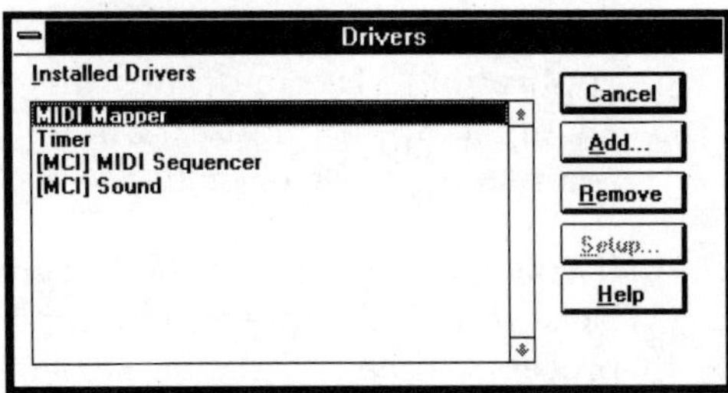

Multimedia driver options

In the dialog box that appears, select the driver that matches your device. If this driver isn't listed, you can select a driver that's compatible with your device or use the device driver the manufacturer provides for use under Windows. To add the manufacturer's driver, select *Unlisted or Updated Driver* from the list of drivers.

Insert the diskette into the disk drive or enter the directory name and disk drive that contains the driver. Once you confirm your actions, the driver is copied to the Windows system directory. Configure the driver in the *...Setup* dialog box, which is automatically displayed.

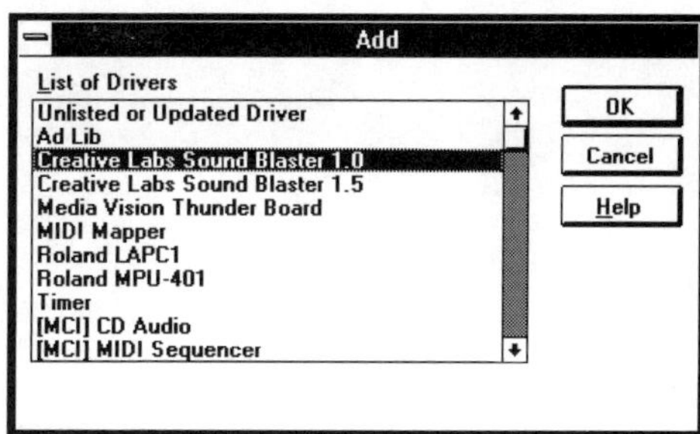

Installing the Sound Blaster driver

The setup varies depending on the driver you install. When you configure a Sound Blaster driver, the *Port* and *Interrupt* settings are adjusted.

Whether the driver works or is properly set up can be tested by assigning notes to certain events with the *Sound* option from the Control Panel. A warm boot must be performed before any changes are activated.

If a device doesn't operate properly, (e.g., if a constant sound is audible with a Sound Blaster card), select the Setup... button again to reconfigure the driver. The same dialog box appears. In most cases, a conflict occurs because of an interrupt overlap. In this case, change the interrupt setting for the appropriate card.

9. Windows Setup

Changing the configuration

During installation, Windows is equipped with the drivers for hardware components, such as the mouse, the screen, keyboard, network, etc. If the configuration changes, you can link individual drivers to Windows in Windows Setup without having to completely install Windows.

Installing applications

Windows Setup automatically links non-Windows applications to the Windows environment. However, some rules must be followed if Windows doesn't find all applications on the hard drive. For a complete description of this procedure, refer to the section on working with applications.

Changing Windows components

Windows consists of numerous individual components that can be added or removed with Windows Setup. Depending on the amount of available memory, you can use Setup to remove the components that you don't use. This option also allows you to create a swap file.

9.1 Using Windows Setup

With Windows it's possible to integrate changes to the hardware without having to reinstall the software. Windows provides a SETUP program for this purpose. This program can be started from the Main group by clicking the Windows Setup icon. While using the Control Panel to install a new printer, you can use Windows Setup to link a new graphics card, another mouse, or set up another network in Windows.

SYSTEM.INI

All changes are stored in the SYSTEM.INI file, which is located in the directory in which you installed Windows. We'll discuss this file's settings in a separate chapter. However, you don't need to make any changes to this file.

Calling Windows Setup

You can start the Windows Setup program from DOS or the Main group under Windows. If you start Windows Setup from DOS, the screen that was displayed the first time you installed Windows appears. If you start Windows Setup from Windows, it appears in a window.

9.2 Installing New Drivers

It's very easy to install new drivers. For example, suppose that you want to replace your old Logitech mouse with a new Microsoft mouse. Simply activate *Setup* by double-clicking its icon in the Main group. Then select *Change System Settings* from the *Options* menu; a window, with the four boxes containing the settings for *Display*, *Keyboard*, *Mouse* and *Network*, appears. Click the box for the mouse to display a list of all available mouse drivers.

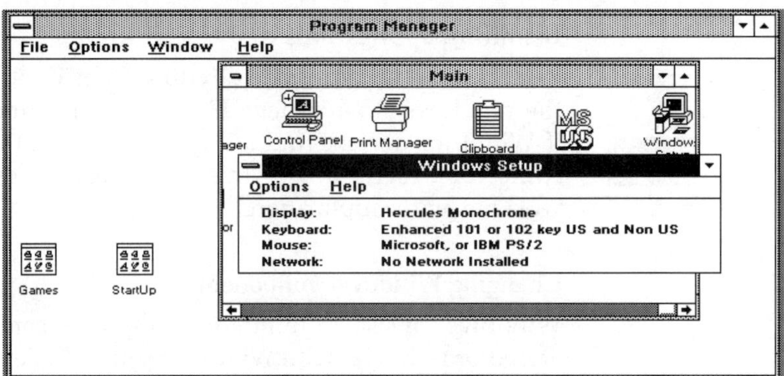

Windows Setup

Selecting drivers

Select the correct driver or one that is compatible to your mouse. After making the necessary changes, confirm your new setting by clicking the OK button. If Windows Setup needs a driver to operate the new device, you'll be prompted to insert the appropriate Windows system diskette. The necessary files are then automatically copied. If the drivers are already on the hard drive in a certain directory, change the default setting for the directory in the dialog box.

After copying and linking the drivers, the Setup program prompts you to restart Windows. Setup does this to enter its changes in the SYSTEM.INI file. However, the entries in this file aren't active until you call Windows. This is why you must reboot the computer after all changes so that your new device can be initialized and run.

Installation under DOS

For example, if you replaced your old Hercules card for a new VGA card, the only way to inform Windows about this change is by starting the Windows Setup program from DOS. The reason why this must be done is obvious. When you installed Windows, the drivers for the Hercules card were installed in Windows. If you install the VGA card, you will no longer be able to start Windows because the card cannot be controlled by the Hercules drivers (unless your VGA card and monitor can emulate Hercules mode).

Change to the directory in which you installed Windows. Usually this is the C:\WINDOWS directory. Call the Setup program by typing SETUP and pressing Enter. The Windows Setup program appears on the screen exactly as it did during the first installation of Windows. Now use the cursor keys to highlight the *Display* box and press Enter to call the list box. Next, select the *VGA* or *VGA with Monochrome Display* option, depending on which screen you're using. After making any other changes to the settings, select *Accept the configuration shown above.*

If Windows needs a new driver to control new hardware components, you'll be asked to insert the appropriate Windows System diskette into the drive. Setup now automatically copies all necessary parts of the program from the diskette. When you restart the computer and call Windows, the changes will be activated.

9.3 Setting Up Windows Components

Windows consists of several individual components, some of which aren't needed to run Windows. For example, Windows can run without the text files that contain supplementary information to the manual, the games, and the applications from the *Accessories* group. These components occupy disk space and, in some instances, are rarely used. Therefore, you can choose to remove them from the hard drive or add only certain ones. In this way, you can save up to 2 Meg of disk space.

Call the *Options/Add/Remove Windows Components...* command to change Windows components.

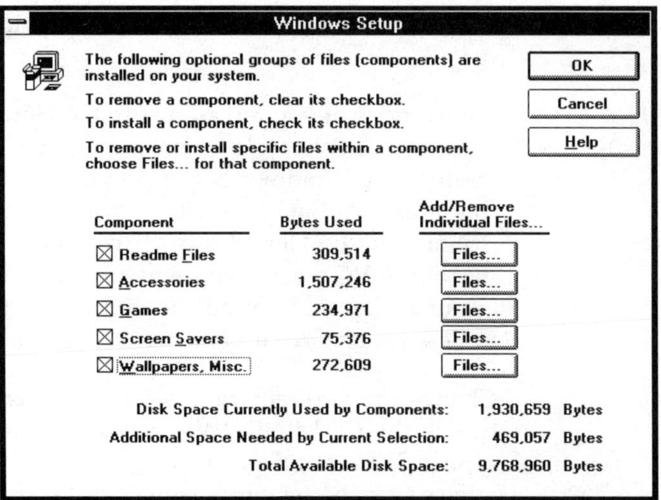

Changing the Windows components

Unless you specify otherwise during the Windows installation, all the components will be saved on the hard drive. This is indicated by the check boxes, which are all activated. Components that aren't checked either aren't on the hard drive or Windows cannot find them.

For example, Windows cannot find components that have been manually copied to a directory other than the original one. Information about the disk space used by the components appears in the lower-right corner of the dialog box.

The middle of the dialog box displays the number of bytes that the activated components occupy on the hard drive. So if you deactivate a component's check box, the number of bytes is reduced.

The components are listed in groups in the first dialog box. These groups, such as the *Readme files* group, consist of several individual files. For more information about the components, double-click the Files... button.

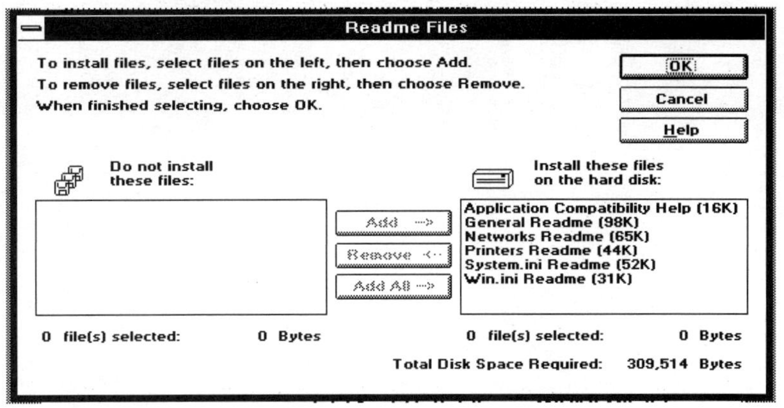

Selecting individual files from the group

Depending on the window (*Do not install...* or *Install these files*) in which you place the files, the components are either installed or removed.

10. Initialization Files

WIN.INI

The WIN.INI file contains the basic Windows settings. All the settings you made on the Control Panel are stored in this file.

CONTROL.INI

The CONTROL.INI file contains color settings for the Windows screen, including the color palette and available patterns.

SYSTEM.INI

The SYSTEM.INI file is the most important initialization file. It contains drivers for the individual hardware components. Windows maintains control in its various modes by using the entries in this file.

PROGMAN.INI

The Program Manager settings are stored in this file. Files used by the Program Manager and application priority settings are listed here.

WINFILE.INI

The WINFILE.INI file contains settings for the File Manager and the Program Manager. Various toggles and confirmation settings are also stored in this file.

10.1 Working with INI Files

Windows generates its own initialization files, which contain program and system settings. These five INI (pronounced "innie") files must be installed in the \WINDOWS directory, or in the same directory as Windows. These files have the extension .INI.

Your last resort

The changes made to the Control Panel are stored in the INI files. An .INI file contains three basic elements: Sections, settings and comments. Here's a sample:

```
[windows]                 ;Section: settings are stored below
spooler=yes               ;Setting: specifies Windows setting
;Enables Print Manager    ;Comment: permits user commentary
```

Earlier versions of Windows used only one initialization file, named WIN.INI. WIN.INI is still important, but its functions have been divided among five files. All INI files are important because some entries, which cannot be made with the Control Panel, can be made directly to the files. (Before changing any INI files, you should be familiar with basic Windows functions.)

In certain situations, the INI files can be invaluable. For example, suppose that you've installed Windows on your computer and want to install a new screen driver to control your new monitor. You accidentally select the wrong driver and now neither driver will display anything correctly. In this case, instead of re-installing Windows, you can change the appropriate setting in the INI file.

In the following section we'll introduce the individual INI files and explain which settings should be made.

To activate changes

When an INI file is changed, the changes won't take effect until the next time Windows is started. Before changing an INI file, create a backup file in the DOS window. To do this, copy the current INI file and give it an *.OLD extension. So, if your system crashes while your changing the INI file, simply return to the original settings by deleting the new files and renaming the .OLD files.

The Notepad and other editing programs

To change an INI file, start the File Manager. Select the INI file you want to change by clicking on it with the mouse or by using the cursor keys. Then select *Run...* from the *File* menu. When the *Run* dialog box appears, press Enter or click on the OK button. The INI file is automatically loaded into the Notepad. You can use any text editor to change the INI files, but you must remember to save the file in the appropriate ASCII format. Some word processors create control codes in their resident format (e.g., Microsoft Word) that cannot be present in an INI file.

Information files

Several files on your Windows diskettes contain additional information about INI files. This information applies to settings that appear only in your INI files (especially SYSTEM.INI) in some hardware configurations. These settings can affect how Windows operates, depending on the hardware configuration. Only Windows users with a grasp of how these settings work should change these settings.

10.2 Working with the System Configuration Editor

Windows contains an undocumented utility called the System Configuration Editor or SysEdit. This utility makes it easy to change the AUTOEXEC.BAT, CONFIG.SYS, WIN.INI, and SYSTEM.INI system files.

All important system files ready at a glance

SysEdit opens all four files automatically; each file is placed in its own window. The window you want to change can then be activated and edited.

The System Configuration Editor is usually located in the \WINDOWS\SYSTEM directory under the name SYSEDIT.EXE. It has its own icon and can be added to the Main window if you frequently experiment with INI files.

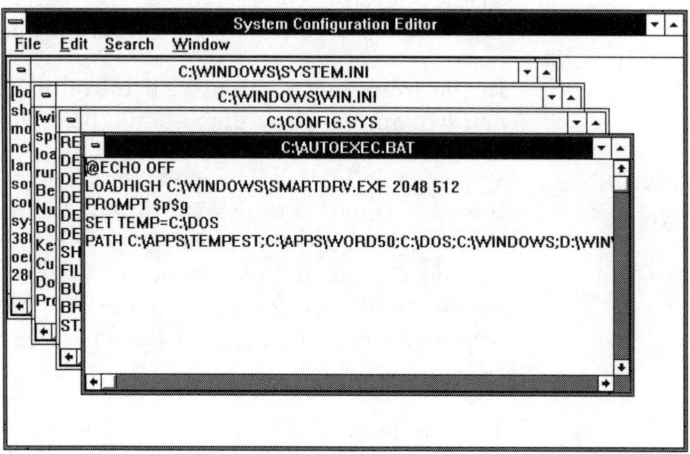

The system editor at work

SysEdit is a dedicated application based on the same premise as the Notepad. A complete search function is available. Simply select the *Search...* command from the *File* menu. Using the Clipboard, you can copy portions of a system file to other applications.

However, you cannot define the files SysEdit automatically opens; it always opens the same four files.

10.3 The WIN.INI File

The WIN.INI file can contain a number of sections and settings controlling application information and system configuration data.

[windows]

This section specifies general Windows settings.

```
load=
```

This setting runs a Windows application in minimized (i.e., icon) form after you start windows. This is useful if you frequently use one particular application. Enter the application name without its extension. Loading Excel as minimized would look like this:

```
load=c:\excel\excel
```

Entering a space between applications in this line lets you load multiple applications.

```
run=
```

Starting an application

This setting runs a Windows application. Enter the name of an application you want opened immediately after Windows starts. You can also specify a file name by including the proper extension in the [extensions] section. This file will be opened automatically when the application is activated.

This option is useful for exchanging information. For example, if you share your computer with a colleague, you can specify that a Clipboard file automatically open when Windows starts. You can use this file to indicate a specific file or to send messages. Also, you could use this option to automatically start the Calendar so that you're reminded of important appointments and plans when you start Windows.

```
run=calendar
```

This entry specifies the file that should be loaded after the application previously indicated starts. For example, if you want to work with an Excel spreadsheet immediately after starting Windows, and then want to load a specific spreadsheet automatically, type the following:

```
run=C:\windows\excel c:\data\file.xls
```

To access files in directories other than the Windows startup directory, enter a complete path name.

```
Beep=yes
```

This setting toggles the computer beep. To deactivate the beep replace *yes* with *no*.

```
Spooler=yes
```

Print Manager

This setting controls Print Manager activity. When you print files, Windows initially sends the files to the Print Manager, which acts as a print buffer. A buffer is an area on the hard drive where the data to be printed can be temporarily stored. Some applications (e.g., PageMaker) take a long time to print. If a file is completely written to the Print Manager, it can be sent from there to the printer. This frees the processor so that it can perform other tasks.

Disabling the Print Manager

If there isn't enough space on your hard drive to print a large file, disable the Print Manager. To do this, replace the *yes* with a *no*. The file is then sent directly to the printer. You cannot use your computer to perform other tasks until the print job is complete.

Remember that if you change this setting while you're working, you must restart Windows in order to activate the change. However, remember to save your WIN.INI file before you reboot.

```
Nullport=None
```

This setting specifies the nullport. If you cannot install a printer port in the system Control Panel because your only port is connected to another printer, install the second printer to a nullport that is simply ignored. Enter the name of the nullport as it should appear in the Control Panel.

```
device=
```

Printer drivers

This setting specifies the default printer driver used by Windows. The following specifies an Apple LaserWriter II NTX (a PostScript printer) attached to COM2:

```
device=Apple LaserWriter II NTX,pscript,COM2:
```

This entry lists the default printer in the order PRINTER (Apple...), PRINTER_DRIVER (PSCRIPT.DRV), COMM_PORT (COM2:). The [devices] section at the end of the WIN.INI file lists valid printers that can be placed in this setting.

```
Documents=
```

This setting lists file extensions of documents (data files) not listed in the [Extensions] section of WIN.INI. All file name extensions listed in [Extensions] are considered documents instead of programs (applications). Documents= lets the user specify additional file extensions for documents.

```
MouseSpeed=1
MouseThreshold1=5
MouseThreshold2=10
MouseTrails=7
```

These settings control mouse operation. The relationship between mouse movement and pointer movement can be adjusted in the Control Panel by selecting *Mouse...* from the *Settings* menu. Additional settings affect the double-click speed and how the mouse appears on LCD screens.

```
NetWarn=1
```

If you've installed a network driver for Windows and are using Windows locally without the network, a warning message appears on the screen. Although the message can be suppressed by setting this parameter to 0, all the network options will also be disabled.

```
BorderWidth=3
```

This entry defines the width of the window border. Any pixel value ranging from 1 to 49 can be used. A value of 1 is the narrowest possible border width.

```
KeyboardSpeed=31
```

This entry specifies the repeat rate of a character continuously pressed on the keyboard. If the character should repeat slowly, enter a value ranging from 1 to 10; if it should repeat quickly, use a value ranging from 20 to 31.

```
CursorBlinkRate=530
DoubleClickSpeed=452
```

Cursor control

These entries affect the double-click speed of the mouse and the cursor blinking speed. These values are measured in milliseconds and should be adjusted in the Control Panel. You can actually see the effects of a setting in the Control Panel.

```
Programs=com exe bat pif
```

This setting lists file extensions of programs (applications). Add program extensions to this setting as needed. Remember to install PIF files in non-Windows applications to adapt the programs to the Windows environment (see Chapter 5 for more information).

```
DeviceNotSelectedTimeout=15
TransmissionRetryTimeout=45
```

These entries specify printer timeout times. After receiving a print command, Windows tries to access the printer within this time limit (in seconds). If the printer is off line, Windows displays an error message. After a timeout period, another attempt is made.

```
ScreenSaveActive=1
ScreenSaveTimeOut=120
```

Screen saver activation

Both entries refer to screen saver activation. The first entry indicates the screen saver status (1 is active). The second entry sets the time, in seconds, that must pass without keyboard entry or mouse movement before the screen saver will appear.

```
DosPrint=no
```

This setting adjusts DOS interrupts for printer output. If you specify *no*, Windows documents print faster because they avoid DOS interrupts. If you print from applications that use DOS interrupts, change the entry to *yes*. This setting can also be adjusted by selecting *Fast Printing Direct to Port* on the Control Panel Printer utility's Connect... button.

```
CoolSwitch=1
```

This setting works with *Fast "Alt+Tab" Switching* and is changed by selecting the Desktop option on the Control Panel. If its value is 1, the function is enabled; if it's 0, the function is disabled.

[Desktop]

This section specifies your Desktop settings.

```
Pattern=(None)
```

This setting identifies the screen background pattern; the default value is no background pattern. If there is a pattern, it's expressed as a string of binary numbers and should be checked from the Control Panel, where individual patterns can be precisely defined. Entries in the Control Panel are taken from a list in the CONTROL.INI file; additional information on pattern creation and modification is included there. The following entry describes the "Diamonds" pattern:

```
Pattern=32 80 136 80 32 0 0 0
```

This pattern translates out to the following pixel layout:

```
     1
     2 6 3 1
     8 4 2 6 8 4 2 1
-------------------------
32       *

80     *   *

136  *       *

80     *   *

32       *

0

0

0
```

```
Wallpaper=(None)
TileWallpaper=0
GridGranularity=0
IconSpacing=75
```

These settings control wallpaper (background) display. Selecting the Desktop icon from the Control Panel lets you make these adjustments. Since Windows supports VGA graphics, you can easily change background patterns. The numbers in these entries were inserted by the Control Panel.

Background pattern

The entry after Wallpaper= indicates the file that contains the colors or background patterns. You can design your own background pattern with Paintbrush and then store it in bitmap format (.BMP). Then, the file name can either be entered here or selected through the Control Panel.

GridGranularity sets up an invisible grid, on which the windows and icons are moved. The maximum setting is 49. With this setting, a window can be placed only on one of the four corners of the screen. The minimum value is 0, which allows a window to move around freely on the screen.

[Extensions]

This section specifies file name extensions. The [Extensions] setting allows you to start files immediately (as you can with WIN.INI) by assigning file extensions to programs.

```
cal=calendar.exe ^.cal
crd=cardfile.exe ^.crd
trm=terminal.exe ^.trm
txt=notepad.exe ^.txt
ini=notepad.exe ^.ini
pcx=pbrush.exe ^.pcx
bmp=pbrush.exe ^.bmp
wri=write.exe ^.wri
rec=recorder.exe ^.rec
```

File name extensions

The first three letters represent the program's default file name extension. This is followed by an equal sign, the name of the program (with its extension) that will be assigned to the extension, a space, a caret (^), and finally the extension is entered again. The caret is a wildcard that enables the correct program to be called whenever any file with that extension is selected.

Excel files

Some Windows applications automatically enter the correct setting in this line when they are installed. Excel, for example, makes the following additions:

```
xls=excel.exe ^.xls
xlc=excel.exe ^.xlc
```

```
xlw=excel.exe ^.xlw
xlm=excel.exe ^.xlm
xlt=excel.exe ^.xlt
xla=excel.exe ^.xla
```

Another possible addition could be:

```
pub=pm.exe ^.pm4
```

This setting would directly call PageMaker files. Add entries as needed for your applications.

[intl]

Country setting

This section contains the country settings made during installation. A country setting includes a currency symbol, a decimal dividing character, the number of digits to be displayed, and other options.

If you work with Windows applications from different countries, watch out for conflicts and be sure that the appropriate country setting is made on the Control Panel. The following listing documents individual settings:

```
sLanguage=enu                       ;Language
sCountry=United States              ;Country
iCountry=1                          ;Country
iDate=0                             ;Date format
iTime=0                             ;Time format
iTLZero=0                           ;Time leading zero
iCurrency=0                         ;Currency display
iCurrDigits=2                       ;Currency digits
iNegCurr=0                          ;Negative currency
iLzero=1                            ;Zero display
iDigits=2                           ;Digits
iMeasure=1                          ;Measurement units
s1159=AM                            ;AM time format
s2359=PM                            ;PM time format
sCurrency=$                         ;Currency
sThousand=,                         ;Thousands separator
sDecimal=.                          ;Decimal point
sDate=/                             ;Date separator
sTime=:                             ;Time separator
sList=,                             ;List separator
sShortDate=M/d/yy                   ;Short date format
sLongDate=dddd, MMMM dd, yyyy       ;Long date format
```

These settings are listed in the same sequence as the options available on the system Control Panel. You should use the Control Panel to make any changes to this section.

[ports]

This section describes Windows' port assignments. The following listing documents these ports:

```
LPT1:=                          ;First parallel port
LPT2:=                          ;Second parallel port
LPT3:=                          ;Third parallel port
COM1:=9600,n,8,1                ;First serial port
COM2:=9600,n,8,1                ;Second serial port
COM3:=9600,n,8,1                ;Third serial port
COM4:=9600,n,8,1                ;Fourth serial port
EPT:=                           ;IBM PostScript port
FILE:=                          ;Print file output
LPT1.OS2=                       ;First OS/2 parallel port
LPT2.OS2=                       ;Second OS/2 parallel port
```

Port settings

Information about installed ports is stored here and adjustments can be made on the Ports section of the Control Panel. An explanation of serial port entries (COM1-COM4) is located in the corresponding section in the Control Panel description.

You can also redirect output to a print file. If you're working on a computer that's not attached to any printer or not attached to the proper printer, this can help solve some problems. Send your output to a print file, copy the file to a diskette, and then print it on another system, for example, with the DOS PRINT command:

```
FILE:=output.prn
```

Setting up print files

Set up your printer driver on the system control panel and also install the connection to OUTPUT.PRN.

You can use any file name, but you must include a .PRN extension. If a name isn't specified, a print request to this port prompts the user for a file name.

You can also assign a print file name directly to a port by entering:

```
LPT1:=output.prn
```

PostScript port

The port EPT:= is available for PostScript printers. If you assign a PostScript printer to LPT1: on the Control Panel, instead of the desired file, a series of PostScript commands may print. In this case, the default printer was configured as a text printer (which is possible with an IBM Pageprinter).

By assigning the EPT port to the Postscript printer, an initialization follows. During this initialization the printer interprets the PostScript commands correctly and accurately prints the file.

OS/2 compatibility mode

If you're running Windows in the DOS compatibility box of OS/2 and want to output to a printer driven by OS/2, you must assign the printer driver to a parallel port with an OS/2 extension.

[Windows Help]

```
H_WindowPosition=[213,160,213,160,0]
M_WindowPosition=[256,49,307,237,0]
```

Help window

This entry records the measurements of the Help window. The X and Y coordinates vary depending on the graphics card resolution. A standard VGA adapter operates with coordinates between 0/0 and 640/480.

[Fonts]

VGA screen fonts

Vector fonts

TrueType fonts

```
MS Sans Serif 8,10,12,14,18,24 (VGA res)=SSERIFE.FON
MS Serif 8,10,12,14,18,24 (VGA res)=SERIFE.FON
Symbol 8,10,12,14,18,24 (VGA res)=SYMBOLE.FON
Small (VGA res)=SMALLE.FON
Courier 10,12,15 (VGA res)=COURE.FON
Roman (Plotter)=ROMAN.FON
Modern (Plotter)=MODERN.FON
Script (Plotter)=SCRIPT.FON
Arial (TrueType)=ARIAL.FOT
Arial Bold (TrueType)=ARIALBD.FOT
Arial Bold Italic (TrueType)=ARIALBI.FOT
Arial Italic (TrueType)=ARIALI.FOT
Courier New (TrueType)=COUR.FOT
Courier New Bold (TrueType)=COURBD.FOT
Courier New Bold Italic (TrueType)=COURBI.FOT
Courier New Italic (TrueType)=COURI.FOT Times New Roman
(TrueType)=TIMES.FOT
Times New Roman Bold (TrueType)=TIMESBD.FOT
Times New Roman Bold Italic (TrueType)=TIMESBI.FOT
Times New Roman Italic (TrueType)=TIMESI.FOT
Symbol (TrueType)=SYMBOL.FOT
```

Fonts

This section lists font files that vary depending on which printers are installed. Some completely Windows-compatible programs automatically make changes during installation (e.g., PageMaker). The next section handles the assignment of TrueType fonts to screen fonts.

[FontSubstitutes]

This section equates generic font names with Windows fonts.

```
Helv=MS Sans Serif
Tms Rmn=MS Serif
Courier=Courier New
Times=Times New Roman
Helvetica=Arial
```

Use the Control Panel to delete or add fonts under Windows.

[TrueType]

This section defines the status of TrueType fonts.

```
TTEnable=1
TTOnly=1
```

TrueType options are defined by selecting the Fonts icon on the Control Panel.

[embedding]

This section lists applications that produce data that can be embedded in other applications. The line contains the type of data, program file reference, and file type.

```
ExcelChart=Chart created by Microsoft Excel, Excel Chart,
           Excel.exe,picture
ExcelWorksheet=Worksheet created by Microsoft Excel, Excel
               Worksheet,Excel.exe,picture
Package=Package,Package,packager.exe,picture
Pbrush=Paintbrush Picture,Paintbrush Picture,
       pbrush.exe,picture
SoundRec=Sound,Sound,SoundRec.exe,picture
```

[Colors]

This section lists different colors in the Windows environment.

```
Background=0 0 128
AppWorkspace=255 255 255
Window=255 255 255
WindowText=0 0 0
Menu=255 255 255
MenuText=0 0 0
ActiveTitle=64 128 128
InactiveTitle=255 255 255
TitleText=0 0 0
ActiveBorder=192 192 192
InactiveBorder=192 192 192
WindowFrame=0 0 128
Scrollbar=192 192 192
ButtonFace=255 255 255
ButtonShadow=128 128 127
ButtonText=0 0 0
GrayText=128 128 128
Hilight=0 0 0
HilightText=255 255 255
InactiveTitleText=0 0 0
ButtonHighlight=255 255 255
```

Colors

These settings control the Windows screen colors. You should use the Control Panel to make any changes because you'll be able to see the actual colors. It's also easier to adjust the different color areas on the screen by using the Control Panel.

The three values that follow each screen element refer to the color intensity of the three basic colors (red, green, and blue). The maximum value is 255 and the minimum value is 0. The intensity of the three values together determines the mixed color that appears on the screen.

[PrinterPorts]

```
PostScript Printer=PSCRIPT,LPT1:,15,45
IBM Graphics=IBMGRX,None
```

Printer setup

This section assigns ports to the printers listed in [devices]. The numbers after each port label represent the amount of time until Windows tries to access the printer again. Set the option in the [Windows] section by selecting the *DeviceNotSelectedTimeout* and *TransmissionRetryTimeout;* options.

[mci extensions]

This section defines multi-media device drivers.

```
rmi=sequencer
mid=sequencer
wav=waveaudio
```

Add entries to this section as needed for devices with other file name extensions.

[Devices]

This section lists installed output devices by printer driver name and port. Active printers are selected from this list.

```
PostScript Printer=PSCRIPT,LPT1:
HP LaserJet III=hppcl5a,LPT3:
```

Make adjustments either with the SETUP program or through the Control Panel.

Program settings

Programs

The previous settings are the default values. If you want to change these values, save them before leaving Windows.

10.4 The CONTROL.INI File

The CONTROL.INI file contains color settings for the Windows screen. Adjust the colors with the Control Panel by selecting *Colors....* You shouldn't change the color options in the CONTROL.INI file itself because you cannot see the changes. However, if you use the Control Panel you'll be able to see the changes.

[current]

This section describes the current color palette.

```
color schemes=Windows Default
```

Other palettes can be chosen from the [color schemes] section.

[color schemes]

This section contains the names of all available color palettes and individual color combinations. Add new color palettes by using the Control Panel. The color sequence follows the sequence of screen elements on the Control Panel. The color values are the basic colors.

[Custom Colors]

This section specifies custom color palette specifications made from within the Control Panel. You can create up to 16 colors with a VGA card. The palette name would then be entered in the [color schemes] section.

[Patterns]

This section specifies all available patterns. The Control Panel accesses this list to create background patterns. Each pattern consists of an 8 x 8 pixel matrix.

```
(None)=(None)
Boxes=127 65 65 65 65 65 127 0
Paisley=2 7 7 2 32 80 80 32
Weave=136 84 34 69 136 21 34 81
Waffle=0 0 0 0 128 128 128 240
Tulip=0 0 84 124 124 56 146 124
Spinner=20 12 200 121 158 19 48 40
Scottie=64 192 200 120 120 72 0 0
Critters=0 80 114 32 0 5 39 2
50% Gray=170 85 170 85 170 85 170 85
Quilt=130 68 40 17 40 68 130 1
Diamonds=32 80 136 80 32 0 0 0
Thatches=248 116 34 71 143 23 34 113
```

With a zero value, the pixel displays the color entered in the *Background* option in the [colors] section. With a value of 1, the pixel displays the color entered in the *WindowText* option in the same section. The following matrix displays a simplified diamond pattern.

```
     1
     2 6 3 1
     8 4 2 6 8 4 2 1
-----------------------
32   0 0 1 0 0 0 0 0
```

```
80    0 1 0 1 0 0 0 0
136   1 0 0 0 1 0 0 0
80    0 1 0 1 0 0 0 0
32    0 0 1 0 0 0 0 0
0     0 0 0 0 0 0 0 0
0     0 0 0 0 0 0 0 0
0     0 0 0 0 0 0 0 0
```

Matrix values are converted to decimal numbers with the calculator. The following values would create the previous pattern:

```
Diamond2=0 24 60 126 126 60 24 0
```

```
      1
      2 6 3 1
      8 4 2 6 8 4 2 1
-------------------------
0     0 0 0 0 0 0 0 0
24    0   0 1 1 0 0 0
60      0 1 1 1 1 0 0
126   0 1 1 1 1 1 1 0
126   0 1 1 1 1 1 1 0
60    0 0 1 1 1 1 0 0
24    0 0 0 1 1 0 0 0
0     0 0 0 0 0 0 0 0
```

[Installed]

This section lists installed available help files, DLLs and fonts, including TrueType fonts. The *yes* setting activates the corresponding entry.

```
3.1=yes
PSCRIPT.DRV=yes
PSCRIPT.HLP=yes
HPPCL5A.DRV=yes
FINSTALL.DLL=yes
FINSTALL.HLP=yes
HPPCL5A.HLP=yes
EPSON9.DRV=yes
UNIDRV.DLL=yes
DMCOLOR.DLL=yes
UNIDRV.HLP=yes
SSERIFB.FON=yes
SSERIFC.FON=yes
COURC.FON=yes
COURD.FON=yes
SERIFB.FON=yes
SERIFC.FON=yes
ARIALB.FON=yes
TIMESB.FON=yes
SYMBOLB.FON=yes
SMALLB.FON=yes
SSERIFD.FON=yes
COURB.FON=yes
```

```
SERIFD.FON=yes
EPSON24.DRV=yes
SSERIFA.FON=yes
COURA.FON=yes
SERIFA.FON=yes
SYMBOLA.FON=yes
SYMBOLF.FON=yes
SSERIFF.FON=yes
COURF.FON=yes
SERIFF.FON=yes
SMALLF.FON=yes
KBDGR.DLL=yes
```

[User installed.drivers]

This section lists all user installed device drivers.

```
LastTime=11414
Wave=sndblst2.drv
MIDI1=adlib.drv
```

You can access this from the Control Panel by selecting the *Drivers...* command from the *Settings* menu, clicking the Add... button and selecting *Unlisted or Updated Driver* from the *List of Drivers* box.

[Screen Saver.Marquee]

This section controls the behavior of your screen saver.

```
PWProtected=1                 ;Password (1=enabled, 0=disabled)
Text=Windows 3.1 Complete     ;Text
Font=Arial                    ;Font type (Arial=Helvetica)
Size=48                       ;Font size in points
BackgroundColor=0 0 0         ;Background color: RGB (=Black)
TextColor=255 0 255           ;Text color: RGB (=Fuschia)
Speed=10                      ;Speed of Marquee (=Moderate)
Attributes=00101              ;Text style (=Bold Italic)
CharSet=0                     ;Character set
```

You can change these settings by selecting *Desktop...* from the Control Panel *Settings* menu.

[ScreenSaver]

This section represents the encrypted Screen Saver password. It's possible to access Windows without using the password to exit the Screen Saver. To do this, delete this setting.

```
Password=7UpvC?
```

[drivers.desc]

This section lists all installed multi-media drivers.

```
midimapper=MIDI Mapper
timer=Timer
Wave=Creative Labs Sound Blaster 1.5
MIDI1=Ad Lib
```

Install a new driver by selecting the *Drivers...* command from the Control Panel *Settings* menu.

[related.desc]

This section specifies related device drivers.

```
Wave=adlib.drv,
MIDI1=
```

10.5 The SYSTEM.INI File

The SYSTEM.INI file contains Windows' hardware settings. Entries that apply to the hardware configuration of your computer are usually specified during installation. Changing this file's contents can be dangerous, because if the entry is wrong, you may have to re-install Windows. However, the fastest way to connect a new mouse or monitor is by changing the appropriate entry in this file.

If you've already attached the new monitor, change the entry under DOS using an editor or word processor. Using the new screen with the old driver may cause problems with the Windows display.

Driver files

File names of available driver files apply to corresponding devices. They are usually saved in the \WINDOWS\SYSTEM directory. To install a device driver not included with Windows, you must start the SETUP program from the operating system.

[boot]

This section lists device drivers available when Windows boots.

```
286grabber=VGAMONO.2GR
386grabber=VGADIB.3GR
```

These are device drivers that are used to display non-Windows applications under Windows, in conjunction with the screen driver listed after the *display=* option. *286grabber* is activated in Standard or Real mode, *386grabber* is activated if you work in 386 Enhanced mode.

```
shell=progman.exe
```

Defining the screen surface

You can choose your starting shell and screen surface. Choose from the following shells:

1. If you usually work with applications and rarely manage your files or work at the operating system level, select the Program Manager. This is automatically loaded when Windows is started with the following:

```
PROGMAN.EXE
```

2. The File Manager should be your shell program if you usually work with files and frequently use operating system commands. You should also use the File Manager if you rarely use an application. Enter the following:

```
WINFILE.EXE
```

If you enter another file name here, system errors may occur. Any Windows program can be called as the screen surface, but with other programs you can exit only by completely quitting Windows.

```
network.drv=Novell Netware 386 or 2.10 and higher
```

This setting refers to the Network program under which Windows has been installed. To change this entry, use the Windows Setup program.

```
language.dll=
```

This setting specifies the language library for language-related functions. To change this entry, select *Language* in the *International* dialog box on the Control Panel. The default setting is US.

```
fixedfon.fon=vgafix.fon
```

This setting defines fixed-width fonts (such as Courier) that are used by Windows applications written for Windows Version 2.x. The same font is also used with Windows 3.0 versions originally written for Windows 2.x. The appropriate entry depends on the screen display option installed during Windows setup.

```
comm.drv=comm.drv
```

This setting lists the name of the serial port driver.

```
sound.drv=mmsound.drv
```

This setting specifies the multi-media sound driver.

```
oemfonts.fon=vgaoem.fon
```

This setting defines OEM screen fonts. These fonts are standard for each graphics card. If you use temporary storage areas, activate the setting and then select either a *Text* display or an *OEM font* display. OEM fonts produce a clearer display.

```
fonts.fon=vgasys.fon
```

This setting specifies the proportional font available in Windows 3.1. The correct setting depends on the screen driver.

```
mouse.drv=mouse.drv
```

This setting specifies the mouse driver accessed under Windows. If you work only with Windows applications, you may remove other mouse drivers from the CONFIG.SYS file or the AUTOEXEC.BAT file to save memory. If you use non-Windows applications (e.g., Word 5.5) under Windows, the mouse may not work properly because this application only supports DOS based mouse drivers.

```
keyboard.drv=keyboard.drv
```

This setting indicates the keyboard driver used under Windows. If you have a special keyboard driver, change the setting in the Windows setup, making the change while working from DOS.

```
display.drv=vga.drv
```

This setting specifies a screen driver. If you set up the wrong screen driver and Windows doesn't run, change this entry to the correct driver so that you don't have to re-install Windows. Also notice that you can use different screen fonts with different screen drivers.

```
system.drv=MS-DOS System
```

This setting specifies the system hardware driver used by your computer. If your computer manufacturer offers its own system driver for Windows, enter its name here.

```
SCRNSAVE.EXE=C:\WINDOWS\SSMARQUE.SCR
```

This setting lists the screen saver file, as defined in the Control Panel.

[keyboard]

This section contains data that controls the keyboard under Windows. Since Windows requires an entry under all values and doesn't use any defaults, you must make all entries through the SETUP program.

```
subtype=
```

This setting defines keyboard functions that aren't standard to the IBM keyboard.

1	2	Olivetti M24 102 keys or AT&T '301' keys
1	4	AT&T '302' keys
2	1	Olivetti M24 102 keys

```
type=4
```

This setting defines the keyboard compatibility value. If an entry isn't made, the standard keyboard is used.

1	AT&T '301' keyboard
2	Olivetti M24 102 key keyboard
3	All AT type keyboards (84 - 86 keys)
4	Enhanced 101 or 102 key US and Non US

```
oemansi.bin=
```

This setting defines the OEM/ANSI code page translation table for systems that don't use the American OEM character set.

```
keyboard.dll=
```

This setting defines non-American keyboards with layouts that aren't compatible with IBM keyboards.

[boot.description]

This section displays options chosen during the Windows installation. Since they are displayed as character strings, you shouldn't make any changes to the existing entries.

```
mouse.drv=Microsoft or IBM PS/2    ;Mouse driver
network.drv=No Network Installed   ;Network status driver
language.dll=English (American)    ;Language DLL
system.drv=MS-DOS System           ;Operating system driver
codepage=437                       ;Codepage
keyboard.typ=Enhanced 101 or 102 key US and Non US keyboards
```

[386Enh]

This section contains settings that control temporary data storage in RAM. These entries are activated only when you run Windows in 386 Enhanced mode. Entries in this section are configured to the computer and can vary depending on the system.

For special configurations, run the ReadMe file SYSINI.WRI and read the available information. Entries in this text file explain the most important options.

```
AllVMsExclusive=false
```

This setting runs all applications in exclusive full screen mode. Other settings in the PIF don't affect this setting. With this setting, from the beginning the current application is given the highest priority. If you often simultaneously start several applications that have equal priority, delete this entry from SYSTEM.INI.

```
AltKeyDelay=005
```

Increase this value, which is measured in seconds, if your application has problems with the keyboard interrupt for the Alt key. This value defines the waiting interval for processing the keyboard interrupt.

```
AltPasteDelay=025
```

This value reports the waiting interval before a character is inserted after the Alt key is pressed. If you encounter problems with an application in connection with the Alt key, increase this value.

```
CGA40WOA.FON=CGA40WOA.FON
```

This entry defines the screen font used to display the 40 x 25 screen with a CGA graphics card.

```
CGA80WOA.FON=CGA80WOA.FON
```

This entry defines the screen font used to display the 80 x 25 screen with a CGA graphics card.

```
CGANoSnow=
```

Set this option to *Yes* to eliminate snow on your screen with a CGA graphics card.

```
device=
```

Depending on your hardware configuration, enter the appropriate device driver on this line to enable cooperation between Windows and your hardware. Make any changes with the Setup program.

```
Display=
```

This entry specifies the screen driver you've installed in the Windows setup.

```
DMABufferIn1MB=no
```

If you encounter problems with an 8-bit card, activate this option by entering *yes*. When activated, DMA (Direct Memory Access) is loaded into the first 1 Meg of RAM.

```
DMABufferSize=16
```

This entry, given in kilobytes, defines the storage capacity to be reserved for DMA. Storage areas above 640K should be used; make the appropriate entry for DMABufferIn1MB.

```
DualDisplay=(between B000:0000 and B7FF:0000)
```

An optional secondary screen adapter can use the area between 640K and 1 Meg. By reserving this address, the adapter stays active. If it isn't reserved, Windows can only use this space with an EGA adapter.

```
ebios=*ebios
```

This entry is identical to "device=".

```
EGA40WOA.FON=EGA40WOA.FON
```

This entry defines the screen font used to display the 40 x 25 screen with an EGA graphics card.

```
EGA80WOA.FON=EGA80WOA.FON
```

This entry defines the screen font used to display the 80 x 25 screen with an EGA graphics card.

```
EISADMA=
```

This setting activates EISA logic by specifying a DMA channel and its size. If a value isn't specified, the system is treated as a normal computer.

Under certain circumstances, this setting can prevent Windows from running in the 386 Enhanced mode. If this is the case, remove this entry.

```
EMMExclude=A000-EFFF
```

This setting excludes an address area to avoid address conflicts between Windows and graphics or network cards that work in the same area. The A000-EFFF setting excludes the area between 640K and 1 Meg. An exclusion prevents Windows from accessing the specified area.

```
EMMInclude=A000-EFFF
```

This setting assigns addressable space before EMMExclude excludes an address area.

```
EMMPageFrame=
```

This setting specifies a starting address after which the first page frame should begin.

```
EMMSize=65536
```

This setting specifies the amount of memory to be used as expanded (mapping) memory. The default value of 65536 frees all system memory for this purpose.

If an application uses all of expanded memory, additional applications cannot use it. In this case, limit the available RAM by entering a size here. A value of 0 disables the use of expanded memory.

```
FileSysChange=
```

If this setting is set to *on*, the File Manager receives a message whenever another application performs a file operation.

```
Global=
```

Entering a device driver in CONFIG.SYS makes it available for virtual use by a local application. If there isn't an entry for this setting, all devices are globally available to all applications.

```
HighFloppyReads=yes
```

If a system crash, caused by a disk drive error, frequently occurs, delete this entry and enter the address E000-EFFF in EmmExclude. The default entry transforms a DMA test function into a read function for the upper area, which prevents problems in some machines.

```
IgnoreInstalledEMM=no
```

If you enter *yes* here, you can start Windows even if your expanded memory manager isn't recognized by Windows. However, you can encounter problems if a RAM-resident program is using expanded memory during the Windows start-up procedure.

```
keyboard=
```

This setting lists the installed keyboard driver.

```
LPT1AutoAssign=60
LPT2AutoAssign=60
LPT3AutoAssign=60
LPT4AutoAssign=60
```

This setting determines how Windows reacts when parallel ports are accessed simultaneously. A value of 0 allows all access, a value of -1 displays a warning message, and a value from 1 10 1000 reserves a time, in seconds, for an active access.

```
MinTimeSlice=20
```

This setting specifies a time, in milliseconds, that is available to each virtual application before the next application receives its turn. Set this value by using the Control Panel.

```
MinUserDiskSpace=500
```

If you frequently work with temporary storage files, this setting defines the size of each file on the hard drive.

```
Mouse=
```

This setting lists the name of the installed mouse driver.

```
Network=
```

This setting lists the network driver if Windows is installed on a network.

```
NoEMMDriver=false
```

If this setting is set to *true*, the expanded memory manager isn't loaded when Windows is started in 386 Enhanced mode.

```
Paging=yes
```

This setting activates RAM paging. If you need space on the hard drive, prevent the use of temporary storage files by entering *no* here.

```
PagingDrive=
```

This setting indicates which disk drive Windows uses for its storage file in 386 Enhanced mode. If there is a permanent swap file (SWAPFILE.EXE), this entry is ignored. If there isn't an entry, Windows tries to set up temporary files in the directory that contains the SYSTEM.INI file. Usually the disk drive with the largest amount of free space should be used. A RAM disk usually offers the best results.

```
SysVMEMSLimit=2048
```

This setting limits the expanded memory that's available to Windows. A value of -1 indicates that all of expanded memory is available, a value of 0 prevents access to expanded memory.

```
SysVMEMSLocked=no
```

If this setting is activated, Windows stores expanded memory on the hard drive.

```
SysVMEMSRequired=0
```

This setting specifies the amount of expanded memory storage area that's needed to start Windows. If no applications use expanded memory, set this entry to 0.

```
SysVMXMSLimit=2048
```

This setting specifies the size of the extended memory storage area that's available to Windows. A value of -1 indicates that all of extended memory is available, a value of 0 completely prevents access to it.

```
SysVMXMSLocked=no
```

If this setting is activated, Windows stores extended memory on the hard drive.

```
SysVMXMSRequired=0
```

This setting specifies the size of the memory area that must be available for the XMS (Extended Memory) driver when starting Windows.

```
TokenRingSearch=true
```

If you're using an IBM computer with a Token-Ring card, activate this setting. If you aren't using a Token-Ring card, remove it.

```
VCPIWarning=true
```

If a non-Windows application tries to access the Virtual Control program Interface (VCPI), an error message appears because Windows doesn't support VCPI. If this frequently happens, set the entry to *false*.

```
WindowUpdateTime=50
```

This setting limits the amount of time in milliseconds between screen refreshments of a non-Windows application in Windows mode.

```
WinExclusive=no
```

When this setting is activated, all of your processor capacity is available to the Windows application in the foreground. If this entry is set to *yes*, other applications cannot run in the background.

```
WinTimeSlice=100,50
```

This setting defines timeslice segments for foreground and background applications. The numbers represent values from 1 to 10000, and the relationship between the numbers is also relevant. Change these values by using the Control Panel.

```
WindowsKBRequired=
```

This setting specifies the size of conventional memory needed for a correct Windows start. Change this setting if you cannot start Windows because there isn't enough memory. If there is no entry, try several values. The value should always be a multiple of 16.

```
windowmemsize=-1
```

This setting reserves space in expanded memory that can be used as temporary storage for programs. It affects working in Real mode with Windows.

Enter a value, in kilobytes, to limit the storage capacity available to a storage area. If you usually start Windows with standard applications that access the expansion areas, enter a value of 0 to prevent Windows access and keep it free for standard applications.

```
local=CON
```

This setting prevents the DOS console buffer from being filled by every virtual machine created.

```
MaxPagingFileSize=
```

Used in SWAPFILE.EXE, this setting specifies an area, in kilobytes, to be reserved for the swap file.

```
COM1AutoAssign=2
COM2AutoAssign=2
COM3AutoAssign=2
COM4AutoAssign=2
```

These settings determine how Windows reacts when serial ports are simultaneously accessed. A value of 0 allows all access, a value of -1 results in an error message, and an entry from 1 to 1000 sets a time, in seconds, that is reserved for each active access.

```
COM1Base=3F8h
COM2Base=2F8h
COM3Base=2E8h
COM4Base=2E0h
```

These settings specify the basic addresses for serial interfaces. These addresses can vary depending on your hardware. Refer to your manual if you encounter problems with the port interfaces.

```
COMBoostTime=2
```

This setting specifies the time, in milliseconds, that's allowed for processing COM interrupts. Errors encountered in data transmission programs can occasionally be avoided by increasing this value.

```
COM1Buffer=128
COM2Buffer=128
COM3Buffer=128
COM4Buffer=128
```

Depending on your protocol, this setting defines the size of the serial interface buffer for data transfer applications. The appropriate value depends on the speed of transmission.

```
COM1Irq=4
COM2Irq=3
COM3Irq=4
COM4Irq=3
```

These settings label interrupt requests to the port, depending on which hardware is being used. If there are conflicts, an IRQ can be deactivated with a value of -1.

```
COMIrqSharing=
```

If you're using a computer with micro channels or EISA logic, change this setting to *true* because the COM1 and COM2 IRQ's are identical with those of COM3 and COM4. For all other computers, change this setting to *false*.

```
COM1Protocol=
COM2Protocol=
COM3Protocol=
COM4Protocol=
```

If characters are lost during data transmission, set the entry to *XOFF* for the appropriate port interface. If problems don't occur with data transmission, an entry shouldn't be made.

[standard]

This section defines settings for Standard mode.

```
NetHeapSize=8
```

If you want to transfer data on a network, use this setting to define a buffer for Windows (measured in kilobytes) for the transmission. On some networks, the default value of 8 should be increased to move the data properly. Storage capacity for other applications are reduced accordingly.

```
Int28Filter=10
```

This setting controls RAM-resident programs such as network drivers. The value indicates a percentage of the INT28H interrupts, in the waiting status of the system. Increasing the numeric value can speed up Windows, but can also interfere with the interaction between Windows and RAM-resident applications. To completely prohibit interrupts, enter a value of 0.

[NonWindowsApp]

```
ScreenLines=25
```

Standard applications

Standard applications are displayed with 25 lines on the screen. If an application (e.g., Word 5.0) uses a different number of lines, this setting can be deactivated.

```
SwapDisk=C:\WINDOWS
```

This setting contains the disk drive and directory that Windows reserves for files. You can enter a RAM disk as the default drive to speed up screen changes. If an entry isn't made, the Windows directory is the default setting.

```
NetAsynchSwitching=
```

If you're working with a non-Windows application in a Windows network environment, you can receive an asynchronous NetBIOS call from the network. If the application that receives the call is in the foreground, it can easily be handled. However, if the call occurs when the application is in the background, a system crash can occur. Entering a 0 completely inhibits calls from the network. Enter a 1 if your applications never receive calls from the network when they're in the background.

10.6 The PROGMAN.INI File

The PROGMAN.INI file contains parameters for the Program Manager. All entries refer to commands on the menu bar of the Program Manager.

[Settings]

This section defines general settings when Windows boots.

```
Window=20 34 595 444 1
```

Size of the Start window

This setting contains the size of the StartUp window. The numbers refer to coordinates of pixels displayable by the current screen driver. If you're using a VGA monitor with an IBM computer, the maximum window size is:

```
Windows=0 0 640 480 1.
```

Your coordinates can vary with other graphics cards, depending on the resolution. The start window is also placed on the screen with this entry.

```
SaveSettings=0
```

Save settings

This setting defines whether you want Windows to save changes on exit. You can enable this option by changing the value to 1, or by selecting the *Save Settings on Exit* command from the *Options* menu of the Program Manager.

```
MinOnRun=0
```

This setting determines whether the Program Manager appears as Minimized (as an icon) after you start Windows. A value of 0 displays the Program Manager as Maximized. A value of 1 displays the Program Manager as Minimized.

```
AutoArrange=0
```

This setting defines automatic icon arrangement. A value of 1 automatically rearranged icons when you reduce a Window's size. A value of 0 means that some icons will be stored beyond the window borders. The sequence of icons is defined in the Order setting of this section.

[Groups]

This section specifies group information.

```
Group1=D:\WINDOWS\access.GRP
Group2=D:\WINDOWS\games.GRP
Group3=D:\WINDOWS\others.GRP
Group4=D:\WINDOWS\windowsa.GRP
Group5=D:\WINDOWS\maingrp.GRP
```

Setting group structures

Grouping structures, which are used with individual files in the Program Manager, are created here during the installation procedure or with the SETUP program. They can be adjusted in the Program Manager. If you've installed Windows on your C: disk drive, but now want to move it to the D: drive, adjust the disk drive and path designations after copying the files. Otherwise, grouping files cannot be found. The order sets the sequence of groups displayed in the *Window* menu of the Program Manager.

10.7 The WINFILE.INI File

The WINFILE.INI file contains settings for the File Manager. However, you should use the File Manager to make any changes.

[Settings]

```
SaveSettings=0
```

Save changes

When you exit the File Manager, you have the option of saving your current settings. Activate this option by selecting *Save Settings on Exit* in the *Options* menu of the File Manager. If a value of 1 is used, this option is activated; a value of 0 deactivates it.

```
dir1=0,0,500,279,-1,-1,1,30,201,1905,246,C:\WIN\SYSTEM\*.*
```

This entry indicates the size of the file window and the disk drive and directory.

```
Face=Times New Roman
Size=10
```

These settings define the font and type size to be used for the file window. Adjust this setting by selecting *Font...* from the *Options* menu.

```
ConfirmDelete=1
```

If this setting contains a value of 1, a confirmation message is displayed before files are deleted. You must then confirm your actions before the file is actually deleted. A value of 0 suppresses the message and immediately deletes the file.

```
ConfirmSubDel=1
```

Delete subdirectory confirmation

If this setting contains a value of 1, a warning message is displayed before a subdirectory is deleted. The subdirectory isn't deleted until the action is confirmed. A value of 0 suppresses the message and immediately deletes the subdirectory.

```
ConfirmReplace=1
```

Move file confirmation

If this setting contains a value of 1, a warning message is displayed before moving a file into another directory. A value of 0 suppresses the message.

```
ConfirmMouse=1
```

Mouse confirmation

If this setting contains a value of 1, a warning message is displayed before a file is moved or copied into another directory with the mouse. A value of 0 suppresses the message.

```
MinOnRun=0
```

Symbol

This setting determines whether the File Manager appears as Minimized (an icon) immediately after Windows starts. If the setting contains a value of 0, the complete Windows screen appears when you start Windows or end an application. If you enter a 1, the File Manager appears as Minimized.

```
Replace=0
```

Subdirectory

If this setting contains a value of 0, a subdirectory opens only one directory window and additional directories are displayed in the same window. If the value is 1, each directory is displayed in a separate window.

```
LowerCase=0
```

Case

If this setting contains a value of 1, directory and file names appear in lowercase. A value of 0 sets the display to uppercase.

```
StatusBar=1
```

File Manager status bar

This setting controls the status display in the directory structure and directory content windows. A value of 0 disables the display and a value of 1 enables the status bar display.

If it's displayed, the number of selected files, the total memory space used, and the total number of files in the current directory are displayed in the lower area of the directory window.

Available memory is then also displayed in the directory structure window.

```
CurrentAttribs=1841
```

This setting specifies the number of files needed to display the attributes you've set up. If the attributes are changed, the new number is written to the drive.

11. The Program Manager

Program Manager screen

The Program Manager consists of the standard workspace for Windows. This is what appears on the screen when Windows starts. The Windows applications are displayed on the screen as icons.

Handling program groups

The Program Manager uses groups to separate applications into similar categories. Besides the Main group, the installation automatically generates the Accessories, StartUp, and Games groups. These contain the standard Windows applications in icon form. A group called Applications contains the other Windows applications.

Starting applications with icons

Applications can be started by double-clicking on their icon or selecting them using the cursor keys and pressing the Enter key.

Starting applications without icons

The Program Manager allows you to start all applications. However, this doesn't apply to only applications that are represented by icons within a group. You can also use the command name to start a program. This is useful for starting DOS programs.

Creating a program group

The Program Manager allows you to place related applications in your own group. So, you can create separate groups for word processors, spreadsheets, databases, and graphics.

Adding applications manually

The Program Manager allows you to add individual applications to any group. A non-Windows application is always started with standard PIF settings. A more complicated application should be set up by Windows' own Setup program, which automatically adds the applications.

11.1 The Program Manager Screen

The Program Manager consists of the standard workspace for Windows. This is what appears on the screen when Windows starts. The Program Manager contains several elements, such as the menu bar, that appear in all Windows applications. Depending on the particular setting, either several open windows or a list of group icons appear.

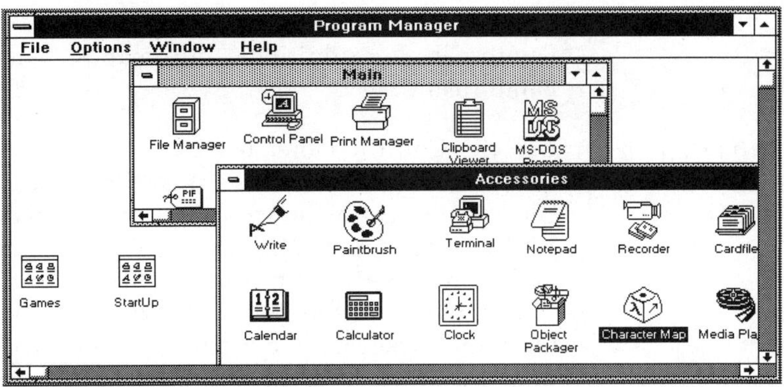

Elements of the Program Manager

The group icons contain the program icons that can be used to call applications. Although the arrangement of the icons within the groups are determined at installation, it's possible to change this arrangement at any time.

The icons act as a way to activate the corresponding applications. If you delete an icon from the Program Manager, the application itself isn't deleted from the hard drive. So, it's possible that an icon will still appear in the Program Manager even though its corresponding application has been deleted. In this case, an error message appears if you try to activate the icon.

The heart of Windows

The Program Manager itself runs inside its own window. Similar to the other windows, this window can be moved, maximized, or minimized. Its base is always the Windows background (desktop). To display the background, reduce the Program Manager to an icon by using the Minimize command from the Control menu.

Something must always appear on the Windows background. At the very least the Program Manager icon always appears. Windows applications that have been activated, such as Write or Paintbrush, run in their own windows on top of the Windows workspace. The Program Manager controls the entire Windows program. So, when its closed, you'll exit Windows. All other windows that are being used by different applications are also closed automatically. This means that the Program Manager has the highest priority.

Structuring the Windows background

You can tailor the Windows background according to your own preferences by choosing among several pictures or drawings that are available as wallpaper or as simple patterns. These pictures appear in the background. All Windows bitmap files can be used as wallpaper. You can also create your own bitmap files by using Paintbrush. For additional information, refer to the chapter on Paintbrush.

Setting up the background

Use the Control Panel to select the desired wallpaper. Select *Desktop...* from the *Settings* menu or click on the Desktop icon. Once you select a file from the *File:* drop-down list box in the *Wallpaper* option, you can choose whether to center the picture or to display it on the entire screen. To center the picture, select the *Center* option button. Some wallpaper pictures automatically fill the entire background, but others are too small to fill the screen. In these instances, you must select the *Tiled* option button, which repeats the picture until the entire screen is filled.

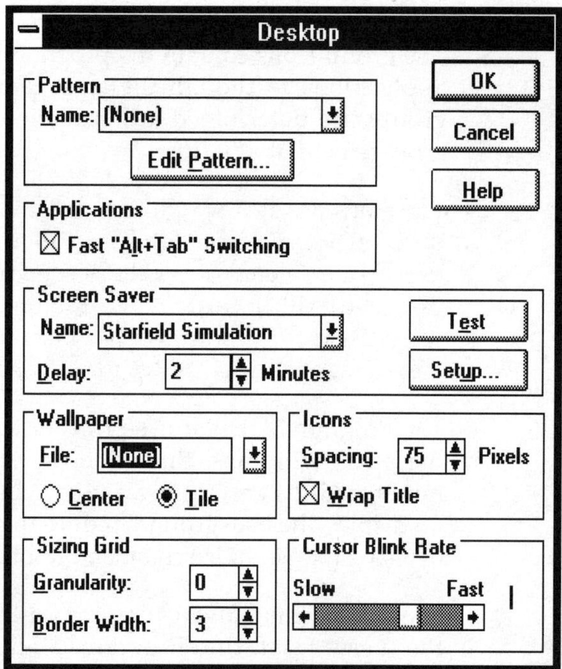

Selecting wallpaper

The following figures show the differences between these two options:

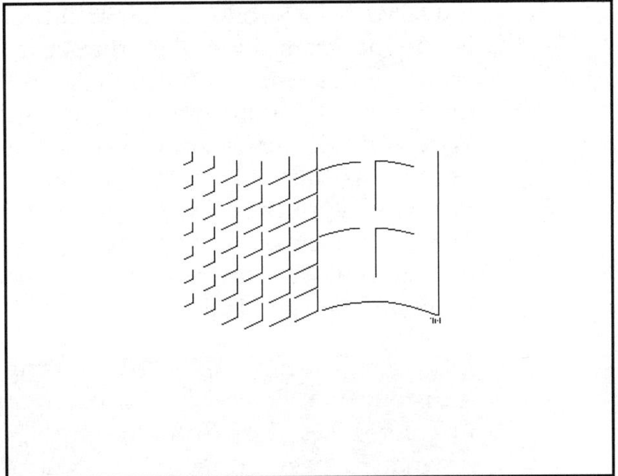

Centered wallpaper

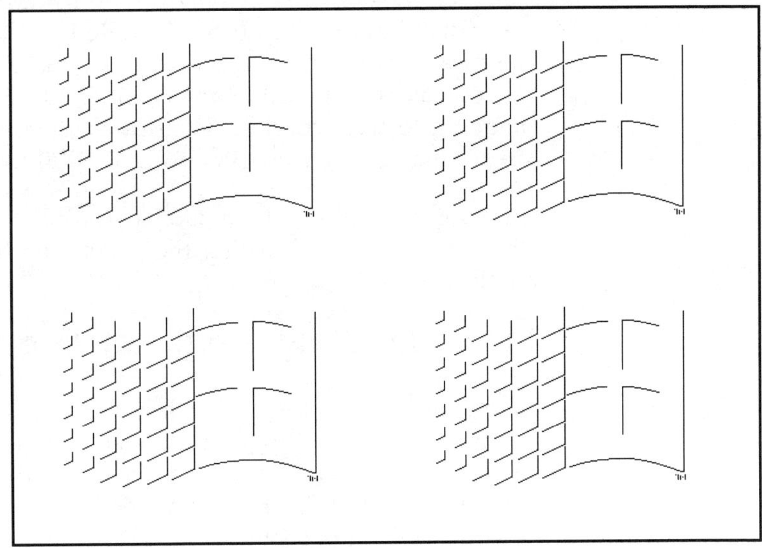

Tiled wallpaper

If you create your own bitmap file with Paintbrush and copy it to the Windows directory, it will then appear in the *File:* drop-down list box in the *Desktop* option.

Selecting a different Main window application

The Program Manager is the heart of Windows. If you close its window, you'll exit Windows and return to the DOS screen. This occurs because of an entry in the SYSTEM.INI file. The entry PROGMAN.EXE follows the SHELL= line entry. PROGMAN.EXE is the program in which the Program Manager resides. By changing this entry, you can make the File Manager, for example, the default window by changing PROGMAN.EXE to WINFILE.EXE. After startup only the File Manager appears. To verify this, minimize the File Manager to an icon. No other Windows application will appear on the Windows workspace. Then if you close the File Manager window, the message about ending your Windows session, which usually appears with the Program Manager, is displayed.

If you perform mostly file management tasks and you're accustomed to the PC Tools environment, you can adapt Windows to conform to this. You can easily run applications (e.g., the Program Manager) from the File Manager.

Creating a runtime version of Windows

Some Windows users always work with the same application. For example, if you only boot Windows to run Microsoft Excel, it may seem that having Windows installed on the hard drive is a nuisance. However, it's possible to simulate a Windows runtime version, as was possible in Version 2.x. For many users, it's annoying to have to close Windows when exiting Excel. In this case, change the SHELL= line to read SHELL=EXCEL.EXE.

However, once this is done, it isn't possible to use any application other than Excel. So, closing the Excel window actually ends the Windows session.

11.2 Handling Program Groups

Following the Windows installation, the first thing that appears on the screen is the Program Manager. In the center of the screen you'll see the Main group window and the program item icons contained within this group. The remaining groups are displayed, as group icons, at the bottom of the Program Manager window.

Besides the Main group, the installation automatically generates the Accessories, StartUp, and Games groups. These activate the standard Windows applications in icon form. If other applications, which are located on the hard drive, were included when Windows was installed or later with the Windows Setup program, another group, called Applications, also appears on the screen.

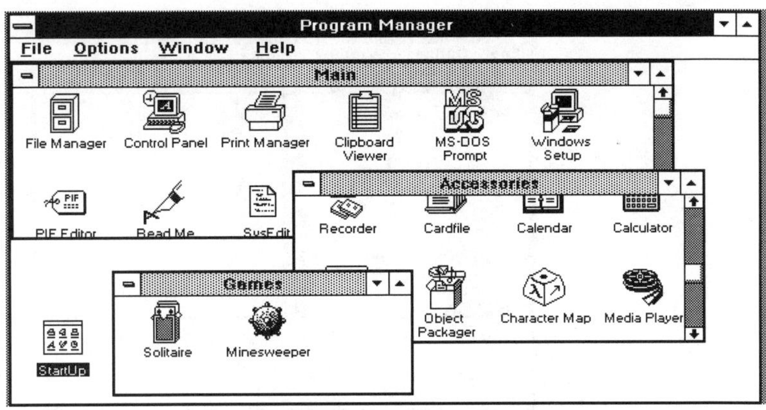

Several opened program groups

Calling a group icon

You can move or resize a window that belongs to a particular program group. To open a group icon, either double-click it with the mouse or with the keyboard, open the *Window* menu and select the desired window. The appropriate window appears on the screen. There may be several opened program groups within the Program Manager; in this case, the active window is indicated by a different-colored title bar. The active window remains in the foreground and no other group window covers it.

Since group windows are components of the Program Manager itself, it's not possible to move them outside the Program Manager's border.

Arranging the groups

Two commands in the *Windows* menu enable you to arrange your group windows so that they are easy to see. The *Tile* command arranges the opened windows so that they're next to each other in the Program Manager. The group that has the most icons occupies the most space.

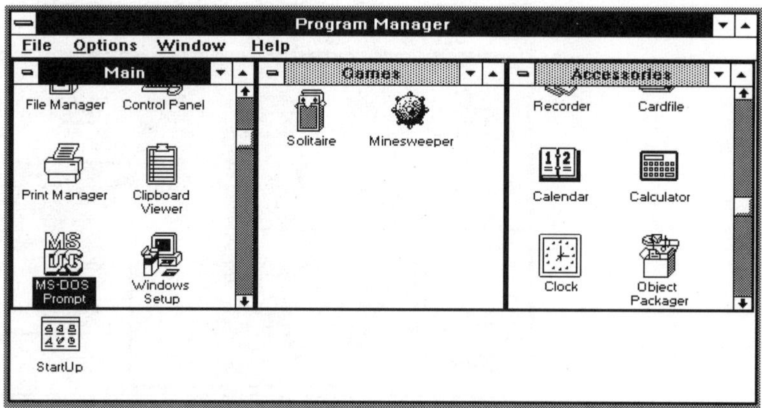

Displaying all groups simultaneously

You can also use the *Cascade* command, which layers all opened windows so that they overlap each other; only their title bars are visible. To place a window in the foreground, click on the window's title bar with the mouse.

Scroll Bar in Group Windows

If a window is reduced to a size that's too small to display all of its icons, scroll bars appear at the right and/or bottom of the window. Use these icons to display all the icons that no longer fit in the window.

Depending on which accessed icons should appear on the screen, the individual groups can be opened or closed, or arranged using the previous commands. However, you should only combine groups that are used regularly. To do this, create a new group and copy the necessary icons into it. Close all remaining groups, leaving only the special group open. This saves memory in addition to providing greater clarity. Remember to save your changes so they are available the next time you run Windows.

Arranging group icons

If the group icons have shifted within the Program Manager window, you can easily move them back to the bottom of the screen. Simply select the *Arrange Icons* command from the *Windows* menu. The icons will be arranged automatically.

The StartUp group

The StartUp group has a special function. Program icons contained within this group are automatically activated at Windows startup and their windows are placed in the background. The Program Manager then appears in the foreground, after all the other applications have been started.

Moving instead of copying

To use this technique to start an application automatically, move the program's icon into the StartUp group. With the mouse, drag the appropriate icon to the StartUp group's icon. You don't have to open the StartUp group itself. If you're using the keyboard, select the *Move...* command from the *File* menu.

Although you could also copy a program icon into this group, moving it is more practical. When a program icon is still visible in its normal working group, it's tempting to activate it at the beginning of the Windows session, even though the StartUp group has already activated it. However, if the icon isn't displayed in its original window, you'll remember that it's now located in the StartUp group.

If you no longer want the application to start automatically, move the icon back to its original location or delete it from the StartUp group if a copy was made.

You can also start applications automatically by adding an entry, after the RUN= line, in the WIN.INI file. However, to do this, you must edit the file. If you later decide to remove these applications, you must edit the file again. Placing a program icon in the StartUp group doesn't automatically produce an entry in WIN.INI. Also, if a program icon has been placed in the StartUp group and in the WIN.INI file, removing it from the StartUp group doesn't automatically remove it from the WIN.INI file. So, be sure that you don't enter the same program name in both places.

11.3 Starting Applications with Icons

To call an application from a group window, activate its icon, whether it's a Windows or non-Windows application. Move the mouse pointer to the proper icon and double-click the mouse.

If you're using the keyboard, first select the icon. Use the cursor keys to move the highlight, which displays the icon title of the active icon in inverse video, to the icon for the application you want to start. Then either press the Enter key or select the *Open* command from the *File* menu.

Setting attributes

Information about how to start the application is assigned to the program icon. Obviously, a name must be assigned to the application. Other attributes, such as a working directory, startup parameters, etc. can be assigned when the icon is created or by using the *Properties...* command from the *File* menu. (We'll discuss this procedure later in the book.)

Remember that a program icon is only a reference to an application instead of the actual application. So, deleting the icon doesn't mean that the application is also deleted from the hard drive. The opposite also applies; a program icon can still be displayed even if the application has been deleted from the hard drive.

Errors at program startup

When using an icon to start an application, occasionally an error message, which indicates that the application wasn't found, appears. It's possible that the application was deleted from the hard drive. In this case, you should delete the program icon with the *Delete* command or the Del key in order to avoid any confusion. If you ever need the application again you must re-install it on the hard drive. The application must be placed in the same directory as before. Otherwise, the current program icon won't start the application.

This brings us to another reason why this error message appears. The startup routine searches for the program name, corresponding to the icon, in the directory assigned to that icon. If the application should have been copied to a different directory, the program icon must be modified. This applies even if there is an all-encompassing path statement in your AUTOEXEC.BAT file. You must also set a path with the *Properties...* command. If a path isn't included for a program name, the search is performed in the Windows directory.

An error message may also result within a network if the application exists on a network server but you haven't logged onto the network. In this case, Windows cannot find the drive or the path, which is identified only when you've logged onto the network before starting Windows.

11.4 Starting Applications without Icons

The Program Manager allows you to start all applications. However, this doesn't apply to only applications that are represented by icons within a group. For example, if you want to use the MS-DOS 5.0 EDIT command to work on a file, you must return to the *DOS prompt*. You can access it directly, along with all parameters, which in this case is the name of the file to be edited. Depending on how often you need such an application, you may want to place it in a group.

Entering the program name

To access the dialog box, in which the program name must be entered, select the *Run...* command from the *File* menu.

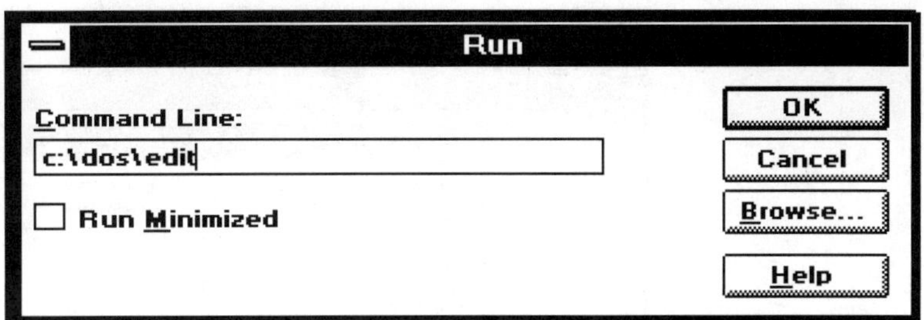

Starting a program

You may enter any name in the command line, including Windows and non-Windows applications. If the application isn't located in the Windows directory, you must specify the correct drive and directory for the application. Otherwise only the Windows directory will be searched. This also applies to applications whose paths are given in the AUTOEXEC.BAT file. Windows will always display an error message if the given application isn't found. Check the spelling of the program name and then check the path. Internal DOS commands such as TYPE cannot be executed; to execute these commands, you must return to the DOS prompt.

Pay attention to the path specification

Besides the program name, and the drive and path specifications, you can enter other required parameters on the command line. When you're editing a file using the DOS EDIT program, notice the path specification of the file to be edited. If the two files aren't located in the same directory, EDIT creates a new file with the same name in its own directory. So, path specifications are important, especially when the file to be edited is located on a different drive.

```
EDIT D:\DATA\ADDRS.TXT
```

This also applies to applications that are started with parameters and allow a specific file to be specified. An example of this is WORD. For this application, one parameter indicates that the application should start in text mode and another parameter specifies a file name.

```
C:\APPS\WORD5\WORD /T D:\TEXTS\LETTER23.DOC
```

Since this entry is long, you may want to represent this application as an icon. Another option is to use the Browse... button, which displays a dialog box that lists all the files that can be started (i.e., the .COM, .EXE, .BAT, and .PIF files).

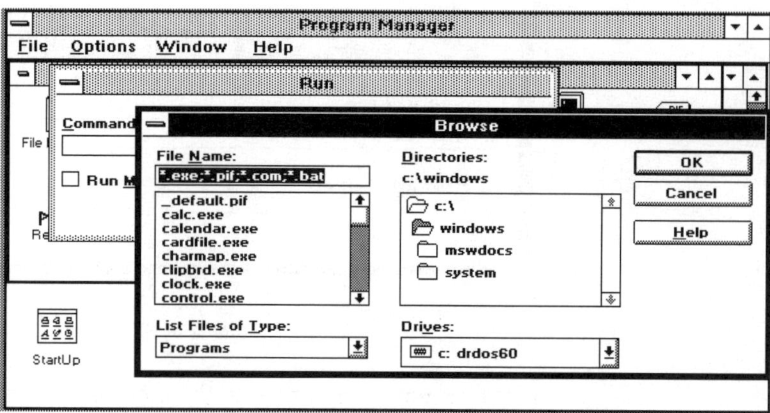

Searching for program names

Choose the drive and directory, in which the application is located. After selecting the program name and confirming it with Enter, the application is automatically entered on the command line, along with its drive and path specifications. You can also enter parameters or file names.

Running applications as icons

To run the application as an icon when it starts, activate the *Run minimized* option. Then use the Task Manager or the Alt + Ctrl key combination to activate the application.

Ending the application

DOS programs that are started in this way remain active until you exit them. For example, if you've been working in the MS-DOS 5.0 EDIT program, the *Exit* command in the *File* menu returns you to the Program Manager. In the Word program, pressing Esc and selecting the *Quit* command returns you to Windows. However, something different happens if you start COMMAND.COM (the DOS command processor) in this way. In this case, several DOS commands may be executed and applications may be started until you run out of memory. COMMAND.COM executes all statements within the MS-DOS Prompt icon.

You can exit the command processor by typing EXIT at the DOS prompt.

11.5 Setting Application Attributes

Information that's needed to run an application can be found behind the program icon. For example, in Word for Windows you may want to immediately access the directory that contains all your text files. Generally, you'll keep these files in a directory other than the default WINWORD directory, although Word for

Windows is configured to always refer to its own directory. Moving through several directories to obtain a specific document file is very time-consuming.

Macros for working directories

This problem occurs in almost every application. Although, in Word for Windows, this problem can be solved by using a macro, this is not the case with many other applications. Here, Windows allocates a working directory that can be accessed immediately after program startup.

When a program is added to a group, the Program Manager sets a program's icon attributes. However, you can change these attributes at a later time. This also applies to the actual icon that Windows automatically creates at installation. To change its attributes, select the icon and select the *Properties...* command from the *File* menu. If you're using the keyboard, press Alt + Enter.

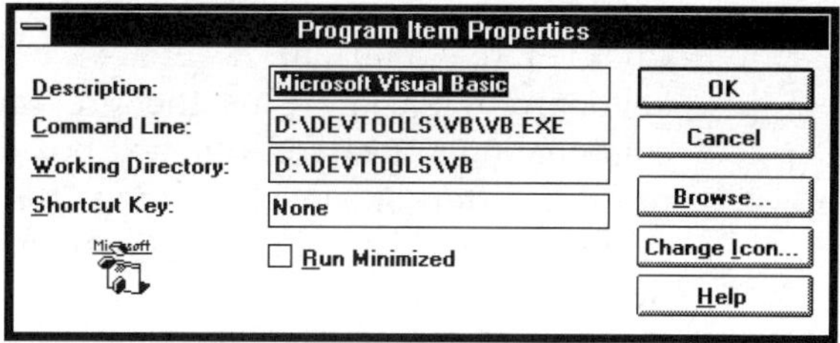

One icon may have many attributes

Changing path specifications

The icon attributes must be changed when the path specifications have changed (e.g., when a particular application has been copied into a different directory). In this case, the application can no longer be started with its icon because Windows searches the specified directory. To correct this, you must enter the proper drive, directory, and program name in the *Command Line* text box. By activating the Browse... button, you can enter the necessary information automatically. Select the drive and directory and then activate the program name. The entry is transferred to the correct line.

Icon specification

The icon's title is defined in the *Description* text box of the *Program Item Properties* dialog box. Icon titles are usually one or two words. However, if you need to use a longer name, use the *Desktop* option from the Control Panel to switch on the *Wrap Title* option. This option automatically wraps a long icon title onto the next line. This saves space in the group and helps keeps your icons organized.

Working directory

We've already discussed the allocation of a working directory. The application refers to this directory after start up. Type the name of this directory in the *Working Directory* text box. You don't have to specify a working directory in this text box for applications that provide an option for specifying this directory.

Activating key combinations

You can assign certain key combinations to applications. These key combinations, called *shortcut keys*, automatically activate the application. The Ctrl+Alt avoids any conflicts with existing Windows key combinations.

Click in the *Shortcut Key:* text box and press a key on the keyboard. This key plus the previously mentioned Ctrl + Alt combination appears in this text box. To replace the previous key, press a different key. By doing this you can generate any key combination. Pressing the Shift key inserts it between Ctrl and Alt. Remember that the key combinations are only valid within the Program Manager. They are ignored within an application.

Assigning additional icons

Program icons usually correspond to a type of application. However, you can change them at any time. Windows provides various icons that you can use as often as you want. Many Windows applications have their own icons, which are usually more elaborate than the Windows icons. It's also possible to use imported icons for other applications.

Icons are assigned to program names

To change an icon, click on the Change Icon... button in the *Program Item Properties* dialog box. The *Change Icon* dialog box appears.

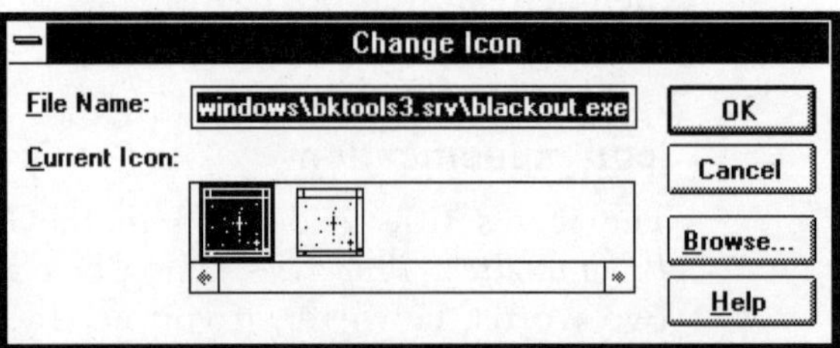

Definite assignment of an icon to a program

The file name of the program and its current icon are displayed. Icons are always assigned to a program name. To change an icon, enter the name of the application that contains the desired icon. For example, if you want to change the icon for the Clock, only the CLOCK.EXE entry and the clock icon appear. If you want to assign the Write icon to the Clock application, type the program name WRITE.EXE in the *File Name:* text box. After a few seconds the Write icon appears. The Program Manager contains the most icons. If you type PROGMAN.EXE in the text box, you'll see an entire row of icons.

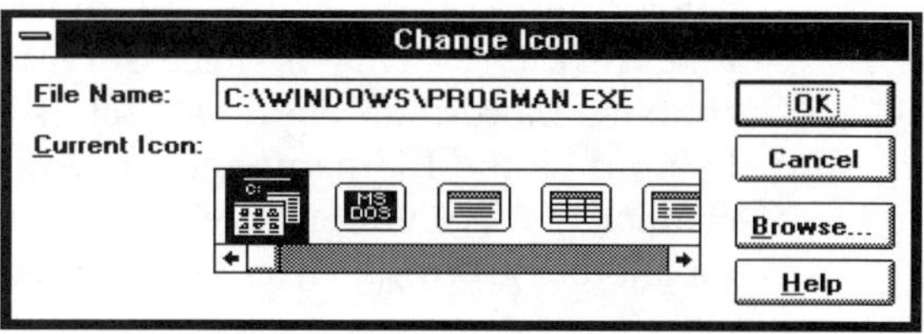

The Program Manager offers the most icons

If you want to assign an icon but you don't know in which directory it's located, click the Browse... button. A file selection window appears in which you can select the appropriate application.

Calling an application as an icon

The *Run Minimized* check box in the *Program Item Properties* dialog box allows you to call an application as a window icon. This icon runs in the background while the Program Manager remains in the foreground. You can use *Switch To...* or the Task Manager to switch the application to the foreground.

This setting is especially useful for the Clock because it enables you to display the time while you're working. Since the Clock shows the correct time even in Minimized form, you don't need to display it as a window. To prevent the Clock from being covered by other windows, activate the *Always on Top* check box in the Clock Control menu.

11.6 Creating a Program Group

So far we've worked with only program groups that were created by Windows. The Program Manager allows you to place related applications in your own group. So, you can create separate groups for word processors, spreadsheets, databases, and graphics.

To create a new group, use the *New...* command in the Program Manager's *File* menu. The *New Program Object* dialog box appears in which you can create a *Program Group* or a *Program Item*. Select the *Program Group* option button and click the OK button. Then the *Program Group Properties* dialog box appears.

A group name should be assigned

In the *Description:* text box, enter the name of the program group you want to create. You should use a name that describes the group's contents. For example, a group that will contain spreadsheet applications could simply be called "Spreadsheets." This group will then be saved under a specific file name with the extension .GRP. You may use a group name other than the one entered in *Description:*, but you must enter the name in the *Group File:* text box. This is necessary when the description name contains more than eight characters. Otherwise, the name would be used as the file name, but it would be cut off after the eighth character. Also, you cannot use a name that's already being used for another group, such as Accessories.

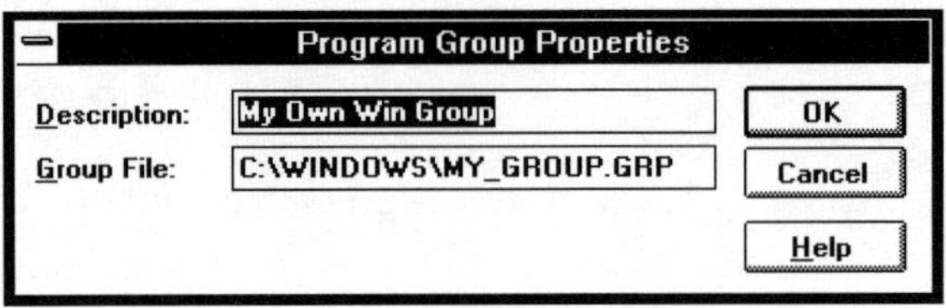

Creating program groups

The newly created group can be added as an icon to already existing applications. You can copy these applications from other groups.

Using group files more often

Group files are entered in the PROGMAN.INI file. The following shows where the .GRP files are located and in which order they are displayed.

PROGMAN .INI entries

```
Order= 2 7 6 5 3 4 1 8
[Groups]
Group1=C:\WINDOWS\MAIN.GRP
Group2=C:\WINDOWS\ACCESSOR.GRP
Group3=C:\WINDOWS\GAMES.GRP
Group4=C:\WINDOWS\STARTUP.GRP
Group5=C:\WINDOWS\MICROSOF.GRP
Group6=C:\WINDOWS\WINBAT.GRP
Group7=C:\WINDOWS\TEST.GRP
Group8=C:\WINDOWS\ARA.GRP
```

The group files contain the applications. This is important to know if you're installing Windows on different computers but still want to keep the same program groups and icons. In this case, simply copy the .GRP files to the Windows directory of the other computers. Of course you must ensure that the applications are stored in the same directories (i.e., that the directories are identically named). Otherwise, individual icons can be matched up using *File/Properties...*. In most cases matching up group files isn't as difficult as creating new ones.

11.7 Moving and Copying Icons

The standard Windows installation process assigns icons to predefined groups. However, the setup may not meet your needs. So, you should configure the icons within a particular group. You can move or copy any icon from one group to another. You can decide whether to retain the original group structure and copy all necessary icons into a single new group, or to modify the existing groups according to your own preferences.

Moving icons

You must select an icon before you can copy or move it. With the mouse, drag the icon from the original group to the new one. Releasing the mouse button assigns the icon to the new group file. It doesn't matter whether the new group is opened or whether it's only displayed within the Program Manager as an icon. You can simply relocate the program icon to the corresponding group icon. To move an icon with the keyboard, select the *Move...* command from the *File* menu or use the F7 key. A dialog box, in which you can define the target group, appears.

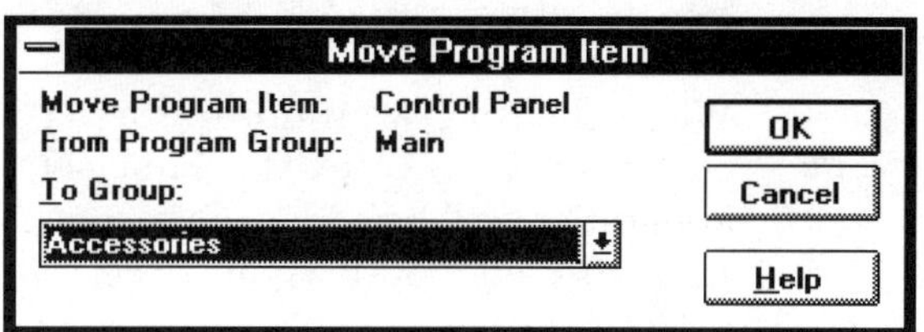

Selecting target group for moving and copying

Use the cursor keys to select the group to which the program icon should be moved. The move is acknowledged and executed through the dialog box. Then the program icon is removed from the original group and inserted into the target group.

Copying icons

The process of copying a program icon to another group is identical to moving an icon. With the keyboard, select the *File/Copy...* command or use the F8 key. With the mouse, copying is performed by dragging the icon while pressing the Ctrl key. Here the icon remains in its group. The cursor still points to it and it can be copied to another group.

Setting application configurations

The *Copy...* command can also be used to perform other tasks. Program icons can even be copied within a group so two (or more) identical icons exist in the same group. This enables you to modify the icons so an application can be started with different parameters or files.

For example, if you activate the Notepad with its normal icon, a temporary file is always created. Suppose that you share the same computer with several people and you've created a Notepad file that contains various messages. Everyone must check this file before using the computer. So, a second icon, which calls this file along with Notepad, must exist. To create this icon, use the *Copy...* command to copy the Notepad icon into the same group and use the *File/Properties...* command to change the description. Add your file name after the program name. Also include the correct path specification if the file is in a directory other than Windows.

11.8 Adding Applications Manually

The Program Manager allows you to add individual applications to any group. A non-Windows application is always started with standard PIF settings. A more complicated application should be set up by Windows' own Setup program, which automatically adds the applications. You could also create a PIF file at a later time.

You can change all entries by using the *File/Properties...* command.

First choose the group

When choosing a group, it doesn't matter whether the group is empty or already exists. First select the group, in which the application will be added. Open the group by clicking on the group icon with the mouse. Again, select the *New...* command in the *File* menu, select the *Program Item* option button and click OK. A dialog box, in which you can specify which application should be transferred, appears. The most important entries are the program's file name and directory in which it's located.

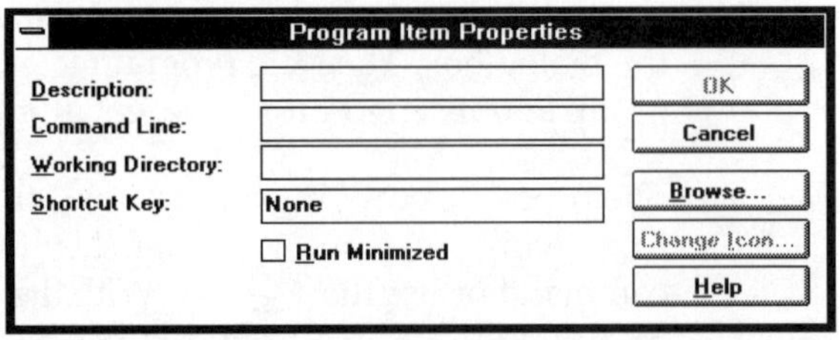

Program Item Properties
Description:
Command Line:
Working Directory:
Shortcut Key: None
Run Minimized
OK
Cancel
Browse...
Change Icon...
Help

Entries for binding a program

Enter the icon's title in the *Description:* text box. If you don't enter a name, the file name, without an extension, is used.

Specifying the program file

Click on the Browse... button if you're not sure which directory contains the program file or whether the file is a .COM or .EXE file. All program files in the current directory are displayed. At the top you'll see a file name extension. If it's *.EXE then only program files with that extension are listed. However, if you would like to see all the .COM files, type "*.COM" in the *File Name:* text box. With the *List Files of Type* list box, you can choose several file types in which to conduct the search. When you find the program file you're looking for, select the OK button. The directory and the name of the program file is automatically displayed in the *Command Line* text box.

Specifying a working directory

A program refers to the working directory after startup. Type the name of this directory in the *Working Directory* text box. You don't have to do this for applications that provide an option for specifying the working directory.

11.9 Adding Applications Automatically

During the Windows installation you're asked whether you want to install applications. If you do, you can specify whether Windows should search for applications either in all drives, one drive, or only one directory. You can restart this procedure at any time to automatically add applications on the hard drive to Windows. Windows lists all the applications it finds. Then you must determine which applications should be transferred. Once this is done, Windows creates the Applications group and assigns corresponding icons to the selected applications. If this group already exists, the new icons are added to it.

You can also assign a program name directly to a particular group. We explained this procedure earlier in this chapter.

Choosing the type of assignment

To start automatic assignments, open Windows Setup from the Main group. Then select the *Set Up Applications...* command from the *Options* menu. In the dialog box that appears, you can select either the *Search for Applications...* option button or the *Ask you to specify an application* option button.

Automatically setting up applications

With the first option, a dialog box, in which you can specify where Windows should search for applications, appears. You can choose a specific path or the entire drive. Then Windows Setup searches for Windows applications as well as non-Windows applications.

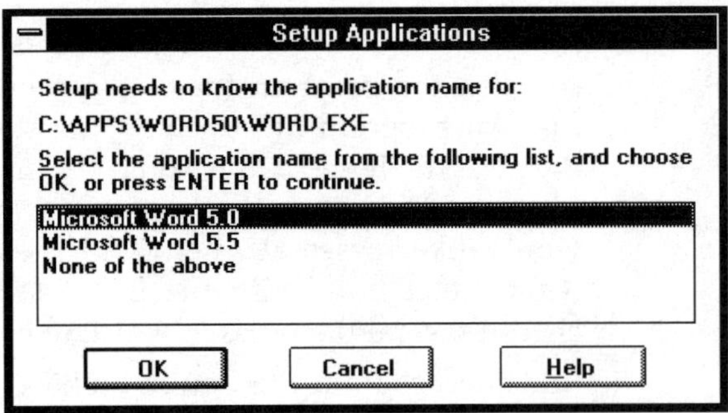

Windows does not always find all programs

Usually all the DOS programs aren't found. Setup finds the more common applications, such as Lotus 1-2-3, Ventura Publisher, and the larger Windows applications. This occurs because Windows has a list of program names inclusive of their standard .PIF file settings. Applications found on the hard disk are compared with the names on the list. If a match occurs and that application is then installed, Windows automatically creates a .PIF file.

This procedure saves a lot of space. In earlier versions of Windows all of the available .PIF files were installed on the hard drive. The chapter on the .PIF Editor contains a list of all the applications that are automatically assigned a .PIF file.

Selecting individual applications

Applications that are found are listed in the left window of the *Set Up Applications* dialog box. All applications that will be automatically set up by Windows must be moved to the right window. You can use either the Add All button to transfer all of the applications or use the mouse to select specific applications and move them to the right window with the Add-> button. Remove any applications in the right window that you don't want to include. You can do this by selecting the application and then activating the <-Remove button. If you select OK, the applications for Windows are set up. The non-Windows applications receive a .PIF file containing standardized settings. These settings should be changed if the application isn't running properly.

Setting up individual applications

Assigning a program to a particular group can be done through *Windows Setup*. If you know the program name and want to assign it to an already existing group, select the *Ask you to specify an application* option button.

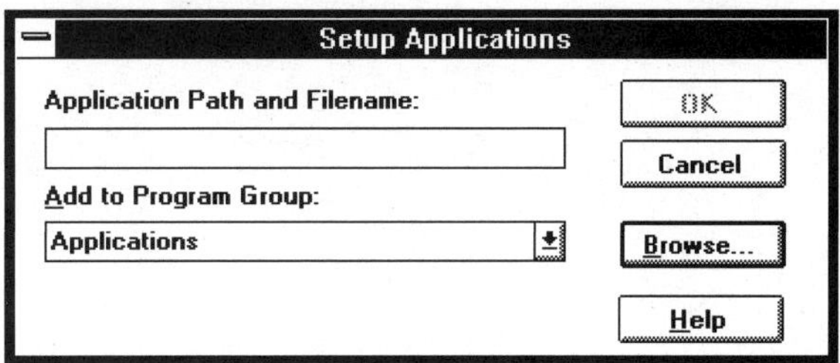

Setting up an individual program

Specify the appropriate program name and directory. If you activate the Browse... button, a file selection window, in which you can enter the program name and the Windows directory, appears. Activate the directory and select the program name from the list. When you select OK, the entry automatically appears in the *Application Path and Filename:* text box.

Change the program icon later

Now select the group in which the icon should appear. A Windows application will be assigned its own icon, but any non-Windows applications receive the default icon which applies to all non-Windows applications. You can change this icon later with the *Properties* command in the Program Manager.

12. Running Applications Under Windows

True Windows applications use interfaces with the screen, printer, mouse, and keyboard that are controlled by the same driver used by Windows. This chapter discusses the similarities between Windows applications and data exchange, how Windows handles non-Windows applications, running multiple applications in Windows, the DOS prompt, and multitasking.

12.1 Windows and Non-Windows Applications

Windows differentiates between two basic types of applications—"true" Windows applications and the non-Windows applications. These applications have different work surfaces and control the hardware peripherals, such as the printer, screen, mouse, etc., differently.

Windows as a basis for applications

Windows has been called an extended operating system. However, this isn't really true because Windows provides a link to the computer's hardware for its applications. For an application to function smoothly, it must be able to activate the individual components of the computer including the screen, keyboard, mouse, printer, interfaces, and drives.

The application includes drivers to control these devices. Windows itself has all the drivers it needs to activate the hardware. At the same time, its user interface enables you (with icons and the mouse) to use all the functions of both the operating system and the hardware.

One driver, many applications

Usually, to install a new graphics card, you must use the Windows Setup routine. This creates a new connection between Windows and the screen, using a different driver. You can use the system controls to select different screen colors, for example. Instead of the driver, only the connection is changed (i.e., you've modified the activation of the graphics card).

Distinguishing Windows applications

Windows applications don't have drivers. Since they're installed on the hard drive, they are dependent upon Windows. These applications use all the Windows resources. For example, to print from an application, you must use the printer driver and, in some instances, the Windows Print Manager. All screen output originates from the Windows graphics driver, etc.

Besides the technical aspects, all Windows applications have identical displays and screen elements because they're developed and programmed according to the same guidelines.

Each additional Windows application uses the same drivers as Windows. This saves memory, increases efficiency, and most importantly, ensures that the screen and printer output remain consistent. A major advantage of using Windows applications is that you can exchange data. Since all Windows applications can access Windows' Clipboard, information can easily be passed among the applications.

Windows applications do not run alone

To verify that Windows applications don't have a screen driver, try to start one of them from the DOS screen. For example, try to start the Windows Clock from DOS by typing:

```
CLOCK [Enter]
```

The following error message appears:

```
This program requires Microsoft Windows
```

Larger programs, such as Microsoft Excel, contain a connection to the Windows kernel. So, the user can start Excel from DOS. This works only if Windows actually exists in executable form on the hard drive. In this case, Windows is started along with the other application, and the Program Manager opens as Minimized.

Almost all the applications included with Windows are Windows applications. This applies to Windows Setup and File Manager as well as Write and Paintbrush. If you're thinking of purchasing new programs for particular tasks, you should consider Windows applications first. There's almost an unlimited variety of applications for an infinite number of tasks.

What software should you purchase in the future?

Windows applications are identified as such on their packages. Many mail order companies also have separate sections in their catalogs for Windows applications and non-Windows applications. You may have to do further research if a product isn't labeled accordingly.

Several manufacturers have begun to offer both Windows and non-Windows versions of their products. If you already own a non-Windows version of a particular application, you should ask your dealer whether a Windows version is available.

Existing applications

Some of the most popular Windows applications are Excel for spreadsheet applications, Word for Windows for word processing, and Superbase for database applications. Pagemaker is a well-known page layout application used in desktop publishing. There are numerous programs for all types of applications.

Shareware and public domain programs also offer a variety of tools and applications. Using these programs can be very economical, since the larger Windows applications can cost hundreds of dollars.

Space prohibits our listing of all the available programs. However, you can refer to the various computer magazines for information on any new Windows applications. Also check whether the magazines have a section for shareware or public domain software.

Non-Windows applications

Windows also allows you to run applications that aren't written specifically for Windows. However, these applications don't offer the advantages of Windows' graphic environment. Non-Windows applications (DOS programs) use the character and line-oriented environment of the DOS operating system.

An important difference between Windows and non-Windows applications is that non-Windows applications run within their own environments. They have their own drivers for controlling the screen, printer, mouse, etc. This applies to all DOS programs. So, the screen or printer output of individual applications may vary because different drivers control the hardware components. It's also difficult to exchange data between individual DOS programs because various formats are used.

Running non-Windows applications under Windows

The most popular non-Windows applications include Microsoft Word, dBASE IV, Lotus 1-2-3, etc. You can start all these applications from Windows. Windows shifts to the background and transfers control of the hardware components to the non-Windows application. For example, if you start dBASE from Windows, dBASE activates its own printer driver for printing databases and program listings. The Windows printer driver cannot be accessed.

Memory isn't the only thing managed by Windows. The Windows kernel is relocated to upper memory to make room for the non-Windows application. The screen is still controlled from the background because there must be a way to switch between dBase and Windows. Since the keyboard must be used to switch between the programs, Windows keeps a few keys allocated to itself while you're working with dBase.

Controlling Windows with .PIF files

Non-Windows applications need a .PIF (Program Information File) file to run under Windows. A .PIF file regulates a program's interaction with the Windows environment. These files determine the range of control given to an application.

Notice how Windows behaves in the background. This helps avoid conflicts that can occur when several programs try to access the same hardware components by using their various drivers. We'll discuss the .PIF files in detail in Chapter 13.

The Windows Setup program provides a way to integrate non-Windows applications into the Windows environment. Setting up the application automatically creates a .PIF file. This applies to all applications that are located on the hard drive after using the *Set Up Applications...* command.

To install a non-Windows application that wasn't recognized by Windows, you must use the *New...* command from the Program Manager's *File* menu. We discussed adding non-Windows applications to the Program Manager in the previous chapter. That chapter also contains a list of the programs, for which .PIF files are automatically created.

Applications and memory use

Now there are various Windows and non-Windows applications, which operate differently. Some programs work with expanded memory and others with extended memory. A similar problem occurs with Windows applications when one program supports Standard mode, and another supports Real mode.

Since Windows uses extended memory more effectively than expanded memory, you should avoid purchasing non-Windows applications that access expanded memory. Otherwise, you would have to partition your main memory, which would affect Windows' performance. For more information on utilizing main memory, refer to the chapter on Windows memory management.

Running non-Windows applications

The way in which Windows displays DOS programs depends on the mode in which Windows is running. A computer based on an 80286 processor can run Windows only in Standard and Real modes (see Chapter 3 for information on Windows startup). In this case, the non-Windows applications run as full-screen applications, which means that they occupy the entire screen.

If instead you have a computer with an 80386 or 80486 processor, you can run Windows in 386 Enhanced mode. Most non-Windows applications can run in a window that contains a Control menu, scroll bar, and title bar.

Exchanging data between windows is easy. We'll discuss working with only non-Windows applications in the 386 Enhanced mode later in this chapter.

Memory problems

If you're working with a non-Windows application that needs more memory than is available, Windows will display a *Not enough memory to run* message. However, there are several ways you can solve this problem.

Closing programs

The simplest method consists of closing all applications that are no longer needed. This also applies to Windows applications. At the very least you should change the applications, including the Program Manager and File Managers, to Minimized form.

Deleting the Clipboard

Check the Clipboard to determine whether it contains anything. You can delete the Clipboard contents, if you no longer need the information stored there.

Full-screen mode

When using the 386 Enhanced mode, be sure to run non-Windows applications in full-screen mode only. This mode uses less memory than window mode.

Changing .PIF files

In the .PIF file you can change entries that affect the application's memory requirements. Otherwise, the default settings for that particular application will be used.

Depending on how many windows and applications are opened and closed during a work session, you can internally reorganize Windows by restarting it. Usually you'll be able to open more applications than before. You can also increase virtual memory by using the system controls.

12.2 Starting Applications

You can start applications in several ways. The best way is to install all your applications (using the Windows Setup program) into a single group, in which they can be found under one icon. Depending on how often you activate a particular application, however, one of the following methods may be more suitable.

Starting from the icon

To start an application contained within a group, open the group window where the applications are displayed as icons. Then activate the desired application by double-clicking on the left mouse button. Alternatively, use the cursor keys to select the icon and then press Enter. You can also select the *File/Open* command from the Program Manager.

Starting from the File Manager

Another way to start standard applications is from the File Manager. Go to the path (or drive) where your program is located and get a file listing. The startup file is identified by the .COM, .EXE, .PIF, or .BAT extensions. Once you've found the correct file, double-click it with the mouse. Using the keyboard, you can select the file with the cursor keys and then press Enter. You can also use the File Manager's *File* menu and select the *Open* command.

Starting with the Run command

Both the Program and File Managers contain the *Run...* command within their *File* menus. When this command is activated, a dialog box, in which you can enter the name of the application you want to start, appears. If you enter only the file name, Windows searches in only the active drive or subdirectory. So, you should either enter the complete path or switch to the proper subdirectory first. The *Run Minimized* check box allows you to set the running application in the background as an icon.

Starting from the DOS prompt

You can also start non-Windows applications by using the *Dos Prompt* icon to activate the operating system's command processor.

However, since this uses additional memory, it's better to activate applications by using one of the other methods. Once DOS has been activated, you'll want to use other applications. Some of the larger applications may cause memory problems.

12.3 The DOS Prompt

Although Windows creates a user-friendly environment, certain tasks can be accomplished only with DOS commands. The File Manager commands provide an easy way to perform various operations pertaining to files and storage media. Unfortunately, these commands leave gaps that can be closed only by manually entered DOS commands.

Calling the DOS prompt

Windows allows you to access DOS directly through the Main group, which contains the *MS-DOS Prompt*. This is the same DOS prompt that appears on the screen when you start the computer or when you call COMMAND.COM (the DOS command processor) via this application. You'll immediately see which screen-exchanging options are available.

Controlling the command processor

COMMAND.COM under Windows runs exclusively as a full-screen application instead of within a window. However, as with other full-screen applications, it's possible to switch to a different application by using the Alt + Tab or Alt + Esc key combinations.

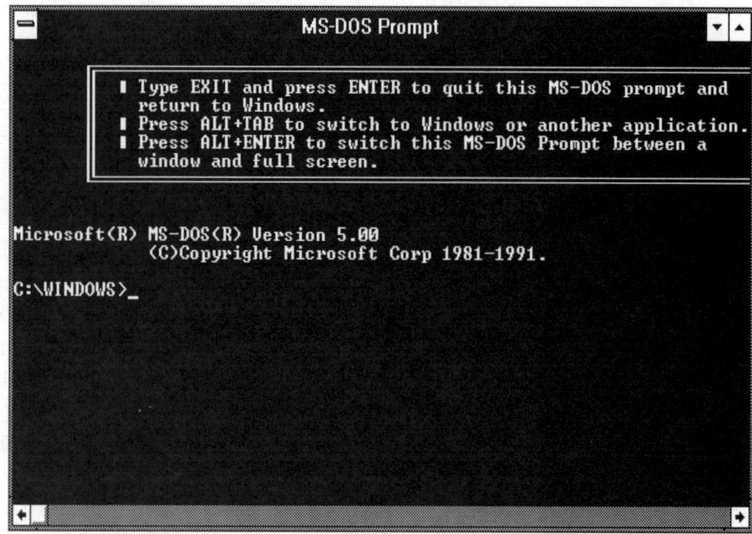

The DOS prompt in Windows

Leaving the DOS prompt

By typing the EXIT command, you can exit the command processor and automatically return to Windows.

Memory allocation for program calling

If there is sufficient available memory, you can start other applications from the DOS prompt that haven't already been installed under Windows. In the Windows directory, Windows has its own .PIF file for the DOS prompt, called *Dosprmpt.pif*.

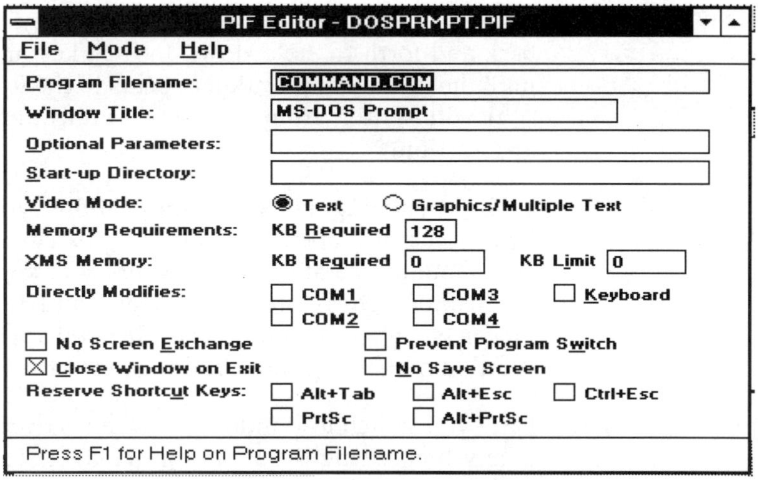

PIF Editor - DOSPRMPT.PIF

File Mode Help

Program Filename: COMMAND.COM

Window Title: MS-DOS Prompt

Optional Parameters:

Start-up Directory:

Video Mode: Text Graphics/Multiple Text

Memory Requirements: KB Required 128

XMS Memory: KB Required 0 KB Limit 0

Directly Modifies: COM1 COM3 Keyboard COM2 COM4

No Screen Exchange Prevent Program Switch

Close Window on Exit No Save Screen

Reserve Shortcut Keys: Alt+Tab Alt+Esc Ctrl+Esc PrtSc Alt+PrtSc

Press F1 for Help on Program Filename.

The .PIF file for the DOS prompt

This file has been set up to allow as much available space as possible in memory. You can change this at any time.

12.4 Running Several Applications

Under Windows, several non-Windows and Windows applications can run simultaneously. The applications are stacked on top of each other. With a key combination, you can switch from one application to another.

When you do this, the application that you want to use is moved from the background to the foreground. The other applications remain in memory; they aren't restarted each time.

Even if you activate a single application, such as Word 5.5, two applications are already running, that application and Windows. Non-Windows applications always run in the background as icons.

Switching between two applications

To switch from one application to another, use the key combination Alt + Tab. For example, if you're currently in Word, this places the Word screen in the background and you'll then see the Windows screen appear. If you press the same key combination again, the Word screen reappears unchanged.

Switching back and forth

The Alt + Tab combination always switches you from one application to the previous application, even if several applications have been started. This key combination always pertains to the active application and the one immediately behind it. If you want to choose a different application to switch back and forth to, hold down the Alt key and press the Tab key until the desired application appears in the foreground. Now Alt + Tab will switch from the new application to the last active application.

Save files before switching

While switching between applications you may accidentally leave some files open. When making extensive entries or changes, you should save all changes before you switch over to the new application. The system may crash and the keyboard may no longer be able to accept entries. If this happens, you cannot load Word into the foreground and then save the files.

Once you switch to Windows, you can activate another application at any time, using the Program Manager. These applications also will appear on the screen in succession.

Switching among several applications

If more than two applications (including Windows) are running, you can use Alt + Tab to switch between individual applications. Hold down Alt and repeatedly press the Tab key; the names of various programs appear in a dialog box in the center of the screen, which can be placed in the foreground. This enables you to find the desired application quickly. However, the *Fast Alt+Tab Switching* option from *Desktop* must be activated. You can determine from Word whether you want to place Windows or Multiplan in the foreground. The application won't be placed in the foreground immediately if it has been minimized to an icon. In this case, you must first select the icon; it will move to the foreground when you release the key.

The key combination Alt + Esc also switches between applications. The Alt key doesn't have to be held down because an application isn't automatically activated if it exists as an icon. When switching among several applications, this key combination activates the applications in a circular pattern. For example, if you've started three applications from Windows and use Alt + Esc repeatedly from within the Program Manager, the following occurs:

Order of switching

Application in foreground	Keyboard entry
Program Manager	Alt + Esc
1st application	Alt + Esc
2nd application	Alt + Esc
3rd application	Alt + Esc
Program Manager	Alt + Esc
1st application	Alt + Esc
etc.	

When switching from a non-Windows application that's running in full-screen mode, each time you press the Esc key either an application or an icon appears in the foreground. When the desired application is reached, release the keys so the application remains in the foreground.

12.5 Program Control with the Task Manager

It's easy to lose track of what's happening on the screen if several applications are open simultaneously. This is usually because too many windows are overlapping. To switch between applications, click on the window border with the mouse or use the key combinations Alt + Tab or Alt + Esc. This always causes a switch from one application to the next.

Although the screen may look unorganized, Windows has everything under control. The Task Manager manages the applications. You can reach this window with the *Switch To...* command from any application window's Control menu. The keyboard command is Ctrl + Esc. To start the Task Manager with the mouse, place the mouse pointer anywhere in the Windows background and double-click.

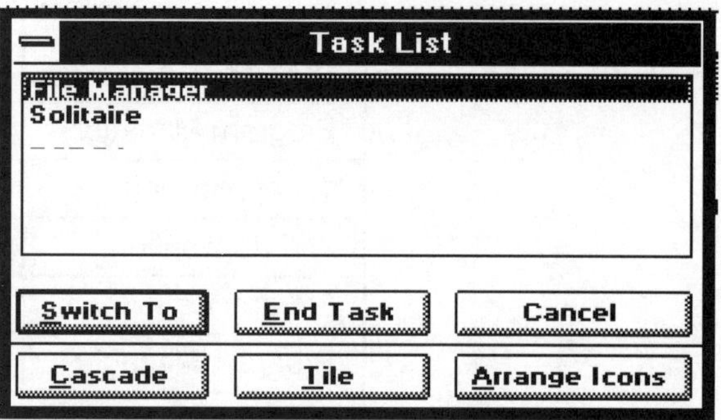

The Task List dialog box

You'll see a list of the currently open applications. It doesn't matter whether the applications are active or displayed as icons. Move the selection bar through the list with the cursor keys or the mouse pointer. The screen exchange option that you finally enter applies to the application you've selected in the list.

Activating applications

By using the *Switch To...* option, you can activate an application. This means that you're opening a window for the application or placing an already-opened window in the foreground. You can also do this by pressing the Tab key while holding down Alt, until the desired application appears in the foreground.

Closing Non-Windows applications

You should always close a non-Windows application with its specific exit command. In the application's Control menu, the *Settings...* command provides a dialog box, in which you can end the program using the Terminate... button. However, doing this may result in data loss for the currently active file. This depends on how the particular application handles its files.

Ending Windows applications

For a Windows application the *Close* command in the Control menu ends the application. If you've made changes to a file with which this application is associated, Windows asks whether you want to save them.

Arranging Windows applications clearly

To arrange all windows on your screen so each title bar is visible, and, therefore, can be activated with a mouse, use the *Cascade* command from the *Window* menu. Then to place an application in the foreground, click on its title bar. However, these functions apply only to Windows applications or to non-Windows applications running within Windows (in 386 Enhanced mode only). Non-Windows applications move to the Windows background as icons.

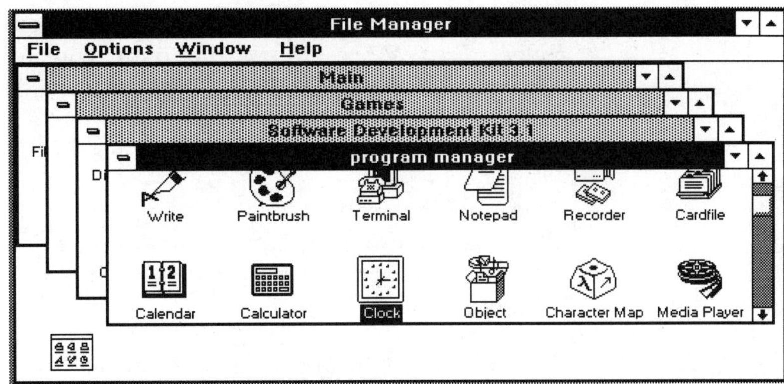

Windows no longer overlap

If there is an icon in the Windows background and only the Program Manager is open, the *Tile* command provides the best arrangement for the Program Manager. All the icons of active applications will still be visible.

Arranging the icon

The *Arrange Icons* command is useful when several windows or icons are on the screen. This allows you to position all icons to the bottom of the screen, starting at the lower-left corner, in case any of them are no longer visible. Non-Windows applications always remain in the background as icons.

12.6 Running Applications in 386 Enhanced Mode

Windows immediately recognizes whether you have a 386 or 486 computer. If you start Windows with WIN /3, Windows automatically switches to 386 Enhanced mode. This mode offers more possibilities for non-Windows applications.

Advantages of the 386 Enhanced mode

The 386 Enhanced mode allows non-Windows applications to run inside a window, which can be changed just like any other window. This also applies to graphic-oriented non-Windows applications such as Microsoft Word 5.0's Print Preview mode. You can operate a non-Windows application inside a window by using the keyboard.

When in the non-Windows application, open the Control menu. Select *Edit/Mark*. Mark the data you want copied to the Clipboard, and press the *right* mouse button. In the Clipboard, the contents are converted to a universal format and can be pasted into another application using the Windows *Edit/Paste* command.

These are basically visual advantages of the Enhanced mode. Actually, a more important advantage is multitasking with timeslice management. We'll discuss this in more detail later in the book.

Problems with applications

Non-Windows applications are started the same way in 386 Enhanced mode as in Standard mode. However, problems can occur with non-Windows applications when they also support your processor's Protected mode. For example, Lotus 1-2-3 Version 3.0 can run as a full-screen application under Windows only if you run Windows either in Standard mode (WIN /S) or Real mode (WIN /R). However, Version 3.1 includes a .PIF file that solves this problem.

Full-screen and window applications

Non-Windows applications under Windows in Standard or Real mode run as full-screen applications. This type of application takes up the entire screen and uses its own drivers to run the printer, mouse, etc. However, Windows in 386 Enhanced mode allows you to run non-Windows applications inside a window.

Key combinations for switching

To run a non-Windows application inside a window, place the application in the foreground and press Alt + Enter. With the same key combination you can change a window application back to full screen. You can preset the mode in the .PIF file. This setting is valid only when the application is first started; the key combination can be used as often as you like.

Word 5.0 in a window

Now a non-Windows application will have the same elements that are used in all Windows applications. However, the Control menu will contain some additional commands.

You can set the window size using the Control menu. With the *Maximize* command, a window will cover the entire screen. However, the application doesn't occupy an entire Windows screen because a DOS application displayed within a window is limited to 25 lines. Windows, however, interprets one DOS line differently, so 25 DOS lines only take up 2/3 of the Windows screen.

Opening the Control menu

You can change a non-Windows application in full-screen mode to window mode by pressing Alt + Spacebar, which opens the Control menu.

Operating non-Windows applications

Non-Windows applications running inside a window are usually controlled with the cursor keys. If the entire application doesn't fit in the current window (e.g., if the window isn't Maximized), you can use either the cursor keys or the mouse to scroll the display. The mouse controls scrolling directly from the scroll bar. With the keyboard, use the *Scroll* option in the *Edit* command of the Control menu. A message appears in the title bar after which you can perform the scrolling with the cursor keys. Pressing Esc at this point returns you to the normal mode and the cursor keys resume their usual function in the program.

The mouse is used by Windows

A non-Windows application running inside a window cannot use the mouse. Since Windows is still in control, the mouse is needed for selecting items within the window. However, in non-Windows mode, in which all applications run as full-screen, you can use the mouse inside your application. In this mode, selective marking isn't possible.

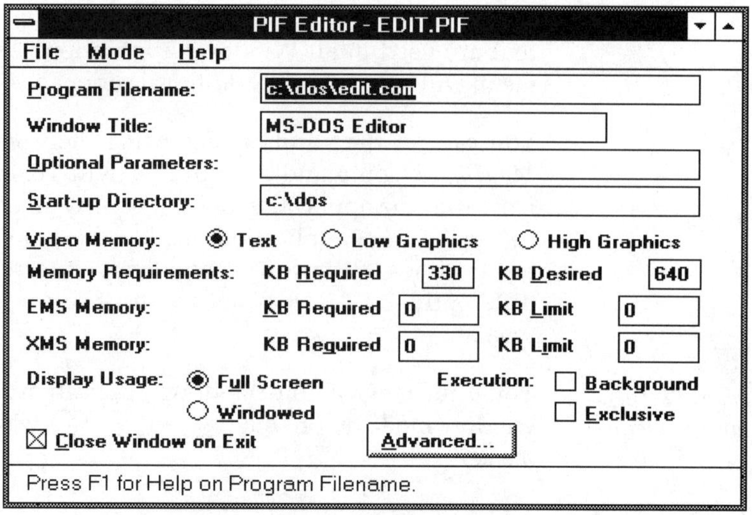

PIF Editor - EDIT.PIF
File Mode Help
Program Filename: c:\dos\edit.com
Window Title: MS-DOS Editor
Optional Parameters:
Start-up Directory: c:\dos
Video Memory: Text Low Graphics High Graphics
Memory Requirements: KB Required 330 KB Desired 640
EMS Memory: KB Required 0 KB Limit 0
XMS Memory: KB Required 0 KB Limit 0
Display Usage: Full Screen Windowed Execution: Background Exclusive
Close Window on Exit Advanced...
Press F1 for Help on Program Filename.

Scrolling using the Control Menu

Exchanging data in window mode

Use a mouse to select data within a non-Windows application that's running inside a window. Simply move the mouse over the area to be selected while pressing the left mouse button. The area changes color and the title bar displays a message indicating that you're in Mark mode.

On the keyboard, use the cursor keys to perform this task. From the Control menu's *Edit* command, select the *Mark* option. To store the selected area in the Clipboard, click the *right* mouse button. Otherwise, select the *Copy* command from the Control menu. Once the selected area has been transferred, the mark mode notification disappears from the title bar and you can continue working normally.

From the Clipboard you can then paste the copied area into another application.

Combining different modes

Suppose that you want to exchange data between two non-Windows applications running in different modes. First start Windows in Real mode with WIN /R, mark and copy the area to be transferred, and save the data from the Clipboard to an appropriate file. Then activate the second application in 386 Enhanced mode and load the previously created file into the Clipboard. You can now enter the contents of the Clipboard into the second application.

Controlling applications

There are various ways to work with several applications simultaneously. Each application is controlled separately with the *Settings* command in its Control menu. You'll find options that may be permanently entered in the .PIF file. The settings remain active only until the application is closed.

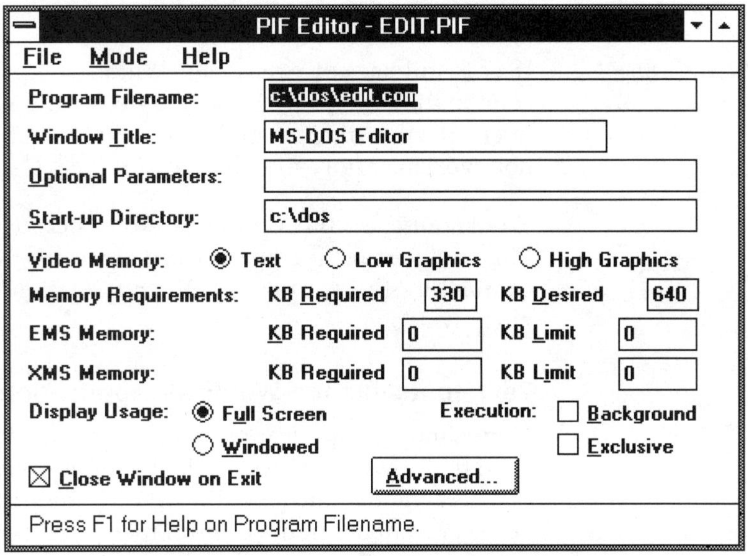

Settings for several applications

Screen options

You can determine whether a particular application should run as a window (*Windowed*) or as *Full Screen*. These settings are entered in the *Display Usage* field. As we mentioned earlier, the key combination Alt + Enter switches between the two modes.

Multitasking options

The *Execution* option allows you to allocate additional CPU time to an important application. Setting the *Exclusive* option suspends all other applications while you're working with this application in the foreground. *Background* allows you to keep an application running in the background while another is in the foreground. Obviously this would be impossible if the current application is running in the *Exclusive* mode. To implement true multitasking in 386 Enhanced mode, you must select the *Background* option in the .PIF files of any applications you want to keep running in the background.

Setting priorities

CPU time is regulated within the *Priority* field, in which relative amounts of time are allocated to each application via time sharing. This field also contains the amount of time allocated under different options. In the next chapter, we'll explain how these values are determined.

Ending non-Windows applications after crash

If you're unable to close your application normally, Windows gives you a chance to exit the application by using the Terminate... option. This option is located in the Control menu's *Settings* dialog box. This is especially useful if your application no longer accepts entries from the keyboard. Try to switch back to Windows, if possible.

Warm start

If you still cannot exit a non-Windows application, use the key combination Ctrl + Alt + Del to perform a warm start. Windows intercepts this function and gives you the option of interrupting the non-working application by pressing Enter.

You should use this option carefully because you may lose data. This can occur if any files are open in the application. After completing the warm start, the application icon reappears in its group window.

Text fonts in non-Windows applications

Non-Windows applications can run under Windows even if they have their own graphics mode. Examples include Word 5.0's Print Preview mode and the WYSIWYG mode of Lotus. With the *Fonts...* command in the Control menu you can change the standard font for a particular application.

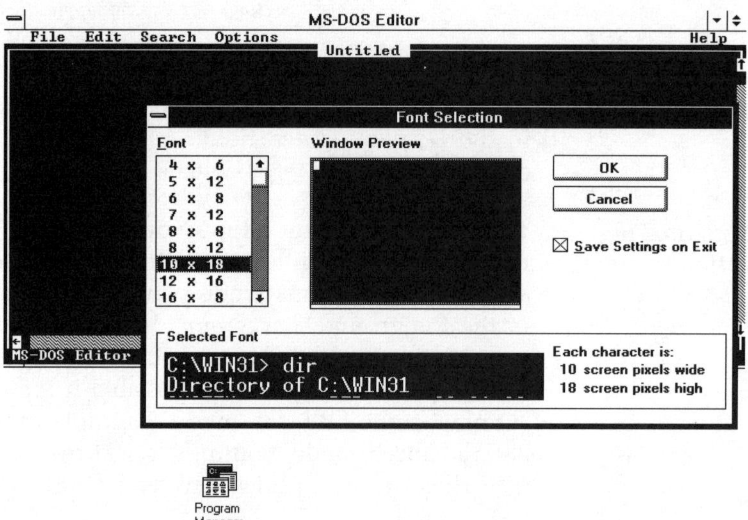

Setting fonts in the DOS window

By selecting a certain font of a particular height and width (in pixels), you can change the appearance of your application on the screen. When choosing a font, remember that window size depends on the font. The current font appears in the bottom window of the dialog box. If you want to keep this font for your next Windows session, use the *Save Settings on Exit* command.

12.7 Multitasking With Timeslices

Windows running in the 386 Enhanced mode uses a multitasking procedure, which is called non-preemptive multitasking. The difference between this system and a true multitasking operating system, such as OS/2, is that CPU time is determined by the operating system instead of the application itself. The OS/2 operating system allocates time to two applications in such a way that they appear to be running parallel to one another. The operating system takes over the flow of control. Windows usually assigns all the time to the application in the foreground. When a second application is started (to be run in the background), it receives time only when the first application releases it.

In true multitasking, the operating system must assume the control and protection of the CPU. This is important because, under Windows, problems can occur with applications that don't follow certain rules. The 386 Enhanced icon in the Control Panel (appears only in 386 Enhanced mode) contains several important options for controlling the Windows multitasking attributes.

With these options you can allocate timeslices to foreground and background applications. In non-Windows applications, you can do this via either the .PIF file or the *Settings...* command in the Control menu.

The CPU determines the timing

Since only one processor serves all applications, the time used to run the applications must be divided. How computing time is allocated determines an individual application's operating speed.

The structure of timeslices

A specific process governs the allocation of timeslices. A timeslice can be subdivided into segments of differing sizes, in which a complete slice represents 100% of the available CPU time.

If only one application is running on a particular computer, it automatically receives the entire timeslice (i.e., 100% of the CPU time). This means that the central processor is occupied exclusively with that application and has no other tasks to perform.

If two or more applications are running simultaneously under Windows, the timeslice (i.e., CPU time) must be divided among them. Two applications receive equal treatment by generating two segments, each comprising 50% of the timeslice.

While rotating the timeslice, imagine a reference point located outside the slice. Segment A and Segment B will take the same amount of time to pass this point, which, in both cases, is exactly half a rotation.

An alternative allocation might be that Segment A (or Application 1) is allotted two-thirds of the timeslice while Segment B (or Application 2) receives one-third. It now takes Segment A twice as long to pass the reference point as Segment B.

PIF Editor - EDIT.PIF

File Mode Help

Program Filename: c:\dos\edit.com

Window Title: MS-DOS Editor

Optional Parameters:

Start-up Directory: c:\dos

Video Memory: (•) Text ( ) Low Graphics ( ) High Graphics

Memory Requirements: KB Required 330 KB Desired 640

EMS Memory: KB Required 0 KB Limit 0

XMS Memory: KB Required 0 KB Limit 0

Display Usage: (•) Full Screen ( ) Windowed

Execution: [ ] Background [ ] Exclusive

[X] Close Window on Exit

Advanced...

Press F1 for Help on Program Filename.

Priority control within the timeslice process

The result of this is that Application 1 runs much faster than Application 2 because the CPU works twice as long on Application 1 as on Application 2, within a preset time frame (one occurrence of the timeslice). So, Application 1 has been assigned a higher priority.

Multitasking for Windows applications

The Windows multitasking options found under the 386 Enhanced icon allow you to assign priorities to your Windows applications. In applications not specially written for Windows, priority values must be set within the .PIF files.

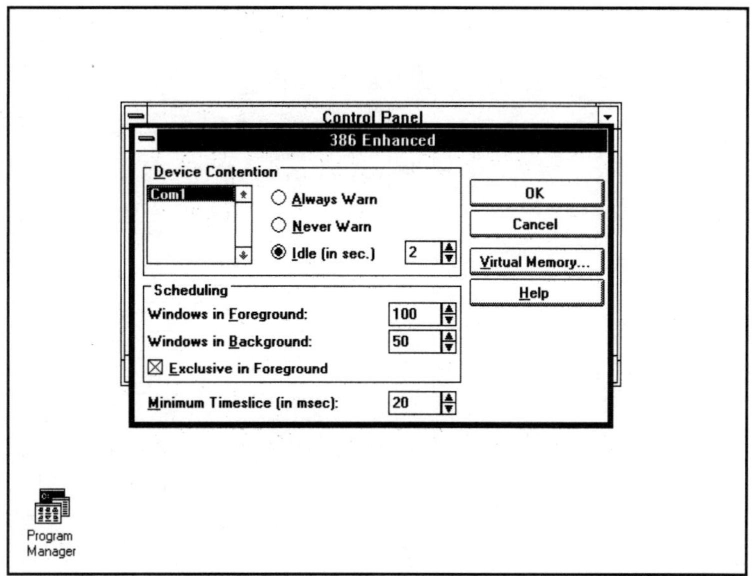

The 386 Enhanced mode dialog box

You can enter values from 1 to 10,000 in the text boxes *Windows in Foreground* and *Windows in Background*. These values alone don't determine the priority of any single application. They must be considered relative to any other values for non-Windows applications that are currently active.

Priority control for non-Windows applications occurs in similar text boxes, which are located in the *Advanced* dialog box of the .PIF Editor. In this dialog box the text boxes are called *Foreground Priority* and *Background Priority*. Here also you can enter values from 1 to 10,000, which once again are meaningless by themselves.

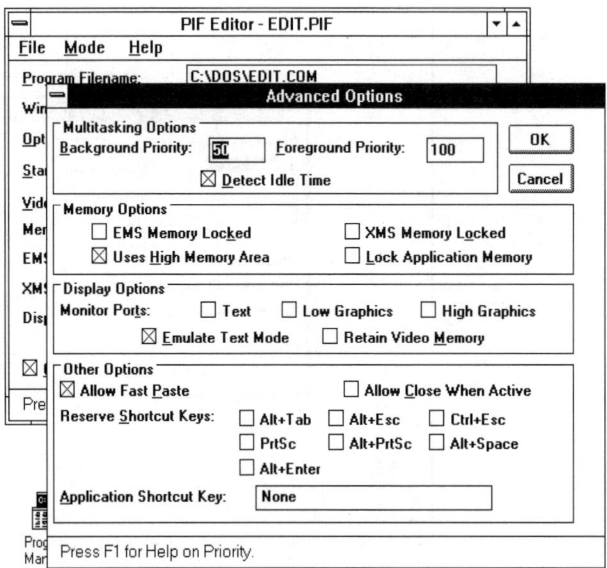

PIF Editor Advanced dialog box

Converting priorities to units of time

In the *Minimum Timeslice* text box of the *386 Enhanced* dialog box, you can enter a value, in milliseconds, that will determine how finely the timeslice must be divided. The values for *Windows in Foreground:*, *Windows in Background:*, *Foreground Priority*, and *Background Priority* (from the PIF Editor) all refer to this minimum timeslice. The default setting is 20 milliseconds. For example, if you enter a value of 100 in *Windows in Foreground*, 100 x 20 milliseconds processing time is allocated to each Windows application, if a Windows application exists in the foreground. Windows transfers control to the next application only after the 2,000 milliseconds have elapsed.

In the previous example we've obtained a total of priority values. If the total is 250, one rotation of the timeslice takes 250 x 20 milliseconds (the default setting). In this way, you can convert relative priority values to absolute units of time.

The highest priority for Windows applications

You can give a Windows application the highest priority. Select the *Exclusive in Foreground* option and all non-Windows applications will be suspended as long as a Windows application remains in the foreground. This setting produces certain segments on the timeslice which are allocated only to Windows applications.

12.8 Priority Control

To allocate time to your applications logically, first you must understand which applications should be running simultaneously, and what tasks the application in the background should be performing.

You must consider the complexity of the individual tasks executed by the computer. For example, if you're working with a word processor, a database, and a spreadsheet simultaneously, you can use a relatively low foreground priority as long as you're entering only text into the word processor.

Text input isn't a difficult task for the CPU. If you perform these types of tasks, then you'll have a lot of processing time left over for more complex tasks in the background. While you're entering your text, the spreadsheet or database applications may be processing inquiries, sorting, indexing routines, or perhaps performing multiple operations.

Example:

Suppose that you've started three applications and have entered standard settings of *Windows in Foreground* equal to 100 and *Windows in Background* equal to 50. The CPU's computing time is then divided as follows:

How are priorities distributed?

A non-Windows application in the foreground with a value of 100, and two Windows applications in the background, each with a value of 50 are running. The total of these values equals 200. So the timeslice must be divided into 200 segments. A hundred of these small segments are combined into one, which is then allocated to the application in the foreground. The remaining 100 segments are equally divided among the two applications in the background.

The result is that the non-Windows application in the foreground receives 50% of the CPU time, while both Windows applications each receive 25%.

Now if you switch to one of the Windows applications, the priorities used by the CPU will shift accordingly.

Changing the application configuration

In this example the non-Windows application has a *Background Priority* value of 50. The two Windows applications each have *Windows in Foreground* values set to 100. Now the sum of all the values equals 250. The 250 segments are then combined into two large segments of 100 each and one smaller one of 50 for the non-Windows application. If these values are represented as percentages, 20% of the available processing time goes to the non-Windows application, while the two Windows applications each receive 40%.

Starting an additional application will further alter the priorities of already-running applications because the total sum of priority values will increase.

Changing priority options while an application is running

You can also change priority options for a non-Windows application if it's running inside a window. To do this, use the *Settings...* command from the application's Control menu.

Windows then displays a dialog box, in which you can temporarily change the .PIF file settings. To make these changes permanent, change the .PIF file itself.

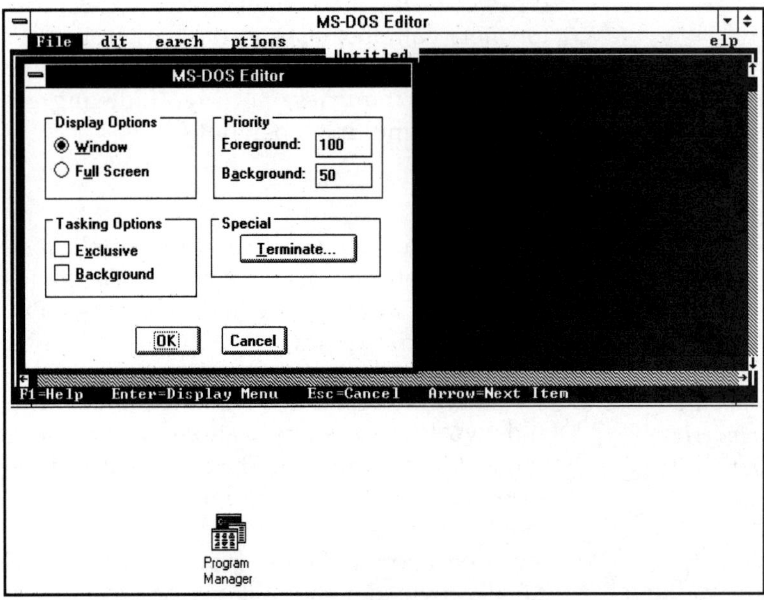

Temporarily changing priorities with the Settings Menu

12.9 Accelerating Screen Swaps

In Windows, swap files delete temporary files, which aren't currently needed, from main memory. This helps free memory for other applications.

Screen exchange in non-Windows applications

Swap files can increase the speed of non-Windows applications. For example, if you've started a non-Windows application, such as Word, and then switch from this program to Windows, the Word screen is automatically saved as a temporary file on the hard drive. This swap file contains all the necessary information that Windows needs to re-create the screen when you switch back again. The standard drive used is the hard drive and the directory is the one in which Windows was installed.

Putting swap files on the RAM disk

This type of swap file needs a certain amount of space on the hard drive. So, if you have two hard drives, you should place the swap file on the drive with the most free space. By doing this, you can also specify a subdirectory created especially for temporary files. However, this method offers only a small advantage in speed.

To solve this problem, simply enter the RAM disk drive as the location for saving temporary files. Because a RAM disk has much faster access to memory than an ordinary hard drive, you can switch from one program to another more quickly. The drive or subdirectory specification is made by adding a line to the SYSTEM.INI file. Either load this file into the Notepad or use the System Editor to move the cursor to the end of the file. You'll find the entry [NonWindowsApp] there. Enter the following line below this entry:

```
swapdisk=[Drive] [Subdirectory]
```

If you're working with a RAM disk, under [Drive] enter the drive letter assigned to it at startup. Otherwise, enter the drive letter or subdirectory that you've planned to use for temporary files.

12.10 Memory-Resident Programs

Another group of applications include memory-resident programs, such as Network Driver and Mouse Driver, and programs such as Sidekick. TSR (Terminate and Stay Resident) applications are either required or simply offer a variety of functions designed to enhance the performance of your computer. Unfortunately, these applications remain in main memory permanently, so the space they occupy is unavailable to Windows.

Allocation to individual units

Memory-resident programs are started, from either the CONFIG.SYS file or the AUTOEXEC.BAT file, when you start your computer. Then they run in the background without requiring any additional input from the user.

For example, many users have a mouse driver in this file. When you start a non-Windows application from Windows and then want to use the mouse, you also need the mouse driver. However, Windows doesn't need this mouse driver because it has one of its own. In this case, you should remove the first mouse driver if Windows is started first. This provides more memory for Windows. Create a batch file for your special application, in which the mouse driver is activated first and then the program is started. You can then ensure that the mouse driver is loaded only when necessary.

Network login

This procedure cannot be used when you want to log onto a network. So Windows can also communicate with the network, you must login before activating Windows.

TSR programs such as Sidekick can manage input, controls, and data processing. They are resident in memory and are started with a hotkey combination.

These programs interrupt your Windows session. At this moment, terminate all other programs that are running, as long as you're still in the screen. You must start memory-resident programs before starting Windows. Then they will be immediately available to you and the operating system. It's possible that TSR programs don't work under Windows when other Windows applications are on the screen. However, you shouldn't encounter problems with non-Windows applications.

Should you use TSR's?

You should always determine the advantages of using a TSR program. Windows already contains many of the functions included in some popular TSR's. These functions can be used with other programs. So, think carefully about installing TSR's under Windows.

13. Adapting Programs With PIF Files

The PIF Editor

PIF Editor

The PIF Editor lets you create new PIF files or edit existing ones. In this chapter we'll discuss how to use PIF files in 386 Enhanced mode and Standard mode.

13.1 Reasons for Adapting Programs

PIF files (Program Information Files) establish the basic contact between Windows and non-Windows applications (or DOS programs). Since non-Windows applications use their own hardware drivers, which are usually located in the same address range as the Windows hardware drivers, PIF files prevent memory conflicts between the two application types.

Also, when you start a non-Windows application from Windows, Windows remains in the background. In order for the non-Windows application to run correctly, Windows must release some memory. Still, there must be a way to switch back from the application, after which Windows again has control.

PIF files prevent conflicts

PIF files determine how a particular non-Windows application interacts with your computer's components. The program controls such things as the memory, screen, and keyboard. Depending on how this is done, it may lead to a direct memory conflict with Windows. PIF files provide options that prevent this kind of overlap and ensure that the program works properly.

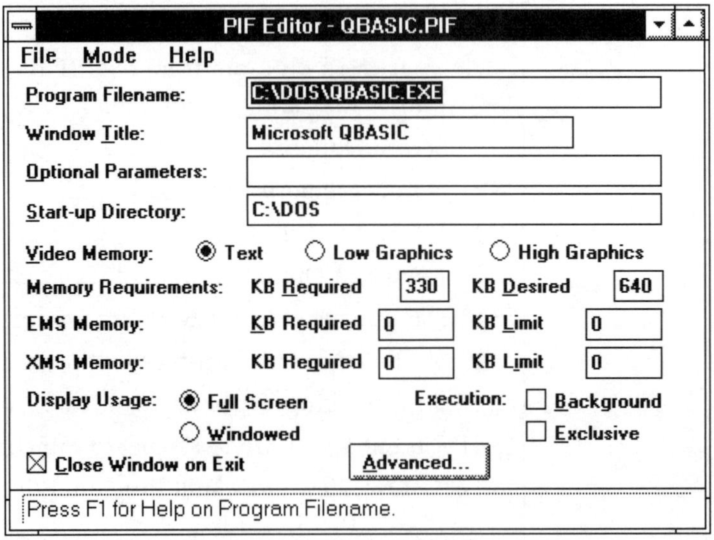

PIF Editor - QBASIC.PIF

File Mode Help

Program Filename: C:\DOS\QBASIC.EXE

Window Title: Microsoft QBASIC

Optional Parameters:

Start-up Directory: C:\DOS

Video Memory: (•) Text ( ) Low Graphics ( ) High Graphics

Memory Requirements: KB Required 330 KB Desired 640

EMS Memory: KB Required 0 KB Limit 0

XMS Memory: KB Required 0 KB Limit 0

Display Usage: (•) Full Screen ( ) Windowed

Execution: [ ] Background [ ] Exclusive

[X] Close Window on Exit Advanced...

Press F1 for Help on Program Filename.

An automatically created PIF file in the Editor

Manufacturer supplied PIF files

Many software manufacturers supply PIF files with their programs to ensure maximum compatibility. Copy the manufacturer's PIF file into the directory containing the corresponding program. Now you'll also be able to start a program by clicking on its PIF file from the File Manager. This works only if you've set up the startup directory properly. If you encounter problems, load the PIF file into the PIF Editor and check the settings.

If you want to run programs, under Windows, that you've written, you may need to create your own PIF files if the default values don't work. This also applies to programs that didn't contain a PIF file originally.

Additional options in 386 Enhanced mode

Windows also differentiates between the various modes in which it can run. Standard mode provides fewer options than the 386 Enhanced mode. Depending on the current mode, the PIF Editor displays different options, which help you create the PIF file. The screen automatically adjusts according to the mode.

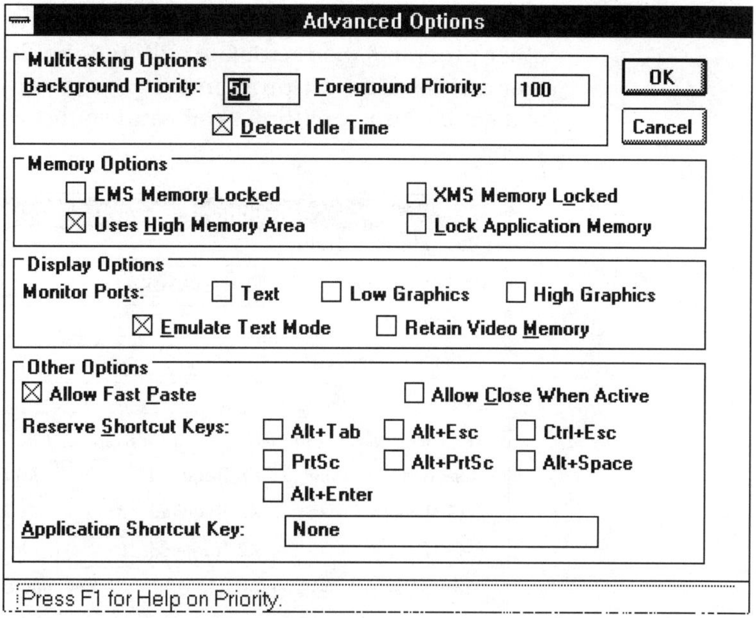

Advanced Options

Multitasking Options
Background Priority: 50 Foreground Priority: 100
Detect Idle Time
OK
Cancel

Memory Options
EMS Memory Locked
XMS Memory Locked
Uses High Memory Area
Lock Application Memory

Display Options
Monitor Ports: Text Low Graphics High Graphics
Emulate Text Mode Retain Video Memory

Other Options
Allow Fast Paste
Allow Close When Active
Reserve Shortcut Keys: Alt+Tab Alt+Esc Ctrl+Esc PrtSc Alt+PrtSc Alt+Space Alt+Enter
Application Shortcut Key: None

Press F1 for Help on Priority.

Additional options in 386 Enhanced mode

In either case you access the same PIF file. Any changes that you made in Standard mode also apply to 386 Enhanced mode.

13.2 Tips on Creating PIF Files

When you configure a Windows application, Windows looks for a file named APPS.INF, which indicates whether this application already has parameters. The program name is compared with the names in APPS.INF, which contains a list of program settings for most applications.

Using the default PIF file

A PIF file won't be created if your program name isn't found. This will also happen if you set up the program with the *New...* command in the PIF Editor.

Windows contains a default PIF file, called _DEFAULT.PIF, that can be used in non-Windows applications. This file, which is located in the Windows directory, contains standardized settings for running a program. First determine how your program runs with these settings. If everything works properly, changes aren't necessary. Create your own PIF files only if you encounter memory or video problems. You shouldn't edit the _DEFAULT.PIF parameters because they apply to all programs that don't have a PIF file of their own.

Some settings used by one program may have a negative effect on other programs. So the default PIF file should contain only values that are valid for all programs. If you must edit _DEFAULT.PIF, make a backup copy first. You can use this copy if you encounter problems.

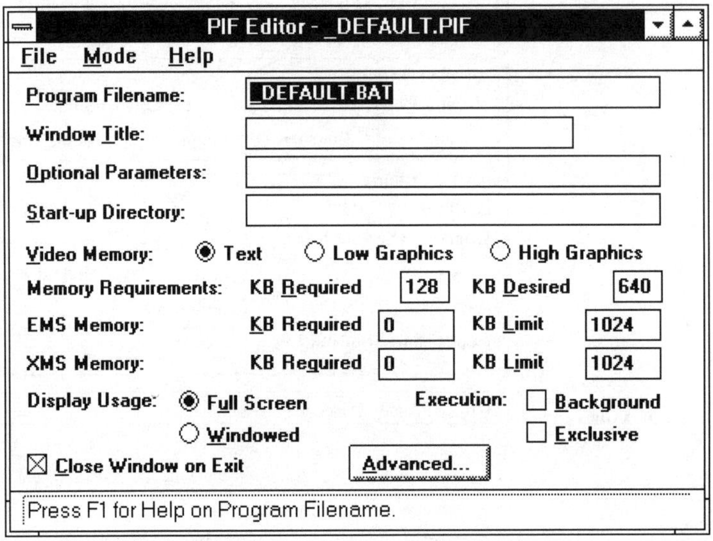

_DEFAULT.PIF in the PIF Editor

Using the PIF Editor

To create your own PIF file, first open the PIF Editor from the Main Group. Then go through the settings described in this chapter. Usually you must experiment with the options before finding the best setting. This especially applies to programs that you've written yourself or poorly documented programs.

You can also check the settings that were made for other programs. Use the APPS.INF file, which Windows uses to create PIF files for well-known applications, as a pattern (refer to the end of this chapter for the contents of the APPS.INF file). First try the settings that are most similar to the ones needed by the program.

The *File* menu contains commands for opening and saving files. If you've edited a PIF file and want to view the results before exiting the PIF Editor, you must save the changes first. Otherwise, your application will start with the old settings.

Testing multiple PIF files

When you're trying different settings, you should create a base PIF file. Save the base file with the *Save As...* command. Use different names for different settings, such as TEST1.PIF, TEST2.PIF, etc. Then start the program using the PIF file and test all the program functions individually. If a problem occurs, try the next PIF file. This enables you to identify any possible errors so that the corresponding setting can be adjusted.

Starting a program from the PIF file

When you start a non-Windows application, Windows searches for the application's PIF file. The PIF file has the same name as the application and a .PIF extension. If the PIF file exists, Windows uses the options contained in that file. Otherwise, Windows executes the program using the _DEFAULT.PIF file.

A program can also be run directly from its PIF file, thus linking the PIF file (instead of the program file) to the Program Manager. This eliminates problems with the search path. Otherwise, the PIF file should be either in the WINDOWS directory or the appropriate program directory. Windows still searches through all the paths specified by the PATH command of the AUTOEXEC.BAT file.

To locate your PIF files quickly, create your own PIF directory and store the files in this directory. Remember to include the new directory in your search path.

13.3 Entries for Calling Programs

Enter the name of the program to be called from the PIF file in the *Program Filename* text box. You don't need to specify a directory if your program and PIF file are located in the same directory as Windows. If you copy the program to another drive or directory, you must change the startup directory entry; otherwise you'll receive an error message and the program cannot be executed. Executable programs include all files with .COM, .EXE and, .BAT extensions.

Program title

Enter the application's title in the *Window Title* text box. In 386 Enhanced mode the name appears in the program window's title bar. Otherwise, press Alt + Tab to switch between applications; the non-Windows application name will be displayed in the title bar.

Program parameters

The *Optional Parameters* text box contains additional parameters that can be given to a program when it's started. This is similar to the startup parameters in Windows that are used in a specific mode. You can start most word processing applications with the last file you edited by entering the file name after the program name. These types of programs can be given various parameters at startup.

If you want to specify anything other than just one parameter or text file, enter a question mark in this text box. A dialog box, in which you can enter any parameter or file name, appears. So, you don't need to change the PIF file each time you want to start the application.

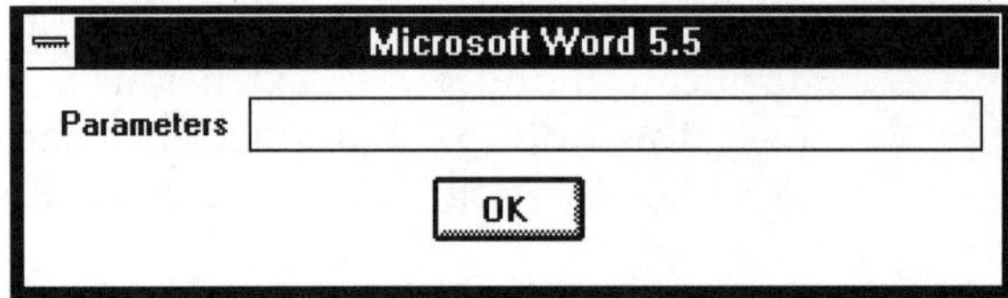

Dialog box for entering parameters

Startup directory

In the *Start-up Directory* text box, enter the drive and directory in which the program is installed. This entry is important; otherwise the program cannot be started from the PIF file. If you try to start a program with an incorrect path specification, an error message appears. Remember to change this entry if you copy the program to a different directory.

13.4 Screen Options

You can use the *Video Memory* option to copy data from your program to the Clipboard. Simply press the Alt + Prt Sc or Prt Sc keys. If Standard mode is active, select *Text* if only text must be transferred or *Graphics/Multiple Text* for graphics and text. If you're in 386 Enhanced mode, select *Text;* if only text must be transferred, *Low Graphics* for lower resolution graphics, and *High Graphics* for higher resolution graphics. Windows then reserves memory; the amount of memory reserved depends on your selection. Remember to select the *Text;* option if you're copying only text; otherwise extra memory, which cannot be used for other purposes, will be reserved.

Using different screen modes

Programs running in different screen modes may create problems with data exchange in the Clipboard while in Standard mode. If this happens, select the *No Screen Exchange* option. Otherwise, incompatible screen modes can lead to errors in data transfer or even cause the system to crash.

Accelerated screen exchange

Suppose that you're working in Standard mode with several non-Windows applications and then switch from one mode to another. Windows saves the screen of the first one so that when you reactivate the application, its screen is displayed properly. Unfortunately, this process is very time-consuming. If the application comes with an independent screen-creating function, you can select the *No Save Screen* option. This provides the best results for your non-Windows applications.

Preventing program switching

The Standard mode *Prevent Program Switch* option prevents you from switching back to Windows while running a non-Windows application. This is done by changing the PIF file. The idea behind this is to allow more memory to be allocated to your application. Once this has been done, you must use the application's own Exit command to switch back to Windows.

Closing a non-Windows application window

The *Close Window on Exit* option causes a non-Windows application window to close automatically when its Exit command is activated (e.g., *Quit;* in Word 5.0). If you don't use this function the window remains open and must be closed separately in the System Menu.

13.5 Setting Memory Options

The value entered in *Memory Requirements* refers to the program size plus the size of the largest data file to be accessed. Usually individual program sizes aren't listed in a manual. In this instance the size refers to the amount of conventional memory needed to run the program instead of to the amount of space the program occupies on the hard drive. Manufacturers always specify somewhat larger values to ensure optimum efficiency.

To avoid allocating too much memory, start with a value of 128K and then gradually increase this value in increments of 16 or 32K. You should allocate a few kilobytes more than necessary; this may help the program run a bit faster. If you enter a value of zero, Windows allocates the entire memory. In some instances this slows down your work with Windows, especially if less memory is actually required. The PIF Editor's default setting is 128K.

XMS memory

The *XMS Memory;* value regulates extended memory. Here Windows can allocate a few bytes of extended memory for use by the application. You can decide the minimum and maximum amounts of memory to be allocated. This maximum amount is sometimes crucial. For example, if you're simultaneously working with several programs that all have access to extended memory, you may encounter problems. However, if each program has a specific range, these types of problems can be avoided.

A value of -1 gives an application the maximum amount of memory available.

13.6 Interface Access

The *Directly Modifies:* section lets you specify access to serial interfaces and the keyboard buffer. These are needed to prevent data loss during simultaneous access.

Serial interfaces

Com1...Com4: If your program is designed for serial data transfer, select the corresponding interface. This would involve programs that support devices such as a serial printer, modem, or serial mouse.

13.7 Keyboard Options

Windows reserves some key combinations for certain functions. Some of the combinations remain active while you're in a non-Windows application, as long as Windows is still running in the background. These are needed for switching between applications because Windows still maintains control over this function. It's possible that your program uses an identical key combination for a different function. In this instance you must decide whether the Windows function or the program function receives top priority.

To give program functions priority, select the key combinations in question so that Windows no longer has control over them. The keys are defined as follows:

Alt + Tab	Switch program (choice of program)
Alt + Esc	Switch program (next program)
Ctrl + Esc	Display program list
Prt Sc	Copy screen to Clipboard
Alt + Prt Sc	Copy current window to Clipboard

This arrangement may prevent you from switching between your application and Windows. If this is the case, you can return to Windows only by exiting the application.

13.8 386 Enhanced Mode Memory Options

PIF options include three different groups of memory requirements. Enter the maximum amount of memory needed by your program in the *KB Desired* option. If the program should run in Exclusive mode (not concurrently with other programs), then enter the maximum value of 640K. Entering a value of -1 allocates as much memory as needed, without exceeding the 640K maximum.

Additional memory

You can also allocate and select expanded memory (EMS) or extended memory (XMS). If both types are available, allocate the memory based on the type of application. Some programs access expanded memory while others use extended memory. You should specify minimum and maximum values; remember that other programs will also use this memory.

Locking memory

Clicking the Advanced... button displays a new set of options that are available only in 386 Enhanced mode. The *Memory Options* lets you lock the memory used by the specified application.

If you activate the *EMS Memory Locked;* check box, you can keep the EMS memory locked and the XMS memory free. Clicking on the *XMS Memory Locked* check box lets you lock the XMS memory and keep the EMS memory free. If you want to prevent your program from using this memory entirely, use *Lock Application Memory.*

The *Uses High Memory Area;* option allows an application to access the high memory area of your computer. High memory is located in extended memory and is accessed by the *HIMEM.SYS;* driver. Activating this option usually doesn't cause any problems. In some cases the high memory area may already be reserved by network drivers prior to the start of Windows and may not be available to the application.

13.9 386 Enhanced Mode Screen Options

There are two ways to run programs in Windows from the *Display Usage* option. You can run the program as *Full Screen.* Most programs function in this mode, including Word 5.0, Multiplan, and Lotus 1-2-3. This mode also saves memory.

The other option, *Windowed,* allows for easier data exchange between programs using the Clipboard. The usual selection commands are available. In a full-screen application, you must use the Alt + Prt Sc combination to copy the screen contents to the Clipboard.

In *Video Memory* you can determine if and how much memory should be allocated for a program's screen output. The more complex the appearance, the more memory is required. You can choose from *Text; Low Graphics* and *High Graphics.* The *Text* option uses the least amount of memory. This also applies to the monitor connections.

In this case, the program's display is controlled directly from the graphics card. Windows should correctly save the screen display of the program when switching between the program to Windows. The *High Graphics* option usually produces the best results. Using the *Retain Video Memory* option from the *Display Options* box frees unused screen memory.

The *Emulate Text Mode* check box allows you to create a faster-running window display.

Accelerating data exchange

Fast data input can save time when you're exchanging data using the Clipboard. The *Allow Fast Paste* option activates the fastest method of data transfer. However, it's possible that your graphics card cannot use this method. If this occurs you must deactivate the option. The *Allow Close When Active* option allows you to finish your work in Windows even if the program is still active.

How your program handles open files is very important. In extreme cases, ending abruptly from Windows can damage files or cause data loss.

13.10 Multitasking Options

If you want Windows to give all available memory to a particular program, use the *Exclusive* option. When this option is active, no other programs can run in the background. Selecting the *Background* option allows a program to continue running in the background at a slower pace (depending on the settings), while you continue working with another program.

Application priorities

With the *Multitasking Options;* you can determine how an application runs, relative to other applications. Enter a value between 0 and 10,000 to assign a foreground priority to your application. The same range of values also applies to the background priority, which can be used only for programs that aren't running in Exclusive mode.

Remember that all other programs also have priority values. They are at least assigned the default settings of 50 (background) and 100 (foreground). Now if you assign a foreground priority of 200 and a background priority of 100 to your application, it receives the most processing time and priority over applications with default settings.

Refer to Chapter 12 for a detailed discussion of timeslicing and the multitasking process.

13.11 386 Enhanced Mode Keyboard Functions

Windows reserves some key combinations for certain functions. Your program may use an identical key combination for a different function. If this occurs you must decide which key combination receives priority (Windows functions or program functions).

To give program functions priority, select the appropriate key combinations so that Windows no longer has control over them. The keys are defined as follows:

Alt + Tab	Switch program (choice of program)
Alt + Esc	Switch program (next program)
Ctrl + Esc	Display program list
Prt Sc	Copy screen to Clipboard
Alt + Prt Sc	Copy current window to Clipboard
Alt + Spacebar	Call application's control menu
Alt + Enter	Places a full-screen application inside a window

Shortcut keys

You can create a shortcut to a program so that pressing a certain key combination moves the application to the foreground regardless of how many other applications are running. This is done with the *Application Shortcut Key* option.

The first key is always Alt or Ctrl. The second key can be a function key, as long as it hasn't been assigned to any other purpose.

To set up a key combination, activate the option and then the keys. The combination is entered automatically. To delete a combination, either use the Backspace key or reset the field to *None* using Shift + Backspace.

13.12 An Overview of Default Program PIFs

Many software manufacturers now supply PIF files with their programs. When combining a non-Windows application with Windows, first check the diskettes to determine whether a PIF file already exists. If it does, copy the PIF file to the same directory as the program files. Call the PIF Editor and change the startup directory as needed. You can then start the program under Windows from its PIF file.

The APPS.INF file

If a PIF file isn't included with the program, determine whether the program is included in the APPS.INF list. This list is the basis of the *Set Up Applications* option in Windows SETUP. The Setup routine will find, on the hard drive, only the programs that are included in the list.

Orientation for PIF files

The APPS.INF file is particularly useful when you're creating a PIF file for a new program and don't know exactly which settings should be used. Find a program that's closest to your program and use the same parameters.

Load the APPS.INF file into a text editor to examine the latest contents of the file. It is extremely important that the entries in the [pif] section are in alphabetical order by an executable filename.

The following is the format of the parameters for the entries in the [pif] section of the APPS.INF file:

```
;  (0) Exe file =
;  (1)  PIF name
;  (2)  Window Title
;  (3)  Startup Directory
;  (4)  Close Window on Exit flag
;  (5)  File from which to extract icon (default is Progman.exe)
;  (6)  Icon number (default is 0)
;  (7)  Standard PIF settings section (default is [std_dflt])
;  (8)  Enhanced PIF settings section (default is [enha_dflt])
;  (9)  Ambiguous EXEs section (Other applications with same EXE name)
;  (10) Optimized PIFs section
;
```

The applications SETUP will appear in the APPS.INF file, which is found in the Windows system directory (e.g. C:\WINDOWS\SYSTEM). The following line shows the location of the parameters in the listing.

```
;0          = 1          2            3 4    5 6  7               8        9  10
123.COM     = 123      ,"Lotus 1-2-3", ,cwe, ,3,std_gra_256,enha_123c
```

The following list is the application that the PIF editor will not find, since these are all standard Windows applications.

```
[dontfind]
   apm.exe
   calc.exe
   calendar.exe
   cardfile.exe
   charmap.exe
   clipbrd.exe
```

```
clock.exe
control.exe
control3.exe
cvpackw.exe
ddespy.exe
dewproj.exe
dialog.exe
dlgedit.exe
drwatson.exe
eqnedit.exe
fontedit.exe
ftp.exe
graph.exe
graflink.exe
heapwalk.exe
imagedit.exe
implibw.exe
jfprint.exe
libw.exe
linkw.exe
lwinhelp.exe
macrode.exe
mapsym32.exe
mcwin.exe
mmsetup.exe
mplayer.exe
msdos.exe
msdraw.exe
mxwin.exe
note-it.exe
notepad.exe
packager.exe
paint.exe
pbrush.exe
pifedit.exe
play.exe
pptgraph.exe
printman.exe
progman.exe
qt.exe
rcppw.exe
rcw.exe
recorder.exe
regedit.exe
regload.exe
reversi.exe
sdkpaint.exe
setup.exe
shaker.exe
shed.exe
sol.exe
soundrec.exe
spooler.exe
spy.exe
stress.exe
swapfile.exe
sysedit.exe
taskman.exe
```

```
tbook.exe
terminal.exe
trans.exe
whelp.exe
win2wrs.exe
winbbs.exe
wincbt.exe
winfile.exe
winhelp.exe
winmine.exe
wintutor.exe
winver.exe
wordart.exe
wpcdll.exe
wpwinfil.exe
write.exe
zoomin.exe
```

14. Data Exchange Between Applications

In this chapter we'll discuss how you can exchange data between applications using the Clipboard for static data exchange, Dynamic Data Exchange (DDE) for linking data to applications dynamically, and Object Linking and Embedding (OLE) for placing objects in applications so that you can retrieve them the next time you start the object's source application.

14.1 Data Exchange Concepts

Each program and each application processes data in a specific format. In this instance the term "format" refers to how the information is created and organized, as well as the form in which the data is stored. Some programs use the same formats to manage information and others use different formats.

Exchanging characters

Being able to exchange data between applications, regardless of the data format, is very important. For example, you can't always place graphic data in a text-oriented application. However, you should be able to transfer straight text data from one application to another.

Data exchange using file formats

One type of data exchange involves external file processing. An application reads in a file's format and converts the file to its own format. The format may also contain style information, such as bold text, for certain words. The receiving application should be able to process this information and display the words in bold text. However, a source application may also be able to save its data in a different format. Although almost every application can store information as unformatted text, usually all formatting is lost. The receiving application reads the unformatted text, which then must be reformatted.

File formats in Windows

This process can be illustrated in Windows with Write or Paintbrush. Write can produce either ANSI text, ASCII text, Write format documents, or Word (DOS) format documents. Word for Windows can also load and generate each of these formats. Paintbrush lets you create or open graphics in BMP format and PCX format. Since it has a filter for displaying this format, Word for Windows can process the PCX file.

Data exchange using the Clipboard

Another data exchange method involves using the Clipboard. The Clipboard is a part of Windows and acts as a mediator between individual applications. The easiest way to use the Clipboard is for data exchange within one application. For example, suppose that you're using Write. If you select a block of text and insert it into another location in the document, the Clipboard is working.

The *Copy* and *Cut* commands place information in the Clipboard and the *Paste* command pastes it back into the document. While a block of text is in the Clipboard, it can be pasted into any other application as long as the application can interpret characters. You cannot paste Write text into Paintbrush. However, you can paste Paintbrush drawings into Write. Since the Clipboard's text area uses a general format, it can easily exchange data. It's also possible to change the format of the text in the Clipboard so that it can be accepted by all applications. This is how you can exchange information between Windows applications and non-Windows applications.

Data exchanged between applications becomes part of the document into which it was pasted. It will be saved along with this document, and will no longer be part of the original application.

Dynamic Data Exchange

Dynamic Data Exchange or DDE acts as a line of communication between applications. It's executed from the Clipboard. Data is copied from a server (source) application to a client (target) application. DDE passes the client application a reference to a variable or a field instead of the actual data. By updating the field, information is taken from the server document and appears in the client application.

After copying a linked file, be sure to maintain the connection properly (e.g., by updating the directory specification for the field entry). Now if the server file is deleted, you'll receive an error message in the client file because a file origin no longer exists.

With dynamic linking, you can decide if and when to make changes to either one of the files.

Object Linking and Embedding

Unlike DDE, Object Linking and Embedding (OLE) copies an object from the server application and places it in the client application. The object (text, graphics, etc.) physically exists in the client file and is stored with it. However, a reference to the server application is still assigned to it.

If you want to make changes to the object, its reference will be activated and the application opens up in the application where the object was originally created. Make the desired changes and close the server application. When you return to the client application, the object (including the changes) will be in the same place you left it.

Using the Object Packager

The Object Packager allows you to create icons that graphically depict this type of link. You can store the link as an icon and then copy it to any Windows application. By clicking on the icon, the corresponding application starts and you can then work on the object. This is helpful because the information isn't inserted permanently but can be recalled when necessary.

With Dynamic Data Exchange, changing server information usually simultaneously affects all documents linked with it. The actual source changes. With an embedded object, you make changes to the object separately. If the same object has been embedded in different applications, making simultaneous changes requires each object to be changed separately.

14.2 Static Data Exchange Using the Clipboard

We mentioned earlier in this chapter that the Clipboard statically copies, cuts, and pastes data. *Copy* or *Cut* transfers the data that's selected in your application to the Clipboard. This temporary memory stores the data only until other data is copied into it or until you exit Windows.

Temporary storage

By using this temporary storage arrangement, you can move the data to another location within your application or to a file that's being processed by a different application. This is done with the *Paste* command. Text and graphics can be copied or duplicated within one or more applications. The data is always sent to the Clipboard.

The Clipboard doesn't have to be active in order to perform these tasks (i.e., you don't need to run the Clipboard to use its capabilities). It functions automatically and is always available.

Calling the Clipboard

Sometimes you must run the Clipboard just like any other Windows application. For example, you must do this to make format changes within the Clipboard or to view the Clipboard's contents. The Main Group lists the Clipboard under the name *Clipboard Viewer*.

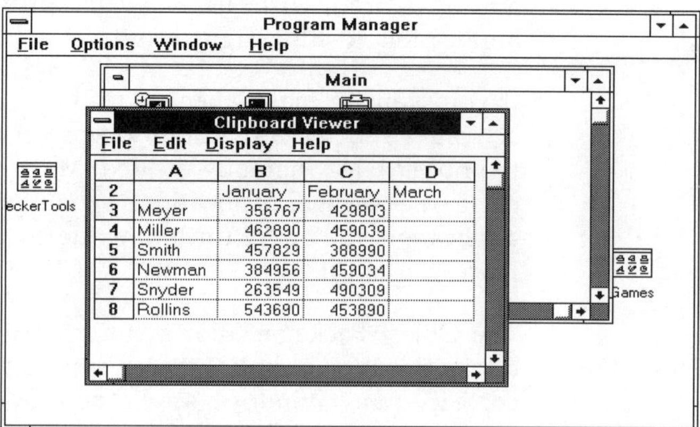

	A	B	C	D
2		January	February	March
3	Meyer	356767	429803	
4	Miller	462890	459039	
5	Smith	457829	388990	
6	Newman	384956	459034	
7	Snyder	263549	490309	
8	Rollins	543690	453890	

Opened Clipboard

The Clipboard will retain its contents until the next *Cut* or *Copy* command is executed. Then the new information overwrites the old. Any information that's stored in the Clipboard is also lost when you exit Windows. This occurs because the Clipboard uses only temporary memory. So, be sure to paste the contents into your application or save the contents under a specific file name.

14.3 Saving the Clipboard's Contents

If you want to use the Clipboard's contents at a later time, save the contents to a file. By doing this you can permanently save the data and use it whenever necessary. Eventually you can create a library for these files that can be accessed from the Clipboard.

Creating a library

The *Save As...* command, which is located in the Clipboard's *File* menu, stores Clipboard data to a file. The dialog box allows you to select the drive and directory in which you want the contents stored. You're asked to enter a file name, which is automatically assigned a .CLP (CLiPboard) extension.

You can specify a different extension, but then you would have to change the description of the file listing. Type a file name and select the OK button to save the file.

Opening Clipboard files

To insert the contents of the Clipboard file into your application (using the *Paste* command), first load the file from the *File* menu with the *Open...* command.

If the Clipboard already contains data, another dialog box asks whether the data should be deleted. If you select OK, the data will be lost. You must determine whether you've copied the data to the Clipboard or actually deleted it from a document. If you aren't sure, then save the current Clipboard's contents to a file. You can always delete the file later.

Now that you've opened the Clipboard file, you can switch back to your application and then transfer the data to your document with the *Paste* command from the application's *Edit* menu.

Deleting contents

To delete the Clipboard's contents, use the *Delete* command in the *Edit* menu. This command deletes the contents of temporary memory instead of the Clipboard file you just opened.

14.4 Changing Formats in the Clipboard

The data passed to the Clipboard is stored in several formats so that it can be available to other applications, which cannot process the original format. Various formats can be used, depending on the type of data that's transferred.

When you move information from one application to another, you can change the format if the automatic format doesn't adequately represent all of the formatting information. However, usually the automatic format is closest to the original format.

Text formats

The *Text* command in the *Display* menu allows you to convert Clipboard text to straight text, which doesn't contain any formatting characters, or to the OEM format (non-proportional font). To display the format that the text had in its original application, use the *Auto* command. You'll also receive the same results with the *Rich Text Format* item, which also retains the original formatting. The *OEM Text* format is generally used for characters that come to the Clipboard from non-Windows applications.

The *Text* format displays the information in a proportional font similar to Helvetica, while the *OEM Text* format is non-proportional, similar to Courier. Both formats recognize tab stops and end-of-paragraph characters.

Depending on the application, information can be represented either in text or graphic format. A good example of this is Excel, in which entries can be processed either as text or graphics. Only formats that the source application is able to use are displayed. So if many formats are available and the current data can only be converted to certain formats, the unusable formats appear in a different color and cannot be selected.

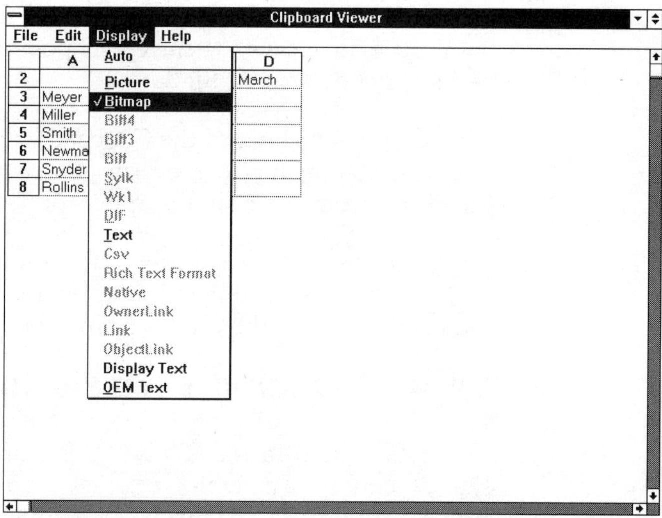

Excel data formats

Graphic formats

If there's graphic data in the Clipboard, the item names in the *Display* menu change. The *Bitmap* and *Picture* commands allow you to represent graphics, which were transferred to the Clipboard, in the corresponding formats.

The *Auto* command returns you to the original format. The *Bitmap* format produces the same display seen in the original application. When pressing Prt Sc to transfer a screen to the Clipboard, the *Bitmap* format is always used.

Texts as objects

In Excel, several formats can be used for graphics in the Clipboard. Even text can be represented in graphic format, so that it can later be inserted as objects in the Excel worksheet.

14.5 Data Exchange in Non-Windows Applications

Exchanging data with non-Windows applications running in full-screen mode is performed differently than between two Windows applications. Since an *Edit* menu isn't available for the data transfer, you must use the Control menu. The procedures for non-Windows applications running in a window differ from those for full-screen applications.

Non-Windows applications running in a window

Let's begin with data exchange in non-Windows applications running in a window. First Windows must be in 386 Enhanced mode. The application's Control menu contains an *Edit* menu with the *Copy* and *Cut* commands. These commands perform the same functions as in a "pure" Windows application.

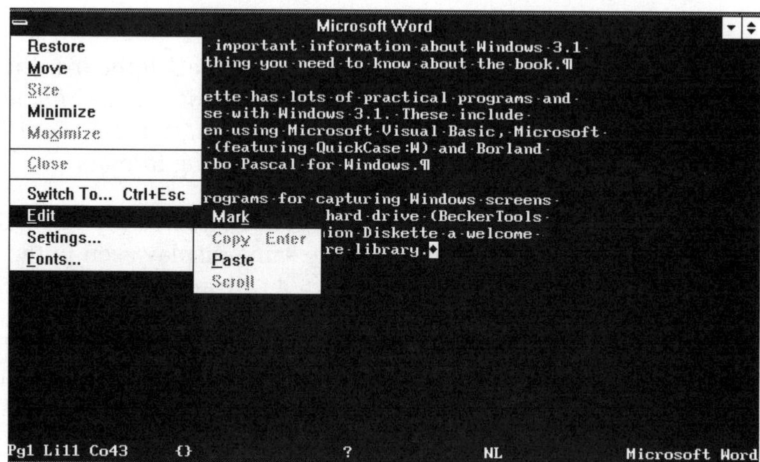

System menu for a non-Windows application

First open the Control menu by pressing (Alt) + (Spacebar). Then select the *Mark* command from the *Edit* menu. Move the cursor to the first character that you want to transfer to the Clipboard. Press and hold the (Shift) key and select the remaining data using the arrow keys. When you're finished, select either the *Copy* or *Cut* command from the Control menu and the data transfer will be performed.

Creating a screen image

To copy the entire screen to the Clipboard, press (Alt) + (Prt Sc). The entire screen, including the window border and any visible portions of the application, are copied to the Clipboard.

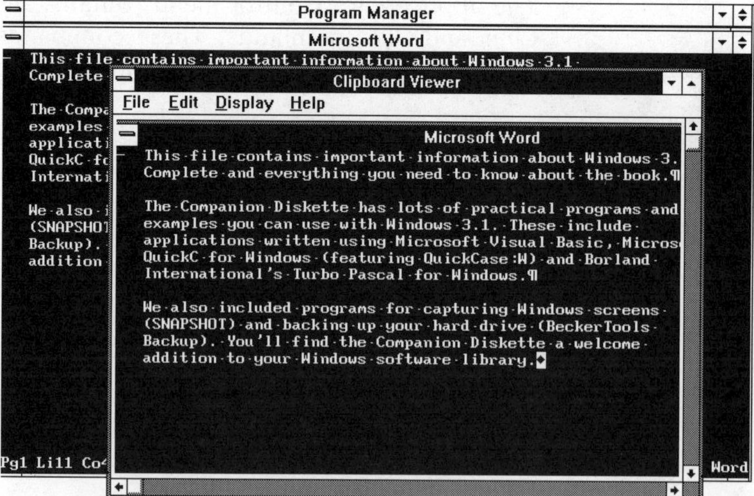

A screen in the Clipboard

Now we'll discuss inserting data in non-Windows applications running in a window. The process is similar to the one used in Windows applications. Place the cursor where you want the data pasted, then select the *Paste* command from the application's Control menu. Since the data is in the Clipboard, you can insert it into any application. If necessary, change the format in the Clipboard.

Non-Windows applications as full-screen only

With non-Windows applications running as full-screen only, it doesn't matter whether Windows is in Standard mode or 386 Enhanced mode.

Hardcopy is the only option

You cannot transfer data selectively from full-screen non-Windows applications to the Clipboard. You must copy the entire screen by pressing the Prt Sc key. Some systems accept only the Prt Sc key, while others accept only Shift + Prt Sc.

Pasting from the Control menu

In these applications, the procedure for inserting data is more complicated. After transferring the data to the Clipboard, start the client application and load the corresponding file. Move the cursor to the place where you want to insert the data. Press Alt + Esc and double-click the icon for the client application at the bottom of your screen. Open the icon's Control menu and select the *Paste* command. This inserts the Clipboard's contents in the file at the current cursor position.

Pasting using the icon

This procedure is necessary because when an application is running as full-screen, a Control menu doesn't exist. So, a full-screen application must be minimized to an icon, since every icon has a Control menu.

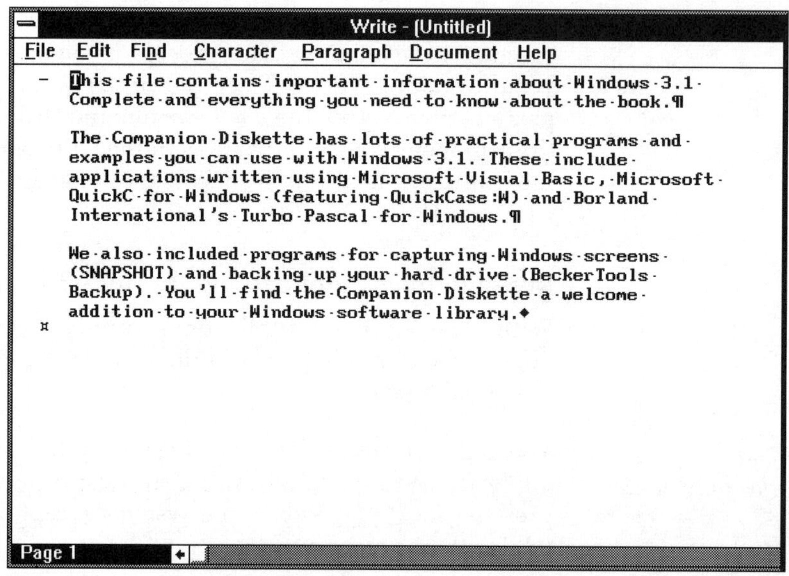

Non-Windows information pasted into Write

14.6 Dynamic Linking Using the Clipboard

The Clipboard makes it easy to dynamically link data between different applications. This process is called Dynamic Data Exchange (DDE). To implement DDE, the appropriate applications must be designed for DDE.

Word for Windows and Excel

Excel 3.0, Word for Windows, and PageMaker can handle DDE. We'll use Write and Excel as examples of typical Windows applications to illustrate the principles of Dynamic Data Exchange.

Linking Write and Excel

To create a link between these programs, move the cursor to the place in the Write document where the Excel worksheet should be inserted. The *Paste Link* command establishes the link between Excel and Write. Be sure that you've already saved both the Write and Excel documents. An Excel worksheet that was created only temporarily and then inadvertently deleted would prevent a link from occurring.

Setting the type of update

An Excel object is usually updated automatically. Change any area of an Excel worksheet and then switch back to Write; the changes will appear in your Write document. To perform a manual update, activate the *Links...* command in the *Edit* menu. You can also set up the same update by double-clicking on the linked object.

The dialog box shows all the links contained within a document. Select either the *Automatic;* or *Manual;* option. With the *Update Now* screen, the object is retrieved from the Excel file and is displayed in the Write document along with any changes you've made. The Change Links... command button allows you to select a new file name in case the name of the linked Excel object has been changed.

Clicking on the Cancel Link command button removes the link and converts the data into a static object.

14.7 Object Linking and Embedding (OLE)

Suppose that you're inserting an object into a document that contains a reference to the server application. This object can be changed at any time. The object and application refer to each other. Also, you have access to all formatting needed to work on the object. As you'll see in this example using Write and Paintbrush, this process can be performed only by applications that support OLE.

The object concept

The OLE process uses the *object* concept, which refers to almost all embedded information. An object may be a drawing from Paintbrush or a worksheet range from Excel.

Run Paintbrush, then run Write. Open the Write file, in which you want to embed a Paintbrush drawing. Move the insertion point to the location at which you want the drawing embedded. Press Alt + Esc to switch to Paintbrush. Create a new drawing or open an existing drawing. Select the drawing, then select *Copy* from the *Edit* menu. While in Paintbrush, save the picture using *Save* from the *File* menu. Press Alt + Esc to switch to Write.

To embed the drawing, select *Paste* from the *Edit* menu. This displays the drawing in the Write document.

Editing an embedded object

If you want to edit an embedded object, select that object by either double-clicking on it or clicking on the object. Then select *Edit Paintbrush Picture Object* from the *Edit* menu. Paintbrush runs and opens the embedded object's file. Edit the object, then select *Update* from the *File* menu to update the drawing.

Select *Exit & Return To...* from the *File* menu. This closes Paintbrush and returns you to the Write file. You can see that the changes have been applied to the embedded object.

14.8 Creating Object Packages

The Object Packager provides a simple way to link or embed information between different applications. The inserted information is represented by an icon, which permits access to this information. Selecting *Package Object/Activate Contents* from the *Edit* menu opens the object in its own application, from which you can view the object or edit it. In this way you can insert placeholders into a document and activate them whenever you need to see the information. You can also assign commands to an object package; so you can double-click on the icon to execute a command.

Dependent on the application

Several options exist for the information that must be inserted. First, only applications that support Dynamic Data Exchange (DDE) or Object Linking and Embedding (OLE) have this process. You can embed or link the objects (i.e., parts of a document) into any other document. However, entire documents can only be embedded, not linked. When working with applications installed prior to Windows 3.1, you can set up icons only by using the Object Packager. You can easily insert object package picture views if you're using the File Manager with applications written for Windows 3.1 (such as the Paintbrush or Write applications included with Windows).

Since Word for Windows and Excel support both processes (DDE and OLE), we'll use them in the following paragraphs to illustrate how the Object Packager works. You must always be able to correctly call up the server applications at any time. Make sure that each application is included in the PATH statement of your AUTOEXEC.BAT file, or an error will occur.

Creating links and embedding

To set up dynamic linking or embedding between two applications, first open the application containing the information (object) to be transferred. If you want to insert a section of an Excel worksheet into a Write document, select the area in Excel and then use the *Copy* command to move it to the Clipboard. Don't close the Excel application.

Object Packager screen

Open the Object Packager from the *Accessories* group. The window contains two windows. The *Appearance* window will display the package's icon, while the *Content* window will display the information needed for packaging.

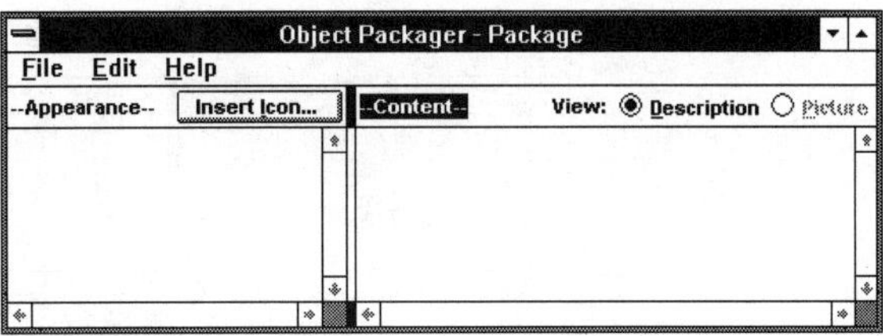

The Object Packager screen

Changing icons and labels

Activate the *Content* field using the mouse or the Tab key. To insert a link into the Object Packager, use the *Paste Link* command in the *Edit* menu.

After doing this, the Excel icon appears in the *Appearance* window and the text *Link to...* and the file name appear in the *Content* window.

If you only want to embed the object, select the *Paste* command from the *Edit* menu. The entry *Copy of Excel Worksheet* appears in the *Content* window. Clicking on one of the View buttons displays the content as either the description (e.g., *Copy of Excel Worksheet*) or as the picture (e.g., the Excel worksheet itself).

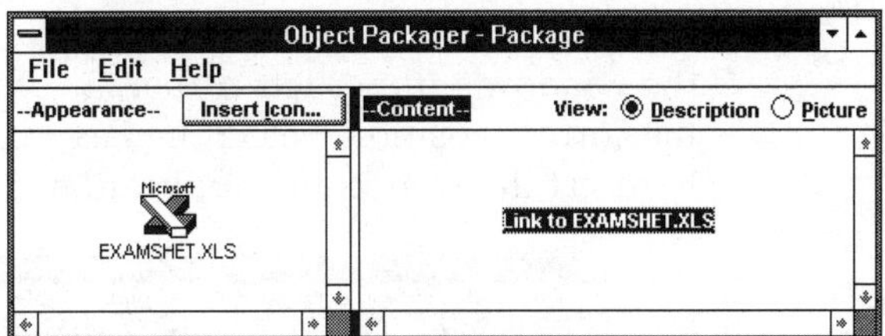

Icon in the Object Packager

Choosing a different icon

To change the icon, first ensure that the *Appearance* window is open. Click on the Insert Icon... command button and select another icon from the list. Click on an icon or enter the name of a file, containing the icon you want, in the *File Name:* text box.

Usually the Program Manager contains the most icons, so that entering PROGMAN.EXE (and path as needed) displays several icons. This icon can be changed at any time.

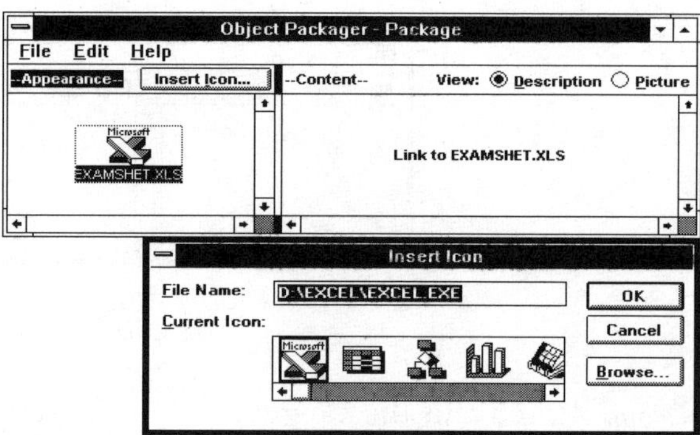

Program Manager icons

You can also change the text below the icon. Ensure the *Appearance* window is active and then select the *Label...* command from the *Edit* menu. Now the package icon can be inserted into an application. The *Copy Package* command moves the icon and its information into the Clipboard.

Inserting the package object

Activate the application, into which you want to insert the package object, and move the insertion point to the desired location (where applicable).

Many applications automatically place the package object icon in the window's upper-left corner. So, you must manually move it to the correct position. Select the *Paste* command from the *Edit* menu to insert the icon in the application.

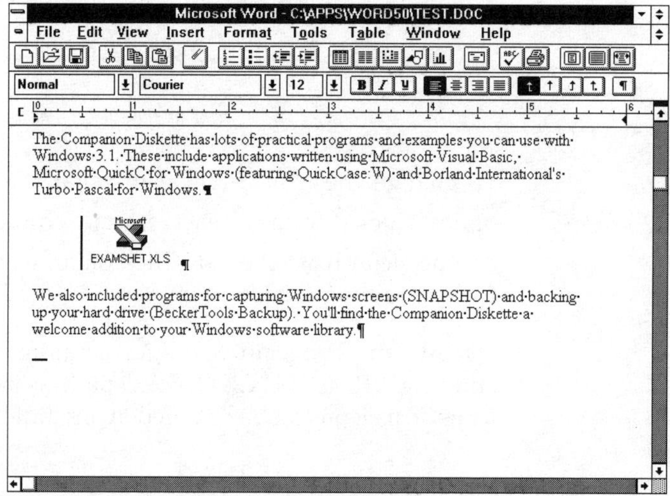

Icon View in Write

You may want to link an entire document, instead of only a portion of a document, with another application. In the Object Packager, select the *Import...* command from *File* menu. In the File Name: list box, select the document that must be linked to the other application. If you select *Copy Package* from the *Edit* menu, the link is placed in the Clipboard, from which you can insert it into the application. However, remember that an entire document can only be embedded, not linked.

Calling and editing a package object

To view the information, double-click the icon with the mouse. Or, to use the keyboard, select the icon and use the *Package Object...* command from the *Edit* menu. Either method activates (opens) the server application and loads the document containing the information. Closing the server application returns you to the client application.

Changes using the Object Packager

To edit the package object, select the icon and use the *Package Object* command from the *Edit* menu. The Object Packager appears. You can start the server application by activating the *Appearance* window and entering the *Edit...Object* command from the *Edit* menu.

Now make the changes in the server application and exit to the Object Packager.

The Object Packager transmits the change to the client application when you select the *Update* command from the *File* menu. Exit the Object Packager to complete the process.

Updating links

When a link is established in the Object Packager, usually an automatic link updating process is produced. This means that changes to an object in the server application are automatically updated.

To change the type of update, for example, to a manual update, open the Object Packager to the object by using the *Edit/Object Package...* command and then enter the *Links...* command from the *Edit* menu.

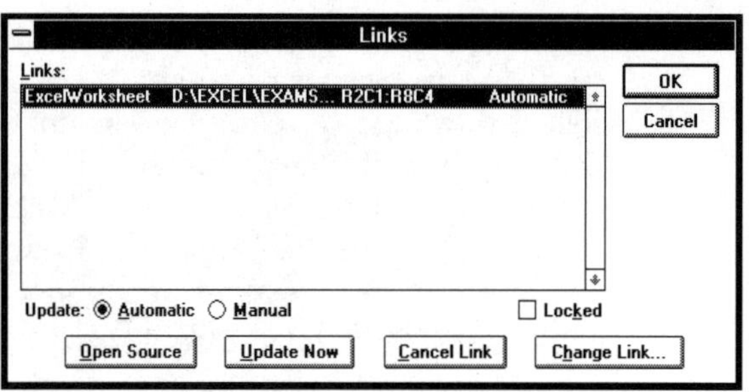

Updating a link

With the Manual and Automatic option buttons you can specify the type of update. This applies only to the link appearing in the *Links:* list box. With a manual setting, the update is performed by clicking the Update Now command button.

This type of update gives the user control over when the changes will occur.

Switching and deleting links

When you click on the Change Link... command button, a File Select dialog box appears. From this box you can select a new drive or directory containing the same file used to define the link. In this instance you would use this function to specify the new location.

The Cancel Link button cancels the link that appears in the field. The package object icon still remains in the application, but is now treated as a static object (i.e., a normal icon). You can enter the server application with the *Edit* command and change the objects yourself.

Assigning general commands

Besides straight linking and embedding, you can also use the Object Packager to create icon based commands. You can call most MS-DOS commands and even other Windows applications.

Use the path specification carefully

Open the Object Packager and then activate the *Content* window. Select *Command Line...* from the *Edit* menu. A dialog box, in which you can enter your DOS command, appears. For example, enter "edit c:\autoexec.bat" to call the DOS 5.0 Editor and edit your AUTOEXEC.BAT file.

Activate the *Appearance* window and click on the Insert Link... command button. Select an icon and click on OK. Select the

Label... command from the *Edit* menu, and enter a label for the icon if desired.

Select *Copy Package* from the *Edit* menu. Switch to the client application and paste this package object into the application.

Now when you double-click this icon, the system calls the DOS 5.0 Editor and loads the AUTOEXEC.BAT file into the DOS 5.0 Editor.

15. The File Manager

The File Manager

You can perform many file and disk operations under Windows with the File Manager. Copying files, creating directories, and formatting diskettes are some of the most important tasks. These operations can be performed quickly and easily with the mouse.

The display format

The desktop of the File Manager provides an overview of drives and directories. It's possible to display more multiple drive windows, with a file window for each drive. This lets you simultaneously display and compare the contents of two different diskettes.

Disk menu

The *Disk* menu of the File Manager contains various commands for working with disks. You can make a system diskette, copy a diskette, and format diskettes. You don't have to specify parameters for the commands in this menu.

15.1 The File Manager Desktop

You can use the File Manager to obtain information about the files stored on your hard drive or diskette. Start the File Manager by double-clicking on the File Manager icon in the Main group.

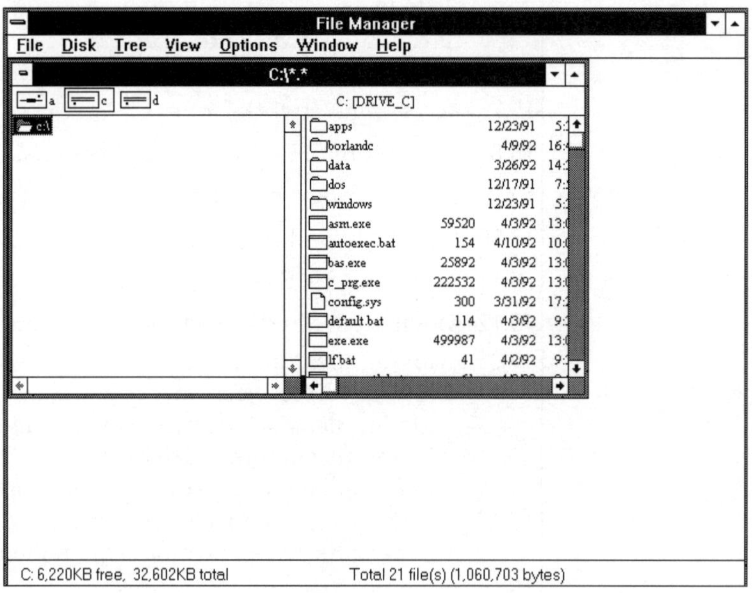

The File Manager window

Displays files

The File Manager window contains a menu bar and displays the directory tree of the hard drive, on which Windows is installed, within a separate window. The directory tree is displayed in a split window. The right half of the window lists the files of the directory currently selected in the left half of the window. Although both halves of the window are linked together, you can modify the display if necessary. The title bar lists the currently selected drive and directory.

Directory icons

The root of the directory tree is displayed on the top. This is the root directory of the current drive. All other directories installed on this drive appear below the root directory. Only the directories of the first level appear in the window. If these directories contain additional subdirectories, the directory icon is marked with a plus sign (+).

You can modify this display. To determine whether these markers are displayed, select the *Indicate Expandable Branches* command from the *Tree* menu. If a minus sign (-) appears in the directory icon, the subdirectories are already displayed. An example of this is the root directory of the current drive. Since you already see all the subdirectories, a "-" appears in the icon for the root directory.

Drive display

The drives are displayed as icons above the directory tree and can be addressed by the File Manager. You can use these icons to display the directories or files of other drives. This is especially useful if you're running Windows in a network. In this instance, the drives of the server are displayed along with the physical drives and can be used normally.

Selecting a window half

Click the mouse to select a window half. The half in which the selection cursor appears is the selected half. Use the Tab key to move the selection cursor with the keyboard.

A status bar appears at the bottom of the display window. This bar provides information about the capacity of the current drive in the left window half and information about the number and capacity of files in the current directory in the right window half. To switch off the status bar, select *Status Bar* in the *Options* menu.

Customizing the Desktop

With the File Manager, you can open more than one directory window. The window can be from the same drive or a different one. This makes it easy to compare directory contents or move files from one directory to another.

To display the contents of another drive in the active window, click the appropriate drive icon. To open a new window for the drive, double-click the drive icon. You can also do this by selecting the *New Window* command from the *Window* menu. To save custom settings that affect the position and display of the windows, select *Save Settings on Exit* in the *Options* menu.

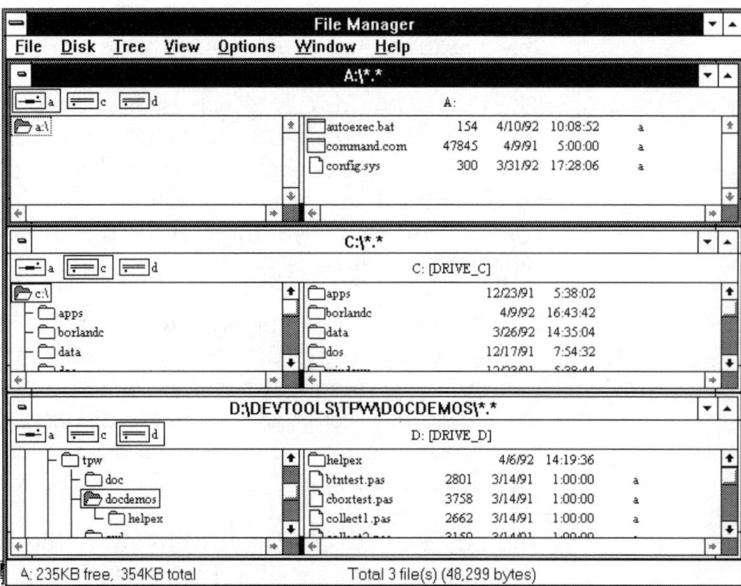

Several windows tiled for comparison

Select *Tile* to arrange all the opened directory windows underneath each other on the screen. If you select *Cascade*, the directory windows will overlap in the display. To place the desired window in the foreground, simply activate its title bar.

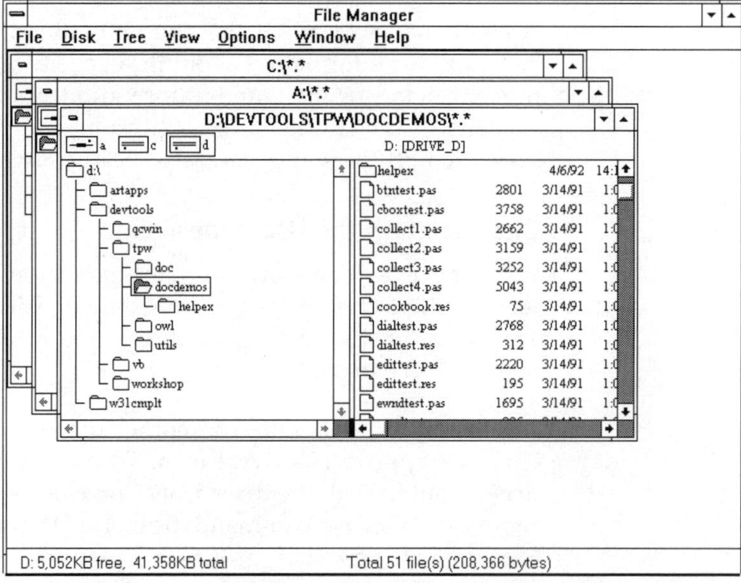

Cascading directory windows

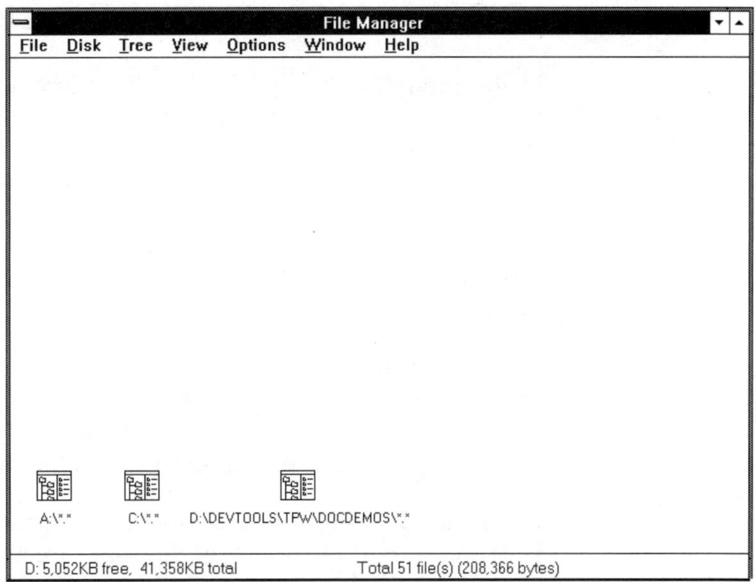

Directory windows displayed as icons

Any directory window that you aren't currently using can be reduced to icons. This setting is useful for directory windows on disk drives. When you make specific settings for displaying diskette contents but a diskette isn't currently inserted in the disk drive, you can shrink the directory window to an icon and call it again when you need it. To do this, use the directory window's Control menu, which contains the same functions as any other Control menu, and select *Minimize*. To arrange the icons, choose the *Arrange Icons* command in the *Window* menu. If you're using more than one directory window, you can move a window to the foreground from the *Window* menu.

Changing the display

You can use the commands in the *View* menu to change the window display. Select the *Tree and Directory* command to display the directory tree and the file list simultaneously. Selecting *Tree Only* displays only the directory tree, while selecting *Directory Only* includes only the file list in the display. If you're using the *Tree and Directory* setting, you can choose the *Split* command to move the split bar between the two windows, which gives one window more space. If you're using the mouse, simply drag the split bar in the desired direction.

Fonts in the File Manager

Use the *Font...* command in the *Options* menu to customize the font used for displaying files. With TrueType fonts you can display file names in any size. Select *Lowercase* to display the file names in lowercase letters.

15.2 Working with the Directory Structure

To become familiar with the directory structure, move the selection cursor to the folder that represents the root directory. Use the direction keys to move to all the branches of the tree. The current directory is also displayed in the upper portion of the window in the line directly below the drive icons. If your directory is large, simply enter the first letter of the directory name you want to select. To obtain the icon for the root directory, type a backslash "\".

Displaying single levels

Since this icon contains a minus sign (-), you can close all the subordinate directories by pressing the [-] key. The subordinate directories are no longer displayed and the "-" has changed to a "+". If you're using a mouse, simply click the directory name.

To display the subordinate directories again, press the [+] key. Then the level directly below the root directory reappears on the screen. Mouse users can simply click the directory name.

Viewing all levels

You can use these functions to expand and collapse not only the subdirectories of the root directory, but also any other branch of your directory tree. To display all the subdirectories of a directory (i.e., without having to move level by level through the tree), instead of pressing [+], press the "*" key. To display all the directories of the drive on the screen, press [Ctrl] + "*". The entire directory tree expands, including all of its branches.

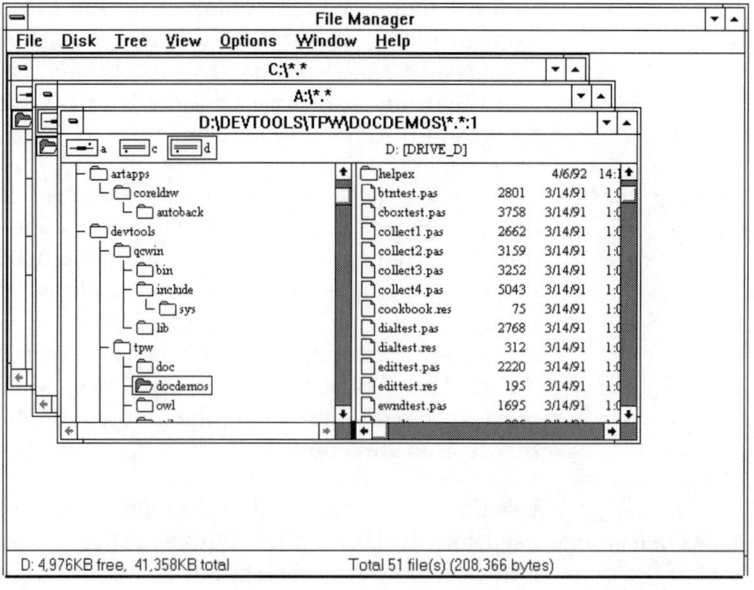

Displaying the directories

Selecting with commands

So far you've learned how to move around the directory tree and open and close its branches. You also learned the keyboard shortcuts for the *Tree* menu commands. The [-], [+], and * keys and the [Ctrl] + * key combination are shortcuts for calling a command from this menu.

Use the *Expand One Level* command to open the next highest directory level of the currently selected directory. Select *Collapse Branch* to close the next highest level of the current directory. Select *Expand All* to open all the directories and select *Expand Branch* to expand all higher directories of the current directory.

15.3 Changing Drives

In the upper-left area of the File Manager window, the drives configured in your computer are displayed as icons. The drive letters for each drive appear below each icon. The directory tree, which the File Manager displays after startup, is always the directory structure of the current drive. If you're in C: (the hard drive), after you activate the File Manager, you'll see the directory tree that you created for this drive.

To receive information about the files and directories on other drives, first you must change to the desired directory.

Changing drives with the mouse

If you're using the mouse, click one of the drive icons and watch as the current directory tree is replaced by the directory structure of the drive you just selected. Clicking the icon once displays the directory tree of the selected drive in the active window. Double-clicking the icon opens a new window and displays the directory tree there.

Changing drives via the drive letters

With the keyboard, you can change drives by pressing a combination of keys consisting of the [Ctrl] key and the letter of the desired drive. For example, pressing [Ctrl] + [A] changes to drive A:. You can also make the drive area active by pressing [Tab] and selecting the drive with the cursor keys. Press [Enter] to read the drive. You could also choose the *Select Drive...* command from the *Disk* menu.

Updating the display

If the file or directory structure on the drive has been changed, these changes may not appear in the display. To ensure that the current contents of the drive always appear in the display, update the display by re-reading the drive. With the mouse, you can activate the drive icon again or press [F5] to enable the *Refresh* command from the *Window* menu.

15.4 Displaying Filenames

Displaying file names in File Manager is similar to using the DOS DIR command. All the files in a directory are displayed on the screen along with their file name, extension, size in bytes, and the date and time they were last modified.

Sorting by name

The list of files is also sorted by file name. Directory entries are identified by folder icons. The System, Read Only, and Archive attributes can also be displayed as additional information. If none of these attributes are set, nothing appears after the file entry.

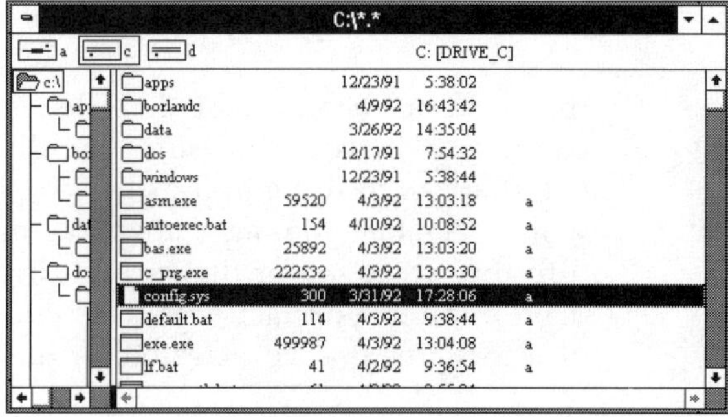

Complete display of file names

Your list of file names probably looks different than the one displayed in the previous illustration. This occurs because of the various settings that can be used to format this list. We'll discuss these settings later in this chapter.

The directory window also provides extensive information about the files of the directory. If the file you're looking for isn't in this directory, there are two ways to change to another directory.

Changing directories

You can use either the keyboard or the mouse to change directories. If you're using the mouse, double-click the directory name to activate the desired directory. This causes the contents of the directory to be displayed in the file window. If the directory window is too small to display all the directories simultaneously, use the scroll bar to place directories outside of the directory window. From the keyboard, press Tab to activate the directory area and use the cursor keys to select the desired directory name. Then press Enter to display the contents of the directory.

Directories in the file list

Subdirectories are marked, in the left area of the file list, with directory icons. The parent directory is represented by an arrow and two dots. You can also activate directories in the file list to display their contents.

Creating directories

Use the *Create Directory...* command to create a directory on your diskette or hard drive. This command is identical to the DOS MD command. To create a directory, first activate the file name window of the directory or select the directory in the directory tree where you want to place the new directory. Then select *Create Directory...* and enter the name of the new directory in the text box of the command's dialog box.

If you create a new directory in a file name window, the new directory entry appears immediately after the command has been executed. If you create a new directory in the window of the directory tree, select *Refresh* from the *Window* menu. The "+" character appears in the parent directory of your subdirectory.

15.5 Changing the File List Display

The display format shown in the previous illustrations is based on the setting that was made after Windows was installed. The file names, their extensions, the size in bytes, the date and time of the last modification, and the various file attributes are displayed in a file name window.

This setting provides the most information about a file list and is the same as the *All File Details* command from the *View* menu.

Display like DOS

You can use the commands in the *View* menu to change the display format. Select the *Name* command to display only the names of the files. The file names are listed below each other and next to each other.

This format is similar to the display of the DOS *DIR /W* command. When this setting is active, the file size, time and date of the last modification, and the file attributes aren't displayed.

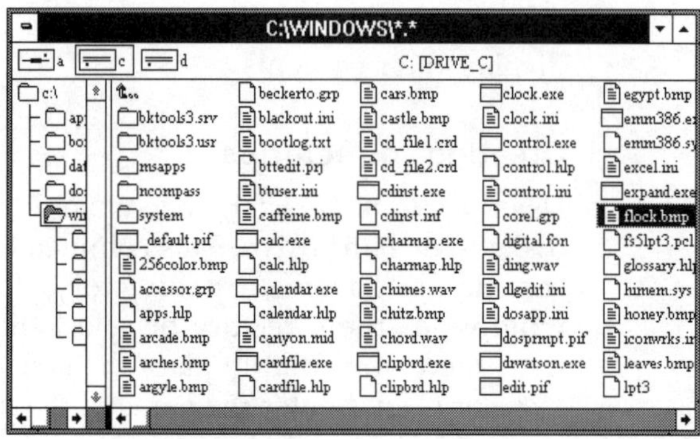

Display of filenames under the Name setting

To display only certain information about your file list, select the *Partial Details...* command to define your own display format.

Partial Details
Details
Size
Last Modification Date
Last Modification Time
File Attributes
OK
Cancel
Help

Selecting display options

After you select this command, a dialog box, in which you can select the information that will be displayed, appears. You can select the following options: *Size*, *Last Modification Date*, *Last Modification Time*, and *File Attributes*.

Custom display

If you activate one or more of the options, the settings will apply for all windows opened on the basis of the current window. However, you can set different display options for any other window.

You can also use the *View* menu commands to determine how the file names will be listed in the window. If you select the *Sort by Name* command, the list is displayed in alphabetical order. The *Sort by Type* command sorts the files in alphabetical order according to their extensions. The *Sort by Size* command sorts the files according to size and *Sort by Date* sorts the files according to their date of creation or the date of the last modification.

Displaying specific files

Use the *By File Type...* command to specify the file types that appear in the display. Before the File Manager executes this command, it displays a dialog box that contains options for specifying the type of file that can be listed. The default settings display all types of files and subdirectories in the file list.

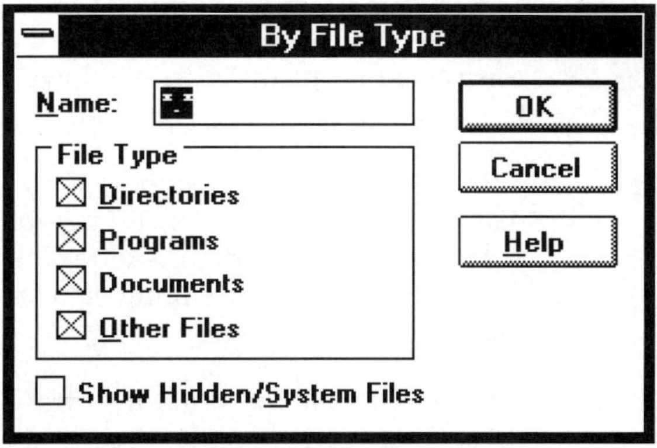

Custom display of file types

For example, to display only program files, select the *Programs* option. All other options are deactivated. All executable files, which have the .COM, .EXE, .PIF, or .BAT extension, are displayed. Select the *Documents* option to display only data files that have been created by programs.

This category includes documents, graphics, .INI files, and Help texts. The listing of files is determined by the entries in the WIN.INI, where file name extensions are allocated to arrange the documents created by programs. If you select the *Other Files* option, only files that aren't included in either the Programs or Documents groups are displayed.

Be careful with system files

If you select the *Show Hidden/System Files* option, the hidden files are displayed. Be careful with these hidden files because they could be the base of the operating system. If system files are deleted, you'll no longer be able to start your computer. System files are indicated by an exclamation point, which appears in the icon.

For example, if you delete a file called 386SPART.PAR, you'll remove the permanent swapfile that Windows uses in 386 Enhanced mode for swapping programs.

15.6 The File Manager Disk Utilities

Besides the file operations we've just described, you can also use the File Manager to perform numerous disk utilities. To perform these operations, use the commands in the *Disk* menu.

Copying disks track by track

At the operating system level, you can use the DOS DISKCOPY command to copy disks. In Windows, use the *Copy Disk...* command to perform this task.

Exact copy

This command creates an exact copy of the diskette in the current disk drive. The entire diskette is copied track by track. The actual database stored on the diskette doesn't affect the length of the copying process or the number of times you're asked to change diskettes.

Unlike DISKCOPY in Windows, first you must switch to the source drive before activating the *Copy Disk* command. After you confirm your selection, a dialog box informs you that all data will be erased from the destination diskette. Click OK to confirm.

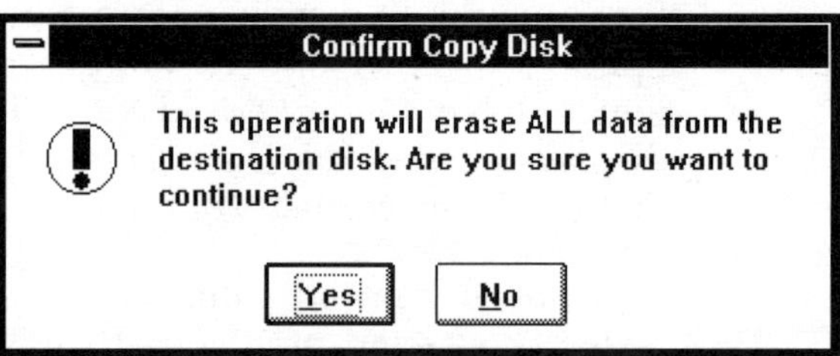

Existing data on the destination disk are deleted

Open the drop-down list box for drives by clicking the arrow to the right of the box. On the keyboard, press Alt+↓ to specify a destination drive. Then press Enter or click the OK button to start the copying procedure.

You can only make copies of diskettes with *Copy Disk....* Also, the source and destination diskettes must be formatted for the same capacity because the copying algorithm works track by track. So a 3.5" diskette formatted for 1.44 Meg can only be copied to a diskette that has the same capacity.

However, it's possible to copy a 3.5" diskette, which is formatted for 720K, onto either a 720K diskette or a 1.44 Meg diskette. Copying 5.25" diskettes is similar. If you have only one disk drive,

Windows will prompt you to insert the destination diskette and source diskette while executing *Copy Disk....*

Labelling a disk

This disk operation is another DOS command that's been incorporated into the Windows user interface. The Windows *Label Disk...* command is similar to the DOS LABEL command. Before using this command, you must change to the drive that contains the diskette to be labelled.

After selecting this command, a dialog box appears. You can enter a name, which contains up to eleven characters, in the text box. If you don't specify a name here, the disk won't have a name or will retain its current name.

Formatting a diskette

Use the *Format Disk...* command from the *Disk* menu to format diskettes. To select a capacity other than the default setting, use the *Capacity:* drop-down list box. For example, to format a double density diskette, that's in a 1.2 Meg drive, at 360K, you must activate this option. Only options that the current drive can process are listed. To name the diskette while it's being formatted, type in a name in the *Label* text box.

To transfer the DOS system files and COMMAND.COM to the diskette while formatting it, activate the *Make System Disk* check box. When this process is complete, you'll have a boot diskette.

Copying system files

To transfer the system files of the currently active operating system to a diskette, use the *Make System Disk...;* command or activate the *Make System Disk* check box in the *Format Disk* dialog box. This command will work only if there are already system files on the destination diskette or if the diskette is blank. So *Make System Disk...* is identical to the DOS SYS command.

15.7 Accessing Network Drives

If you work in a network, you can access all the drives on this network if you know the password and path name of the drive. If you make a connection to the network before starting Windows, Windows will automatically find all existing network connections and display the network drives as separate icons. In this case, the File Manager automatically receives additional functions.

Depending on the type of network, the commands and dialog boxes listed in the following paragraphs may vary. Verify this information by checking with your network supervisor or referring to the network manual.

Connecting to a network drive

To make a new connection to another network drive, activate the *Network Connections...* command. In the dialog box that appears, you must specify the drive letter, path name, and, if necessary, the password. The command only appears if Windows is running in a network environment.

Windows assumes that you want to use the next free letter as your drive letter. However, you can also select a drive letter from a list of available letters. Then specify the path for the drive. In the *Current Drive Connections* dialog box you can choose the path to the server in which the corresponding drive is installed using the Browse... button.

Searching for drives

To add this new connection to the list, activate the *Add to Previous List* check box before clicking the Connect button. If you're working in a network that allows you to scroll through the drives, you can also click the Browse... button in the *Network Drive Connections* dialog box.

After clicking this button, the *Network - Disk Resources* dialog box appears with a list of all available drives and all shares of the currently selected directory. Shares are areas of a drive that can be accessed by several users.

To make a connection to a share, first you must select the drive on which the share is located. Click OK to open the *Connect Network Drive* dialog box and click OK to make the connection.

To end a connection to a drive, use the *Disconnect Network Drive* command. It's only possible to disconnect from one drive. If necessary, you must change drives before selecting this command. Then select the drive from which you want to disconnect. Before access to this drive is closed, a confirmation message appears. Click OK to confirm the message.

15.8 Associating Files with Applications

The *Associate...* command assigns a file to an application that will be used to edit the file. For example, you can use *Associate...* to assign all files ending in .TXT to a word processor so that these files can be edited. There are already some default settings for files created by Windows applications. For example, all files with the .BMP extension are assigned to Paintbrush, all files with the .CLP extension are assigned to the Clipboard, all files with the .WRI extension are assigned to Microsoft Windows Write (the Windows word processor), etc. The defaults have already been activated from the WIN.INI file.

Steps without association

This method reduces the number of steps that are needed to edit a file with the matching application. To work without Windows or to edit files without associating them, do the following:

1. Start the application that you want to use to edit a file, such as a drawing or document.

2. For Windows applications: Select the *Open* command from the *File* menu of the application, change to the correct directory or drive if necessary, and click the OK button. For applications that aren't programmed to run under Windows, you must load the desired file with the appropriate command after changing to the proper directory or drive.

3. Edit the file.

Steps with association

By using *Associate...* to assign a group of files to an application, you can automate one of the steps listed in the previous procedure. So, you must perform only the following steps:

1. Select the file to be edited in the file window of the File Manager.

2. Select *Open* or *Run...*, press Enter or double-click the file name. The application *associated* with the file automatically starts and loads the file you selected.

3. Edit the file.

You associate a file with an application by its file name. Since most applications automatically give extensions to files when they are created, simply associate the extension to the application once. Then you'll be able to load and edit all files created by that application under Windows as we previously described. You can automate the call of the application with *Associate...*.

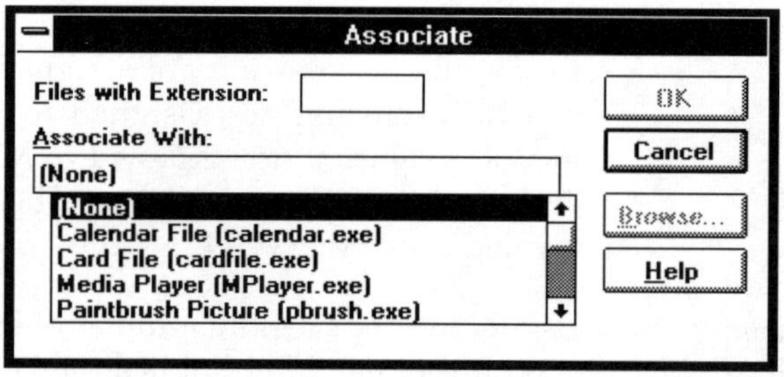

Associate

Files with Extension:

Associate With:

(None)

(None)
Calendar File (calendar.exe)
Card File (cardfile.exe)
Media Player (MPlayer.exe)
Paintbrush Picture (pbrush.exe)

OK

Cancel

Browse...

Help

Assigning an application to the active file

In the *Files with Extension* text box, specify the file extension you want to associate with an application. Select the application from the *Associate With:* list. If the application doesn't appear in the list, click Browse... to associate an application from the *Browse* dialog box.

Entry in the WIN.INI

Once you associate files, which have a specific extension, with an application, the association is permanent. This occurs because of the entries made in the WIN.INI file. A section of WIN.INI, called [Extensions], records which extensions are associated with which applications. The following is an example of the [Extensions] section from a WIN.INI file:

```
[Extensions]
cdr=coreldrw.exe ^.cdr
Corel Draw
cal=calendar.exe ^.cal
Calendar
crd=card.exe ^.crd
Cardfile
trm=terminal.exe ^.trm
Terminal
txt=d:\word\word.exe ^.txt
MS-Word
ini=notepad.exe ^.ini
Notepad
pcx=pbrush.exe ^.pcx
Paintbrush (PCX-Format)
bmp=pbrush.exe ^.bmp
Paintbrush (Bitmap-Format)
wri=write.exe ^.wri
Write
rec=recorder.exe ^.rec
Recorder
frm=fm.exe ^.frm
FormMaster
xls=excel.exe ^.xls
Excel (Worksheets)
xlc=excel.exe ^.xlc
Excel (Charts)
xlw=excel.exe ^.xlw
```

```
Excel (Workspaces)
xlm=excel.exe ^.xlm
Excel (Macros)
```

15.9 Calling Programs and Files

You can start applications from the File Manager. To do this, activate the program file from the file list. For example, to start Word for Windows, change to the directory in which WinWord is installed and start Microsoft Word for Windows by double-clicking the WINWORD.EXE program file. If you're using the keyboard you can select the program file with the cursor keys and press Enter to start it. When you exit the application, you automatically return to the File Manager. You can also switch to the File Manager while you're working with the application.

To display the File Manager as an icon while an application is active, select *Minimize on Use* in the *Options* menu. This setting saves disk space and should always be activated.

Starting from a file

If you used *Associate...* to associate the files with an application, you can use the same procedure to start an application from a document file. In these instances, you can simply double-click the filename. The application associated with the file will start along with the file.

Starting with Run

You can also use the *Run...* command to start an application. After activating *Run...*, a dialog box appears. In the *Command Line* text box specify the name of the program file you want to start. If this program file is in the current directory, simply specify the file name. To start an application that's in a different directory, enter the file name and the complete path name in the text box.

Loading a file when starting an application

If a file isn't associated with an application, there is another way to use *Run...* to load a file. The only difference is that you include the name of the file you want to edit in the text box, separated by a space. If the file you want to load is already associated with an application, simply enter the file name. This procedure only works with programs that accept file names as parameters.

15.10 Printing a Text File

The *Print...* command in the *File* menu of the File Manager is identical to the DOS PRINT command. When this command is activated, the selected file is printed on the default printer. However, if there are any control characters in the text they are ignored because the selected file is simply copied to the corresponding port without using a printer driver.

Outputting print files

Print... can also be used to print files that have been prepared for output on a printer and contain the appropriate control characters. Print files are used, for example, when you're working on a computer that doesn't have a printer or has the wrong printer. In such cases you can redirect the printer output to a print file instead of the printer. The control characters and formatting characters are interpreted, along with the selected printer driver, and written to the file.

Later when you're working with a computer that has the correct printer, simply copy the file to the appropriate port to have it formatted and printed out with the correct page breaks.

15.11 Searching for Files

If a directory contains numerous files or if you're not sure in which directory the file is located, use the *Search...* command from the *File* menu to locate a file.

Searching in the directories

If you want to search only one directory, change to this directory before activating *Search*. Then select *Search...* and enter the name of the file in the *Search For* text box in the *Search* dialog box. You can also use the MS-DOS wildcard characters (? and *). To search the entire drive, activate the *Search All Subdirectories;* check box before clicking OK.

After confirming the command, Windows begins the search. If the search is successful, a window opens displaying the results of the search. For example, if you were searching for a file name within a directory, this name, along with the complete path specification, is displayed in this window. If you used wildcards in your search, all the files that fulfill the criteria are displayed with the complete path specification.

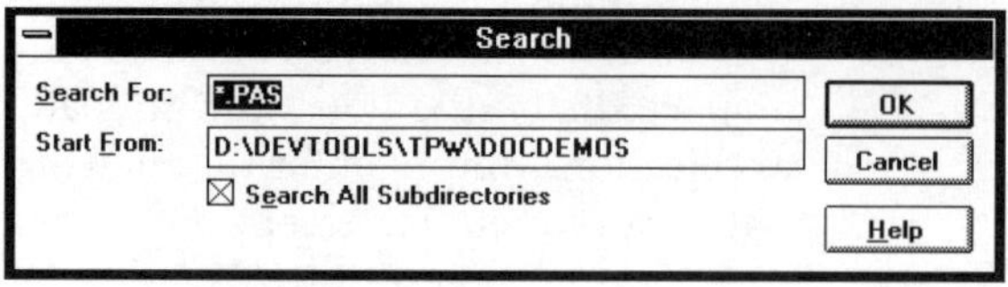

Specifications of a search for a file

If the search was unsuccessful, Windows displays an error message. The file names found by *Search...* can now be processed with the commands of the *File* menu. Since the *View* menu commands cannot be accessed when the *Search Results* window is active, you cannot change the display of the file names.

Search results in the window

You can also display the *Search Results* window as an icon. To do this, use the *Minimize* command from the window's Control menu. After selecting this command, an icon named *Search Results* appears at the bottom of the File Manager window.

15.12 Moving Files and Directories

Windows also provides a command for moving files. Select *Move...* to move a file from one directory to another directory or drive. Instead of being copied, the file is transferred. There are two steps to the *Move...* command:

How files are moved

1. Copying the source file to the destination drive or directory.

2. Deleting the source file.

Moving files

To move a file or directory to another directory, select the source file or source directory. Then select *Move...* from the *File* menu. You can also press F7.

Now a dialog box appears with two text boxes for specifying the source and destination. If you select the files you want to move before activating the command, Windows will make the appropriate entry in the *From:* text box, which specifies the source.

You must enter a path specification in the *To:* text box. This indicates the directory to which the selected file or directory should be moved. If you didn't select the files before activating the command, you can do so now in this dialog box. After making the appropriate entry, either press Enter or click the OK button to execute the command.

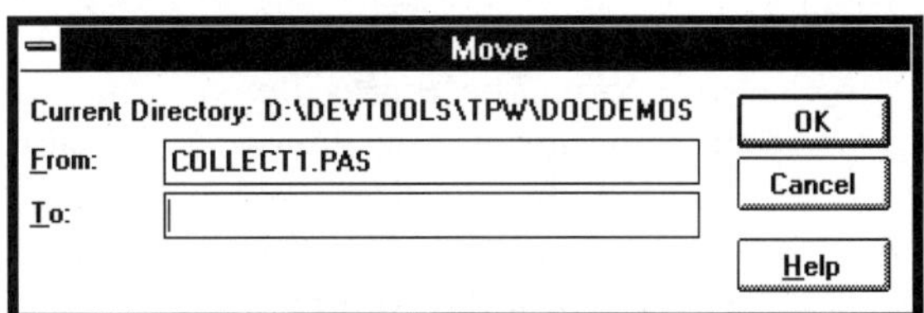

Move dialog box

After Windows executes the command, it doesn't display a message. However, the source file or source directory no longer exists because the *Move...* command deletes the source.

Moving directories

When you move entire directories, all the subdirectories contained in the source directory are included in the move. The directories affected by the move are created as subdirectories of the destination directory and then deleted from the source directory.

Moving files and directories with the mouse

Although *Move...* is a useful command, it's even faster and easier to move files with the mouse. First click on the file or directory that you want to move. Then hold down the mouse button. Drag the icon for your file or directory (while holding down the mouse button) across the screen. You must drag the icon to the icon for the destination directory and release the mouse button.

You cannot move everywhere

While dragging the icon with the mouse you may cross areas in which the icon turns into a circle and slash icon. This means that you cannot release the mouse button in these areas to move the files represented by the icon you're dragging.

The circle and slash icon appears whenever the mouse pointer is located outside of the file name window or directory tree. If you accidentally release the mouse button in these areas, the screen doesn't display an error message. Instead, the drag and drop operation you started is canceled.

Moving more than one file

Moving several files from a directory is similar to moving a single file or an entire directory. The only difference is the way the files are selected before *Move...* is activated.

To select more than one file, first select one file and then hold down the Shift key. Then simply move the cursor or click the mouse to select additional files.

Size display of selected files

In the status bar at the bottom of the File Manager you'll see information about how many files you've selected and how many bytes of memory capacity these files will occupy in the destination directory. The *Status Bar* option must be enabled to display this information. If you haven't yet enabled this option or you want to disable the display, select the *Status Bar* command from the *Options* menu. When this option is enabled, a checkmark appears to the left of the command.

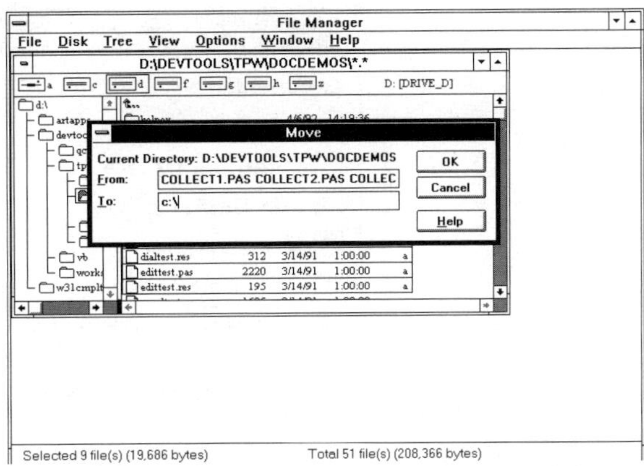

Moving more than one file

After all the files to be moved have been selected, you can move them with *Move*. If you're using the mouse, simply click on the selected file block. Hold down the mouse button and move the icon, which now represents several files, to the destination directory.

Moving files to other drives

You cannot move files or directories to other drives. However, if you try to do this, you won't receive an error message because *Move...* doesn't actually move the files/directories. Instead, it copies them to the selected drive.

Besides this exception, the procedure is the same as moving objects within a directory. If you want to drag an icon to another drive with the mouse, you don't need to open a new directory tree for this drive. Instead, you can drag the icon to one of the drive icons at the top of the directory tree window.

Confirmation message during mouse operations

Moving an entire directory also means deleting a directory (i.e., the source directory). So, after you activate this command, a dialog box, which asks whether you really want to delete the subdirectory, appears. This confirmation message protects you from accidental deletion. To switch on/off all the File Manager confirmation messages, activate the check boxes of the *Confirmation...* command in the *Options* menu.

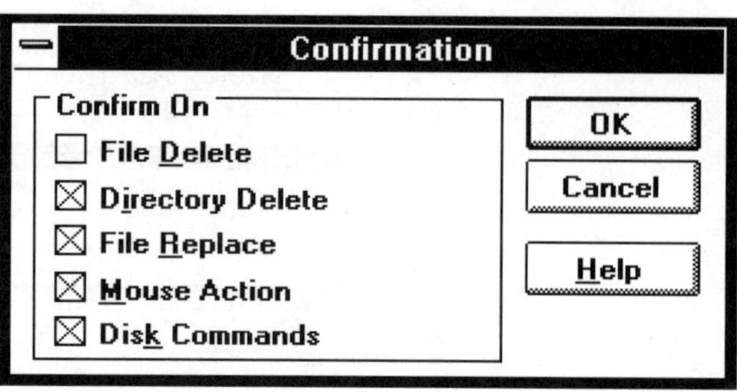

Confirmation dialog box

To eliminate the confirmation messages, make the necessary changes in the *Confirmation* dialog box. In this dialog box you can determine which file operations (if any) display confirmation messages.

Activate the *Mouse Action* check box to protect file operations, which are initiated by mouse actions, with confirmation messages. You should switch on this option because mistakes can happen very quickly when you're moving files.

For example, you could release the mouse button over the wrong destination directory.

Another confirmation option that's important for *Move* is called *Directory Delete*. When this check box is active, you're asked whether you want to delete each subdirectory of the source directory when moving directories.

15.13 Copying Files And Directories

Use the *Copy...* command to copy files and directories. The procedure for using *Copy...* is the same as all other file operations. First select the file or directory you want to copy, then select *Copy...* and specify the destination in the *Copy* dialog box.

After entering all the necessary specifications, press Enter or click the OK button to execute the command. If you didn't select the files you want to copy before you activated the command, you can also select files in the *Copy* dialog box.

As long as the files you're copying don't exist in the destination directory under the same name, *Copy* executes without displaying any messages.

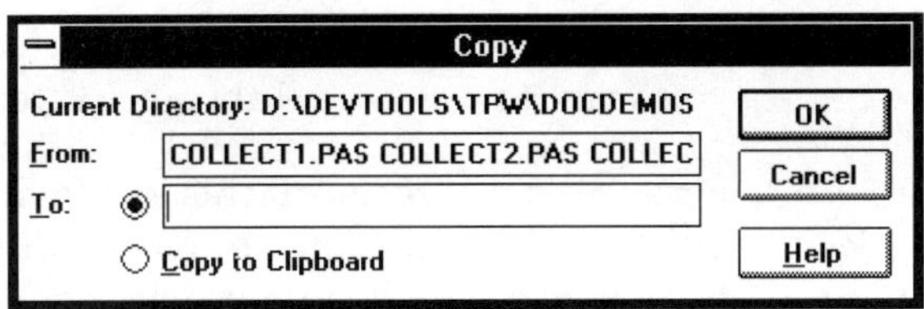

Specifying the source and destination

Copying files and directories with the mouse

If you're using the mouse, copying files and directories is similar to moving them. When you move files, you must only click on the files and hold down the mouse button to drag the icon. To copy files by using the mouse, you must hold down both the mouse button and the Ctrl key. Other than pressing the Ctrl key, the steps for both operations are identical.

If you select the *Copy to Clipboard* option, the selected files are placed in the clipboard. However, this option is only useful for files that can be displayed in the clipboard.

Copying more than one file

To copy more than one file, simply select all the files before activating *Copy*. For more information, refer to the "Moving more than one file" section, which was presented earlier in this chapter.

Confirmation messages when copying files

Depending on the settings you make in the *Confirmation* dialog box, confirmation messages may also appear when you copy files and directories. For example, if you copy files, which already exist under the same name in the destination directory, Windows displays a dialog box that asks whether you want to replace or overwrite these files. However, this confirmation message appears only if the *File Replace* option is activated in the *Confirmation* dialog box. If this option isn't switched on, files in the destination directory with the same name as the ones being copied are overwritten without any prompt for confirmation.

15.14 Deleting Files and Directories

In Windows, use the *Delete...* command to delete files and directories. Again, you can select the files and directories you want to delete before activating the *Delete...* command. If you don't select these files or directories before activating the command, you can specify them in the *Delete* dialog box.

Unlike the DOS DEL command, you can also delete subdirectories with *Delete....* You can even delete subdirectories containing file or subdirectory entries. To do this, select the name of the directory you want to delete and then activate *Delete....*

Confirmation messages when deleting files

Because the effects of this command are permanent, the *File Delete* check box found in *Options/Confirmation...*should always be switched on when your deleting files. This option displays each file name you're deleting, giving you an opportunity to exclude this file from the delete operation or cancel the command completely.

When you delete directories, the *Directory Delete* option is important. When this option is activated and you delete a directory, which still contains subdirectories, Windows asks whether you want to remove each subdirectory from the directory tree.

Both options should be activated before using *Delete....*

15.15 Renaming Files and Directories

As you'll learn in this section, the *Rename...* command of Windows does much more than the DOS REN command. First, we'll discuss what the two commands have in common. Both REN and *Rename...* are used to change file names. You can use wildcards, which enable you to change only file extensions or a specific letter within the file name.

Rename... also lets you select files or directories you want to rename before you activate the command. However, you can also specify the old and new names of the file(s) or directory(ies) in the dialog box after activating the command.

File name conventions

You can also change the names of directories, regardless of whether the directories are empty or already contain entries. The Windows file and directory names conform to the MS-DOS conventions.

File names can contain a maximum of eight characters and have extensions of up to three characters. Extensions are separated from the file name by a period. Directory names can also have a maximum of eight characters but cannot have an extension.

15.16 Changing File Attributes

The *Properties...* command from the *File* menu is another new function in the Windows File Manager. This command allows you to change or set file attributes. We'll briefly explain file attributes, including what they are, how to set them, and why they are important for files.

Properties for QCSTEP4.EXE

File Name: QCSTEP4.EXE
Size: 15,476 bytes
Last Change: 4/17/92 9:36:18
Path: D:\W31CMPLT\PROGRAMS

Attributes
☐ Read Only ☐ Hidden
☒ Archive ☐ System

OK
Cancel
Help

The file attribute setting

The Archive attribute

The first attribute we'll discuss is the archive attribute. This attribute indicates whether the current version of the file has already been backed up with the DOS BACKUP or XCOPY command.

The operating system automatically sets the archive attribute when a file is created and each time it's changed. This enables users to back up only those files that have been changed or created since the last backup. When BACKUP and XCOPY create a backup copy, they automatically reset the archive attribute of the files they're backing up. In this way, users can recognize which files are currently backed up and which ones aren't.

If you want to intervene in this process, you must set or clear the archive attribute, which is represented by an A. Under DOS, the ATTRIB command is used to set file attributes; under Windows, the *Properties...* command performs the same tasks.

The Read Only attribute

The Read Only attribute protects a file from accidental deletion or write accesses. A file set with this attribute (represented by an R) can only be read, not changed or deleted. However, this attribute doesn't provide true protection, because anyone who's familiar with the DOS ATTRIB command or the *Properties...* command can clear this attribute and change or delete the file. So this attribute prevents only accidental changes or deletion.

If you try to delete a file with a set Read Only attribute, the Access denied" error message appears and the procedure is aborted. The *Delete...* command from the File Manager only asks whether you want to delete the write protect file. If you answer yes, it will also remove this file from your directory.

The Hidden attribute

If the Hidden file attribute is activated, the file name won't be displayed when the DOS DIR command is executed. The File Manager won't display these files either unless the *Show Hidden/System Files* check box is activated in the *By File Type* dialog box.

This attribute prevents files, whose names don't appear in the display, from being easily deleted. This is true as long as you work exclusively in this operating system. Even if you enter DEL *.* under MS-DOS, files with the Hidden attribute won't be deleted. This means that it would be impossible for you to delete the two system files, MSDOS.SYS and IO.SYS, without previously clearing the Hidden attribute.

The *Delete...* command from the File Manager is more powerful because it doesn't stop at Hidden files. For example, if you enter the command, *Delete *.** for the root directory of your boot drive, both system files would be deleted if you ignore any confirmation messages. This is another reason why you should also use the *Directory Delete* and *File Delete* confirmation options.

The System attribute

The System attribute can also be affected by the *Properties...* command. This attribute is useful only to the DOS SYS command, which is used to transfer system files (files with a set system attribute) from one drive to another. For this reason, never set this attribute for a file unless it's necessary; otherwise memory problems can occur when you transfer system files to their reserved place on a diskette/hard drive.

We described how to display a file's attributes in the section on the *Partial Details...* command in the *View* menu.

The *Properties...* command is self-explanatory. After you activate this command, a dialog box, containing four check boxes, appears. Each of the attributes we described can either be set or cleared.

This command affects the files that were selected before it was activated. So, you must select those files, whose attributes you want to change, before activating *Properties...*.

16. Printing With Windows

Installing printer drivers

Windows uses printer drivers to fully use all the options of the connected printer. The printer drivers provide Windows with the necessary information for controlling the options. To use a new printer, you must install the printer model in Windows from the Control Panel.

Printer configuration

Before printing a document, you can set the formats and printer driver options under which the document must be printed. Among these are the position of the paper, font cartridges, or the graphics resolution of the printer.

Print Manager

The Print Manager is a printer spooler program that you can use to continue working in Windows during printing. Printed output is temporarily stored on the hard drive and printed using the timeslicing technique.

Managing the print queue

If the Print Manager places several files in a print queue, you can use the Print Manager to change the order of printing, add new print jobs, or delete existing jobs. You can also change the assigned priority.

16.1 General Printing Information

Since Windows takes over control of the printer, the settings for the printer are valid for all Windows applications. This is useful because the printer output is the same for all Windows applications.

Using printer drivers

Every printer has specific options that affect printer output and quality. Laser printers have paper cartridges or double bins, while dot matrix printers use continuous feed paper. Windows also manages the use of different fonts or special graphics capabilities for all printers.

Printer driver options

Windows uses printer drivers for this purpose. Printer drivers are files from which Windows takes information about the printer being used. The installed fonts, type of printer output, and setup of paper cartridges are all described in printer drivers.

Printers are installed during Windows installation or later from the Control Panel. You can install new printer drivers and make changes to existing ones from the Control Panel. So, you don't have to go to the Control Panel to set options, such as using a certain kind of paper bin. Almost all Windows applications contain the *Printer Setup* command. This command sets printer options from within the application.

Printing from non-Windows applications

To print from non-Windows applications that are started from Windows, use the printer driver of the application. Windows itself doesn't have any influence on the printer output of non-Windows applications.

Screen fonts and printer fonts

There are two ways Windows can print a document. It can use the fonts built into the printer. This is the fastest method of printing because it doesn't require any font conversion. The other method involves printing documents in graphics mode. If the printer only has a few fonts available, you can print the Windows screen fonts in graphics mode. However, this slows down printing significantly.

If you use printer fonts in a document, Windows may not be able to display these correctly. Windows works with screen fonts that are independent of printer fonts. When you use printer fonts, Windows represents them with the screen font that most closely matches the printer font.

Using the Print Manager

The Print Manager redirects printer output to a buffer so that you can continue working while you're printing. The hard drive acts as a buffer so that when you use the Print Manager the file is first placed in a special area of the hard drive. The file isn't sent to the printer until the system is free again. Windows then divides the system resources between the Print Manager and the current application, which causes the application to slow down slightly. By setting priorities for the printer and the application in the *Options* menu, you can divide the processor time equally between the Print Manager and the application, or assign more processor time to either the Print Manager or the application.

Disabling the Print Manager

The fastest way to print is to disable the Print Manager. When you do this, the output is then sent directly to the printer without being sent to the hard drive. However, you must wait until the printer is finished before you can continue working with the current application. If your printer has large amounts of buffer memory, disable the Print Manager—the printer buffer already acts as a spooler.

If you've already printed under Windows (e.g., with Microsoft Windows Write), then you automatically used the Print Manager. The Print Manager runs in the background. This means that it writes the file you want to print to the hard drive and then sends it to the selected output device (printer or plotter). This enables you to continue working on your computer while your file is being printed.

16.2 Installing and Configuring Printers

Activate the Control Panel to install a printer driver. Double-clicking the Printer icon or selecting the *Settings/Printer...* command starts the installation or configuration routine for printer drivers to be used by Windows and Windows applications. If you used this option to change settings, you don't have to restart Windows because all changes become active immediately.

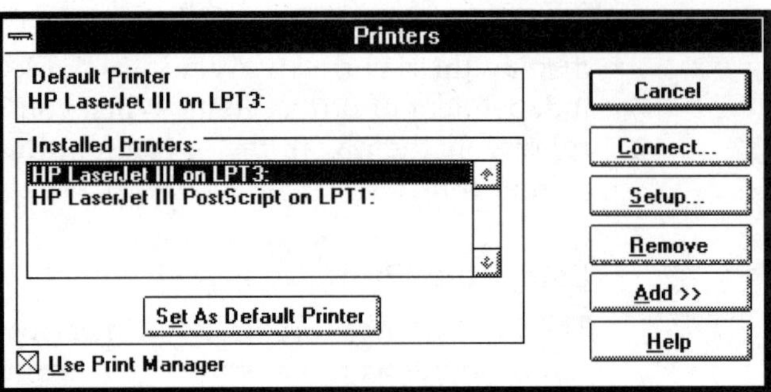

A listing of all installed printer drivers

To delete a printer driver from the list, select the Remove button. This removes the driver from the list, but doesn't delete it from the hard drive. Printer drivers are located in the Windows system directory under the .DRV extension.

Setting the default printer

The current default printer is displayed in the *Default Printer* box. The default printer is the printer to which a file is sent after you select the *Print* command in a Windows application. To use a different printer as the default printer, select the name of the installed printer driver from the list and click the Set As Default Printer button. The name of the new printer now appears in the *Default Printer* box.

No need to restart

Now any printer output under Windows will use the new printer driver. The setting remains active until another printer is specified as the default printer.

Use Print Manager

Activate the *Use Print Manager* check box to determine whether the files to be printed on the default printer are first placed in temporary storage on the hard drive by Print Manager or immediately sent to the printer.

With larger print jobs, sometimes the Print Manager shouldn't be used. For example, it's a good idea to work without Print Manager if there isn't enough free space on the hard drive to temporarily store a large file.

There are some disadvantages to using this method. You cannot work with your computer until the complete file has been sent to the printer and the print job isn't displayed in the print queue.

Installing new printer drivers

To install new printer drivers, click the Add >> button. The dialog box increases and a list of all available Windows printer drivers is displayed in a list at the bottom. Select the appropriate printer driver for your printer and click the Install button.

If your printer model isn't included in the list, refer to your printer manual to determine whether your printer is compatible with one of the models listed. If it is, select the printer driver of the compatible model. If this doesn't work, try each of the drivers until you're satisfied with the results.

Drivers are located on the Windows diskettes

After clicking *Install*, Windows prompts you to insert the appropriate Windows setup diskette, which contains the printer driver you selected, into a disk drive. You must do this so that Windows can copy the selected printer driver to the correct directory. When Windows is finished copying, the newly installed printer driver is entered and highlighted in the list of installed printer drivers. If you've already copied the contents of the Windows diskettes or the printer drivers to your hard drive, change the entry for the appropriate drive or directory.

Assigning a printer port

To assign a port to the printer or set the timeouts, click the Connect... button.

Another dialog box appears. You can assign a port to an installed printer in this dialog box. Windows then directs the printer output to this port. Select the proper port for your printer from the *Ports* list box.

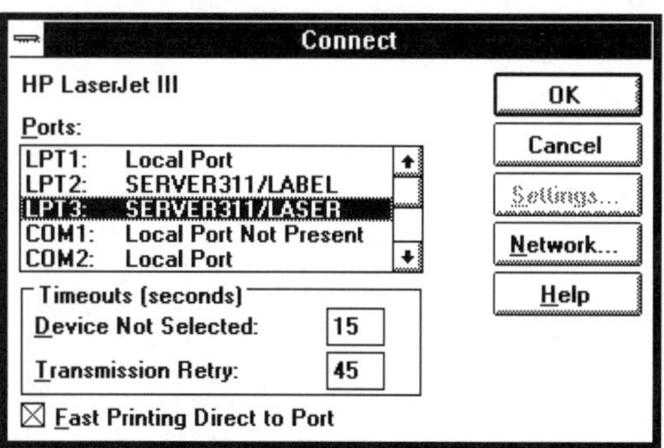

Assigning the port

If you're working with two printers (e.g., a dot matrix and a daisy wheel printer), you can assign the same port to both of them (e.g., using a data switch box). Windows lists the ports in the *Ports* list box, followed by references to ports not present, as needed. You can change the serial port settings by clicking the Settings... button.

Printing to a file

You may want to install a second printer driver so that you can print to a file. Then you could send output to a typesetting machine. Assign the FILE port to the second printer. In this case, Windows asks for the name of the print file you're creating every time you output to this printer. The print file contains the printer-specific control characters in addition to text or graphics.

Activating the PostScript Interpreter

In addition to the parallel ports, there are also COM1: - COM4: ports available for serial data transfer to the printer, and an EPT port. The EPT port drives the IBM Personal PagePrinter (a PostScript printer).

Activate the *Fast Printing Direct to Port* check box so that Windows prints as fast as possible. In this case, Windows sends the output directly to the port, bypassing the DOS printer interrupts.

The other settings in this dialog box apply to the timeouts that you want to set for your printer. In the two text boxes, type the number of seconds you want to elapse before Windows declares a timeout, and before Windows retries transmitting the data.

To open another dialog box to make detailed settings about the paper format or paper tray, click the Setup... button. For example, if you're using a laser printer with a double paper tray, then you must specify the proper tray. If you change paper trays frequently, you should use the Recorder to create a macro for this purpose.

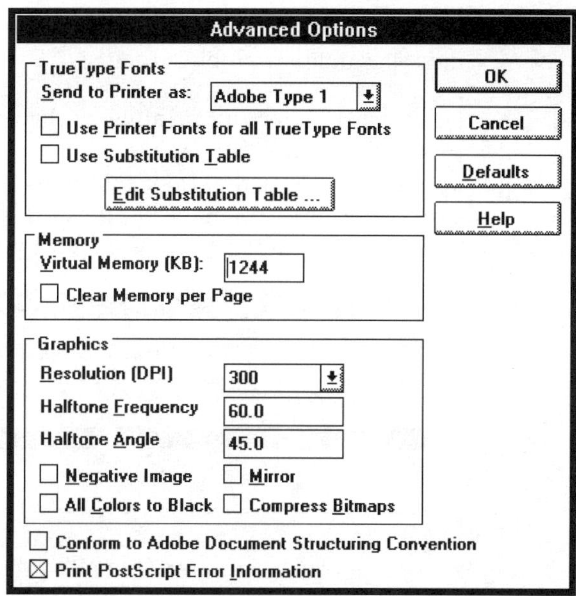

Printer options for a Postscript laser printer

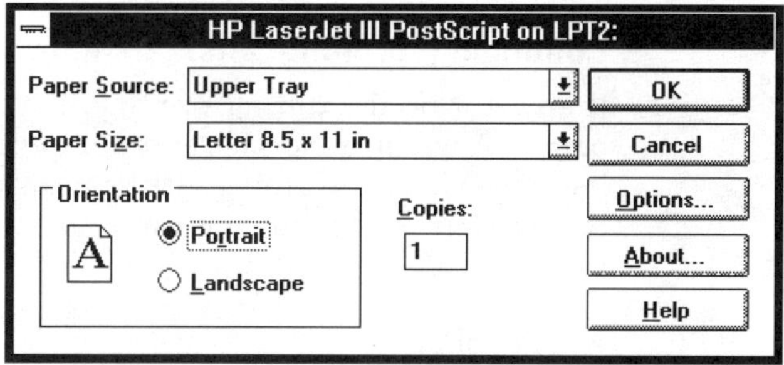

Printer options for an HP Laserjet printer

If an application has its own *Printer Setup* command, you can change the printer settings with this command. For example, an application may have its own controls for printing in Portrait (high) or Landscape (wide) format. The new settings remain active and are valid when you access a different application. This means that the settings are universally available under Windows. So, you should always check your settings before printing.

16.3 Use Print Manager

If the *Use Print Manager* check box in the *Printer* dialog box is active and you use the *Print* command, the Print Manager automatically sends the file or document to the printer. Since the

Print Manager works in the background, you won't receive any messages unless a problem occurs.

Using the Print Manager to control printing

However, to interrupt printing or change the order of files, you can place the Print Manager in the foreground like any other application from the Task List. During printing, the Minimized icon of the Print Manager appears in the Windows desktop. You can also activate the Print Manager by clicking this icon.

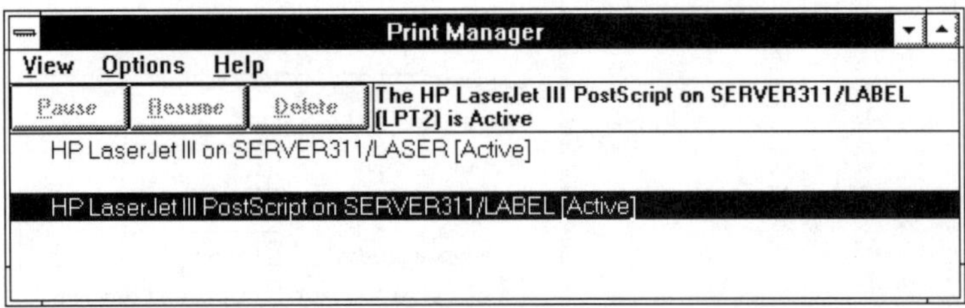

The Print Manager desktop

You can use the buttons and menu commands to control printing. In the following sections, we'll explain these options.

Continuing printing after an interruption

If an error occurs during printing, the Print Manager interrupts output. A warning message appears, indicating that output is being interrupted. This warning also appears when the printer output cannot start. The following can cause the printer to interrupt or fail:

Common printing errors

- Out of paper
- Printer cable loose
- Paper jam in printer
- Internal printer print spooler full

If you detect mechanical errors, they must be repaired. If you can't find anything wrong, simply switch off the printer, wait a few seconds, and then switch it back on. This clears the printer's internal buffer and puts the printer back in ready mode. Doing this usually solves the problem.

Resuming printing after an interruption

Once the problem is solved, press Enter to remove the message from the screen and use the *Task List* dialog box (*Switch To...* from the Control menu) to place the Print Manager in the foreground. Here you can read the percentage figures to determine how much of the printing process is already completed. Press the Resume button to activate Print Manager again and continue the interrupted print job.

If this doesn't help, switch off both the printer and the computer and wait ten seconds. Switch on the printer first, then the computer. When you switch on the computer, a signal is sent to the printer port during the automatic hardware test. This places the printer in ready mode. Activate Windows and print the document again.

Printing several files

You can print several files sequentially. To do this, select the files within the File Manager in the order in which you want them printed and then select the *Print* command. Print Manager then creates a print queue, whose files are printed in sequence. If you're printing from one application, use the *Print* command several times to fill the waiting queue.

Print jobs in the queue

All the files in a print queue that haven't been printed yet are listed below the printer status message in the list of print jobs. Use the direction keys to move the selection cursor within this print queue.

Displaying the current print job

The print job currently being processed is indicated by a small printer icon. For each print job, the date, time, size of the print file, the application from which you're printing, and the name of the document being printed are displayed. Windows also displays the percentage of the current print job that's already completed. To toggle the display of the print time, print date, and file size, use the *Time/Date Sent* and *Print File Size* commands from the *View* menu.

For more information about a selected print job, refer to the upper-right corner of the *Print Manager* window. You can determine whether a file is being printed or is waiting to be printed. You can also determine whether the printer has stopped or an error has occurred (e.g., no paper, printer off line).

Changing a position in the print queue

Except for the print job currently being processed, the print jobs in a print queue have consecutive position numbers. The sequence in which the files are printed is also determined by these position numbers.

To move a print job up within the print queue, you must change the order of the print jobs. To do this with the mouse, move the mouse pointer onto the print job you want to advance. Press and hold the left mouse button. Drag the entry to the desired position, then release the mouse button.

Windows exchanges the positions and numbers of the print jobs affected by this operation. With the keyboard, select the print job you want to move, hold down Ctrl, and press the direction keys to move the job to the desired position.

16.4 Setting Print Manager Options

Use the *Low Priority*, *Medium Priority*, and *High Priority* commands from the *Options* menu to determine the amount of processor time that should be used for processing the print jobs while you work with other applications.

Setting priorities for printer output

The *Low Priority* command assigns more processor time to the applications than to the Print Manager. *Medium Priority* assigns an equal amount of processor time to the applications and the Print Manager. *High Priority* assigns more processor time to the Print Manager than to the applications.

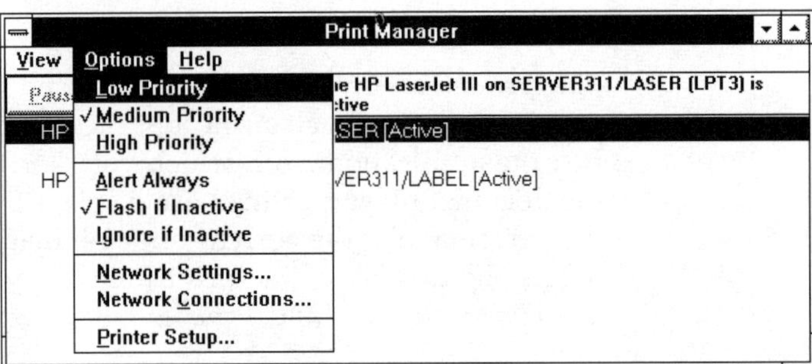

Controlling print to the advantage of the application

Handling print jobs

The three command buttons below the Print Manager's menu bar can be used to modify the processing of the current print job. To stop the print job that's currently printing, click the Pause button.

After selecting the printer you want to stop and clicking this button, the printer stops and the Print Manager displays *is Paused* as the status of the printer.

Resuming a paused print job

To resume printing the current print file, click the Resume button.

Deleting a print job

If you notice that you're printing a document that you don't want to print, you can remove this print job from the print queue by selecting it and clicking the Delete button. If you exit the Print Manager without printing all the files in the queue, the remaining print jobs are deleted.

The Print Manager as an icon

When the Print Manager is displayed as an icon, it automatically closes after the printing process is complete (i.e., after the last file has been printed). However, if the Print Manager is running in an open window, it remains active after the file has been printed.

In this case, the Print Manager behaves like any other Windows application. It displays messages on the screen if an error occurs and prompts you to insert another sheet of paper if you selected Manual Feed.

Controlling Print Manager

Use the following commands from the *Options* menu to control the Print Manager: *Alert Always*, *Flash if Inactive*, and *Ignore if Inactive*.

If you select *Alert Always*, the Print Manager immediately displays a message on the screen whenever user input is needed. *Flash if Inactive* specifies that the icon or title bar of an inactive Print Manager window will flash and emit a warning beep when necessary.

The *Ignore if Inactive* command suppresses all information from the Print Manager when errors occur and the Print Manager is only an icon or an inactive window on the screen. In this case, the printer stops and you won't know what happened until you activate Print Manager again.

17. Write

Microsoft Windows Write provides various features that can help with almost all your daily writing tasks. The Windows Clipboard simplifies certain functions, such as deleting, copying, and moving text.

In this chapter we'll discuss how Write interacts with the Clipboard and TrueType fonts, how to format text using the formatting ruler and tabs, how to print a document using Write, and how to exchange data between Paintbrush, Word for Windows, and Write.

17.1 The Write Window

Write is a word processor that can be used for everyday writing tasks. Write also allows data exchange with other Windows applications. If you're familiar with Word for Windows, you'll notice that, except for a few features (e.g., print merging), Write has many of the features included in Word for Windows.

Double-click the Write icon in the Accessories window.

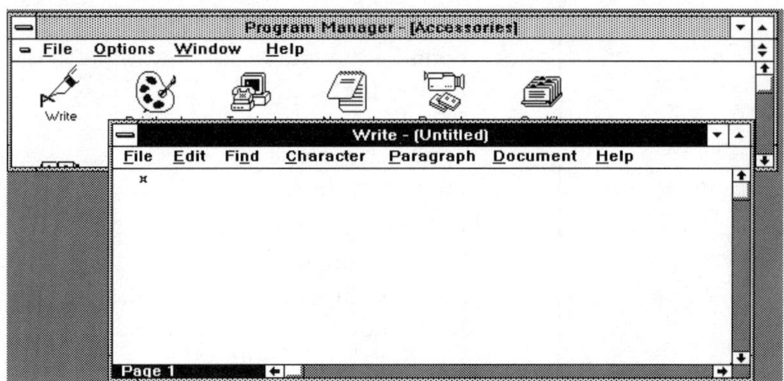

Elements of the Write window

The title bar displays the program name and the name of the currently active document. If you're working on a new document and haven't assigned a name to it yet, "*Untitled*" appears in the title bar. Once you assign a name using *Save* or *Save As...*, it will appear in the title bar.

Page breaks

The page number of the current page is displayed in the lower-left corner of the Write window. The current settings for page margins and format will determine when a new page begins. The » character in the left margin indicates a page break. The left margin is called the *selection area*, because the user can select parts of a document using the mouse. When you move the mouse pointer into the selection area, it changes to an arrow that slants to the upper-right.

The formatting ruler

The formatting ruler can be displayed by selecting *Ruler On* in the *Document* menu. By using the mouse you can manipulate the appropriate icons and markers on the ruler to format paragraphs.

17.2 Creating a Document

When you start Write, an empty writing area appears. You can immediately begin to create your document. The size of the area available for typing depends on the *Page Layout...* settings, which are located in the *Document* menu. The page margins are specified here. The desired page orientation (portrait or landscape) is selected in the *Print Setup...* dialog box. Before starting to type a document, you should adjust these settings as needed since they affect the text format and the printed layout.

The Page Layout

Under *Page Layout...* you can set the size of the margins between the text and the edges of a printed page. Before entering the settings, determine which unit of measurement is currently active (*inch* or *cm*). The selected unit applies to all measurements in Write. This unit is indicated on the ruler.

To assign the first page of your document a page number other than 1, use the *Start Page Numbers At:* text box (see later in this chapter for more information on page number assignment).

Portrait and landscape orientation

The page format is set using *Print Setup...* from the *File* menu. In the dialog box that appears you can choose between *portrait* and *landscape* orientation. Depending on the type of printer, various page sizes can also be selected. The margins specified for a Write document are measured relative to the physical dimensions of the page as defined by these formatting selections.

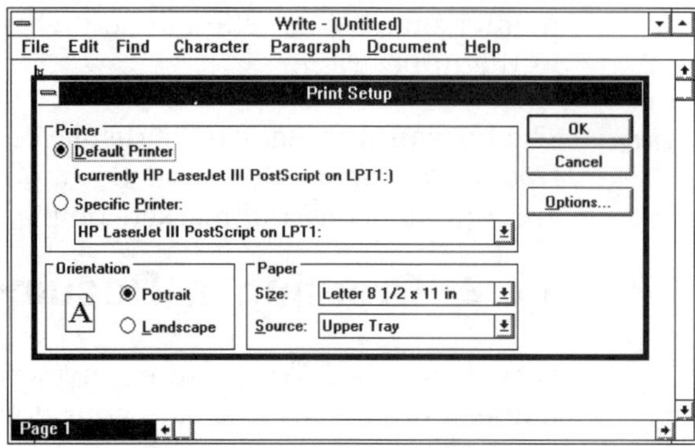

Setting the page format

Entering text

Write begins with an empty screen so that you can immediately begin to type your document. As you type, notice that when a word no longer fits at the end of the current line, it automatically moves to the start of the next line. This process is called *word wrapping*. The number of characters that fit on a line is determined by the size of the margins defined for the page. All the entered text is assigned to one paragraph until you press Enter. To enter a blank line, simply press Enter again. A blank line is treated as a separate paragraph.

Practice text

To experiment with Write, type the following text, including the errors:

Dear Mr. Russmann,

In spite of the current high demand for my pygmy quial, I muft return the recent orderrr you sent me of Abacus QuailFeed. After discovering my Sales Manager recently skipped off with my spouse and most of my quial, I discovered that I owe you for no less than two unpaid orders. Please contact the following organization for the $1200.00 I owe you:

The Online House Bank - A Division of Angst S & L

Acct. No.: 2345678

Keyword: Quial

I thank you for your time, and await your response.

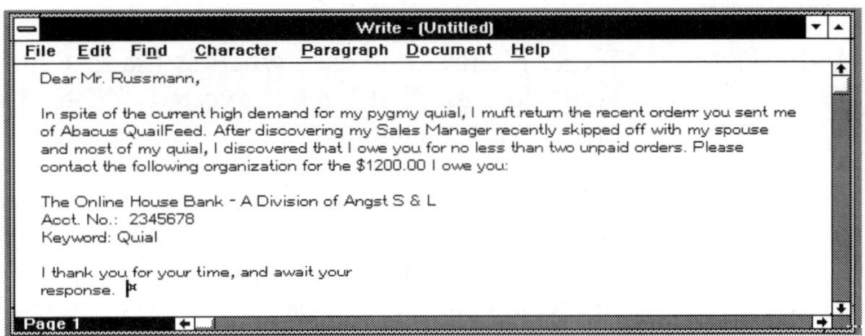

Text display in Write

17.3 Saving a Document

You should save your text at regular intervals. This stores all the changes you've made since the previous save, and prevents any significant data loss in the event of a power outage or system crash. When entering or changing extensive sections of a text, you should save after every page. The *Save* command is located in the *File* menu.

You can assign the *Save* command to a function key by creating a macro.

Save

If you've just started a new document, only a temporary file name has been used internally. Above the menu bar you'll see the word "*Untitled*" where the file name usually appears. In this case, the commands *Save* and *Save As...* are identical.

When either one of these commands is activated, you'll be asked to enter a file name. Try to use meaningful names when naming files, especially text files, so that you can identify the files without activating them. You don't have to enter a file name extension. All Write files are automatically given the .WRI extension. For our example, use the name QUAIL.WRI and press Enter.

Making a backup copy

When you click on the *Backup* box in the *File/Save As...* dialog box, Write generates a copy of your file with a .BKP extension before each actual save. This copy reflects the status of the current Write file when it was last saved (i.e., before the most recent changes). If you later need to revert to the previous version, simply load the backup file.

It's easier to change the system file in Write if the *Text Only* option from the *Save File as Type:* list box in the *Save As...* dialog box is active. This option deletes all the formatting from the text.

ASCII and ANSI text

When you load an ASCII file containing certain characters into Write, the program asks whether the text should be converted to Write format. If it isn't converted, Write displays black blocks instead of the characters.

This phenomenon occurs because Word and Windows use different character sets. Word (like many other non-Windows programs) uses the *extended ASCII* (American Standard Code for Information Interchange) character set. This was originally a 7-bit character set comprised of 128 characters, which didn't include foreign characters. Extended ASCII is an 8-bit code set of 256 characters, which includes the foreign characters.

The *ANSI* (American National Standards Institute) character set is a standardized coding method for screen output and keyboard input. All Windows applications use this character set.

When assigning file names, remember that Windows usually refers to the directory from which it was started. If you work with numerous text files, you should organize them according to subdirectories. In this case, you must activate the appropriate subdirectory before saving a file.

Once a file name has been assigned, you can perform subsequent saves with the *Save* command from the *File* menu. The program will then store the text immediately without asking for a file name. It simply assumes the current file.

Occasionally you'll want to base a new text on an existing one and still keep the old one in its original form. In this case, you must use the *Save As...* command to store the revised version under a new file name. If you save it under the old name, the previous version will be overwritten.

17.4 Selecting Characters and Paragraphs

Before correcting the errors in our practice text, you should understand a procedure that's important to cutting, copying, and pasting text. This procedure involves selecting a certain portion of text, which is designated as a block. The command you activate will affect this block of text.

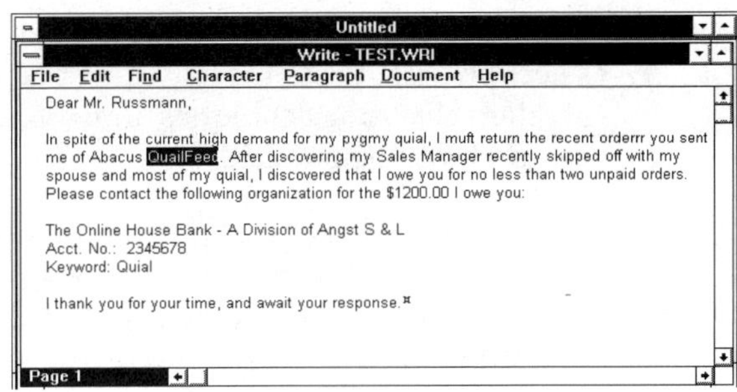

Selecting text is the basis of formatting

Place the mouse pointer on the word *QuailFeed* in the second line of the second paragraph. A double-click displays the word in inverse video (white on black). Try doing this with other words. You'll see that this technique always selects only an individual word.

Now place the mouse pointer to the left of the word *QuailFeed* and press and hold the mouse button. Drag the mouse pointer to the end of the line and release the mouse button. The entire line is selected.

Selecting multiple portions of a text

In the same way you can select several lines by dragging the mouse pointer up or down. Don't be afraid to experiment with this technique.

Now place the mouse pointer to the left of the first line of the first paragraph. The mouse pointer changes to an arrow that slants to the right. As we mentioned earlier, this area is called the selection area.

Click once to select the entire line. To select several consecutive lines, drag the pointer down to the last line of the section you want to select.

Try another method of selecting an area between two random points. Position the mouse pointer in front of the word *current* and click once. Now place the pointer after the word *that* in the fourth line of the first paragraph. Press the Shift key and click again. The entire area is selected.

The selection area

This also works in the selection area except that only entire lines or paragraphs can be selected. To select a paragraph, move to the selection area next to the paragraph to be selected and double-click the mouse button.

Selecting the entire document

To select the entire document, move the mouse pointer to the selection area, press the Ctrl key, and click once. Experiment with all the selection techniques until you're familiar with them and can perform them quickly.

Selecting with the keyboard

You can select text without the mouse by using the keyboard as follows: Using the cursor keys, position the insertion point at the beginning of the area to be selected. Hold down the Shift key and press the → cursor key. The text is selected as the mouse pointer moves. If you press the ↑ key, part of the previous line is also selected. The selection ends at the position where the → key was last pressed.

17.5 Editing Functions in Write

Delete

It's easy to delete text in Write. Position the insertion point before the middle *r* in the word *orderrr*. Press the Del key to delete the *r* to the left of the insertion point. The rest of the line automatically shifts back one position to the left. Now press Backspace to delete the *r* to the right of the insertion point. The remainder of the line again shifts one position to the left.

Deleting text

It's also easy to delete larger portions of your document, such as several letters, words, or even paragraphs.

Select the phrase *After discovering my Sales Manager recently skipped off with my spouse and most of my quial,* (including the space following the comma). Now select the *Edit* menu and the *Cut* command. This cuts the selected text and the remaining text shifts to close the gap. You could achieve almost the same effect by selecting an area and pressing the Del key. The difference between the two methods is that the *Cut* command stores the cut text in the Clipboard, while the Del key completely deletes the text.

Undoing a command

Before continuing with the delete function, try the following. Select the *Edit* menu again and select the *Undo* command. This restores the sentence to its original form. *Undo* cancels the last command that was executed. If you cannot undo that command, the *Undo* menu item appears ghosted (gray). When this occurs, you must make the correction manually.

17.6 Copying and Moving Text

Two other block operations that Write can perform on any group of characters, words, or paragraphs are *copying* and *moving* text. When you copy, the text is inserted in the new location but also remains in the original location. If you move text, it's removed from its original location and inserted in the new location.

The Clipboard

The *Cut*, *Copy*, and *Paste* commands in the *Edit* menu are used to perform these tasks. These commands are also assigned key combinations so that they can be accessed quickly.

An example

Move the insertion point to the end of the last paragraph and press Enter. Select the paragraphs that contain the desired text. Move the mouse pointer to the blank line you just created. Press and hold Shift and Alt, and click the mouse. The paragraphs move to the new location. The text below the insertion point moves down to make room for the inserted text.

Create a blank line after the last paragraph of the document by pressing Enter. Select the paragraph that begins with the phrase *I thank you for your time....* Move the mouse pointer to the blank line you just created. Press and hold Shift and Alt, and click once with the mouse. The paragraphs move to the new position. Delete any excess blank lines you may have created.

When using the commands from the menu bar, you must *Cut* the text to be moved. This places it on the Clipboard. Then *Paste* it from the Clipboard to the new position.

A similar procedure is used to copy text. This time use the *Copy* command to copy the selected text from the document into the Clipboard. In this procedure, the selected text also remains in the document. To insert the text from the Clipboard in a new location, use the *Paste* command.

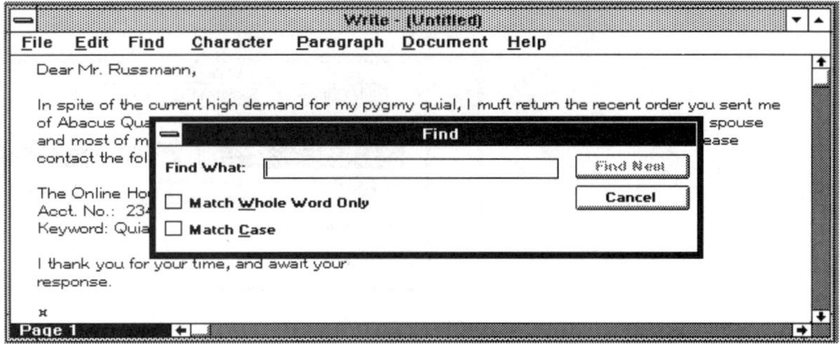

The copy function saves work

Combining files

Often you'll want to combine texts that already exist as files on your hard drive or floppy diskettes. To do this, you must start Write twice and place the two windows next to each other.

Start Write, then adjust the window so that it occupies the left half of the screen. If you don't already have Write running with the QUAIL.WRI file, start Write and open the QUAIL.WRI file.

Select the entire file. Then select the *Copy* command from the *Edit* menu. Now switch to the left window and select *Paste* from the *Edit* menu. You can switch between the two windows, bringing the appropriate source file or files into the right window and copying the desired portions to the left window by using the Clipboard.

17.7 Finding and Replacing Text

As you can see, we deliberately misspelled the word *quail* in the QUAIL.WRI document. Although Write doesn't have a spelling check feature, it does have find and replace capabilities.

Search functions

Activate the *Find* menu and select the *Find...* command. A dialog box, in which you can enter a search text of up to 256 characters, appears.

The question mark is a *wildcard* character (it represents any character) that's used in a search text. For example, if the search text is *?ate,* Write will find *date, late, rate,* etc. To find text that includes spaces, paragraph marks, tabs, and page breaks, the following special characters must be used:

^w	Space
^t	Tab
^p	Paragraph mark
^d	Page break

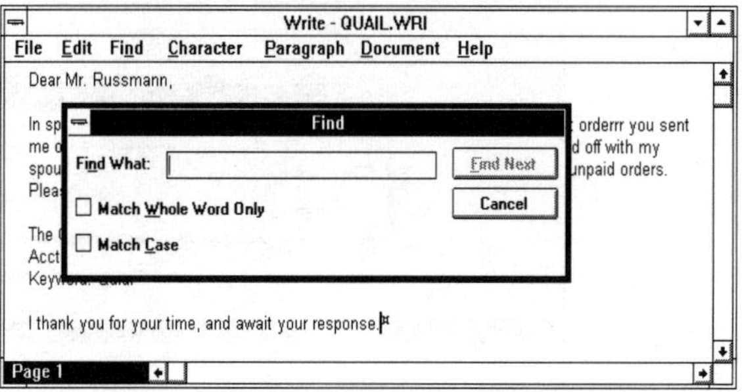

Searching is easy

Activate the *Match Whole Word Only* check box if you want to find the search text only when it occurs as a separate word. Otherwise, for example, the search text *date* will find *dated, candidates,* and *mandate.*

Select *Match Case* to locate only text that has the same capitalization as the search text. For example, if you clicked this check box and the search text is *date*, Write won't find *Date*.

Find Next

The search process begins when you click the Find Next command button. Close the dialog box and edit the found text if desired. You can use the *Repeat Last Find* command to locate any additional occurrences of the text.

Replacing text

The *Replace...* command in the *Find* menu allows you to automatically change the located text.

Enter the appropriate search text (quial) and replacement text (quail), then request the desired action. *Replace* replaces the currently selected text and continues the search. *Replace All* automatically changes every occurrence of the specified text in the document. *Find Next* locates the next occurrence of the text. *Close* ends the process.

17.8 Formatting Characters

As its name implies, *formatting* involves putting characters, paragraphs, or areas of a text into a certain format. There's a difference between character and paragraph formatting. *Character formats*, such as boldface, italics, and various font sizes, affect individual characters. So, every character in a word can have a different character format.

Paragraphs with character formats

Obviously, an entire paragraph can have the same character format. So, the term *paragraph* simply refers to a certain number of characters. However, a *paragraph format* refers to attributes that apply to an entire paragraph. For example, *Left justification* is a paragraph format.

Character formats

To assign a particular format to one or more characters in a document, first you must select the characters. Remember that character formatting applies to only characters that are selected.

Applying character formats

Select the title of the text and open the *Character* menu. The character formats which are available in Write are listed. If you select *Bold, Italic,* or *Underline* the title will be displayed in the corresponding format. *Superscript* and *Subscript* are normally used in scientific writing. These styles represent raised and lowered characters, respectively, in relation to the normal print line and enable you to represent formulas, such as H_2O.

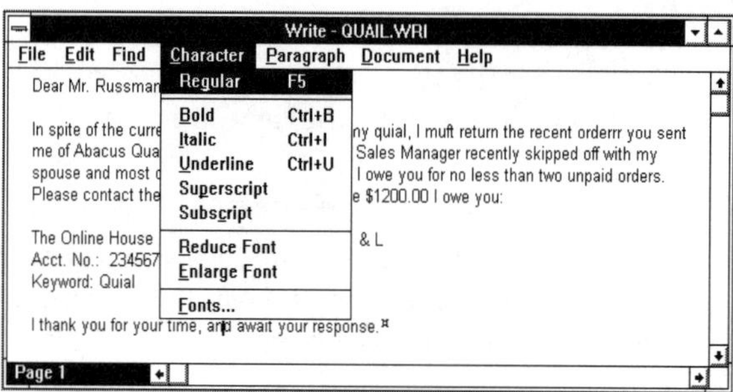

Use the Character menu to format text

To restore normal formatting, select the text again, open the *Character* menu and select *Regular*. You can also select the text and press F5. All special character formatting will be canceled.

Fonts

The *Fonts...* command provides three different types of fonts. To choose the various font types, select the text area, select the *Character* menu, and the *Fonts...* command.

Three font types are used in Write:

Printer fonts

Printer fonts can be produced on the selected printer because they're installed with the printer itself. These are also known as resident or hard fonts. It's important that Windows uses a compatible printer driver. Changing the printer driver may change the number and types of printer fonts that are available.

Fixed screen fonts

These fonts represent the printed text on the screen. Since the number of screen fonts is limited, similar printer fonts are often represented by the same screen font in Write. This also applies to the font size because screen fonts are available only in fixed sizes.

TrueType fonts

TrueType fonts can be set to any size. The desired character sizes can be displayed both on the printer and on the screen. The advantage of TrueType fonts over fixed printer fonts is that characters of every size are computed from a single font file, while each size of printer font has its own file.

Printer fonts are faster

If you use printer fonts, your text will print out faster than with TrueType fonts because the fonts are resident in the printer. Internal calculation isn't needed to generate the desired character.

If you're using a printer with only a few fonts available (e.g., a 9-pin dot matrix), both font types can be printed in graphics mode. Although this improves print quality, the printing speed decreases.

Font families

There are two types of fonts: *proportional* and *non-proportional*. The difference lies in the width of the individual characters. Another basic font distinction is between *serif* and *sans serif*. This relates to the appearance of the characters:

This is a serif font, and so is this, but this is sans serif.

Since these names will change depending on the printer, we'll use the generic font names. The differences between the four basic font groups are as follows:

Courier

Courier is similar to the type found on a typewriter. This font has non-proportional characters. This means that every letter has the same amount of space on the printed line, even though the *i*, for example, is narrower than the *m*. This font is usually listed as Courier and Courier New.

Times Roman

Times Roman is a proportional serif font. Serifs are the small hooks and edges on the characters. This type of font is used in this book. You'll find this font listed under names like Times, Times Roman, Times New Roman, and Tms Rmn.

Helvetica

Helvetica is a proportional sans serif (without serifs) font. It has an unadorned, straight, and smooth style. The headings in this book appear in Helvetica. You'll find this font listed under names like Arial, Univers, and Helvetica.

Symbol

Symbol isn't actually a font type in the same sense as those previously described. It's a different character set that includes many special symbols, such as Greek letters.

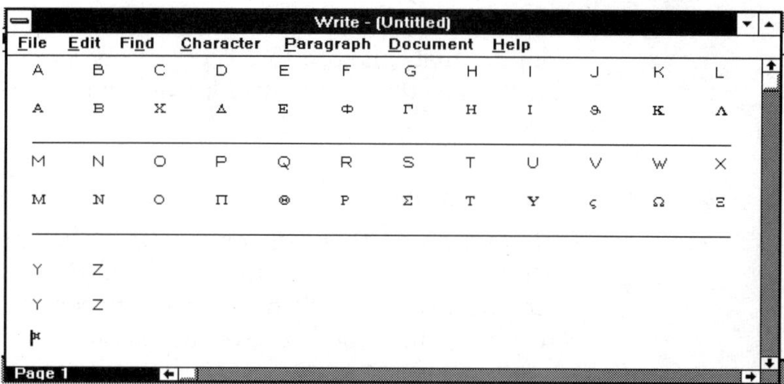

These keys generate the Symbol characters

In Chapter 8 we explained how to load additional font types using the Control Panel. As we mentioned earlier, the number of font types available, except for TrueType fonts, depends on the selected printer. The *Fonts...* command in the *Character* menu lets you choose from the fonts that are available for the current printer.

Changing font height

To change the point size (the height of the letters in a text), select the *Fonts...* command from the *Character* menu. Here you can specify an exact value for the size. The selection list shows the available options.

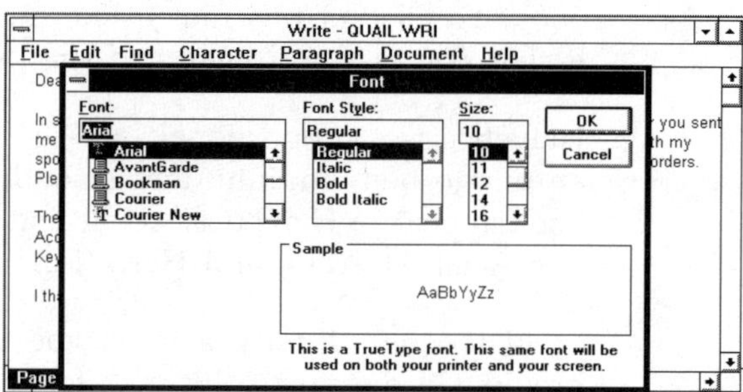

Lots and lots of fonts

Fonts designated with a printer symbol can be generated by the active printer driver. Those indicated with the prefix *TT* are TrueType fonts.

Changing font sizes

Each of the fonts specified here can be assigned another available point size by selecting the appropriate value.

An easier way to change font sizes for selected text is to use the *Reduce Font* and *Enlarge Font* commands in the *Character* menu. These commands change the font according to the next available point size.

17.9 Formatting Paragraphs

Paragraph formatting is always applied to one or more paragraphs. In this case, a paragraph is the area between two paragraph marks.

Pressing Enter defines a paragraph mark. As you type your text, it automatically advances to the next line because of the word wrap feature. Don't press Enter until you want to begin a new paragraph. The cursor then jumps to the start of the next line, and whatever you enter from that point on belongs to the new paragraph until you press Enter again.

Blank lines

When you press Enter twice, you create a blank line (a paragraph without any characters). Unfortunately, unlike Word for Windows, Write doesn't display the paragraph end marks.

Cursor placement in the paragraph

To apply a format to a specific paragraph, first you must select the paragraph. If you select more than one paragraph in succession, the formatting applies to all of them. Since paragraph formatting applies to an entire paragraph, selecting any part of one is equivalent to selecting the entire paragraph. So you only have to place the cursor somewhere within the paragraph to be formatted.

To apply a paragraph format, select the desired paragraph or paragraphs and select the appropriate format from the *Paragraph* menu.

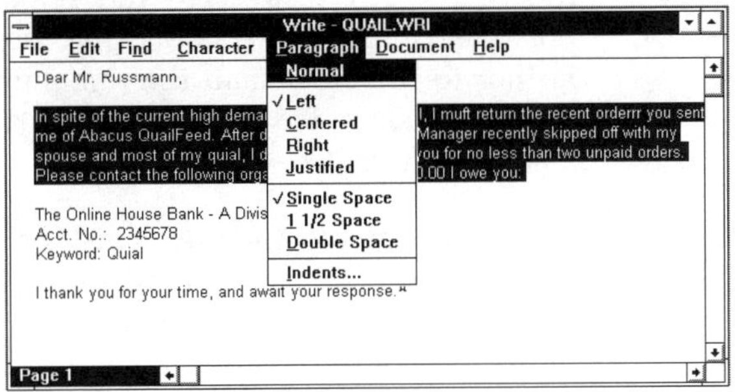

The Paragraph menu items

The following formats are available:

Text alignment

Normal

The selected paragraph is left-justified and single-spaced.

Left

The selected paragraph is left-justified (i.e., text is aligned at the current setting for the left margin). Letters are usually formatted as left-justified.

Centered The selected paragraph is aligned according to an imaginary vertical axis between the left and right margin settings. The first and last character of any given line are located an equal distance from the left and right margins, respectively.

Right The selected paragraph is right-justified. Text is aligned at the current setting for the right margin.

Justified The selected paragraph is aligned at both the left and right margins. This format is normally used in books.

Line spacing

Single Space This is the closest spacing between successive print lines of the selected paragraph.

1 1/2 Space An extra half-line of space separates two successive print lines of the selected paragraph.

Double Space An extra line of space separates two successive print lines of the selected paragraph.

Indentation

The *Indents...* command allows you to specify how many inches or centimeters the selected paragraph should be indented from the current left margin (the *Left Indent:* text box) and from the current right margin (*Right Indent:* text box). The first line can also be indented with respect to the remainder of the paragraph. A positive value in the *First Line:* text box indents the first line farther to the right than the remaining lines. Entering a negative value will extended the first line farther to the left. This is called a hanging indent.

Numbering paragraphs Many documents include a list of numbered paragraphs. The numbers appear as hanging indents before the text. To create numbered paragraphs, first type the paragraph number. Then tab to the left indent position for the paragraph. (In our example this will be 1 inch.) Now you can enter the text. The *Indents...* values for this example are *Left Indent:* 1" and *First Line:* -1".

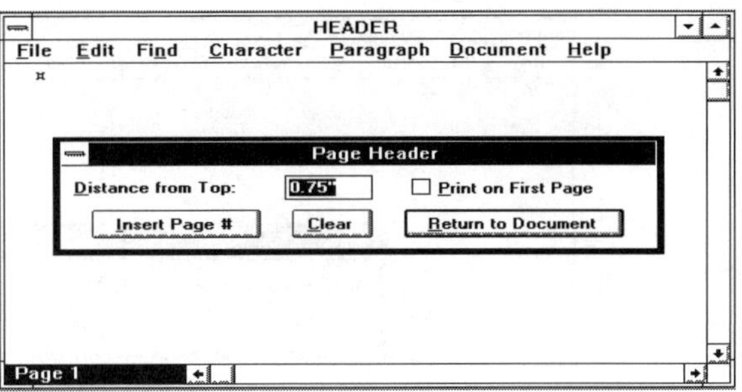

Paragraph formatting

By using this type of formatting, you can emphasize important passages and make your documents look more professional.

Headers and footers

Now we'll discuss formatting features that affect an entire document instead of individual characters or paragraphs. With these features, you can insert headers and footers, including page numbers, into every page of your document.

You can use headers and footers for displaying titles, page numbers, copyright notices, and any text that's repeated throughout a document. Headers and footers are located between the upper and lower text margins and the physical edges of the page. If you use them, be sure that there is enough space for them in the document. To do this, set the text margins accordingly. The following procedure for creating a header also applies to footers.

Remember that headers and footers aren't displayed on the screen. They appear only when the document is printed.

The Header dialog box

To create a header, select the *Header...* command in the *Document* menu. The text of the header is entered separately from the other text and has its own window. In the dialog box, specify the desired distance from the top of the page and whether the header should appear on the first page of your document. You may not want the header to appear on this page if it's a title page or a table of contents.

The header is entered and formatted like other text. Click the document window to close the dialog box and then type the header. When you're finished, activate the dialog box and select the appropriate action.

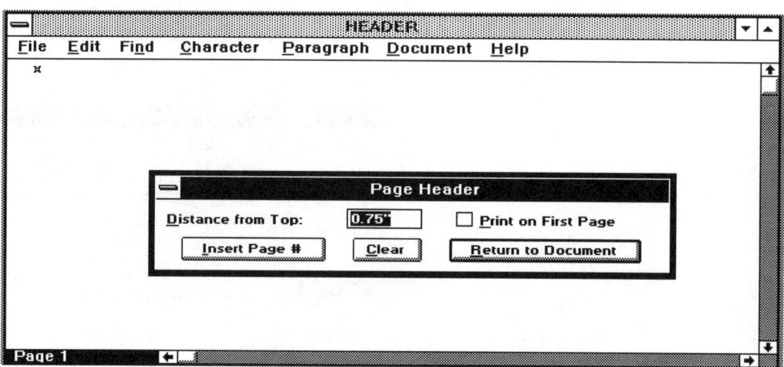

The Header dialog box

Clear deletes the header. *Return to Document* saves the header and restores the normal document window.

Inserting page numbers

It's easy to number your document pages automatically. The page number is expressed as a variable in either a header or footer.

The page number variable

To insert page numbers in a header, select the *Header...* command in the *Document* menu. Click *Insert Page #* in the dialog box. The word (page) appears in the text area. This indicates a variable that's replaced by the actual page number when your document is printed. This procedure can also be used to insert page numbers in a footer.

You can format page numbers by applying the desired formatting features (font, size, etc.) to the (page) field just as you would to non-variable text.

Setting the starting page

For a large project, such as a book, you should make each chapter a separate document. In this case, you should number the pages consecutively from one document to the next. The *Page Layout...* dialog box under the *Document* menu lets you specify the starting page number for a document. For example, if the first chapter ends with page 4, type 5 in the *Start Page Numbers At:* text box for the second chapter. The current page number appears in the lower-left corner of the Write window.

17.10 The Formatting Ruler

There's an even easier way to format paragraphs with the mouse in Write. The formatting ruler represents the various line spacing and alignment formats as icons. Simply select the paragraph you want to format and click the appropriate icon. The new format is immediately applied. This ruler is also helpful because it indicates the scale of measurement across the page.

To display the formatting ruler, select the *Ruler On* command in the *Document* menu.

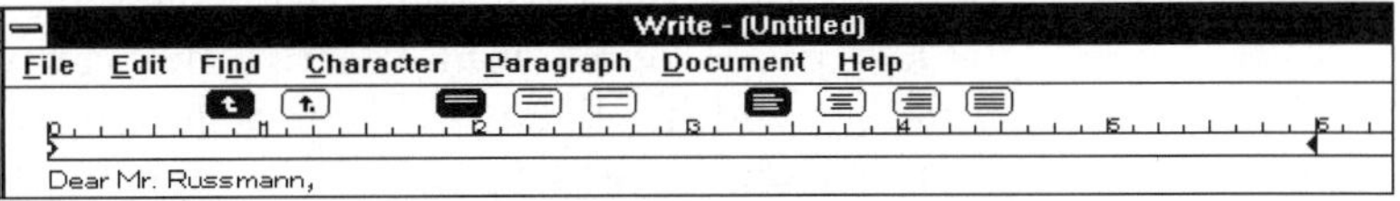

The formatting ruler is a convenient helper

The ruler icons

The first two icons represent tab stops. The left icon indicates a left-aligned tab and the right one a decimal tab. We'll discuss tabs in more detail in the next chapter. The three icons in the center represent the line spacing options (single spacing, 1 1/2, and double spacing). The last four icons represent paragraph alignment. Again from left to right, the formats are left-aligned, centered, right-aligned, and justified.

Using indent markers

Symbols called *indent markers* also appear on the ruler, just below the measurement scale. They show the indentation settings for the current paragraph. Three indent markers are available. Left and right paragraph indentation are indicated by triangular markers at the corresponding positions. The first line indent marker appears as a small dot, which may overlap the left indent marker.

Now try to use the ruler to change paragraph indentation settings. Place the insertion point within the paragraph to be changed and then drag the indent markers to new positions. Practice changing all three settings and observe the results.

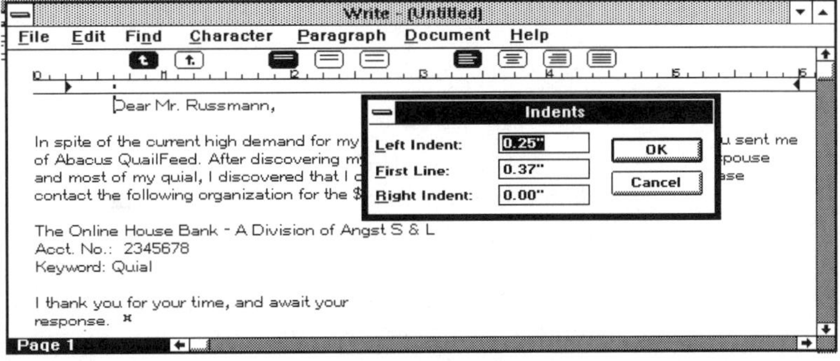

The indent markers

The new settings will be displayed in the *Indents...* dialog box.

17.11 Tab Stops

Tab stops define columns of text at fixed intervals across a page. This is especially useful for creating tables and lists. When using a non-proportional font, such as Courier, you can separate columns by typing spaces between them. However, it's difficult to do this with a proportional font because the various characters have different widths. Even if you can get your columns to line up perfectly on the screen, they'll be uneven when you print them. This occurs because the printer and screen fonts aren't actually identical.

Defining tab stops

To solve this problem, Write provides two kinds of tab stops. The normal tab defines a left-alignment position for text. A decimal tab is used to align columns of numbers with decimal points.

Open a new document. To set tab positions, select the *Tabs...* command in the *Document* menu. The *Tabs* dialog box allows you to specify up to twelve tab positions. Enter 1.5 in the first *Positions:* text box. Press Tab and enter 4 in the second *Positions:* text box. This sets the tabs in inches.

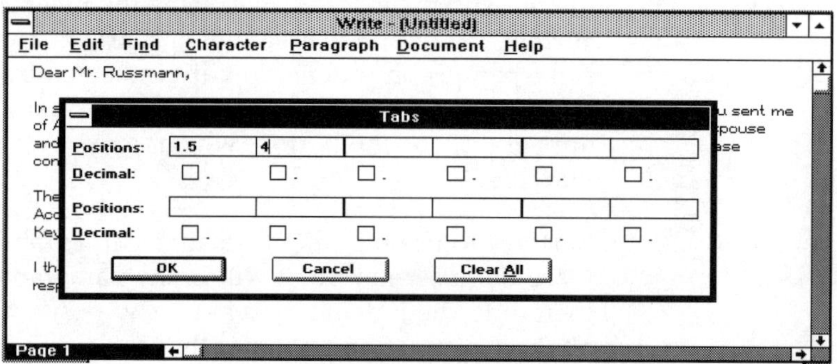

Defining tab stops

A table created with tabs

Once this is done, the tab settings will apply to the entire document. Individual paragraphs cannot be assigned their own tab settings.

To see the tab positions, display the formatting ruler. The tabs are represented as arrows under the measurement scale.

Tabs and the formatting ruler

You can also change tab settings by manipulating the arrow icons on the formatting ruler. To reposition an existing tab, simply drag the arrow to the left or right. To create an additional tab, first click the appropriate icon above the ruler. The tab on the left is a normal left-aligned tab and the other (with a dot) is a decimal tab. Then click the desired position on the ruler scale.

Now you can use your tabs to create a table. For example, we entered the following information in Write:

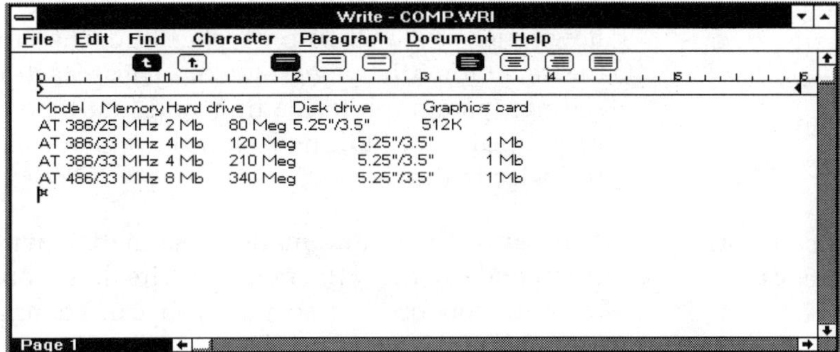

However, we want the information to appear in a table. By using the arrow icons on the formatting ruler, we can display the information in a table. Make certain to press Tab between each column in the table.

Once this is done, the table will appear similar to the following:

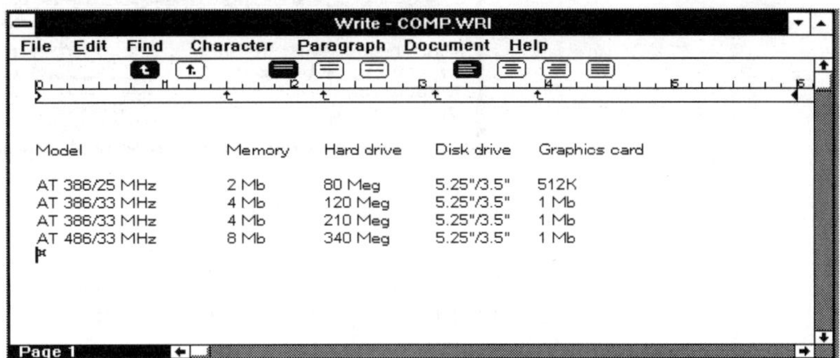

A completed table in Write

Clearing tabs

To erase all tab settings, select *Clear All* in the *Tabs* dialog box and click the OK button. You can also delete individual settings by clicking the appropriate position and pressing the Del key.

With the ruler, you can clear tab settings by dragging individual tab arrows up or down off the ruler until they disappear.

17.12 Printer Output

How text is printed on the page depends on the specified page margins and formatting features.

Defining page breaks

Write automatically repaginates (breaks into pages) any document that is longer than one page. Several factors determine how much text will fit on a page and, therefore, how Write will create automatic page breaks. These factors include margin settings, paragraph formatting, and font type and size. Automatic page breaks are indicated with the » character, which appears in the selection area.

Moving page breaks

You can activate automatic repagination with the *Repaginate...* command in the *File* menu. Write lets you interact with the repagination process so that you can change breaks that were inserted by the program. To use this option, activate *Confirm Page Breaks* in the *Repaginate* dialog box.

At each automatic page break, you're asked to confirm the break or reposition it. You can move the page break up. However, since the minimum lower margin cannot be removed, you can lower the page break only if you've already raised it.

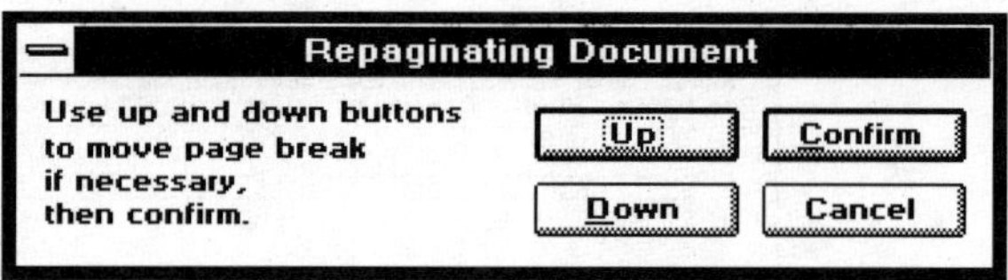

Confirming page breaks

You can also insert manual page breaks anywhere in your document. Simply place the insertion point at the desired location and press Ctrl + Enter. A manual page break appears as a dotted line across the screen.

You must also tell Write what type of paper you're using, the type of paper feed (e.g., continuous), and the desired orientation (portrait or landscape). This is done with *Print Setup...* under the *File* menu.

Starting to print

To start printing, select *Print...* in the *File* menu. A dialog box asks for the *Print Range*. *All* prints the entire document, *Selection* prints only selected text, and *Pages* prints the specified pages.

Printing part of a document

If you want to print only a certain portion of your document, Write lets you specify a range of pages. To use this option, click on the *Pages* option button. Enter the *From:* (first) and *To:* (last) page numbers of the range to be printed. You can also use the *Selection* option button, which prints only the text that's selected in the document.

If the area you want to print isn't located on the current pages, you may want to reposition the page breaks temporarily. For example, suppose that you need to see the last few lines of one page and the beginning of the next. Instead of printing two full pages, you can insert manual page breaks before and after the desired passage. These page breaks can be removed after printing. You can also select only the paragraphs you want to print and click the *Selection* option button in the dialog box.

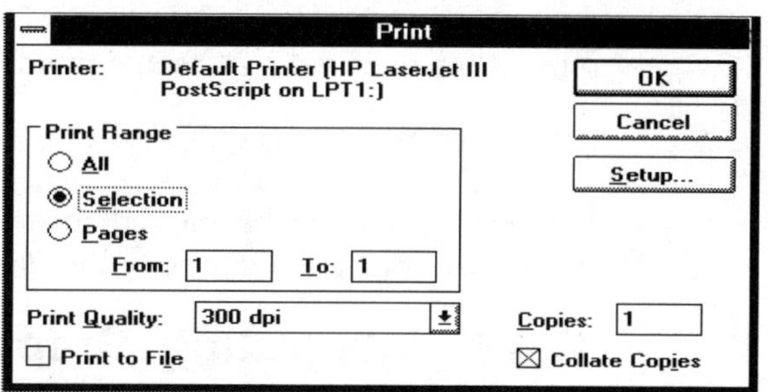

Printing selections

Setting print quality

The quality of the printed output varies depending on the printer. This especially applies to graphics printing. Quality depends on the resolution of graphic output, which is measured in dots per inch. This also affects the printing of text, since TrueType fonts, for example, are printed on dot matrix printers in graphics mode. Usually, a higher resolution means better print quality but slower printing speed. You can choose the desired *Print Quality* in the *Print* dialog box. Only resolutions that are supported by the currently selected printer driver are listed.

Making copies

You can print multiple copies of your document by specifying the appropriate number in the *Copies:* text box of the *Print* dialog box. Some printers support collation of copies. This means that the first copy of the complete document will print first, followed by the second complete copy, etc. Without collation, all copies of a specific page are printed together.

Printing errors

If you encounter problems when printing, there may be several causes. Determine whether the printer is switched on, is online, and has paper. Also verify that you're using the correct port and printer driver. If you need to install a new driver, save your text and close Write. Then run the Control Panel from the *Main* window.

Printing on another printer

If you want to print your document on a printer that's connected to a different computer, you must use that printer's driver to print your text. This ensures that you're using the correct fonts and formatting capabilities. Don't forget to switch back to your own printer driver when you're finished.

Creating print files

If Windows isn't installed on the computer from which you want to print, use the Control Panel to direct the printer driver to *a file* instead of a physical port. Then activate the *Print...* command on your own computer. You'll be prompted for a file name. Then the document will be written to the file with all the necessary formatting and control characters. This file can be printed on the other computer by the DOS command:

```
COPY <PRNTFILE> LPT1:
```

If the output must be passed to a file with the current printer driver, you must activate only the *Print to File* check box.

17.13 Integrating Graphics

You can use graphics to enhance your documents and clarify information. Write offers several ways to incorporate graphic objects, which include pictures, screen snapshots, and spreadsheet tables.

Usually, any element that can be placed on the Clipboard can be inserted into a Write document. The Clipboard provides capabilities for modifying the graphic format. Once the graphic is placed in a document, only the position and size can be changed.

The OLE principle

Graphic objects can also be *embedded* in a document by using the principle of Object Linking and Embedding (OLE), which is available under Windows 3.1. In this procedure, an object created in an application that supports embedding (such as Excel or Paintbrush) is inserted into your Write document, along with instructions about the object and its source application. The object and instructions become a physical part of the document.

Later you can change the object from within Write by double-clicking it. Write opens a window from the source application and loads the object into it, so that you can make the desired changes. After saving your changes, close the application. You're automatically returned to Write, where the object has been replaced with the updated version.

Dynamic Data Exchange

Another way to incorporate information into Write documents from other sources is through Dynamic Data Exchange (DDE). This procedure logically links data from a supporting application (the source) to your document (the destination), but the data itself isn't physically placed in the destination. Changes made to the source are applied automatically to the destination or when you manually request them in Write.

See Chapter 14 for more information on OLE and DDE.

Pasting graphics from the Clipboard

A graphic (e.g., a Paintbrush picture) must be copied to the Clipboard before it can be pasted into a document. Select the item in the source application and place it in the Clipboard by selecting the *Copy* command from the *Edit* menu. This procedure is the same in all Windows applications. Pressing the Prt Sc key copies the entire screen to the Clipboard.

In your Write document, move the cursor to the place where you want to insert the graphic. Select *Paste* from the *Edit* menu.

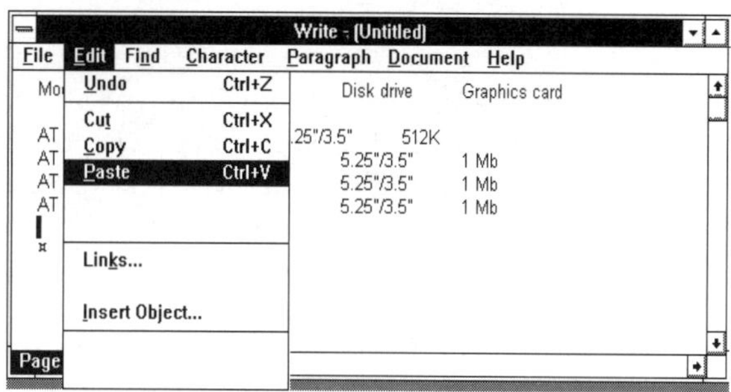

Using the Paste command to insert a graphic from the Clipboard

The graphic will appear in your document and any subsequent text will be moved down.

Pasting graphic formats

The *Paste Special...* command lets you define the format in which the object must be inserted. The available formats are the same as the ones that can be changed in the Clipboard. This is a fast way to specify the format without going through the Clipboard.

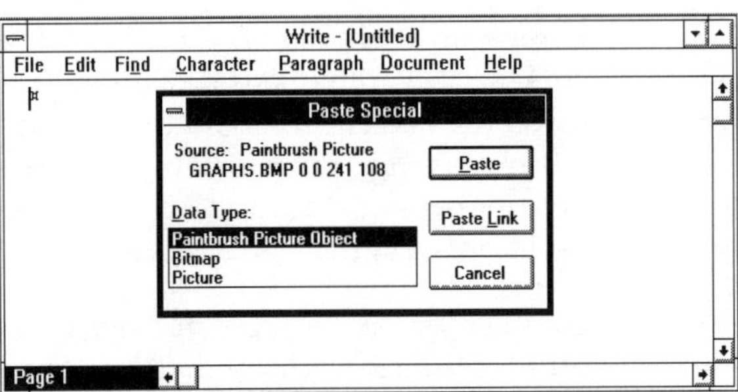

Changing the format of a pasted graphic

Using paragraph formats

Once a graphic is inserted using the Clipboard, it belongs to your document and is no longer linked to its source. If you want to edit it, you must cut it, edit it in the server application, and paste it again with the Clipboard.

Repositioning graphics

A graphic's position, size, and alignment can be changed in Write. First select the graphic by clicking it with the mouse. When you select a graphic, it's inverted on the screen, similar to selected text. The graphic can now be handled like a normal paragraph. It can be copied or moved with the *Cut, Paste,* or *Copy* commands and aligned with left, right, or centered paragraph formatting.

Move Picture in the *Edit* menu allows you to position the selected graphic horizontally. Use the mouse or the arrow keys to move the cursor; the graphic will follow. If you're using the keyboard to move the picture, press Enter to lock the picture into position. To move the graphic down, simply insert blank lines above it.

Resizing graphics

To change the dimensions of a graphic, use the *Size Picture* command in the *Edit* menu. Use the mouse (without pressing the mouse button) or the arrow keys to move the cursor to a side or corner of the graphic frame. As you continue moving past this point, the frame will expand accordingly. When it reaches the size you want, click the mouse button or press Enter. Notice that you can adjust the height and width separately. You must retain the original proportions to avoid distorting the graphic.

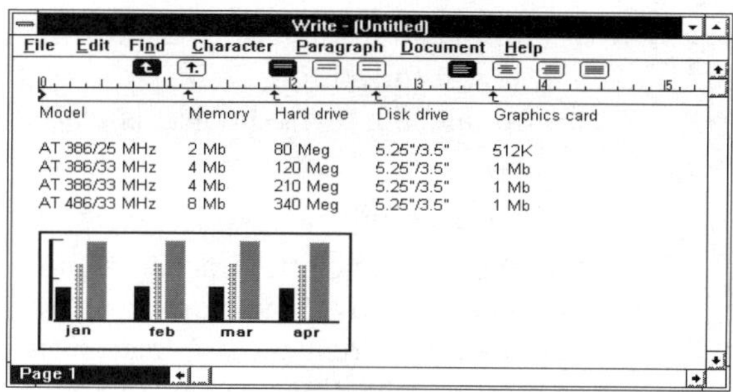

Inserted and formatted graphics

Embedding objects

When you insert an object, which includes instructions about its source application, into your document, the object can later be changed at any time. Besides the additional capabilities we'll now describe, all the formatting options discussed in the previous section are also available for embedded objects.

To embed an object, select the *Insert Object...* command. You now have a selection of programs that support the OLE concept.

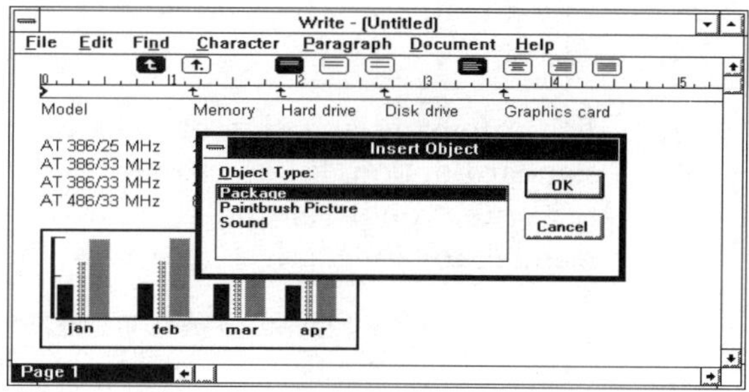

Choosing an application for creating an object

The application you select will be opened and you can create an object or load one that already exists. This could be, for example, a Paintbrush drawing, Excel worksheet, or Object Manager package. With the *Exit* command, the application is closed and the object is embedded at the current cursor position in the Write document.

Changing an object

To change an object, double-click it with the mouse. Or use the keyboard to select it and choose the command *...Object*. This command's complete name depends on the object's source application.

The application then opens and the object is automatically loaded and ready for editing. When you exit the application and confirm the update, the revised object is placed in your document.

Creating links

Linking is a way of cross-referencing information from one file to another. The information resides only in its original source application. When the application is changed, any reference to it in other applications can be changed automatically. You can also choose to update a particular reference only when you request it.

To create a link, you must be in an application that supports the linking process. Excel is an example of such an application. To link an Excel spreadsheet to a Write document, select the desired data in Excel and copy it to the Clipboard. (Under Excel an embedded object can also be linked. This provides all the possibilities of both features.)

Linking with Excel

In Write, move the cursor where you want to insert the spreadsheet. Use the *Paste Link...* command to establish the link between the Excel file and the Write file. Before doing this, be sure that both files have been saved. If your Excel spreadsheet is only a temporary file and is later deleted, the link will obviously be lost.

Updating links

The automatic updating of links when a source is changed is the standard option. If you change the table in Excel and switch back to Write, you'll see the changes in your document. To specify manual updating, select *Links* from the *Edit* menu.

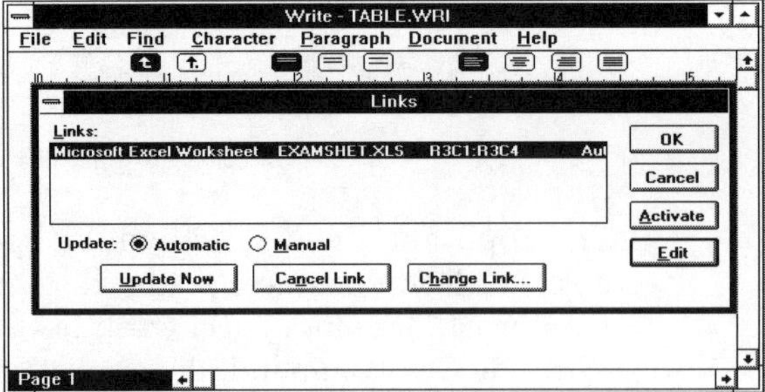

Updating links

All links contained in the document appear in the dialog box. For a selected link, you can specify either *Automatic* or *Manual* update.

If you've specified manual update, the Update Now button applies any source changes to the destination document. If the source name has been changed, click on the Change Link... command button and enter the new name.

When you select *Cancel Link,* the information remains in your document but can no longer be updated from the source because the link is broken.

17.14 Processing Other Formats

In this section you'll find information that you'll need to process Word for DOS files in Write or vice versa.

Reading Word files

Word provides true word processing capabilities, such as print merging, hyphenation, and a thesaurus. Unfortunately it's more difficult to use than Write, which is completely Windows-compatible and extremely user-friendly. So, each program has its own advantages and disadvantages. Most likely you'll want to exchange your files between these programs.

Determining the available fonts

Before exchanging data between Word and Write, remember that each program has its own fonts. For example, suppose that you load a Word file into Write, which doesn't recognize the Word file's fonts. These fonts are automatically converted into a Write-specific font (e.g., Tms Rmn).

Let's try to load a formatted Word document. Start Write and select *Open* from the *File* menu. Enter the full file name of the Word document in the dialog window. When you click the OK button, the following appears:

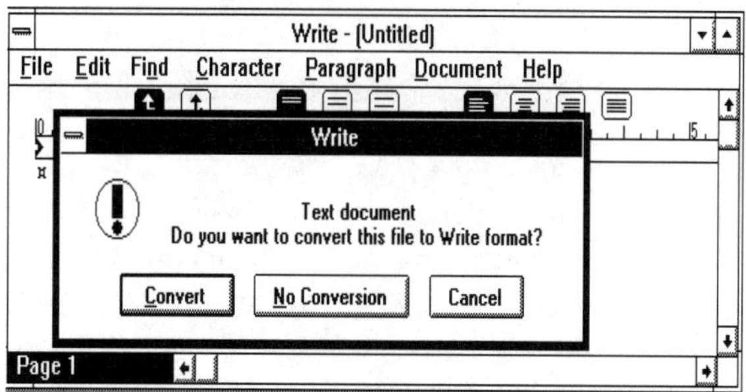

Converting a Word file

You must either convert the document, load the file without converting it, or cancel your command. Click the Convert button. The text is converted from Word format to a Write format and appears on the screen.

Selecting conversion type

When you open an unformatted Word file, you can either convert the file, not convert it, or cancel the command. You should convert the file if it was created outside the Windows environment. Otherwise, some characters, such as the German umlauts, won't be translated correctly. Don't convert if the text was created under Windows.

Some special Word features that aren't recognized and supported by Write will be lost in the conversion process. The following is a brief list of what is and is not converted.

Features converted from Word

Converted:

```
Paragraph formats
Paragraph end marks
Boldface
Italics
Underline
Superscript
Subscript
Some footnote elements
Tabs
```

Not converted:

```
Automatically inserted page numbers
Margin settings
Section formatting
Headers and Footers
Line spacing (triple- and higher become double-spaced)
Strikethrough
Double underline
Large type (as a formatting function)
Protected intervals
Automatic hyphenation
Style sheets
```

You can change the formatting in Word style sheets to direct formatting so that, during the conversion to Write format, the formatting is preserved. To do this, select your entire text from within Word. In the *Format/Character...* menu, choose a character format that isn't used in your text (e.g., strikethrough). From this menu, choose *No* in the corresponding field. Now when you close this dialog box, the character formatting of the style sheet will be converted to direct formatting.

Converting printer formats

You must use the same procedure for paragraphs. In the *Format/Paragraph...* menu, select a paragraph format that isn't used in your text and select *No* in the corresponding field. The paragraph formatting of the template is converted to direct formatting. Now you can save the document and load it to Write.

From Write to Word for DOS

Finally, we'll briefly describe how to use your Write files in Word. Open the file in Write and remove any graphics (Word cannot process these). Then select *Save As...* from the *File* menu. From the *Save File as Type:* list box, select the *Word for DOS (*.DOC)* option. This converts the document to Word format. When you open the document in Word, paragraph and text formatting are present and you can use all Word functions on your text.

If you select the *Word for DOS/Txt Only* option, the document's formatting is deleted.

18. Paintbrush

Drawing with Paintbrush

Paintbrush is an excellent drawing program for creating color graphics. The actual drawing is done with the left mouse button. Place the drawing tool on the drawing area by pressing this button and then move the tool around by moving the mouse.

The drawing tools

A professional drawing is more than a simple sketch. Paintbrush offers various tools and patterns that help you create different types of drawings. For example, you can use cutout tools, an airbrush, erasers, a paint roller, brushes, curves, and lines.

Viewing your drawing

When you load an existing drawing into Paintbrush, only a portion of the entire drawing area is displayed on the screen. A color palette and toolbox occupy part of the available drawing area. You can remove either or both of these to enlarge the drawing surface. The *View/View Picture* command removes other elements of the window. Only the drawing itself remains, as it would appear when printed or saved. From the *View* menu, you can *Zoom Out* to get a complete overview of your drawing or *Zoom In* to enlarge a smaller section for detailed work.

Text processing

Paintbrush lets you add text to your drawing in a variety of fonts, styles, and sizes. The attributes of your Paintbrush text must be set before the text is added. Once it's pasted into your drawing, text is displayed and manipulated as a bitmapped graphic; it can no longer be changed as in a traditional word processing application.

Additional functions

The *Pick* menu lets you flip, invert, or tilt a defined cutout (i.e., an area selected with the Scissors or Pick tool).

Making a screen copy

It's often useful to make a copy of a Windows screen that can be incorporated into another application, such as a word processor document. Press the Prt Sc key on your keyboard. This copies the entire screen image to the Clipboard. You can then paste the image into Paintbrush for editing. You can even automate the process with macros (see Chapter 23 for information on the Recorder, and on creating macros).

Printing

You can easily print part or all of your drawing on the installed printer. You can choose from a variety of layout options, including headers and footers.

18.1 The Paintbrush Window

Microsoft's decision to include the Paintbrush application in Windows 3.0 set a standard that has become widely accepted in the area of pixel-oriented graphics. Although the Windows version is slightly scaled down from the standard version of Paintbrush (e.g., it doesn't have a scanning function), Windows Paintbrush fulfills all the essential requirements of a complete drawing and painting package.

Paintbrush formats

Besides the Paintbrush-specific .PCX format, which is widely used in the DOS world, Paintbrush recognizes the Microsoft Windows Paint (.MSP) format available under Windows Versions 1.x and 2.x. So the graphics formats are compatible throughout all Windows versions. Bitmap (.BMP) format is the default Paintbrush format for Windows 3.1.

Creating custom backgrounds

The bitmap format is suitable for creating your own Windows backgrounds. The Windows wallpaper patterns, which are located in the Control Panel, consist exclusively of bitmap files. If you want to customize your Windows screens, you can create your own wallpaper design in Paintbrush as a bitmap file.

The Paintbrush icon, which is located in the *Accessories* group, is a painter's palette. Although the Paint program in older versions of Windows worked only in monochrome mode even if the system had a VGA card, Paintbrush provides brilliant colors. To start Paintbrush, double-click the palette icon.

The Paintbrush window is divided into five areas.

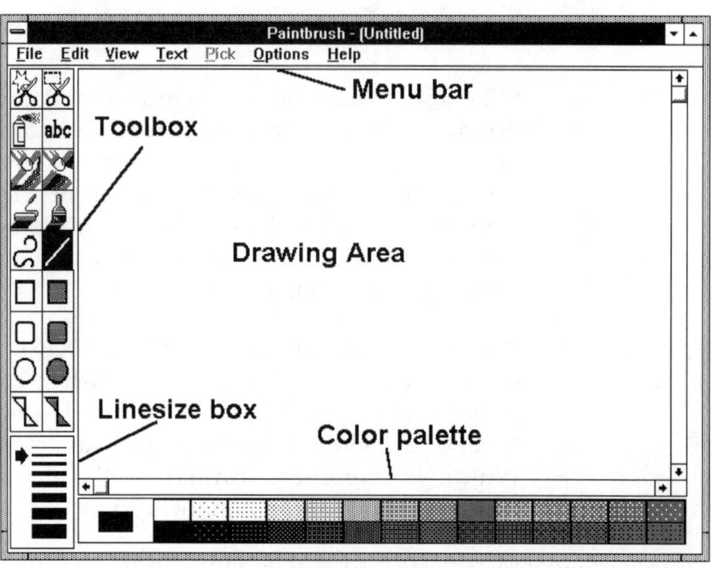

Elements of the Paintbrush screen

Drawing area

The Paintbrush components

The central element of the window is the drawing area. Depending on the size settings used, this area may not display the entire drawing surface. In this case, scroll bars are displayed along the right and bottom edges. These are used to display more of the drawing surface.

Menu bar

Above the drawing area is the menu bar, which contains all the Paintbrush commands.

Color palette

At the bottom of the screen is the color palette, which contains 28 colors. The current color, which is used for all the figures and text you apply to your drawing, is displayed to the left of the color palette. You can change the current color at any time by double-clicking the desired color within the palette. You can even mix colors to create your own custom palette.

Toolbox

Just as an artist needs brush, pencil, and charcoal, a Paintbrush user needs the tools displayed to the left of the drawing area to sketch, shape, and erase. This part of the window is called the Toolbox.

Linesizes

In the lower-left corner of the Paintbrush window is the Linesize box, which displays the available widths for the drawing stroke or outline of the various tools and shapes. An arrow indicates the currently selected width.

☞ From the keyboard you can select any area by using the Tab key.

18.2 Drawing with Paintbrush

A practice picture

After starting Paintbrush, an empty drawing area appears on the screen. The default selections (thin line, black color, and brush tool) are automatically activated. Inside the drawing area the mouse pointer is displayed as a dot whose size is determined by the current drawing width. You can adjust this size by using the Linesize box. The mouse pointer, or brush in this case, is moved with the mouse or direction keys. Actually you should use a combination of both of these methods; use the mouse for coarser movements and the direction keys for finer ones.

The brush

The actual drawing is done with the left mouse button. Pressing this button places the imaginary brush on the canvas and allows you to guide the brush with the mouse. However, you must have a very steady hand to draw precise lines with the mouse. For more accurate results, use the keyboard. Press the Ins key to place the brush on the drawing surface. Now draw a line by moving the brush with the direction keys.

For example, if you press the → key twice, the brush moves two pixels to the right. If you hold down the → key, the brush continues drawing while moving at an increased speed.

Release the Ins key to lift the brush from the canvas. Practice using the brush so that you become familiar with the basic drawing procedure.

The same technique is used in working with the other Paintbrush tools.

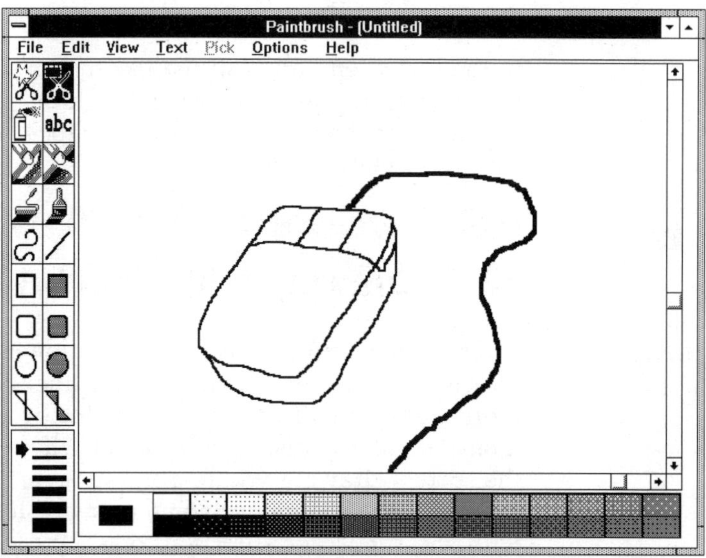

A freehand drawing of a mouse

Cursor coordinates

For exact positioning of the brush or any other tool, you can use the *Cursor Position* command from the *View* menu. This opens a small window that displays the current X and Y coordinates of the cursor position, relative to the upper-left corner of the drawing area. The window can be repositioned as desired and closed using its Control menu when the coordinates are no longer needed.

18.3 The Drawing Tools

Paintbrush provides various tools and shapes to help you create professional-looking artwork. To select a tool, click on it in the Toolbox. The tool's background color changes to indicate that it's active. The mouse pointer changes, depending on the item selected. The following tools and shapes are available in the Toolbox:

Tools and shapes

Scissors

The Scissors tool is used to select a cutout that must be moved or copied to another area of your drawing. The Scissors tool draws a line around the desired cutout. The area can then be dragged with the mouse or placed in the Clipboard with the *Cut* command from the *Edit* menu. Unlike the Pick or selection rectangle described later, the Scissors can cut an irregular contour around an object. So, this tool is especially useful for deleting items from your drawing.

Pick (selection rectangle)

This tool is used with the *Cut* and *Copy* commands to place rectangular cutouts into the Clipboard. These cutouts are then inserted into another location with the *Paste* command. To mark a cutout, drag the mouse from the upper-left corner to the lower-right corner of the desired area. A rectangular frame appears to mark the selected area. You can quickly and easily make selections with this tool.

Airbrush

This tool sprays the drawing area with the current color. Press the mouse button to apply the spray and move the mouse to direct it. If you click the mouse once in place, a circular pattern of colored pixels, similar to a checkerboard, appears. The slower you drag the mouse, the closer together these patterns appear and, therefore, the denser the spray.

Text Tool

This tool works in with the *Text* menu to insert text into a drawing. First select a font in the appropriate size and style and then position the cursor in the drawing area where you want to place your text. When you click the mouse, the cursor changes to a blinking vertical line. Now you can begin typing the text. You can change the text as long as the blinking cursor is active. Once you click to a new position, the letters can no longer be edited as text. To delete or change them you must edit them as pixel graphics like any other object in your drawing.

Color Eraser

This tool erases a color from a drawing or pattern. From the Color Palette, select the color you want to erase. Then drag the mouse over the desired area. Only the selected color is removed (i.e., replaced with the background color). Everything else in the drawing area remains unchanged.

Eraser

The Eraser clears all colors and patterns from the drawing area. Hold down the mouse button and move the cursor over the area to be erased. The selected linesizewidth determines the size of the Eraser cursor and the precision of the erasing process. To erase with the maximum precision, zoom to the pixel level and paint the individual pixels with the background color.

Paint Roller

The Paint Roller fills a solid object or enclosed background area with the currently selected color. Position the cursor within the area to be filled and press the mouse button to apply the color.

Brush

Use the Brush to paint strokes of the currently selected drawing width and color.

Curve

With this tool, draw curved lines of the selected width and color. Mark the starting point with the mouse button and drag the mouse to the other endpoint of the desired curve. A straight line will connect the two endpoints. Then release the button, move the mouse to the apex of the desired curve, and press the button again. The connecting line will curve toward the apex. Clicking the left mouse button a second time will fix the curve. Before the curve is fixed, you can erase it by clicking the right mouse button. You can also move the mouse pointer at this time to create an S-curve instead of erasing the line.

Line

This tool draws a straight line between two points. Anchor the starting point by pressing the left mouse button and dragging the pointer to the other endpoint of the desired line. Releasing the mouse button fixes the connecting line. Since a line, like everything else in your drawing, consists of pixels, angled lines may produce "jaggies" (jagged edges in the line).

Shapes

The shape tools produce the contours of various geometric figures to help you draw outlines and solid shapes. The shape figures are the Box, Rounded Box, Circle/Ellipse, and Polygon. As with other drawing tools, the width of the contour line is determined by the currently selected drawing linesizewidth, and its color is determined by the currently selected color. Each of the four available shapes has two variants, which appear in pairs on the Toolbox panel. The left variant produces an outline contour only. The right one fills the outlined shape with the desired color.

Similar to the Line tool, the Box, Rounded Box, and Circle/Ellipse shapes are drawn by dragging the mouse. The Polygon tool works somewhat differently. Use this tool to construct a closed contour consisting of any number of line segments. Place the mouse pointer at an initial starting point and drag to draw the first line segment. Release the mouse button, then drag the pointer to the end of the next line segment.

One click causes the new segment to appear. Continue in this way with the rest of the desired polygon. Double-clicking closes the figure by connecting the last segment to the starting point.

Before closing the contour, you can erase it using the right mouse button.

18.4 Loading and Saving Drawings

Saving a drawing

As we mentioned earlier, Paintbrush starts with an empty drawing area, ready to begin a new drawing or load an existing one for changes. When your drawing is finished it can be saved as usual with the *Save* and *Save As...* commands in the *File* menu. A list box allows you to specify the graphic format to be used for storing your drawing. The *16-color bitmap (BMP)* format is the Windows default. Windows wallpaper, for example, is stored in this format.

If you want to use your drawing as a wallpaper pattern, store it in bitmap format, then use the Control Panel to select it (see Chapter 8). The wallpaper patterns provided with Windows can, like any normal drawing, be opened and edited in Paintbrush.

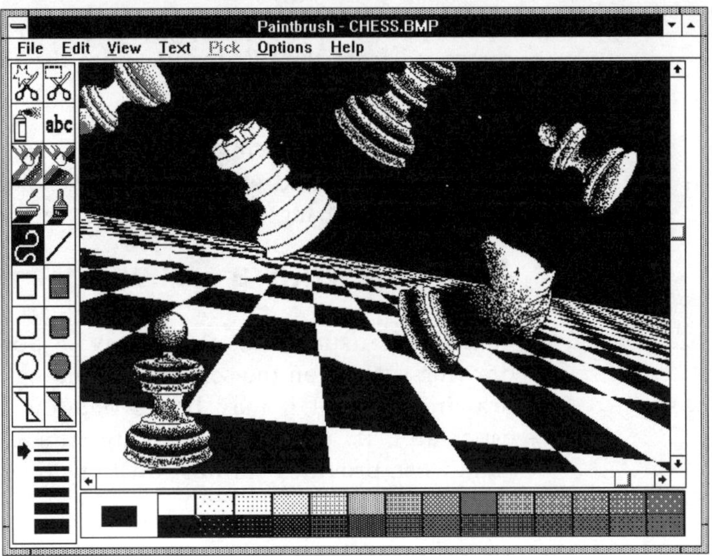

Loading a wallpaper pattern

Interchanging graphics

Some applications require that you save your file in .PCX format. Most standard DOS programs that use graphics can interface with .PCX files. This is the format used by the original Paintbrush program. If you want to place your drawing in a Word document, for example, you should use .PCX format when saving the file. To use a non-standard graphics format, open the *Save File as Type:* list box and select from the available choices, which include .PCX and four bitmap formats.

The Paintbrush formats

The four available bitmap formats are as follows:

Monochrome bitmap

16 Color bitmap

256 Color bitmap

24-bit bitmap

These options determine how colors are represented in your graphics files. The format you choose affects the file size. So the same drawing in *256 Color bitmap* format is about ten times as large as when stored in *Monochrome bitmap* format. Usually the first two formats are suitable for most needs, with *16 Color bitmap* format for graphics that are displayed on a color monitor and *Monochrome bitmap* format for black-and-white graphics.

Loading a Drawing

To load an existing drawing into Paintbrush, choose the *Open...* command from the *File* menu. From the file selection list, choose the file you want to load.

To create a new drawing, choose *New* from the *File* menu. If you select this command when a drawing is loaded, a dialog box lets you save your changes before clearing the drawing area.

18.5 Viewing a Drawing

Paintbrush usually displays only a portion of the available drawing surface on the screen. Depending on the dimensions of a drawing, part of it may be beyond the borders of the screen, especially if you're displaying the Palette and Toolbox. Paintbrush provides various functions that help you display your drawing.

Adjusting the drawing area

To expand the drawing area, remove the Palette or Toolbox using the *View* menu. The currently selected tool and color remain active in this mode so you can continue to work on your drawing. The *View Picture* command from the *View* menu uses the entire screen to display an overall view of the entire drawing. All other elements of the window are removed, including the menu bar. You should use this mode only for viewing or making a screen copy (you cannot edit the drawing in this mode).

Pressing the Prt Sc key copies your drawing to the Clipboard, from which it can be pasted into Write or other applications.

Zooming

The *Zoom In* and *Zoom Out* commands are important for pixel-oriented graphics programs. When you select the *Zoom In* command, a rectangular frame appears in the drawing area. Position the frame around the area to be enlarged and press the mouse button. The framed area expands to fill the entire drawing area and is covered with a grid. The selected rectangle also appears, in its normal size, in the upper-left corner of the drawing area.

The grid separates the enlarged section into individual pixels, which are manipulated separately. This enables you to work on your drawing with precise detail. Click a pixel to paint it with the current color. Only the Brush and Paint Roller can be used in this mode. *Zoom Out* returns the drawing to normal view. Choosing *Zoom Out* from normal view reduces the drawing to give you an overview of the entire image.

18.6 Text Processing

Adding text

To add attractive text elements to your Paintbrush drawings, use all the available Windows fonts. Using Paintbrush to work with text is slightly different from using a word processor. You must determine the desired font attributes beforehand. You cannot change them once you have added the text to your drawing, as you would in a word processor. This is because Paintbrush treats text as graphics, instead of as character strings.

Choosing fonts

Since it's not as easy to change font attributes in a drawing as in a word processor document, think carefully before choosing these attributes. Once the text is converted to graphics, letters become groups of pixels like all the other elements of your drawing.

An example

Select the Text tool from the Toolbox. The cursor is displayed on the drawing surface as a blinking vertical line. Position the line where you want your text to appear and click the mouse button. Notice that all text entered in Paintbrush drawings will remain aligned starting at the cursor position.

Enter a few words or letters. The text is displayed according to the currently selected *Font, Size* and *Style*. You can change these attributes, by using their respective menus, until you click to a new position or select a different tool. These actions permanently fix the text as a graphic element in your drawing, so it can no longer be edited or corrected with the usual word processing features (e.g., the Backspace key). To edit this text, you must first use the graphics tools to cut it out, color over it, or erase it from the drawing, and then retype it.

Using TrueType fonts

The following illustration shows the various styles that are available under the Paintbrush *Text* menu. You can use all the TrueType and fixed screen fonts that are in every Windows application. Printer fonts aren't included because all the text is converted to pixels and printed in graphics mode.

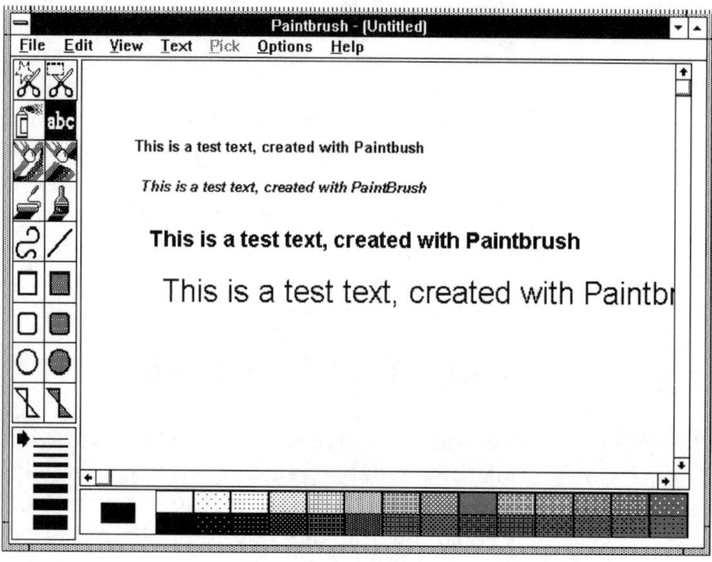

Paintbrush Fonts

Fonts and sizes

When you select a font type, you also specify the particular size that you want to use. These are shown in the *Font* dialog box. A preview area displays examples of the selected type in various sizes. TrueType fonts are scaleable, which means that they are available in almost any point size. Fonts that are listed only in specific point sizes are fixed screen fonts.

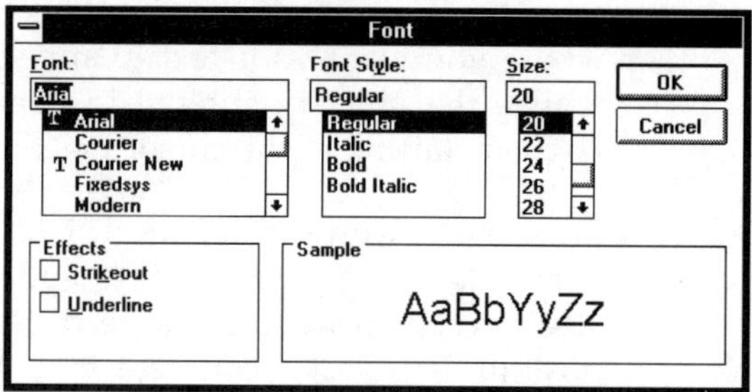

Selecting and defining fonts

Font styles

The font styles available in Paintbrush are the same as those used in Write. With the corresponding commands, you can display text in *Bold, Italic,* or *Underline,* or a combination of these. Also, all the previously mentioned styles can be combined with either the

Shadow or *Outline* command, but not with both. The *Regular* command sets all styles back to their standard settings.

If you want to use certain text attributes or fonts from a different word processor in your drawing, you can try incorporating them using the Clipboard.

18.7 Changing Colors and Line Attributes

The Paintbrush Color Palette contains an array of the most frequently used standard colors. You can design your own combinations if the standard palette isn't suitable. Each color on the currently displayed palette can be modified individually, and any palette combination can be stored under a separate name. So, you can design a variety of palettes for different uses. You can also work on a given drawing with first one palette and then another to utilize additional colors. However, remember that using more than 16 colors requires an expanded format (*256 Color bitmap* format), which means that your file will be several times as large as with 16 colors.

Modifying colors

You can double-click any of the current palette colors to change it. A dialog box with scroll bars for the three color components (red, green, and blue) appears. This also occurs if you select the *Edit Colors...* command from the *Options* menu.

Change the color by scrolling the individual components to mix them in varying degrees. As you make your adjustments, the result is shown to the right. Click OK when you're satisfied with the effect. With the *Save Colors...* command, you can save your custom-mixed color palette in a file for later use. The extension .PAL is automatically appended to such files. Choose *Get Colors...* when you want to use the palette on other drawings.

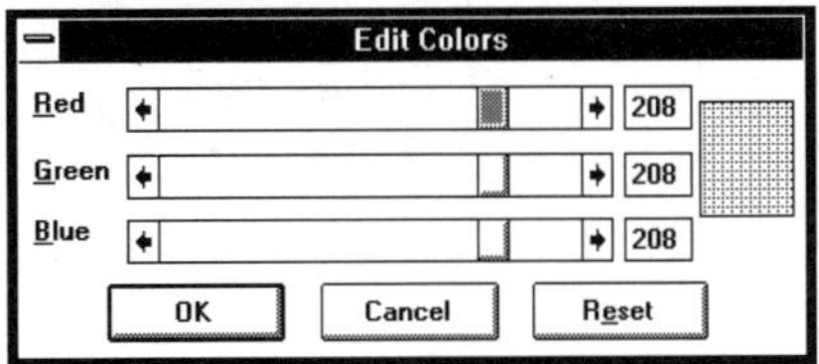

Create your own custom palettes

Brush widths and shapes

Paintbrush provides eight linesize widths, which apply not only to the Brush, but also to other drawing tools. The Brush can also be selected in a variety of shapes, which can be accessed via the *Brush Shapes* dialog box under the *Options* menu. Besides the standard square shape, you may choose from an octagon or lines at various angles. Experiment with the different brush shapes to determine what effects you can create.

18.8 Working with the Clipboard

In the chapter on the word processing program Write, we described how Paintbrush graphics can be inserted into other Windows applications by using the Clipboard. This allows you to illustrate your Write documents, for example, with the drawings you create in Paintbrush. It's also possible to take existing graphics from other programs and place them in Paintbrush so that they can be edited.

The Clipboard

The Clipboard uses the Scissors and Pick tools from the Toolbox. When either of these is used to select an area within the drawing, the *Edit* menu's *Cut, Copy,* and *Paste* commands become available. These commands are the same in all Windows applications.

Transferring complete drawings

The *Copy To...* and *Paste From...* commands provide another alternative. After selecting these commands, you'll be prompted for a file name. The file you specify replaces the Clipboard, so it can be used as a permanent storage place for graphic elements.

You can save frequently used elements in individual files and insert them, when needed, in new drawings. If you frequently create graphics, which contain the same elements, you should develop a symbol library to save time.

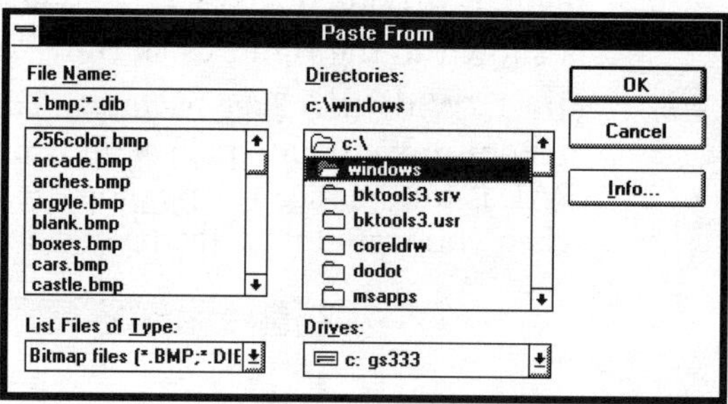

Pasting symbols

Undoing mistakes

An especially useful function is located in the *Edit* menu. The *Undo* command lets you correct a mistake by removing the effect of the previous action. When an action can no longer be undone, this command is displayed as ghosted and cannot be used.

18.9 Additional Functions

Paintbrush provides additional functions that affect only the areas of a drawing that are selected with the Scissors or Pick.

These areas are called cutouts. These functions are located under the *Pick* menu. If an area isn't currently selected, the menu cannot be accessed and will appear dimmed.

Pick

Pick menu commands affect only the area that's currently selected with the Scissors or Pick. The effects of these commands can depend on the proportions of the selected area surrounding the object. For example, the *Flip Horizontal* command flips the selected cutout symmetrically from side to side along its central axis, while *Flip Vertical* flips it upside down. The farther an object is from the center of the cutout, the more it will be displaced by these functions.

Another function for editing a selected area is *Inverse*.. This command changes the foreground color within the selected area to the background color and vice versa.

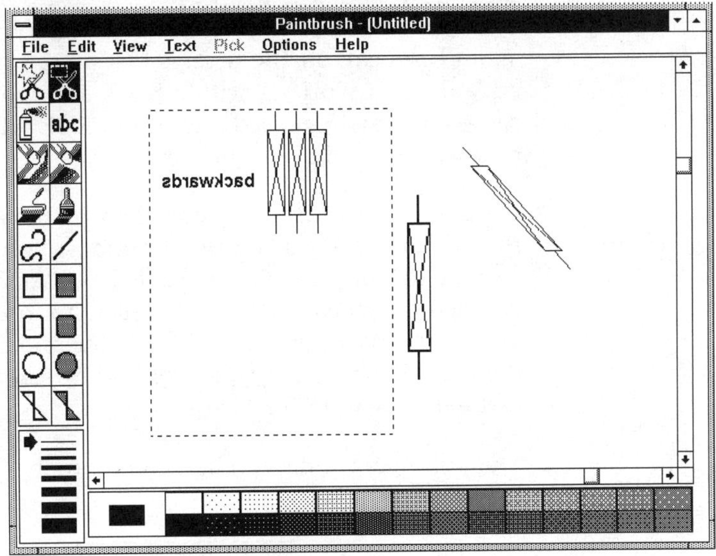

Objects that have been altered using the Pick menu

The *Tilt* and *Shrink + Grow* commands offer additional options for manipulating objects. Again, a cutout area must first be defined, as previously explained. Then, if the *Shrink + Grow* command is activated, a rectangle can be drawn wherever you want the selected cutout to be placed in the drawing area.

The dimensions of the cutout are adjusted to fit the rectangle. Drawing a smaller rectangle shrinks the cutout and drawing a larger one enlarges it. When this command is activated, a checkmark appears next to it in the menu. The function remains active until it's selected again and the checkmark is removed.

The *Tilt* command operates in a similar way. When this command is checked, the selected cutout can be skewed to any angle. To do this, tilt the rectangle after it's drawn at the new location.

The *Clear* command in the *Pick* menu can be used in conjunction with either *Tilt* or *Shrink + Grow*. This clears the original cutout area when the corresponding function is executed.

18.10 The Layout of the Drawing Area

Defining the drawing layout

Several commands can be used to define the layout of the drawing area. The surface itself is a rectangle whose dimensions can be specified in the *Height* and *Width* fields of the *Image Attributes* dialog box.

When specifying these dimensions, observe the currently active measuring unit. The available choices are inches *(in)*, centimeters *(cm)*, and pixels *(pels)*. You can also specify whether your drawing should appear on the screen in *Colors* or *Black and White*. The advantage of working with a black and white display is that you see your drawing exactly as it will look when printed, unless, of course, you have a color printer.

Headers and footers

Other layout features are controlled by the *Page Setup...* options in the *File* menu. By using these options, you can add headers and footers to your drawings. Each has a maximum length of 256 characters, which is usually much more than can actually fit within the page borders. The header and footer entry boxes are quite small. Use the Home, End, and direction keys to scroll longer text entries within the boxes.

The following control characters can be used in headers and footers:

&d	Enter the current system date
&t	Enter the current system time
&f	Enter the current file name
&p	Enter the current page number
&l	Left align text that follows
&r	Right align text that follows
&c	Center text that follows

An example

To display the page number at the right margin, the date at the left, and a title in the center, format a header as follows:

```
&l&d&cTitle&r&p
```

The remaining fields in the *Page Setup* dialog box are used for setting the page margins. Remember the currently selected unit of measurement.

18.11 Making and Editing a Screen Copy

Taking snapshots

Sometimes you may need to create a screen snapshot, which is a hardcopy image of a screen that can be used in another application, such as a word processor. The illustrations in this book were created in this way by using Windows itself. You no longer need a special hardcopy program to capture and edit screen images. Simply press the Prt Sc key. If you must capture numerous screens in separate files, automate this procedure by using the Recorder.

Using Monochrome display

If you want to print your screen images in black and white, you may want to set your display color scheme to monochrome before generating the screens to be copied. This produces greater contrast between the adjacent areas than by simply choosing the *Black and White* setting for *Image Attributes* in Paintbrush. Although the *Black and White* setting will convert colors to gray scale values, this usually results in some loss of contrast because different colors may have the same gray value.

First run your application to create the desired screen image. Pressing P will capture the entire screen image and copy it to the Clipboard. The Alt + Prt Sc combination copies only the contents of the active window.

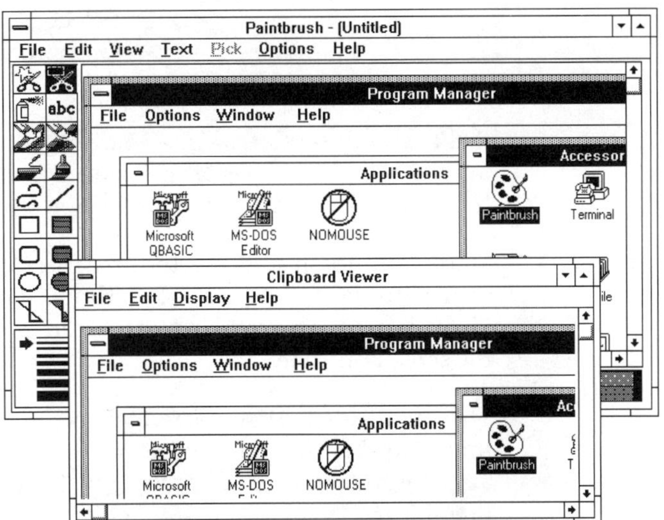

A screen copy on the Clipboard and in Paintbrush

Editing screen images in Paintbrush

To edit the screen image, start Paintbrush and set the units to *pels* under *Image Attributes...* in the *Options* menu. The drawing surface should be set to the same resolution as the graphics card (for our example, this is 640 x 480 pixels). Then select *Zoom Out* from the *View* menu to transfer the screen image file from the Clipboard. Now select the *Paste* command from the *Edit* menu twice.

The screen image will appear in Paintbrush, covered by a grid. When you select *Zoom Out* from the *View* menu, the picture returns to full size and the grid disappears. The image can now be saved as a .PCX file and accessed from many other applications.

Automating with macros

With the help of the Recorder, we assigned two macros to function keys to automate this process. First the image units are changed to pixels and the storage format option is changed to .PCX manually.

Macro 1 (assigned to F3):	Call Paintbrush (by icon) Open *View* menu Select *Zoom Out* Open *Edit* menu Select *Paste* Reopen *Edit* menu Reselect *Paste* Open *View* menu Select *Zoom In* Open *File* menu Select *Save As...*
Macro 2 (assigned to F4)	Open *File* menu Select *New* Open Control menu Select *Minimize*

Before recording the macros, you should place the Paintbrush icon in the lower-left corner of the screen. This is important because the first macro later starts the application found at this position.

Executing the macros

Start Paintbrush and set the image units to pixels and the file format to .PCX. Minimize Paintbrush and place this icon in the lower-left corner of the screen. Load the macro file and initiate the screen printing.

Then activate the first macro by pressing F3. The image is placed into Paintbrush and you're asked for a file name. Type the appropriate name and press Enter. Run the second macro by pressing F4 to clear the drawing area and minimize Paintbrush to an icon in the lower-left corner. Now you can start the next screen capture.

18.12 Printing

Before printing, you should activate *Print Setup...* to ensure that the correct printer and printer options are specified. This is the same procedure used for other Windows applications. You must do this only if you always use the same printer.

Printer output

When you're ready to start printing, select *Print...* from the *File* menu. Before the drawing is sent to the Print Manager, a dialog box allows you to specify certain printing parameters.

One of these parameters specifies the quality of output desired, which affects the printing speed. You can select either *Draft* for a quick test copy or *Proof* for the finished product. *Proof* uses the highest resolution available for your setup, requiring considerably more time to produce than the *Draft* output.

Printing partial drawings

Another parameter lets you choose whether to print all or only a part of your drawing. If the *Partial* setting is activated, when you begin to print, you'll be asked to frame the area of your drawing you want to print. A *Scaling* parameter in the dialog box can be used to reduce or enlarge the drawing or portion sent to the printer. For example, if you enter 25%, your output is reduced to one-fourth the actual size. You can also enlarge the output.

To print multiple copies, type a number in the *Number of copies* text box.

Finally, the dialog box contains a check box for the *Use Printer Resolution* parameter. This allows you to use the different resolutions supported by the current printer. The higher the printer resolution, the slower but more precise is the output.

19. Notepad

Editing

Notepad provides basic editing features for creating and modifying text files that don't have control characters. Notepad works only with the ANSI character set.

Inserting the Date and Time in a Text

You can easily add the date to your documents by using the Notepad's *Time/Date* command.

Searching for Text Strings

Notepad has a search function that finds a specified string of characters in your text. This is a fast way to find specific information in long documents.

The Time-Log File

You can record your daily activities in a log for future reference. Each time you open your log to record an entry, the current date and time are automatically added.

19.1 Editing Text

Notepad is a basic text editor that can be used to create and change small text files. You can use it to edit all system files (i.e., files containing the ANSI character set) created under Windows. These include, for example, the Windows .INI files. Files in ASCII format (e.g., AUTOEXEC.BAT) should be edited only if they don't contain graphic characters.

When you start Notepad from the Accessories group, an empty notepad appears. You can begin typing text immediately or open an existing text file.

The entry area

Over 1000 characters can be entered on a single line. However, this many characters cannot be displayed within the borders of the screen. As you exceed the display width, the Notepad page scrolls to the left to make room for more characters. Your horizontal position within the Notepad surface is indicated by a scroll bar along the bottom of the window.

Creating line returns

To limit your text to the width of the window, activate the *Word Wrap* command from the *Edit* menu. The program adjusts the line length to fit within the current window borders by inserting "soft" line returns between words as needed. If you resize the window later, the line returns will be repositioned accordingly. So, you can "wrap" the text to fit any size window, so that it's always visible and easily edited. A check next to the *Word Wrap* command indicates that this option is active.

You can also end any line with a fixed or "hard" return by pressing Enter. If the window is later narrowed so that this line is only a few words too long, it will be broken with a soft return and only the remaining few words will appear on the next line. The hard return then places subsequent text on the third line.

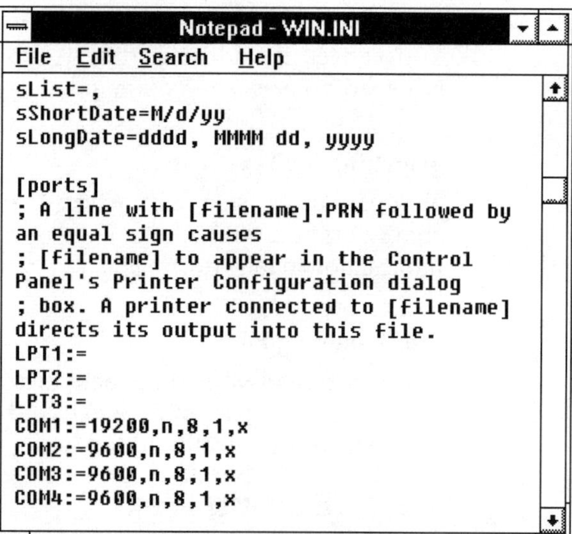

Word wrap in a document

Creating tables and lists

Text is displayed in Notepad by using a nonproportional system font. So, spaces can be used to separate columns in lists or tables.

However, it's much faster to use the Tab key. This indents text by moving the insertion point to a fixed column position.

To exchange text with a second document, simply start a second Notepad window and open both text files simultaneously.

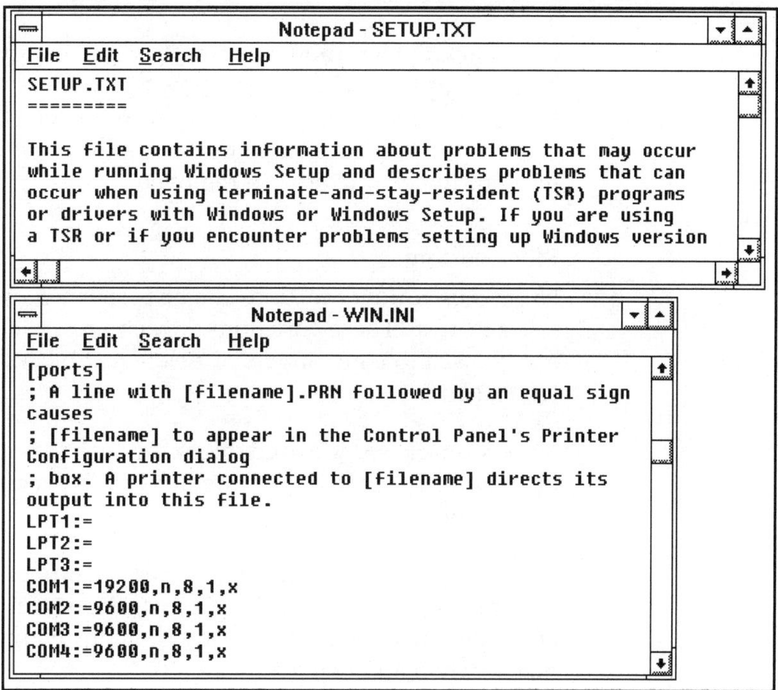

Two Notepads for exchanging text

You can easily transfer any section of text between the documents by using the Clipboard. Select the text to be copied from the first window and activate the *Copy* command from the *Edit* menu. Then activate the second window, move the insertion point to the place where you want to insert the text, and activate *Paste.*

19.2 Editing Functions

Notepad contains all the editing functions that are needed to process text. These functions can be divided into two categories: special keys on the keyboard and commands in the *Edit* menu.

The delete keys

Notepad operates in Insert mode. This means that when you move the insertion point between two characters and start typing (or insert information from the Clipboard), the new data is inserted at the insertion point position. Any text that follows the insertion point is shifted to the right.

To replace a single character, you must delete the original and insert the new one. You can delete characters by using the Del and Backspace keys.

First, click the left mouse button to place the insertion point at the desired position. Then use Backspace to delete the character to the left of the insertion point or Del to delete the character to its right. To delete several characters, simply hold down either key until all the characters are removed.

Block editing

Numerous editing functions can be performed on an entire section of selected text. These functions, which are called block operations, can be used to copy, move, or delete text blocks of any size in your Notepad document.

Simply mark the desired block of text by using the mouse or keyboard. The editing command that's executed will affect the entire block of text.

The *Copy* command from the *Edit* menu places a copy of the selected block in the Clipboard. You can insert this block anywhere in your document by moving the insertion point to the new location and using *Paste*.

If you want to remove the block from its original position before moving it to another location, use the *Cut* command instead of *Copy*.

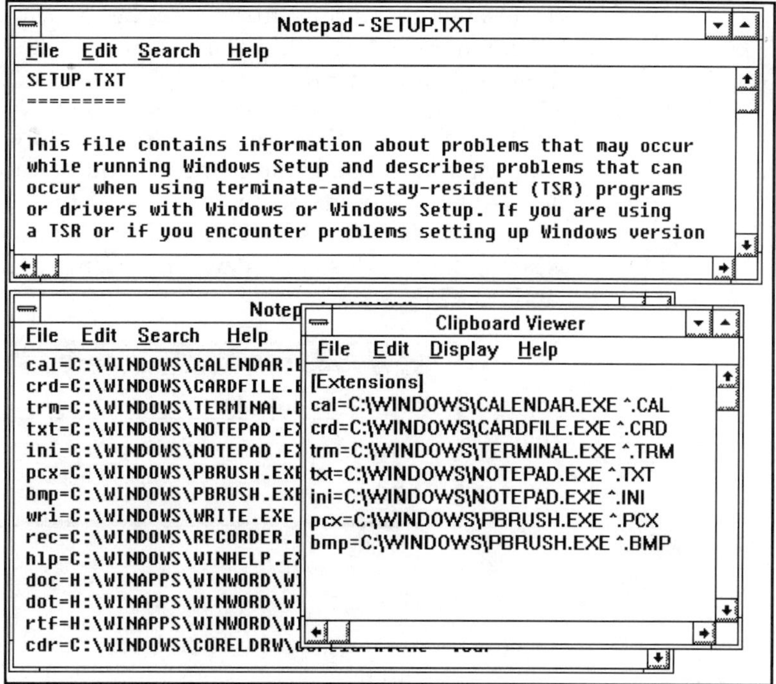

Copying paragraphs with the Clipboard

To delete a block of text, mark the area to be removed and press Del. *Select All* selects the entire document. By using this command, you can easily incorporate an entire text file into another file using the Clipboard.

Undoing the last command

Usually it's possible to cancel an edit operation. To do this, use the *Undo* command from the *Edit* menu. *Undo* removes the effects of the previous command and restores the text to its original condition. If the previous operation cannot be canceled, *Undo* is displayed as dimmed.

19.3 The Search Function

Notepad can search for a particular string of characters within a text. When the search is successful, the located string is displayed in reverse video.

The *Search* menu enables you to locate information in a large document quickly. As you type, you can insert special character sequences to mark places, to which you'll want to return. Then, to locate these places, use these sequences as search text. The search process can be performed either forward or backward within a text.

Initiating the search

To locate a text string, first move the insertion point to the place where the search should begin. Then activate the *Find...* command from the *Search* menu.

In the dialog box that appears, type the word or character string you want to locate. If the search should be case-sensitive (i.e., the located text should match the case of the search text), activate the *Match Case* check box. If you don't specify a case-sensitive search, the search string "date", for example, would return "Date" and "DATE".

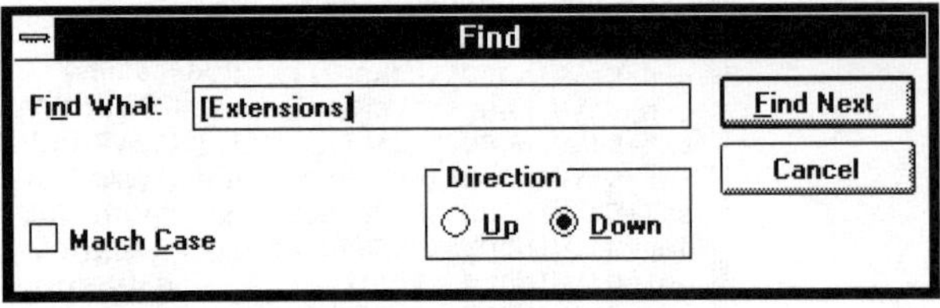

The Find dialog box

The search process

Once started, the search function returns the first occurrence of the specified search text. This means that a search for the word "date" would also find "outdated".

Use *Find Next* if you want to know whether your text contains other occurrences of the search text.

Setting the search direction

The search function usually proceeds forward from the insertion point position to the end of your document. You can reverse the direction by selecting the *Up* option button in the *Find* dialog box.

19.4 Including the Time and Date

With Notepad, you can easily add the date and time to your documents. This helps you determine whether the information in a document is current.

Current time

To insert the current time and date into your document, move the insertion point to the place where you want to insert this information and select *Time/Date* from the *Edit* menu.

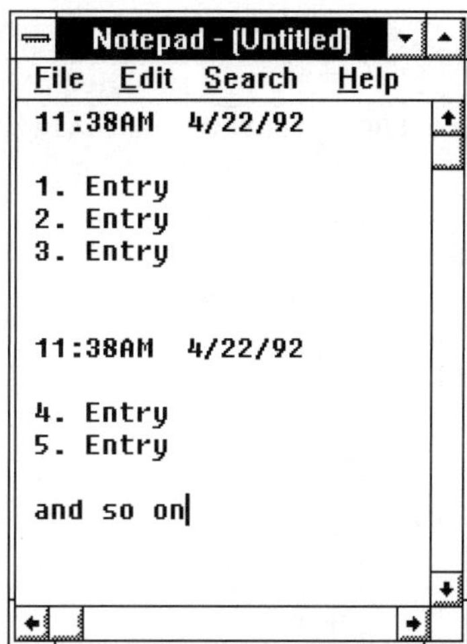

Entering the Time and Date in a Notepad file

The current system time and date are inserted in your document. If they are incorrect, you can reset them by using the Control Panel. If your computer doesn't have a realtime clock, this must be done each time you start the computer.

Changing the display format

The format used to represent time and date depends on the International settings that were selected during installation. These can also be changed using the Control Panel. If you change them temporarily, remember to restore their normal settings because other Windows applications that use the system time and date will be affected by the changes.

19.5 Creating a Time-Log File

You can record your activities in a time-log file that you create and update in Notepad. When you finish a task or want to record an idea, open the log and make a new entry. Each time you do this, Notepad automatically adds the current time and date. The time-log provides a convenient and accurate chronological record of your activities and observations.

Defining a time-log file

Open a new document file or an existing one that must be used for logging your time. With the insertion point at the beginning of the first line, type *.LOG*. This designates your file as a time-log.

Save the file and then open it again. Windows now appends the current time and date to the end of the file each time it's opened. Your entries are recorded chronologically and stamped with the time and date.

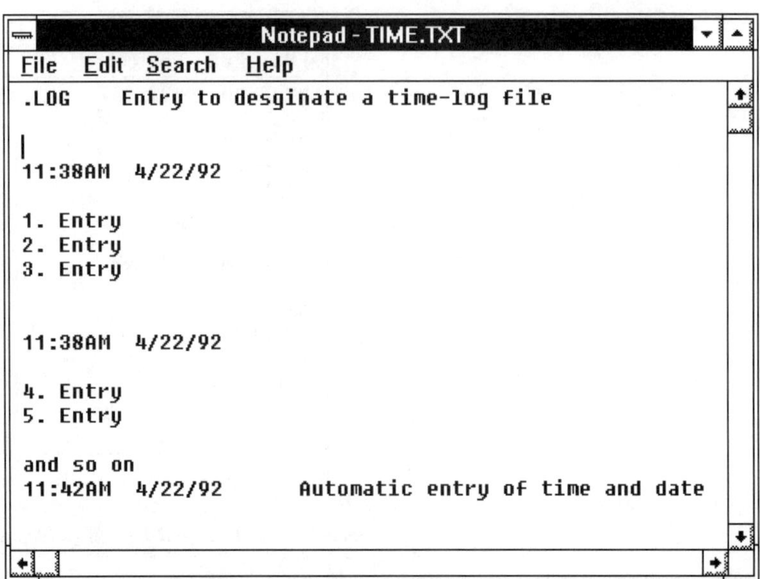

Entries are kept chronologically

Since the log time/date-stamp originates from the system date and time, it uses the same formatting options that were described in the previous section. These options can be set using the Control Panel.

19.6 Saving and Opening Files

Notepad starts with an empty page, on which you can immediately begin typing to create a new document. Until you save your new document to a disk file, the information is stored in a temporary work area that's accessible only to the system.

Saving documents

When you save a new file for the first time, the *Save* and *Save As...* commands work identically. With either one, the *Save As...* dialog box appears and requests a file name. If you don't want to save your document under the current path, select the appropriate directory from the list of available directories. Then enter a name for your file. A file extension isn't necessary because Windows automatically assigns the .TXT extension to Notepad files.

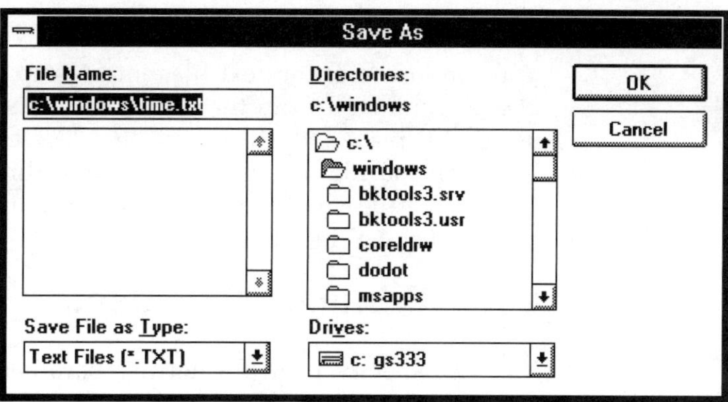

Entering a directory and file name

Save your file at regular intervals while you're working to avoid data loss in case of a power failure.

When changing a file that has already been named and saved, use the *Save* command to update the previous version. A dialog box won't appear. For existing files, use *Save As...* only if you want to save the new version as an additional file under a different path or name.

Starting a new document

To start a new document, activate *New* from the *File* menu. The Notepad page is cleared and the old file name is removed from the title bar.

If you haven't saved your chances for the previous document, a dialog box, asking if you want to do so, appears. This also occurs when you try to close Notepad without having saving your work.

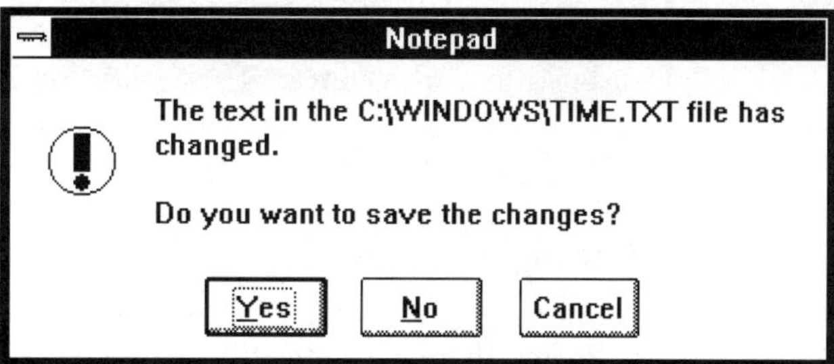

Request to save your changes

Overwriting files

If you reply to the *Save As* dialog box with a file name that already exists, Windows asks if you want to replace the existing file. If you want to update the existing version with your changes, answer Yes. Otherwise, answer No and enter a new name.

Opening files

You can load existing text files into Notepad for editing with the *Open...* command from the *File* menu. The file selection window usually displays only files with the .TXT extension. To display a list of all the file names in the current directory, select *All Files (*.*)*. If the file you want appears in the list, you can open it by double-clicking the name.

19.7 Printing Documents

You can specify page formatting parameters for printing your Notepad documents. These parameters include margins and page layout information, as well as headers, footers, and page numbers. Use these settings to organize long documents.

Control characters for headers and footers

Page margins and headers and footers are set using the *Page Setup...* command from the *File* menu. Headers and footers can contain the following control characters:

&d	Enter current system date
&t	Enter current system time
&f	Enter file name
&p	Enter current page number
&l	Left-align text that follows
&r	Right-align text that follows
&c	Center text that follows

Suppose that you want to print your document with a header on every page and the page number on the right, the date on the left, and a title in the center. The following header will do this:

```
&l&d&cImportant Notice&r&p
```

Starting to print

To start printing, select *Print* from the *File* menu. A dialog box indicates that printing will begin. If you want to halt the process, click the Cancel button.

Printing proceeds according to the various parameters that were set by the *Page Setup...* and *Print Setup...* commands. *Print Setup...* parameters include the paper size and page orientation.

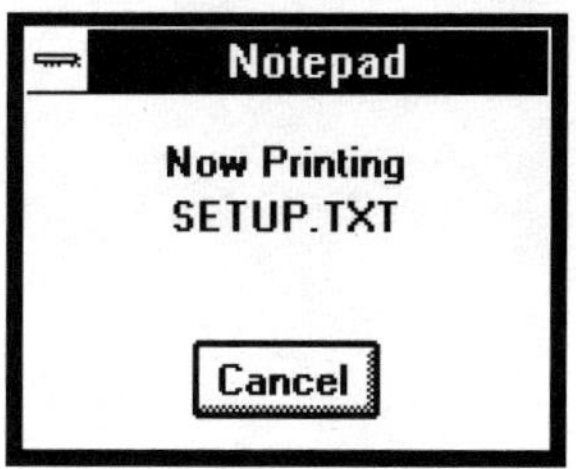

Page formatting

If more than one printer is connected, be sure that you select the proper one. Otherwise, the text may not print correctly. Use *File/Print Setup...* to specify the desired printer driver.

20. The Calendar

Calendar

Marking special days

You can indicate special occasions and events by using five different symbols to mark the appropriate days in Month view.

Entering appointments

Appointments that were entered in Notepad can be easily transferred to the appropriate Calendar page.

Defining special times

You can schedule an appointment at any time of the day. Besides full-, half- and quarter-hour intervals, special appointment times can be defined as needed.

The alarm

Calendar has an alarm clock to help you remember important appointments. If you set the alarm, you'll see and hear a reminder of your appointment at the scheduled time.

Appointment overviews

You can create several calendar files to organize your schedules by category. It's possible to display your calendar a day at a time, or to display an entire month. Appointments can be deleted for an entire day or several days.

20.1 The Calendar Window

Do you want to start planning your birthday celebration for the year 2000? In Windows' Calendar, it's easy to manage your appointment schedules. You can record and view appointments for any day from January 1, 1980 to December 31, 2099.

Special calendar files

You can organize your schedules according to the type of activity or occasion by creating a separate calendar file for each one. For example, you can create one calendar to record vacations, another to keep track of birthdays, and another for your job or business.

Once you schedule an appointment, you can set an alarm that will remind you to keep it. The alarm appears on the screen and can also emit a sound.

Starting calendar files directly

Usually when you start Calendar, Windows assumes you'll be using a new file. If you always work with the same Calendar file and want it to load automatically when you start Calendar, use the *File/Properties...* command from Program Manager to add your file's name behind the Calendar program. Actually several calendar files can be assigned to their own icons in a group.

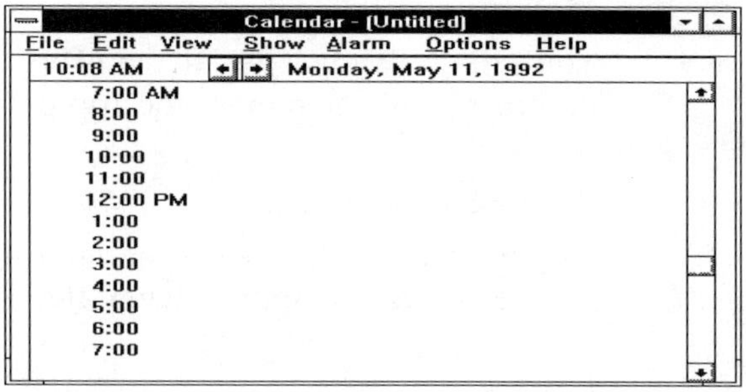

The Calendar window

The Day view

The initial Calendar screen shows a time schedule for a single day, similar to a page from an appointment book. This is called the Day view. At the top, you should see the current date and time. These values are taken from the system date and time. If they aren't correct, they can be reset with the Control Panel.

Setting the date and time

Each time you open a calendar file, the appointment page for the current date is displayed. Appointments that were already entered for this date are displayed beside the scheduled times.

The Day view is one of two modes, in which the Calendar is used. In the other mode, which is called Month view, you can display an entire month on the screen at once. To activate this mode, select *Month* from the *View* menu.

To switch between viewing modes quickly, double-click the date that appears at the top of the page in either mode.

Calendar - [Untitled]
File Edit View Show Alarm Options Help
10:11 AM Monday, May 11, 1992
May 1992

S	M	T	W	T	F	S
					1	2
3	4	5	6	7	8	9
10	> 11 <	12	13	14	15	16
17	18	19	20	21	22	23
24	25	26	27	28	29	30
31						

The month at a glance

Month view displays an entire month in a traditional calendar format; dates and days of the week are displayed. When you switch to this mode from Day view, the day you were viewing remains the selected date and is highlighted on the calendar page. This date also appears on the top line.

20.2 Selecting the Date

When you open a calendar file, you're automatically located at the current date and time. By using shortcut keys and commands, you can easily move around in Calendar. So you can quickly schedule appointments or determine the day of the week for a specific date.

Movement keys

While in Month view, you can move back or ahead one month by using the PgUp and PgDn keys. The selected date remains the same as you page from month to month. Holding down either of these keys repeats the action so that you can rapidly page back or ahead in time. The repeat key rate for your keyboard is adjusted in the Control Panel.

You can also use the scroll bar to page from month to month. Using the mouse, click the right scroll arrow to page ahead and the left scroll arrow to page back.

Within the month, you can select a different day with the direction keys on your keyboard, or by clicking the day with the mouse.

Moving in Day view

While in Day view, you can move to the different time periods by using either the direction keys or the mouse. In this mode, the PgDn and PgUp keys scroll the appointment schedule for the selected day. To move to the next or previous day, use Ctrl + PgUp and Ctrl + PgDn.

Movement commands

The commands in the *Show* menu are also used for moving around in the Calendar. These commands are available in both viewing modes, and although their exact actions differ depending on the mode, they are essentially the same in principle. In Month mode, the *Next* command displays the following month, and the *Previous* command displays the previous month. In Day view, these commands display the following day and previous day, respectively.

Selecting the current date

To return directly to the current date from any other date, select *Today* from the *Show* menu.

Specifying a date

The *Date...* command from the *Show* menu takes you directly to any date you specify. A function key provides an even faster way to use this option. The *Date...* command is assigned to the F4 key.

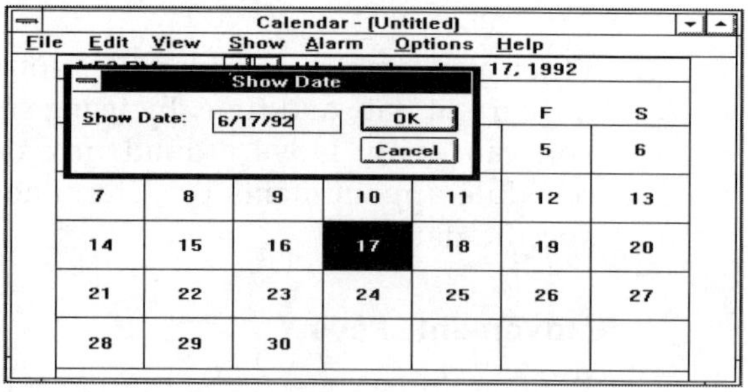

Calling a date quickly

The date you specify must be within Calendar's available time span (i.e., the years 1980 to 2099). Otherwise, an error message appears.

20.3 Marking Special Days

To designate certain days in the Month view, mark them with special symbols. Five different symbols can be used to indicate different types of activities or occasions. This is the maximum number of symbols that can be assigned to one date.

Assigning marking symbols

To mark a special day on the displayed month, use the direction keys or mouse to select the desired date. Then choose *Mark...* from the *Options* menu. The *Day Markings* dialog box appears.

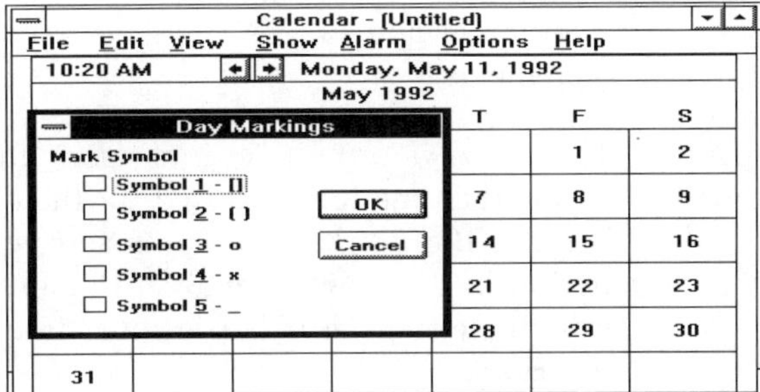

Selecting a day marking

Five different marking symbols, from which you can choose one or more to assign to the selected day, appear. The symbols you assign will then appear on the Month view's calendar page.

You can assign a specific meaning to each symbol. By doing this, you'll automatically know the various types of special occasions or specific activities that are occurring within any month. For example, you can assign the symbols as follows:

Defining symbol meanings

Symbol 1	[ ]	Appointment
Symbol 2	( )	Meeting
Symbol 3	o	Telephone call
Symbol 4	x	Birthday
Symbol 5	_	Personal

Use the buttons to select the icons you want to place in the box for the current day. Marking month view with these symbols gives you an overview of the entire month.

Double-clicking to Day view

After assigning symbols to special dates in Month view, you may want to record a detailed description of the events in Day view's appointment schedule or scratch pad. To switch to Day view, double-click any desired date.

20.4 Configuring the Day View

To enter a detailed appointment, you must switch to Day view. A scheduled activity can be entered after each time period. Before you begin recording appointments, you should configure the appointment calendar to the requirements of your schedule. Configuration changes are made using the *Day Settings...* command from the *Options* menu.

The default setting lists times at one-hour intervals. So you can indicate appointments and activities in full hour increments. The interval setting can be changed if you want to use shorter time increments.

Defining the time interval

The *Interval* option buttons from the *Day Settings* dialog box define the time interval used for the daily appointment schedules. Besides the default one-hour setting, 30-minute and 15-minute option buttons are available. Remember that if you use the 15-minute setting your list is four times as long as with full hour intervals.

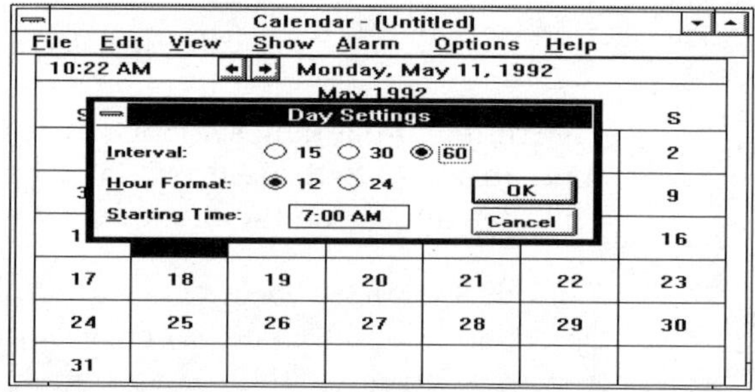

Changing the time interval

Time format

The same dialog box lets you choose between 12-hour and 24-hour time. Most U.S. users prefer the 12-hour format, unlike users in countries where the 24-hour format is standard.

You can also change the first time displayed on your appointment schedule from the default setting of 7:00 AM. With one-hour intervals, the standard appointment schedule page shows times from 7:00 AM to 8:00 PM. If your day begins earlier, you may want to change the *Starting Time* text box to 6:00 AM, for example. Your appointment calendar page will then show all times from 6:00 AM to 7:00 PM. Scroll the page up or down to display appointments outside this range.

Defining special times

You can make an appointment entry for each time listed on your schedule. It's also possible to list additional special times that don't occur at the selected intervals.

To schedule an appointment at a special time, choose the *Special Time...* command from the *Options* menu.

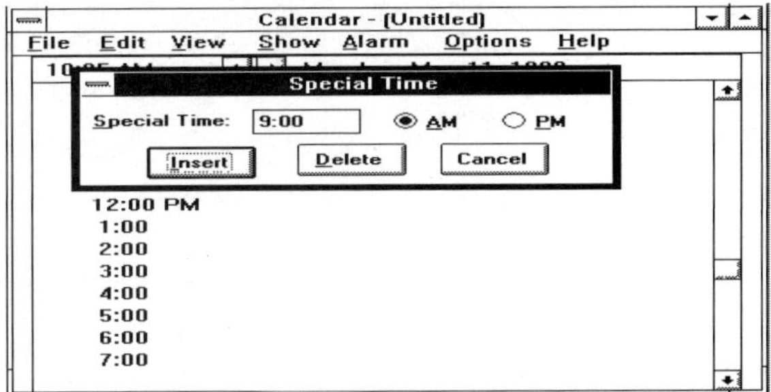

Entering a special time

In the dialog box that follows, enter the desired time in hours and minutes (e.g., 9:00) and, if using the 12-hour format, select *AM* or *PM* as needed. Then click the Insert button. If the format of your time entry is invalid, an error message appears.

Proper entry format

Unlike the settings we just discussed, a special time is defined for a specific day only. If it should apply to a range of dates, you must repeat the process for each date individually.

Deleting special times

Use the *Special Time...* command to delete special times from your schedule. Select the time you want to delete, choose the *Special Time...* command, and click the Delete button in the dialog box. Only special times can be deleted in this way.

20.5 Entering Appointments

There are two ways to enter an appointment. Simply select the appropriate time, then either type the desired text or transfer it from Notepad using the Clipboard.

Entering appointment information

To select a time, click the desired line with the mouse or move the cursor by using the direction keys. Now you're ready to enter the text. You don't need to limit the text to the displayable page width. However, if you exceed this width, you may want to type the most important data first so it's automatically seen when the page is later displayed. You can then use the direction keys or scroll bars to display the remaining text.

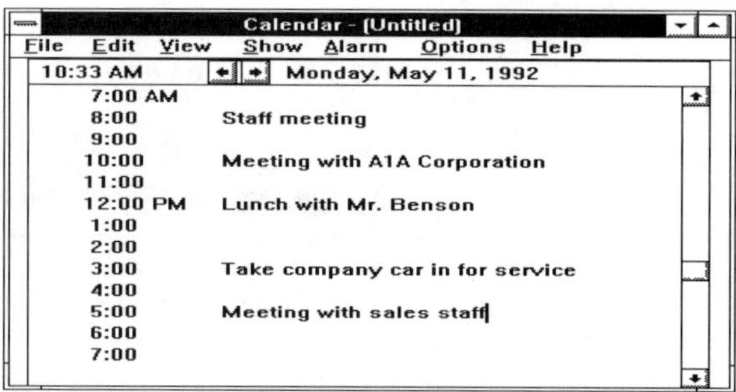

Comprehensive information for the day

If you schedule the same event frequently, you can create multiple entries of the same text by using the Clipboard. Simply select the desired text and then activate *Copy* from the *Edit* menu. Then the text can be pasted to another location.

The scratch pad

For a quick overview of a day's most important activities, record these activities in the scratch pad. This is a separate area at the bottom of the page. Place the insertion point on the scratch pad by clicking with the mouse or pressing the Tab key. On the three lines that are provided, you can record any important information you'll need for this day.

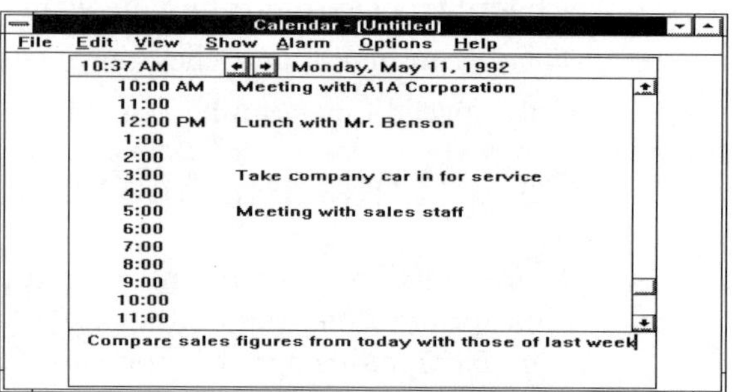

Entering priorities on the scratch pad

The scratch pad notes will also appear when this day is selected in Month view.

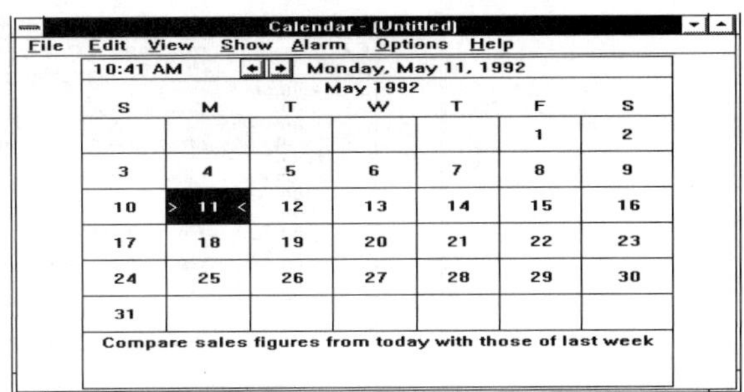

The scratch pad notes appear in Month view

Deleting appointments

When your scheduled activities have occurred or have been canceled, you may want to delete them from your calendar. You can delete a single appointment or those of an entire day or range of days.

To delete a single appointment, select the entry in Day view and press Del or use *Cut* from the *Edit* menu.

Deleting appointment days

You can delete all appointments for a day, week, month, or any range of dates you choose. The *Remove* command in the *Edit* menu performs this function.

In the *From* and *To* fields of the *Remove* dialog box, enter the starting and ending dates of the desired date range. To delete the appointments for a single day, leave the *To* field blank.

20.6 The Alarm

You can use the Calendar to remind you of important tasks that must be performed on time. By setting an alarm, you'll see a message or hear a beep at the specified time.

Setting the alarm

Place the cursor on the appointment for which you want to set the alarm. Choose *Set* from the *Alarm* menu. After you confirm the command, a small bell appears in front of the time. If you later want to remove the alarm, select *Set* again. A checkmark appears next to the *Set* command when this option is activated. Selecting the command then removes the checkmark, showing that the alarm is no longer set.

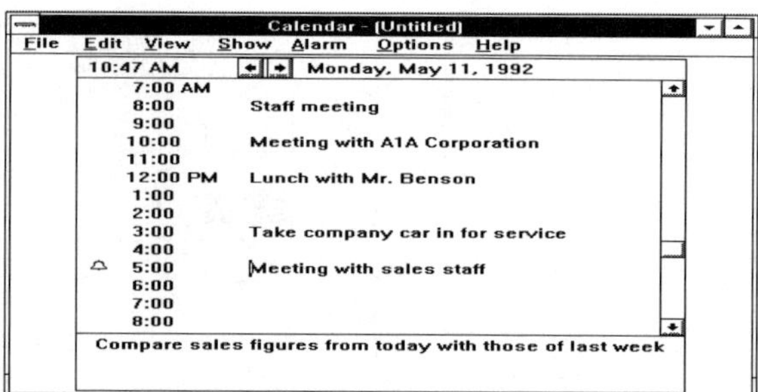

The alarm is set

When the alarm time is reached, a tone sounds and the title bar or Calendar icon starts to blink. So, the alarm sounds even when Calendar isn't running in the foreground. You should then load it and open the appropriate calendar file.

Viewing the appointment

When the alarm goes off, you can activate Calendar. A dialog box, appears displaying the text for the scheduled appointment.

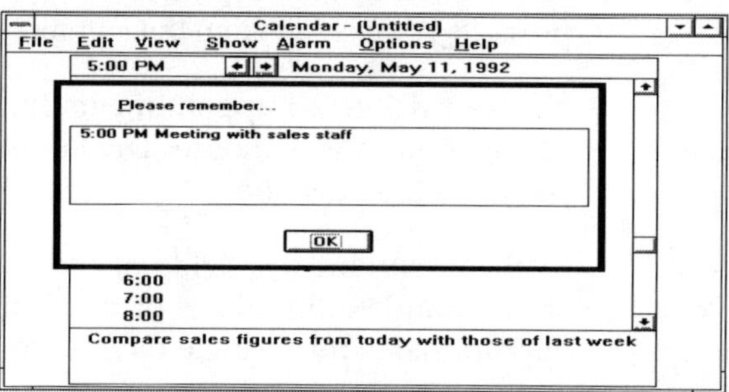

Displaying an important appointment

Setting the optical signal

If the tone that sounds is annoying, you can disable it under *Controls....* To do this, deactivate the *Sound* check box and the then press OK. The dialog box for the scheduled appointment will appear on the screen.

Alarm controls

The alarm can sound early to give advance notice of a scheduled appointment. Select *Controls...* from the *Alarm* menu, then enter a number from 0 to 10 in the *Early Ring* text box to specify the desired number of minutes.

Switching off the alarm

When the Calendar window is activated and the *Alarm* dialog box appears on the screen, press the OK button or Enter to switch off the alarm.

If the Calendar window isn't active, the title bar or Calendar icon blinks. First activate Calendar and then switch off the alarm as previously indicated.

20.7 Saving and Loading Calendar Files

Calendar starts with an empty appointment page. If you want to create a new calendar file, you can start typing your appointments immediately. This information is stored in a temporary work file. To save this information permanently, you must save it to a disk file.

Saving calendar files

The first time a new calendar file is saved, the *Save* and *Save As...* commands are identical. With either one, the *Save As...* dialog box appears and requests a file name. First select the appropriate directory from those listed if you don't want to save your calendar file under the current path. Then enter a name for your file. A file extension isn't needed. Windows automatically assigns the extension .CAL to calendar files.

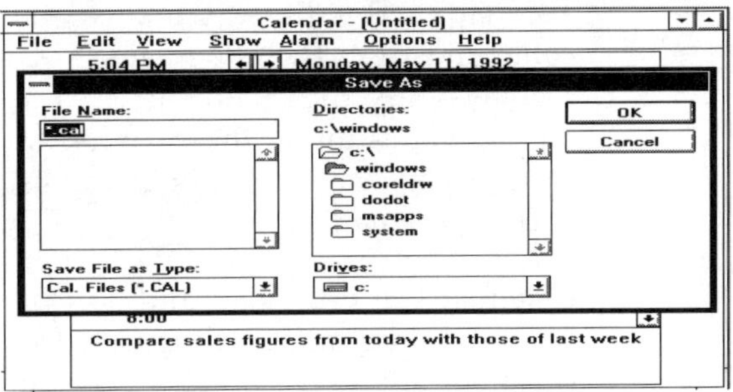

Entering the directory and file name

You should save your calendar file at regular intervals so that you don't lose any data because of a power failure or a computer crash.

When changing a calendar file that has already been named and saved, use the *Save* command to update the previous version. A dialog box won't appear. For existing files, use *Save As...* only if you want to store the new version as an additional file under a different path or name.

Starting a new calendar file

When you're finished editing an old calendar file and want to start a new one, select *New* from the *File* menu. The calendar page is cleared and the old file name is removed from the title bar.

If you didn't save your changes to the old calendar file, a dialog box now gives you the opportunity to do so. This also occurs when you try to close Calendar without first saving your changes.

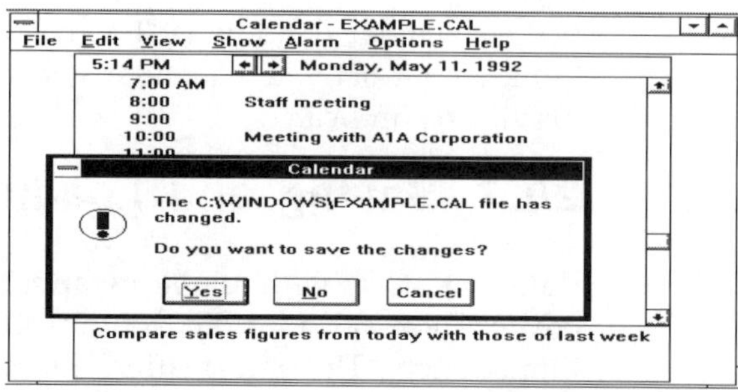

Request to save your changes

Overwriting files

If you enter an already existing file name in the *Save As* dialog box, Windows asks whether you want to replace the existing file. If you want to update the existing version with your changes, click on Yes. Otherwise, click on No and enter a new name.

Opening files

To load and edit existing calendar files, select the *Open...* command from the *File* menu. The file selection window usually displays only files with the .CAL extension. To display a list of all file names under the current directory, choose *All Files (*.*)*. If the file you want appears in the list, you can open it by double-clicking the name.

Calendar can only load and edit files that were created with the Calendar program. Cardfile files, for example, cannot be opened in Calendar. If you try, you'll receive an error message.

After changing a calendar file, you can easily compare it to the previous version. Simply start a second Calendar window and open the file again. You could also select the name of your old calendar file in the File Manager, which also automatically starts the program. (Be sure that the WIN.INI file has the proper entries.) Now you can compare the old and new versions side by side in two separate windows.

20.8 Printing Calendar Pages

You can print pages from your calendar files just like you print other documents. Headers, footers, and page numbers can also be added.

Control characters for headers and footers

Page margins, headers, and footers are set using the *Page Setup...* command from the *File* menu. Headers and footers can include the following control characters:

&d	Enter current system date
&t	Enter current system time
&f	Enter file name
&p	Enter current page number
&l	Left-align text that follows
&r	Right-align text that follows
&c	Center text that follows

To add a header, which shows the page number on the right, the date on the left, and the title in the center, enter the following:

```
&l&d&cAppointments&r&p
```

Starting to print

You can print the appointments for a particular date or a range of dates. Choose *Print...* from the *File* menu. In the *From:* and *To:* text boxes, enter the beginning and ending dates for the range you want to print. To print the appointments for a single day only, leave the *To:* text box blank.

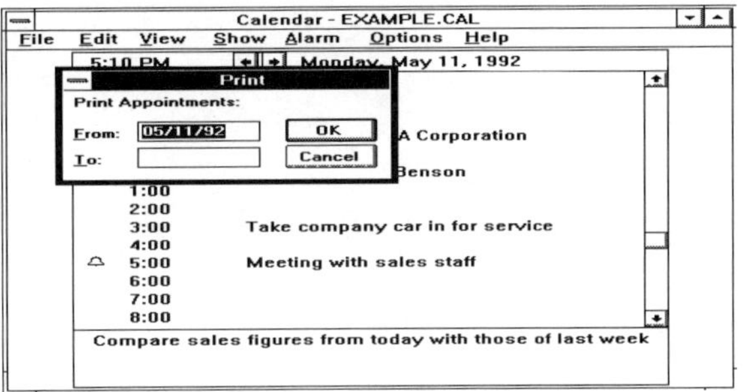

Selecting a print range

The printing is performed according to the settings specified under the *Page Setup...* and *Print Setup...* commands. These parameters include the paper size and page orientation.

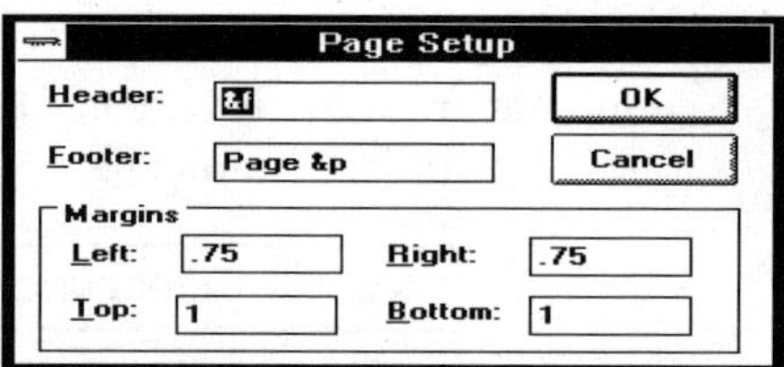

Setting for page setup

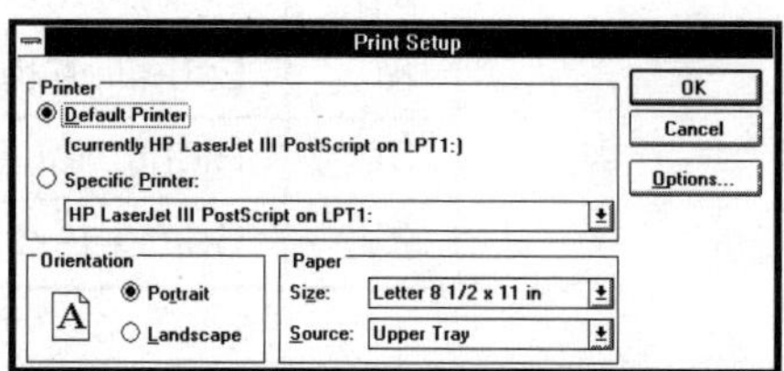

Setting printer options

If more than one printer is connected, ensure that the proper one is selected. Otherwise, the text may not print properly. Use the *Print Setup...* command to specify the desired printer driver.

21. Terminal

Terminal programs let you access different types of communication, such as local Bulletin Board Systems (BBSes) and multiple-user commercial online services. These communication methods can be accessed with phones and modems. You can send and receive programs, check on the latest news, and meet new people by using these communication capabilities.

In this chapter we'll discuss the Terminal application that's included with Windows. You'll learn how to prepare the Terminal for telecommunications, make a connection, send and receive data, store and print data, and reassign function keys.

21.1 Preparing Terminal

Terminal operation usually follows the same pattern. After you start the Terminal, you must set or verify the modem settings and communication parameters. You then select the *Phone* menu to make the connection to another computer. Files are sent and received through the Transfers menu.

When your telecommunication session is complete, select the *Phone* menu to disconnect your modem from the other computer. Use the *File* menu to save the terminal parameters that were set during this session.

Configuration

A modem is required

First, you'll need a modem (modulator/demodulator). A modem modulates a computer signal so that it can be sent over two wires (phone lines). Then a receiving modem demodulates the signal so it can be decoded by the receiving computer. This way computers can talk to each other and easily exchange data.

A modem can be purchased as a card that fits into your PC or as an external box that attaches to your PC with a cable. Baud refers to the speed of data transfer that the modem can handle. Although 1200 baud modems are quite inexpensive, 2400 baud modems are faster and don't cost much more than the 1200 baud modems. Check with you dealer to determine what type of modem your computer contains, if it contains a modem.

When you start Terminal for the first time, a dialog box appears asking for the default serial port. The serial port is also referred to as a COM or communications port. You must specify which serial interface (COM1-COM4) is connected to your modem. Check with your dealer to see which port your modem uses. Remember that mice, printers, or plotters may already be using most of your serial interfaces. If you don't want to remove one of these peripherals, you may have to buy another serial interface card for your system, or explore other device connections (e.g., a bus mouse instead of a serial mouse).

If a free interface isn't currently available, you can't use Terminal at the moment. Select the *None* option, exit Terminal, and skip to the next chapter.

Declaring terminal type

The first step consists of informing the Terminal program of the necessary settings. Select *Terminal Emulation...* from the *Settings* menu. Three options are available. The *TTY (Generic)* option emulates a standard teletype (TeleTYpe). The *DEC VT-100 (ANSI)* and *DEC VT-52* terminals were standards devised for Digital Equipment Corporation host terminals. The VT-100 terminal supports text attributes, such as bold and color text.

The *Terminal Preferences...* command from the *Settings* menu specifies screen display options such as font, number of columns, cursor display, and foreign language translations of characters.

Setting Columns

The *Terminal Preferences* dialog box lets you select either 80 columns or 132 columns on your screen display.

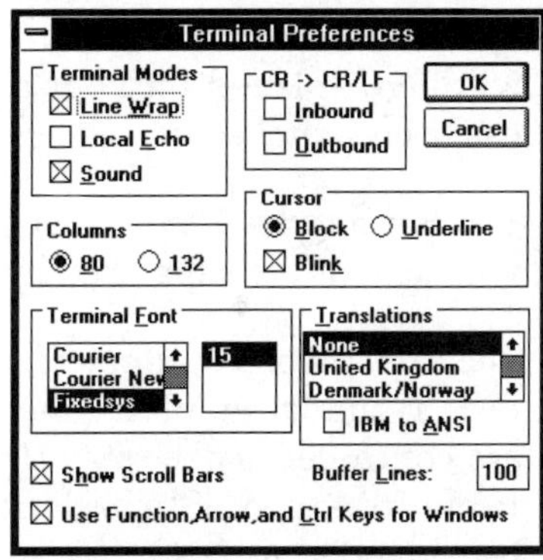

Terminal Preferences dialog box

Different terminal fonts can be selected in this dialog box (these may vary from system to system). The font size is determined by the number to the right of the font.

The cursor can be displayed as a block or an underline, and can be displayed as blinking or constant (the blinking makes the cursor easier to see).

Line feed and carriage return

Depending on how the remote computer sends or receives data, you can send or receive carriage returns with or without line feeds by clicking the *Inbound* or *Outbound* check boxes. The carriage return resets the cursor or printhead to the beginning of the line.

Buffer Lines

The *Buffer Lines:* check box determines how many lines Terminal stores in its buffer before replacing them with new ones. This may be important if you're connected with an online service.

You can enter values between 25 and 999. The buffer defaults to a value of 100.

Line Wrap

If you select the *Line Wrap* check box, the cursor immediately jumps back to the first column when it reaches the 80th column. Otherwise, the character in the 80th column would be overwritten by every newly received character. You must select this option if you're using an 80 column terminal but are receiving data from a 132 column terminal. Otherwise, the characters received after the 80th column would be lost.

Local Echo

Click on the *Local Echo* check box only if the computer to which you're connected operates in half-duplex mode. This means that it cannot simultaneously send and receive data. When this check box isn't activated, the characters you enter won't appear on your screen.

If the remote computer operates in full-duplex mode, your messages will be displayed on your screen when the *Local Echo* check box has been switched on.

Sound

The Sound check box activates the system speaker. In this case, your actions are supported by a beep.

Translations

The *Translations* option lets you send and receive foreign language text. Terminal emulates the European 7-bit character sets, which are controlled by the ISO (International Standards Organization). If the IBM to ANSI check box is activated, ASCII characters will be converted to ANSI characters.

Terminal Font

The *Terminal Font* option tells Terminal which font to use. If the remote computer doesn't support the same font, display problems will occur.

If the *Show Scroll Bars* check box is enabled, scroll bars are displayed in the Terminal window. Disabling this check box removes the scroll bars.

Key function

If the *Use Function, Arrow,* and *Ctrl Keys for Windows* check box is enabled, these keys can be used for Windows control. When this check box is disabled, these keys can be used to control online services or BBSes.

Setting communication parameters

The second step in preparing for telecommunication lies in setting communication parameters. To do this, select the *Communications...* command from the *Settings* menu.

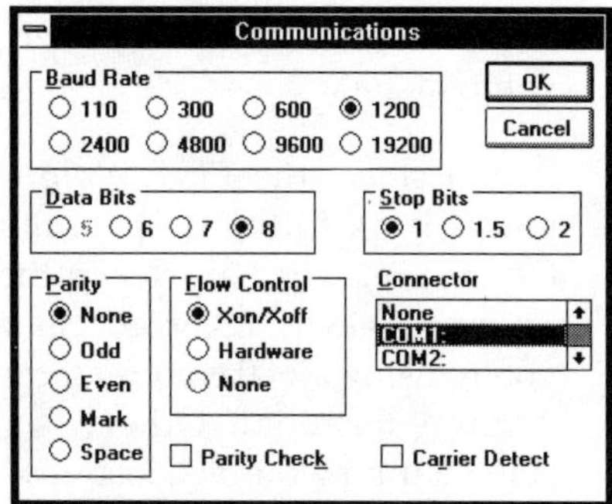

Communications dialog box

All the communication parameters you select must match those of the remote computer (except the COM port through which communication is taking place). This ensures error-free communication.

Communication Parameters

Many of these options depend on the settings for your modem or the settings for the remote computer. Consult the required publications, or your online service's documentation, and change the options accordingly.

Baud Rate

The *Baud Rate* option indicates the speed at which the data is transmitted. The transmission rate is measured in Baud; 1200 Baud and 2400 Baud are frequently used speeds. Check you modem's documentation to determine the speed at which your modem operates.

If you connect two computers with a null modem cable, a higher Baud rate can usually be accessed. Simply remember that both sender and receiver must be operating at the same Baud rate.

Parity

Parity checking provides an additional bit with a transmitted byte, checking for communication errors. Although parity checking is rarely performed, Terminal provides the *Even*, *Odd*, *Space*, *Mark*, or *None* options.

Data Bits

The *Data Bits* options allow you to set the number of data bits per byte to 6, 7, or 8 bits. Selecting the *7* option button transmits characters in the original 128 character font (a setting rarely used today). Selecting the *8* option button allows the transfer of a complete byte, which permits the transmission of the ASCII 256 character font. The default value is *8*.

Stop Bits

The *Stop Bits* option specifies the number of stop bits inserted between two characters. You must include at least one stop bit. More stop bits increase the integrity of the transmission, but may decrease the speed of the communication. The default value is *1*.

Flow Control

When data is sent from the computer to the modem, the buffer may overflow. This occurs because of the slower transmission speed of the phone lines. To prevent an overflow, the flow of data must be stopped. Terminal provides two options: *Xon/Xoff*, in which the modem uses two control characters to control data flow, and *Hardware*, in which the remote computer dictates data flow using hardware lines. Select *None* if overflow control isn't needed.

Enable the *Parity Check* check box if you want transmission errors to be documented.

Enable the *Carrier Detect* check box if you want Terminal to detect the modem signal sent when the connection is made between two systems.

21.2 Transmission by Modem

If you want to work with a modem, the Terminal program will request additional settings.

Setting the Modem type

Select the *Modem Commands...* command from the *Settings* menu. This dialog box contains a number of defaults for three popular modems (Hayes, MultiTech, and TrailBlazer). If your modem isn't listed, select the closest one (usually Hayes) and enter the commands from your modem's documentation.

Once the modem commands are established, you'll want to call a remote computer. Select the *Phone Number...* command from the *Settings* menu. Enter the phone number in the *Dial:* text box. Enter the entire number, including area code. You may enter the area code, exchange, and number with or without hyphens.

Phone Connections

You may also have to begin the phone number with a 1 or 9, depending on where you live. This single digit can be followed by a comma, which delays dialing for two seconds. This may be useful for international calling.

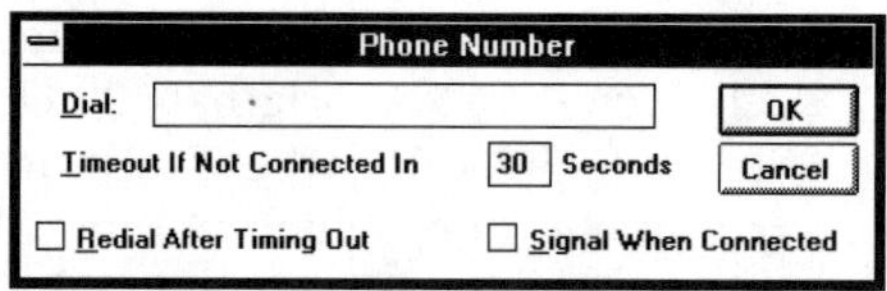

Phone Number dialog box

You can use hyphens to separate numbers so that the numbers are easier to read (the modem ignores these hyphens when dialing).

☞ If you're using a null modem cable, with a direct connection to the remote computer, instead of a modem, leave the *Dial:* text box blank.

Signal when connected

If the *Signal When Connected* check box is activated, a beep is emitted when a connection has been made.

The *Timeout If Not Connected In* option specifies how long Terminal should wait for a response from the remote computer before disconnecting. The default of 30 seconds can be increased to 256 seconds.

Entry for foreign numbers

It may take a long time to connect to a computer in a foreign country. It's also possible that a timeout may occur because of line noise or a busy signal. The modem disconnects after a certain period of time. Enabling the *Redial After Timing Out* check box instructs Terminal to dial the number again after timing out.

Saving and Loading Terminal Settings

Your terminal should now be prepared for communication. Before you call a BBS or an online service, save the current settings.

Select the *Save As...* command or the *Save* command in the *File* menu. Enter the name of the BBS or remote computer.

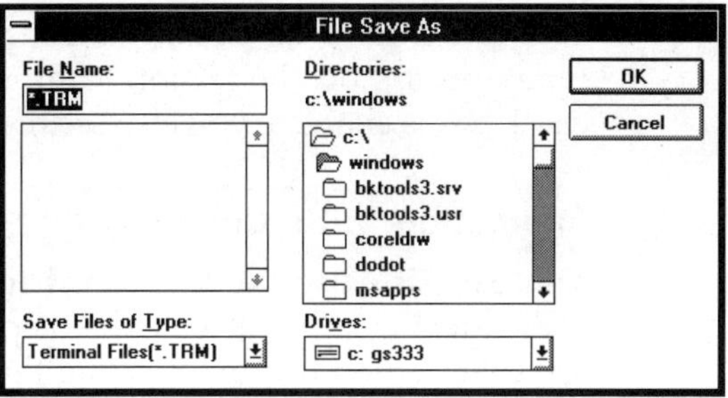

Save dialog box (.TRM default extension)*

Click OK to save your parameter file on diskette or hard drive. These settings remain in effect.

Loading a parameter file

Select the *Open...* command from the *File* menu to load a parameter file. If you select this command, Terminal lists all files, in the current directory, that have the .TRM extension. Select the file you need and click OK. This file configures your terminal to the previous settings.

21.3 Connecting and Disconnecting

Select the *Dial* command from the *Phone* menu. Terminal dials the desired computer or online service.

Check settings on error

If this connection isn't made, check the options you selected in the *Settings* menu.

After you received all requested data, or the remote computer has disconnected, you should terminate the connection.

Terminating a connection

To do this, first enter the exit or log off command, recognized by the remote computer, from your keyboard. This may be BYE, OFF, or EXIT, or you may have to press the G key (for "goodbye") or L key (for "logoff"). After the remote hangs up, select the *Hangup* command from the *Phone* menu. If you're working with a modem, a proper disconnect is important.

Remember, with paid services or long distance phone calls, every minute that your phone is off the hook costs money.

21.4 Sending Data

After a connection has been made, the data can be transmitted in several ways.

Keyboard entry

You can enter data directly through the keyboard. All data you type appears on the remote computer's screen. If the *Local Echo* check box is enabled, you also see the data on your own screen.

Interacting with Clipboard

You can also use the Clipboard to send text. If you previously copied text from Write or the Notepad into the Clipboard, you can send the copied text by selecting the *Paste* command from the *Edit* menu.

Placing data in the Clipboard

When you receive data, you can copy it to the Clipboard after selecting it on the screen by using the *Copy* command from the *Edit* menu.

Sending text files

Terminal allows you to send (upload) complete files. Before you can send a text file you must select a *transfer protocol*. Select the *Text Transfers...* command from the *Settings* menu. If you select the default of *Standard Flow Control*, the protocol set in the *Settings/Communication...* command is used for the transmission.

Set line wrap

Enabling the *Word Wrap Outgoing Text At Column:* ensures that the transmitted text wraps at a specific position on the line. Set this to the receiving terminal instead of your own system. For example, the text box for this option must contain 131 to accommodate a 132-column terminal.

Sending text files a character at a time

If the text file should be transmitted one character at a time, click the *Character at a Time* option button. Another option group appears in the middle of the dialog box. Here you can specify the interval at which single characters can be transmitted, either through character echo or, in the case of the *Delay Between Characters* option button, in tenths of a second.

Instead of verifying transmission, this setting only determines the speed. If you want character transmission to wait until character echo occurs, click on the *Wait for Character Echo* option. This method is slow and is rarely used.

Sending text files a line at a time

Select the *Line at a Time* option button to transmit text one line at a time. Like the *Character at a Time* option button, this option allows time intervals in tenths of a second.

The *Wait for Prompt String:* option lets you test for complete transmission of the preceding line. After the line is sent, this setting instructs the system to wait until the next line can be transmitted.

Prompt string

In the *Wait for Prompt String:* text box, enter the prompt string the Terminal should expect. Terminal defaults to the end-of-line code ^M.

If the acknowledgment of transmission is interactive instead of automatic, you must enter the character string supported by the remote system in the *Wait for Prompt String:* text box.

To send the text file, select the *Send Text File...* command from the *Transfers* menu. A dialog box appears, from which a text file can be selected.

Line feed

You can either end each line with a line feed after each carriage return or remove each existing line feed. Select *Append LF* or *Strip LF*.

Click on the [OK] command button to start transmission. The bottom line of the Terminal window displays the file name being transmitted. You'll also see a bar that indicates the progress of the transmission. Click on the [Stop] command button to stop transmission or the [Pause] command button to pause transmission. The [Pause] command button then changes to the [Resume] command button; click on this button to resume transmission.

View ing text files

The *View Text File...* command displays the selected text file in the Terminal window. If the entire text cannot fit in the Terminal window, the text scrolls. Click on the [Stop] command button to stop display or the [Pause] command button to pause display. The [Pause] command button then changes to the [Resume] command button; click on this button to resume display. Once the entire file is displayed, you can scroll up or down the Terminal window using the scroll bars. However, remember that the scroll bars must be activated by using the *Terminal Preferences...* command from the *Settings* menu. To clear the Terminal window, select *Clear Buffer* from the *Edit* menu.

Sending binary files

Use the *Send Binary File...* command from the *Transfers* menu to send any file other than an unformatted ASCII text file. For example, you must select this command to send any formatted Word for Windows document and any program files.

Transmission protocol

Before you can send a binary file, you must specify the transmission protocol (the method of transfer). Select the *Binary Transfers...* command from the *Settings* menu. There are two protocols available: XModem/CRC and Kermit.

The XModem/CRC protocol is generally used in personal computer communications that use eight bits per byte (e.g., BBS communication). Kermit (named by Columbia University developers after Kermit the Frog) is used for communication with mainframe computers, which transmit seven bits per byte.

After you select a protocol and click OK, you can select the *Send Binary File...* command from the *Transfers* menu. Select the name of the file you want transferred.

Click on the OK command button to start transmission. The bottom line of the Terminal window displays the file name being transmitted, and a bar indicates the progress of the transmission. Click on the Stop command button to stop transmission.

21.5 Controlling Transmission

You can also stop sending a binary file during transmission by selecting the *Stop* command from the *Transfers* menu.

Handshake controls the buffer

Any incoming data that's received after you select this command are stored in the buffer. When the buffer is full, data can be lost if the connection isn't configured for handshaking (see the *Communications...* command from the *Settings* menu). If you selected the *Xon/Xoff* option, the system sends an Xoff to stop receiving.

After you stop transmission, you can scroll through the received information in the buffer using the cursor keys, the PgUp and PgDn keys, or you can click on the scroll bars. Click on Resume to continue receiving information in the buffer.

Earlier in this chapter we discussed the *Terminal Preferences...* command from the *Settings* menu. The *Buffer Lines:* text box determines the number of lines allocated to the buffer. Setting the *Columns* option to 80 and typing 25 in the *Buffer Lines:* text box reduces the amount of time needed for receiving data after you select Stop.

21.6 Storing Data

You can receive files and store the information for later recall.

Check transmission protocol

Before receiving data, you must specify the correct transmission protocol, as you did for sending files. (Review the earlier sections of this chapter.)

Once you've established the transmission protocol, select the *Receive Text File...* or *Receive Binary File...* command from the *Transfers* menu. Enter the file name under which the data should be stored.

Set the type of reception

Three check boxes provide file receipt options in the *Receive Text File* dialog box. The *Append File* check box appends the data to be received to an existing file.

The *Save Controls* check box allows you to receive ASCII files containing control characters and retain these control characters instead of stripping them from the received file.

The *Table Format* check box changes two or more consecutive spaces in the file being received to a tab.

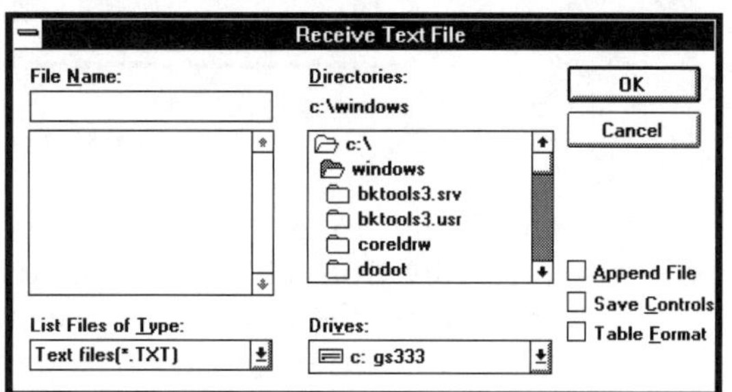

Receive Text File dialog box

21.7 Printing Data

You can send text directly to a printer. Before starting transmission, select the *Printer Echo* command from the *Settings* menu. If a checkmark appears beside the command, it's enabled;

otherwise it's disabled. *Printer Echo* starts the Print Manager when active.

Exiting Terminal

The *Exit* command from the *File* menu exits Terminal. If you changed something in the *Settings* menu, Terminal will display a dialog box asking if you want to save changes. Click Yes to save changes for later recall, No to abandon changes, or Cancel to return to Terminal.

21.8 Function Key Assignment

You can assign frequently used Terminal commands to function keys. With four separate function key levels available for function keys F1 through F8, you can have a total of 32 custom function keys.

You can reassign the function keys by selecting the *Function Keys...* command from the *Settings* menu. Clicking on the *Keys Visible* check box displays the function key assignments in the bottom border of the Terminal window. You can display only one level of eight function keys at a time.

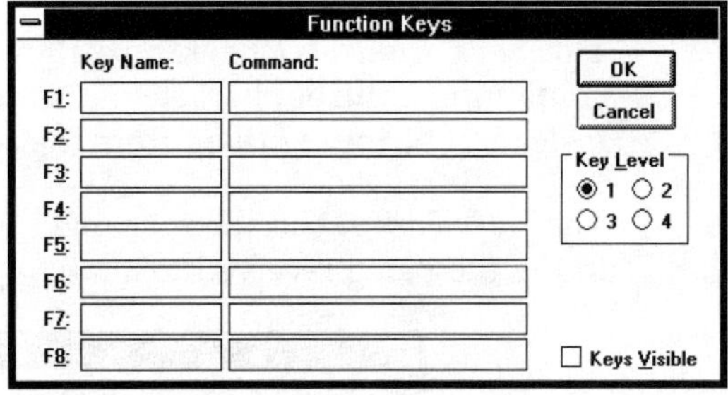

Function Keys dialog box

Eight fields appear for each level. The keys are numbered sequentially from F1 to F8. Click on one of the *Key Level* option buttons to set the level. Enter a name for a key in the *Key Name:* text box, then press Tab to move to the *Command:* text box. You can specify commands by using the following command codes:

Command codes `^L1...^L4`

This code switches key levels from a specific function key.

`^$B`

This code sends a break code to the remote computer.

`^A..^Z`

These codes represent the control codes from Ctrl + A to Ctrl + Z.

`^$C`

Executes the *Dial...* command from the *Phone* menu.

`^$H`

Executes the *Hangup* command from the *Phone* menu.

`^$D<x>`

Delays the Terminal connection for x seconds.

21.9 Making a Null-modem Cable

We'll conclude this chapter by providing instructions on how to make your own null-modem cable for connecting two PCs through their serial ports. These PCs can be in the same building, but not necessarily in the same room. This can be useful for exchanging data between two computers.

This data transmission cable consists of two DB25 connectors, which are connected with a 7-line cable. Since this cable is for serial transfer, the cable can be of virtually unlimited length.

Pin assignments

Solder the pins in the following order:

2	3	TXD->RXD	(sender->receiver)
3	2	RXD<-TXD	(receiver<-sender)
4	5	RTS->CTS	(Handshake one direction)
5	4	CTS<-RTS	(Handshake other direction)
6	20	DTR->DSR	(function control)
20	6	DSR<-DTR	(function control)
7	7	GND	(ground)

Because of the symmetrical pin assignment, it doesn't matter which end of the cable is inserted into the computer. Before buying the two DB connectors, make sure that your serial interface is compatible with a DB 25 connector.

22. The Cardfile

In this chapter, we'll discuss the Cardfile. You'll learn what the Cardfile is and what it does, how to search for and change data, how to combine multiple files, and how to print a list for review.

22.1 The Cardfile Screen

Start Cardfile from the *Accessories* group. A blank card, similar to a standard file card, appears on the screen. You can enter information on two different areas of this card.

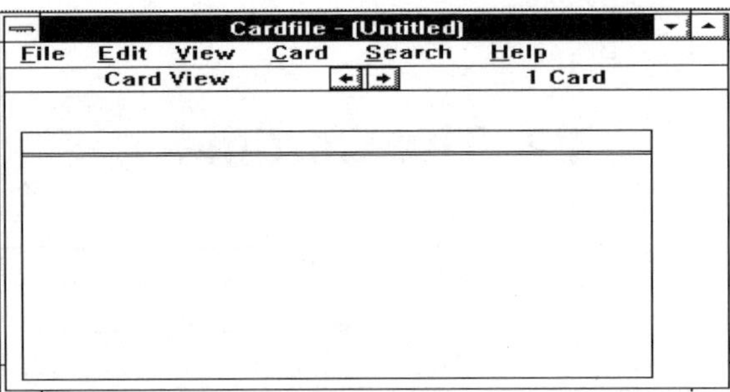

The Cardfile

The index line

The index line contains the card title. You can use the index line information to find cards quickly because Cardfile displays cards in index line order when *List View* mode is active. For example, if you use the Cardfile for telephone numbers, the index line should probably contain the last name of the individual listed on the card. If you want the Cardfile to sort by telephone number when in List mode, the index line should contain the telephone number.

The information area

The information area, which is located directly below the index line, comprises the largest part of the card. Enter the information, to which the index line refers, in this area. You can type this data in any location in the information area.

The Cardfile has text entry and editing features similar to other Windows applications. For example, you can use the *Find...* command from the *Search* menu to locate a specific text in one of the cards.

To insert text and pictures in cards, use the Clipboard. Cardfile also supports Dynamic Data Exchange (DDE) and Object Linking and Embedding (OLE).

Cardfile view modes

You can display Cardfile information in one of two modes. The first mode is Card View, which is the default mode. When Card View is active, the cards in the file are displayed as cascaded. This displays the index line for all cards except the one in the front of the group. Click on a card's index line to move that card to the foreground. Select the *Card* command from the *View* menu to enable this mode.

List View

The second mode is List View, which alphabetically displays the index lines for all cards. You can move up and down in the list by using the mouse pointer, the ↑ and ↓ direction keys, and the PgUp and PgDn keys. Since no other information is displayed, this mode is only useful for viewing index lines. Select the *List* command from the *View* menu to activate this mode.

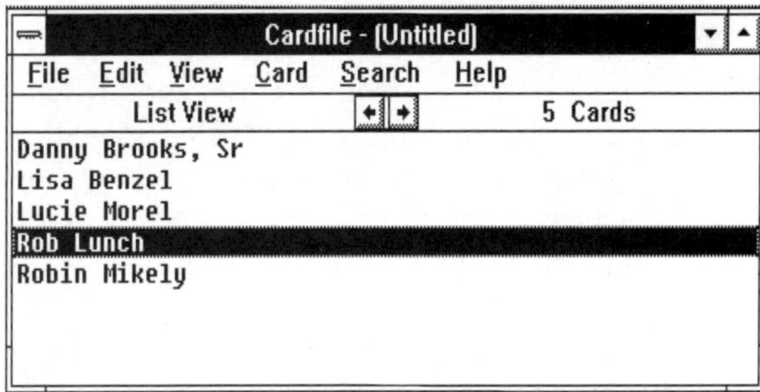

List View

Selecting a card

You must move a card to the foreground before you can write data to it or edit existing data. To move a card to the foreground in Card View mode, click on the index line of the desired card or use the PgUp and PgDn keys.

22.2 The Index Line

With the index lines, you can easily find information in Cardfile.

Editing an index line

Select the *Index...* command from the *Edit* menu or press the F6 key to edit an index line. When in List View mode, you can double-click any index line to edit it. However, when in Card View mode, you can only double-click the index line in the foreground card for editing.

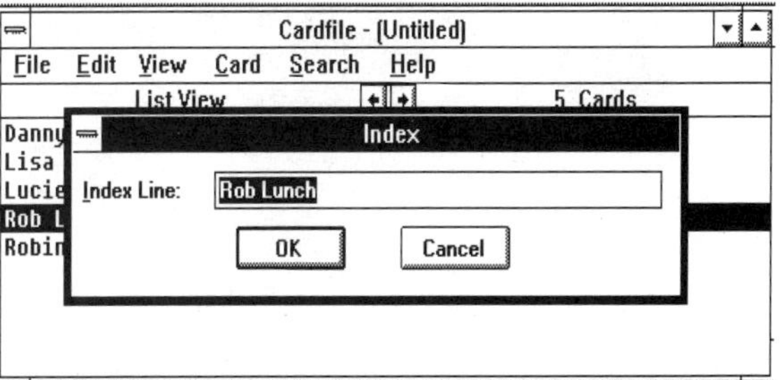

Editing an index line

Now you can enter any words, separated by spaces, into the index line. For example, you can enter names in the left margin of the index line, insert spaces, then enter the telephone numbers corresponding to the names. Cardfile beeps when your input exceeds the amount of space allocated for the index line (the spacing isn't WYSIWYG). Click OK to display your input on the index line of the current card.

Editing the index line

To edit the index line, place the desired card in the foreground and select *Index...* from the *Edit* menu. The current contents of the index line are selected and displayed in the text box. You can delete the entire line by pressing the Del key. If you only need to edit individual characters, use the cursor keys to move the insertion point to the desired position.

After you enter or edit the index line and either click OK or press Enter, the insertion point moves to the information area.

22.3 The Information Area

The information area uses the same editing features as many word processors. You can move the insertion point by using the direction keys or the mouse and edit text.

Moving the insertion point

The insertion point first appears in the upper-left corner of the information area. Pressing the Enter key moves the insertion point to the beginning of the next line. The Backspace key deletes characters to the left of the insertion point. Pressing Home and End moves the insertion point to the beginning and ending of the current line, respectively. The Tab key generates a tab that contains eight spaces.

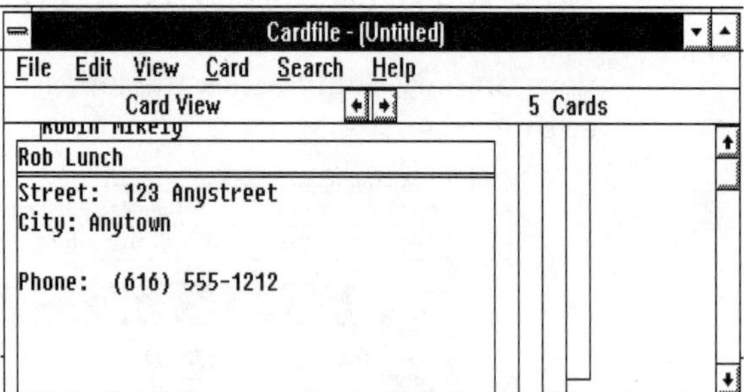

Positioning text on the card

When you enter similar information in a file, you should place specific information in the same position on each card. This ensures that you'll find information in each card quickly and easily. For example, you should enter the most important information first so that the information that's less important will appear at the bottom of the card.

Also, you may want to add field names for each item. These items can then be found by using the *Find...* command from the *Search* menu. Once you establish the format for one card, you may want to make copies of that card by using the *Duplicate* command from the *Card* menu.

22.4 Editing Cards

Cardfile provides various features that simplify creating and editing cards. You can copy and paste data to a card by using the Clipboard.

Copying information

To copy information to another card, select the information you want to copy. Then select *Copy* from the *Edit* menu to copy the selected information to the Clipboard, or select *Cut* from the *Edit* menu to remove the information from the current card.

Move the insertion point to the place where you want to copy the Clipboard's contents. Then select the *Paste* command from the *Edit* menu.

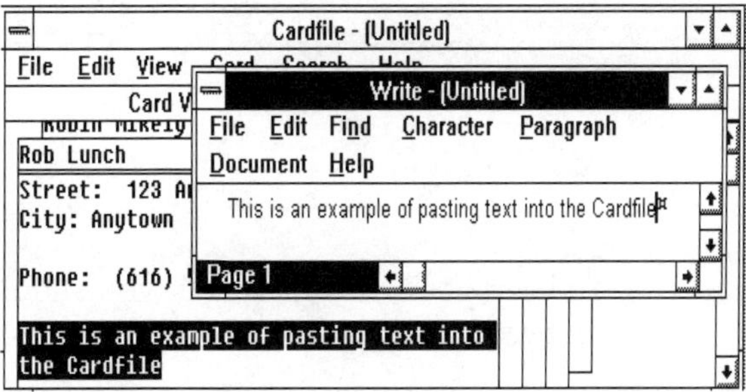

Inserting text from Write into the card file

You can also cut, copy, and paste data from the information areas of cards to other Windows applications that are able to accept text or pictures.

Restoring a card

Suppose that you've edited a card, but have decided that you want to restore the previous version. If you haven't saved your changes yet, select the *Restore* command from the *Edit* menu. This restores the original appearance of the card.

Undo

If you discover that you've made an error immediately after editing a card, and you haven't changed to another card, select *Undo* from the *Edit* menu to undo that edit.

Adding a new card

You can add new cards to a file. Select *Add...* from the *Card* menu to add a new card. In the dialog box that appears, type the index line data for the new card. When you press Enter or click OK, a new card, containing the index line information you just typed, appears.

Duplicating cards

Earlier in this chapter we mentioned that you can duplicate cards by using the *Duplicate* command from the *Card* menu. Select the card you want to copy (move it to the foreground). Then select *Card/Duplicate*. A new card, which contains the same information as the original card, appears.

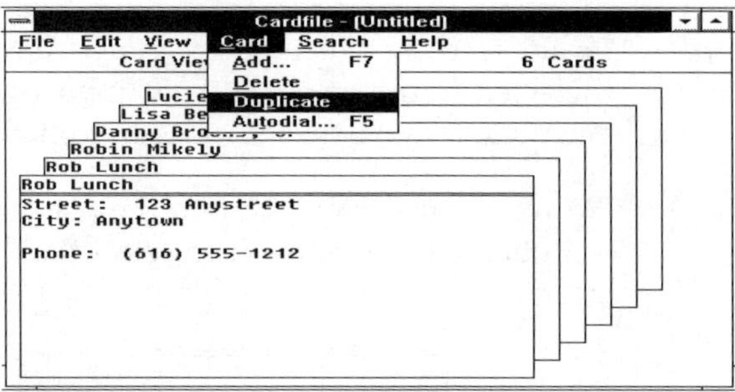

Duplicating cards

To keep your file organized, you should establish a structure in the first card of a new file and then duplicate this card as needed.

Deleting a card

If you no longer need a card, you can delete it. Place the card in the foreground and select the *Delete* command from the *Card* menu. A dialog box prompts for confirmation of deletion. Click on OK to delete the card.

22.5 Editing Pictures

The Cardfile can store pictures as well as text. You can paste pictures from the Clipboard, link pictures to Cardfile using dynamic data exchange (DDE), or embed pictures using Object Linking and Embedding (OLE).

Creating pictures with the scanner

Since Cardfile now accepts pictures, you can even include scanned images (e.g., snapshots) on cards, as well as names and addresses. Scanners, which convert photographs, clip art, etc., into pixel based files, are fairly inexpensive. You may want to purchase a scanner with Windows-based scanning software.

Pasting pictures from the Clipboard

After scanning, load the picture into a paint program (e.g., Paintbrush). Select the picture and copy it to the Clipboard by using the *Cut* or *Copy* command from the *Edit* menu. Now switch to Cardfile and select the *Picture* command from the *Edit* menu. This tells the Cardfile that the next item to be pasted is a picture file. If the *Text* menu item was marked, you cannot load the picture currently stored in the Clipboard. Cardfile checks the Clipboard format before allowing the paste. Move the card, in which you want to paste the picture, to the foreground and select the *Paste* command. The picture appears on the card.

Changing the size of the picture

Usually the card is too small to accept the entire picture. Use the direction keys or the mouse to scroll the picture around the card until the portion of the picture you want to view is visible. We recommend that you estimate the card size and resize the picture from within the paint program before pasting the picture in Cardfile. After positioning the picture, select the *Text* command from the *Edit* menu to make the picture permanent on the card.

Combining text and pictures

A picture can be placed in a card at any time. Select *Picture* from the *Edit* menu to switch to picture mode. Now the picture can be moved with the mouse or the direction keys. If a card already contains text, the picture overlaps the text. Then you must move the picture, by using the direction keys or the mouse, to a location where the text is unaffected by the picture.

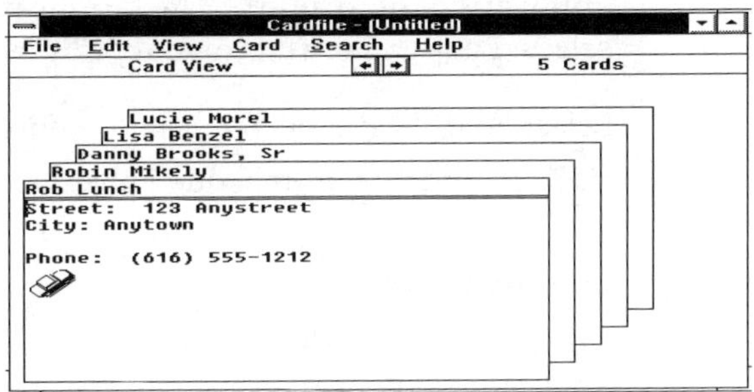

Combining text and picture on one card

Text can also be inserted on a card that already contains a picture. Switch to text mode and paste the text. The text will overlap the existing picture.

Inserting objects

If you're inserting an object in your document, which has a reference to its original application, the object can be changed at any time.

To insert a picture as an object, select the *Insert Object...* command from the *Edit* menu. You can now select from applications that support the OLE concept.

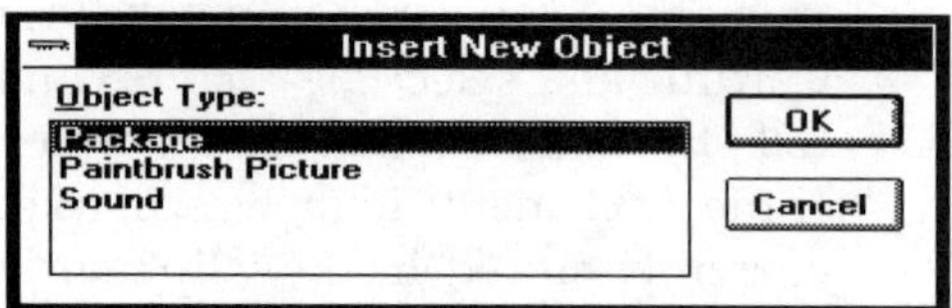

Applications for inserting an object

Select an application and click OK to start the application. Now you can create an object within the application. This object can be a Paintbrush drawing, an Excel worksheet, or a packaged object from the Object Packager. After creating the object, select *Exit* from the *File* menu. This closes the application and inserts the object in Cardfile.

To insert an existing object, switch to the application, from which the object was created. Open that object's file. Mark the object and select *Cut* or *Copy* from the *Edit* menu. Switch to Cardfile and select the card into which you want the object pasted. Select *Picture* from the *Edit* menu, then *Paste* from the *Edit* menu.

Editing an object

Double-click an object to edit it. You can access the object from the menus by marking the object and selecting *Edit...Object* from the *Edit* menu (the menu item changes, depending on the object's application of origin). The application runs, and opens the selected object file. You can now edit the object.

Select *Exit*. A dialog requests confirmation of the update. Click OK to update the embedded object and return to Cardfile.

Inserting links

Links in a file display objects that were created by using applications other than the current one. If you edit the object in its own application, the link can update the current application, either manually or automatically.

Links can be used only in applications that support Dynamic Data Exchange (DDE). Microsoft Excel supports DDE. Run Excel, create a worksheet, and save it (this is extremely important). Select the worksheet and copy it using *Copy* from the *Edit* menu. Switch to Cardfile.

Connection with Excel

Select the card into which you want to paste the Excel data link. Select the *Paste Link* command from the *Edit* menu. This pastes the Excel data and establishes a link between Excel and Cardfile. Ensure that both the Cardfile document and the Excel document were already saved. If the Excel worksheet wasn't saved, an update won't occur.

Setting the type of Actualization

Dynamic Data Exchange defaults to automatic update. If you edit the worksheet in Excel and switch back to Cardfile, Windows performs the update automatically. If you want to use manual updating, select the *Link...* command from the *Edit* menu. Click on the Manual option button and click OK to change updating to manual mode.

Click on the Update Now button to update the link from the Excel file. Click on the Change Link... button to replace the current link with another file. Click on the Cancel Link button to cancel the current link. The object is converted to a static object, which means that it remains in the card, but won't be updated.

22.6 Finding Information

Cardfile lets you find specific data in the information area. You can also access cards based on the contents of the index line.

Search only in Card View mode

The commands used in searching are effective only in Card View mode. Although you can go to index lines from within List View mode, you can view the results only after switching to Card View mode.

Go to index line

To find an index line, select *Go To...* from the *Search* menu, or press F4. The *Go To....* command is similar to flipping through a set of actual file cards in search of a heading.

Going to the index line

Type the search string in the *Go To:* text box and click on OK to perform the search. You can type all or part of a string. For example, if you're searching for the name Anastasia, simply type *Anas*, or *stas*, or even *tasia*. Remember that the *Go To...* command isn't case sensitive (i.e., it will find either *Anastasia* or *anastAsia* if you type *anastasia* as a search string). Also, *Go To...* accounts for spaces (i.e., it will not find *An ast asia* if you're searching for *Anastasia*).

Go To... performs its search from front to back. The card corresponding to the first index line containing the search string is moved to the foreground.

Finding information area data

Use the *Find...* command from the *Search* menu to find data in the information area. This command searches the information areas of cards for the search string, ignoring the information listed in the index line.

Search character sequences

Type the search string in the *Find What:* text box. Unlike *Go To...*, this dialog box provides various options for text searching.

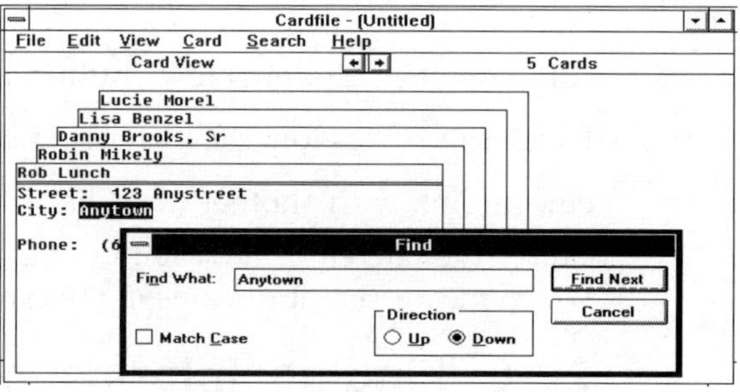

Defining search parameters

You can type entire words or parts of words in the *Find What:* text box. Also, you can specify whether the *Find...* command should use case sensitive searching and specify the direction of the search. Click on the Find Next button to search for the search string. The *Find* dialog box remains on the screen during the search. Each time the *Find...* command encounters an occurrence of the search string, you can click Find Next to continue. Click Cancel to exit the search.

Independent dialog box

You can still access all Cardfile commands (except *Find...*) while the *Find* dialog box is displayed on the screen. Use the System menu to close that dialog box or click Cancel.

Selecting *Find Next* or pressing F3 finds the next occurrence of the search string.

22.7 Merging Card Files

Cardfile lets you merge two or more files into one file. The merged file is sorted into alphabetical order. The original card files remain unchanged if you store the new, merged card file under its own name.

Using card files with the same layout

The *Merge* command is most useful with multiple files that contain similar information (e.g., two customer files for different areas). Cardfile can handle a maximum of 1,260 cards. Every card has space for a 40 character index line and a 440 character information area.

Maintaining the original file

To merge multiple files, open the first file you want to use as the target file. This can be a new file or an existing file. Select the *Merge...* command from the *File* menu. The *File Merge* dialog box lists available .CRD files. Click on a file name and click OK. Cardfile loads the selected file into the target file.

Copy the content of other files, as often as you want, into the current card file. You can even merge the target file into itself.

22.8 Modem Control

If you have an autodial modem connected to your system, you can use the *Autodial...* command from the *Card* menu to dial your telephone. Ensure that your modem is properly connected and the communications parameters have been set correctly.

Move the card, containing the number you want dialed, to the foreground, mark the phone number, and select *Autodial...* from the *Card* menu.

Including the area code

If you don't select a phone number, Cardfile searches for the first number that resembles a telephone number. If you want to include an area code, you must separate the area code from the rest of the phone number by using a dash (not a space or a slash).

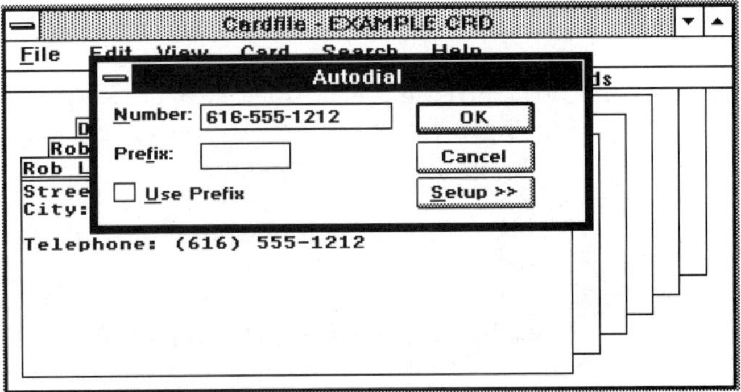

Accessing the first number on the card

Marking a special number

The search begins in the index line. The first phone number that's found appears in the *Number:* text box of the *Autodial* dialog box.

To dial another number from the card, mark this number before selecting the *Autodial...* command. You can edit the number that appears in the *Number:* text box or enter another number.

If the phone number to be dialed requires a prefix (e.g., 1) or an area code, enter this number in the *Prefix:* text box. This prefix can apply to dialing another area or simply dialing out of the office telephone system.

This prefix remains in the system for all subsequent calls of the *Autodial...* command. Clicking the *Use Prefix* check box dials this prefix on every call.

Modem setup

Click the Setup >> command button to configure the system to your modem. When you click Setup >>, the dialog box expands to display option groups containing different modem parameters. You can specify the dialing type your telephone system uses, the serial port to which your modem is connected, and your modem's baud rate.

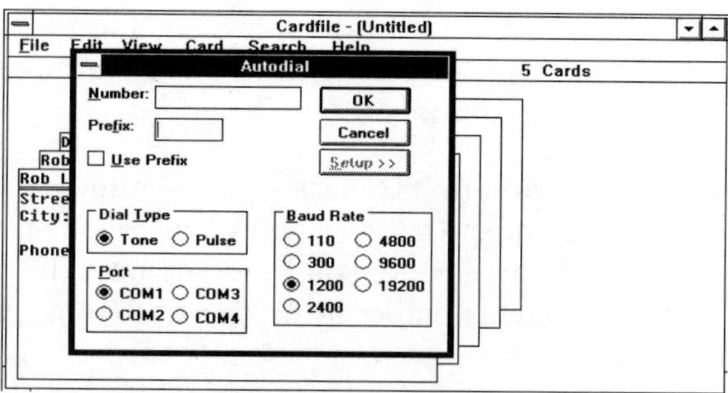

Modem setup

Dialing system of the phone

If your telephone makes a clicking noise while dialing, you're using a pulse system. If you hear a series of beeps while dialing, you're using a tone system.

Serial port

This option specifies the serial port to which your modem is attached.

Baud rate

The baud rate refers to the data transmission speed of your modem.

When all settings are correct, click OK to continue.

22.9 Saving and Loading Cardfile Data

When you first call Cardfile, the screen displays a blank card. You can start creating a new file immediately. The information you type here is stored only in RAM. So, you must save the file to the hard drive or a diskette for later use.

Saving new card files

If you're storing a new document for the first time, the *Save* and *Save As...* commands have the same effect. Both commands display the *Save As* dialog box. Enter a file name and the directory, in which you want the new file saved. Cardfile automatically appends the .CRD extension to these files.

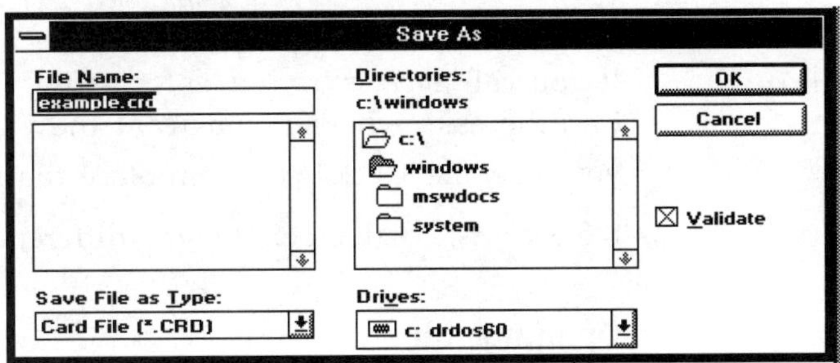

Directory and name input

As you edit, save your work regularly. This will prevent data loss in case of a power outage or a system crash.

If you're editing an existing file, select *Save* from the *File* menu. This saves the file under the current name. If you want to save the file to a different directory, or save it under a different name, select *Save As....* Cardfile will prompt you for a name. Enter the new name or directory and click OK.

Creating a new file

Select *New* from the *File* menu to create a new file. This displays a single blank card.

If you select this command when you're still in a file to which you've made changes, a dialog box appears, asking whether or not you want to save the changes. Click Yes to save the changes, No to close the file without saving the changes, and Cancel to return to the current file. The same dialog box appears when you select *Exit* from the *File* menu.

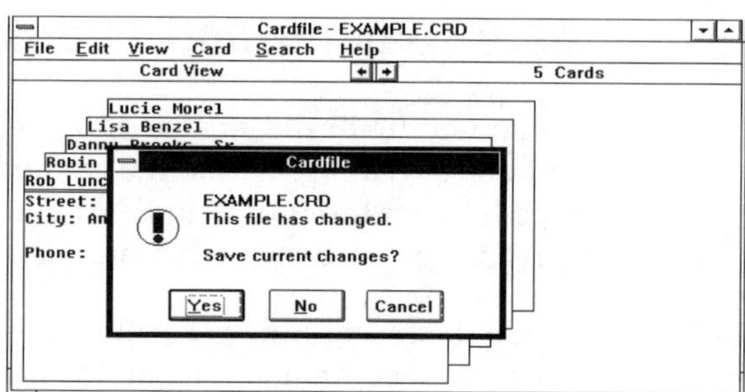

Confirm before saving

Overwriting files

If you call *Save As...* and enter a file name that already exists, Cardfile asks whether you want the existing file replaced with your new file. Click Yes to replace the file and No to return to the *Save As...* dialog box. Enter a different name and click OK.

Opening files

The *Open...* command from the *File* menu lets you open and edit a previously stored Cardfile. Normally the *File Name:* list box displays only files with .CRD extensions. If you want to change to another extension, select the file from the *List Files of Type:* drop-down list box. Selecting *All Files (*.*)* displays all file types. Select a file and click OK to open that file.

Remember that Cardfile can open or edit only files that were created by Cardfile. So, you can assume that Cardfile cannot edit files created using the Calendar. If you try to load a Calendar file, an error message appears.

Windows lets you easily compare an edited file with an older version. Open a second Cardfile window by calling Cardfile again. To do this, either double-click an icon or use the File Manager. Then you can click between windows and view each file.

22.10 Printing Card Files

Cardfile generates card records that are ready for printing. You can specify the paper size, margins, header data, and footer data.

Control characters for headers and footers

Headers and footers make longer documents easier to read. Select the *Page Setup...* command from the *File* menu to specify margins, as well as the data you want printed in the page header and footer. Cardfile provides the following control codes for headers and footers:

&d	Display current system date
&t	Display current system time
&f	Use current file name
&p	Use current page number
&l	Left-align the following text
&r	Right-align the following text
&c	Center the following text

To help you understand how this works, we entered the following in the *Header:* text box and removed existing text from the *Footer:* text box. This header prints the system date left-aligned, a centered text, and the current page number right-aligned:

```
&l&d&cImportant Information&r&p
```

Printing

You can print all the cards in the file, or just one card. Changing to List View mode allows you to print all data using the *Print All* command from the *File* menu. If you want to print one card, change to Card View mode, move the card to the foreground, and select the *Print* command from the *File* menu.

The parameters set in the *Page Setup...* and *Print Setup...* commands specify the printed page size and format.

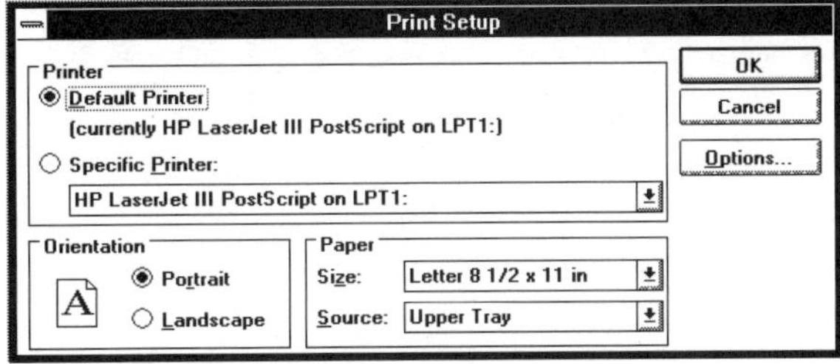

Setting printer parameters

If you have multiple printers on your system, ensure that the correct printer driver is selected before printing. Use the *Print Setup...* command to check the printer driver.

23. The Recorder

Recording a macro

The Recorder helps you generate macros, which enables you to perform multiple commands with a single keystroke. In this chapter we'll show you how to create new macros for Windows, edit existing macros, and merge multiple macros.

23.1 Operating The Recorder

The Recorder lets you record and store groups of command sequences. When these sequences are stored in a macro file, they can be used in future Windows sessions as executable routines. These routines can be called with key combinations.

Automating actions

Macros can be written for all Windows applications. It's even possible for several Windows applications to interact. With a macro, it's possible to start the Cardfile from the word processor Write, then select a certain name from the card file, and copy it, using the Clipboard, to a letter that's being created in Write.

Controlling macro execution

Actions performed with the keyboard and the mouse can be recorded in a macro. The execution of a macro can be limited to the application, under which the recording was made. A macro can also be available to all applications. However, the recorded input must also apply to the current application at the time of the macro call.

We'll use an example to clarify the Recorder's requirements and procedures.

Consider ions before recording a macro

Before recording a macro, determine what the macro should do. For our example, the key sequences that are recorded will open a window for all groups of the Program Manager and display them next to each other in the Program Manager window. Then the Program Manager window will be maximized to its full size.

Also, the starting position on the display screen must be well-defined when the macro is being recorded or called. At this point, we assume that, except for the Program Manager, no other window has been opened and all program groups are displayed only as icons. To follow our example, your screen should look similar to the following:

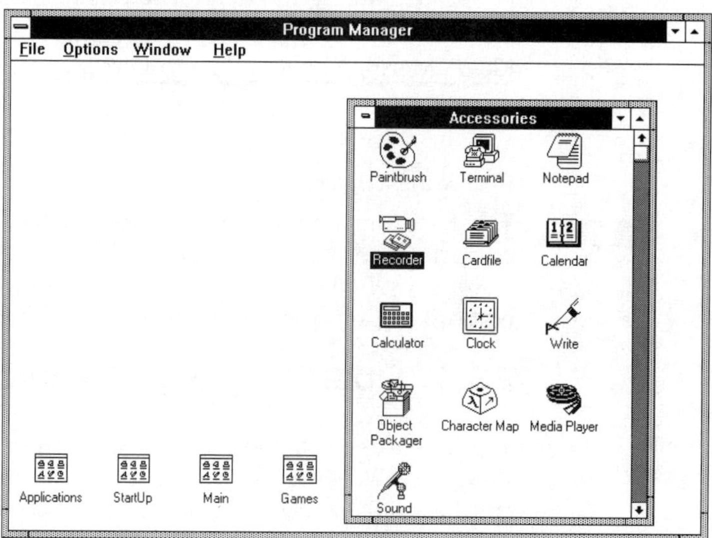

This is the way your screen should look before the call of the Macro recorder

23.2 Recording a Macro

Start the Recorder from the Accessories group. The *File*, *Macro*, *Options*, and *Help* menus appear in the Recorder's menu bar. To start a recording, select the *Record...* command from the *Macro* menu.

Once this command is activated, a dialog box, which requests a series of entries, appears. These document your macro. In this dialog box, type the information that's later used to identify the macro (i.e., to call the recorded macro).

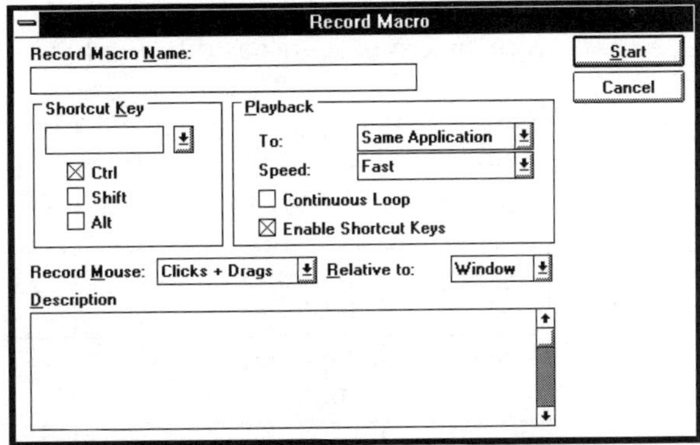

The Record Macro dialog box

You can assign a name to the macro that will be recorded. This name can have a maximum of 40 characters and can briefly describe what the macro does. Use this name to activate the macro.

Key combinations

You can also assign shortcut key combinations to the macro. To do this, combine any key on your keyboard with the Ctrl, Shift, and Alt keys. Which of these three keys should be part of the key combination is determined by which check boxes are activated.

This key can be entered in the *Shortcut Key* text box or selected from the drop-down list box, if it's a function key or a special key.

You can enter either a name or a key combination for calling the macro. We recommend that you use both of these since both appear in the Recorder window when you load the macro file. The name describes the function of the macro, which is called using the key combination.

The name for our example macro is "All Groups in the Program Manager" and the key combination is Ctrl + P.

Documenting a macro

To add other information about complex macros, enter a detailed description in the *Description:* text box. This description can be almost any length.

All additional settings, which can be made here, refer to the recording or reproduction of the macro to be recorded now.

Click on the Start command button. The Recorder window is minimized to a blinking icon. This means that the "Recording" process has begun. Any operations that are performed are recorded and can be activated later with the key combinations you specified. Try to avoid entry errors as much as possible, so that your macro executes as effectively as possible later.

Entering an example macro

Now you see only the Program Manager's window. To keep this example simple, we'll only make inputs by using the keyboard. Type the following key combinations sequentially:

Alt+W	(opens Window menu)	1	(opens Group 1)
Alt+W	(opens Window menu)	2	(opens Group 2)
Alt+W	(opens Window menu)	3	(opens Group 3)
Alt+W	(opens Window menu)	4	(opens Group 4)
Alt+W	(opens Window menu)	5	(opens Group 5)
Alt+ Spacebar	(opens Program Manager system)	X	(selects the Maximize command)
Alt+W	(opens Window menu)	T	(selects the Tile command)

Terminate macro recording

Click on the blinking Recorder icon or activate the key combinations Ctrl+Pause (<Break>), to interrupt the macro recording. A dialog box, in which you can save the macro, cancel the recording, or resume the recording, appears.

Storage options for the macro

Click the Save Macro button and then the OK button. The Cancel Recording option button should be activated only if you made an error and want to delete the entire recording. With the Resume Recording option button, you can continue the interrupted recording where you left off.

After you select *Save Macro* and click on OK, the dialog box disappears and the Recorder remains as an icon at the bottom of the window. To test whether our macro works, first restore the initial conditions at the beginning of the recording. Close all group windows and return the Program Manager window to its normal size.

Now you can call the macro you just created. Open the window of the Recorder by double-clicking on the minimized Recorder icon.

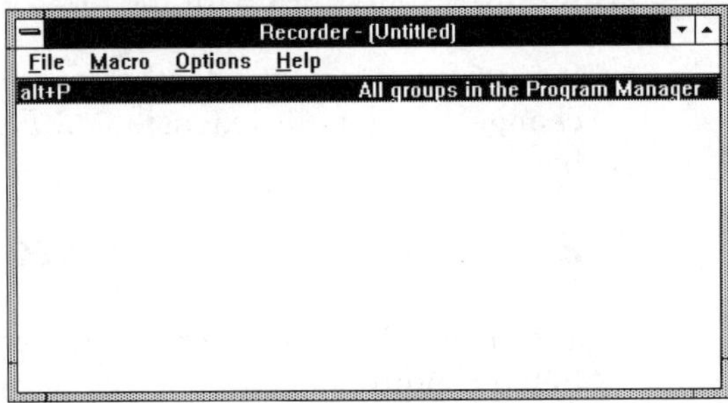

The first macro in your macro file

The first line of the Recorder window contains an entry for the macro that was just recorded. This entry contains the shortcut key combinations and the name of the macro. This name isn't the file name under which this macro is stored. Instead, it's only the name of one macro in a file, which hasn't been named yet.

If you examine the title bar of the window, you'll see that only *Untitled* is displayed as the name of the loaded file. This means that your macro hasn't been saved in a file. If you want to save the macro in a file, you should do so immediately.

23.3 Saving and Opening Macros

To save your macro in a file, select the *Save* or *Save As...* command from the *File* menu. A dialog box, in which you can enter a file name for the macro file, appears. You can also specify the drive and directory for the macro file.

Enter any name in this dialog box. The Recorder automatically assigns the .REC file extension. This also associates the file with the Recorder. If necessary, you can use another file extension. However, you should use the .REC extension because any other extension name won't be associated with the Recorder.

Opening a macro file

To work with existing macro files, first you must open them. This is the same process that's used to open documents in a word processor. To do this, select the *Open...* command from the *File* menu. A dialog box, which asks which macro file should be loaded, appears.

This dialog box is identical to the Open dialog box of the *Open...* command in other Windows applications. A list of files in the current directory is displayed. This list contains only files that have the standard extension for this application. For the Recorder, only files with the .REC extension are displayed.

Be careful if you used other extensions. In this case, you must change the default extension *.REC for the file name in the text box.

23.4 Running a Macro

To ensure that the macro works properly, you must restore the initial condition on your screen at the time of the macro recording. Then press the key combinations that you assigned to the macro. For our example macro, this is Alt+P.

If you receive different results, try again. Make sure that you're starting with the same conditions that existed during the beginning of the recording.

Call by name

It's also possible to activate a macro by using its name. Restore the initial condition again and open the window of the Recorder. If you recorded additional macros, first select the macro to be called by using the mouse click or the direction keys.

Selecting a macro in the list

Select the *Run* command from the *Macro* menu to execute the selected macro. The Recorder is displayed as an icon and the Program Manger window appears in the foreground. All recorded operations should be automatically performed by the macro.

If the result is still incorrect, delete the macro and start a new recording.

Deleting a macro

If a macro recording is incorrect or the recorded macro is no longer needed, you can easily remove the macro from a macro file.

Select the macro in the Recorder window and select the *Delete* command from the *Macro* menu. The Recorder displays a dialog box which asks if the selected macro should be deleted. Once you click OK, the macro is deleted from the currently loaded macro file.

23.5 Changing Macro Properties

If you want to change the properties of a recorded macro, for example by entering a detailed description for a macro, you can do this with the *Properties...* command from the *Macro* menu.

After this command is selected, you can edit and change some settings and information that you made before the beginning of the macro recording.

Changing the control of the macro

Here you can assign another name, change the shortcut key combinations, modify the description of the macro, or add a description. You can also influence the playback settings. Information about the mouse operations in this macro appear above the Description field; this information cannot be changed.

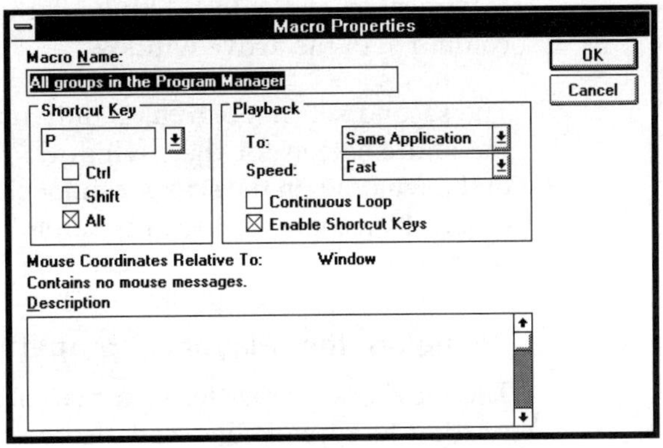

Changing the properties of macros

For our example macro, we are told that the mouse operations are relative to movements in a window, but no mouse operations were recorded.

These settings are made during the recording. Since we only recorded a very simple macro, we were satisfied with the default settings and didn't change them.

Record Mouse operations

The three default settings that affect the recording of mouse movements are located in the Record Mouse drop-down list.

The first setting is *Ignore Mouse*. This means that, while a macro is being recorded, any operations you perform with the mouse won't be recorded.

The second setting is *Clicks+Drags*. With this setting, only the mouse operations, which occur while the mouse key is pressed, are recorded. For example, this occurs when the mouse is clicked on a specific object or when an object is dragged to another window.

The third setting is *Everything*. With this setting, all mouse operations, even those performed without a depressed mouse key, are recorded and repeated when the macro is called.

Positioning the mouse pointer

Another setting involves the area relative to the movements of the mouse pointer. You have two options.

Coordinates determine the position

The *Window* setting is the most popular setting because the mouse movements are usually oriented in the area that contains the window of the active application. The position of the window on the screen isn't important. The mouse operations are converted into a type of coordinates. Think of these coordinates as "line 4 / column 5" of the active window.

The second setting, *Screen*, is only useful for applications that use the entire screen for their window. With this setting, the position of the window on the screen cannot change and no errors, which are caused by a changed screen position, can occur during the execution of the macro.

Changing the Playback properties

The playback properties of a macro, such as execution speed and relation to applications, can also be changed. For example, before recording and for a stored macro, you can determine whether the macro can be called for only one application (namely for the application with which it was recorded) or for all applications. Use either the *Same Application* or *Any Application option*.

Reference of the macro command

With the *Same Application* setting, the commands refer to the application with which the macro was recorded. This means that if, during the recording, the *Maximize* command was selected for the Program Manager, this command will be executed only for the Program Manager. If this application isn't available at the time of the macro call, an error message is displayed.

If you selected the *Playback To Every Application* setting, the Recorder will at least try to execute the recorded operation with the currently active application. If the recorded commands don't exist, the macro cannot execute properly and an error message will appear or a series of warning beeps will sound.

Changes in the execution speed

For ordinary macros, which automate frequently-used command sequences, you can select the *Fast* setting for the execution speed. This allows Windows to execute the recorded commands as fast as your computer permits.

For macros that represent a demonstration of certain procedures and run in an endless loop, use the *Recorded Speed* setting. Remember that the steps that are automatically executed should be slow enough so that they can be followed by the user.

Automatic repetition of macro executions

To create a demonstration macro, the recorded macro must be repeated automatically. To do this, activate the *Continuous Loop* setting, which is located in the *Record...* or *Properties...* dialog box. You can specify this setting either before or after the macro is recorded.

Nesting macros

The last option, which can be changed, is the *Enable Shortcut Keys* setting. This means that the macro recording can call other macros with key combinations. If this option is switched on, it's possible to call a macro from inside another macro, similar to a subroutine.

For example, the following program structure is possible: macro-1 calls macro-2, macro-2 calls macro-3, macro-3 calls macro-4, etc. However, you can use only 5 nesting levels.

Nesting is only possible if you allow the Recorder to record such key combinations. If you switch off this option from the beginning (before the beginning of the recording), it isn't possible to nest macros because the input of the key combinations for the macro call is ignored.

If you disable the *Enable Shortcut Keys* check box later, this has no effect, because only the operations that are initiated by the called macro are recorded instead of the key combinations.

Changing the default settings

If, while you're working with the Recorder, you notice that the default settings don't meet your requirements, you should change them to create your own custom macro recording environment. To change these default values, use the *Preferences* command from the *Options* menu.

In the dialog box that appears, you can determine which values should appear in the *Record...* command dialog box. Mark the proper option buttons or select the content of the input fields from the appropriate drop-down list fields.

You can set the default options for *Playback To:*, *Speed*, *Record Mouse*, and *Relative to:*.

Suppress termination of a macro

To prevent the termination of a macro that was called, such as a demonstration macro, it's possible to disable the Ctrl+Pause (<Break>) key combinations. To do this, use the Ctrl+Pause (<Break>) command, which switches these key combinations on or off. If this option is active, a checkmark appears beside it. If the termination capability has been disabled, the macro can be stopped only by resetting the computer.

When a macro is terminated in this way, data may be lost if open files weren't closed properly, which usually isn't possible in an endless loop.

Suppressing a macro call briefly

Suppose that, while working with the Recorder, you want to work with another application briefly. If this application uses the same key combinations that you assigned to your macros, you can suppress the call of a macro through these shortcut key combinations. So, you don't have to exit the Recorder to access other applications.

To do this, use the *Shortcut Keys* command from the *Options* menu. With this command, you can switch the macro calls on or off. If a checkmark appears to the left of the command, it's activated.

Minimizing the Recorder during execution

The last option in the *Options* menu is *Minimize On Use*. This option allows the window of the Recorder to remain open after the start of a macro. The Recorder window is automatically reduced to a minimized icon when you call a macro.

23.6 Merging Several Macro Files

While working with the Recorder, you'll probably generate several macro files.

Store macros according to applications

Perhaps you've organized your macros so that the ones that belong to a certain application are assigned to a specific file. So, all the macros that you recorded for working with Write are stored in a file named WRITE.REC and all macros that apply to the Calendar are located in the CALENDAR.REC file, etc.

Although this system is useful when you need a specific macro, you'll encounter problems if you're simultaneously working with the Calendar and Write. Every time you want to call a macro for a specific application, first you must load the macro into the Recorder.

Creating a complete macro file

To solve this problem, use the *Merge...* command from the *File* menu. With this command, you can merge the contents of two or several macro files into one file. Later, you must load only this one file to obtain access to macros for several applications simultaneously.

First create a new macro file with the *New* command from the *File* menu. This file will hold the contents of all the individual macro files. When you've completed this step, you can select the *Merge...* command. A dialog box, similar to the *Open...* command dialog box, appears.

Here, you can select the files from a list of the files in the current directory. The content of these files will be copied into the newly created macro file. Select the correct macro file and click on OK to merge the file into the current macro file.

As you can see, the macros that were in the existing files now appear in the window of the Recorder in your new macro file. This procedure can be repeated for all macro files that should be merged with the new file. The original files remain unchanged and the content of the new file isn't overwritten, but extended, through the merging of old files.

24. The Clock

Display of the time

The Clock displays the current system time and the current system date. The setting of the correct time and the date occurs through the system control.

Analog and digital clock

The Clock can be displayed as analog or digital.

Individualized display

You can change the display of the clock according to your preferences. Besides the two modes (analog or digital), the font and the display of the date or the seconds can be controlled.

24.1 Calling and Viewing the Clock

The Clock accessory in Windows enables you to display the time and date. You can select the display mode that's used. Activate the Clock from the *Accessories* group. In the *Settings* menu the display mode is controlled with the *Analog* and *Digital* commands.

In the analog time display, the date appears in the title bar of the clock window. For the digital time display, the date appears below the time.

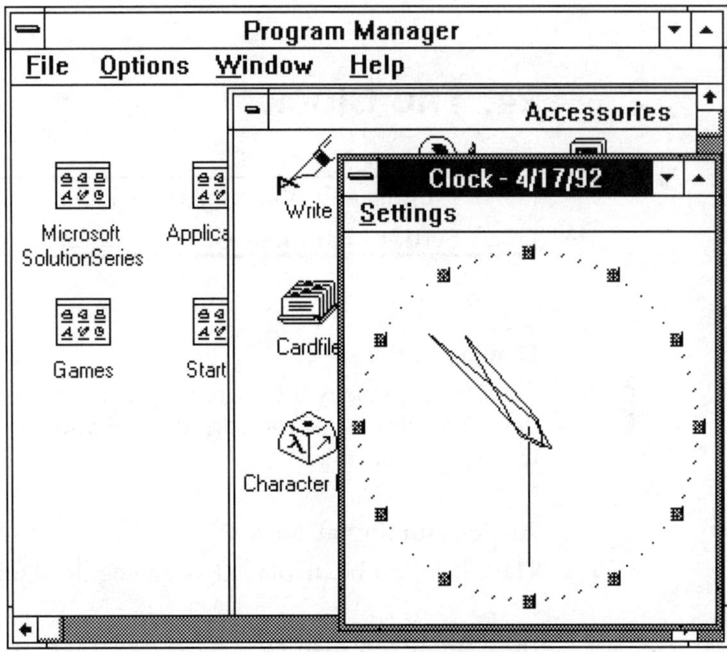

Analog time display

You can increase the size of the window so that it fills the entire screen. However, the Clock window usually interferes with the display of other applications. For this reason, you should display the clock as an icon. Since the application continues to run, and the time is clearly visible on the minimized icon, you should ensure that the window of your application doesn't cover the lower portion of the screen.

If you want the Clock to always appear as a minimized icon in the foreground, select the *Always on Top* command from the Control menu of the Clock window.

Correcting time and date

The time display of this clock depends on the system time of your computer. If the wrong time or date is displayed, set either or both with the help of the system control.

24.2 Setting Parameters

The time display, the date display, and the seconds display can be modified in different ways, according to your needs.

Setting seconds and date

If the seconds are displayed, the second hand appears in the analog clock and the seconds display appears in the digital clock. In this case, the *Seconds* command is marked with a checkmark. If you select this command, the checkmark will disappear and the seconds will no longer be displayed.

The *Date* command operates in the same way. If this command has a checkmark, the date appears in the analog clock's title bar, or below the digital clock's time display. If you select the command, the checkmark is removed and the date display is suppressed.

Suppressing the title bar

If you want to suppress the title bar, select the *No Title* command. This provides more space for the clock in the window. If you've chosen the analog clock display, the date display also disappears. To reactivate the title bar, double-click the *Clock* window with the mouse, or press the Esc key.

Display font

If you're operating the Clock in digital mode, you can change the display with the *Set Font...* command. This assigns a new font to the display. The *Font:* list box lists the available fonts.

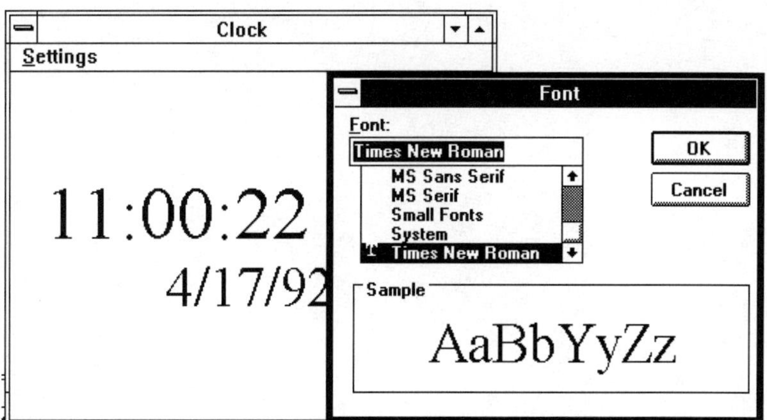

Digital clock with customized font

25. The Calculator

The Standard Calculator

Calculator

The Windows Calculator in the Standard display has all the functions of a normal calculator. This includes the four basic math functions, square root, percentages, and reciprocals. Memory storage functions are also provided.

The Scientific Calculator

With the enhanced display of the Scientific Calculator, many operations from technical and scientific fields can be performed. This includes statistical and trigonometric functions. It's also possible to represent values in different number systems.

Automated calculations

With the Clipboard, comprehensive calculations can be written on a page of the Notepad and then read into the calculator. Using the key codes for calling the proper function, the input is calculated immediately.

25.1 The Standard Functions

We'll only briefly explain the individual functions because they are too complex to discuss in detail in this book. However, you must know what functions are available and how the Windows calculator operates.

Standard Calculator functions

The Standard Calculator is basically a normal pocket calculator. It's useful because it can be displayed on the screen along with other applications. For example, you can use the Notepad to create a text document containing numbers that must be added together. If you activate the Calculator, you can perform these additions while Notepad is still displayed on the screen.

The results can be copied directly from the calculator into the text document or a Paintbrush picture. Calculations that appear in text or pictures can be performed automatically on your calculator; you don't have to enter any numbers.

Activating the Calculator

Double-click the *Calculator* icon from the Accessories group. The Calculator, which has several basic functions and a memory, can be used with a mouse or the keyboard. To use the mouse, simply click on the keys that you want typed. The keyboard contains the number keys 0 to 9. If you're using the keyboard, simply press these keys to type numbers into the Calculator.

Performing calculations with the keyboard

To activate the various functions, press the following keys:

sqrt	@	Square root
%	%	Percentage
1/X	r	Reciprocal value
=	=	Equals
+/-	F9	Changes the sign
.	.or ,	Decimal point
Back	Backspace	Delete rightmost digit
CE	Del	Clear entry
C	Esc	Clear calculation
MC	Ctrl+L	Memory Clear
MR	Ctrl+R	Memory Recall
MS	Ctrl+M	Memory Store
M+	Ctrl+P	Add value to memory

After you start the Calculator, the content of memory is zero. You can then add or subtract in the memory. You can also display or delete the memory contents.

25.2 Entering Calculations

Sometimes you must perform calculations in applications. For example, this can occur when you're writing bills using a word processor. Although some word processors can perform basic calculator functions, more complex calculations can be performed with the Calculator and the results can be copied into the text.

Syntax of formulas

Formulas can be pasted directly into the calculator by using the Clipboard. After the calculation, the result can be inserted into the document using the Clipboard.

During automatic calculations, the numbers must be in the proper order. The numbers can be separated only by characters, which the calculator recognizes as operations. If you're using the calculator with the keyboard, you activate these characters to perform an operation. Also, there cannot be any control characters in the formula. However, spaces and line breaks between the values or operands are allowed.

Type the desired formula in the document and select all the values that should be calculated. Only the selected values are used in the calculation. Copy the values into the Clipboard and then insert them into the Calculator. The Calculator immediately begins to read the values and to interpret the key codes. After the values are read, the last value appears in the display. When you press the [=] key, the result is calculated.

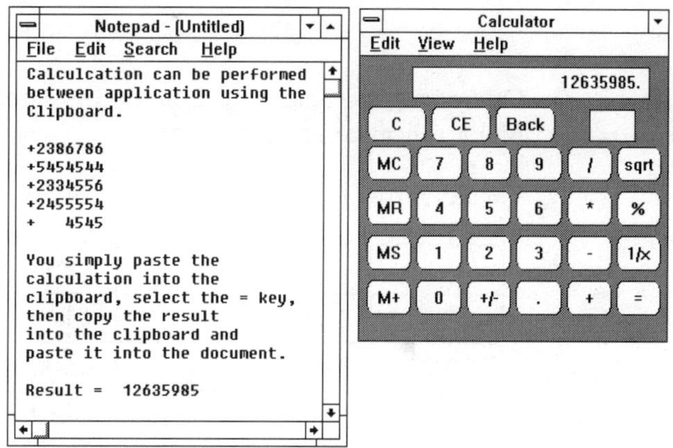

Transmitting formulas from a document

Select the *Copy* command to copy the results displayed in the calculator window. Then, in the text, move the insertion point to the location where you want to insert the result. When you select the *Paste* command and press the [Enter] key, your calculation is complete.

25.3 The Scientific Calculator

The *Scientific* command in the *View* menu switches the Calculator into Scientific mode. This mode provides more mathematical functions.

The Scientific Calculator has trigonometric, statistical, and scientific mathematical functions. This calculator also has a 14-digit display area, which has a three place exponential display.

If you enter more than 14 numbers, the calculator display changes to scientific notation.

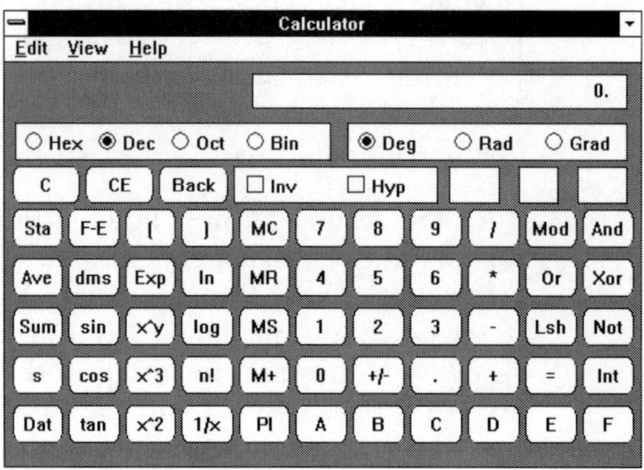

The Scientific Calculator

Operation using the keyboard

Operating the Scientific Calculator with the keyboard may seem like a nuisance at first.

The Scientific Calculator uses the following buttons and keys:

(	(	Open parenthesis.
)	)	Close parenthesis.
And	&	Logical AND.
Int	;	Display integer part of value. Inv+Int displays the fraction of a decimal number.
Lsh	<	Binary shift left. Inv+Lsh shifts right.
Mod	%	Modulo division (remainder) of x/y.
Not	~	Logical NOT.
Or	|	Logical OR.
Xor	^	Logical exclusive OR.

Number systems

The calculator can also convert between number systems that aren't based on the decimal system. The hexadecimal system and the binary system, which are used by computer programmers, are examples of this type of system. To select a number system, use the option buttons in the upper-left area of the calculator.

The following settings are possible:

Hex	F5	Hexadecimal (base 16): Range $-2^{31}-1$ to $2^{31}-1$
Dec	F6	Decimal (base 10)): Range -9.99999999999999e-307 to 9.99999999999999e+307
Oct	F7	Octal (base 8): Range $-2^{31}-1$ to $2^{31}-1$
Bin	F8	Binary(base 2): Range $-2^{31}-1$ to $2^{31}-1$

When a number system is selected, the previously entered number is immediately converted to the new number system. The calculator then accepts only input allowed by the currently active number system.

Converting numbers

The option buttons to the right of the number system option buttons are the display formats for the Hexadecimal, Octal, and Binary number systems. The following settings are possible:

Dword	F2	Full 32-bit representation of value.
Word	F3	Display lower 16 bits of value.
Byte	F4	Display lower 8 bits of value.

Statistical functions

The scientific calculator also provides statistical functions. To activate these functions click the *Sta* button. A separate dialog box appears. Move the *Statistics Box* dialog box so that the entire calculator display is visible. The *Statistics Box* is used to create statistics that are based on several values. These values are listed in the *Statistics Box*.

If the *Statistics Box* is still active, select the RET button to switch to the main calculator and retain the *Statistics box* entries. Enter the first value, which is the basis for your statistic. Select the Dat button to place the value in the *Statistics Box*. Enter as many additional numbers as needed, repeating the same procedure. The number of entries depends on the memory capacity of your computer. After all the values are in the *Statistics Box*, you can use the following functions. The result will appear in the calculator display.

Statistical functions

The Scientific Calculator contains the following statistical functions:

Ave	Ctrl+A	Average. Inv+Ave returns average of squares.
s	Ctrl+D	Standard deviation (population parameter=n-1). Inv+s calculates standard deviation with population parameter of n.
Sum	Ctrl+T	Sum of value list.
Sta	Ctrl+S	Activate statistics box.
Dat	Ins	Place number in Statistics Box.

Trigonometric functions

The Scientific Calculator also contains the following trigonometric functions:

Inv	i	Use inverse function for sin, cos, tan, PI, x^y, x^2, x^3, ln, log, Ave, Sum and s.
Hyp	h	Set hyperbolic function for sin, cos and tan.
cos	o	cosine.
Inv+cos		arc cosine.
Hyp+cos	h	hyperbolic cosine.
Inv+Hyp +cos		arc hyperbolic cosine.
Sin	s	Sine.
Inv+Sin		Arc sine.
Hyp+Sin		Hyperbolic sine.
Inv+Hyp +Sin		Arc hyperbolic sine.
tan	t	Tangent.
Inv+tan		Arc tangent.
Hyp+tan		Hyperbolic tangent.
Hyp+Inv +tan		Arc hyperbolic tangent.
Deg	F2	Trigonometric degree input (decimal system).

Rad	F3	Trigonometric radian input (decimal system).
Grad	F4	Trigonometric gradient input (decimal system).
dms	m	Number display in degree-minute-second format (degree display). Inv+dms converts degree-minute-second number to degrees.
F-E	v	Toggle scientific and normal notation. The Scientific Calculator switches to scientific notation if the user enters a number larger than fifteen digits.
ln	n	Natural logarithmbase e). Inv+ln calculates e^x (x=current number).
log	l	Common logarithm (base 10). Inv+log calculates 10^x (x=current number).
n!	!	Factorial.
PI	p	PI (3.14...). Inv+PI displays PI*2 (6.28).
x^y	y	x raised to y power. Inv+x^y calculates the y root of x.
x^2	@	Square current number. Inv+x^2 calculates square root of x.
x^3	#	Cube current number. Inv+x^3 calculates cube root of x.

26. The Windows Games

Taking a break with Windows games

As you know Windows contains many useful programs and utilities that help you increase your productivity. However, the Windows developers also included some games that can be used without leaving the Windows environment. The games Solitaire and Minesweeper provide instant recreation when you need a break from your work.

Solitaire

The Solitaire game is identical to the actual card game of the same name. The object is to gather all the cards into their own suits, from the Ace to the King.

Minesweeper

In this game, you must try to find all the mines in the minefield as quickly as possible. To do this, you must locate squares that don't contain mines and mark the squares that do contain mines. The number in the upper-left corner indicates how many mines are adjacent to the square that's clicked.

26.1 Solitaire

Solitaire is a popular card game that's played with a pack of fifty-two cards. The deck of cards contains four suits named Diamonds, Hearts, Spades, and Clubs. Each suit contains thirteen cards. Traditionally the Hearts and Diamonds are red and the Spades and Clubs are black. The sequence of cards in a suit is from Ace (value one), through the numbered cards, such as two, three, etc. to ten, followed by Jack, Queen, and King.

Arrangement of the cards

When you run the Solitaire game, you'll see a deck of cards open in the upper-left corner of the window. To the right of this deck are four suit stacks. The cards of each suit (Clubs, Spades, Hearts and Diamonds) are placed in these stacks according to the sequence Ace (low) to King (high).

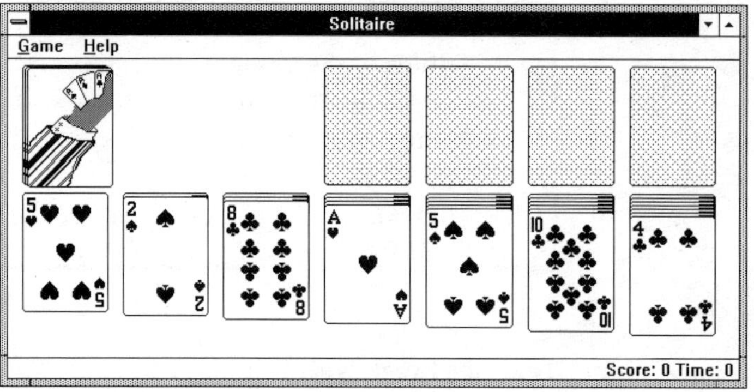

The cards never lie!

Seven row stacks are located below the deck and the suit stacks. Depending on where a card is located, additional playing cards may be located beneath it. Starting from the left of the screen, no cards appear under the first card that's displayed. The second card has one card hidden below it. The number of cards hidden below the top card increases as you move to the right of the screen.

Rules of the game

The object of this card game is to collect the entire deck of cards according to suit and according to the sequence Ace to King. The first card that can be placed on one of the suit stacks, either from the deck or the row stacks, must be an Ace. This is followed by the two (or Deuce) from the same suit. These suit stacks are filled with their respective suits until all of them have a king on top. At that point, you've won the game and a special graphics display appears on the screen.

Cards that are face up can be placed either on the row stacks or directly on the suit stack.

To deposit the cards on the row stacks or suit stacks, add cards to these stacks from the deck. Also, after moving the top card to a suit stack or another row stack, you can turn over a card that was hidden in a row stack.

Row stacks

Row stacks are created in descending order with alternating black and red cards. For example, if a red nine of Diamonds or Hearts is visible on a row stack, it can only be placed on a black ten (Clubs or

Spades) of another row stack. Then you can turn over the top card of the row stack, from which the visible card was removed. When none of the visible cards can be moved, you can turn over a new card from the deck in the upper-left corner.

If an Ace appears, you can move it to one of the suit stacks. Then the proper Deuce (Deuce of hearts on Ace of hearts, etc.) can be deposited on the Ace.

End of the game

The cards are uncovered according to a random number generator. So, often you won't be able to make another move. When this occurs, you must start a new game.

To make Solitaire more challenging, you can play against the clock.

The Solitaire commands

Start the game by clicking on the Solitaire icon. The window that opens contains the deck and the four suit stacks. There are seven face-up cards displayed on the row stacks. As we mentioned earlier, the individual row stacks contain different numbers of cards.

Before starting the game, you can set the Solitaire options. The *Game* menu contains the commands that control the game.

When you activate the *Deal* command, new cards are dealt. You can chose this command after you've reached a dead end and want to start the game with new cards.

The *Undo* command reverses the last move you made. If, after moving a card, you realize that you could have made a better move, you can restore the original condition with this command and make a different move with the card.

The *Deck...* command displays the *Select Card Back* dialog box, which lets you set the pattern on the back of the card. You can choose from several designs.

To move a card, hold down the left mouse button while dragging the mouse pointer to the desired location. Aces can be moved from the deck or row stack to the suit stack by clicking on the card twice with the mouse. To display a face down card, which was revealed on a row stack after the top card was dragged away, click on it with the mouse.

Determine scoring

To set the method of scoring, activate the *Options...* command. The scoring and type of play are set as follows:

Standard scoring

You receive ten points when a card is moved to one of the four suit stacks. When a card is turned over in the row stacks, 5 points are added. If the *Timed game* check box is selected, 2 points are deducted after every thirty seconds.

Vegas scoring

With this scoring method, the player starts each game with a stake of minus 52 dollars. This wager is reduced when you deposit a card in one of the four base fields for 5 points. This reduces the deficit and the player increases the stake.

If the *Keep score* check box is selected, the stake or deficit is used in the next game.

26.2 Minesweeper

After you start the Minesweeper game, a playing field appears on the screen. The surface of the Minesweeper consists of four elements. The largest part is the actual playing surface, which is divided into numerous squares. The number of hidden mines is displayed in the upper-left corner of the playing field. The playing time is displayed on the right. The middle button is used to restart the game if you hit a mine. You can also restart the game by pressing the F2 function key or activating the *New* command from the *Game* menu.

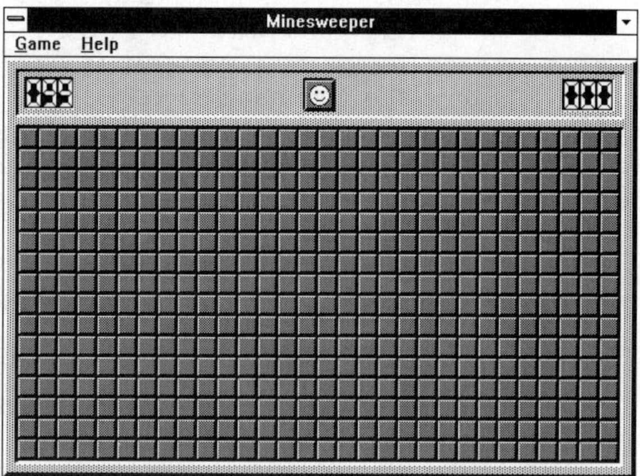

The Minesweeper for experts

Purpose of the game

The object of the game is to locate all the squares that don't contain mines. Click on a square with the mouse to uncover it. Uncovering the first square is based on luck. If a mine is hidden there, the game ends. If the square doesn't contain a mine, the square will display information about the locations of additional mines in the surrounding squares.

Uncovering the next field

A number, which indicates the number of mines in the bordering squares, appears in the uncovered square. You should imagine an area as a square with a 3 x 3 matrix. So, if there's a 1 in the middle of the matrix, only one mine is in the immediate vicinity. The number 2 indicates two mines, etc. The following illustration shows how the mines can be located around a certain number.

Possible positions of the mines

Through a combination of the displays, you can determine which squares contain mines or which do not. If, for example, a 1 appears in two neighboring squares, they probably point to the same mine. However, depending on the displays in the surrounding squares, this may not be true.

All fields point to the same mine

In some cases, only luck can help you avoid the mines. If you know a square contains a mine, mark it with the right mouse button. This disables the mines. At the end of the game, all mine fields must be marked.

Marking the mines

If you're sure that a mine is hidden behind a square, mark this field by pressing the right mouse button. You can choose between two types of markings with the *Marks (?)* command.

If a checkmark appears before the *Marks (?)* command, when you double-click on a field with the right mouse button, the field is marked with a question mark. Use this mark when you aren't absolutely sure that the square contains a mine. If a checkmark doesn't appear before the command, the square is marked with a flag symbol. Marked fields cannot be uncovered. The marked mine is subtracted from the score. If you continue to click on a marked square with the right mouse button, you can change the marking.

Setting the degree of difficulty

The degree of difficulty of the game is determined by the number of the mines in relation to the number of fields. The size of the playing field and the number of mines can be defined. You can set the degree of difficulty in the *Game* menu.

Beginner

For the beginner, a playing field with 8 x 8 (64) fields is displayed. This field contains 10 mines.

Intermediate

The intermediate players use a playing field with 16 x 16 (256) fields, which contain 40 mines.

Expert

The experts use a playing field with 16 x 30 (480) fields, which contain 99 mines.

You can create your own playing field by using the *Custom...* command. You can specify the number of horizontal and vertical squares. Depending on the input, the *Minesweeper* window increases or decreases. You also set the number of the mines in the dialog box. Then the mines are distributed over the playing field with the help of a random number generator.

If you want to make the changes in the default fields, select, for example, the *Expert* command and then *Custom....* The currently used data appear as the default in the dialog box. If you only want to increase or decrease the number of the mines, simply make the entry in the proper text box. In this case, the size of the field isn't changed.

The maximum number of mines that can be set depends on the number of squares. You cannot set 80 mines if you only have 70 active squares. If you specify a number that's too large, the highest possible number of mines for the number of the fields is used.

Monochrome Display

The playing field can be displayed in monochrome. If you want to use this setting, select the *Color* command. If a checkmark appears before the *Color* command, the color display is active. Removing this checkmark activates monochrome display.

Displaying the high scores

The *Best Times...* command displays a dialog box that contains the best results for each degree of difficulty. If new game conditions should be specified, erase the existing ones with the Reset Scores button.

27. The Character Map

Selecting the character set

This application displays a complete list of all available characters installed in Windows. The display of the characters depends on the font selected. When a character is selected, the key or key combination that is used to display the character in an application is also displayed.

Using special characters

Characters can be copied individually or in groups from the Character Map to the Clipboard. Using this technique, special characters can be easily copied into the text.

27.1 Selecting Characters

Character Map, which is an application from the Accessories Group, displays the Windows character set. The Character Map provides an overview of all the characters of the ANSI character set that are used by Windows. This also makes the characters, which usually aren't on your keyboard, accessible. Depending on your keyboard and keyboard driver, you may have more or fewer characters directly accessible on your keyboard.

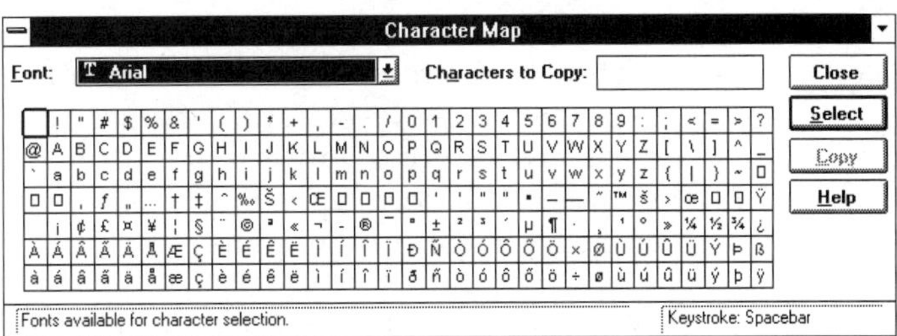

The Arial font

Unlike normal fonts, the Symbol character set provides a series of symbols that can be used in various documents. You can also use the foreign language characters without having to install the country specific character sets.

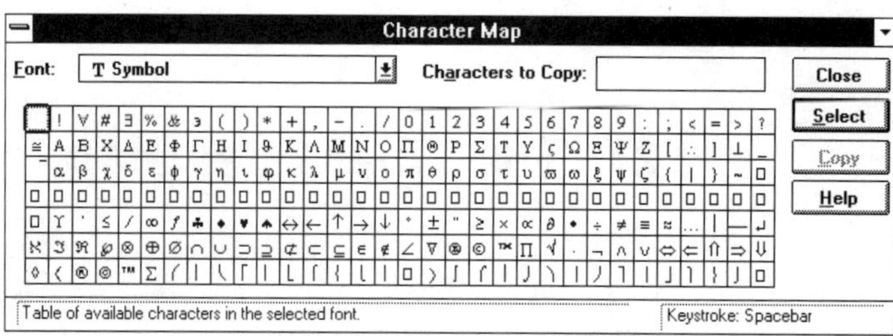

The Symbol font

Before you select a character, you should select the desired font. Use the *Font:* drop-down list box. The fonts displayed are installed screen fonts and TrueType fonts. When you've selected a font, click on the displayed characters with the mouse. If you hold down the mouse key when you select a character, the character is enlarged. You can also move around the Character Map using the direction keys.

27.2 Copying Characters

There are two ways to insert special characters and symbols into your documents. First, you can copy selected characters from the Character Map into the Clipboard and from there paste them into the proper application. Second, you can select the character in the Character Map, and remember the key combination used to display the character.

When a character is selected in the Character Map, the key combination for it appears in the lower-right corner of the *Character Map* window. Some characters can be generated in the normal way with a single key, and others must be generated with a combination of keys.

Numeric keypad

If you want to display a character that isn't located on your keyboard, you must enter its character code using the Alt key and the numeric keypad. The Character Map doesn't have to be displayed in order to do this. You can display these characters from any Windows application. However, this always selects the character in the current font.

To display the special characters, press and hold the Alt key, then type the numbers of the character code on the numeric keypad. If you use the numbers in the top row of keys on the "normal" keyboard, the characters won't be displayed.

Copying characters into the Clipboard

If you want to enter a complete character sequence into another application by using the Clipboard, first select the sequence in the Character Map. Select the characters to be pasted and then press the Enter key to place them in the *Characters to Copy:* text box. Repeat this process until the desired character sequence appears in this text box. Click the Copy button to copy the contents of the *Characters to Copy:* text box to the Clipboard.

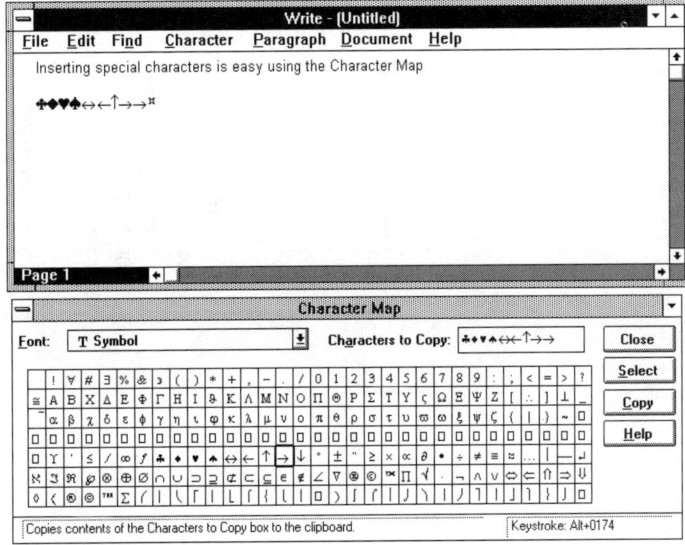

Pasting characters in Write with the Clipboard

The following table of high bit ASCII characters is very helpful when it's displayed on the screen. To create the desired character, first find it in this table. While holding down the Alt key, press the keys on the numeric keypad for this combination. For example, to create the Umlaut "ü", keep Alt depressed while activating the 1, 2, and 9 keys of the keypad.

The following table shows the high bit ASCII characters:

	0	1	2	3	4	5	6	7	8	9
110										
120									é	ƒ
130	Ä	ë	è	ê	î	ì	É	æ	Å	ò
140	ö	ô	Ç	ü	â	╛	«	Ö	Ü	ÿ
150	₧	¥	╪	à	å	ó	ú	┤	₧	─
160	ç	Æ	ù	£	û	ä	╖	╝	└	┌
170	¬	½	¼	┴	╟	╚		▒	█	│
180	┤	╡	╢	╥	╕	╣	║	╗	╝	╜
190	╛	┬	└	┴	┬	├	─	┼	╞	╟
200	╚	╔	╩	╦	╠	═	╬	╧	╨	╤
210	╥		╘	╒	╓	╫	╪	┘	┌	┘
220	■	>	<	■	a	º	Γ	╣	π	σ
230	╡	T	Φ	Θ	╜	╢	░	┐	e	∩
240	=	▒	│	█	║	║	╓	┼	í	Ñ
250	Ñ	╞	ⁿ	²	▪					

28. Multimedia With Windows

What is Multimedia?

Multimedia refers to taking audio and video data from outside sources (video recorders, CD drives, etc.) editing this data, and combining this data using the computer.

Special drivers must be linked to Windows before external multimedia devices can be used. To do this, double-click the Drivers icon from the Control Panel.

Sound Recorder

Use the Sound Recorder with a special sound card to record sounds or music and mix them into a new file. You can change sequences through special effects.

Media Player

The Media Player controls external drives, such as video recorders and CD-ROM drives. You can use the Media Player to play back recordings or sequences in specific situations.

Sound

You can use a sound card to replace the Windows warning beep with any sound file.

It's also possible to assign sound files to specific Windows events.

28.1 Introduction to Multimedia

The term Multimedia refers to an application that contains different aspects of various programs. It's an attempt to combine the different means of communication and audio/visual presentation in the computer into one software package.

MIDI applications

Companies have been developing multimedia products for some time. These products include compact disk players and sound cards. Professional MIDI (Musical Instrument Digital Interface) applications make it possible to mix sounds in the computer and replay the new sound file on high-fidelity equipment. Using CD-ROM drives in professional databases (e.g., encyclopedias) is also part of multimedia.

Hardware and software companies are still devising their own standards independently, so universal adoption of one standard hasn't yet occurred. However, some standards have been accepted; we'll discuss these later in this chapter.

Multimedia uses

Multimedia can be used in various ways. For example, multimedia is well-suited for visual information, such as databases and tutorials.

A good example of this is the Microsoft Encyclopedia, which allows the user to run special animations on given topics, or request background information through its interactive structure. Microsoft also offers a Multimedia Extension that is available only on CD-ROM.

However, this software can be used only in connection with a sound card (e.g., the Sound Blaster Pro from Creative Labs) and a CD-ROM drive. This Windows software is indirectly guiding other companies in the same direction. Many manufacturers supply conversions of the control software for use under Windows.

The leading hardware and software companies are trying to develop computer standards. The hardware standard was developed under the term MPC (Multimedia PC).

The minimum requirement is a 16 MHz 80286 system with 2 Meg of conventional memory and a VGA card. In addition, the computer must have an internal CD-ROM drive and a supported audio card.

Audio cards

The Sound Blaster Pro card and the CompuAdd Multimedia Option Card are examples of audio cards. The CD-ROM rounds off the Multimedia Kit, and contains the Multimedia Extension from Microsoft.

Along with drivers for controlling the devices, the Multimedia Extension contains a complete window as well as the Multimedia Development Kit, which programmers can use to create their own multimedia applications or expand existing ones. Programming is done in C, but it's also possible to use Visual Basic routines.

There is also an author system so that you can create multimedia applications without knowing programming languages. The CD also contains a complete programmer's manual, including a guide to creating your own applications.

Sound Recorder and Media Player

The Sound Recorder and Media Player applications, which are standard parts of the Accessories group beginning with Windows Version 3.1, were both taken from the Multimedia Extension.

Unfortunately, you won't be able to do anything with those applications unless you have additional hardware, such as an audio card, or a CD player, or a MIDI sequencer. In some cases, users will have sound cards that were created for use with computer games.

If you hook up a loudspeaker, you can make realistic sound effects, provided the game supports sound cards. Generally, the Windows Sound Recorder can address almost all of these sound cards.

Until recently, sound under Windows was limited to assigning digitized sounds to specific events (Windows startup, error message, etc.) as warning beeps.

However, you can use the Sound Recorder to mix and modify the sound files. Also, some cards allow you to plug in a microphone, which then allows you to create voice input and output. For example, you could record the phrase, "Good Morning, Captain," save the phrase to a sound file, then assign this phrase to the Windows Start event.

Every time you start Windows, the system will play, "Good Morning, Captain," in the voice used to record the original sound, through the connected speakers.

28.2 Linking Device Drivers

Linking must be done first

Before using an external multimedia device, you must link it. Before purchasing cards or drives, refer to the manufacturer's specifications about which entry is needed in the AUTOEXEC.BAT and CONFIG.SYS files. This is important so that the device is recognized by the computer when you boot it up.

It's impossible to list all the general rules because manufacturers configure their devices differently. Generally, the devices have an installation or configuration program on the diskettes that's included with each device.

The necessary drivers must be linked to Windows in order to use a multimedia card, such as a sound card (AdLib or Sound Blaster), or to control CD-ROM drives.

Successful installation of a driver is the prerequisite for using the Media Player and Sound Recorder applications. Install your driver from the *Drivers* dialog box. After activating the icon, a list of all installed drivers appears in a dialog box.

Installing the Sound Blaster card

To install another multimedia device, you must add its device driver to the list. First, install the device in the computer. For example, if you were installing the Sound Blaster II card, you would plug it into a free expansion slot on the computer. Then hook up a loudspeaker or a microphone to the card. Click the *Add* button in the *Drivers* dialog box to select the proper driver from the list.

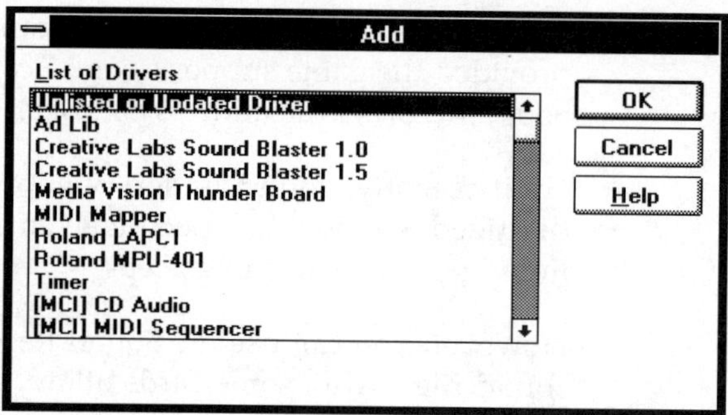

Selecting Multimedia drivers

Using other drivers

Select the driver that matches your device. If it doesn't appear in the list, you have two options. You can select a driver for a device that's compatible with your device. Otherwise, the manufacturer usually encloses drivers that you can link to Windows.

To do this, select the *Add Unlisted Or Updated Driver* option from the list. Windows then prompts you to insert the appropriate diskette in the drive or specify a directory or drive that contains the driver.

After confirmation, the driver is copied to the Windows system directory. Before that, Windows automatically displays the *Setup* dialog box, in which you must configure the driver.

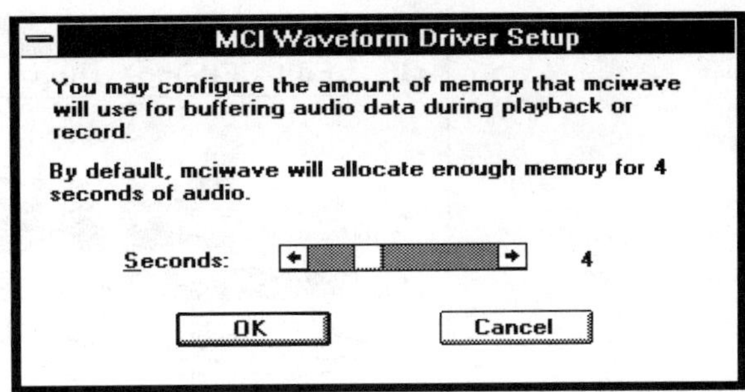

Setting up the [MCI] Sound driver

The setup can vary depending on the installed driver. If you set up the Sound Blaster driver, the *Port* and the *Interrupt* are set.

To determine whether the Sound Blaster driver functions have the proper settings, first restart the computer to initialize the card or device.

Then assign sounds to specific events by selecting the *Sound...* command from the Control Panel's *Settings* menu.

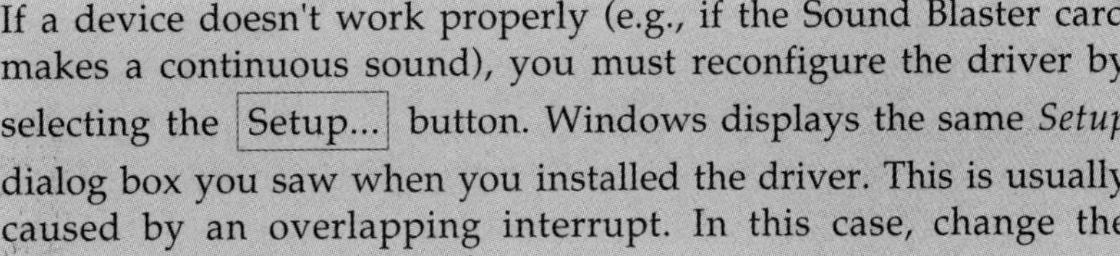

If a device doesn't work properly (e.g., if the Sound Blaster card makes a continuous sound), you must reconfigure the driver by selecting the Setup... button. Windows displays the same *Setup* dialog box you saw when you installed the driver. This is usually caused by an overlapping interrupt. In this case, change the interrupt setting on the card.

28.3 The Sound Recorder

You can digitize sounds from audio sources and save them as a file with the Sound Recorder. You can also mix several sound files to a single file and modify sounds in their structure.

Obviously, it's also possible for the Sound Recorder to play back sound files. A sound file can be up to 60 seconds in length.

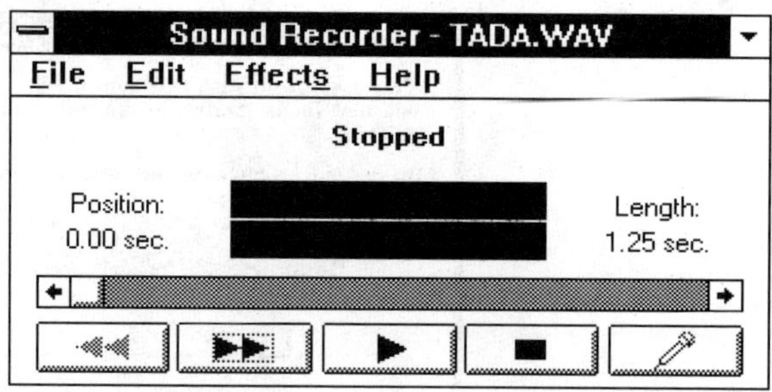

The Sound Recorder desktop

The buttons of the Sound Recorder

The Sound Recorder desktop contains buttons similar to those on a cassette recorder. The buttons have the following meanings:

<<

The Rewind button. Click this button to move the position pointer to the beginning of the sound file. The position within the file is indicated by the scroll bar and the wave box.

>>

The Forward button. This button is for fast-forwarding in the sound file. The position pointer is placed at the end of the sound file. The wave box and the scroll bar both indicate the current position.

>

The Play button. Select this button to play back the sound file. To search for a specific position within the sound file, to use a certain effect, or to insert another file, play back the file to determine the position acoustically.

■

The Stop button. Use this button to stop the file from fast-forwarding, rewinding, or playing back. You can determine the current position from the scroll bar or the wave box.

Determining the position within a sound file

As we mentioned, the scroll bar determines the position within a sound file. To insert or mix another sound file in a specific place on the file, it's important to know the exact position.

The wave box

The scroll bar is connected to the wave box. At the beginning of a sound file, the wave box is at 0.0 sec. The length of the entire file is specified to the right of the wave box. You can set the position in the file with the scroll bar by dragging the scroll box to the desired position or by clicking the scroll bar arrows.

If you're using the keyboard, use the direction keys to move the scroll box distances of 0.1 seconds. You can also determine where you are in the sound file from the graphic display, which represents sounds as wavy lines.

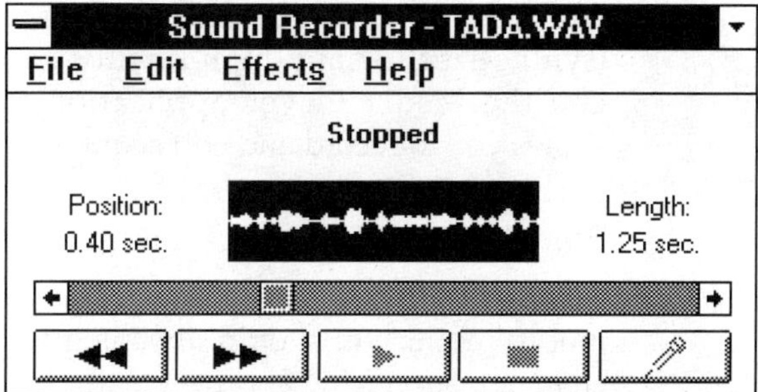

Graphic display in the Wave box

Creating a sound file

To create a sound file, open the *File* menu and choose the *New* command. You don't have to do this if you just started the Sound Recorder. In this case, a file hasn't been loaded yet so you can start working immediately.

If a sound file is being processed when you select *New;* a message will ask whether you want to save any changes that were made.

Once you answer this message, you can work with the new file. You can edit only one file at a time. Even if you're mixing files, only one file, which can be saved under a new name, is being created.

To use an existing file, select *Open...* from the *File* menu. Since the Sound Recorder can process only files in wave format, all the files with the .WAV extension appear in the dialog box. Select the desired file and perform the necessary changes.

If you made changes to a file but you don't want to save these changes, select *Revert...* from the *File* menu. The file will remain unchanged.

Recording from external sources

The button containing the microphone icon is only active if a microphone is connected to the sound card. You can either create a new file for spoken input or mix the spoken input into an existing file.

After determining the place in the file where you want to begin recording voice input, activate the Record button. All input will now be recorded from the microphone. To stop recording, select the Stop button.

Use the same procedure if you connected a MIDI device (synthesizer) or any high-fidelity component to the sound card. Use the Media Player application to control the devices. This allows you to record and edit sequences from any CD.

Editing sound files

Use a new name

Before creating a sound file from several other sound files and modifying it, you should always give this file a new name. If you change a sound file and save it under the same name, the original contents of the file are overwritten.

You can manipulate sound files in various ways by using the commands from the *Edit* and *Effects* menus. While the commands of the *Effects* menu apply to the entire file, the commands of the *Edit* menu apply to only a specific position within the file.

To insert another file in a sound file, use the scroll bar or the buttons to move to the place where you want to insert the new file.

If you're at the beginning of the file, the contents of the new file are placed in front of it. You can add the contents of the inserted file to the end of the existing file by moving to the end of the file.

So when you play back the file, the sounds are played in sequence. If you insert a new file in the middle of the current file, when you play the file back, the sounds of the original file will be interrupted by the sounds of the inserted file.

Inserting another file is useful if you want to expand spoken output by more words. For example, if you recorded the sequence "Good Morning, Captain," you can add whatever you want to the sequence (up to 60 seconds in length).

Increasing the sequence

There are two ways you can increase the sequence to "Good Morning, most illustrious Captain." You can play the file until you pass the word "morning" and record the new sequence "most illustrious" from the microphone.

Unfortunately, with this method, when you record, it deletes everything beginning at the current position. So you must re-record the last part of the sentence. This can be a problem if the end of the sentence is very long.

In this case, it's better to open a new file, record the sequence "most illustrious", and insert it in the proper place in the original file.

Deleting an area

If you want to delete areas from the beginning and end of the file you want to insert, for example, to remove unnecessary empty space, use the appropriate commands from the *Edit* menu.

To delete an area at the beginning of the file, move to the place in the file where the sequence you want to use begins and select *Delete Before Current Position*. Follow the same procedure to delete the area after the current position.

Define the position and select *Delete After Current Position*. You must answer a confirmation message before the area is deleted. The length of the file is shortened by the length of the deleted sequence. This enables you to limit the size of the sequences you want to insert.

Unlike inserting a file at a certain position, mixing a file causes both sequences to run parallel, beginning at the place the new file was inserted. To mix a file, move to the place in the original file where you want the inserted file to overlap the original sequence.

The original file doesn't increase in length unless it's shorter than the inserted file. If it's shorter, then the rest of the inserted file is added to the original file.

Using effects

Increasing volume

The Sound Recorder provides a few effects for modifying sound files. The *Increase Volume (by 25%)* command increases the volume of a sequence by 25%. To return the volume to its normal level, select *Decrease Volume*.

Double the playback speed

You can also double the playback speed of a file by activating *Increase Speed (by 100%)*. Select *Decrease Speed* to return the file to normal speed.

Echo effect

Select *Add Echo* to create an echo effect. The echo applies to the entire file. Selecting *Reverse* plays the file from back to front. You can only reset these commands by choosing *Revert...* from the *File* menu.

This restores the file to its previously saved status. When you use *Revert...*, remember that you're also canceling other changes.

Sound files as objects

You can embed sound files in other applications either as packages, with Object Packager, or as objects using the appropriate command (see Chapter 14 for more information). By embedding sound objects in text documents or tables, you can provide Help support in spoken output.

To connect the Sound Recorder to *Object Packager*, import the file you want to transfer and select *Copy* from the *Edit* menu. The icon for the Sound Recorder is now in the Clipboard.

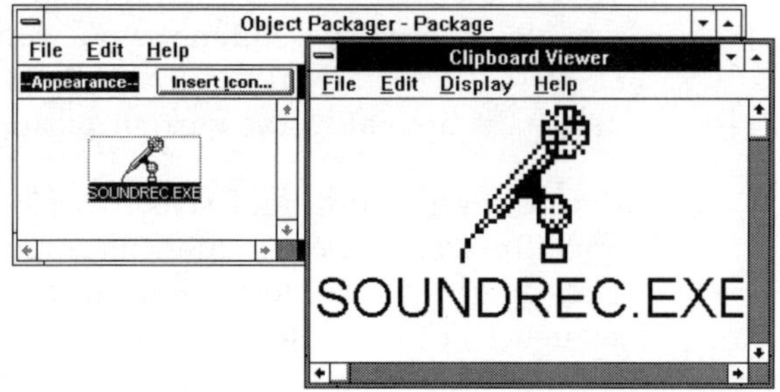

The Sound icon in the Clipboard and in Object Packager

Activate *Object Packager* and click on Insert Icon... . Object Packager then links the sound icon and the active sound file.

Sound Objects in documents

28.4 The Media Player

Media Player is an application that's used to control external multimedia devices. It also controls sequence playbacks. A sound card is needed for connecting the external devices and making output.

Device types

Media Player recognizes two kinds of devices. Simple devices, such as an audio CD player, can be controlled only by the buttons. Pressing the buttons plays back the information contained in the device. For example, CDs can be played from a connected CD player by pressing the Play button on the Media Player.

However, with multiple devices, such as a synthesizer hooked up to the MIDI port, you can play back files to control the devices.

Selecting a device

From the Control Panel, select *Settings/Drivers* to install devices. We described this procedure earlier. After installing the drivers, restart Windows to initialize the devices.

Then go to the *Device* menu of the Media Player and select the device you want to use. If the device is a simple one, you won't be able to select *Open* in the *File* menu. You'll only be able to use the buttons to control the device.

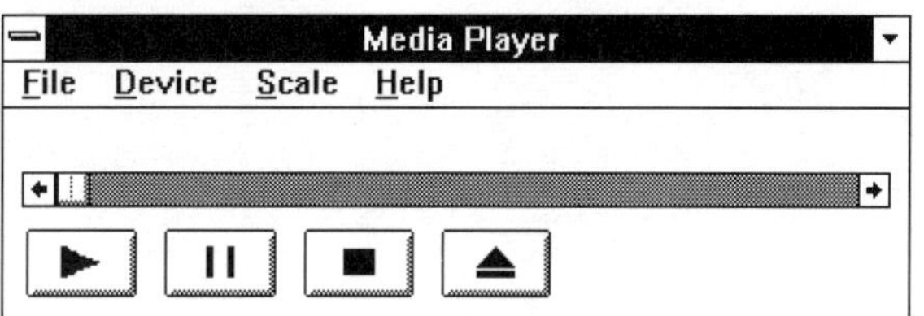

The Media Player

When you select a driver for a compound device, the *Open...* command is active and you can load a file to play on the device. In the list, compound devices are followed by an ellipsis.

Controlling a device

There are four buttons for controlling a connected device. Use the scroll bar to move around in the control file. Depending on the device, you can set either the Time scale or the Tracks scale in the *Scale* menu by selecting *Time* or *Tracks*. You should use the Tracks scale if you're playing CDs and use the Time scale if you're playing sound files.

Play

Select the Play button to play a sound file or CD.

Pause

Use the Pause button to interrupt play. Select the button again to resume playing from the same position.

Stop

Select the Stop button to stop playing a sound file or CD. Selecting Stop works even if the Pause button is selected.

Eject

You can only use this button on devices that have an eject function. For example, if you select Eject, a CD will be ejected from a CD player. You can only use this function when the device is stopped.

29. Windows And MS-DOS 5.0

Windows vs. MS-DOS

In a sense, Windows and MS-DOS 5.0 (called MS-DOS in this chapter) are competitors. For example, the MS-DOS Shell's Program List area and File List area offer text-oriented alternatives to the Windows Program Manager and File Manager.

In this chapter we'll discuss how MS-DOS and Windows coexist. Once you understand this, you'll see how you can optimize Windows and MS-DOS, and minimize conflicts in disk and memory access.

29.1 Using Windows with MS-DOS

Windows 3.1 and MS-DOS work well together. Since both are Microsoft products, they contain the XMS memory manager HIMEM.SYS and the 386 memory manager EMM386.EXE.

However, it's possible to refine and optimize this cooperation between Windows and MS-DOS. When installing either product, you may need to decide whether your PC should be Windows-oriented or MS-DOS-oriented. For example, if you plan on using Windows often, you'll want the Windows mouse driver running when you start the computer. If you prefer MS-DOS, you may want to run the mouse driver as needed, instead of including it as a device driver.

MS-DOS applications

Calling MS-DOS based applications from Windows can be difficult and sometimes impossible. For example, some tape drive backup programs won't work from Windows and hard drive optimizers shouldn't be used from within Windows.

One option consists of either selecting the best possible compromise between Windows and MS-DOS during installation or working with different system files and simply switching between the two files when necessary.

In this chapter you'll learn how to maximize your productivity with Windows and MS-DOS.

Compared with the competition

MS-DOS versus DR DOS 6.0

Let's compare MS-DOS 5.0 with its main competition, DR DOS 6.0 from Digital Research. From our experience, DR DOS 6.0 works well with Windows 3.1 in all available operating modes only if you avoid using certain DR DOS memory management options (i.e., memory expansion and the high memory area). However, you can use these options in MS-DOS without any restrictions.

You may have a system that contains DR DOS 6.0 and Windows 3.1. To learn how these two systems can coexist, refer to the next chapter.

29.2 Optimum Installation on Different Systems

There isn't a single optimal solution for installing MS-DOS and Windows. The installation depends on the system and your own requirements. In this section, we'll provide some suggestions for installing Windows on different systems.

Installing on an 80286 with 1 Meg total RAM

80286 with 1 Meg

An 80286 with 1 Meg total memory is the minimum system requirement for Windows 3.1. It's may be possible to install Windows 3.1 on an XT system, but the 80286 machine is the minimum suggested by Microsoft.

The memory must be distributed properly (640K of RAM and 384K of extended memory). We suggest the following:

- Be sure that the CONFIG.SYS file contains the following lines, so that DOS and Windows can use high memory:

```
DEVICE=HIMEM.SYS
DOS=HIGH
REM other lines of the CONFIG.SYS
```

- Avoid using a RAM disk or a cache program, such as SMARTDRV.EXE, from WINDOWS. This further reduces the amount of memory available for DOS and Windows.
- Use as few memory resident programs (e.g., mouse drivers) as possible. These programs also reduce the amount of available memory.
- If you need a special memory resident utility program (e.g., PC Tools DeskTop), avoid running it from AUTOEXEC.BAT as a resident program. Instead, start Windows, open a command interpreter from Windows, and start the program as a DOS task. This reserves memory for Windows applications and other DOS tasks.

The following system files illustrate good interaction between DOS and Windows on an AT with 1 Meg of RAM:

CONFIG.SYS for AT with 1 Meg

```
REM CONFIG.SYS for PC/AT (286) with 1 Meg
DEVICE=C:\WINDOWS\HIMEM.SYS
SHELL=C:\DOS\COMMAND.COM /E:300 /P
FILES=20
BUFFERS=20
BREAK=ON
STACKS=0,0
DOS=HIGH
```

AUTOEXEC. BAT for AT with 1 Meg

```
REM AUTOEXEC.BAT for PC/AT (286) with 1 Meg
PATH C:\DOS5;C:\BAT;C:\WIN
PROMPT $P$G
SET COMSPEC=C:\DOS\COMMAND.COM
SET TEMP=C:\TEMP
SET TMP=C:\TEMP
VER
```

Memory:

This configuration provides about 610K of free conventional RAM under MS-DOS. Also, the MEM command informs you that MS-DOS is in upper memory and 32,760 bytes of XMS memory are still available. Windows can make excellent use of this memory for Standard mode.

Incidentally, Windows allocates 478K of memory for Windows applications, which isn't actually that much. However, if you access a command interpreter from Windows, about 581K is allocated.

Installing on an 80286 with 2+ Meg total RAM

80286 with 2 Meg

For an 80286 with 2 Meg or more total RAM, you could use the same settings as in the configuration described above for 1 Meg. While this gives you almost no advantage under DOS 5.0, your Windows applications have more memory at their disposal and DOS applications could use XMS memory if necessary, depending on the DOS application.

However, a portion of the memory could be used for increasing speed on slower hard drives. You could also use a small portion of memory for a RAM disk, especially if there are more than 2 Meg of total memory available. Remember that Windows will use the additional XMS memory without any problems. However, unlike setting up a RAM disk or cache, which also fully utilizes DOS applications, you won't have much memory for working with DOS applications.

Now let's discuss memory options. In MS-DOS 5.0 you can use RAMDRIVE to create a RAM disk or use the SMARTDRV.EXE cache program from Windows to set up a buffer for hard drive accesses. In either case, you'll lose some memory.

CONFIG.SYS with RAMDRIVE

```
REM CONFIG.SYS for PC/AT (286) with 2 Meg and with RAMDRIVE
DEVICE=C:\WINDOWS\HIMEM.SYS
SHELL=C:\DOS\COMMAND.COM /E:300 /P
FILES=20
BUFFERS=20
BREAK=ON
STACKS=0,0
DOS=HIGH
DEVICE=C:\DOS\RAMDRIVE.SYS 320 /E
```

☞ If you forget the /E switch in RAMDRIVE, the RAM disk will be placed in conventional memory and only 296K will remain. This isn't enough memory for most programs.

This CONFIG.SYS provides an especially fast drive with a new drive letter. You only lose 2K of conventional memory, so there are still 616K conventional memory available. On a 2 Meg 80286 you'll still have 1024K of XMS memory for Windows in Standard mode.

This very fast drive is ideal for swapping temporary files in Windows. It works much faster than swapping data on a slow hard drive. Add the following line to your AUTOEXEC.BAT file (assuming that your new drive is D:):

```
SET TEMP=D:\
```

AUTOEXEC. BAT with SMARTDRV

```
C:\WINDOWS\SMARTDRV.SYS 320
```

If you use this line in the AUTOEXEC.BAT, SMARTDRV will use 320K of extended memory for temporarily storing hard drive data. This decreases available conventional memory much more than RAMDRIVE, leaving only 604K of conventional memory. On a 2 Meg 80286 you still have 1024K of XMS memory for Windows in Standard mode.

80386SX with 1 Meg total RAM

A typical 386SX computer has 1 Meg of total RAM. So, you must fully utilize this memory and swap as many system areas and device drivers to extended memory as possible. With only 1 Meg, it's not possible to operate Windows 3.1 in 386 Enhanced mode, so you should provide as much memory as possible for Standard mode and DOS:

CONFIG.SYS for 386 SX with 1 Meg

```
REM CONFIG.SYS for 386 with 1 Meg
DEVICE=C:\WINDOWS\HIMEM.SYS
DEVICE=C:\WINDOWS\EMM386.EXE NOEMS
SHELL=C:\DOS\COMMAND.COM /E:300 /P
FILES=20
BUFFERS=20
BREAK=ON
STACKS=0,0
DOS=HIGH,UMB
```

AUTOEXEC. BAT

```
REM AUTOEXEC.BAT for 386 with 1 Meg
PATH C:\DOS5;C:\BAT;C:\WIN
PROMPT $P$G
SET COMSPEC=C:\DOS\COMMAND.COM
SET TEMP=C:\TEMP
SET TMP=C:\TEMP
LOADHIGH DOSKEY
VER
```

Memory:

This configuration provides about 615K of free conventional memory under MS-DOS. Not only is this a lot of memory, but several programs were loaded beyond the 80286 configuration with the same amount of free conventional memory. This was made possible by extra system memory, called upper memory, which was provided by EMM386.EXE. Calling EMM386.EXE supplies the appropriate information:

```
MICROSOFT Expanded Memory Manager 386, Version 4.44
Copyright Microsoft Corporation 1986, 1991

EMM386 successfully installed.

Expanded memory services unavailable.

  Total upper memory available  . . . . . .     0 KB
  Largest Upper Memory Block available  . .     0 KB
  Upper memory starting address . . . . . .  C800 H

EMM386 active.
```

Calling MEM /C shows the distribution of the drivers and MS-DOS throughout memory:

```
Conventional Memory:

  Name                Size in Decimal        Size in Hex
-------------       ---------------------   -------------
  MSDOS                11712       ( 11.4K)       2DC0
  HIMEM                 1184       (  1.2K)        4A0
  EMM386                8896       (  8.7K)       22C0
  COMMAND               3056       (  3.0K)        BF0
  FREE                    64       (  0.1K)         40
  FREE                630256       (615.5K)      99DF0

Total FREE:           630320       (615.5K)

Upper Memory

  Name                Size in Decimal        Size in Hex
-------------       ---------------------   -------------
  SYSTEM              172064       (168.0K)      2A020
  KEYB                  6208       (  6.1K)       1840
  DOSKEY                4144       (  4.0K)       1030
  FREE                   128       (  0.1K)         80
  FREE                 32560       ( 31.8K)       7F30
  FREE                 46928       ( 45.8K)       B750

Total FREE:        79616       ( 77.8K)

Total bytes available to programs (Conventional+Upper):
709936   (693.3K)
Largest executable program size:
630128   (615.4K)
Largest available upper memory block:
46928   ( 45.8K)
```

MS-DOS is located in high memory. HIMEM, EMM386, and a small portion of COMMAND.COM are in conventional memory. Upper memory contains the remaining drivers, KEYB and DOSKEY, and the system.

Unlike the 80286 configuration described earlier, the drivers are in extended memory, so they don't reduce the conventional memory. Much memory is still free in upper memory, which enables you to load other drivers or TSR programs with DEVICEHIGH or LOADHIGH without decreasing the conventional memory.

Expanded memory and page frames

It's important to prevent EMM386.EXE from allocating expanded memory. Otherwise, the necessary page frame would waste 64K of valuable memory and you would have problems running Windows in Standard mode. The page frame is a special memory area that's needed for swapping memory in expanded memory.

80386DX with 2+ Meg total RAM

After setting up upper memory and high memory on a 386 computer with 1 Meg of memory, almost no extended memory is available as XMS memory. So there's no need to worry about using memory. However, if your system contains 2 Meg or more, we recommend running Windows in 386 Enhanced mode.

The NOEMS option

If you use the configuration listed above for a computer with 1 Meg total memory, you get XMS memory as additional free extended memory.

This is possible because the NOEMS option was specified after EMM386. Since this prevents EMM386 from configuring expanded memory (EMS memory), a page frame between 640K and 1 Meg isn't needed.

However, if you frequently work with programs that require expanded memory, you must omit the NOEMS option so you get the rest of the free memory as expanded memory.

Optimum setup of Windows in 386 Enhanced mode

In 386 Enhanced mode, you use basically the same settings you did for Standard mode. Don't set up expanded memory. With SMARTDRV, remember to specify a minimum cache size as the second parameter.

Otherwise, Windows can request the entire cache memory for its own use (and will quickly do so). If this happens, the hard drive speed decreases.

CONFIG.SYS for 386 with 4 Meg

```
REM CONFIG.SYS for 386, 4 Meg and Windows
DEVICE=C:\WINDOWS\HIMEM.SYS
DEVICE=C:\WINDOWS\EMM386.EXE NOEMS
SHELL=C:\DOS\COMMAND.COM /E:300 /P
FILES=20
BUFFERS=10
BREAK=ON
STACKS=0,0
DOS=HIGH,UMB
```

SMARTDRV.EXE and minimum cache memory

Finally, the AUTOEXEC.BAT should be linked to the SMARTDRV.EXE cache program by adding the following line:

```
LOADHIGH C:\WINDOWS\SMARTDRV.EXE 1024 256
```

The above line configures the cache program SMARTDRV.EX with 1024K of standard memory and 256K of minimum cache memory.

The value 10 was used for BUFFERS in CONFIG.SYS, because this buffer is only needed for disk drives; SMARTDRV.EXE buffers the hard drive. SMARTDRV.EXE can loan all the cache memory, except for the minimum amount specified, to Windows.

More memory by optimizing the sequence

Occasionally, you can access more memory for applications by changing the sequence of drivers and programs loaded with DEVICEHIGH and LOADHIGH.

To do this, use MEM /C to see which programs could be loaded in upper memory and which ones are in conventional memory.

Sometimes a relatively small program can occupy a large block of upper memory. This prevents a larger program from loading into that block. By changing the driver sequence, you can usually change this situation so that a larger program can be loaded into upper memory instead of a smaller program.

More memory by using additional areas

Create a boot diskette

By default, EMM386.EXE doesn't use the E000H—EFFFH to create a page frame for expanded memory or as upper memory. By creating a special boot diskette, you can experiment with allocating this area.

Format a diskette as a system diskette by using the following MS-DOS 5.0 command:

```
FORMAT A: /S
```

Copy the AUTOEXEC.BAT and CONFIG.SYS files to that diskette. Also, copy important DOS commands, such as

QBASIC.EXE, EDIT.COM, UNFORMAT, FDISK, etc. to this diskette.

Edit the CONFIG.SYS file on the hard drive by adding the following line:

```
DEVICE=C:\WINDOWS\EMM386.EXE NOEMS I=E000-EFFF
```

If you have a VGA card, you can also open up an additional area for upper memory, which varies with the color or monochrome display.

If you make this change and have problems after rebooting, you can still try to use parts of the memory area by decreasing the size of the maximum area.

For VGA color monitors

If you have a color monitor, the B000H—B7FFH area can be used for upper memory:

```
DEVICE=C:\WINDOWS\EMM386.EXE NOEMS I=B000-B7FF I=E000-EFFF
```

For VGA monochrome monitors

If a monochrome monitor is installed instead of a color monitor, the B800H—BFFFH area can be used for upper memory:

```
DEVICE=C:\WINDOWS\EMM386.EXE NOEMS I=B800-BFFF I=E000-EFFF
```

In both cases you can gain 32K of extra upper memory for device drivers if you don't encounter problems.

If you make a mistake and the system crashes during bootup, insert the boot diskette, reset the system, and edit the CONFIG.SYS file on the hard drive.

If the problems continue, copy the boot diskette's CONFIG.SYS and AUTOEXEC.BAT files to the hard drive and start over.

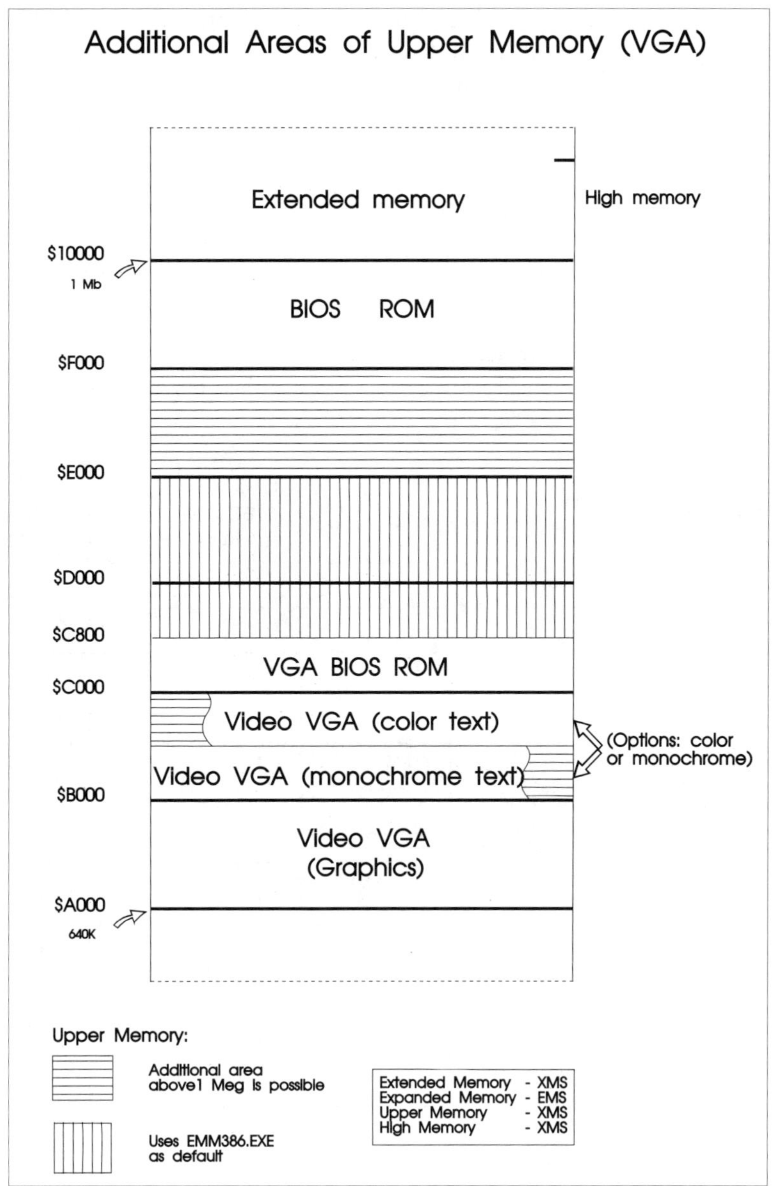

Extra upper memory

The above illustration shows the location and characteristics of upper memory.

By default, EMM386.EXE uses only the area from C800H-DFFFH with the setting NOEMS on a VGA graphics card, which provides only 96K of upper memory. In many cases, this isn't an adequate amount.

By allocating the area from E000H-EFFFH, you can gain an additional 64K, which gives you a total of 160K of contiguous upper memory.

Since most 386 systems probably have a VGA card (especially for using Windows 3.1), you can gain 32K of upper memory depending on the kind of monitor you use.

You can clearly see that this 32K area is separated by the VGA BIOS from the remaining block of upper memory.

Since memory areas are always specified in hexadecimal notation, the following is a short list that should help you understand this notation:

Table of notations

Memory block	Hexadecimal memory address (K)	Decimal memory address (K)
0	0000	0
1	1000	64
2	2000	128
3	3000	192
4	4000	256
5	5000	320
6	6000	384
7	7000	448
8	8000	512
9	9000	576
10	A000	640
11	B000	704
12	C000	768
13	D000	832
14	E000	896
15	F000	960
16	10000	1024 = 1 Meg

29.3 Installing for Easy Switching Between DOS and Windows

If you use DOS and Windows equally, you should set up two basic file systems and switch from one to the other as needed.

To set up the option for switching:

Before switching, some preparations are necessary:

Set up system files for the switch

- Copy the existing system files to your DOS and Windows directories. If possible, use files that haven't been modified or customized in any way:

```
COPY C:\CONFIG.SYS C:\WINDOWS
COPY C:\AUTOEXEC.BAT C:\WINDOWS

COPY C:\CONFIG.SYS C:\DOS
COPY C:\AUTOEXEC.BAT C:\DOS
```

- Create two batch files, called GODOS.BAT and GOWIN.BAT, in your batch directory. These files are used for switching between DOS and Windows. First, create the version for DOS, using a text editor, a word processor, or the DOS COPY CON command:

```
REM GODOS.BAT
@ECHO OFF
ECHO Switching to DOS configuration.
COPY C:\DOS\CONFIG.SYS C:\
COPY C:\DOS\AUTOEXEC:BAT C:\
ECHO Now reboot the system.
```

It's just as easy to create the Windows batch file:

```
REM GOWIN.BAT
@ECHO OFF
ECHO Switching to Windows configuration.
COPY C:\WINDOWS\CONFIG.SYS C:\
COPY C:\WINDOWS\AUTOEXEC:BAT C:\
ECHO Now reboot the system.
```

If you use different names for the directories, use those names instead of C:\WINDOWS and C:\DOS.

On the basis of this structure, you can begin to customize the system files. You can base your custom files on the suggestions we presented in the previous section. The following is our recommendation for a CONFIG.SYS for Windows and a CONFIG.SYS for DOS on a 386 with 4 Meg:

CONFIG.SYS for using DOS

```
REM CONFIG.SYS for 386/4 Meg using DOS
REM Store in: C:\DOS\CONFIG.SYS
DEVICE=C:\DOS\HIMEM.SYS
DEVICE=C:\DOS\EMM386.EXE RAM I=D000-EFFF
DEVICEHIGH=C:\DOS\SETVER.EXE
SHELL=C:\DOS\COMMAND.COM /E:1000 /P
FILES=30
BUFFERS=10
BREAK=ON
DEVICEHIGH=C:\DOS\MOUSE.SYS
DEVICEHIGH=C:\DOS\SMARTDRV.SYS 2048 /A
DOS=HIGH,UMB
```

The special features of this CONFIG.SYS enable you to use expanded memory and upper memory (RAM parameter in EMM386.EXE). Also, the DOS environment memory in SHELL= is set to a high value (/E:1000).

Without Windows, you must use a DOS mouse driver to use a mouse pointer in DOS programs. SMARTDRV.SYS receives 2048K of expanded memory to speed up hard drive accesses; the remainder is available to application programs.

Many compatible mice encounter problems with the Microsoft mouse driver, MOUSE.SYS, unless a switch on the mouse is set to the "Microsoft compatible" setting. Another way solve this problem is to switch off the computer, switch it back on (Ctrl + Alt + Del or Reset isn't sufficient), and hold down the left mouse button for 1 to 2 seconds.

CONFIG.SYS for using Windows

```
REM CONFIG.SYS for 386/4Meg using Windows
REM Store in: C:\WINDOWS\CONFIG.SYS
DEVICE=C:\WINDOWS\HIMEM.SYS
DEVICE=C:\WINDOWS\EMM386.EXE NOEMS I=D000-EFFF
DEVICEHIGH=C:\DOS\SETVER.EXE
SHELL=C:\DOS\COMMAND.COM /E:300 /P
FILES=30
BUFFERS=10
BREAK=ON
DOS=HIGH,UMB
```

Then add the following line to your AUTOEXEC.BAT:

```
LOADHIGH C:\WINDOWS\SMARTDRV.EXE 2048 512
```

Since the CONFIG.SYS for a Windows system doesn't use expanded memory (NOEMS), it's able to allocate more upper memory. Also, the CONFIG.SYS has a significantly smaller environment memory (/E:300) and doesn't use the DOS mouse driver, MOUSE.SYS. The line SMARTDRV.EXE in the AUTOEXEC.BAT file also obtains additional information about the minimum cache memory that Windows cannot swap.

When making these or similar changes, remember to transfer the changes made to the current system files in the root directory to the DOS or Windows system files in their subdirectories. For example, if a newly installed program expands the path of the AUTOEXEC.BAT in the root directory, this change will be overwritten by the AUTOEXEC.BAT from the C:\WINDOWS directory the next time you switch to Windows (with GOWIN). You must enter the changes manually in both versions of the AUTOEXEC.BAT files.

If necessary, you can easily determine whether any changes were made by an installation program. Simply use the FC command for comparing files. For example, if you switched to Windows, the system files in the root directory should be identical to those in C:\WINDOWS. Then, determine if there are any differences:

```
FC C:\CONFIG.SYS C:\WINDOWS\CONFIG.SYS
```

Your screen will look similar to the following:

```
Comparing files C:\WINDOWS\CONFIG.SYS and C:\CONFIG.SYS
***** C:\WINDOWS\CONFIG.SYS
FILES=30
BUFFERS=10
BREAK=ON
***** C:\CONFIG.SYS
FILES=30
BUFFERS=20
BREAK=ON
*****
```

FC displays the line that has been changed (BUFFERS) as well as the previous and subsequent lines, so you can easily see the change (in this case, 20 instead of 10). To accept this change, you must enter it manually in C:\DOS\CONFIG.SYS and C:\WINDOWS\CONFIG.SYS. Repeat the same procedure of comparing and updating for the AUTOEXEC.BAT.

29.4 Device Drivers and CONFIG.SYS

Now we'll show you how to improve your PC system configuration for DOS and Windows.

Problems with installation programs

Has this ever happened to you? You run SETUP for Windows 3.0 and a message states that some of the device drivers in the CONFIG.SYS file are incompatible. SETUP offers you the option of updating some old device drivers (usually MOUSE.SYS and HIMEM.SYS). You confirm this action.

Later, you install Word 5.5, whose SETUP program also gives you the option of updating the existing mouse driver. You confirm this action also.

However, when you use MS-DOS 5.0, the SETUP program informs you that it has automatically updated some device drivers. You may be wondering what will happen to the device drivers when you upgrade to Windows 3.1.

Although user-friendly installation packages are very helpful, they can also disrupt system files.

Earlier we explained how a 386 with MS-DOS 5.0 installed for optimum memory management has a CONFIG.SYS that can provide up to 50K more conventional memory, with the drivers arranged in the proper order. However, if another installation program adds its own drivers and replaces existing ones, problems can occur.

If you're not sure whether you have control over your PC or if it's taken on a life of its own at your expense, look at the CONFIG.SYS file. This section explains the important device drivers. Once you understand how CONFIG.SYS works, you can eliminate anything that's unnecessary and perhaps even get some extra speed out of your system.

Starting without the CONFIG.SYS file

It used to be much easier

The CONFIG.SYS file didn't always exist on the PC. Before this file, if you needed to update your keyboard for a different country, you had to run the SELECT command. This command would write new code for keyboard access to AUTOEXEC.BAT from DOS diskettes.

Now, the installation programs included with MS-DOS and DR DOS create independent, complex configuration files. Unfortunately, most PC users don't actually understand how these files work. The settings made in these files determine how a PC performs. However, redundant and unnecessary command lines are time-consuming when the system is started. This wastes memory and hinders performance. The incorrect settings can reduce the performance of your computer by up to 50 per cent.

The proper settings in CONFIG.SYS are extremely important when you run Windows 3.1 and MS-DOS 5.0. To better understand this, let's take a look at how a PC system starts.

How a PC starts

Boot sector, IO.SYS and MS-DOS.SYS

The BIOS in the PC's ROM first checks the computer's components. Then it searches drive A: for a boot sector. If a diskette isn't in drive A:, the BIOS searches drive C: for the boot sector and loads the boot sector if found. The boot sector contains disk information and a boot program that searches for two hidden system files.

In MS-DOS, these files are called IO.SYS and MSDOS.SYS. Since the BIOS cannot identify subdirectories until after startup, these two files must exist in the root directory, and the first two entries of the directory must ensure correct loading. The BIOS passes control of the operating system to these two files after loading.

CONFIG.SYS

Now MS-DOS should be configured to the existing hardware. MS-DOS searches for the CONFIG.SYS file in the root directory, and processes the configuration commands contained in the file. This file adds drivers (usually with the SYS extension) to the system and specifies settings for file handling (i.e., the number of buffers and number of files that can be processed simultaneously).

The command processor COMMAND.COM

COMMAND.COM is the part of MS-DOS that maintains contact with the user and executes commands. The command processor loads and starts from the root directory. The SHELL command lets you specify an alternate command processor from within CONFIG.SYS (e.g., the Norton Utilities command processor). This command interpreter then starts instead of COMMAND.COM and can also be located in a subdirectory.

AUTOEXEC.BAT

COMMAND.COM searches for a batch file called AUTOEXEC.BAT, and then executes the commands contained in this file. The AUTOEXEC.BAT file must be located in the root directory. Once this is done, MS-DOS is ready to accept commands and displays the prompt to indicate that it's ready.

So, CONFIG.SYS executes early in the startup phase of the computer. As a result, this file can call an extended memory driver, which makes extended memory available to applications. You cannot abort CONFIG.SYS.

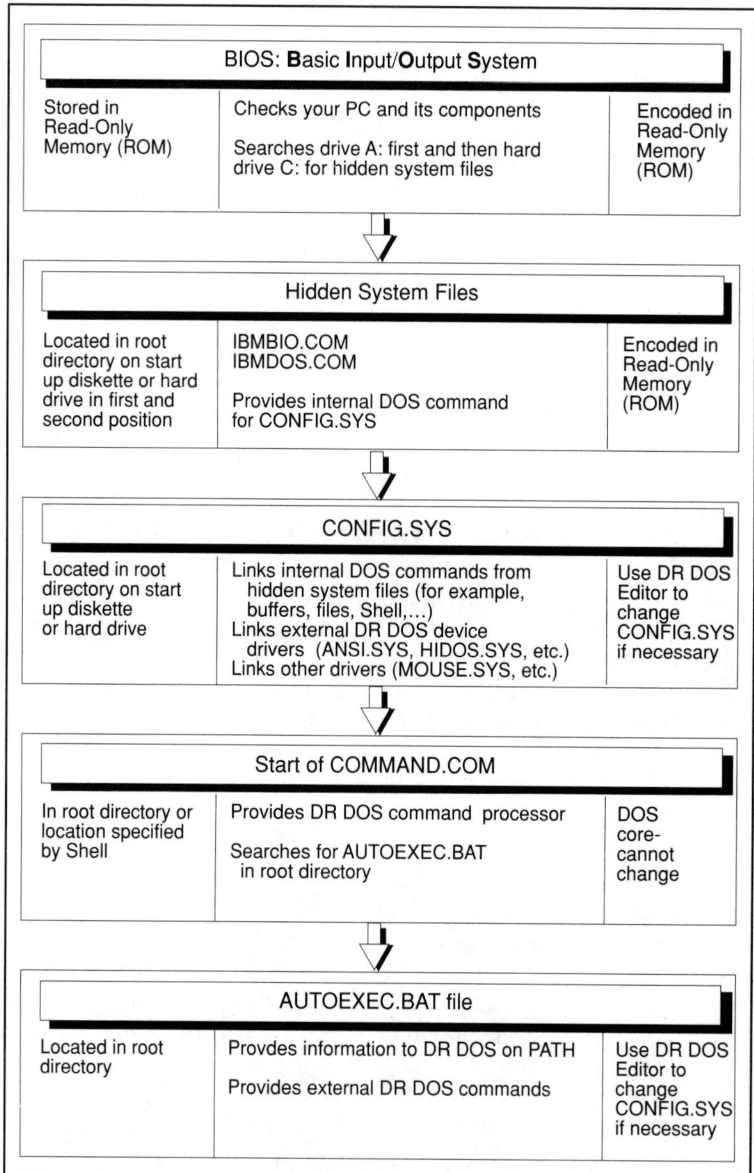

Booting a PC

The above illustration shows the different steps involved in booting a PC system. You can clearly see where the user can begin controlling, or rearranging, the rest of the process.

The BIOS (Basic Input/Output System), which is stored in the ROM of every PC, checks all components and searches for the hidden system files.

These hidden system files are part of the operating system (e.g., of MS-DOS 5.0). They're responsible for making the internal DOS commands available, which enables the CONFIG.SYS file to be executed.

Next, CONFIG.SYS itself is processed. This is also the first step at which the user can intervene.

Then the root directory of the start drive is searched for the COMMAND.COM file as the operating system's command processor.

Make adjustments to COMMAND.COM by assigning parameters to COMMAND.COM using the AUTOEXEC.BAT file.

When this process is completed, the operating system is accessible to the user. He/she can enter DOS commands at the prompt or use a graphical user interface, such as Windows or the MS-DOS Shell.

What are device drivers?

The CONFIG.SYS file has two main functions. It specifies important settings during startup and calls several devices by using programs called device drivers.

Software adapters

Device drivers control and configure access to the hardware (they could be called software adapters). Instead of addressing the hardware directly, MS-DOS addresses the device drivers. MS-DOS can be adapted to different hardware through various device drivers.

Some built-in device drivers (e.g., diskette and hard drive control) are included with MS-DOS, but the user must load other drivers from disk.

For example, the KEYB device driver adapts MS-DOS to foreign keyboards.

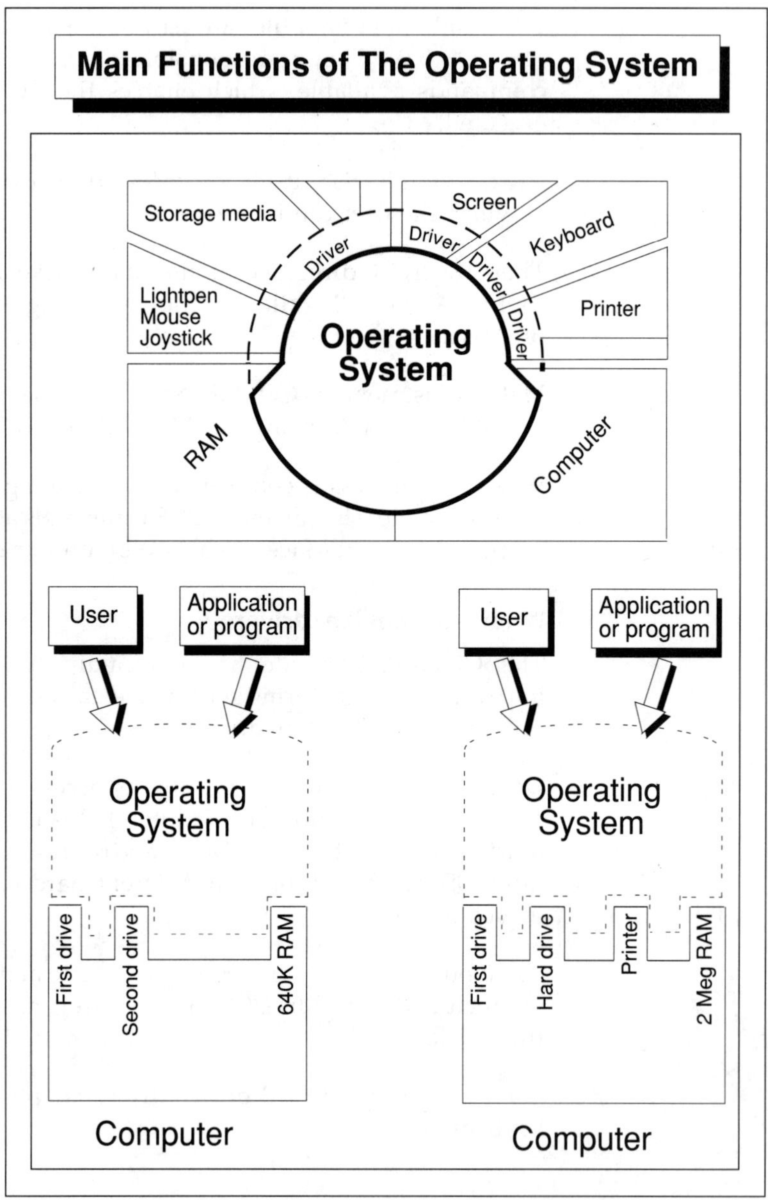

Basic operating system functions

The above illustration describes the basic tasks of an operating system in two different respects:

1. The operating system ensures that the actual computer can communicate with memory (RAM) and peripherals in an organized manner. Drivers play a major role in this process. They permit the user to adapt the operating system to the PC components. Some drivers

reside in the operating system while others are in the CONFIG.SYS file.

2. The lower portion of the illustration shows the significance of the operating system and the use of different devices. For example, with the help of the operating system and special drivers, the computer can access different drives, screens, printers, etc.

The SYS extension

By updating a driver, you can improve or adapt the system without making direct changes to MS-DOS. For example, if keyboards change, all you'd need is a new keyboard driver to update MS-DOS. Most device drivers have the SYS extension and can be called from CONFIG.SYS.

When you connect a new device to your PC, you may also have to inform MS-DOS of this fact. For example, you cannot use a mouse until you first run a mouse driver.

Edit CONFIG.SYS carefully

Be very careful when making changes to the CONFIG.SYS file, because errors could lead to the PC malfunctioning. If serious errors occur from within CONFIG.SYS, MS-DOS may not finish booting the system. If this happens, you may not be able to correct the CONFIG.SYS file.

In Section 29.2 you created a system diskette. Copy AUTOEXEC.BAT and CONFIG.SYS to this diskette. Edit CONFIG.SYS from your hard drive. If you make an error, you can boot from the diskette, copy CONFIG.SYS from the diskette to the hard drive, and start over. Also, we recommend that you make a backup copy of the CONFIG.SYS and AUTOEXEC.BAT files on another diskette for emergency use.

CONFIG.SYS commands

CONFIG.SYS is a text file. So, if you load it into a text editor or word processor, you can view the lines of text in this file. In this section we'll discuss the different commands you may find in your CONFIG.SYS file. We'll show which settings decrease the amount of memory available, so you know which command lines to check when you're searching for more memory for your programs.

We'll use only brief descriptions. For more information on each CONFIG.SYS command, refer to MS-DOS specific books, such as *DOS 5.0 Complete* from Abacus.

The following lists the command, its function, and memory requirements:

BREAK
Checks or changes DOS' break option by pressing Ctrl + C (no memory requirements).

BUFFERS
Determines the number of read/write buffers for data exchange between diskettes and hard drives (decreases conventional memory by 532 bytes per buffer and decreases the processor speed).

COUNTRY
Makes country-specific settings (date and time format, decimal separator) (no extra memory requirements).

DEVICE
Installs a device driver (decreases memory according to driver).

DEVICEHIGH
Installs device in upper memory (better memory use than DEVICE).

DOS
Determines how DOS will use high memory and upper memory (makes more free memory possible).

DRIVPARM
Sets parameters for drive (no memory requirements).

FCBS
Sets the number of file control blocks, like FILES but older, outdated convention (reduces memory, can usually be omitted).

FILES
Maximum number of opened files (reduces memory by 64 bytes per file).

INSTALL
Loads programs in resident memory (reduces memory depending on specified program).

LASTDRIVE
Determines the number of drives (hardly reduces memory).

REM
Defines a comment line (no memory requirements).

SHELL
: Loads command interpreter (reduces memory only if you use /E as a parameter for environment memory).

STACKS
: Memory for hardware interrupts (reduces memory if you specify >0, usually you can specify STACKS=0,0), only needed when error messages occur.

Device drivers in CONFIG.SYS

The DEVICE command lets you access a series of drivers from CONFIG.SYS:

ANSI.SYS
: Screen controls (changing the screen and colors, reassigning keys)—the MODE command uses ANSI.SYS for changing screen resolution (e.g., 43 line display).

COUNTRY.SYS
: Country-specific table for the COUNTRY command.

DISPLAY.SYS
: Screen font tables (only necessary when using code pages).

DRIVER.SYS
: Device driver for drives, used to redefine existing drives (capacity, format).

EGA.SYS
: Device driver that stores EGA card settings for later recall (doesn't apply to VGA cards); installing EGA.SYS before MOUSE.SYS saves memory.

EMM386.EXE
: Device driver for expanded memory, converts extended memory to expanded memory on 386s (e.g., Microsoft Word 5.5).

HIMEM.SYS
: Device driver for XMS memory (extended memory, high memory, and upper memory).

KEYBOARD.SYS
: Different keyboard layouts for KEYB.

PRINTER.SYS

Character set tables for IBM printers (only necessary when using code pages).

RAMDRIVE.SYS

MS-DOS RAM disk (called VDISK.SYS in PC-DOS).

SMARTDRV.SYS

Driver for hard drive acceleration (cache program).

The SMARTDRV.EXE cache program that's included with WINDOWS 3.1 can be installed using AUTOEXEC.BAT.

Other driver programs listed in your CONFIG.SYS file correspond to a special device or program. One hard drive installation utility uses its own special driver. If you remove these drivers, your hard drive will stop working.

The CONFIG.SYS settings influence your computer's performance. Let's discuss the more common settings.

Adapting the date and currency format

Use the COUNTRY command to adapt MS-DOS to different countries' notations. For example, use the following setting for Germany:

```
COUNTRY=049,437,C:\DOS\COUNTRY.SYS
```

Without this setting, the date and time notation defaults to U.S. format (e.g., MM-DD-YY).

Speeding up general drive access

Buffers are an area of conventional memory that MS-DOS needs for read and write operations during data transfer. Each buffer occupies 532 bytes of memory. The BUFFERS setting varies depending on the system. The more buffers you allocate, the faster you're able to access diskettes or hard drives, but the less memory you'll have available for applications. On a system with 640K memory and a hard drive, the following entry in CONFIG.SYS is appropriate:

```
BUFFERS=25
```

The buffers occupy 13K in RAM. If you don't specify enough buffer space with the BUFFERS command, your hard drive and diskette accesses could become very slow.

If you use SMARTDRV.EXE for Windows, you should set BUFFERS to 10, since SMARTDRV.EXE controls temporary storage, and any additional buffers would only cost time and memory.

Setting the number of open files

Many applications expect more than eight files (the MS-DOS default) to be open simultaneously. You can use the FILES command to change this number. For example, the following entry in the CONFIG.SYS file is more suitable:

```
FILES=25
```

Each increase in FILES requires 48 bytes of memory, so FILES=25 requires 1200 bytes, or slightly more than 1K.

Some database programs require an even larger value (e.g., 30). Either refer to your application's documentation or increase the value if you receive an error message stating that no more files can be opened.

Setting the number of logical drives

MS-DOS can manage five drives with the letters A-E by default. If you want to define more drives, use LASTDRIVE to increase the number. You must do this if you redefine drives (with SUBST) or want to split a hard drive into several partitions. To be able to use eight logical drives with the letters A-H, enter the following command in CONFIG.SYS:

```
LASTDRIVE=H
```

State the last valid drive's letter instead of the last valid drive's number.

Specifying the command interpreter

Usually MS-DOS loads the COMMAND.COM program from the root directory of the current drive as the command processor. SHELL specifies a different path or file name. If the command interpreter is located in the DOS subdirectory, use the following line:

```
SHELL=C:\DOS\COMMAND.COM /P
```

This command serves three different purposes:

- To use a command interpreter from a subdirectory, decrease the number of files in the root directory:

```
SHELL=C:\DOS\COMMAND.COM /P
```

- To use a command interpreter with a different name:

```
SHELL=C:\NEWCMD.COM
```

- To increase the environment memory (see below). The following line creates an environment memory of 512 bytes (see below):

```
SHELL=C:\COMMAND.COM /P /E:512
```

The path and name of the command interpreter specified here should match the COMSPEC value found in the AUTOEXEC.BAT file.

Make sure you specify the /P switch, so that the command interpreter loads permanently.

Determining the system environment size

MS-DOS notes important information in the system environment. If the default size is insufficient, you can increase it with the SHELL command. 512 bytes are sufficient for most applications, so the line in the CONFIG.SYS file should be expanded to:

```
SHELL=C:\DOS\COMMAND.COM /P /E:512
```

By using this line, you can prevent error messages during intense environment variable access (e.g., in batch files).

You must specify /P in order to load the command interpreter permanently. Otherwise, the AUTOEXEC.BAT file won't execute when you reboot. Also, entering EXIT crashes your system.

Many environment variables can be used, especially if you use a network. In such cases, reserve about 1000 bytes using the following:

```
SHELL=C:\DOS\COMMAND.COM /P /E:1000
```

Adding screen and keyboard controls

The ANSI.SYS driver adds ANSI screen and keyboard capabilities to your system. Add the following line to CONFIG.SYS (adjust the path as needed—our ANSI.SYS driver is in our DOS directory):

```
DEVICE=C:\DOS\ANSI.SYS
```

Redefining the keyboard in DOS

ANSI.SYS provides additional keyboard controls and extended screen functions in DOS. This is useful if you frequently work with the DOS prompt from within Windows.

Enter the following to display a more detailed header from within ANSI.SYS:

```
PROMPT $e[s$e[f$e[7m$t$h$h$h$h$h$h o'clock $d
$p$g$e[K$e[u$e[0m$p$g
```

This displays the following on your screen:

```
| 12:49 o'clock Thu 05-02-92 C:\MISC\BAT>   |
```

To display the original prompt, use:

```
PROMPT $p$g
```

We'll present an example that shows you how to redefine the keyboard layout with ANSI.SYS, using the F9 and F10 function keys.

This example is especially useful to users who are frustrated because MS-DOS forgets the old directory when you change to a new one. If you've just been in a directory, called C:\TEXTS\PERSONAL\LETTERS\1992, and had to change to C:\TEMP, returning to the old directory can require a lot of keystrokes.

You can use a special trick to save the current directory (C:\TEXTS\PERSONAL\LETTERS\1992) to a function key together with the CD command. The following batch file called SAVEDIR.BAT automatically handles this after the call.

Enter the following batch called SAVEDIR.BAT (include the two lines after the PROMPT commands):

```
@REM SAVEDIR.BAT
@REM Saves current directory on F10
@SET OLDPROMPT=%PROMPT%
@PROMPT $e[0;68;"CD ";"$p";13p

@PROMPT $e[5A

@SET PROMPT=%OLDPROMPT%
@SET OLDPROMPT=
```

Now type the following command line. You can now call SAVEDIR.BAT from the F9 key:

```
PROMPT $e[0;67;"SAVEDIR";13p
```

This causes the system prompt to disappear, but the command line has been accepted by ANSI.SYS. To restore a prompt, enter:

```
PROMPT $p$g
```

You can also include this definition in the AUTOEXEC.BAT if necessary. ECHO must be switched on, so you can type the following lines:

```
REM regular AUTOEXEC.BAT lines precede this
ECHO ON
@PROMPT $e[0;67;"SAVEDIR";13p

@ECHO OFF
REM regular AUTOEXEC.BAT lines follow
```

Now if you want to record the current directory (i.e., C:\TEXTS\PERSONAL\LETTERS\1992), simply press F9. Then you can change directories as usual, for example, by entering CD C:\DOS. To return to the saved directory, simply press F10.

SAVEDIR.BAT is incompatible with DOSKEY, the program used for editing command lines. Pressing F9 after starting DOSKEY results in a prompt to enter a line number.

If you'd like more information about DOS applications, read *DOS 5.0 Complete*, available from Abacus. Also, similar keyboard tricks can be performed in Windows by using the Recorder.

Speeding up file access

If you frequently need certain files, FASTOPEN can help you access them faster. This is especially useful when you use database programs, or even Windows. If you have a hard drive and 640K of RAM, use the following command in CONFIG.SYS to configure FASTOPEN for tracking 100 files:

```
INSTALL=C:\DOS\FASTOPEN C:=100
```

Defining additional drives

MS-DOS recognizes connected disk drives and operates them in a specific way. To run a drive with a different capacity, use the DRIVER.SYS device driver.

For example, if you want a 3.5" drive B: configured to 720K instead of 1.44 Meg, add the following to the CONFIG.SYS file:

```
DEVICE=C:\DOS\DRIVER.SYS /d:1 /f:2 /H:2 /S:9 /T:80
```

After the next warm boot, MS-DOS reports an additional driver and specifies the drive letter under which drive B: can be used as a 720K drive. Drive B: continues to be available under B: as a 1.44 Meg drive.

If the DRIVER.SYS file isn't located in the root directory, you must specify the complete path.

Don't be surprised if you find two identical lines in an AT's CONFIG.SYS file:

```
DEVICE=DRIVER.SYS /D:0 /F:0

DEVICE=DRIVER.SYS /D:0 /F:0
```

Both command lines create a new 360K drive (because of /F:0) based on the existing A: drive (defined by /D:0). This computer, for example, has two new drives, D: and E:, which automatically format diskettes at 360K capacity. This example clearly shows that you cannot use /D to specify the drive number or drive label. MS-DOS automatically finds the next available drive label.

Using conventional memory as a RAM disk

You can significantly speed up diskette accesses by using a part of conventional memory as a RAM disk or virtual drive. The RAMDRIVE.SYS device driver performs this task.

Add the following line to your CONFIG.SYS file to enable the RAM disk:

```
DEVICE=C:\DOS\RAMDRIVE.SYS
```

The next time you start the PC, you'll have a new drive under the registered drive label. It has a capacity of 64K and can hold 64 files or directories. This information is displayed after the PC starts up. The memory used for the RAM disk is taken from conventional memory, so applications might not have enough memory under certain conditions.

In PC-DOS 5.0 the driver is called VDISK.SYS instead of RAMDRIVE.SYS.

If you have extended memory, add the /E switch to the RAMDRIVE command to allocate extended memory for the RAM disk instead. This reduces the load on conventional memory. To use the 384K of extended memory, which is available on many 80286 machines with 1 Meg of total memory, add the following line to the CONFIG.SYS file:

```
DEVICE=C:\DOS\RAMDRIVE.SYS 384 /E
```

The RAM disk can also use expanded memory for data storage if you add the /A switch as a parameter. If you have 1024K of expanded memory available, the following command allocates all this memory as a RAM disk:

```
DEVICE=C:\DOS\RAMDRIVE.SYS 1024 /A
```

We'll go into more detail about using a RAM disk with Windows later. Generally, cache memory is more useful than a RAM disk.

Speeding up hard drive access

If your computer has extended memory or expanded memory, you can significantly increase hard drive access speeds by using the SMARTDRV.SYS cache program. When entering the SMARTDRV command in your CONFIG.SYS file, specify how much extended memory you want to use for temporary storage. Without this specification, MS-DOS allocates 256K. To allocate 1024K of extended memory for temporary data storage, include the following line in your CONFIG.SYS file:

```
DEVICE=C:\DOS\SMARTDRV.SYS 1024
```

Use the /A switch to allocate expanded memory instead of extended memory. The line would then read:

```
DEVICE=C:\DOS\SMARTDRV.SYS 1024 /A
```

We mentioned that the Windows SMARTDRV.EXE cache is installed through AUTOEXEC.BAT. Since some applications don't work with SMARTDRV.EXE, we first explained how to install the MS-DOS cache program SMARTDRV.SYS. However, if you don't run such programs, install the Windows SMARTDRV.EXE cache from the AUTOEXEC.BAT file as follows:

```
C:\WINDOWS\SMARTDRV.EXE
```

Except for /A, you can use the same parameters for this cache program that you used for SMARTDRV.SYS (SMARTDRV.EXE cannot access expanded memory). So to allocate 1024K of extended memory for temporary storage of data, your line in AUTOEXEC.BAT should look like as follows:

```
C:\WINDOWS\SMARTDRV.EXE 1024
```

If you prefer expanded memory, you must use SMARTDRV.SYS.

We'll discuss SMARTDRV.EXE in more detail later.

Using the MS-DOS BREAK command

Use the MS-DOS BREAK command to determine whether the user has pressed Ctrl + C to cancel a command. Add the following line to CONFIG.SYS to enable BREAK:

```
BREAK=ON
```

You can also change the setting later by entering BREAK ON or BREAK OFF from the DOS prompt.

A sample CONFIG.SYS file

The following is a sample CONFIG.SYS file for MS-DOS in the root directory of the C: drive:

```
DEVICE=C:\DOS\ANSI.SYS
FILES=20
BUFFERS=20
SHELL=C:\COMMAND.COM /P /E:500
INSTALL=C:\DOS\FASTOPEN C:=100
```

Special features of Windows

Although the Windows installation program provides a very comfortable Windows configuration, it drastically changes your CONFIG.SYS file.

Windows removes CONFIG commands

Windows adds entries to the CONFIG.SYS file during installation, but also adds REM to some entries, changing those entries into inactive lines. If other programs require this memory expansion, problems will occur the next time you reboot your PC. Now let's look at the most important features of a CONFIG.SYS file when used with Windows 3.1.

Always make backup copies of AUTOEXEC.BAT and CONFIG.SYS before running any installation programs and keep a boot diskette available (see Section 29.2 for instructions on making a boot diskette). Some programs reset the computer after installation, and if the installation program corrupted or rewrote your existing CONFIG.SYS file, you won't be able to inspect it or make changes to it. So, study the changes the program makes to your system files and remember that not all of those changes are useful.

Changes suggested by Windows

Windows lets you decide whether changes should be made to these system files. If necessary, you can undo the changes made by Windows or make your own changes. By doing this, you may avoid some of the problems we discussed in the previous paragraph.

1. HIMEM.SYS: To run Windows 3.1 in standard or 386 Enhanced mode, you must install HIMEM.SYS. Usually, the required command line for this is:

```
DEVICE=HIMEM.SYS
```

2. Since Windows works with multiple files, set the number of files that can be opened simultaneously to a large value (e.g., 25 or 30):

```
FILES = 25
```

3. Windows uses the hard drive extensively for data storage and swapping data from conventional memory. So speeding up data transfer also speeds up Windows. Often, the SMARTDRV.EXE utility program should be included in the AUTOEXEC.BAT file, because it's especially optimized for interaction with Windows. However, avoid SMARTDRV.EXE if you have a 286 with only 1 Meg of memory or a 386 with 2 Meg, since the acceleration will be canceled by the slowdown caused by an insufficient amount of memory for Windows.

Minimum and maximum cache memory

You must define both the minimum and maximum amount of memory SMARTDRV can use under Windows. Suppose that you have a 286 with 2 Meg of extended memory, and you want to use a minimum of 256K and a maximum of 1024K for SMARTDRV. Add the following command line to the AUTOEXEC.BAT (HIMEM.SYS must already be active in the CONFIG.SYS file):

```
C:\WINDOWS\SMARTDRV.EXE 1024 256
```

If you don't use much memory for Windows applications or you haven't started Windows, this accelerates data transfer to the hard drive. If Windows requires a lot of memory for applications, it can still "borrow" memory from SMARTDRV. This virtually cancels error messages because of insufficient memory.

If you work with such a setting for SMARTDRV, set BUFFERS to a smaller value (10). This enables you to save memory and avoid duplicating data in temporary storage.

Setting the CONFIG.SYS file for DOS 5.0

CONFIG.SYS should also be optimized for MS-DOS. That's why you should make the necessary preparations to improve the CONFIG.SYS file before installation.

XMS Specification

1. Beginning with MS-DOS 5.0, all programs and drivers should access extended memory according to the XMS specification. MS-DOS 5.0 includes the HIMEM.SYS driver for this purpose. Without it, neither RAMDRIVE nor SMARTDRV will use extended memory. HIMEM.SYS should appear in the first line of the CONFIG.SYS file (or it should at least precede all programs that use extended memory).

2. You can define how MS-DOS uses extended memory with the new DOS= command. Only two settings are possible on a 286, DOS=HIGH or DOS=LOW. In the first case, DOS moves partially to the first 64K of high memory, thus creating more space in conventional memory. As a result, approximately 580-590K of conventional memory is available on a computer with a normal setup.

```
DEVICE=C:\DOS\HIMEM.SYS
DOS=HIGH
```

On a 386, you can also enable EMM386.EXE to allocate reserved memory areas between 640K and 1 Meg for drivers and TSR programs. MS-DOS will use this memory completely if you add the ,UMB (Upper Memory Block) parameter to the DOS= line. The CONFIG.SYS file must then include the following lines:

```
DEVICE=C:\DOS\HIMEM.SYS
DEVICE=C:\DOS\EMM386.EXE NOEMS
DOS=HIGH,UMB
```

Instead of DEVICE, use the new command called DEVICEHIGH. This loads drivers into the reserved area between 640K and 1 Meg. Of course, this is impractical for HIMEM and EMM386 since these two programs make the reserved memory possible in the first place.

This computer setup usually provides 620 to 630K of conventional memory.

Special features of Windows 3.1

If you used a memory manager like EMM386 with Windows 3.0, certain settings would only allow the use of Windows in Real mode. This minimizes Windows' potential. However, with MS-DOS 5.0 and Windows 3.1, you can also run Windows in Standard mode and 386 Enhanced mode if you use EMM386.EXE and expanded or upper memory.

```
REM CONFIG.SYS for MS-DOS 5.0 and Windows on 386s
DEVICE=C:\WINDOWS\HIMEM.SYS
DEVICE=C:\WINDOWS\EMM386.EXE RAM
DOS=HIGH,UMB
```

This problem no longer occurs with the combination of MS-DOS 5.0 and Windows 3.1. You can install upper memory and expended memory, and run Windows in Standard mode and 386 Enhanced mode without any problems. However, it's important that you have as much XMS memory available as possible. Windows only uses this memory for its own work.

WINA20.386, which Windows 3.0 required in the root directory of the start drive, is no longer needed if you run Windows 3.1.

If you can do without expanded memory, you can also gain more upper memory, since you don't have to install the 64K page frames required for expanded memory. Specifying NOEMS after EMM386.EXE not only gives you much more upper memory, but also provides much more conventional memory in many cases, because it allows you to load other device drivers and TSR programs in upper memory.

29.5 Hard Drive Optimization for Windows

Not long ago, a 20 Meg hard drive was considered a very large storage medium, and many users wondered how they could fill such a big disk.

Time, technology, and Windows have changed this situation. Both Windows and its applications require a lot of hard drive space. These applications also generate large files. Because of this, problems and errors can quickly occur because hard drive installation and partitioning wasn't considered.

Unfortunately, this will occur regardless of the amount of data your own hard drive can hold. So, let's discuss how you can perform some preventive maintenance on your hard drive capacity.

Reasons for cleaning up the hard drive

Cleaning up your hard drive helps prevent three major problems:

- User loses track of files
- Drive speed too slow
- Insufficient disk space

Besides solving these problems, there are several other advantages to organizing your hard drive. For example, it's much easier to back up data. Also, if you carefully plan where to place programs and data, you can decrease the amount of data that must be backed up.

As we mentioned earlier, Windows places considerably higher demands on the existing hard drive than MS-DOS does. So, to work efficiently with Windows, you must have a hard drive with at least 10 Meg free capacity and an average access time of 20 ms. If you run Windows on systems with less free capacity or slower hard drives, the execution speed usually decreases.

However, by improving the setup and use of the hard drive, you can significantly increase Windows' performance. In this section we'll discuss how you can optimize your hard drive.

Preparations

This section contains techniques you can use to improve the performance of the hard drive. However, some of these procedures could lead to problems and errors in extreme cases. So, you should back up back up your data before trying any of these measures. If you haven't backed up in a long time, this would be a good time to perform a complete backup of your hard drive. Otherwise, at least back up the data that has changed since the last backup by using the MS-DOS BACKUP command with the /M switch.

You can find more information on data security in Section 27.9.

Creating a boot diskette

Before backing up data, make a boot diskette. If you can't boot from the hard drive and you don't have a boot diskette available, you won't be able use RESTORE to restore the backup. When you create the boot diskette, copy as many "important" MS-DOS commands to this boot diskette as possible. These commands should include FDISK, RESTORE, SYS, FORMAT, and UNFORMAT.

Step 1: Check hard drive partitioning

Many hard drives with more than 30 Meg capacity are still divided into two partitions and several "logical" drives (drive letters). This occurs because, prior to Version 4.0, MS-DOS could manage only drives with a maximum of 32 Meg capacity. So a 40 Meg hard drive had to be divided into a drive C: with 32 Meg and a drive D: with 8 Meg. If you had an 80 Meg hard drive, two 32 Meg drives (C: and D:) and one 16 Meg drive (E:) were needed.

Partitions are no longer necessary

Anyone who is running MS-DOS 5.0 no longer needs these partitions. However, many users have kept them because any change would result in data loss on the hard drive. Then a complete backup would be needed.

Dividing the hard drive into two partitions with logical drives does have one advantage. If the data on one drive are accidentally destroyed, the other drives usually aren't affected. Unfortunately partitioning has only disadvantages. For instance, you must back up each partition because BACKUP and other data security programs can only back up a single drive at a time. The NCD (Norton Change Directory) command that lets you change to any directory also stops at that border between drives. Also, partitioning into several drives usually wastes space because if you have 1.5 Meg on each drive, you don't have enough room to install a program with 2 Meg on either drive.

So if you want to clean up your hard drive and the data have been backed up, you should think about repartitioning the hard drive. Back up your data, if you haven't already done so. Then you'll need MS-DOS (Version 4.0 and up), a boot diskette, and the MS-DOS FDISK command.

Using FDISK

If you select option 3 in the main menu and press Enter, and then 3 for *Delete Logical DOS Drive(s) in the Extended DOS Partition* and press Enter, you'll see all defined logical drives displayed on the screen. You can then specify the drive letters or press Esc to return to the main menu. After you enter the drive letter, you're prompted for the disk volume label. Here you must enter a name that can be displayed by the MS-DOS VOL command. If the drive doesn't have a name, simply press Enter.

After a confirmation prompt, the drive definition in the display is marked as "deleted". After the last logical drive in the extended DOS partition has been deleted, a message on the screen indicates that no logical drives are defined. Press Esc to return to the main menu.

Next you must delete the extended DOS partition. To do this, select option 3 in the main menu and press Enter, and then 2 and press Enter, for deleting an extended DOS partition. After that, a confirmation prompt appears. Press Y. Then a message appears on the screen. Press Esc to return to the main menu.

All partitions and drives are removed

Finally, you're ready to delete the primary DOS partition. Select option 3 (Delete partition or Logical DOS Drive) in the main menu of FDISK and press Enter. Then choose menu item 1, *Delete Primary DOS Partition.* A confirmation prompt follows which you must confirm by pressing Y. Then the following message appears:

```
Primary DOS Partition deleted
```

Also, the current status of the hard drive is displayed.

Creating a primary DOS partition for the entire hard drive

To use the entire hard drive under MS-DOS as one drive, you must create a single, primary DOS partition. This is relatively easy to do.

To create the partition, select <1> in the main menu of FDISK, for *Create DOS partition or Logical DOS Drive* and press Enter. Then enter a <1> for *Create Primary DOS Partition* and press Enter again.

Creating a DOS partition

Answer the prompt for the maximum size of the DOS partition with Y and press Enter. MS-DOS now treats the entire hard drive as one drive. Since no other partitions are possible, FDISK ends here.

Insert the boot diskette into the drive and press Enter. Use FORMAT C: /S to format the hard drive and then use RESTORE to place your data back on the hard drive.

Step 2: Organize the directory structure

Although you can do without subdirectories on diskettes, this isn't possible on hard drives. Obviously, you cannot keep more than 511 files or directories in the root directory of a hard drive.

Path specifications of no more than 63 characters

Another limitation of hard drives applies to path specifications. A path can have a maximum of 63 characters. Since a file name and extension require 11 characters, a total of 52 characters can be used for directory specifications. If you use names with 8 characters and no extensions, you can have 6 to 7 directory levels. However, any levels above five are difficult to read.

We recommend following these rules for your directory structure:

- Separate different programs by installing them in different directories. This minimizes problems caused by files that have the same name, and minimizes problems in upgrading programs.

- Keep only necessary files in the root directory of the hard drive. The only necessary files are AUTOEXEC.BAT and CONFIG.SYS. You can start by loading the command interpreter from the \DOS subdirectory with:

```
SHELL=C:\DOS\COMMAND.COM /P
```

Expand lines, such as DEVICE=ANSI.SYS, to the following in the CONFIG.SYS file:

```
DEVICE=C:\DOS\ANSI.SYS
```

Decreasing the number of files in the root directory makes it easier to organize your hard drive. This also increases MS-DOS's execution speed because DOS doesn't have to examine all the file entries when it searches for subdirectories.

Separate programs and data

- Keep programs and data separate. So, you'll only need to back up the entire hard drive after major changes (e.g., reinstallation of programs). Otherwise, simply back up the few data directories, which doesn't take very long. For example, usually you won't have to back up the WINWORD directory, which contains the Word for Windows word processor. However, if you store Word for Windows documents in a directory named \DOCS, you should back up this directory frequently.

  There is a disadvantage to using this procedure. When starting Word for Windows, the WINWORD directory is usually the default directory, so you must change directories to open a document.

Solution:

Mark the WINWORD icon in the Program Manager and select *File/Properties....* In the dialog box that appears, type your Word for Windows path in the command line and C:\DOCS as the working directory. This sets the proper file directory as the default.

You can use this trick for almost any application, in which you want to keep program files and data files separate. Of course, you can also use the options available in each application to set the data directory.

- If you edit several types of data and want to keep the types separate, do the following:

  Create a single directory, called \DATA. Use subdirectories to separate the different types of data: \DATA\DOCS, \DATA\DBFS, \DATA\WKSHEETS or, if you want to organize according to subject, \DATA\PERSONAL, \DATA\COMPANY, etc. Then simply include the data from this directory in your regular backups:

```
BACKUP C:\DATA\*.* A: /S
```

Basic directories: DOS, TEMP and BAT

- Every hard drive should contain the following basic directories: DOS, TEMP, and BAT. The \DOS directory contains all the DOS commands and additional files (drivers with the SYS extension and help files). So, when you install a new version of DOS, you can update and replace the files more effectively. Also, defining a search path in the AUTOEXEC.BAT file makes it possible to find the DOS commands at any time:

```
PATH C:\DOS
```

The /TEMP directory is used for temporary data storage. You should place all the data, that's only needed temporarily, in this directory. Many of your applications can also place temporary data in this directory. To do this, add the following command line to your AUTOEXEC.BAT file:

```
SET TEMP=C:\TEMP
```

Programs, such as DOS and Windows 3.1, will then place temporary files in this directory. This is helpful because any temporary files that were created because of program errors or crashes will be saved in one location. To clear your TEMP directory, enter the following line in your AUTOEXEC.BAT file:

```
DEL C:\TEMP\*.*
```

Finally, place all of your small batch files and utility programs in the \BAT directory. To easily update the batch files, extend the search path for these programs to the following:

```
PATH C:\DOS;C:\BAT
```

You're probably wondering how you can create such a well-organized directory structure. It's relatively simple to copy drivers from the root directory to a DOS directory, then add the path specification to the DEVICE= command in CONFIG.SYS.

Utility programs, such as the File Manager, can be especially useful for improving the directory structure. You can use these programs to move files (copy and then delete them from the original location) and rename and move directories (including the data in those subdirectories). You can use this option for moving to change the directory structure later (e.g., add the \DOCS directory to the \DATA directory, resulting in \DATA\DOCS). It's best if you point with the mouse to the \DOCS directory, hold down the left mouse button, and move the directory to the \DATA entry in the directory structure.

Step 3: Make room by deleting files

Many computer users aren't satisfied with their hard drives and believe they need drives with more memory. Unfortunately, larger hard drives are expensive. However, there are alternatives to purchasing a larger hard drive.

The simplest solution is to delete unnecessary data from the hard drive. The following are some suggestions:

Deleting duplicate files

All double and triple copies of files and programs can be deleted. If you don't work with special program directories and the appropriate search paths, you can quickly copy programs to more than one directory so that they are always available. In reality, however, you only need one mouse driver, etc. If you keep all your DOS files in the DOS directory and all other utilities in the \BAT directory, and you've defined the appropriate search path in the AUTOEXEC.BAT, you can delete all the extra versions.

Using the File Manager to search

How do you locate multiple copies of the same programs and files? Although the File Manager in Windows 3.1 can search an entire diskette or hard drive for files and display them in a window, unfortunately the files are sorted according to directories. So, you cannot bypass all directories and sort alphabetically. However, sorting alphabetically would help you find multiple copies of files in different directories.

Sorting files alphabetically

If you're using DOS 5.0 with the MS-DOS Shell, you can select the *View/All Files* command from the menu. All the files on the entire hard drive are sorted alphabetically and listed. This enables you to quickly find double and triple versions of a file. For each file, the MS-DOS Shell displays numerous functions and the directory path, so you can effectively delete the duplicate files.

You can also use the Windows 3.1 File Manager to search for multiple copies of a file. Select *Search* from the *File* menu. A dialog box appears, in which you can enter the name of the file in *Search For:*, and the root directory in *Start From:*. The screen then displays every occurrence of this file on the entire directory. Unfortunately, you cannot use "*.*" as your file specification because files are sorted by directory.

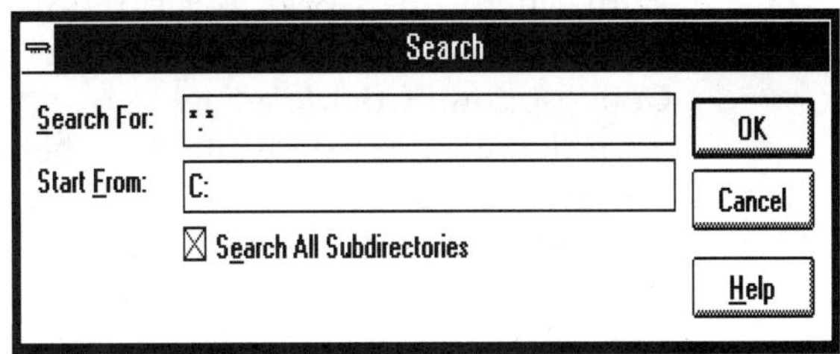

Using Search... to search for multiple copies of a file

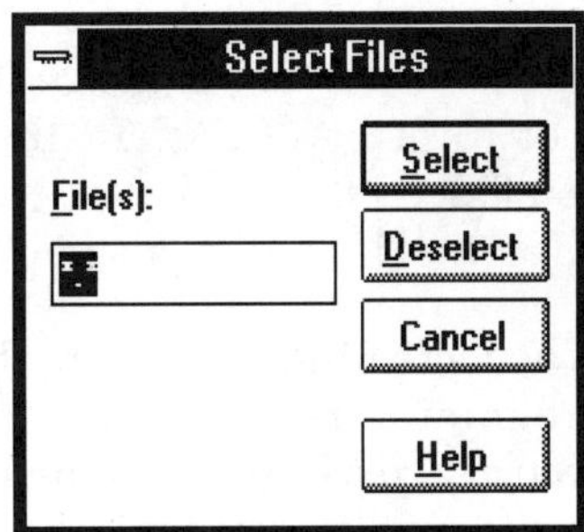

The Select Files... dialog box

Deleting BAK and TMP files

Deleting backup files

You can also free a lot of space on the hard drive by deleting file versions you no longer need. You should also delete temporary files (i.e., files with the .TMP or .$DB extension), which the program creates during your work and sometimes doesn't delete, and backup (BAK) files. Carefully search your hard drive for these files and delete them.

Don't delete these files if the program to which they belong is still active.

If you ever use CHKDSK to check the hard drive, you may also find some files named FILE????.CHK (numbers may appear instead of question marks) in the root directory.

These files are created because of errors on the hard drive and can also be deleted.

Some programs make backup copies of the previous file version when you save. Word automatically assigns the .BAK extension to these files, which can occupy much space on the hard drive.

Don't delete the .BAK files while you're using Word. Instead, delete these files when you're finished with the files and you've quit a program and returned to DOS.

With Microsoft Works for Windows, you can specify whether Works saves the last version of a file by selecting the Backup Copy option of the *File/Save As...* command. Works files usually have default file extensions that begin with the letter "W" (WPS for texts, WKS for tables, etc.), while the backup copies have extensions that begin with the letter "B" (BPS, BKS etc.). These files can also accumulate over time, occupying a lot of space on the hard drive. So, you should delete all duplicate versions of a file regularly.

For example, to delete files with the B* extension (BPS, BKS, etc.), use the *File/Search...* command from the File Manager and simply enter *.B* under *Search For:*. Under *Start From:*, enter the root directory (C:\). In the new dialog window that appears, you'll see all the files matching this description. You can easily select the desired files and delete them by pressing Del.

Deleting older program versions

When creating space on the hard drive, don't forget the old program versions that you're keeping on the hard drive for security reasons. This usually occurs when you upgrade an application. For example, you may have upgraded to Word 5.5, but kept Word 5.0 in a separate directory in case of any problems. If errors and problems occur, you can always return to the older version.

However, once you've established that the new version works properly, you should delete the older version. First compress the old version (more on this later) and store it on diskettes before deleting it from your hard drive.

Step 4: Compress files

If you still don't have enough hard drive space after deleting all unnecessary data, there are other ways to create space. Windows 3.1 requires about 7.5 Meg, but Windows applications (e.g., Word for Windows, Excel, and Works for Windows) also demand large amounts of disk space.

Data compression programs

Data compression programs, which are also called archiving utilities, can provide a solution. As the name suggests, a data compression program compresses one or more files into a smaller unit, without losing the contents of the file(s). The file cannot be accessed in compressed form, but can be accessed once it's decompressed.

Compression programs use elaborate mathematical algorithms to do this. For example, if a file contains the number 0 one thousand times in a row, the data compression program notates that the number 0 occurs one thousand times, instead of notating the thousand occurrences of the number. So, we need only two bytes for the number of times the number occurs in the file (1000), and one byte for the number itself (0). This represents a saving of 99.7 percent.

Compression to 30%

The more a data compression program wants to compress, the longer it takes because it must examine the file to find places where it can save space. However, such programs can reduce any data to an average 30-50% of the uncompressed file size. Also, many single files can be compressed into one new file. This also reduces the space required for files because even a 1-byte file occupies 4096 bytes on a typical hard drive.

The most important compression programs are called PKXARC, PKZIP, and LHARC. These programs differ slightly in compression rate and runtime performance. We'll show you an example using LHARC:

Suppose that there are several files in the \DATA\1992 directory that you won't need again for several weeks. Change to the \DATA\1992 directory and start the compressor with:

```
LHARC M 1992.LZH
```

This command compresses all the files in the current directory and places them in an archive file called 1992.LZH. Then it deletes all the uncompressed files. The M switch represents Move (compress the files, then delete the originals).

If you want to keep the originals, use this command:

```
LHARC A 1992.LZH
```

This adds the files to the compressed file, and gives you the option of deleting the originals manually.

Later, when you need the files again, you can use the same program to extract (decompress) them. To do this, call LHARC from the \DATA\1992 directory as follows:

```
LHARC E 1992.LZH
```

The E (Extract) command extracts the compressed data. The archive file containing the compressed data isn't deleted, so you must do this yourself with DEL.

The following are two tips about data compression:

- You don't have to compress all the files in a directory. LHARC A 1992.LZH instructs LHARC to compress all the files in the directory. If you want to compress only certain files, you can specify the file name(s). The following command compresses all .XLS files in the directory:

```
LHARC A 1992.LZH *.XLS
```

- File compression also requires a certain amount of space on the hard drive because the compression program always creates the compressed file first. So, to compress 1 Meg worth of files, you should have at least 512K free on the hard drive. After compressing the data and deleting the uncompressed files, though, you should have about 1 Meg available (512K from before, 512K saved by compression).

Here's one last tip on deleting older versions of programs. Before deleting them from the hard drive completely, compress them in their directory. Then keep them in their directory for awhile. Frequently users notice that they still need certain data or programs from the older program, such as a printer driver or mouse driver. Then you can extract this file from the compressed data and copy it to the new program directory. Delete the old version only after you've worked without it for a long time.

For example, to extract only the MY.PRD printer driver for Word from 1992.LZH, type the following:

```
LHARC E 1992.LZH MY.PRD
```

Determining the contents of the archive file

If you're not sure which files are in an archive file, call LHARC with only the name of the archive file:

```
LHARC 1992.LZH
```

Beginning with Version 6.0, PC Tools can also display different archive files from PC-SHELL if you select the *File/Quickview* command.

By following these tips, you should be able to postpone buying a new hard drive just on Windows' account for some time, even if you decide to purchase the latest version of Windows in the next couple of days.

29.6 Optimum Memory Management

Most users know that there are different kinds of memory. Many computers with 2 Meg total memory have less than 500K free after starting up. In this section we'll discuss some practical solutions for memory management, so that you can maintain as much free memory on your computer as possible. Unlike the earlier section on memory use, we'll provide basic information instead of sample configurations. So, you'll be able to customize any system file.

Have the boot diskette you created in Section 29.2 available, in case you make any errors while configuring the system.

The absolute basics:

First we'll explain the terminology we'll be using throughout this section:

Conventional memory
: Memory below 640K, available for MS-DOS applications.

Extended memory
: Memory available for 80286, 80386 and 80486 computers, beginning at 1 Meg (1024K).

Expanded memory
: Also called EMS. Memory that can be used by any computer, inserted into the available memory in small portions called memory pages. The 64K area into which the memory is inserted is called a page frame.

High memory
: Special 64K memory, beginning at 1 Meg, that can be used directly by some programs, such as MS-DOS 5.0 and Windows.

Upper memory
: Memory in free areas between 640K and 1 Meg (memory located where you ordinarily find hardware extensions, video memory, and the BIOS ROM).

XMS memory
: A special standard for extended memory, represented above all by HIMEM.SYS, required by more programs. XMS memory contains extended memory, upper memory, and high memory.

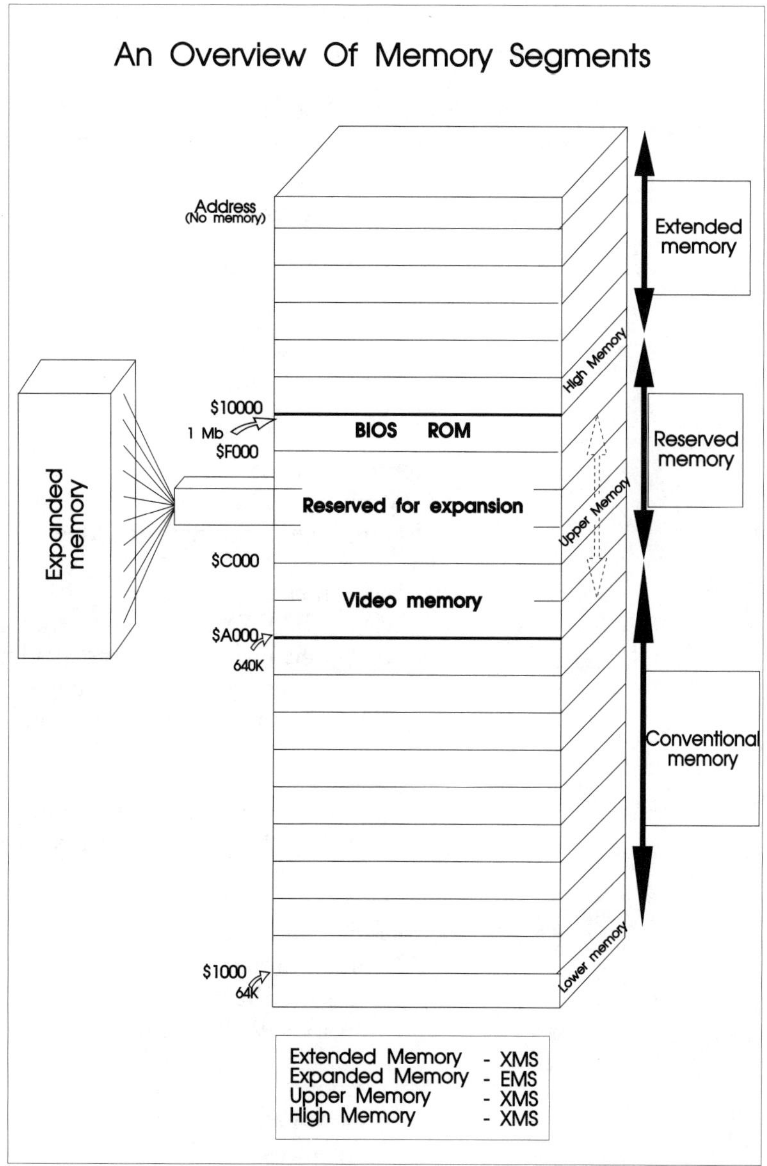

An overview of memory division

The above illustration shows the basic division of the PC into different memory areas. First, note the rough division into three categories:

0 - 640K
    Conventional memory

640K - 1 Meg
    Reserved memory (high memory, upper memory)

1 Meg - 16 Meg
Extended memory

Expanded memory lies outside of this number assignment, giving the PC access to a special area in memory called a page frame.

Along with these larger categories, there are also names for areas with special characteristics:

The first 64K of conventional memory are referred to as "Lower memory". Reserved memory is divided into BIOS ROM, video memory, and hardware extensions.

The first 64K in extended memory are called high memory.

Unfortunately, different memory types have different names in different versions of DOS. Therefore, we compiled different terms for the two most important DOS versions, MS-DOS 5.0 and DR DOS 6.0:

Address (K)	MICROSOFT	DRDOS
0 to 640	Conventional memory	Conventional memory
Over 1024	Extended memory	Extended memory
?	Expanded memory	Expanded memory
1024 to 1088	High memory	High memory
640 to 1024		Upper memory
0 to 64		Lower memory

Table of different memory terms

How to save memory

Minimum memory requirements

On a computer without any extended memory (and without any setting in the system files), there is approximately 578K of memory (592848 bytes) with MS-DOS 5.0. While this value may vary depending on the computer (number of drives, etc.), this is the approximate maximum value possible.

There are several tips and tricks you can use to provide more memory for DOS programs. However, often these tips and tricks depend on the type of computer and its layout.

Another way to provide more memory is by not wasting memory. To provide as much memory as possible for applications, use only as much memory as is absolutely necessary. Large CONFIG.SYS and AUTOEXEC.BAT files and many loaded utility programs consume precious memory.

Obviously, the commands that are used depend on a person's needs. So, we'll show you which commands in the system files don't require any memory, and how much you can use through specific settings.

Commands without memory requirements

You can use these commands without worrying about memory.

BREAK
: Determines when DOS processes can be canceled.

COMSPEC
: Command interpreter environment variable.

COUNTRY
: Country-specific characters and notation.

ECHO
: Enables/disables message display.

PATH
: Defines a path.

PROMPT
: Defines the prompt character.

REM
: Defines comment lines.

SET
: Defines environment variable.

VER
: Checks version.

VERIFY
: Verifies data written to disk.

SHELL
: Specifies command interpreter.

Although you could lose a couple of bytes specifying environment variables, such as COMSPEC or PROMPT, these few bytes usually aren't important.

How much memory do the commands and settings require

Memory requirements in detail

The following paragraphs introduce the most important commands and settings for the CONFIG.SYS and AUTOEXEC.BAT files, with the required memory and the limitations. You'll also find a list of less frequently used MS-DOS commands, which could appear in the system files. Use this information to learn how to conserve memory so that more memory is available for applications.

By using some "economy settings" (e.g., BUFFERS=1) you can even go below the minimum value without altering CONFIG.SYS and AUTOEXEC.BAT. However, this slows down or restricts the PC, so you shouldn't actually use this setting.

APPEND
: Search path for files; with APPEND you can set a search path for files (PATH only sets a search path for programs). APPEND uses 9280 bytes of memory, because part of APPEND stays resident in conventional memory.

BUFFERS
: Number of buffers for working with diskettes and hard drives; each additional buffer allocates 532 bytes in memory and can store 512 bytes of information, so it has 20 bytes of management information. If a value isn't specified, MS-DOS determines the number of buffers according to the existing hardware. Fifteen buffers allocate about 7980 bytes. Although you can save almost all of this memory by specifying BUFFERS=1, you must sacrifice a considerable amount of speed.

DEVICE
: Installs device drivers; memory requirements depend on the loaded device driver. If possible, use DEVICEHIGH on a 386.

EMM386.EXE
: Device driver for memory management and allocation of EMS and UMB. While this driver allocates 8896 bytes in memory, it can provide considerably more free memory. The driver is only necessary and practical on 80386 and 80486 computers with extended memory and requires HIMEM.SYS.

FASTOPEN
: Speeds up access to files that have already been accessed. Part of FASTOPEN remains resident in

memory, occupying at least 3680 bytes. FASTOPEN notes specific information about a file and requires 48 bytes in memory for each file.

FCBS
: Sets the number of file control blocks; this corresponds to an older version of FILES. Each of the 4 default File Control Blocks allocates 64 bytes, while each additional File Control Block would also use 64 bytes. Unlike FILES, FCBS is no longer important today.

FILES
: Sets the maximum number of opened files; each opened file requires 64 bytes of management information. You cannot specify a value less than 8. If the value for FILES is too low, MS-DOS sends an error message.

GRAFTABL
: Loads graphics character set; after calling this program, ASCII characters from code 128 and up can also be displayed in graphics mode. Calling GRAFTABL reduces conventional memory by 1296 bytes.

GRAPHICS
: Loads graphics print program; after starting this program, hardcopies of the screen can also be created in graphics mode. The program requires 5968 bytes in memory.

HIMEM.SYS
: A device driver for XMS memory. HIMEM.SYS occupies 1184 bytes in memory, but is indispensable for memory management for Windows and many other programs. The driver is only necessary on 80286, 80386, and 80486 computers with extended memory.

KEYB
: Selects keyboard layout; KEYB is necessary only for adapting your system to foreign keyboards. It occupies 6320 bytes in memory.

LASTDRIVE
: Defines the maximum number of possible drives; 80 bytes for each additional drive letter. The default is LASTDRIVE=E, so LASTDRIVE=F decreases memory by 80 bytes.

PRINT

Installs a printer; with PRINT you can set up a print queue so you can continue working with your computer during printing jobs. The resident part of PRINT allocates 5808 bytes in memory for this. We recommend using the Windows Print Manager instead of PRINT.

RAMDRIVE.SYS

Installs a RAM disk; RAMDRIVE is a resident program that emulates a disk drive. This program requires 3424 bytes of memory, and also requires HIMEM.SYS. If the data are stored in conventional memory instead of extended memory, a great deal more memory is lost (at least an extra 64K). So, you should always create a RAM disk in extended memory.

SETVER

SETVER must be enabled as a device driver in the CONFIG.SYS file if MS-DOS 5.0 should report a different DOS version than 5.00. You'll lose 400 bytes by making this entry.

SHARE

Permits multi-user operation; SHARE only needs to be loaded if you're running a network (or under certain circumstances within multitasking operations) and requires 6320 bytes by default.

SMARTDRV.SYS

Device driver for speeding up hard drive accesses by placing the data in temporary storage; a part of SMARTDRV remains resident in memory, requiring 15552 bytes as well as HIMEM.SYS. If the memory for temporary storage is also in conventional memory, the memory requirements are considerably higher (at least 256K). That's why you should only use extended memory for SMARTDRV.

SMARTDRV.EXE is the cache program that's included with WINDOWS. It has the same requirements as SMARTDRV.SYS. However, it uses slightly more memory (around 26K). However, if you work with Windows frequently, you should still use this cache program.

STACKS

Memory for hardware interrupts; usually MS-DOS works with the default value of STACKS=4 for 4 interrupt buffers. However, you can almost always set the value STACKS=0,0, which provides 1872 bytes.

Seldom used commands

Along with these commands and drivers that frequently occur in the system files, there are also some other ones that aren't required as often. We'll only briefly mention their memory requirements because they only play a minor role in Windows operation:

ANSI.SYS

Device driver for screen and keyboard; ANSI.SYS uses 4208 bytes of memory. However, it's almost useless for Windows operation, unless you plan to use the command area frequently under Windows and use ANSI.SYS to assign the function keys with useful routines.

ASSIGN

Changes the drive label; ASSIGN uses 1680 bytes of memory and is mainly ignored by Windows.

COMMAND

Starts the command interpreter. Although one command interpreter requires much more space in memory, each additional COMMAND.COM occupies only 3184 bytes in memory because large parts of the original command processor can be used. Because of this memory saving technique, the command interpreters used, beginning with MS-DOS 5.0, must be identical.

JOIN

Assigns a path to a (pseudo) drive; requires no memory, but is also ignored by Windows.

MODE

In redirecting a serial port to a parallel port, a resident portion of MODE is loaded, requiring 496 bytes in memory. Other MODE commands only set devices and don't require any memory. In Windows, it's better to use the Control Panel to set printer ports.

NLSFUNC

Loads country-specific information; NLSFUNC uses 2880 bytes of memory; you should use the Control Panel to make these settings.

SUBST

Assigns a drive to a directory. While SUBST doesn't require any memory, it's ignored by Windows.

Summary:

By eliminating unnecessary drivers or settings that are too large for certain system values you can save some memory.

Memory management solutions

If you experiment with memory management, you'll continually either receive error messages or even crash the computer.

Solution:

Creating a boot diskette

Keep the boot diskette that you created in Section 29.2 handy. If you haven't created one yet, do so now. Insert a blank diskette in drive A: and type the following:

```
FORMAT A: /S
```

Once the system has formatted the disk and copied the system files over, copy the following files over to your boot diskette:

```
AUTOEXEC.BAT
CONFIG.SYS
DOS\QBASIC.EXE
DOS\SETVER.EXE
DOS\EDIT.COM
DOS\FDISK.EXE
```

If your CONFIG.SYS file on the hard drive crashes, insert the boot diskette in drive A:, and reset the system. Once the system boots, correct the errors in the CONFIG.SYS file on the hard drive, remove the boot diskette, and reset the system again.

If a serious error occurs while the AUTOEXEC.BAT file is executing, you can insert the boot diskette and reset the system, or simply reset the computer and press Ctrl + C to abort AUTOEXEC.BAT. The latter method means that you won't have a search path for the MS-DOS commands.

Problem: Programs dependent on other DOS versions

Here's another problem: You start the PC from a boot diskette, but programs that require a certain version of DOS no longer function.

Solution: SETVER

In MS-DOS 5.0 you can use certain programs meant for other versions of DOS by simulating another DOS version. To do this, use the MS-DOS SETVER command.

However, there are two parts to this adjustment: First the driver must be started in the CONFIG.SYS each time because a device driver and the version table in the hidden system files must be expanded by the new value.

If you created a boot diskette in such a situation, there are three things you must have:

1. The MS-DOS SETVER command must be included on the boot diskette.

2. The CONFIG.SYS file on the boot diskette must contain the following entry:

```
DEVICE=SETVER.EXE
```

3. Also, you must update the version table of the diskette which contains the different DOS version numbers for special programs. Either use the SETVER command or call the MS-DOS SYS command from the hard drive, which already contains the proper version table. The current data are automatically used.

29.7 MS-DOS, Windows and Data Security

Data can disappear or be accidentally erased over a period of time, so backing up data is a necessity for many users. In this chapter, we'll provide some tips and tricks that will save you time and effort in backing up data.

An example of data loss

A large portion of one of our books was almost lost when the network server reported a "hard disk controller error." When we checked our tape streamer backups, we found that one was a backup that was six months old and one was a current backup of another book.

We worked from partial backups and diskettes to try to reconstruct the lost data. During this reconstruction, the repair shop called to tell us that the hard drive had been repaired, and that the data on the hard drive was intact. The book reached the publisher on deadline, but we learned a painful lesson.

This experience should illustrate the importance of making proper, timely backups. The following are some tips and tricks for backing up data.

Minimizing backup time

Remember that you want to keep the backup time as short as possible. However, you should realize that restoring data that's lost will take much longer than backing up the data. Many new tape streamers operate by this principle: High-speed, frequent data backups with longer time periods for restoration.

How it works

The following illustration shows a data backup procedure that guarantees much protection without requiring a lot of time. When combined with virus protection measures, this procedure should provide almost perfect data protection.

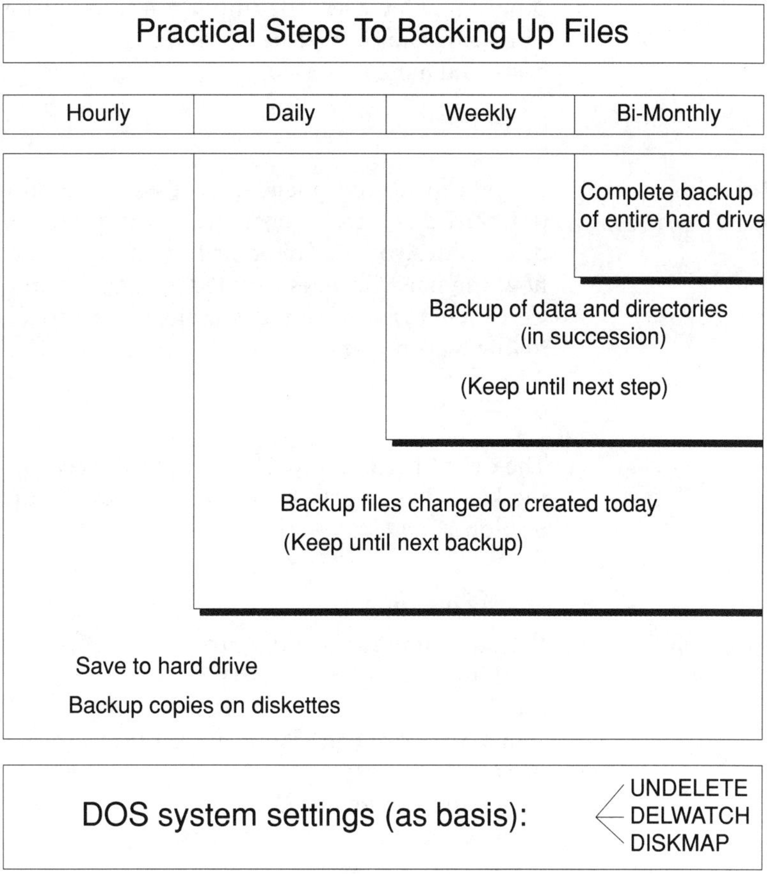

Practical Steps To Backing Up Files

Hourly	Daily	Weekly	Bi-Monthly
Save to hard drive Backup copies on diskettes	Backup files changed or created today (Keep until next backup)	Backup of data and directories (in succession) (Keep until next step)	Complete backup of entire hard drive

DOS system settings (as basis): UNDELETE, DELWATCH, DISKMAP

An overview of data security

Basis:

Basic protection with MIRROR

Use the basic DOS options of data protection, especially MIRROR. MIRROR can preserve information about a hard drive or diskette, the partition table, and the deleted files. This information simplifies data restoration and ensures that the data will be completely restored.

Procedure:

To protect the system area of the C: drive from accidental destruction, add the following command line to your AUTOEXEC.BAT file to enable MIRROR:

```
MIRROR C:
```

To include protection from accidental deletion of files on both drive C: and drive A:, you can load part of MIRROR as a TSR program, which records important information about deleted files. This can make restoring deleted files with the UNDELETE command more successful:

```
MIRROR C: /tC /tA
```

Protecting the partition table

Despite protective measures, it's still possible for all the data of the hard drive to be destroyed if the partition table on the hard drive is destroyed. This partition table contains information about how the hard drive is divided into one or more partitions (drives C:, D:, etc.). To protect this table, save it to a diskette by using the following command:

```
MIRROR /partn
```

The only time you must repeat this procedure is when you change the hard drive partitioning (e.g., if you followed the procedure in Section 29.5).

Hourly backups

Don't run SHARE

We recommend backing up the file on which you're currently working once every hour. You can do this using file options (e.g., the *Transfer* menu in Word 5.0, or the *File/Save As...* command in Word 5.5). You can also use the Windows File Manager to do this because you can copy the file without exiting the executing program. However, SHARE cannot be running simultaneously. SHARE would notice the multiple access to one file and display an error.

Also, another program cannot access the same data. For example, you couldn't select *File/Save* in Word 5.5, then copy the same file to diskette during that save, using the File Manager.

Two backups

It's also important that you alternate between two backups. Save to the first diskette the first time you back up data, then save to the next diskette on the next backup. This way you're still covered if both the original and one backup are destroyed.

Daily backups

At the end of every work day you should back up all new and edited files. The BACKUP command performs this task. Sometimes you can use wildcards (*.DOC) to help select files.

Procedure:

To save all data that have been changed since the last backup to diskettes, use the following command:

```
BACKUP C:\*.* A: /S /M
```

Use wildcards to limit the backup to specific files. For example, to back up only the Microsoft Word DOC files that have been changed since the last backup, use the following command:

```
BACKUP C:\*.DOC A: /S /M
```

Using ATTRIB

There is a disadvantage to backing up the .DOC files using this method. The BACKUP command ignores all glossary files, style sheets, and illustrations. You want these files backed up, but you don't want the .BAK files. You can bypass the BAK files in the backup by changing the archive bits in all .BAK files using the ATTRIB command. The BACKUP command then views the .BAK files as unchanged. The following commands perform a complete backup of all files except .BAK files:

```
ATTRIB C:\*.BAK /S -A
BACKUP C:\*.DOC A: /S /M
```

You could generate a batch file containing these lines and assign it an appropriate icon in the Program Manager. Then you can start the batch file from Windows by double-clicking the icon.

Weekly backups

Backing up the entire directory

At the end of the week, use the BACKUP command to back up the entire directory, including all of its subdirectories. If the data are in several different directories, then more work is involved and you must use this backup procedure for several directories.

Instead, you should change the directory structure so that all the data are located in one data directory. To do this from MS-DOS, you could use COPY to copy directory contents to a new directory, use DEL *.* to delete the contents from the old directory, and then remove the old directory with RD.

Since this involves many steps, we recommend using the Windows 3.1 File Manager, because it can move directories. To do this, select the desired directory in the Directory Tree. Press and hold the mouse button, and drag the selected directory to its new position in the Directory Tree. You may have to open two windows to do this, if the two directories cannot be displayed together.

You should also you two set of diskettes for your weekly backups. Alternate between each set of diskettes each week.

Procedure:

To back up a complete data directory called C:\DATA, use the following command:

```
BACKUP C:\DATA A: /S
```

If the data are located in more than one directory, you must use several command lines. There are two tricks for simplifying and automating the process:

- Create a batch file with the commands needed to back up the data directory.

Adding backups together

- Append multiple data directories by using the /A switch with BACKUP. The following is a sample batch file:

```
REM Batch file for weekly backup
BACKUP C:\TEXTS\LETTERS\*.* A: /S
BACKUP C:\LETTERS\PERSONAL\*.* A: /S /A
BACKUP C:\PICTURES\FIG\*.* A: /S /A
```

In the first line, BACKUP prompts you to insert the first backup diskette, while in the following command lines the command prompts you to insert the last diskette. Since this backup will probably only require one diskette, all you have to do is confirm. This also applies to the remaining commands.

To restore the data, specify the desired files and directory with RESTORE. The command will notice that data were added and includes those data in the restoration.

6 month backups

The total backup

Every few months, or after upgrading an application, you should perform a complete backup of the hard drive (i.e., the root directory and all subdirectories). Again, use two different sets of backups and alternate them. For example, use diskette set 1 when you back up data on January 2nd, then diskette set 2 when you make backups on July 2nd. Return to set 1 the next January 2nd.

Procedure:

This procedure is simple, but requires the most time and the most diskettes. Incidentally, MS-DOS 5.0 automatically formats unformatted diskettes when the diskette capacity matches the drive capacity. The following backs up drive C:'s data to diskettes placed in drive A:

```
BACKUP C:\ A: /S
```

Summary:

We hope this section provides some information that can help you avoid a disaster. Remember that the saying, "Better to be safe than sorry," applies to backing up data.

Overview: DOS data security commands

The following overview shows the most important DOS commands for backing up or restoring data, and their most frequently used parameters:

ATTRIB
: Changes file attributes.

+A/-A
: Use +A and -A to set the archive attribute for one or more files. When you save with BACKUP, the attribute is cleared (archive attribute not set = File is backed up) and set by DOS when the file is changed. Use +A to set the attribute yourself as "not backed up."

/S
: Use /S to include files in subdirectories.

The following is an example:

```
ATTRIB *.BAK -A
```

The above example marks .BAK files as "backed up." The next time you back up the system using BACKUP /M, the process will be faster and will require fewer diskettes.

BACKUP
: Backs up all specified files from source drive to target drive:

/S
: Includes subdirectories in the backup.

/M
Backs up only files that have changed since the last backup.

/A
Existing backup not deleted, appends newly backed up files.

The following is an example:

```
BACKUP C:\DATA A: /S /M
```

The above example backs up all files with a set archive attribute (= changed since last backup) from C:\DATA, including all subdirectories, to A:.

MIRROR
Backs up system information.

/Partn
Backs up the partition table to diskette.

/TDr
Loads deletion-tracking program for drive Dr.

The following is an example:

```
MIRROR C: /Ta /Tc
```

RECOVER
Tries to restore a file as much as possible, omitting defective parts. **Caution:** Specify files only. Don't specify a drive.

The following is an example:

```
RECOVER A:\PROGRAM.BAS
```

RESTORE
Restores data backed up with BACKUP.

/S
Includes subdirectories.

/M
Restores only changed files.

/N
Restores only files that no longer exist.

/P

Prompts the user before restoring write-protected, hidden, or changed files.

/D

Only displays restoration process, so you can check the possible results.

The following is an example:

```
RESTORE C:\DATA A: /S /M
```

29.8 MS-DOS Diskette Formatting

The MS-DOS 5.0 FORMAT command is a very flexible command. Even if you have infinite hard drive space for your Windows files, you'll still occasionally need formatted diskettes.

DOS can undo formatting

If you have MS-DOS 5.0 and use FORMAT A: to format diskettes, you already have many advantages compared to someone using an older version of DOS. MS-DOS automatically tries to preserve existing diskette data on formatted diskettes. You can then unformat the diskette if you accidentally format a diskette containing important data.

However, this option depends on a number of factors. If you don't know about these factors, you won't be able to use UNFORMAT. FORMAT has many options to make formatting easier and more convenient.

Special features in Windows

Compared to formatting a diskette from DOS, this process has some special features in Windows.

Multitasking while formatting

- On a 386 computer running in 386 Enhanced mode, multitasking is allowed while formatting diskettes from within Windows. You can work on another task while formatting a diskette.
- Unfortunately, you cannot utilize many of the options available in MS-DOS 5.0. The most serious disadvantage is that you can't use the /Q (quick format) switch in Windows.

Formatting with File Manager

Because of these disadvantages, you should format diskettes from within MS-DOS. You can still format diskettes from Windows, but the MS-DOS FORMAT command is more flexible.

What happens when you format diskettes with MS-DOS

Blank diskettes are simply magnetic media without any information. The first time you format a diskette, the formatting process divides the diskette into tracks and sectors. Then FORMAT verifies the diskette (checks it for readability). Finally, the system areas needed by DOS are created (boot sector, root directory, and file allocation table).

If you have a diskette that's already formatted, and you want to reformat it, you can use this diskette. If the diskette has already been formatted once in this way and the user wants to format the diskette again, it doesn't have to be divided into tracks and sectors again. MS-DOS implementations, starting with Version 5.0, provide various formatting alternatives.

- If the diskette is still unformatted, MS-DOS formats it at the highest possible drive capacity (1.2 Meg on a 5.25 inch high-density drive, or 1.44 Meg on a 3.5 inch high-density drive).

Backup copy of the system areas

- If the diskette has already been formatted once and you want to format it again with the same capacity, MS-DOS can limit itself to verifying the diskette and creating new system areas. Since the actual data (letters, addresses, programs) don't have to be destroyed, MS-DOS creates UNFORMAT information (a backup copy of the system areas) and hides this information on the diskette. This UNFORMAT information will let you restore the information stored on the diskette before this formatting session.

- If the diskette has already been formatted once and you want to format it again with a different capacity, MS-DOS must delete all information from the diskette before dividing the magnetic media into tracks and sectors. This makes it impossible to undo the formatting with UNFORMAT. The system informs you of this, and you can proceed with the format or abort the program.

Storing UNFORMAT information requires space on the diskette. The FORMAT command won't offer this option on diskettes that contain large amounts of data. A 1.2 Meg diskette requires about 12K of data for storing UNFORMAT information.

Quick formatting diskettes

MS-DOS verifies (checks) an entire formatted diskette for readability before creating system areas on the diskette. This readability applies only to readable elements of the diskette. Bad sectors are marked as such, so the free space on a newly formatted diskette can change from diskette to diskette.

If a diskette is reformatted, MS-DOS verifies it and creates the new system areas based on that verification. While this process is faster than formatting for the first time, it's still time-consuming (about one minute for a 1.2 Meg diskette).

Quick formatting doesn't verify

If you only want to remove all existing data from a diskette, you don't have to verify it in the process. The /Q (quick format) switch deletes existing data from the diskette, generates an UNFORMAT file, and creates new system areas. The following command formats a previously formatted diskette in a few seconds:

```
FORMAT A: /Q
```

You cannot change capacities when you use the /Q switch, because the division into tracks and sectors must be changed. Whenever possible, save time by using the /Q switch. You can easily replace the "normal" Format command (with Verify) with Quickformat (without Verify) by adding the following command line to your AUTOEXEC.BAT file:

```
DOSKEY FORMAT=FORMAT.COM $* /Q
```

Use macro capabilities

This loads a special command line editor into resident memory. This editor also has macro capabilities. Whenever you enter FORMAT at the DOS prompt, the system will remove FORMAT from the line and replace it with FORMAT.COM /Q. The $* instructs the system to place all other specified parameters here.

For example, if you type the following command:

```
FORMAT B: /S
```

DOSKEY changes the command to this:

```
FORMAT.COM B: /S /Q
```

Deleting old data during diskette formatting

Occasionally you won't want MS-DOS to make data retrievable on a formatted diskette. For example, perhaps important or personal data, such as tax information, is saved on a diskette. Eventually, you'll no longer need this information. However, if you format the diskette, someone else can retrieve and view the information by using the UNFORMAT command.

Protection through FORMAT A: /U

MS-DOS 5.0 provides an option for formatting a diskette in the same way MS-DOS formatted diskettes up to Version 4.01 (completely overwriting data and verifying new tracks and sectors). The /U (unconditional) switch performs an unconditional format, generating new tracks and sectors on the diskette, without generating UNFORMAT information. To format a diskette unconditionally in drive A:, type the following command:

```
FORMAT A: /U
```

Be extremely careful when using /U because once you've formatted with this parameter, it will no longer be possible to restore the data on the diskette.

Volume labels and serial numbers

After formatting a diskette, MS-DOS automatically prompts you for a volume label for the diskette. The Windows File manager automatically displays this "electronic labeling." Pressing Enter instructs the system not to add a volume label name.

Electronic labeling

The MS-DOS LABEL command lets you add a volume label to a hard drive or diskette at any time, or change the existing volume label. The DIR command displays the volume label name at the beginning of the directory display.

The volume label name can contain a maximum of eleven characters. Unlike file names, this name can also contain spaces. You should assign meaningful names to your diskettes. So, you can view the volume label name of a diskette by using the VOL command, and have some idea of what's on a diskette without viewing the entire directory.

Volume serial number

MS-DOS 5.0 doesn't use diskette names to distinguish between different diskettes. Instead, it uses a special volume serial number, which is assigned when the diskette is formatted. This number consists of two four-digit hexadecimal numbers. MS-DOS uses this number to determine when diskettes are changed.

The date a diskette was created is also important because you cannot tell by the data stored on the diskette. The data keep their original date when copied to the diskette. To easily determine this information, creating a directory, called DATE, on the diskette by using the MD command. (You could also use a different directory name).

Since this directory receives the same date and time information as the files, you could use DIR from DOS or the Windows File Manager to easily determine the creation date.

Formatting a hard drive

It's often a good idea to change your hard drive's structure before installing Windows. There are times when you must do this after installation. For example, formatting the hard drive may be necessary after a powerful virus attack. Or, you may have to take your PC to the shop, and you don't want any unauthorized personnel viewing your personal files.

The FORMAT command can also format a hard drive if it's divided into one or more partitions by FDISK. FORMAT recognizes errors on the hard drive and bypasses these defective portions for later use.

Formatting a hard drive can be intimidating. However, in certain situations, you'll want to reformat a hard drive without making changes to the partitions. For example, this can be useful when you must take the computer to the repair shop and you want to remove all data from the hard drive beforehand. Or a software error has caused such a serious error in a drive's structure, that you can't eliminate it with CHKDSK, and you must reformat the hard drive.

If the hard drive is divided into several partitions, you must format each one using the FORMAT command. When you do this, back up your data first. Call FORMAT and specify the drive letter previously displayed. You must format the first drive with the /S (system) switch so the computer can be started from this drive:

```
FORMAT C: /S
```

If the operating system (the hidden system files) isn't on the hard drive yet, and there is no system diskette with these files in drive A:, FORMAT prompts you to insert a DOS diskette into drive A: and confirm by pressing Enter.

Confirm the following security prompt with Y and Enter. Then the screen displays the percentage of formatting completed, counting from 0 to 100. When the formatting process is complete, you must specify a name for the hard drive. This name can be up to eleven characters in length and can contain spaces. You can also press Enter to avoid specifying a name.

Special options for diskettes

Changing the capacity

Users don't always want to format diskettes with the maximum possible capacity. You can format double density (DD) 5.25" diskettes with 360K in a 1.2 Meg drive by specifying the /F: (format) switch and the exact capacity. For drive A:, the line would be:

```
FORMAT A: /F:360
```

On a 3.5" drive with 1.44 Meg, you can format double density diskettes with 720K capacity by specifying /F:720. On the new

2.88 Meg drives, you can use a specification of /F:1440 to format at 1.44 Meg capacity.

How to create a system diskette

We've mentioned how to create a boot diskette, from which you can boot the system. You may have to create such a diskette if you cannot boot from the hard drive, or if you're experimenting with CONFIG.SYS and AUTOEXEC.BAT.

Let's examine the problem more closely. When you make changes to the CONFIG.SYS or AUTOEXEC.BAT configuration files, you may make an error while editing the files and the computer may not boot because of those files.

If you don't have a boot diskette available, you don't have access to the bad files.

Frequently, though, this isn't enough by itself, and you must still copy important files to the diskette. However, don't copy the AUTOEXEC.BAT and CONFIG.SYS files directly to the diskette, because the path specifications used in those files may not apply to the diskette. In an extreme case, using the original files of the hard drive on a diskette could prevent the computer from starting up from the diskette (especially when the CONFIG.SYS SHELL command is used incorrectly). That's why you should save the two system files under different names (A.BAT and C.SYS or something similar).

Formatting a diskette as a system diskette

To copy the operating system to a new diskette during formatting, use the /S (system) switch. This copies two hidden files (IO.SYS and MSDOS.SYS) and the COMMAND.COM command processor to the diskette, leaving less room on the diskette for data.

To prepare a diskette in drive A: as a system diskette, type the following command:

```
FORMAT A: /S
```

If the diskette has a lower capacity than the drive you're using, you must also specify the correct capacity using the /F: switch.

To format a double-density (360K) diskette in a 1.2 Meg drive as a system diskette, type the following:

```
FORMAT A: /S /F:360
```

Using SYS to create a system diskette

System diskette without formatting

To use a diskette that already contains data for booting the computer, you must prepare it by copying the system files onto the diskette.

You cannot do this with the COPY command because the system files must be located at the beginning of the root directory on the diskette. This isn't possible with COPY.

The SYS command copies the files to the beginning of the diskette's root directory. Then it's no longer absolutely necessary to format the diskette with the /S switch.

However, ensure that there's enough room on the diskette for these files. The SYS command copies the two MS-DOS system files and the COMMAND.COM file to the diskette in the specified drive.

These files occupy about 120,000 bytes. If the diskette to which you want to copy the two system files and COMMAND.COM is in drive A:, the command line must look as follows:

```
SYS A:
```

You can use a system diskette prepared in this way to start up the computer. To do this, place the system diskette into drive A: and switch on the computer.

The following illustration combines all the MS-DOS 5.0 formatting options.

It also shows what happens to data stored on the diskette during the process:

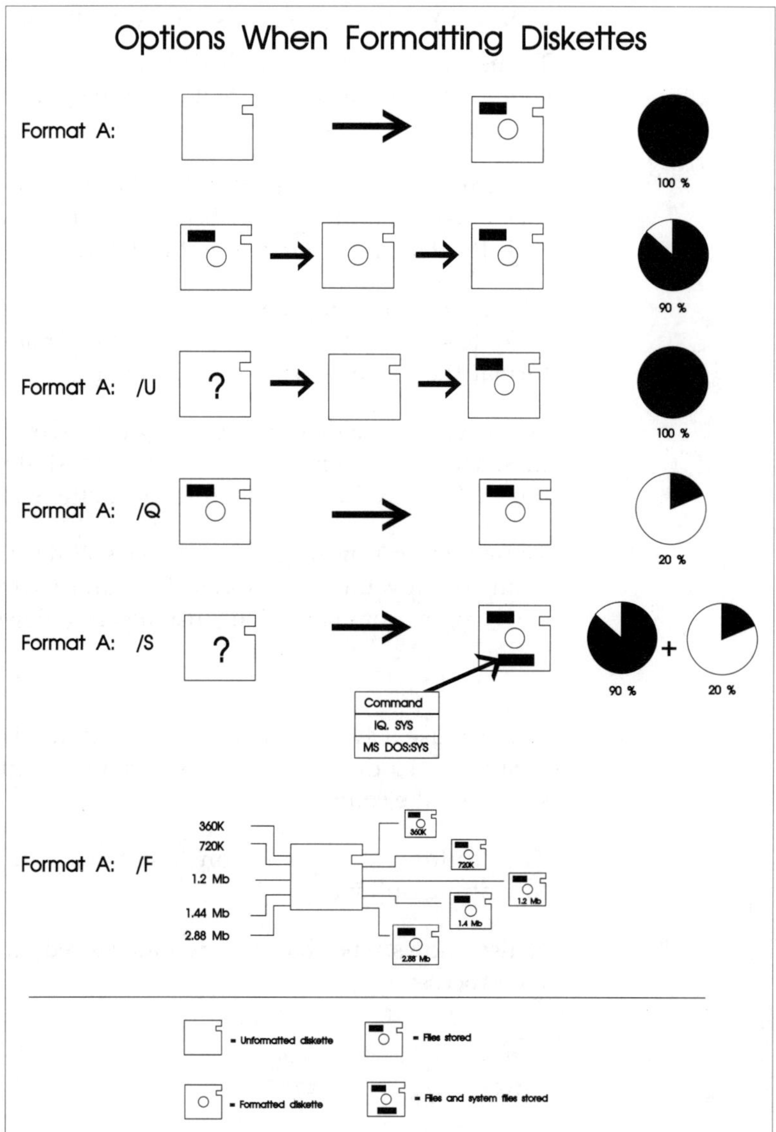

Formatting options with MS-DOS 5.0

The above illustration shows the various options for formatting diskettes. Unlike older versions of DOS, when you format a diskette directly, it's no longer completely remagnetized. Instead, the existing format is used (if possible) and verified. Then FORMAT creates a new system area based on what was available at the time. A diskette is only "remagnetized" when it's formatted for the first time or formatted at a different capacity.

/U:

This switch performs an unconditional format. Any data the diskette may have contained are lost.

/Q:

This switch performs a quick format, without checking the existing magnetization. As a result, DOS only takes 20 percent of the time that's usually required for formatting.

/S:

This switch formats the diskette as a system diskette, which is capable of booting the computer. After formatting, the /S switch copies the system files needed for booting to the diskette.

/F:

This switch formats at a different capacity than the maximum capacity of the drive. You cannot use the UNFORMAT option after selecting this switch, if the capacity is lower than the maximum.

Restoring data from accidentally formatted diskettes or hard drives

Prerequisites for UNFORMAT

If you accidentally format a diskette or hard drive and would like to restore the data, this is possible as long as you haven't:

- Used /U (unconditional formatting).
- Changed the capacity.
- Saved data to the diskette/hard drive since formatting.
- Ignored the warning message stating there is not enough room for a backup.

If you haven't don't any of the above, you can use UNFORMAT to restore the status of the diskette/hard drive prior to the formatting.

You should be more careful with UNFORMAT than with FORMAT. UNFORMAT truly restores the "old" status. So, if you changed the contents since the last formatting, these changes will be lost. However, if some of the data areas on the diskette have already been overwritten, UNFORMAT may not be able to restore the diskette/hard drive to its old status.

To restore a formatted diskette in drive A:, type the following command:

```
UNFORMAT A:
```

After inserting the diskette, whose contents you want to restore, UNFORMAT displays the information it found. You must answer a security prompt before the command restores the old status of the diskette.

Summary:

The MS-DOS FORMAT command provides so many features that you should definitely consider using it, especially since some very important and interesting options for preparing diskettes aren't available in Windows itself. The time you save in your daily work using MS-DOS can be used for other tasks.

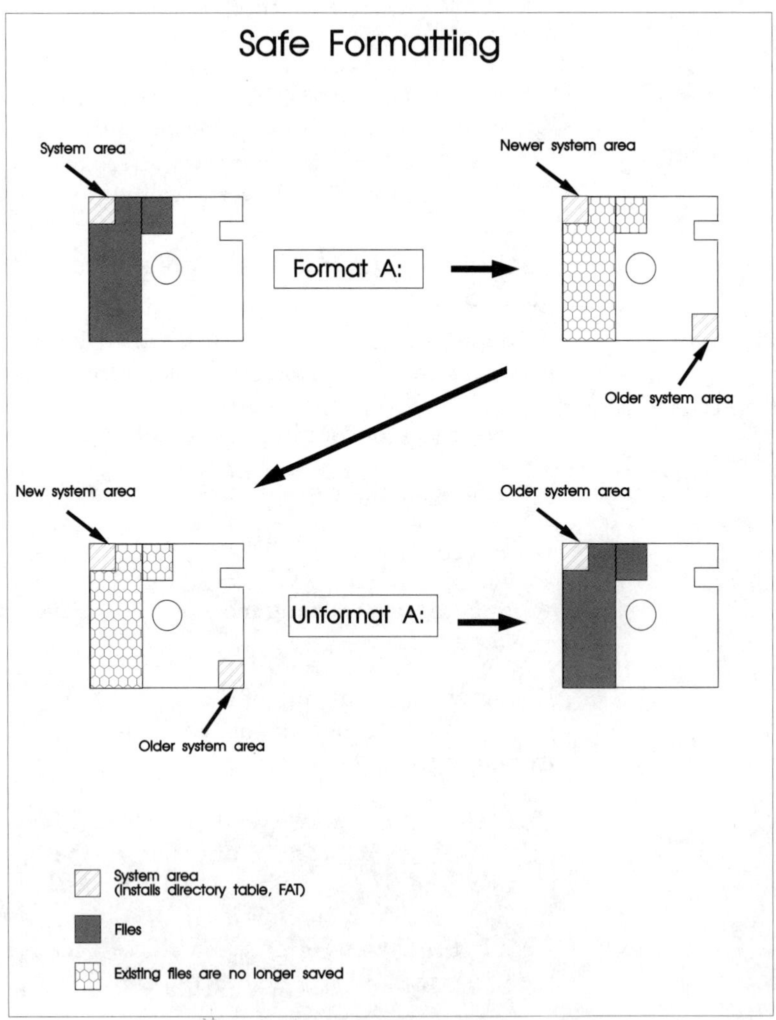

Safe formatting and data restoration

The above illustration shows the basic processes for "safely" formatting a diskette and restoring the data.

DOS saves the old system area as hidden and creates a new system area. If you save data to the diskette now, the saved system area would be overwritten, along with the existing data, which are no longer saved. The diskette appears to be blank.

UNFORMAT removes the newly created system area from the diskette and restores the old one from the saved data. Now the data still available on the diskette are again visible and protected.

What the Windows File Manager does better

Although formatting diskettes with the prompt is more flexible, there are some tasks that can be performed more quickly and easily with the File Manager:

Advantages and disadvantages of the File Manager

- Quick formatting a diskette is much faster with the Windows 3.1 File Manager. The process takes only five seconds, as compared to eleven seconds from DOS. To do this, select *Format Disk...* from the *Disk* menu and enable the *Quick Format* check box.

- There are also some advantages to using the File Manager for first-time formatting or formatting with /U (Windows 3.1's default setting). Since the process takes a certain amount of time, on an 80386 computer you can do something else (multitasking), and Windows will automatically enable the File Manager after formatting is finished. The File Manager then informs you of the results, so you don't have to wait for the formatting process to end before working on another task.

Windows slows down considerably in diskette accesses, including diskette formatting. The reason for this is that a track must be completely formatted before another application can receive control. This slows down Windows and other applications.

29.9 Windows and Disk Drives

The better Windows can interact with the existing disk, the better Windows will work. Naturally, the hard drive is the most important factor. This section shows some options for improving the way Windows works with diskettes and hard drives.

Active and passive acceleration

You can divide methods of acceleration for hard drive accesses through software into two categories:

Active software methods

BUFFERS, FASTOPEN, Cache

These methods permanently change the way the hard drive is accessed. For example, BUFFERS lets you use buffers, or even make cache memory, out of a large memory range. Programs like FASTOPEN can also store information about the positions of files on the hard drive.

So the next time you open the file, the system already knows the file's position. This eliminates the need to search for the file. These methods are called active because the acceleration method requires processing time, or memory, or both. Basically, you lose something when you use these methods (more on this later).

Passive software methods

Unlike the active methods, passive methods are used only once, or used occasionally, as separate operations, The passive methods don't require resources during the actual processing time on the PC. However, passive methods require time.

Defragmentation and directory structure

Passive methods, such as defragmentation, are ideal for those times when you don't need to use the PC. You can run a defragmentation program overnight, instead of switching off your PC. Running the PC a few hours longer won't hurt the PC and you don't lose any time. With passive methods, it's important that the user doesn't have to intervene at regular intervals (change diskettes, answer prompts, etc.).

Using a cache to buffer the hard drive

Although hard drives access data much faster than disk drives, larger files and memory intensive processes still require a certain amount of time.

High speed hard drives exist, but they're quite expensive, and few are available for 80286 and 80386 machines.

The basic principle of acceleration

Use the hard drive as little as possible

There are ways to speed up access to the slowest hard drives. One method is to use the hard drive as little as possible. This might sound silly at first, but you can actually allocate memory for the purpose of storing hard drive data.

A program that performs such allocation is called a cache (pronounced like "cash").

RAM is faster than the hard drive

A cache program temporarily stores information read initially from the hard drive. This information is placed in a cache in conventional memory. The next time an application needs that information, it's read from RAM instead of from the hard drive.

If no more room exists, an application must make space in the cache as needed. Older data, or seldom used data, can be removed from this space.

Most cache programs only place information from read accesses in temporary storage. Data are always written to the hard drive. This protects the data, because written data aren't saved until they are saved to the hard drive.

Acceleration through BUFFERS

MS-DOS already has the capacity for temporary storage. The BUFFERS= line in your CONFIG.SYS file specifies the number of 512-byte buffers MS-DOS should use for temporary data storage.

If there isn't a specification in the CONFIG.SYS file, MS-DOS chooses a value depending on the particular PC system. However, usually this value is too small.

We recommend the following setting for a computer with a 30 Meg hard drive:

```
BUFFERS=30
```

This change isn't activated until the next time you start the PC. You'll notice the change by an increase in hard drive speed.

99 BUFFERS provide only 50K

However, the possibilities for MS-DOS with BUFFERS are limited for many reasons. First, the maximum value you can specify is 99, providing only 50K for cache memory.

Also, the system that replaces old information with new isn't very effective. That's why special cache programs can considerably improve the effect.

Acceleration through a cache program

SMARTDRV is the Windows cache

Windows includes one of these special cache programs. This program is called SMARTDRV.EXE. It's installed using the AUTOEXEC.BAT file.

You can only use extended memory with SMARTDRV. Unlike buffers, SMARTDRV does the following:

- The WINDOWS 3.1 SMARTDRV.EXE program can only use extended memory. For example, 80286 machines with 1 Meg of memory can use 384K as cache memory, of which the SMARTDRV utility program itself requires 26.624 bytes in conventional memory.

  Available RAM decreases only slightly. On an 80386 you can also install high memory, and SMARTDRV.EXE can then be loaded into this reserved memory. So, conventional memory isn't affected.

- SMARTDRV replaces older cache contents with newer ones according to a clever system. So it's possible that the necessary data will actually be in temporary storage.

Use SMARTDRV only with extended memory

As the amount of more memory available to a cache program increases, so does its effectiveness.

However, if the PC doesn't have extended memory, this memory is lost as RAM. Beginning at a certain boundary, larger applications cannot be loaded.

The speed advantage of a cache program can also vanish if it's a smaller size because memory intensive applications must frequently swap information from RAM to the hard drive. This wouldn't be necessary if the RAM were completely available.

So, you can use SMARTDRV only when there's additional memory available as well as conventional memory.

The following illustration shows how a cache operates.

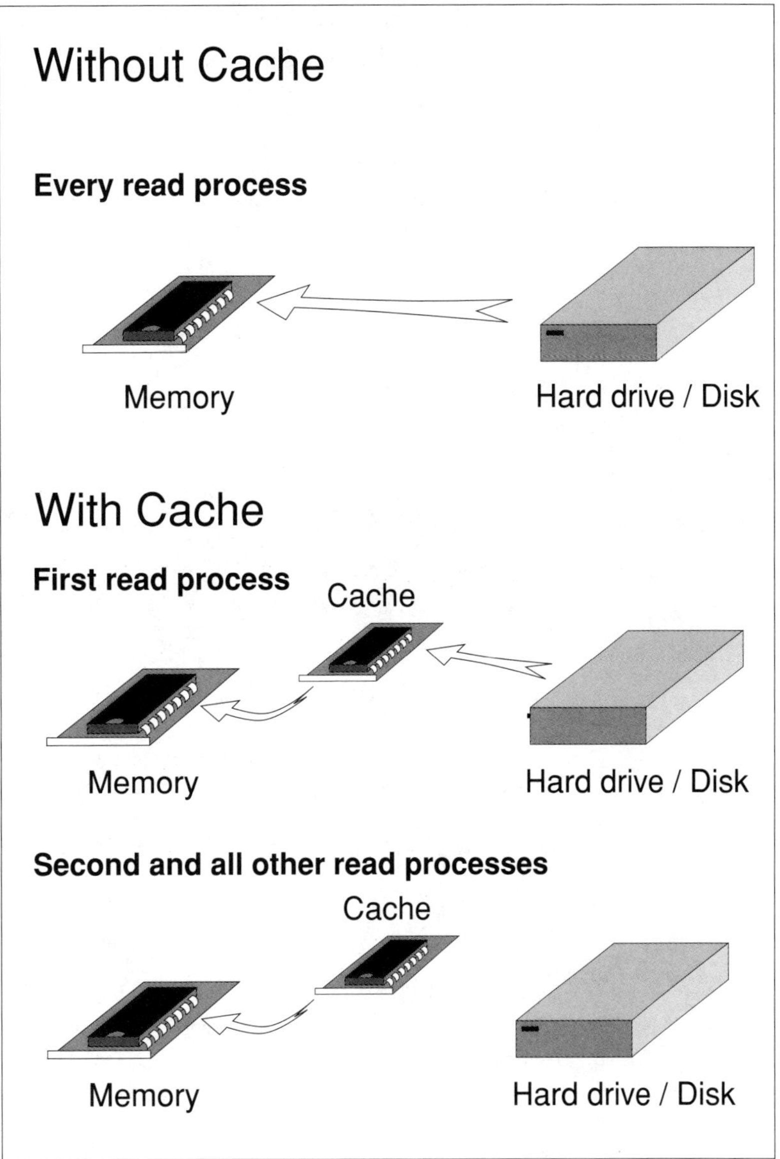

How a cache works

Without a cache, the system reads the hard drive or diskette for information. This process is time-consuming.

With a cache, the system reads the hard drive or diskette for the information, the first time the information is needed. As the information is loaded, the RAM allocated by the cache receives the information.

As a result, the next time the information is needed, the system reads the information from the cache instead of the hard drive or diskette.

Using a cache in extended memory

SMARTDRV.EXE, the cache program provided with WINDOWS 3.1, must be installed in the AUTOEXEC.BAT file, unlike earlier versions of SMARTDRV. To use extended memory for temporarily storing data and programs, simply specify the memory size in kilobytes. On an 80286 machine with 1 Meg of memory, you could use the 384K of extended memory by entering the following command line in the AUTOEXEC.BAT:

```
C:\WINDOWS\SMARTDRV.EXE 384
```

An XMS driver must exist to manage extended memory (e.g., HIMEM.SYS in the CONFIG.SYS file). Also, HIMEM.SYS reserves the first 64K of extended memory as high memory, so there will be 64K less memory available as XMS memory for the cache.

If you run Windows in 386 Enhanced mode, you should also use a second value to specify the amount of memory by which Windows can reduce the cache. In the example above, Windows could borrow the entire 384K from SMARTDRV if it were running in 386 Enhanced mode. If you don't want Windows to borrow any memory at all, specify the same value in the second parameter:

```
C:\WINDOWS\SMARTDRV.EXE 384 384
```

Tip: An expanded memory cache under DOS

SMARTDRV.EXE doesn't support expanded memory. If you still want to access expanded memory, use SMARTDRV.SYS from MS-DOS 5.0. Adding the /A parameter instructs SMARTDRV.SYS to use expanded memory for the cache. To use 256K of expanded memory for temporary storage and acceleration, type the following command in your CONFIG.SYS file:

```
DEVICE=C:\DOS\SMARTDRV.SYS 256 /A
```

Remember that the MS-DOS 5.0 SMARTDRV.SYS file must be installed in the CONFIG.SYS file in a line following the DEVICE command, which specifies the expanded memory manager.

If you're using the EMM386.EXE device driver on an 80386 system to emulate expanded memory, don't allocate this simulated expanded memory to SMARTDRV, because this would unnecessarily reduce the access speed to this memory. Reduce the expanded memory by the amount you want to use for the cache and allocate this memory as extended memory. Besides, Windows works better with its own cache program, SMARTDRV.EXE, and this program can only use extended memory.

An example

Suppose that you converted 1 Meg of XMS memory and all the extended memory to expanded memory. To do this, you used the following line in the CONFIG.SYS file:

```
DEVICE=EMM386.EXE 1024
```

Now you would like to use 512K for temporary storage with SMARTDRV. Reduce the expanded memory to 512K and call SMARTDRV in the AUTOEXEC.BAT file using the parameter 512:

```
CONFIG.SYS      DEVICE=C:\WINDOWS\EMM386.EXE 512
AUTOEXEC.BAT    C:\WINDOWS\SMARTDRV.EXE 512
```

This allocates 512K of extended memory for temporary storage, leaving 512K of expanded memory available for applications. If Windows can only borrow a maximum of 256K of the cache memory, the second line must read:

```
C:\WINDOWS\SMARTDRV.EXE 512 256
```

Remember that the second parameter specifies the minimum amount of memory left over for the cache, instead of how much memory Windows can borrow.

If you use SMARTDRV to speed up access to the hard drive, set the number of buffers (BUFFERS) to 10.

How much of an improvement through SMARTDRV

You'd probably also like to know much SMARTDRV improves your hard drive, so you can determine whether you want to use it. We tried the different options on a computer and measured the times for each option. We used an 80286 with 12 MHz, 3 Meg of extended memory, and a relatively fast hard drive with 19 milliseconds access time and 50 Meg memory capacity.

We used the DR DOS 6.0 cache program, SUPERPCK, in the comparison. For more information on SUPERPCK's options, refer to the chapter on DR DOS 6.0.

Process	No cache	SMARTDRV 2048 512	SUPERPCK /S:2048 /L:512
WORD 5.5 (1st)	5.5s	5.1s	5.5s
WORD 5.5 (2nd)	5.2s	2.6s	3s
CHKDSK (1st)	15.7	14.5	17.83
CHKDSK (2nd)	15.0	12.3	13.5
WIN (1st)	24.15	16.8	15.3
WIN (2nd)	23.0	16.8	9.8

Although the results are only estimates, some patterns are obvious:

Speed advantage of a cache program

Once you call an application program, such as Word 5.5, for the second time, the speed advantage of a cache program; is obvious. It's remarkable that in the CHKDSK test, not only does the cache program, SUPERPCK, slow down the process the first time (17.8 instead of 15.7) but also still requires 13.5 the second time, although the hard drive wasn't accessed.

Perhaps the CHKDSK command itself was the cause, working as a brake. It's also interesting that SUPERPCK can significantly improve execution speed, at least in starting Windows, and clearly beats the Windows cache, SMARTDRV.SYS.

Summary

As you've probably noticed, the results aren't very impressive. On the average, the acceleration from 2 Meg of cache memory is significantly below the factor 2.

The comparison works a little better when the hard drive is slower. However, systems with slower hard drives don't usually have 2 Meg of extended memory available.

Acceleration with FASTOPEN

Using FASTOPEN lets you speed up repeated access to files and directories. Usually MS-DOS has to search the directory structure of the hard drive when a file or directory is needed.

FASTOPEN notes the exact position

FASTOPEN records the exact position of a file or directory on the storage medium, so it can be directly accessed the next time. This is especially useful for working with applications that frequently open and close files.

These programs include databases and word processors, which instead of preserving the entire document in RAM, relocate part of the document to the hard drive (Word 5.5).

To speed up repeated file accesses, specify the drive and desired number of files after FASTOPEN:

```
FASTOPEN X:=nnn
```

In the example, "X" represents an existing hard drive and "nnn" represents the number of files. For example, the following command allocates up to 50 file positions for the C: drive:

```
FASTOPEN C:=50
```

FASTOPEN can also place the file positions in expanded memory if you include the /X switch:

```
FASTOPEN C:=50 /X
```

You should add the line to the AUTOEXEC.BAT file so that FASTOPEN is available as soon as you boot the computer.

FASTOPEN requires about 48 bytes for each file that it notes. So the example line above leaves 2,400 fewer bytes of RAM or expanded memory, without including FASTOPEN itself.

FASTOPEN cannot be used with programs that optimize file positions on the hard drive. These programs include SE.EXE from Norton Utilities and COMPRESS from PC Tools. Also, don't call FASTOPEN from Windows.

Advantages of a RAM disk

Part of conventional memory (RAM) can be used as a disk drive or hard drive for data storage. This requires a special device driver, called RAMDRIVE.SYS. If the driver isn't in your root directory, specify the drive and path in the following command lines as well.

In PC-DOS 5.0, the driver is called VDISK.SYS.

A RAM disk is fast

A RAM disk (or virtual drive) is much faster than a disk drive or a hard drive because no moving parts or hardware communicates with the RAM disk. Data access occurs almost as quickly as direct access to conventional memory.

The time difference that occurs stems from the small amount of memory management handled by the RAM disk program. As a result of this, you can considerably speed up many data intensive processes by storing the data on the RAM disk.

The data stored in a RAM disk are lost each time you restart the computer. Remember to save these data to the hard drive or a diskette before switching off the computer. Otherwise, on the RAM disk keep only data that won't be changed and that's also located on a diskette or the hard drive.

RAM disk features

A RAM disk has the following special advantages and disadvantages compared to disk drives and hard drives:

Advantages of a RAM disk

The most important advantages of a RAM disk result from the great speed with which the computer can access the memory. This is significantly higher than the speed of hard drives, which is already fast.

The advantages of a RAM disk

- Programs load quickly from a RAM disk. If you need to use a program often, copy it to the RAM disk and load it from there. You may want to expand the search path by adding the drive specification of the RAM disk. This should appear first in the search path, so programs are loaded from the RAM disk first. For example, if D: is the drive letter of the RAM disk and MS-DOS is in the C:\DOS directory of the hard drive, the search path in the AUTOEXEC.BAT should be structured as follows:

```
PATH D:\;C:\DOS
```

- Data can be retrieved from the RAM disk much faster than from a diskette or hard drive. If you use the same files frequently, copy them to the RAM disk and then load them from there. Since the contents of the RAM disk are lost when you reset or switch off the computer, avoid editing data in the RAM disk.

- Many programs work with temporary files, in which information is stored briefly. Frequently, such programs place these temporary files in a special directory when you define TMP or TEMP as an environment variable, which contains the desired directory as its contents. If you configure a RAM disk as a storage space for temporary files, the speed of the program can be significantly increased.

  For example, to have Word 5.5 place all temporary files on RAM disk D:, you must type the following command before calling Word:

```
SET TMP=D:\
```

To have Windows do the same, you must also enter this command:

```
SET TEMP=D:\
```

- It's best if you add this line to the AUTOEXEC.BAT file. With this command line, you're setting TMP and TEMP as environment variables.

Disadvantages of a RAM disk

The biggest disadvantages of a RAM disk stem from the fact that the data are being placed in the memory of the computer (RAM), instead of a "real" storage medium (diskette/hard drive):

The disadvantages of a RAM disk

- When you switch off the computer, press the Reset button or press Ctrl + Alt + Del. If a serious program error occurs, the data in the RAM disk are lost forever. So, editing or making changes to data in the RAM disk is dangerous. You should store only those data in the RAM disk that are also stored on a diskette or hard drive.

- Since the RAM disk is completely empty each time you restart it, first you must copy data or programs to the RAM disk when you begin working with it. This is why you should place data in the RAM disk only if you'll use it frequently.

- If you don't have extended memory or expanded memory, the memory used for the RAM disk directly affects conventional memory. Even with a RAM disk that has 256K memory (less than the capacity of a 360K diskette), most large applications will no longer have enough memory available, and will abort with an error after startup.

  PCs without extended memory should have no more than 128K memory reserved for the RAM disk. Even with this small amount of memory, there can still be problems. So in practice, if your computer has a hard drive, but no extended memory, avoid using a RAM disk.

A RAM disk is no alternative

Usually, it's not a good idea to have a RAM disk if you use Windows frequently. Instead, you should make all the memory directly available to Windows. Then Windows will seldom, or never, relocate data and programs.

Having a RAM disk makes sense if you have a lot of total memory and only rarely work with Windows. Then you could set up a RAM disk in the following way:

```
DEVICE=RAMDRIVE.SYS Size Sector Entries Switch
```

Use this command to set up a RAM disk from within the CONFIG.SYS file. Among other things, you can specify the memory size when setting up the RAM disk.

If you don't make any specifications, default values, which aren't suitable for Windows, will be used.

Size
: Set the memory size of the RAM disk in kilobytes here. At least 16K are required, while the highest permissible value is 4,096K = 4 Meg. If you don't specify anything, a setting of 64K is used.

Sector
: Set the sector size here. 128 bytes is the default value; the following values are permitted: 128, 256, 512, and 1,024. We recommend using 512.

Entries
: Set the number of root directory entries here. You can choose from 4 to 1,024 entries, while the default is 64. We recommend either 64 or 128.

Switch

/A
: Use expanded memory for the RAM disk.

/E
: Use extended memory for the RAM disk.

You cannot use the /A switch and the /E switch simultaneously.

More ways to speed up access

Along with the active options of the cache and the RAM disk, there are also passive options for speeding up access to diskettes and hard drives.

Order through directory structures

- To improve data access speed, maintain the hard drive's basic structure.
- Keep as few files as possible in the root directory. Place directories there, instead of files. MS-DOS must search all entries in the root directory before it can use the data in a subdirectory. If 120 files precede the desired subdirectory, the search will take that much longer.

- Structured directories are good, but access time increases dramatically when you start going beyond five levels. To minimize access time, keep your directory tree fairly "flat" (see the illustration below).

- When you set up a new hard drive, create the directory structure first, then copy files onto the hard drive. So the subdirectory entries are at the beginning of the directories, preceding the file names. This enables MS-DOS to find the subdirectories more quickly.

- Organizing the AUTOEXEC.BAT search path by sequence can help MS-DOS find frequently used commands more quickly.

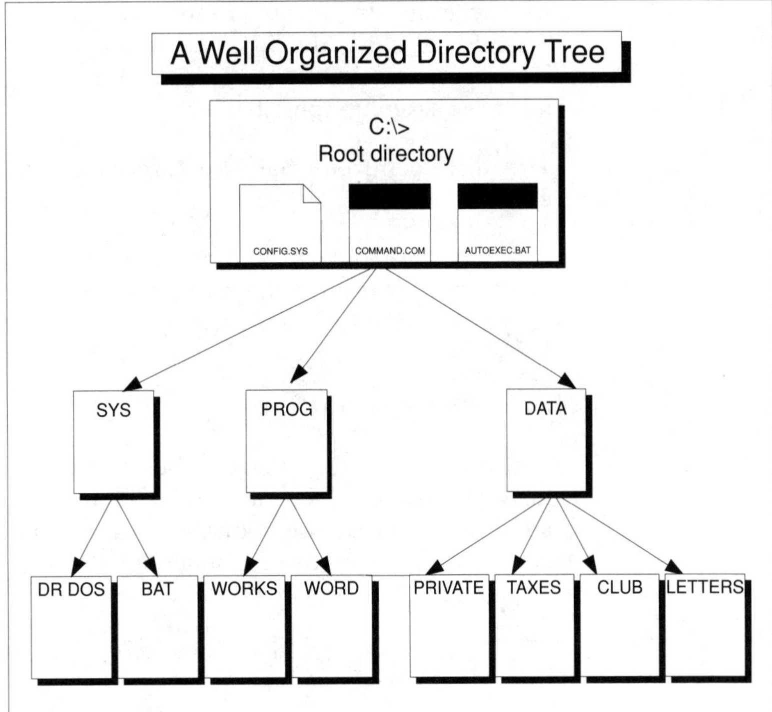

An optimized directory tree

The above illustration shows an optimized directory structure on a hard drive. The basis is the root directory, which is available immediately after formatting.

The root directory should only contain important system files like AUTOEXEC.BAT, CONFIG.SYS, and COMMAND.COM. There are three subdirectories as well as the three system files. The SYS directory contains all the other system specific files.

These system specific files include transient commands and operating system utilities (found in the DOS subdirectory), and batch files (found in the BAT directory). You could also create a directory, for temporary files, which is stored in the SYS subdirectory under the name TEMP.

The PROG subdirectory contains subdirectories in which applications and other programs are stored (WIN and WINWORD).

The DATA directory contains files generated by applications and other programs. The subdirectories in the DATA directory will vary depending on the user's needs.

In our example, we have subdirectories named PERSONAL, TAXES, CLUB, and LETTERS. This arrangement simplifies backing up data. Only the DATA directory and its subdirectories must be backed up consistently.

This directory tree's flat structure makes data access quick and easy.

If you decide to create the directory for temporary files in SYS, inform Windows and other programs by adding the following lines to your AUTOEXEC.BAT file:

```
SET TEMP=C:\SYS\TEMP
SET TMP=C:\SYS\TEMP
```

Merging files

You can also reduce the number of files wherever possible by merging multiple files into larger single units. For example, write all your business correspondence as one multiple-page file. Use your word processor's outline mode, if possible, to keep the letters organized.

✍

Use Word's outline mode to Move through a document. If necessary, use specific key code entries to separate parts of the file, and use your word processor's *Search* command to find the correct entry.

Using compression programs

We discussed LHARC earlier in this chapter. You can use LHARC (or the newer version, named LHA) to create archived files. One archived file contains multiple files that are compressed into one compact unit.

Although you must unpack an archive before you can access the desired file, compressing seldom used files and subdirectories until they're needed will save considerable disk space.

Setting an optimum interleave

A computer system cannot automatically read data from the hard drive at the speed at which the data are transported through the rotation of the drive on the read/write head.

On a typical hard drive (capacities up to 80 Meg) with 17 sectors of 512 bytes per sector, 510K of data must be processed per revolution (3600 revolutions per minute -> 60 revolutions per second) and transferred to conventional memory.

Since the average 80286 can only manage half or less, the computer needs two or more hard drive revolutions to read an entire track. This problem also affects the sector sequence in a track.

If the sectors actually followed each other sequentially, the next logical sector would have passed underneath the read/write head by the time the hard drive is again ready to read and process data. Then the hard drive must wait about one revolution before it can read the next sector.

Although this takes "only" 0.02 seconds, this is a long time for a fast drive, and leads to a considerable loss of speed. That's why there's a special technique for reading and processing the data as quickly as possible: interleave.

The interleave technique arranges the sectors in such a way that the next numbered sector is separated from the previous numbered sector. Ideally, the controller will be ready for data transfer when the read/write head is above the appropriate sector.

The interleave factor specifies how many sectors appear between two numerically consecutive sectors. An interleave factor of 1 means that the sectors follow one another, without any sectors in between. A factor of 3 means there are two sectors between one sector and its numerical successor.

So, an interleave factor of 3 gives the computer more time to transfer the data from the sector it is currently reading before the next sector is directly underneath the read/write head.

Common interleave factors for PC/XT systems are 5 or 6, while standard 80286 machines usually have an interleave of 2 or 3. Only 80386 and fast 80286 machines with very quick hard drive controllers can manage an interleave factor of 1.

It's important to match the interleave factor to the speed of the computer and controller. On fast 80286 machines you occasionally find: "1:1 Controller", which means the controller has an interleave factor of 1, so the sectors follow each other directly and can still be read and processed immediately.

Hard drive controllers can also place one or more sectors in temporary storage. The more data the controller is able to store, the better the computer is supported in data transfer.

Remember that setting an interleave factor that is too large (3 instead of 2) only leads to a slight decrease in speed (the hard drive only has to wait one sector for the right sector with the next number).

However, setting an interleave factor that is too small (2 instead of 3) results in a much greater loss of speed. In this case, the current sector has passed before the hard drive could read and process it, forcing the hard drive to wait another entire revolution.

The user determines the interleave factor (the sequence of sectors in a track) during low-level formatting. It's difficult to change this factor because hard drive data may be destroyed.

However, some special utility programs (e.g., CALIBRATE in Norton Utilities 6.0) let you optimize the interleave factor without data loss. To do this, these programs read a hard drive track to memory, reformat this track with a different interleave factor, and write the data back to the track.

Optimizing file distribution

Hard drives slow down as they fill with data, and as the user deletes and generates data. Let's examine how MS-DOS stores data on a hard drive, then we'll give you some solutions to the problem that exists.

Data is stored contiguously on an empty hard drive. This means that the controller writes data to one track of the hard drive until that track is full, then it writes data to the next track.

Since a hard drive usually contains two disk platters with two read/write heads for the top and bottom, as many as four tracks can be written before the read/write heads move to other areas. Tracks that can be processed without moving the heads are called cylinders.

On a typical hard drive with 17 sectors per track, 8704 bytes (17x512) fit on one track. So the four tracks of a cylinder can accommodate 34816 bytes. The PC can read or write a file of 34K or less without having to move the read/write heads during the process.

When a file is distributed consecutively over the sectors so that no unnecessary waiting times occur, that file is stored *optimally* on a track.

Files become fragmented over a period of time

However, actually files are constantly deleted and stored on the hard drive. For example, this happens when you make changes to a document and then save it again. When a file is deleted, the empty areas are used later to store new data.

However, if the new files to be saved are larger than the amount of free contiguous space, the file must be distributed over several free areas. So, the file is stored on different areas of the hard drive.

When you read or write to such files, the head must constantly travels to new tracks in order to access other parts of the file. This slows down the hard drive considerably.

This process worsens when a hard drive is almost full. When this happens, the free space consists of several small areas, onto which the files must be distributed. This is why data should never occupy more than 80 or 90 percent of a hard drive's capacity.

To determine this amount for your hard drive, figure your hard drive capacity, subtract a tenth of that, then subtract that same figure to determine the 80 percent rule. For example, if you have a 20 Meg hard drive, the formula would be: 20 - 2 - 2 = 16 Meg.

Defragmenting

Utilities called disk optimizers arrange hard drive files in optimum sequence. You'll find these disk optimizers packaged with utilities such as BeckerTools (Disk Optimizer), the Norton Utilities (SD.EXE), and PC Tools (COMPRESS.EXE).

Although some of these utilities can take hours to optimize a large hard drive, they run entirely by themselves. So, you can leave your computer unattended. You should use a disk optimizer when you won't be needing your computer for awhile.

Preparations and requirements for optimizing

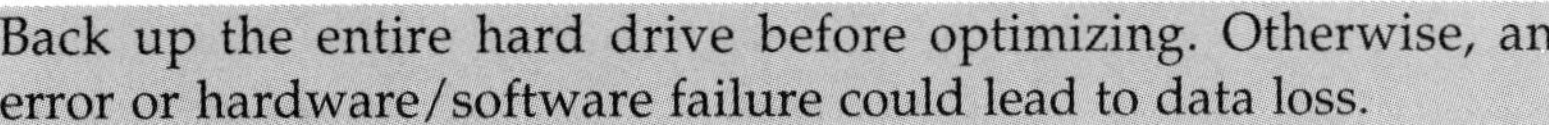

Back up the entire hard drive before optimizing. Otherwise, an error or hardware/software failure could lead to data loss.

Remember that optimizing the hard drive interferes with the hard drive's internal structure. The optimizing program changes directory order and the file allocation table. It also reads data and rewrites the same data in contiguous order.

If the optimizing program cannot complete the process (e.g., a power outage occurs), data integrity could be damaged. Because of this internal intervention, optimizing programs cannot be run from within Windows or with TSR (Terminate and Stay Resident) programs.

Before running an optimizer, you must check for and eliminate all errors on the hard drive. Run CHKDSK to do this. CHKDSK /F fixes errors that are found on the hard drive.

Requirements for defragmenting

Do the following before optimization:

- Make a current backup of the hard drive.
- Use CHKDSK to check the hard drive for possible errors. Use CHKDSK /F to correct any errors.
- Exit to DOS if you're in Windows, or any other multitasking environment. Also, if any TSRs are running, exit them as well. Only the optimization program should be running as a single task.

Once this is done, you can start the optimization program.

However, you don't necessarily have to perform all these safety measures before calling the optimization program. Instead, many optimization programs let you display the current status of a hard drive.

Then if you discover that the fragmentation isn't too severe, you don't have to run the optimization program. So the safety measures aren't necessary.

The best time to optimize your hard drive is the end of the work day. Before leaving for the day, run the optimizer and leave the power switched on.

30. Windows And DR DOS 6.0

In the previous chapter we discussed running MS-DOS 5.0 and Windows together. In this chapter we'll discuss the differences and special features of running DR DOS 6.0 with Windows.

We won't repeat all the elements, which are almost identical to MS-DOS 5.0. Instead, we'll explain only the special features that are related to DR DOS 6.0. The sections on backing up data, formatting, and cleaning up hard drives/diskettes also provide some useful information.

30.1 Windows and DR DOS 6.0 Basics

DR DOS 6.0 and Windows 3.0 worked well together. This is because DR DOS was intentionally set up to work with Windows. For example, the memory management program, EMM386.SYS, contained a special /WINSTD switch for operating Windows in Standard mode. Also, the cache program SUPERPCK could lend cache memory to Windows by using the PCKWIN.SYS driver. However, there could be problems with the current version of Windows (3.1), because the early versions of DR DOS 6.0 weren't completely compatible with Windows 3.1. We'll discuss some of these problems and some solutions.

The fastest solution is an upgrade to the latest version of DR DOS 6.0. Online services that include Digital Research user support (e.g., Compuserve Information Service) have an update available that users can download, and by the time this book is published, Digital Research should have a completely Windows compatible DR DOS 6.0 available.

Even after the actual installation, you can call Windows Setup and make changes to the system settings. You can easily avoid some problems related to memory usage by answering the appropriate question.

DR DOS and Windows in Standard mode

To do this, you must also select special settings so that everything functions properly when you run Windows 3.1 and DR DOS 6.0 together.

For example, when optimizing diskettes/hard drives or increasing hard drive capacity with SuperStor, you must make some settings manually so that DR DOS 6.0 works with Windows 3.1.

In the following sections we'll briefly discuss the special features of running DR DOS 6.0 and Windows and offer some solutions. Then, we'll discuss special topics, such as memory management, in detail.

Installing DR DOS 6.0 and Windows

Before installing Windows under DR DOS, remember the following: First, you can install Windows only if extended memory is available. Under certain circumstances, you can encounter problems if this memory is provided by HIDOS.SYS. In the simplest case, the correct XMS driver for installation is automatically used during the Windows Setup program. However, the Windows Setup program could abort with an error message, informing you that the XMS driver isn't compatible. Then you can continue the installation only after doing the following:

- Find a file called EXPAND.EXE on the WINDOWS installation diskettes and copy it to your hard drive.
- Find the installation diskette containing the HIMEM.SY_ file and copy this file to your hard drive also.
- Now you can unpack the HIMEM.SY_ file with the following command line:

```
EXPAND -R HIMEM.SY_
```

- The unpacked file is now available under the name HIMEM.SYS and you must link it to the CONFIG.SYS file with the following line:

```
DEVICE=HIMEM.SYS
```

- If necessary, insert the name of the corresponding directory in front of the name of the XMS driver.

- At the same time, remove the HIDOS.SYS driver from the file. To do this, simply place a REM in front of the corresponding line, the entry should look like this:

```
REM DEVICE=HIDOS.SYS
```

- Now reboot the computer; you'll be able to use the Windows installation program.

Windows and DR DOS 6.0 each have elaborate installation programs that can change the AUTOEXEC.BAT and CONFIG.SYS system files. Unfortunately, some of the changes can lead to complications.

What Windows changes during installation

Windows tries to insert the memory management program, HIMEM.SYS, into CONFIG.SYS. It also inserts the Windows driver, SMARTDRV.EXE, into AUTOEXEC.BAT as a hard drive cache. Although Windows can use HIMEM.SYS together with DR DOS, the SMARTDRV.EXE cache program isn't prepared to work with DR DOS. So, when you install this program and call an external command, your computer will crash. Be sure to remove this cache program from your AUTOEXEC.BAT file.

What DR DOS 6.0 changes

DR DOS enters either HIDOS.SYS or EMM386.SYS in the CONFIG.SYS file as memory management programs. You can also determine a cache program in SETUP. Then DR DOS will load PCKWIN.SYS in the CONFIG.SYS file for working with Windows along with the actual cache program, SUPERPCK. For better cooperation between Windows and DR DOS, use both the DR DOS memory program and the DR DOS cache program.

X

You should use the following procedure: If possible, first install Windows and then install DR DOS. If you must install Windows again, check the changes Windows made to the CONFIG.SYS and AUTOEXEC.BAT files and, if necessary, remove the lines containing HIMEM.SYS and SMARTDRV.EXE from these files. Use the DR DOS 6.0 memory management program and hard drive cache. To do this, after changing the CONFIG.SYS file, start the DR DOS 6.0 SETUP program and reconfigure the memory management and cache program.

The various terms for memory types

If you try to combine the various capabilities of memory management from Windows and DR DOS, you'll always encounter the same problem. Microsoft and Digital Research use different terms for the various types of memory. For example, the Microsoft term "High Memory" means "Lower part of extended memory" in DR DOS 6.0. So, we've included the various terms of MS-DOS 5.0, Windows 3.1, and DR DOS 6.0 in the following table:

Address (K)	Microsoft	DR DOS	Special
0 - 640	Conventional Memory	Conventional Memory	
> 1024	Extended Memory	Extended Memory	XMS
?	Expanded Memory	Expanded Memory	EMS
1024-1088	High Memory	High Memory	XMS
640-1024	Upper Memory Block	Upper Memory	XMS
0 - 64		Lower Memory	

Table of various memory terms

Memory management and Windows in Standard mode

EMM386.SYS /WINSTD

If you must run Windows in Standard mode, you must use the /WINSTD option in DR DOS with EMM386.SYS. If you configure memory management via SETUP and use the setting for 80386 memory management (EMM386.SYS) with MemoryMAX, you must remember the following:

- Answer "YES" to the question about running Microsoft Windows in Standard or 386 Enhanced mode. Although some special options of the DR DOS 6.0 Memory Manager (high memory and upper memory) won't be available, you won't be able to operate Windows in Standard mode otherwise. Also, under no circumstances can you set up upper memory, load some programs into upper memory, and then disable upper memory with MEMMAX -U.

- Don't activate the "Use Unneeded Video Memory as RAM" setting. It's possible to run Windows when this setting is activated if you disable this memory with MEMMAX -V before starting Windows. However, if you forget to do this, you'll encounter problems, such as crashing the computer. So, if you use Windows frequently, leave this setting disabled.
- Disable the conversion from extended memory to expanded memory. To do this, choose NO for LIM 4.0 EMS Support. Windows cannot work in Standard mode if a portion of the memory is used as expanded memory EMS.

If you don't want to follow these requirements, use the DR DOS 6.0 option of choosing between different configurations. To do this, in CONFIG.SYS, insert the appropriate prompt options for changing the settings when you run Windows in Standard mode.

If necessary, you could also use several CONFIG.SYS files for different modes of operation. For example, you could create two files called CONFIG.DR6 and CONFIG.WIN and use ? to set up a prompt in the actual CONFIG.SYS file that uses CHAIN to add the special CONFIG file.

We'll discuss the options for switching between different system files in more detail in the section called "Installation for switching between DR DOS and Windows."

Memory management for expanded memory and Windows

Windows uses memory differently, depending on the various Windows operation modes. So, we cannot provide a general explanation. In Windows 3.0 Real mode, you could only use expanded memory with conventional memory. Since Windows 3.1 no longer has Real mode, you should convert as little extended memory as possible to expanded memory. You can even eliminate expanded memory entirely when you no longer use any applications that require only conventional memory and expanded memory.

Prerequisites for Standard mode

In Windows 3.1 Standard mode, don't emulate expanded memory. If you run Windows in 386 Enhanced mode, Windows will use only conventional memory and XMS memory. Windows can simulate expanded memory for application programs on its own. If you convert extended memory into expanded memory with the programs in DR DOS 6.0, leave enough extended memory for Windows. If you don't have a lot of extended memory (2 Meg), don't use EMM386.SYS for memory conversion. Instead, start programs that require expanded memory (such as Word 5.5) from Windows in 386 Enhanced mode.

Windows and using video memory with DR DOS

Obviously Windows cannot work with DR DOS if DR DOS makes the video memory, which is reserved for graphics display, available as conventional memory. Since Windows works exclusively in this graphics mode, it needs the memory for the screen display.

So if you work with Windows, be sure to switch off the "Use Unneeded Video Memory as RAM" setting in SETUP under 80386 memory management (EMM386.SYS).

30.2 CONFIG.SYS and AUTOEXEC.BAT Samples

The following sample files show typical system files for optimum cooperation between Windows and DR DOS 6.0.

Sample files for an AT/286 with 1 Meg memory

If you have an AT with a 286 processor and 1 Meg of total memory, carefully use the available options because the available resources are limited. The following system files show a sample configuration with a lot of available conventional memory.

CONFIG.SYS for a 286

```
REM CONFIG.SYS for a 286 with 1 Meg
DEVICE=C:\SYS\DRDOS\HIDOS.SYS /B=AUTO
HIDOS=ON
SHELL=C:\SYS\DRDOS\COMMAND.COM C:\SYS\DRDOS\ /P /E:300
FILES=30
HIBUFFERS=25
BREAK=ON
FCBS=0,0
FASTOPEN=0
LASTDRIVE=E
HISTORY=ON, 256, OFF, OFF, OFF
COUNTRY=049,,C:\SYS\DRDOS\COUNTRY.SYS
```

AUTOEXEC. BAT for a 286/AT

```
@REM AUTOEXEC.BAT FOR A 286 WITH 1 MEG
@ECHO OFF
PATH C:\DRDOS;C:\BAT;C:\PROG\WORD55;C:\WIN
SET DRDOSCFG=C:\DRDOS6
CD \DRDOS
BREAK ON
MODE CON RATE=32 DELAY=1
VERIFY OFF
PROMPT [DR] $P$G
IF NOT "%TEMP%"=="" MD %TEMP% >NUL
SET TEMP=C:\TEMP
SET TMP=C:\TEMP
```

```
ECHO ON
```

A 286 configured in this way has 619K of available conventional memory and 320K of available extended memory as XMS memory. Windows operates in Standard mode.

Memory type	Total bytes (K)	Available (K)
Conventional	655,360 (640)	641,344 (626K)
Lower extended	65,520 (64)	7,368 (7)
Extended	393,216 (384)	0 (0K)
Extended via XMS		327,680 (320K)

If you don't work with Windows, you can also use SUPERPCK to set up cache memory and use all the available XMS memory for it:

```
SUPERPCK /EM /S:320 /P
```

Then you'll receive the following information about the memory you've just set up:

```
Super PC-Kwik(R) Disk Accelerator, DRI Edition, Version 4.04
Copyright 1986 - 1991 Multisoft Corporation, All Rights Reserved.
Program licensed exclusively for use on a single computer.
Unrecognized character(s) ignored: M
Subset of program (SUPERPCK.SB7) loaded.

 Following is a list of the parameters in effect:

  /D- Generic support of diskette transfers.
  /H+ Advanced support of hard disk transfers.
  /B+ Perform batch copies to/from cache.
  /O- Standard algorithm for advanced support.
  /Q- Return DOS prompt normally.
  /T+ Track buffering using a 17-sector buffer.
  /V+ Use volume change hardware.
  /W+ Check write requests for redundancy.
  /&U- Cache is not loaded in High Memory.
  /L+     160K reserved for lending.
            0K on loan.
          160K available.
  /EM     320K Extended memory cache has been set up as follows:
                      Conventional        Extended
       DOS/Resident       144K               64K
       PC-Kwik             31K              320K
       Available          465K            2,048K
       Total              640K            2,432K
Caching is now enabled.
```

Although you lose 31K in conventional memory via the cache program, 320K in extended memory is used to speed up access to diskettes/hard drives.

While working with Windows though, you should use the cache memory because the available memory is already limited.

Sample files for a 386 with 8 Meg of memory

Obviously, the situation is quite different for a computer with a 386 processor and 8 Meg of total memory. First, you can and should run Windows in 386 Enhanced mode. Also, you can definitely set up cache memory because there is enough available memory to do this. You can also enable high memory, which makes much more conventional memory available. The following system files show a sample configuration with a lot of conventional memory still available (626K).

CONFIG.SYS for a 386

```
REM CONFIG.SYS for a 386 with 8 Meg memory
SHELL=C:\DRDOS\COMMAND.COM C:\DRDOS\ /P /E:800
DEVICE=C:\DRDOS\EMM386.SYS /F=NONE /B=FFFF /R=AUTO
HIDOS=ON
HIDEVICE=C:\DRDOS\PCKWIN.SYS
HIDEVICE=C:\MOUSE.SYS

FILES=30
HIBUFFERS=10
BREAK=ON
FCBS=0,0
FASTOPEN=0
LASTDRIVE=E
HISTORY=ON, 256, OFF, OFF, OFF
COUNTRY=001,,C:\DRDOS\COUNTRY.SYS
```

AUTOEXEC. BAT for a 386

```
@REM AUTOEXEC.BAT FOR A 386 WITH 8 MEG MEMORY
@ECHO ON
PATH C:\DRDOS;C:\BAT;C:\PROG\WORD55;C:\WIN;C:\DBASE4
SET DRDOSCFG=C:\DRDOS6
C:
CD \DRDOS6
SUPERPCK /EM /S:2048 /L:1024 /EP /&U+
BREAK ON
MODE CON RATE=32 DELAY=1
HILOAD KEYB GR+
VERIFY OFF
PROMPT [DR] $P$G
IF NOT "%TEMP%"=="" MD %TEMP% >NUL
SET TMP=C:\TEMP
SET TEMP=C:\TEMP
ECHO ON
```

A 386 computer with 8 Meg of memory configured in this way has over 626K of conventional memory and you can run Windows in 386 Enhanced mode:

	Total bytes (K)	Available (K)
Conventional	655,360 (640)	641,344 (626K)
Upper memory	151,422 (148)	120,400 (118K)
Lower extended	65,520 (64)	8,853 (7)
Extended	7,340,032 (7168)	0 (0K)
Extended via XMS		6,963,200 (6800K)

30.3 Special Features for Disk Drives and Hard Drives

Windows and DR DOS cannot conflict with one another in handling diskettes/hard drives either. So you should consider the following problem areas:

Permanent swap files and SuperStor

In 386 Enhanced mode, Windows can simulate RAM by swapping part of the data and programs to a location on the hard drive. This is also the reason why *Help/About Program Manager...* in the Program Manager displays more free memory space in 386 Enhanced mode than is installed on the computer.

To increase access speed to files, you should allocate part of the hard drive as a permanent swap file, instead of the temporary files that are otherwise necessary. Also, there are fewer temporary files left in a system crash if Windows always uses the same area on the hard drive for swapping.

You can determine whether a permanent swap file is installed by opening the Control Panel program in the Main group. Since a permanent swap file is only important in 386 Enhanced mode, the *386 Enhanced...* menu item is also only available in this mode. You can run this option by double-clicking its icon or selecting the menu item. A dialog box appears, in which you can enable the Virtual Memory... button. Information about the swap file is located under *Current Settings*. The current settings are displayed here, including the *Drive*, the *Type* (Permanent, Temporary), and the *Size* of the swap file in kilobytes.

Setting up a swap file

To set up a swap file in Windows, select the Change >> button. Now you're ready to set the desired values under *New Settings* for the *Drive*, the *Type* (Permanent, Temporary), and the *New Size* in kilobytes. You should use the recommended value (under

Recommended Size) and confirm this by pressing Enter. A security prompt appears, asking whether you want to accept the changes. Select Restart Windows to automatically accept these values. Otherwise, select Continue to cancel the settings. In this case you don't need to restart Windows.

Remember that Windows cannot create any swap files if you operate the entire hard drive as a SuperStor drive at an increased capacity. So, if you plan to run Windows in 386 Enhanced mode, don't let SuperStor manage the entire hard drive. Reserve between 5 and 10 Meg of the hard drive capacity when you install with SSTOR. If you're converting the C: drive to a SuperStor drive, you can then specify the disk space on your new D: drive with 5 - 10 Meg to be used as a permanent swap file.

First use the DR DOS DISKOPT command to optimize drive D: so you have the largest amount of contiguous space possible on this drive. Windows can only use a contiguous area of the hard drive as a permanent swap file for 386 Enhanced mode.

Windows and cache programs

Windows places greater demands on the hardware than DR DOS. This also applies to access time and data transfer. To speed up your work with Windows, you can use a cache program, if you have enough memory.

Windows adds a cache program, called SMARTDRV.EXE, in AUTOEXEC.BAT during installation. However, this cache program doesn't work with DR DOS, so you should definitely remove it from the AUTOEXEC.BAT and use the SUPERPCK program from DR DOS instead. Like SMARTDRV, SUPERPCK can also loan part of the cache memory to Windows. However, SUPERPCK can loan cache memory to other programs in DR DOS.

Setting up SUPERPCK

The best way to install SUPERPCK is to use the DR DOS SETUP program. Select the Super PC-Kwik Disk Cache setting in DiskMAX and set any other options after closing the screen. Answer the first question, "Do You run Microsoft Windows in Standard or Enhanced mode?" with "Yes" and leave the other settings as they are, since SUPERPCK itself uses the best settings.

☞ The installation program also immediately installs the Windows interface, PCKWIN.SYS, in the CONFIG.SYS.

Optimizing diskettes and hard drives

The same principles that applied for MS-DOS 5.0 also apply for DR DOS. Please refer to the appropriate passage in the chapter on MS-DOS.

SUPERPCK, DISKOPT, and DELWATCH

Use SUPERPCK from DR DOS instead of SMARTDRV.EXE to buffer the hard drive. You can use the DR DOS DISKOPT program to optimize the file distribution on the hard drive. So you don't have to use special tools, such as SE.EXE (Speed Disk, Norton Utilities) or COMPRESS.EXE (PC-Tools). You should use DISKOPT because it can also optimize SuperStor hard drives and consider files secured by DELWATCH.

Although DISKOPT might take up to an hour to optimize the files of a relatively full 80 Meg hard drive, it runs independently. So you can leave the computer unattended.

Preparations and requirements for optimization

Before optimizing, you must back up the data. If you're working with a hard drive, this means that you must back up the entire hard drive. Otherwise, hardware or software errors or failures could lead to data loss.

DISKOPT changes internal data structures

The warning above is important because when you use DISKOPT to optimize the hard drive, the internal structure of the data storage unit is affected. DISKOPT will change the internal structure of the directories, continually make changes to the File Allocation Table, and read much of the data of the hard drive and write them to another location. If DISKOPT cannot finishing executing such a process (e.g., because of a power outage), the integrity of the data is damaged. Since DISKOPT intervenes in the internal structure of the hard drive, you cannot run DISKOPT as a task in TaskMAX, as a program under Windows, or along with other TSR programs.

Before using DISKOPT, ensure that all hard drive errors have been detected and, if possible, corrected. The best way to check for errors is to use the CHKDSK command. Also, DISKOPT will check the internal structure of the hard drive. If DISKOPT detects an error, it indicates this with a warning and aborts. Use CHKDSK with the /F option to correct the error. Because this is so important, we've included a summary of the requirements for using DISKOPT:

Requirements for optimization

- You should have a current backup of the hard drive.
- Use CHKDSK to check the hard drive for possible errors. Use CHKDSK /F to repair any errors.

- Program managers, such as TaskMAX, Windows, or Quarterdeck's DesqView, should not be running. DISKOPT must be the only task accessing the drive.

However, you don't necessarily have to perform these security measures before calling DISKOPT. The optimizing program can also display the current status of a hard drive. Then if you discover that the fragmentation isn't serious, you may not need to run DISKOPT. So obviously you wouldn't need to perform the security measures either.

A good time to use DISKOPT to optimize your hard drive is when you're finished working on the PC for several hours or the rest of the day. Instead of switching off your PC, start DISKOPT. To cancel DISKOPT before it's finished optimizing, simply press Esc.

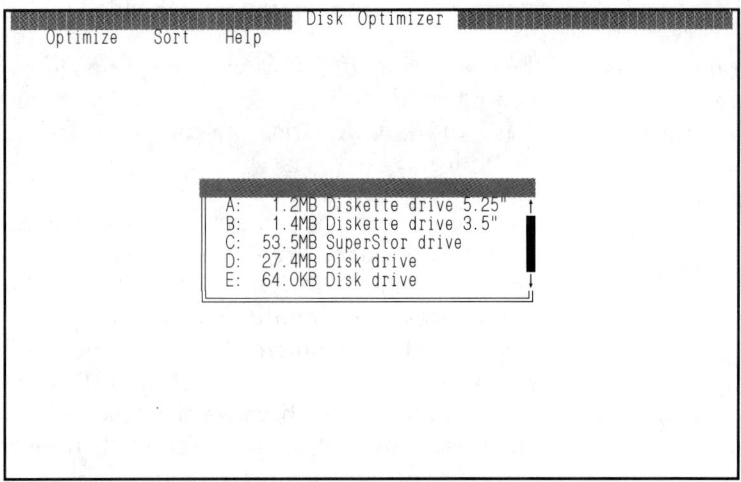

Available drives

Starting DISKOPT

After typing DISKOPT to start the optimization program, a list of all the available drives for optimization appears. Pseudo disk drives aren't included in the list.

Use the cursor keys to select the desired drive and press Enter to activate the drive. You could also specify the drive when starting the program:

```
DISKOPT C:
```

After you specify the drive, the optimization program reads the internal structure of the stored data and displays it on the screen. The character "X" represents an immovable area (cluster) of the hard drive (either a system file or defective area of the hard drive), the dots represent occupied areas, and the patterned areas represent free clusters.

Determining the file sequence

You can also determine the sequence of the file entries on the hard drive. DR DOS can change the position of the elements in a directory (we'll call them directory entries). This term refers to an element in the particular directory, instead of to a subdirectory.

Sorting directory entries

Usually the directory entries for the subdirectories are placed at the beginning and the directory entries for the files are placed at the end. This arrangement speeds up work with subdirectories because the program quickly finds the subdirectories. You can also use the Sort menu to determine the sequence of the file entries. By default, DR DOS 6.0 places the subdirectories at the beginning of the directory and the files at the end, so you only determine the sequence of the directory entries (subdirectories and files). The following settings are possible:

Name
: The directory entries are sorted alphabetically according to name. The subdirectories appear first, followed by the files.

Extension
: The directory entries are sorted by extension. If subdirectories also have extensions (DATA.DAT, TEXTS.91), then they are also sorted alphabetically by extension.

Date
: The entries are sorted by date, with the most recent files at the end.

Size
: The files are sorted by size, with the smallest files at the beginning.

Clusters
: The files are sorted by their starting clusters. This accelerates the optimization process.

Unsorted
: Directory entries aren't sorted. This means that the entries remain in the existing order.

The optimization of the sorting sequence is performed separately from the actual optimization of the data. This allows you to change the sequence of file entries in seconds on an optimized hard drive. DR DOS needs to change only the directory entries, instead of the actual data. Sixteen of these directory entries fit into a sector with 512 bytes, so to sort 160 directory entries, the program must read only 10 sectors. The data could even be numerous megabytes, if each file had an average size of 100K.

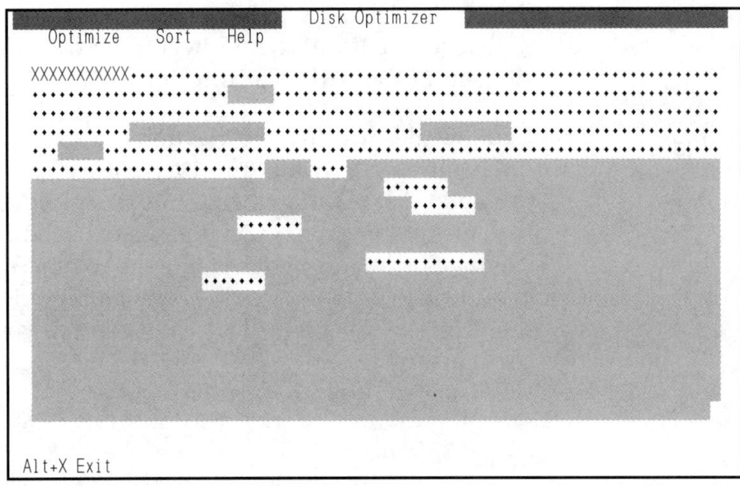

A logical drive before optimization

Starting the optimization

After selecting the drive, you can start optimizing the disk by selecting *Optimize disk* in the *Optimize* menu (Alt+O). The purpose of optimization is to combine free areas and those areas on the disk that are occupied by data. The clusters of single files are also combined into one block. You can watch this process on the screen.

After optimization starts, the individual directories are first sorted, then the optimization of the actual data begins. You can easily follow the different processes of optimization. Optimized clusters change the character that displays them to a small circle, while the writing of a cluster is represented by a "W".

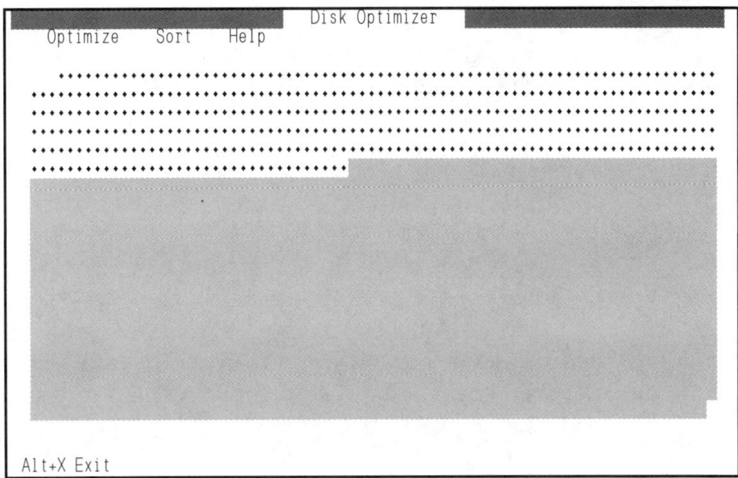

A logical drive after optimization

Several factors determine how long the optimization process will take. On an ordinary 40 Meg hard drive the process takes about 10-20 minutes on an AT, if the files haven't been optimized for a long time. Upon completion, DISKOPT displays the message: "Optimization complete." All the data are in one contiguous block in the top of the screen, while the free areas are at the bottom of the screen. After you select "OK", the optimization program returns to the DOS prompt.

If there are still "gaps" after optimization

You may be wondering about the gaps shown in the display of the distribution of data on a drive. Actually, the optimization program won't fill in all of these gaps. This occurs because DISKOPT doesn't move system files.

For example, if you define a swap file in Windows, it's automatically assigned the "System" attribute. So DISKOPT won't move it. The two system files IBMBIO.COM and IBMDOS.COM, in the root directory, aren't moved either.

If possible, before optimizing try to delete all system files (except the DR DOS system files in the root directory). In Windows, remove the swap file before optimization (see description above) and then recreate the swap file after optimization.

Finding system files

It's also possible that some of the "System" files on the hard drive don't even require this attribute. To display all of the "System" files on hard drive C:, use the XDIR in the following way:

```
XDIR C:\*.* +S /S /P
```

+S indicates display files with a set system attribute, /S indicates that the subdirectories should be included, and /P indicates that the screen output should be stopped automatically after every page. To clear the system attribute of the TEST.DAT file in the TEMP directory for optimization, use the following command line:

```
ATTRIB C:\TEMP\TEST.DAT -S
```

Never clear the system attribute of IBMBIO.COM and IBMDOS.COM in the root directory. Also, be very careful with copy-protected programs that can only be installed a certain number of times on the hard drive. It's better to remove such a program before using DISKOPT and reinstall it afterwards.

After DISKOPT is finished, you can only use UNDELETE to recover deleted files that have been protected with DELWATCH.

Windows and TaskMAX

Both Windows and DR DOS 6.0 have a program switcher. While Windows is designed to run simultaneously with several programs (multitasking), TaskMAX only switches between programs and can have one active program at a time. You shouldn't use both program switchers. It's not even possible to run TaskMAX from Windows since TaskMAX must be loaded from the first command processor that's loaded. However, you should also avoid starting Windows from TaskMAX. Instead, exit TaskMAX and then start Windows.

It is possible to start Windows from TaskMAX. However, then you wouldn't be able to switch to TaskMAX from Windows so you couldn't use other programs in TaskMAX. To do this, you must exit Windows completely. If you start Windows from TaskMAX, you can start more than one program in Windows, but you shouldn't do this. At least don't start any programs in Windows that have already been started in TaskMAX.

30.4 Installation for Switching Between DR DOS and Windows

When you install DR DOS 6.0 and Windows, you could try to find a happy medium that's acceptable for both programs. But if you don't want to make the difficult compromise between optimum DOS requirements and optimum Windows requirements, you can simply install two different systems and switch back and forth between them. To do this, set up two different sets of system files and switch between the two configurations.

Unlike MS-DOS 5.0, you can switch between different configurations and even run the standard configuration after a short delay.

CONFIG.SYS for a 386 with switching option

The following CONFIG.SYS sample file works with three different configuration blocks:

CONFIG.SYS for a 386 with switching option

```
REM CONFIG.SYS for a 386 with 8 Meg memory
REM Switching option DR DOS/Windows
REM After 10 seconds, use DR DOS configuration

ECHO Use DR DOS                      = 1
ECHO Windows in Standard mode        = 2
ECHO Windows in 386 Enhanced mode = 3
ECHO Please press 1-3
TIMEOUT 10
SWITCH DRDOS, STAND, ERW
EXIT

:DRDOS
SHELL=C:\DRDOS\COMMAND.COM /P /E:800
DEVICE=C:\DRDOS\EMM386.SYS /F=AUTO /B=FFFF /V /R=AUTO
HIDOS=ON
HIDEVICE=C:\MOUSE.SYS

FILES=30
HIBUFFERS=10
BREAK=ON
FCBS=0,0
FASTOPEN=0
LASTDRIVE=E
HISTORY=ON, 256, OFF, OFF, OFF
COUNTRY=001,,C:\DRDOS\COUNTRY.SYS
ENTER

:STAND
SHELL=C:\DRDOS\COMMAND.COM /P /E:300
DEVICE=C:\DRDOS\EMM386.SYS /F=NONE /B=FFFF /WINSTD /R=AUTO
HIDOS=ON
HIDEVICE=C:\DRDOS\PCKWIN.SYS
FILES=30
HIBUFFERS=10
BREAK=ON
FCBS=0,0
FASTOPEN=0
LASTDRIVE=E
HISTORY=ON, 256, OFF, OFF, OFF
COUNTRY=001,,C:\DRDOS\COUNTRY.SYS
ENTER

:ERW
SHELL=C:\DRDOS\COMMAND.COM /P /E:300
DEVICE=C:\DRDOS\EMM386.SYS /F=NONE /B=FFFF /R=AUTO
HIDOS=ON
HIDEVICE=C:\DRDOS\PCKWIN.SYS
```

```
FILES=30
HIBUFFERS=10
BREAK=ON
FCBS=0,0
FASTOPEN=0
LASTDRIVE=E
HISTORY=ON, 256, OFF, OFF, OFF
COUNTRY=001,,C:\DRDOS\COUNTRY.SYS
ENTER
```

If DR DOS gets to the place with the SWITCH command, you can select the desired subroutine by entering its number. In our example, if you wanted to run the subroutine called "STAND", you would press 2. If you press Enter or 1, the DR DOS subroutine will be processed.

By inserting TIMEOUT 10, we instruct DR DOS to wait only a certain amount of time for the user to enter a selection. After this time has elapsed, the first option is automatically selected.

The ENTER command must come at the end of the subroutine; otherwise DR DOS outputs an error message. After the subroutine is finished, the CONFIG.SYS file continues after the line with the SWITCH command.

It's also important to ensure that the program doesn't run into the subroutines at the end. Otherwise you'll receive a continuous error message, since DR DOS encounters "Enter" without first receiving a GOSUB or a SWITCH. This is why you should always insert the EXIT command at the end of the main program.

AUTOEXEC.BAT for a 386 with switching option

You can also define a different AUTOEXEC.BAT for each of the three possible work situations. The mechanism is essentially the same.

AUTOEXEC. BAT for a 386 with switching option

```
@REM AUTOEXEC.BAT FOR A 386 with switching option
REM Switching option DR DOS/Windows
REM After 10 seconds, use DR DOS configuration

ECHO Use DR DOS                      = 1
ECHO Windows in Standard mode        = 2
ECHO Windows in 386 Enhanced mode    = 3
ECHO Please press 1-3
TIMEOUT 10
SWITCH DRDOS, STAND, ERW
GOTO END

:DRDOS
@ECHO OFF
PATH C:\DRDOS;C:\BAT;C:\PROG\WORD55;C:\DBASE4
SET COMSPEC=C:\DRDOS\COMMAND.COM
SET TMP=C:\TEMP
```

```
SET DRDOSCFG=C:\DRDOS
C:
CD \DRDOS
SUPERPCK /EM /S:4096 /L:2048 /EP /&U+
BREAK ON
MODE CON RATE=32 DELAY=1
VERIFY OFF
PROMPT [DR] $P$G
SET TEMP=C:\TEMP
IF NOT "%TEMP%"=="" MD %TEMP% >NUL
ECHO ON
ENTER

:STAND
@ECHO OFF
PATH C:\DRDOS;C:\BAT;C:\PROG\WORD55;C:\WIN;C:\DBASE4
SET COMSPEC=C:\DRDOS\COMMAND.COM
SET TMP=C:\TEMP
SET DRDOSCFG=C:\DRDOS
C:
CD \DRDOS
SUPERPCK /S:2048 /L:1024 /EP
BREAK ON
MODE CON RATE=32 DELAY=1
VERIFY OFF
PROMPT [DR] $P$G
SET TEMP=C:\TEMP
IF NOT "%TEMP%"=="" MD %TEMP% >NUL
ECHO ON
ENTER

:ERW
@ECHO OFF
PATH C:\DRDOS;C:\BAT;C:\PROG\WORD55;C:\WIN;C:\DBASE4
SET COMSPEC=C:\DRDOS\COMMAND.COM
SET TMP=C:\TEMP
SET DRDOSCFG=C:\DRDOS
C:
CD \DRDOS
SUPERPCK /EP /S:2048 /L:1024 /&U+
BREAK ON
MODE CON RATE=32 DELAY=1
VERIFY OFF
PROMPT [DR] $P$G
SET TEMP=C:\TEMP
IF NOT "%TEMP%"=="" MD %TEMP% >NUL
ECHO ON
ENTER

:END
ECHO Finished...
```

When you work with this configuration file or a similar one, you can no longer configure your system with SETUP because SETUP automatically removes the selection option.

31. Windows In The Network

Windows 3.1 can run with a network. In this chapter we'll describe the advantages and features of this capability.

This chapter isn't a general discussion of the advantages and disadvantages of working with a network or a detailed explanation on how to use a network. Instead, we'll show examples of everyday work with Windows on an existing network. Also, we'll provide some tips and tricks for optimizing Windows on the network.

If you're unfamiliar with networks, in the first section you'll find information on network basics. Obviously, you must install a network before using the Windows network options. So we'll provide some general information about network operation.

We specifically refer to Novell NetWare in this chapter because many consider it the current standard in networks.

31.1 What is a Network?

Networks enable you to exchange data between different computers quickly and easily. For example, worldwide networks make weather data, currency rates, and similar data available all over the world.

Also, local networks, called LANs (Local Area Networks), allow different computers from the same network to use existing hardware components, such as printers and hard drives.

Depending on their capacities, networks place special demands on the programs used in them. You must ensure that two different users don't change the same data simultaneously: The programs being used must be *network compatible*.

Essentially, the programs must include *file locking*. This is a protective mechanism for locking a file being edited by another user.

Local networks differ in three ways:

- Arrangement of individual components.
- Transmission media and techniques.
- Access procedures.

Different network types

Two computers and a cable

The simplest solution is to exchange data between only two computers, which are connected by a cable. Prices for the necessary equipment start at approximately $150.00. This is ideal for data transfer between a desktop computer and a laptop or notebook computer.

Although this is an easy way to exchange data between computers, we won't discuss this option in detail because there's isn't an actual procedure for access protection.

Programs such as Windows or Superbase support networks with their own "network operating system" and access protection like Novell networks or the Microsoft LAN Manager.

Another method involves several computers, which are networked in star, ring, or bus formation. In the star formation, all the PCs (called workstations) are connected to a powerful main device (called a server) in the shape of a star.

In the ring network, all the computers are connected to a cable that's a closed ring. On a bus-shaped network system, the ends of the ring are open.

The advantages and disadvantages of the different formations depend on the different data exchange options. For example, in a star network, each workstation can exchange data directly with the server, but must make a detour through the server to contact another workstation.

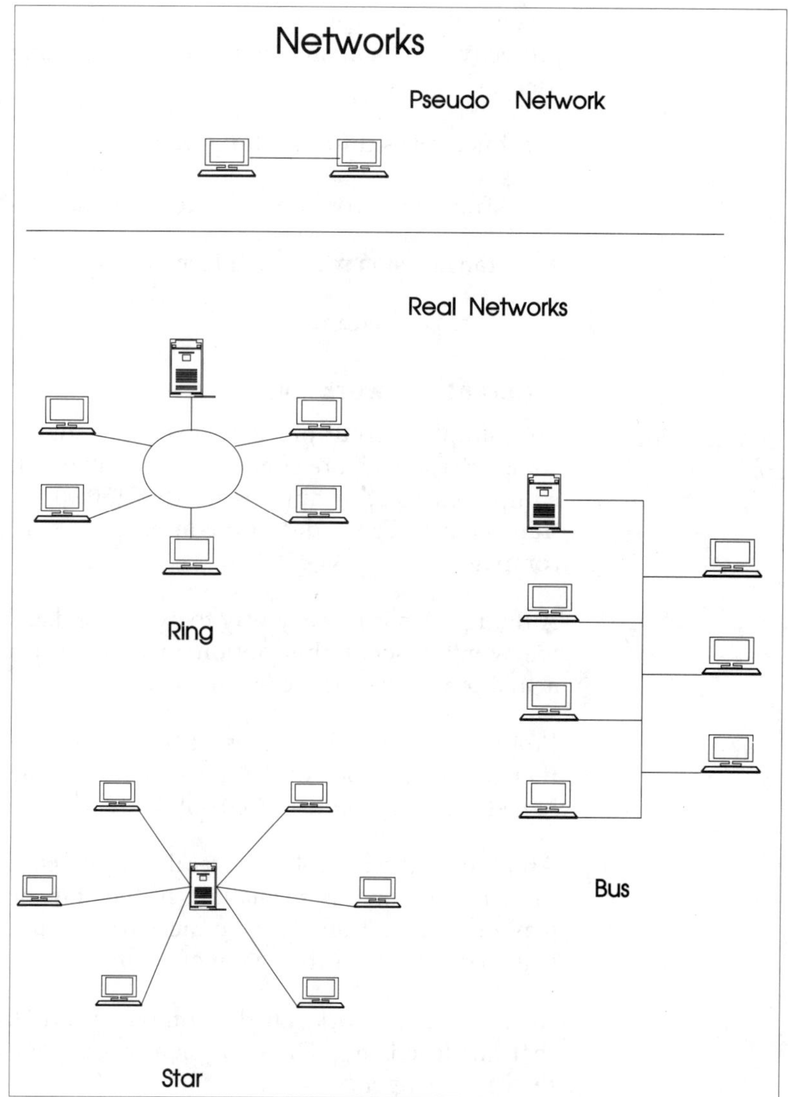

Different network types

In the ring network, however, data are sent from one computer to the next, running in circles. The disadvantage of using this network is that if a single workstation breaks down, the connection is severed. The star network, for example, is very time-consuming and expensive because it requires many more cables and can also disrupt work in an office.

Advantage of a network

The special advantage of a network is that the server (usually the most powerful computer in the network) stores programs and data, while the workstations can access the programs and data stored in the server. This makes it relatively easy to keep data up-to-date.

There's no need to worry that a computer will have an outdated copy of the data or more than one copy of the data.

Also, the workstations themselves can much less powerful than the server, and can even work in the network without a hard drive or disk drives if the server can handle all data and programs. Special boot ROMs exist, so you can modify a PC to boot from the network exclusively.

Networks also provide the option of making other computer services available for all workstations connected to the network. For example, print servers print the incoming print jobs from all the workstations on the connected printer, or a workstation equipped with a fax machine.

31.2 Network Basics

Lately, networks have been receiving a lot of attention. Why are so many PC users becoming interested in this technique? What are the advantages and disadvantages of networks?

Why more users have more than one computer

The number of users with two or more computers is steadily increasing. We'll use two examples to explain this trend.

File sharing

One example is the steady expansion of networks in business. In the business world, several employees of a company access the same software and data. For several years, it's been common practice to have all users on the network accessing common databases.

Also many users now have more than one computer at home. This results in typical networking problems and requirements, even if the user doesn't immediately see potential problems. There are several reasons for this:

- You may buy a new computer after a couple of years but don't want to sell your old one because it's obsolete. Also, having a second or even third computer is ideal for performing experiments, playing computer games, etc.

- In addition to your computer, you purchase a laptop or notebook computer. As a result, you must constantly update the data on the desktop and portable systems.

- Your computer is in the repair shop for a long period of time. Meanwhile, you buy another computer so you can continue to work. However, when the old computer returns from the repair shop, eventually it isn't used.

- Perhaps you want two PCs so if one breaks down, your work won't be interrupted while the computer is being repaired.

Data transfer causes problems

Once you have more than one computer, you'll quickly notice that moving data back and forth between computers can cause serious problems:

- You must be extremely careful if you have the same document or file on more than one computer. When you update one version, you must also update the other one. If you forget to do this, you may accidentally work with the older version of the file.

- Frequently, the desired program or file isn't available on the computer you're currently using. For example, suppose that you're working on one computer and want to look up something on another one. This isn't possible if the other computer doesn't have the necessary program.

- It's very time-consuming to use diskettes to exchange data or programs between computers. Transferring data by diskette is especially inconvenient if the data won't fit onto one diskette (this usually occurs with graphic files and documents). If this occurs, the data must either be copied to several diskettes using BACKUP or compressed with a special compression program, transferred to the other computer by diskette, and then decompressed again.

- Using a null modem cable with the appropriate software (such as LapLink) is also rather slow when you're working with large amounts of data. For example, it takes an average of 10 to 15 minutes to transfer 2 Meg. During this time you cannot use either computer.

Fortunately, network technology can help solve these problems.

Networks defined

According to our definition, a network must have the following components:

- At least two computers hooked up to a cable. At least one of the computers acts as the server and contains programs and data.

- A special network software program. This is the network operating system, which manages data and provides access protection.

Cheap networks

Unlike our definition, many modern "networks" are simply low-priced methods of connecting two or more drives by cable. This type of network makes the drives of one computer available on the other computer under new drive specifiers. Windows usually doesn't offer special support for these networks, which don't provide true data access control. You cannot organize work under Windows in true network fashion by using these cheap networks.

Actually, along with the components we mentioned above, there are a few more necessary components, such as:

- An operating system that you can use in the network. For example, you could use MS-DOS 5.0 or DR DOS 6.0.
- Programs capable of working in the network. Generally this means that your word processor must do more than simply write, save, and print documents. It must also deal with access rights, and be able to distinguish between several different users. We'll explain the details more thoroughly later.

System manager

- A user in the network that's responsible for managing and installing the network. The better this person installs the network, the more smoothly the users will be able to work in the network and the more all other users will profit from working on the network. This person is called the *system manager*.

What are the advantages of a network?

Perhaps you're wondering about the advantages of a network. Obviously simple data transfer isn't the only advantage. Actually, a well-installed network provides several important advantages:

Working on Projects

- A network makes it possible for several persons to work on a project. For example, it's very easy to access a common database.
- Data redundancy (i.e., multiple copies of the same data on different computers) wastes resources. Also, it's possible that someone might accidentally edit an outdated version of a file or that several people might have different versions of a file.

Data security

- A network provides a simple and relatively inexpensive means of data security. On single computers with independent hard drives, users must either back up data to diskettes (a lot of time and effort) or each computer must have a tape streamer installed for tape backups (a lot of money). With a network, only the server's hard drive must be backed up. This can be easily done by using a single tape streamer.

Communication options

- The communication options available within a network are excellent. Not only can a user send a message to another network user, it's also possible to send a message to an entire group of users.

  As a result, every member of this work group automatically receives the message. It's also possible to create electronic mailboxes, in which messages are kept for those users who aren't logged into the network and therefore cannot receive their messages.

  All the options mentioned here are prerequisites for optimum teamwork and can significantly increase the productivity of a work group.

Supervision

- The supervisor can easily monitor the individual users on the network. For example, the supervisor can determine which user is accessing particular programs and data, and how long the user has been logged into the network.

  A supervisor can also determine which programs and libraries a program such as Windows uses. If you examine the startup process, you'll definitely be surprised at how many files and drivers Windows opens and uses during its start phase:

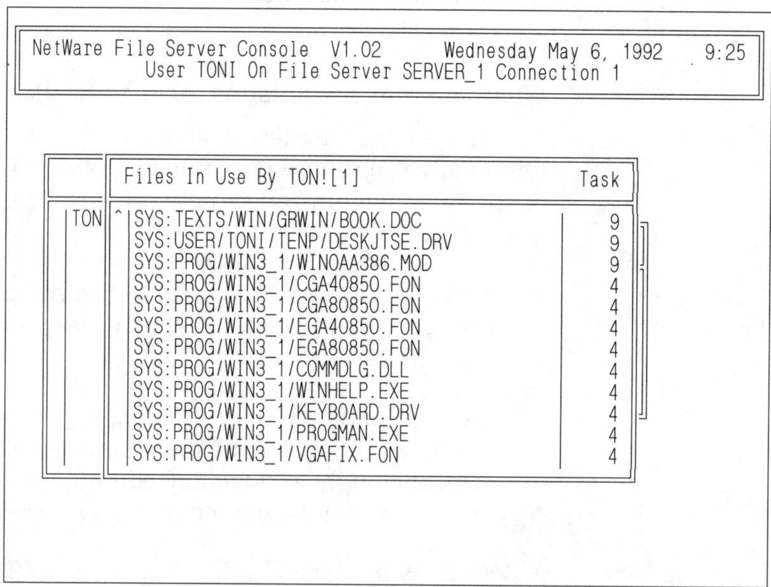

```
NetWare File Server Console  V1.02      Wednesday May 6, 1992    9:25
         User TONI On File Server SERVER_1 Connection 1

Files In Use By TON![1]                          Task
TON  SYS:TEXTS/WIN/GRWIN/BOOK.DOC                 9
     SYS:USER/TONI/TENP/DESKJTSE.DRV              9
     SYS:PROG/WIN3_1/WINOAA386.MOD                9
     SYS:PROG/WIN3_1/CGA40850.FON                 4
     SYS:PROG/WIN3_1/CGA80850.FON                 4
     SYS:PROG/WIN3_1/EGA40850.FON                 4
     SYS:PROG/WIN3_1/EGA80850.FON                 4
     SYS:PROG/WIN3_1/COMMDLG.DLL                  4
     SYS:PROG/WIN3_1/WINHELP.EXE                  4
     SYS:PROG/WIN3_1/KEYBOARD.DRV                 4
     SYS:PROG/WIN3_1/PROGMAN.EXE                  4
     SYS:PROG/WIN3_1/VGAFIX.FON                   4
```

Everything can be monitored in the network windows

Peripheral devices

- A network enables users to make better use of peripheral devices. With the proper planning, all network participants can use a network printer, modem, or fax.

Cut costs

- In many cases, installing the right network with a high powered server allows you to cut costs on workstation computers. Instead of installing an 80 Meg hard drive in each workstation computer for Windows 3.1, choose a server with a 200 Meg hard drive and install Windows and all other necessary programs on the server. The workstations won't need hard drives.

Data protection

- It's easy to protect computer programs and data from destruction as well as unauthorized use. For example, in a well-organized network, it's safe to allow an inexperienced person to use a workstation because he/she doesn't have the access rights to delete or destroy data.

- Also, you can prevent unauthorized users from accessing confidential data. So, you can take a network server to the repair shop without worrying about anyone reading your business reports or copying private data from the hard drive.

It's also very easy to determine whether a program has "crashed" or is still running properly.

What are the disadvantages of a network?

The following are the disadvantages of using a network:

Hardware costs

- The necessary network hardware can be very expensive. For example, a file server should be at least a 386 with a large hard drive (100 Meg or more) and have 4 Meg or more of memory. Also, you actually need another computer because the file server should be used exclusively for networking (dedicated), instead of being used as a workstation. If a program on the server crashes the server, the network connection is severed and unsaved data is lost.

Expensive extra capacity

- The more security you want in the network, the greater the hardware costs. Since all data are available only once on the workstation and a second time on the server, it's a good idea to rely on more than just the installed hard drive. You should not only install a very secure (i.e., expensive) hard drive, but also use *mirroring*. This involves installing a second, identical hard drive on the computer and always writing the data from the network operating system (such as Novell NetWare) to both hard drives. In read operations, both databases are read and compared. If there are differences or one of the hard drives breaks down due to a hardware defect, you can still read the data from the second hard drive and continue working with it.

Uninterruptible power supply

- Usually if a solo computer in MS-DOS crashes because of a power failure, no serious damage occurs. However, if this happens to a server on a network, considerable data loss can occur. In a network, you cannot quit working without properly *running down* the server (saving all data correctly). So you also need an uninterruptible power supply (UPS). This is a large battery that can maintain power for 15-30 minutes when a power outage occurs. The more computers protected by this battery power, the more expensive the UPS. Reasonably priced batteries for just the server start at about $170.

High costs

- The costs for the network operating system are also high. The more speed and performance you want, the more expensive the operating system. The price also depends on the maximum number of users. An operating system that manages only up to 5 workstations is much less expensive than an operating system that manages 100 workstations.

Expensive network software

Usually software is available in two versions: an inexpensive version for one computer or the more expensive network version. However, you can save money if a network version for five users costs "only" twice as much as the version for one computer, because then five users can work with one program.

- To fully utilize a network, you need special network software. The software must be network capable. This means that the programs must have a protective mechanism for locking a file currently being edited by another user (file locking;), or locking the data record currently being edited in a particular file (record locking).

Training period

- Learning how to use a network requires additional time and money. Although there are numerous books on common application problems, the information on networks is usually theoretical and doesn't help solve practical problems. Sometimes the only choice is expensive training or an expensive maintenance contract.

Supervisor

- Usually a solo PC user can handle data maintenance. However, in a network, a supervisor should handle the basic tasks and setups. Regardless of whether or not this is the supervisor's only task, the process is time-consuming.

What are the requirements?

Once you decide to use a network, you must know the network requirements. You may already be familiar with some of the following terms.

Server

A server must be at least an 80286 machine with 2 Meg of memory. However, such a server would be completely overwhelmed by Windows, so we recommend a computer with at least a 386DX processor and 25 MHz, a 100 Meg hard drive, and at least 4 Meg of memory. The server doesn't need a mouse or VGA card, since you should run it only as a dedicated server (no DOS/Windows operation). A reasonably priced Hercules Graphics Card should be sufficient.

After installation, you can even remove the keyboard and monitor from the server. If you need to enter or display something, borrow a monitor and keyboard from a workstation.

By not having a keyboard and monitor for the server, you can prevent someone from accessing the network through the server and entering dangerous commands, such as MONITOR, SHUTDOWN, etc.

Workstations

The workstations don't have to be as powerful as the server. For example, reasonably priced 386SX computers with 4 Meg of conventional memory are almost as powerful as 25 MHz 386DX models if the server is able to provide rapid data transfer due to sufficient dimensioning. 80286 machines aren't ideal as workstations because the necessary network program takes up about 60K of memory. This significantly decreases available conventional memory. However, 386s with MS-DOS 5.0 can relocate the network drivers in reserved memory (Upper Memory), leaving 600K and more available conventional memory despite the network.

Network cards

In a network, the network cards plugged into the server and the workstations handle the actual data transfer. That's why network cards, along with the server hard drive, are important to the total performance of the network. Anyone who chooses the cheapest (usually also the slowest) network card won't be able to enjoy the high data transfer rates in Windows. You should use a 16-bit card for the server, while fast 8-bit cards can be used for the workstations.

Cabling

Although the cabling of the computers isn't that expensive,

the special cables and plugs also require special tools. You should have cables made. Also, be sure to provide as much slack as possible. This is important if a workstation is transferred to another location. The cables must also be equipped with special seal resistors.

Network cables are sensitive

Network cables are sensitive in two ways. Remember this when you're planning the location of your workstations. Don't place the cables where they could be run over by a chair with casters. Interrupting a single connection while the network is running can cause a malfunction in the network.

For correct data transfer, a network needs closed cables. If the cables are accidentally disconnected, data transfer can no longer be guaranteed.

Network operating system

As we mentioned earlier, you need a special network operating system for the server (and its programs on the workstations). Novell NetWare is an accepted standard with a high performance level. For example, the 80286 Version 2.15 works without any problems on an 80386 with 3-5 computers under Windows. The special 80386 Version, 3.11 offers even more power and speed. There are a number of other products, of course, such as the LAN-Manager, which is based on OS/2.

Operating system

It's not possible to equip all computers with one network operating system. The server and the workstations still need a DOS. Windows also needs a DOS as a base operating system, on which a different, more specialized system can be placed.

Which DOS version you select depends on your hardware and personal preferences. We recommend MS-DOS 5.0 and DR DOS 6.0 because both of these DOS versions use special techniques of memory management to solve the constant problem of memory space on network computers.

On 80386s, both DOS versions let you move the network drivers to Upper Memory. DR DOS can even do this on 80286s with NEAT or SCAT chip sets so DR DOS has the advantage on 80286s.

Security

We recommend using an uninterruptible power supply and a tape streamer for data security. There are also other security measures, such as mirroring. However, these can be very expensive.

Usually when a server breaks down because of a defect, the entire system will no longer function. This means that you never realize how many necessary programs and data are located only on the server until the server crashes.

If this occurs, you can get help from the dealer by signing a maintenance contract or you can use a removable hard drive and a second PC as a "replacement server." In an emergency, you can remove the removable hard drive from the defective server and place it in the replacement server. However, this eliminates a workstation, and the hardware must also be installed properly so the replacement can function as a server.

Quality

By now you probably realize that cutting corners on a network's quality and performance is the wrong way to economize. If you want to start a network but also want to save money by purchasing cheap components, you should avoid networks. Novell has a very good reason for labeling only high quality hardware "Novell capable."

Why Novell?

Of course there are several operating systems for using Windows in the network. However, there are also a number of reasons for using Novell NetWare.

Novell is the standard

- Novell has set a standard for efficient PC networks. Its experience has contributed to its success.
- Novell is constantly being upgraded so you don't have to worry about not being able to adapt your network operating system to new hardware and software. For example, in the beginning there were problems with existing Novell versions and Windows 3.0. However, Novell users quickly received updates, and the updates have been incorporated into today's current versions, 2.2 and 3.11.
- Novell is supported by many programs. This applies to both Windows and applications (e.g., Superbase).
- With Novell, you're more likely to get competent help and advice in solving problems than you would with any other network operating system.

Our basis for examples and tips

The following section deals with a bus network.

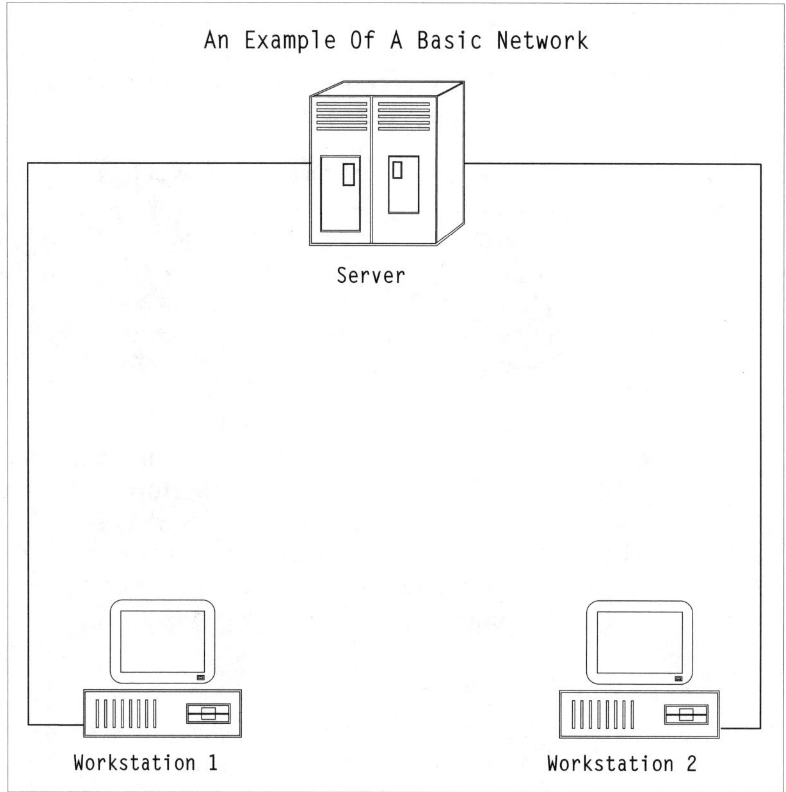

A simple network

The above illustration shows the basic principle of a network and the simplest network configuration. There is a server and one or more workstations, which are connected to the server by special cables. This makes it possible for all workstations to access the programs and data of the server; the programs and data need to be present only once on the server's hard drive. This helps preserve data integrity because all workstations use the same database.

The examples and processes in this section are based on a Novell network using Version ELS Level II Version 2.15. The procedure may differ slightly for other versions of Novell. However, the essential steps, processes, and problems are almost identical.

However, a network offers many more options than you see in our simplified form. For example, you can use different operating systems on the workstations: One station can use MS-DOS 5.0, while the other station can use OS/2 V1.3.

Workstations are also able to provide services for all network participants. For example, they can provide more than one print server or one communication server that provides communications and fax capabilities in the network. The following illustration shows this type of network:

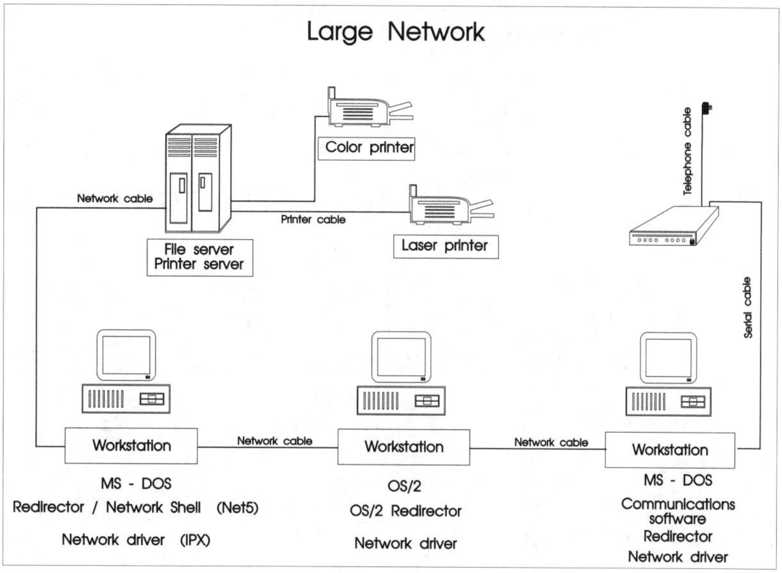

Network with workstations, server, printer ,and modem

This illustration shows a network with three workstations; one of these workstations assumes special tasks. The file server in the upper-left is a central element and also functions as a print server. It's connected directly to the printers (a color printer and a laser printer) by a printer cable.

The file server is connected to the three workstations at the bottom level by network cables. One workstation is running under MS-DOS, the second one is running under OS/2, and the third station on the far-right is also running under MS-DOS. This workstation also has all the communications software.

In addition, this workstation has the serial cable to the modem, from which the telephone cable is hooked up to the public phone system.

Of course, the two different operating systems, DOS and OS/2, also require different network drivers and network shells (redirectors).

31.3 How to Install a Novell Network

Installing a network is much more complicated than installing MS-DOS on a single PC. Even if you're already working with an installed network, you should still review the installation process. This may help you find a solution when you encounter problems.

Overview of the steps

Installing a network involves several necessary and important steps. Some of these steps are very time-consuming.

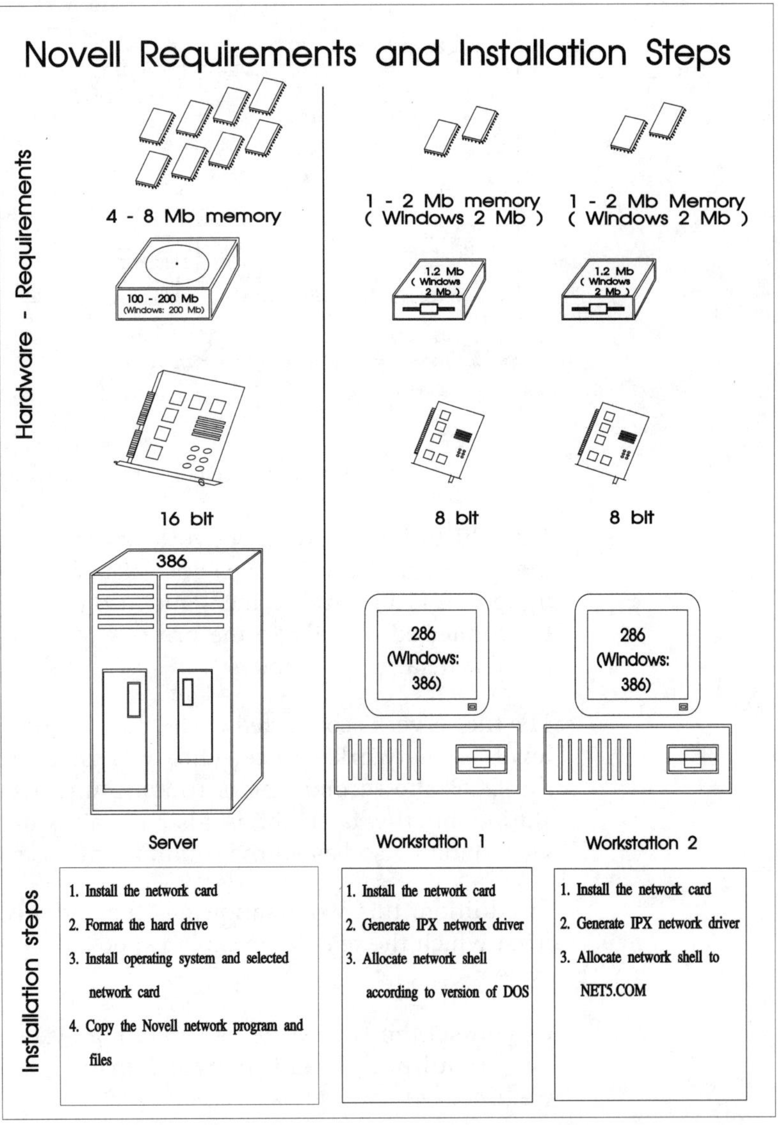

Installation steps

The above illustration shows the requirements for installing a Novell network. The illustration distinguishes between the necessary hardware components for the server and the workstations. As you can see, the server places more demands on the hard drive and memory than the workstations.

The illustration also contains a list of each installation step. The steps for the server and the workstations also differ significantly.

Hardware and software requirements

All the hardware and software requirements must be fulfilled.

Hardware requirements

- An 80286, or even better, an 80386 with at least 2 or 4 Meg of memory for the server (we recommend a 386DX with 25 MHz and 4 Meg of memory).
- A hard drive with at least 80 Meg for the server (we recommend 200 Meg with an access time of less than 20 ms).
- A network card for the server (we recommend a 16-bit card).
- For each workstation, a PC with at least 640K of RAM and a network card.

Software requirements

- A network operating system (Novell 2.2 or 3.11, or Microsoft LAN Manager).
- An operating system for the server (Either MS-DOS 5.0 or DR DOS 6.0, or if you use Microsoft LAN Manager, OS/2).
- An operating system for each workstation. However, you need only a base system of hidden system files and a command interpreter if DOS is installed on the server.

Preparing the server

Installing the server and workstations

Installing the server consists of:

- Installing the network card in the server (installing and selecting addresses and interrupts).
- Formatting the hard drive.
- Installing an operating system for the server and selected network card.
- Copying the Novell network programs and files to the server.

Preparing the workstations

Installation measures for each workstation consist of:

- Installing the network card (installation and selection of addresses and interrupts).
- Generating, or creating, the IPX network driver for the special workstation and network card.
- Allocating the network shell, depending on the version of DOS (NET3.COM for MS-DOS 3.3, NET4.COM for MS-DOS 4.0, NET5.COM for MS-DOS 5.0). These network shells are also often called redirectors, because they check accesses to DOS and redirect them to the network when a network drive appears in the access. DR DOS 6.0 registers as DOS Version 3.3, so you have to use the NET3.COM director for this version of DOS.

Windows 3.1 includes new programs and files for IPX and NETX. Replace the old files NET3.COM, NET4.COM or NET5.COM with NETX.COM from Windows 3.1 and have the supervisor generate a new IPX.COM file from IPX.OBJ if these network drivers are old. IPX.OBJ should have a version number greater than 3.10.

You can easily determine which version you have by entering IPX /I:

```
Novell IPX/SPX  v3.10 (911121)

(C) Copyright 1985, 1991 Novell Inc.  All Rights Reserved.

LAN Option: Western Digital EtherCard PLUS EC  v3.08
(901101)

Hardware Configuration: First Software Configured Adapter
```

The network shell should also be at least Version 3.25. Otherwise, you should use the shell from Windows 3.1. The advantage of using the Windows shell is that it works with all common versions of DOS.

```
NetWare V3.25 BETA VERSION 04 - Workstation Shell (911204)
(C) Copyright 1991 Novell, Inc.  All Rights Reserved.
```

Logging in

Registering to the file server

To be able to log in (register to the file server), after booting the computer, you'll need IPX and NET?. The question mark represents a particular number, depending on the DOS version being used. In the example, we have NET5.COM for MS-DOS 5.0. Also, you must change to the network drive and start the LOGIN command. Then specify the user name and the password.

Then, a workstation must have a boot diskette or a hard drive. You should include the necessary command lines in the AUTOEXEC.BAT file:

```
IPX
NET5.COM
F:
LOGIN
```

Installing the network

The supervisor always logs in first, without specifying a password. In this state, the network is almost unprotected and not yet installed. So you should determine a password for the supervisor immediately. You can use the SYSCON program to do this. Also, similar to a local hard drive, the necessary directories must be created and the programs and data installed.

Back up the hard drive to diskettes as soon as possible. You can back up the entire network hard drive with the NARCHIVE or LARCHIVE command, if you have enough diskettes available. To back up 80 Meg of data, you'll need about 70 1.2 Meg diskettes.

How to set up directory structures

You should set up directories on your hard drive to create order. This is especially true for a network hard drive, since several different users will be accessing it. More importantly, a proper directory structure can simplify and speed up both data backups and access to data. You can increase access speed to data on the hard drive by creating a simple structure that allows you to find files more quickly.

Directory tree and later access rights

You should also combine the subdirectories into a "branch" when you establish the directory tree. Later, this will simplify the task of assigning access rights. It's much easier to lock users out of an entire directory tree than it is to lock 20 different subdirectories.

- Save as few files in the root directory as possible. Instead, place directories there. This will make it easier to keep track of data. It's much easier to find your way around the root directory when only 10 directories appear on the screen instead of 120 files.

- Also, while deep directory structures starting at the fifth level might be well-structured, when you want one of those directories you must move through all of the directories above it. So, it's better to have a flat directory tree (see the illustration below).

- When you install a new hard drive, create the directory structure before copying files to the hard drive. This places the subdirectories in front of the files at the beginning of the directory, so you can find them more quickly.

Arranging the directory tree

Novell has several default directories that it automatically creates on the hard drive during installation. The following is a listing of the directories:

SYSTEM
: Contains programs and data that are important for the supervisor.

LOGIN
: Contains programs and files for logging in to the file server.

MAIL
: Contains additional subdirectories for each user and for defined groups. The name of each subdirectory consists of "random" number and letter combinations; only the supervisor has a 1 as his or her directory name. For example, the MAIL directory might look as follows:

```
F:\
├---MAIL
|    ├---1
|    ├---20007
|    ├---10004D
|    ├---11005D
|    ├---120065
|    ├---13006F
|    ├---170079
|    ├---180085
|    ├---1A0091
|    ├---A0031
|    ├---B0051
|    ├---C0041
|    └---D003B
├---SYSTEM
...
```

PUBLIC
: The PUBLIC directory contains all the necessary and practical commands users will need. This directory is similar to the DOS directory on the "local" hard drive of a PC that isn't connected to a network.

Along with these Novell default directories, you should also create additional directories that are useful for basic partitioning. Later, this will make the directory tree much easier to read in the Windows File Manager. For example, you could create the following directory tree:

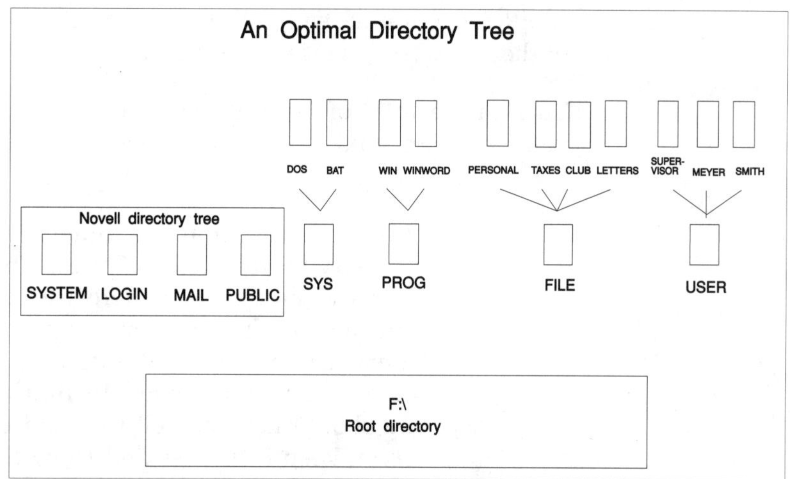

An ideal directory tree

The above illustration shows a directory tree whose structure is ideal for working in a network.

First the Novell default directories (SYSTEM, LOGIN, MAIL and PUBLIC) branch off from the root directory (F:\). None of them (except MAIL) have any additional subdirectories. Now the user should create four subdirectories, which (except for MAIL) don't have any subdirectories. Then the user should create four subdirectories, from which all the other directories branch, resulting in a flat structure (preventing unnecessary browsing through directories).

The SYS subdirectory contains all the important directories and data for operating the system. The DOS directory branches off from SYS. You should also place a directory for custom batch files here.

The PROG subdirectory contains the Windows directory and the different program directories (in the example we only included WINWORD).

The DATA subdirectory is important for everyday backups, because it contains all the user data files. These files are usually changed frequently. In the example, there are four subdirectories on the third level (PERSONAL, TAXES, CLUB, and LETTERS). This division depends on individual circumstances.

To the far right is the USER directory, which contains the data and controls that are important for working with the network. In our example, there are three subdirectories branching off from

USER. One is for the supervisor and two subdirectories are for users of the workstations (Meyer and Smith).

There are a total of three levels in our model, preventing long paths through subdirectories and their data.

User defined directories

SYS
: This directory contains other programs and files necessary for the system. For example, you could place the DOS subdirectory here (for all accessible DOS commands). Also, you could create a BAT directory for batch files and tools. We don't recommend copying these files to the Novell PUBLIC directory because you should keep Novell files and DOS files separate, as you keep DOS files and batch files or custom files separate from each other. As we'll explain later, you should write-protect the Novell directories and at least the DOS directory. It will be much easier to do this if you follow our procedure.

PROG
: Place program directories in this directory. In our example, we had WIN for Windows and WINWORD for Microsoft Word for Windows. You should keep different programs in different directories and separate the programs from the program data. This makes it easier to back up the data.

DATA
: You should also create several directories for data. There are two ways to organize them. Either create directories according to subjects (such as LETTERS, TAXES, PERSONAL) or organize the data according to their programs (TEXTS, ICONS, PICTURES). How you organize your data depends on the programs you use.

USER
: If there are several users in the network, each one should have his/her own directory. It's best if you organize them as subdirectories of a USER directory. Doing this simplifies working with Windows and the user-specific Windows files. Besides, by backing up the USER directory tree, you can easily secure all user-specific settings.

☞ In the beginning, only the supervisor has access to the directory structure. To give a new user access to a directory, you must first define it. This is why you should organize partial directory trees in advance so a user can have read or read/write access rights to several directories that belong together .

How to install data and programs on the server

After setting up the directory tree you must set up the basic structure of programs and data on the hard drive. Now it's a matter of filling the structure with the proper contents.

Installing data on the server

Installing data is relatively easy. Simply copy diskettes from a connected workstation to the server in the desired data subdirectory. If the data were previously stored on a single PC and this PC is now connected as a network workstation, you can simply log in from this computer and copy the data to the server with the XCOPY command:

```
XCOPY C:\DATA F:\DATA /S
```

You could as easily use the File Manager of Windows 3.1. To do this, start the File Manager, select the DATA directory in the directory tree, and enter F:\DATA as the destination directory after choosing *File/Copy...*, or open two directory trees and drag the C:\DATA directory to the server's DATA directory.

Installing network-capable programs

Installing network-capable programs is relatively easy. After creating a suitable program directory as a subdirectory of F:\PROG, start the installation program. However, with most programs you must choose installation in the network before or during selection of the installation options.

Call the Windows Setup program with the /A switch to install all files and programs on the server. Then, set up each workstation with SETUP /N.

The same procedure is used with Microsoft Word 5.5. First, you must install all files on the server with the installation program. Then you can install the program for each user on the network with the /USER parameter.

However, you could also:

- Perform a normal single user installation in the F:\PROG\WORD directory of the server.
- Then copy the user-specific files MW.INI, SCREEN.VID, STANDARD.TBS, STANDARD.STY, etc. to a user directory such as F:\USER\MEYER.
- Use SET to set the environment variable MSWNET55 for each user in the user's subdirectory.

The following is the command line for the Word files in the F:\USER\MEYER directory for the user MEYER:

```
SET MSWNET55=F:\USER\MEYER
```

It's best to place such command lines in the AUTOEXEC.BAT (workstation-specific) or in the LOGIN script (user-specific). We'll discuss both procedures later.

☞ The first time Word is called in the network, you must use WORD /N. After that, Word notes this setting in the MW.INI file and you can then call Word in the usual way, without parameters or with a file name.

As much write-protection in the network as possible

If possible, write-protect the program directory of a network-capable program. This prevents the program from being accidentally deleted or changed. Also, you should declare the files in the program as shareable (accessible to more than one user). You can do both tasks with the Novell FLAG command. For example, to label the Word files as described, use the following command line:

```
FLAG F:\PROG\WORD\*.* S RO
```

This line states that all the files in the WORD directory should be set to Shareable and Read Only.

☞ To handle whole directory trees with all their files, use the SUB option with FLAG.

Installing non-network programs

You can also install non-network programs on the server, as you would on a local hard drive of a single PC. Since the programs aren't network-capable, they can only be used by a single user.

However, problems can occur. For example, every time MEYER changes the screen settings of the program, the settings of his colleague, SMITH, also change because the program cannot manage different user settings. Also, a non-network program will barely be able to cope with limited access rights to a directory or file. While Word 5.5, which is network-capable, displays the following message upon access to a file being used by another user:

```
Another user is currently editing the file:
F:\DATA\TEXTS\LETTER.TXT
```

(and some files automatically open in Read-Only mode), another program may display the message

```
File cannot be opened
```

or

```
Hard drive/diskette full
```

In most cases, you can avoid these problems by not installing files and programs from non-network applications or by at least declaring them as non-shareable with FLAG. You might also install the program for the network and then declare all the program files, including the INI files, as Read-Only. Then the different users can't change and save the program settings.

Numerous non-network Windows programs enter most of their settings in the WIN.INI file. The big advantage to this is that the programs become at least partially network-capable, since if Windows is correctly installed in the network, each user works with his own WIN.INI, and, as a result, also works with his own program settings.

Why install Novell for users?

Creating a data backup

After installing most of the data and programs on the server, you should make a data backup. Although you'll probably improve and optimize the backup mechanism later, you should back up your existing work at least once. Using a streamer (tape drive) makes backing up especially easy.

Today there are many devices that you can install into a workstation like a disk drive and then quickly back up 40 - 200 Meg of data onto a tape. If you're performing a complete backup, simply insert one tape after the other until you've backed up everything.

Why not let all the users work as supervisors?

You might consider allowing all network participants to log in as supervisors. Apparently, there's an advantage to doing this. You save yourself the aggravation and time of assigning access rights for all the necessary directories to each user. You might be tempted to do this because when you install a new user (see below), he or she only starts out with minimal access rights to the server. So, the user can hardly do any work with the server.

You could also solve this problem by setting up directory trees containing all directories with common access rights or by simply defining a group, specifying access rights for the group in general, and then adding the individual users to the group.

However, there are serious disadvantages to not having various users:

- Security
  One especially serious disadvantage is the loss in security. The supervisor has unlimited access to all resources. So, if everyone is a supervisor, very important files can be deleted. For example, the LOGIN file, which is used to log into the network, can be destroyed. It's much better if the actual activities in the network are performed with only limited access rights and the supervisor only logs in to the network as the supervisor when the appropriate activities are called for, such as changing access rights.

- User differentiation
  If all the users log into the network as supervisors, the network and network programs will no longer be able to differentiate between different users. This would cancel out a very important requirement for working with such programs: differentiating between different users with individual settings.

- Login script
  You can define a startup script for every user, similar to the AUTOEXEC.BAT on a PC with MS-DOS. For example, this permits each user to install a series of automatic processes to make networking easier. Or, the supervisor could start a "safe shell," such as a DOS shell with limited options or the Novell shell for an inexperienced network participant. This is only possible if different users are defined on the network.

How to set up Novell for users

As we mentioned, after setting up the basic options in the network, the supervisor shouldn't perform his/her own work with programs as the supervisor. Instead, the supervisor should create the appropriate user IDs.

Supervisor password

After installing the server, the default setting has the supervisor without any password. You should change this as soon as possible. If you haven't assigned a password to the supervisor yet, do so before installing any other users:

Defining a supervisor password

We assume that you've booted up the network and logged in as supervisor on the file server. Now start the SYSCON installation program. If there is no search path, you can also change to the \PUBLIC directory beforehand.

After calling SYSCON, use the cursor keys to select the *User Information* menu item and select the entry called *SUPERVISOR* in the list of user names. Then enable *Change Password* in the *User*

Information window. After typing in the password (case isn't important), you must enter the password a second time to verify there aren't any typing mistakes, because the characters aren't displayed when you enter passwords for security reasons.

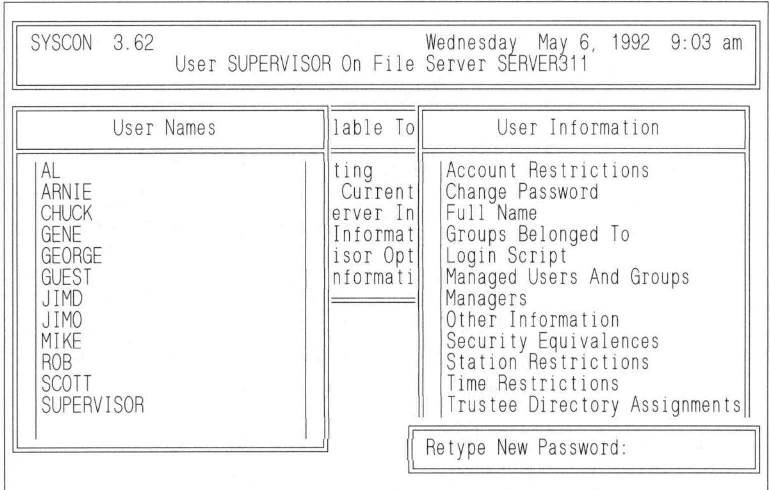

A password for the supervisor

If both password entries match, you can exit SYSCON by pressing Esc several times (or by pressing Alt + F10) and answering a security prompt. Then you return to the system prompt.

Don't forget your password. Either write it down and keep it in a safe place or store it in your safe or a safety deposit box at the bank. Without this password, it's almost impossible to continue the installation on the network.

Sample definition of a new user

You also use SYSCON to set up the file server for new users. However, before you begin creating user IDs, you should understand the individual steps involved and read about the advantages of groups and how to install them. Defining several users is a time-consuming process, which you should simplify and standardize as much as possible to avoid problems.

We want to set up a user named MILLER and use it as a general user ID for our examples.

Adding a new user ID

Here are the steps for defining a new user:

Start SYSCON and select the menu item called *User Information*. A list of all existing user ID's appears. Press Ins to insert a new ID.

If nothing happens when you press Ins, you're not logged in as supervisor. Since only the supervisor can define new users, you should press Esc several times to exit SYSCON, log out by entering LOGOUT, and log back in as supervisor with the correct password.

Then you're prompted to enter the *User Name:*. Type in MILLER here and press Enter. A second later the new user appears in the alphabetical list of user ID's; now the process is completed.

When you exit SYSCON now, you or someone else can login on this file server with the new user ID, MILLER. By default, there is no password and access rights are minimal. However, we recommend that you at least specify a password and expand the minimal access rights slightly. Right now, the new user MILLER can only open files from the \LOGIN and \PUBLIC directories and use and change files in MILLER's special MAIL subdirectory. However, this subdirectory doesn't contain any files yet.

Creating the user password

To assign a password to MILLER, select it in the list of User IDs and press Enter to enable it. Then go to the *User Information* window. Select *Change Password* and press Enter. After entering the password, you must enter it a second time to verify that you didn't make any typing errors. This is important because, for security reasons, the characters aren't displayed when you enter passwords. If both password entries match, you can exit SYSCON or assign access rights.

There are several rules for assigning passwords. Most of these rules refer to what you cannot do. Although we won't discuss this in detail, we've listed the most important rules below:

Rules for passwords

- A password should be at least five characters long and should be different from the user name.
- Any passwords that occur to you quickly will also be quickly discovered by others, such as the first names of your family members, your birth date, etc. Carefully select a password and store it in a safe place.

Displaying existing access rights for MILLER

If you really want to work with the new user ID, MILLER, then you must at least assign it more access rights in the network. Later in this chapter we'll discuss the problems involved and the many options that are available. For now, we just want to take a look at the initial situation and how to create two new access rights for MILLER:

Select *Trustee Directory Assignments* in the *User Information* window for MILLER. A new window appears, displaying the directories on the left and the access rights on the right:

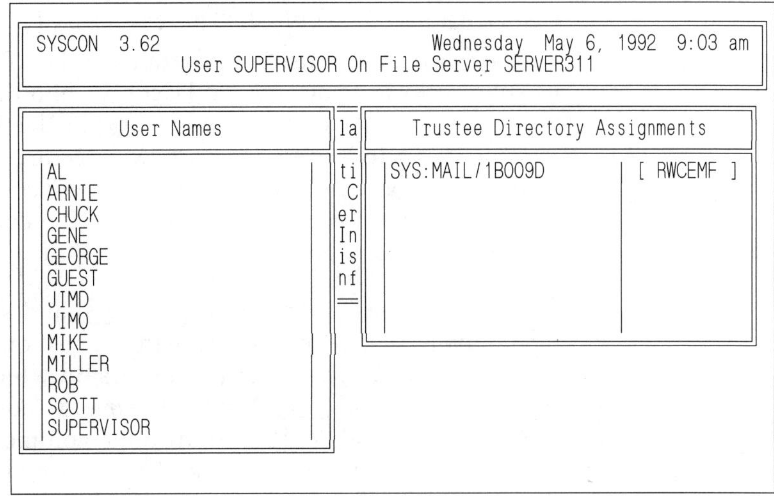

Access rights for MILLER

At the moment, MILLER only has rights in the two default directories, \PUBLIC and \LOGIN, and in a directory called SYS:MAIL/1B009D. MILLER's access rights are displayed in brackets on the right:

Access rights and their definition

R Allows the user to read from a file opened with (O).

W Allows the user to change or write to a file opened with (O).

C Allows the user to create new files.

E Allows the user to erase files.

M Allows the user to rename files, change and delete file attributes, and change directory names.

F Allows the user to scan files (not their contents) in the directories. If a user doesn't have this right, entering DIR would result in the message "File not found", without any explanation stating the reason.

There's one more access right that's missing, which is why there is an empty space in the brackets:

A Access Control is the most powerful right in a directory and enables the user to create and remove subdirectories and assign access rights to other users.

Changing access rights for programs and data

To allow MILLER to use the programs in the \PROG directory and its subdirectories, you must at least give him the Read, Open, and Search rights. To do this, press Ins in the *Trustee Directory Assignments* window to enter a new directory in the list of access rights. A new window, *Directory In Which Trustee Should Be Added*, appears. You can directly enter the complete path of the directory in this window.

However, it's easier simply to press Ins and select the directory interactively (i.e., step-by-step with suggestions displayed on the screen). A *File Servers* window appears, in which you confirm the server by pressing Enter. Next, a *Volumes* window appears. In our example, we press Enter to confirm the volume SYS:. This opens a new window called *Network Directories*, with the available directories:

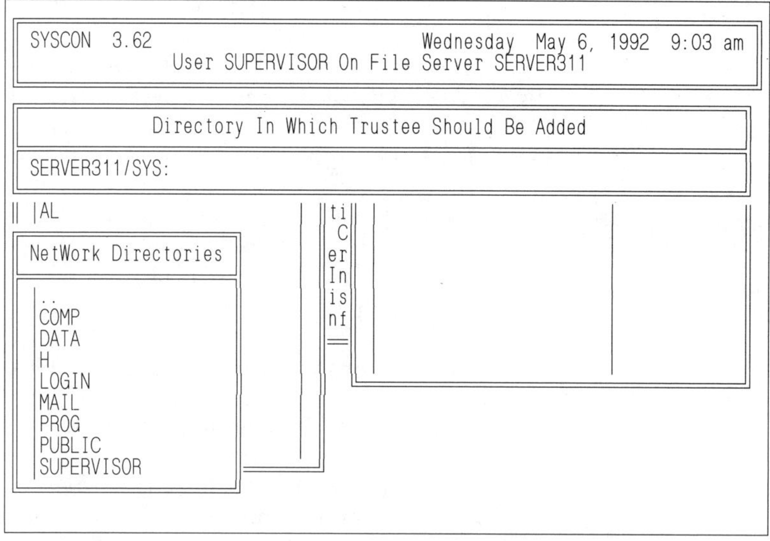

Selecting a new directory

The *File Servers* option stems from the possibility of installing more than one server in a network. Volumes correspond to the partitions in DOS (i.e, the option of dividing a hard drive into several areas).

Standard rights ROS

To select the \PROG directory as the first directory, move the highlight to this directory and press Enter. This also causes the directory name to appear in the *Directory In Which Trustee Should Be Added* window. Now press Esc to finish the process of defining directories for the user. This causes the *Network Directories* to disappear. The *Directory In Which Trustee Should Be Added* window now contains the correct path (in our example SERVER311/SYS:PROG) and can be closed by pressing Enter. Novell automatically adds the standard rights, *Read, Open, and Search* to the directory. These are sufficient for the program directory, since it allows the user to find and use the programs.

We also want to add the \DATA directory to the list of directories, but expand the rights. Follow the same procedure you used for \PROG to add the \DATA directory with the default rights. Press Ins to insert, press Enter to go one level deeper in the directory structure or confirm a selection, press Esc or .. to go one level higher, or complete the process of selecting directories.

After the directory is inserted in the *Trustee Directory Assignments* window and highlighted, press Enter to start changing the access rights. This displays all the available rights on the screen; in this case the *Read, Open,* and *Search* rights. To revoke a right, press Enter to enable it and answer the confirmation message. However, since we want to insert new rights, we press Ins instead. A new window appears with the rights that haven't been granted for this directory:

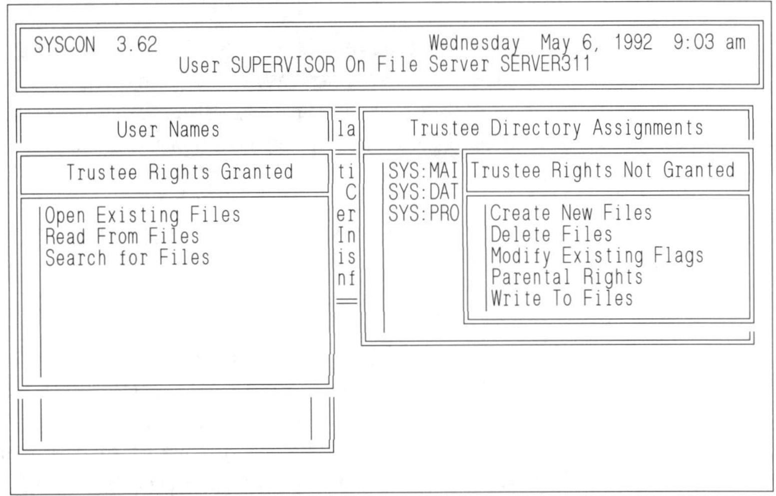

Granting additional rights to a directory

We want to grant at least all the rights necessary for editing data (i.e., *Create, Delete,* and *Write*). Press Enter to enable *Create New Files*. The window disappears and the new right is added to the *Trustee Rights Granted* list of available rights. Repeat this process for the other two rights, *Delete* and *Write*.

To end the process of granting rights, press Esc; the changes remain in effect. If you're satisfied with the current settings, press Esc to return to the main menu or exit SYSCON directly by pressing Alt + F10 and confirming the security prompt.

Defining the properties of several users through groups

As you can probably imagine, setting up many users can be very time-consuming for the supervisor. That's why Novell gives you the option of combining the identical properties of several users into one group.

For example, you could define access to the \PROG and \DATA directories for a group named TEXTS and then simply enter several users as members of the TEXTS group. Or you could define a group named CAD and grant the group access rights to the designing program and the current drawings.

Besides eliminating a lot of work for yourself, there are two advantages to doing this:

Advantages of a group

- You don't have to enter the new access rights for every user whenever you make changes (such as adding new directories).
- You don't have to worry about forgetting to make changes for one user, so users who are working on the same projects have different access rights. What works for Meyer as a member of the TEXTS group will also work for Smith.

In our example, you'll revoke the access rights to the two directories, \PROG and \DATA, from user MILLER and define them in a new group called TEXTS.

We'll start by creating the new TEXTS group in the SYSCON main menu. Press Enter to enable *Group Information*. The *Group Names* window appears with all the existing groups. Novell automatically created a group called *Everyone* during installation. Every user is automatically a member of this group. However, we want to add a group called TEXTS so we press Ins.

We enter TEXTS in the *New Group Name* window and the new group is added to the *Group Names* list. By selecting this group and pressing Enter, we get the *Group Information* window. Here we can define access rights with *Trustee Directory Assignments*, jas we can for one user.

After defining both directories (as described above for MILLER), we still must install MILLER as the first member of this group. This is very easy. With the TEXTS group activated, select the *Member List* entry in the *Group Information* window. A new window, called *Group Members*, appears.

This window doesn't have any entries yet. Pressing Ins displays a new window called *Not Group Members*. Select MILLER from this window. Once you press Enter, MILLER will be a member of the group and you can press Esc to exit.

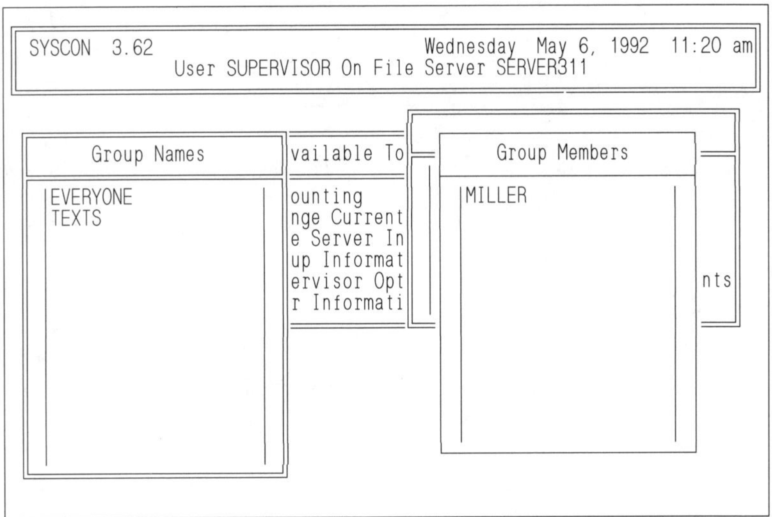

MILLER becomes a member of the TEXTS group

Finally, you can revoke the rights defined for MILLER, since he will now be granted those rights as a member of the TEXTS group. To do this, select the *User Information* entry from the main menu of SYSCON, and then select MILLER in the window that appears. Then the *User Information* window appears, in which you can enable the *Trustee Directory Assignments* menu item.

Then the window with the defined directories appears. You can select the two lines you added earlier by using the direction keys and then press Del:

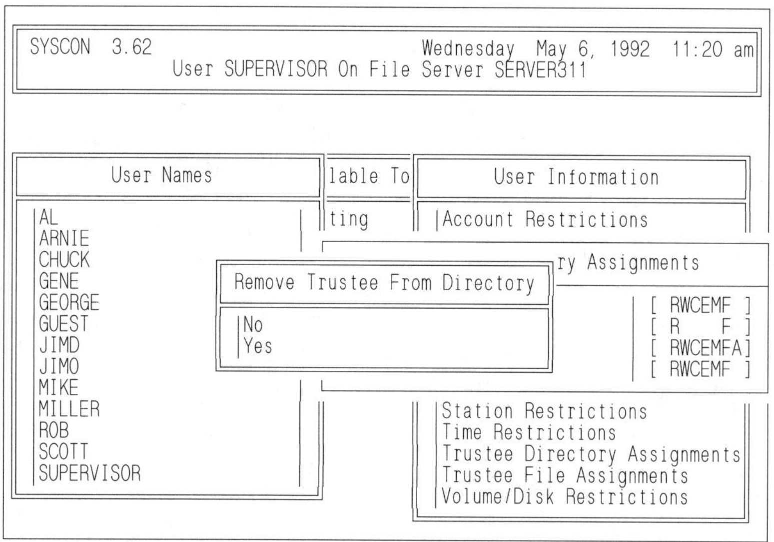

Pressing Del *to revoke an access right*

After confirmation, the access rights definition is deleted.

The change becomes effective immediately, but Novell only checks access rights for a directory when you change to it. In other words, someone could select a directory called \DATA, to whose files he has no access right. If the supervisor then grants him the appropriate right, he still cannot access the files in the \DATA directory. Novell won't check the access rights and allow the user access to the files in this directory until the user leaves and changes back to the directory with CD.. and CD DATA.

Minimum access rights and what you need for work

Novell only grants minimum access rights for a new user. These rights are:

- To search, open, and read files in the \PUBLIC and \LOGIN directories.

The MAIL directory

- Also, every user gets a special subdirectory in the MAIL directory for storing user-specific data. Included among such data is a login script, containing a sequence of batch-like commands similar to the AUTOEXEC.BAT.

However, with these access rights, a user can only experiment on the server; the new user cannot edit or delete any files.

To be able to start programs, he or she needs at least the same rights (Search, Open, Read) for the program directories. Besides that, he/she needs a directory, in which he/she can save the data of the programs. Generally the user needs the rights to create, modify, and write for this directory.

In Windows 3.1 you can distribute programs and data in such a way that the actual main part of Windows is present in one directory, for which only the basic rights (Search, Open, Read) are necessary. However, since Windows must create and change a multitude of files (such as the .INI files or .GRP files for group information), and it does so for every single user, there is also a Windows directory that is different for each user. It contains user-specific data such as the WIN.INI with its many settings; the Program Manager manages the .GRP files there, etc.

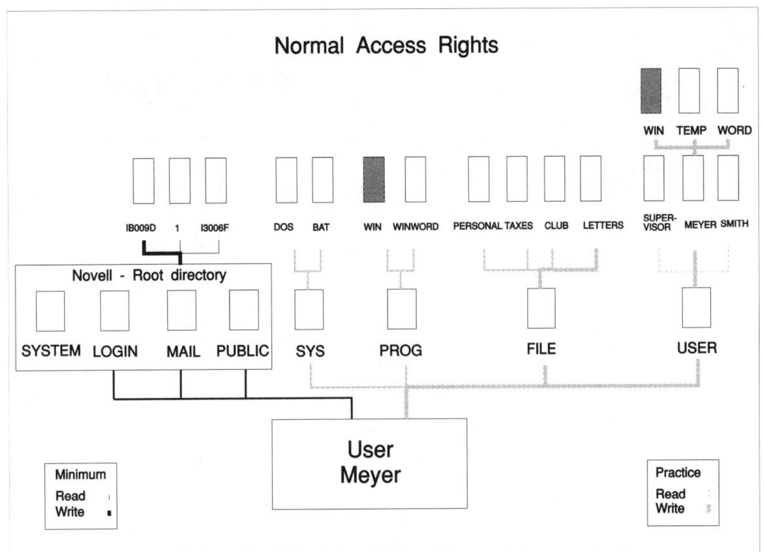

Minimum and practical access rights

The above illustration shows the difference between the minimum access rights necessary and those rights that are actually necessary for daily tasks. It also distinguishes Search/Read rights and Write/Change rights.

With minimum access rights, Meyer can login on the system but cannot do anything else. The most Meyer can do is start the SYSCON program from the \PUBLIC directory or call help with HELP.

That's why the second group of lines shows the rights that are actually necessary. Windows, for example, is divided into a non-changeable part (\PROG\WIN) and a part that can be changed by the user (\USER\MEYER\WIN). Of course, the majority of the Windows programs and files are in the \PROG\WIN directory and must be accessible for all Windows users.

31.4 Installing DOS in the Network

While the main focus of this chapter is setting up and optimizing Windows 3.1 in a network. Having DOS properly organized is an important requirement. Besides, the setup options within DOS (such as the CONFIG.SYS or AUTOEXEC.BAT) can be combined excellently with the options in Novell (such as the login scripts).

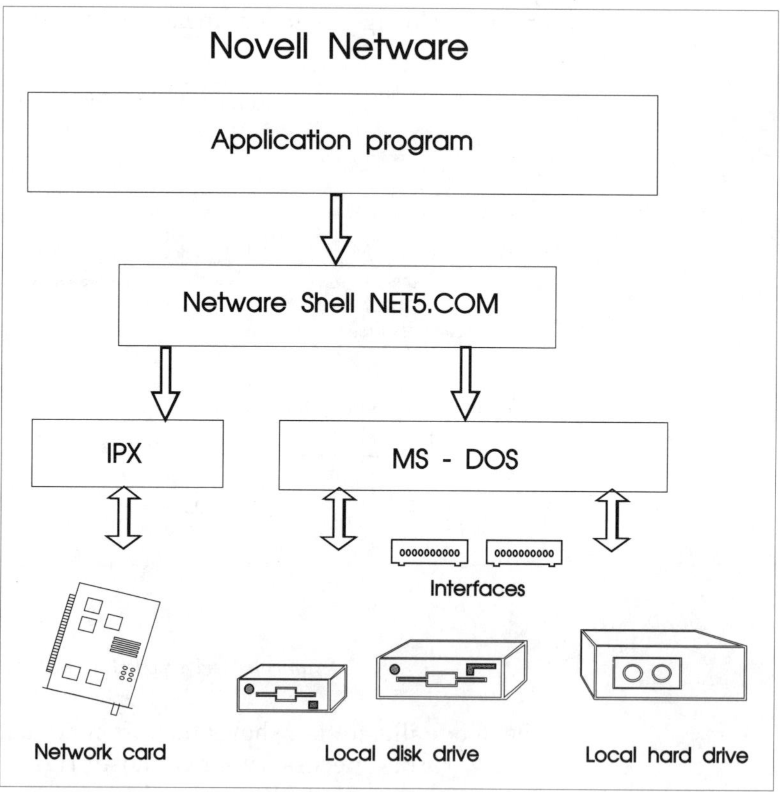

How DOS and Novell work together

The above illustration shows the cooperation between MS-DOS, which is normally used as a stand-alone operating system, and the special Novell network operating system.

If the user calls an application, it results in accesses to devices, such as disk drives and printers, while the program is running. The network shell started on the stand-alone computer switches between the application program and MS-DOS. It checks all accesses and either passes them on to MS-DOS (right track), or sends them to the server using IPX and the network card, where the network operating system (not shown here) takes care of the rest.

Because of its ability to filter and redirect accesses to the drive letters of the network, the network shell is often referred to as the redirector.

Which directories to install for users

Choosing the right directories and directory structures is an essential requirement for effective data backups and optimum work. If several users are working on one project, you must be able to lock the files being edited, but you must also be able to exchange the results as quickly as possible.

Directories for projects

It's especially easy to solve this problem on a network-capable database, such as Superbase, because the smallest access unit of a database is a data record. It's important to have a directory, such as F:\DATA\SBDATA, to which all users working on a project have access. After defining the project participants as a group in Novell (see our example of the TEXTS group), you can define an access right for the group and enter the project participants as group members.

This is different if you're working with a word processor, such as Word 5.5 or Word for Windows. In this case you should use one or more common project directories and take advantage of the Summary Info in Word 5.5 or Word for Windows to identify the location of the documents in the network.

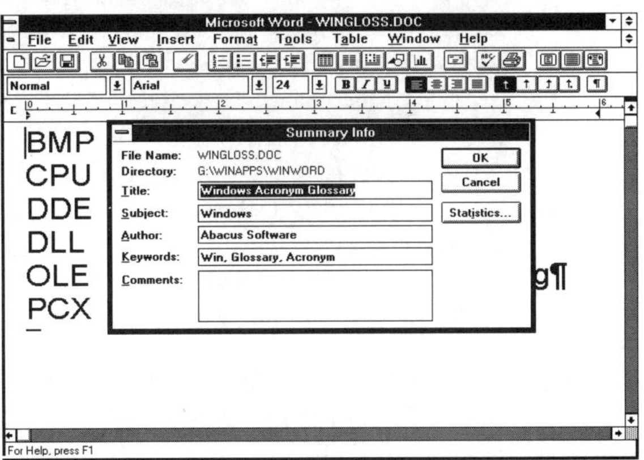

Word for Windows Summary Info configured to the network

Accessing USER directories

Of course, you'll also create directories in which each user can store personal data. For example, users could store the .INI files or even .PIF files or wallpaper for the Windows Desktop in such a directory. For example, a practical solution is to create the necessary subdirectories in a directory called \USER:

```
F:\USER\MEYER
F:\USER\SMITH
...
```

It's important that each user have full access rights to his or her directory, and also have read rights to other users' directories. Meyer, for example, can do as he pleases in the MEYER directory. However, in the F:\USER\SMITH directory, Meyer should at least be able to view files and file contents.

Often a user will discover that someone else made a change (e.g., to Windows) that the user would also like to set. To do this, the user must copy a few lines from the WIN.INI file to his or her own .INI file, or else copy a clever .PIF file to the user's own directory. However, users shouldn't be able to change or delete another user's personal files.

Temporary directory for data exchange

It's important to have a directory for temporary data storage and data exchange. It's best if you create a directory called \USER\TMP, to which all users have read/write access.

Now, if MEYER wants to send a text to SMITH, he would first copy it to \USER\TMP and then inform SMITH that the text is in that directory. All the network participants should understand that files can be stored only temporarily in this TMP directory.

☞ This TMP directory should be different from the DOS directory for temporary files, which you define for DOS with SET TEMP=. Otherwise, many programs would place temporary data there, making it almost impossible to delete files. Imagine if someone entered DEL *.* in the directory for temporary files to delete all the files and Windows or Word crashed a little later. However, with different users that wouldn't be so easy to do, because the network wouldn't allow files, which are currently being used, to be deleted.

How to install DOS on the server

You could also place MS-DOS directly on the server. To do this, install an appropriate directory (like F:\SYS\DOS) and copy the DOS files to it.

Setting up the workstations

However, you cannot boot the workstations from this DOS directory because while the workstations are booting, they don't have any connection to the network (unless there is a boot ROM on the network card). However, you can at least start each workstation from a diskette with the operating system and after the network drivers automatically load, access the file server for the remaining DOS commands. Instead of the diskette, you could also use local hard drives on the workstations.

The files on the start diskette could look as follows for a workstation under Novell 2.15:

```
REM CONFIG.SYS
SHELL=COMMAND.COM /E:1000 /P
DEVICE=HIMEM.SYS
DEVICE=EMM386.EXE NOEMS
DOS=HIGH,UMB
DEVICEHIGH=SETVER.EXE
FILES=30
BUFFERS=30
BREAK=ON
```

These command lines install MS-DOS in High memory with a command interpreter that has 1000 bytes of environment memory. In addition, EMM386.EXE installs Upper Memory without EMS (for professionals: this omits the page frames). This makes more High memory available for loading the network drivers.

```
@REM AUTOEXEC.BAT
@ECHO OFF
LOADHIGH IPX
LOADHIGH NET5
F:
LOGIN
PATH F:\SYS\DOS;F:\SYS\BAT;F:\USER\MEYER;F:\PROG\WIN
SET COMSPEC=F:\SYS\DOS\COMMAND.COM
SET TEMP=F:\USER\MEYER
SET TMP=F:\USER\MEYER
PROMPT $P$G
```

First, the IPX network driver and the NET5 network shell start up, and the file server is available after LOGIN. Then you can use PATH to install search paths. The search path for the command interpreter can be directed to the network's DOS directory (of course, there must be a valid COMMAND.COM file in this directory) and the temporary directories are defined as environment variables.

If the computer has a hard drive, you could set up the temporary directories on the local hard drive, which takes the burden off the network.

If you're interested in optimum installation of MS-DOS or DR DOS for a network and Windows, with an emphasis on memory and disk optimization, refer to the appropriate chapters in this book. We'll concentrate only on general installation.

Protecting the DOS files through write-protect

After installing DOS on the server, you should protect it from being accidentally overwritten by users. To do this, either don't grant the users any write rights to this directory, or set the appropriate write-protect attribute for the files. We recommend the latter solution, because it allows you to exclude special files (such as the .INI files) from write-protection. In certain cases it's absolutely necessary to exclude files from write-protection (see below).

Be careful with .INI files

Be careful with programs that save changes in special files (such as the DOSSHELL.INI or PCSHELL.CFG). Such programs can have considerable difficulty if they are unable to write to these files. The programs won't always just display an error message; occasionally they'll even crash.

So, for these programs (usually non-network programs), don't revoke write access in general. Instead, grant the users the right to delete and write to these directories, but then set the write-protect attribute for all the files except the .INI files.

For example, here's what you could do with the DOS directory and the TEXTS group:

1. Enable the TEXTS group from SYSCON and insert the following access rights for the F:\SYS\DOS directory:

```
SYS:SYS\DOS                    [RWOCD S ]
```

This makes it possible for all members of the TEXTS group to read, write, open, close, delete, and search for files in the DOS directory.

2. Use the Novell FLAG command to set the file attributes to Shareable and ReadOnly.

```
FLAG F:\SYS\DOS\*.* S RO
```

3. Then set the attribute for all .INI files to ReadWrite and NonShareable.

```
FLAG F:\SYS\DOS\*.INI NS RW
```

You can change the file attributes only if you're the supervisor or have the right to modify in this directory. Since the TEXTS group wasn't granted this right, only the supervisor can change the attributes.

You can even use this trick for the entire directory tree, \PROG. You should also consider other extensions as .INI files, such as SYS for CDCONFIG.SYS of CorelDraw. To set all files to Shareable and ReadOnly in directories beginning with \PROG and including subdirectories, use the command line:

```
FLAG F:\PROG\*.* NS RW SUB
```

"SUB" represents subdirectories.

How to determine special settings for users

As you can see, there are numerous installation options within a network. However, we haven't presented all the options. For example, with Novell you can easily make custom settings for different users. The supervisor can do this or any user can also change and refine the settings. These setting options, for example, refer to:

- Installing special search paths for the user
- Automatically starting programs
- Defining special environment variables that manage the various network programs

Now we'll provide a few introductory examples. We'll explain other, more interesting options when we discuss optimum installation of Windows for the different users.

The function of AUTOEXEC. BAT and CONFIG.SYS

The two system files, AUTOEXEC.BAT and CONFIG.SYS, play an important part in installing the workstations. The necessary device drivers and system settings are defined in the CONFIG.SYS, while the AUTOEXEC.BAT usually contains a definition of the system prompt and specifies the start of the IPX network driver and NET5, the network shell.

However, these functions and processes are user-independent. Regardless of who logs in on a workstation, the same CONFIG.SYS and AUTOEXEC.BAT will run. This process isn't a limitation if Meyer can only login on workstation 1 and Smith can only login on workstation 2. A network is actually much more flexible.

Perhaps Meyer has a 3.5" disk drive for using different types of data on workstation 1, but only has 4 Meg total memory and an 80386 computer without a mathematical coprocessor. If he wants to edit an extensive drawing with CorelDraw, he can trade places with Smith, login on the more powerful 80486 with 8 Meg of memory as MEYER and continue his work there without any restrictions. There is a special technique for doing this: login scripts, which are very important for optimally installing Windows 3.1.

The function of the login script

In Novell NetWare, a login script is a special startup file, in which any user can create his/her own special work environment. Unlike the AUTOEXEC.BAT file, this login script executes as soon as the user is logged in on the network. So it's independent of the starting process of the PC, which results in access to the network.

The login script can determine an entire series of activities. The most important ones are:

- Defining a special name for the user/workstation.
- Defining search paths for programs and commands.
- Starting programs automatically.
- Defining special environment variables that manage the various network programs.

Now we'll provide some introductory examples. We'll explain other, more interesting options when we discuss optimum installation of Windows for the different users.

How to create a login script

Use the SYSCON program to create a login script for a user. This program contains a built-in editor for creating and editing the login script:

Don't change the supervisor's login script until you have enough knowledge and have created a backup user for the supervisor. If you make an error in the supervisor's login script, it may prevent a valid connection to the network. Since only the supervisor can change the supervisor's login script, the error leads to a dead end.

So, you should create a user who has the same access rights as the supervisor and receives the same password (e.g., user SV).

To install this second supervisor, you must create the user as described above. Then select *User Information* in the SYSCON main menu and choose the user, to whom the access rights should be assigned (in our case, the new user SV), from the list of *User Names*. Then select the *Security Equivalences* entry in the *User Informations* menu and press Ins. In the *Other Users And Groups* list that appears you'll then see all the defined groups and users. Select *Supervisor* and press Enter to accept the selection. Then press Alt + F10 to exit SYSCON.

After taking these safety precautions, it's safe to change the supervisor's login script as well. However, you still should practice on another user or on a test user first. This advice is based on the fact that Novell uses a default script; a login script isn't created for the user. As soon as this happens, the default script is no longer processed.

To create a login script for a user named MILLER, use the following procedure:

Call SYSCON and select the *User Information* entry in the main menu. After selecting MILLER from the *User Name:* list, choose the *Login Script* entry under *User Information*. If there isn't a login script for the user (as we assume), you can decide whether you want to use another user's login script: *Read Login Script From User*. The name of the current user, MILLER, is suggested. If you confirm this suggestion by pressing Enter, a blank editor screen appears, *Login Script For User MILLER*.

You could also specify an existing user to load his login script as a default.

Now you can enter a script in the editor window.

Here's a sample login script:

```
REMARK Login script for user MILLER
MAP F:=SYS:
COMSPEC=F:\SYS\DOS
DOS SET MSWNET55="F:\USER\MILLER"
DOS SET WINDIR="F:\USER\MILLER"
DOS SET TEMP="C:\TEMP"
DRIVE F:
MACHINE="MILLER"
EXIT "\PUBLIC\MILLER"
```

This sample login script works in the following way:

REMARK
: Introduces a comment line and prevents Novell from paying attention to the rest of the line.

MAP
: Represents a drive letter to a path on the server. In this case the first volume on the server can be used as F: (volume = partition under DOS).

COMSPEC
: Defines the path and file name of the command interpreter.

DOS SET
: Sets system variables, similar to the MS-DOS SET command. In the login script, a TEMP directory for DOS and Windows and a directory for user-specific

WORD and Windows files called F:\USER\MILLER are specified.

DRIVE
Switches to the specified drive.

MACHINE
Defines a name for the computer.

EXIT
Ends the login script and executes the specified batch file or program. In the example, the MILLER.BAT batch file contains further commands. There can be a command of up to 14 characters (including the path specification) after EXIT.

After entering the lines, press Esc. A prompt then appears (*Save Changes*), asking whether you want to save the input or changes. After confirming this prompt, press Alt + F10 to exit SYSCON and login again as user MILLER to try out the login script. A batch file called F:\PUBLIC\MILLER.BAT should be present.

How to change a login script

To modify an existing login script, use the same procedure you would to create a new login script. However, the existing script will appear without the option of selecting a user name.

You can use Del and Backspace to delete characters, and select a block of text by pressing F5 and moving the cursor keys. Press Del to delete a block and press Ins to insert it elsewhere in the text.

To save the changes you've made, press Esc and confirm the security prompt.

Unfortunately, you cannot easily insert several lines from one script into another script, because only one script can be loaded at a time. You can press F5 to switch on selection mode, use the direction keys to select the desired lines, and press Del to delete them. However, then you must press Ins to insert the lines back in the script, call the second login script, and insert them in the first login script. So, exchanging several passages between two login scripts can be very time-consuming.

Instead of doing it this way, you can start two command interpreters in Windows and use the SYSCON command in both. Use *Edit/Copy* to copy lines, and *Edit/Paste* to paste them from the Clipboard into the other script. By using the Clipboard, you can use the mouse to cut out files, go to the word processor, and continue working.

A login script's minimum contents

You should at least use the MAP instruction, as shown in our example, in a custom login script. Without it you cannot access the server. If you don't create a special script file, Novell uses a default login script. This assigns the letter to the network drive. If you create a custom login script, the automatic allocation is omitted.

You can also change your login script without being logged in as supervisor. The only time you must login as the supervisor is to change other users' scripts.

31.5 Installing Windows in the Network

This section discusses the requirements for using Windows 3.1 in the network.

What does Windows have to offer in the network?

There are several advantages to installing Windows 3.1 in a network:

- The most important advantage is the many options offered by Windows. These include memory management, data exchange, multitasking, etc. Why do without these options in the network?

- Windows requires a lot of memory on the hard drive, and most Windows applications occupy a lot of disk space. If you install the same applications on each network computer, a lot of hard drive space is used. You can solve this problem by installing Windows and Windows applications in the network because the programs are stored only once on the server's hard drive.

- Windows supports powerful, expensive hardware. A network is an easy way to use an expensive PostScript printer with other users.

- Windows provides a series of special network functions. For example, the Print Manager can easily access the print queue of a print server. Also, you can connect with other file servers from Windows, and even instruct Windows to recreate the connection every time Windows starts up.

Requirements for running Windows in the network

There are a few requirements for running Windows in the network. Also, there are some aspects that you should consider before installing a network.

- You need a Windows compatible network. Check the following list to determine which networks are suitable:

```
3Com 3+Open LAN Manager           3Com 3+Share
Banyan VINES 4.0                  IBM PC LAN-Manager
LAN Manager 1.x                   LAN Manager 2.0 Basic
LAN Manager 2.0 Enhanced          Microsoft Network
Novell Netware
```

Windows also supports other network types if they have a driver for Windows.

- You need a file server with a relatively large, fast hard drive. You should use a fast 80386 with 4-8 Meg of memory and a hard drive. If you plan to work mainly with Windows applications, this hard drive should be at least 200 Meg, with access times of less than 17 ms.

- You should have identical or similar workstations if you want users to be able to login from different workstations. If possible, each workstation should have a 40 Meg hard drive and VGA card and monitor.

- You must complete some licensing documentation for running Windows (legally) in the network. Check the Microsoft Licensing Agreement provided with Windows.

How to install Windows for the network

There are two steps for installing Windows in the network. First, perform a complete Windows installation on the server, including all drivers and data. This way, you can set up workstations with entirely different drivers. The complete installation requires about 18 Meg of hard drive space on the file server.

Then perform a custom installation for each user. To do this, install Windows in a special directory for each workstation or user. This installation takes up about 300K per user.

How to install Windows on the server

Installing Windows on the server is easy, if you have enough disk space and the proper access rights. Copy all the Windows diskettes to the server and decompress the files (this makes all the disk data available, saving you the trouble of switching diskettes when changing the configuration later).

SETUP /A

Start the Windows Setup installation program with SETUP /A (for network administrator) and specify a directory on the server, such as F:\PROG\WIN, as the destination for the installation. Then insert the diskettes in the drive, one after the other. The

Windows Setup program copies the files to the file server and decompresses them.

Windows occupies approximately 18 Meg of memory. Then you can perform the installation for the individual workstations, or users.

How to install Windows on the workstation

To install Windows from a workstation, login on this workstation as a user. In our description, we'll again use MILLER as our user name. You'll need a special user directory for installation. It's best if you use your own user directory on the server, such as F:\USER\MILLER or a subdirectory of this directory: F:\USER\MILLER\WIN. Doing this enables you to login from another workstation and still work with your own Windows data and settings.

You could also use a directory from your own local hard drive as a user directory, for example, C:\WINDOWS. However, we'll use F:\USER\MILLER as our sample directory in the following paragraphs.

SETUP /N

Use the special parameter, /N (for Network), to start the installation program. If you still haven't defined a search path to the general Windows directory on the server, do this now and start SETUP with the complete path specification: `SETUP /N`.

```
F:\PROG\WIN\SETUP /N
```

You can also change to the directory on the server containing all the Windows files, F:\PROG\WIN, and start the installation program from there.

Answer the prompt for the destination directory for installation with F:\USER\MILLER (or whatever user directory you're installing).

☞ Don't accidentally choose the server directory containing all the Windows data.

Then a screen appears with a listing of the hardware and software components determined by Windows. In most cases, Windows will identify the elements correctly, so you continue by pressing Enter.

After you press Enter, the user data are copied or generated and Windows automatically starts up for the rest of the installation. You're also prompted to install a printer, have the installation program search the hard drive for programs that will then be automatically available in Windows, and have Readme files displayed on the screen.

The default setting for all three selection options is "Yes"; you should accept these default settings.

After you press Enter to complete the screen, Windows copies the user files and builds the groups and programs in the Program Manager on the screen so they are easy to follow.

Changing the system files

Then the AUTOEXEC.BAT and CONFIG.SYS system files are changed. We don't recommend letting Windows automatically change them. Instead, display them beforehand and check them or make the changes manually.

We recommend doing this because Windows makes some changes to the system files that are practical only if the user always logs into the network from the same workstation. If this isn't the case, it's better to make changes and settings in the login script of the user, instead of in the AUTOEXEC.BAT.

We'll explain which changes Windows wants to make and how to combine them with the user login script later.

Also, SETUP enters files on the server as drivers in the CONFIG.SYS, but these aren't available yet because the workstation isn't connected with the network yet. However, you won't have this problem if Windows installs the user data in a C:\WINDOWS directory on the local hard drive.

After completing installation, you should reboot the computer. If you want, Windows will also do this for you.

After logging in to the network as a user, you can start Windows 3.1 by entering WIN.

The following illustration shows Windows as an operating system attachment working with Novell as the network operating system, with multitasking (here with three programs).

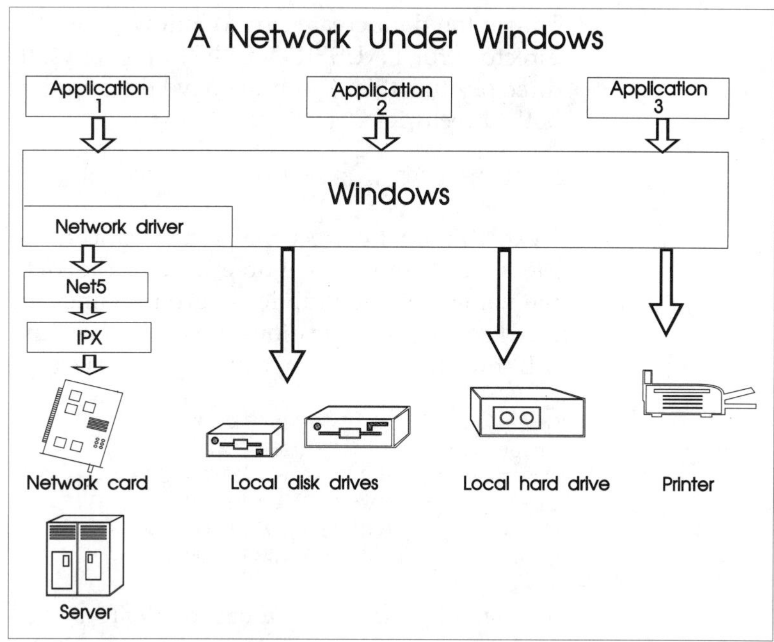

How Windows and Novell work together

At the top level are the programs with which the user works directly (in this case, applications 1 through 3). Only Windows organizes their cooperation as well as contact to the peripheral devices (disk drives, hard drive, printer). Windows is above a network drive connected to the network shell (here Net5) and the IPX network driver. The latter makes the connection to the server via the network card.

Compared to the illustration "How DOS and Novell work together", this illustration also clearly shows that Windows decision structures come before the network shell. So, Windows has more control over the entire operation.

Simplified installation for several users

If you have to install Windows in this way for several users, the process can be rather time-consuming. However, you can also speed up and simplify the process if you fulfill a few requirements.

Copy the user files

It's easy to install Windows again if the connected workstations are very similar, for example, if they have the same monitors and video cards.

Then you copy the files in the user directory created by Windows to the new user directory and adapt the path specifications in the INI files.

To use the data created by Windows from the F:\USER\MILLER directory for F:\USER\MEYER, first copy all the files to the new directory (for this, you must have the appropriate access rights for both directories):

```
XCOPY F:\USER\MILLER F:\USER\MEYER /S
```

Correct the path specifications

Next, you must correct the path specifications in the WIN.INI and PROGMAN.INI files. For example, the path specifications and file names for the individual group names are in PROGMAN.INI file. The path specifications must be placed in the new directory so MEYER isn't constantly changing SMITH's groups.

```
Group1=F:\USER\MEYER\MAINGROU.GRP
Group2=F:\USER\MEYER\MISC.GRP
Group3=F:\USER\MEYER\WINDOWSA.GRP
Group6=F:\USER\MEYER\ACCESSOR.GRP
Group7=F:\USER\MEYER\GAMES.GRP
Group8=F:\USER\MEYER\MEYERWOR.GRP
```

You should use the Notepad or Write to make the changes. The automatic search and replace function is also useful.

Using a special file as a default

Although normal Windows installation is usually fast and easy, when you install several users much of the installation can be time-consuming and too interactive (you must answer numerous questions and confirm lots of settings).

Setting up a new version of Windows by copying user-specific data also requires changing paths afterwards as well as write access to all the appropriate user directories. Actually, only the supervisor should have this access.

This is why Windows 3.1 also offers a special installation based on a file in which the essential settings are stored. This way you don't have to make the interactive input necessary for installation yourself, and can even call the installation program from a batch file.

The procedure for installation is as follows: First, create the special definition file, then start the Windows installation program with a special parameter and specify the name of the definition file. Windows will then use the data from this configuration file.

Of course, you can also easily install Windows on several different computer systems by using several definition files. You must place the files in the directory to which the user has read and write access rights, so the Windows installation works.

The SETUP.INF file

You'll find an example of such a definition file, called SETUP.SHH, in the Windows directory. Suppose that you wanted to use this file to install Windows for a user and all of the Windows data and programs including the SETUP.SHH file are in the F:\PROG\WIN directory. Then use the following command lines:

```
F:
CD \PROG\WIN
SETUP /H:SETUP.SHH /N
```

☞ You can also use this procedure when you don't want to install a network version of Windows. To do this, omit the /N switch. However, in this case, installation will be interactive unless you don't have to insert all the diskettes one after the other. In other words, you should place the Windows files in a special directory.

Structure of the SHH file

Here's what the structure of the file should be:

[sysinfo]

Along with the "showsysinfo" variable, [sysinfo] determines whether the setting screen should be displayed during installation. This causes the settings to display, giving the user an opportunity to change them. Possible settings are "yes" or "no".

```
showsysinfo=no
```

[configuration]

You can define and set the various devices that are available here. If you don't specify a device, the installation program will automatically determine the values. You can take the possible notations from the SETUP.INF file in the Windows directory. If you are upgrading an existing Windows version (such as 3.0), the installation program partially ignores entries for the hardware, taking the existing defaults instead. To prevent this from happening, you can place an exclamation point in front of the setting:

```
machine = !ibm_compatible
```

You could use the following definitions for the [configuration] area:

```
machine =
display =
mouse =
network =
keyboard =
language =
kblayout =
```

You will find the specific entry options under each definition in the SETUP.INF file. For example, for "machine" you would find the following information:

```
machine=
ibm_compatible
ast_386_486
at_and_t
everex_386_25
hewlett_packard
ibm_ps2_70p
ibm_ps2_140sx
ncr_386sx
nec_pm_sx+
nec_prospeed
toshiba_1200xe
toshiba_1600
toshiba_5200
zenith_386
```

[windir]

Enter the directory in which you want to install Windows here. The installation program automatically updates existing versions.

```
C:\WINDOWS
```

[userinfo]

If you're installing Windows on a stand-alone computer, you enter the name and company here. If it's a network installation, the name and company will be ignored. The first setting is mandatory; if you don't specify anything, you'll be prompted to do so during installation. Both entries can be up to 30 characters long and must be placed in quotation marks if the entries contain spaces.

[dontinstall]

Define components here that you don't want to install. The possible components are:

```
accessories
readmes
games
screensavers
bitmaps
```

By default, Windows installs all the components.

[options]

You can set additional options for the installation here. These options are: display readme files (on-line documents), automatic installation of applications, and start Windows tutorials at the end of installation.

Possible settings are:

```
readonline      Display Readme files
setupapps       Set up existing applications (interactive)
autosetupapps   Automatic setup of all applications on the
                hard drive without any prompts
tutorial        Starts the tutorial after installation
```

[printers]

You can place values for the printer after this key term. These values are also listed in the CONTROL.INF file after [io.device]. You can also find the values for the port under [ports]. You must specify one of these after the printer:

```
"HP DeskJet 500",LPT1:
```

[endinstall]

Determine settings for the end of installation after this key term. For example, you can determine how the AUTOEXEC.BAT and CONFIG.SYS files should be changed and what happens at the end of installation.

configfiles="modify", "save", "save, Name1, Name2"

Determines whether the files will automatically be modified or whether the suggestions are saved in two special files called CONFIG.WIN and AUTOEXEC.WIN or in two files that you define.

endopt = "exit", "restart", "reboot"

Determines whether the installation program returns to DOS, restarts Windows, or even reboots the computer. The last option, "reboot", isn't available if you use /N to install a network.

The following sample file, MEYER.INF, installs Windows in the network for a user called MEYER. It should be saved in his user directory, F:\USER\MEYER. You should start the installation program from the Windows program directory, \PROG\WIN, with the following line:

```
SETUP /H:F:\USER\MEYER\MEYER.INF /N
```

```
; SETUP file for MEYER
; VGA, Network

[sysinfo]

showsysinfo = yes
```

```
[configuration]
machine = ibm_compatible
display = vga
mouse = ps2mouse
network = novell
keyboard = t4s0enha
language =  enu
kblayout = nodll

[windir]
c:\windows

[userinfo]
"user's name"
"company name"

[dontinstall]
games

[options]
readonline

[printers]
"HP DeskJet 500"

[endinstall]
configfiles = save
endopt = exit
```

Remember that with a network installation, all the Windows files are unpacked in a directory on the file server, such as \PROG\WIN. The WIN.SRC, SETUP.INF, and CONTROL.INF files are also located there. You can take the terms for the settings from these files.

Other setting options

Along with using SYSCON to install users directly and installing Windows for one user, there are several other setting options. Setting up environment variables in the AUTOEXEC.BAT or in the login script are two of the most important options.

Determining an area for swapping (temporary files or swap file) or having programs automatically start in Windows are also important for your later work in the network. Now we'll present some typical optimization and setup options.

Determining temporary directories

When you install Windows, you determine the directory for temporary files through an environment variable. When Windows or other application programs must store information temporarily, the information is stored in the appropriate directory instead of in the Windows directory.

Selecting the right directory for this not only affects the processing speed, but can also ensure that the network is organized.

For example, if the user cannot write or make changes to the directory for temporary data, you won't be able to save any temporary data and Windows will soon display error messages or have memory problems.

To determine the temporary directory, define an environment variable in the following way, usually in the AUTOEXEC.BAT file:

```
SET TEMP=F:\USER\MEYER\TEMP
```

In this case, the temporary data would be saved in the specified directory on the file server. Of course, these hard drive accesses place a burden on the network.

If the workstations have their own local C: hard drives, you should place the temporary files there:

```
SET TEMP=C:\TEMP
```

If you often notice that data garbage collects in this temporary directory (i.e., temporary files continue to exist there after programs crash and take up more of your hard drive capacity), you can use an easy, safe method to delete these data. To do this, insert a line in the AUTOEXEC.BAT file. Don't delete the files when Windows has already been started.

```
SET TEMP=C:\TEMP
ECHO After pressing Y, existing
ECHO temporary files in %TEMP% will be ECHO deleted
DEL %TEMP%
```

This prompt gives you the option of stopping the process, if necessary, so you can use the temporary files to reconstruct an error.

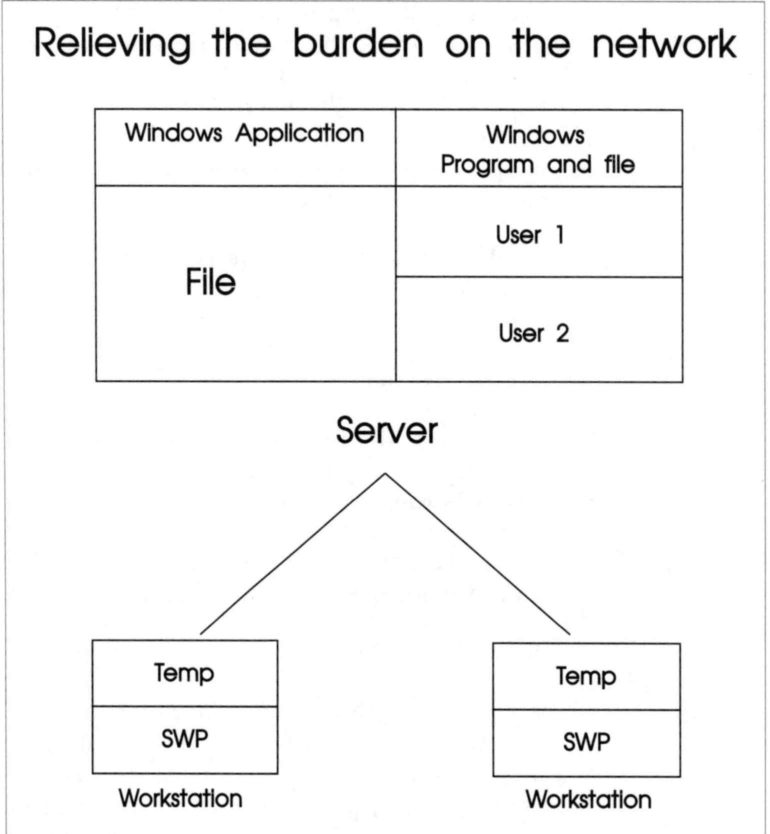

Taking the burden off the network

The above illustration shows a distribution of data and programs in the network that takes as much of the burden as possible off the network.

However, a user still has optional access from any workstation because the user-specific configuration data continue to be available on the file server.

Windows itself is on the file server along the individual settings for each user. The applications and their data files are also on the server, easily and directly available to all of the users.

However, the temporary files (Standard mode) and any possible permanent swap files are on the local workstations. If Windows must swap or reread data to switch from one application to another, this occurs on the local hard drive, which takes the burden off the network.

Temporary swap files or a permanent swap file?

There are some disadvantages to managing temporary data in separate temporary files. On a very fragmented hard drive, the files can be spread out over the tracks so accesses become extremely slow.

Although you can correct and improve this condition through optimization programs, as soon as you work with the data, the new order quickly disintegrates. Also, the optimization takes a long time.

Another disadvantage is that temporary files will remain stored on the hard drive if Windows crashes in mid session. These stored files can accumulate, taking up large amounts of hard disk space.

Although we showed you a way to eliminate "data garbage" earlier, not all programs will use a directory for temporary data.

In Windows you can also set up a permanent swap file, which is optimally placed (not fragmented) on the hard drive. This eliminates the limitations and problems we just discussed.

However, such a swap file also occupies the reserved part of the hard drive, and you must be sure that this reserved part of the hard drive is both large enough and contiguous.

The following illustration shows the essential differences between storage in a permanent temporary file and in variable files.

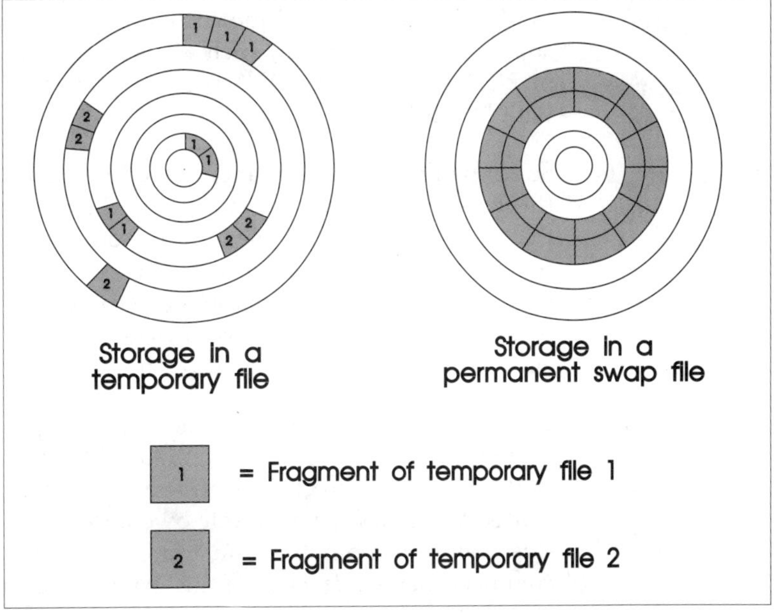

Temporary files and a permanent swap file

Variable files are fragmented

When a variable file is created (both file 1 and file 2 in the illustration), it's usually "fragmented" (i.e., the data aren't in sequence, but instead are "scattered" on the hard drive). This fragmentation will slow down access to this file. Although you can use tools to eliminate fragmentation, it will return eventually.

Windows automatically creates a permanent swap file contiguously; the swap file cannot be fragmented either. Accesses from Windows are faster. However, the memory reserved for the swap file is also permanently assigned (two cylinders in the illustration), so it cannot be used for other programs or data.

You cannot specify the hard drive on the file server for storing temporary files. Windows only suggests local hard drives in the Control Panel dialog window for *386 Enhanced Virtual Memory.*

When you install Windows in the network, you can use the existing local hard drive resources to take the burden off the network. All data that don't have to be exchanged between the workstations and the server can relieve the network and significantly increase the speed of other, unavoidable accesses.

Optimizing Windows through a permanent swap file

First, be sure you have a local hard drive on the workstation. Then create a sufficiently large swap file. You may have to use a utility program beforehand to improve the arrangement of the data on the hard drive so a large enough contiguous area is available. MS-DOS 5.0 doesn't include such a program, so you must rely on a supplementary product, such as Norton Utilities (SD, SpeedDisk) or PC Tools (Compress). A program called DISKOPT is included with DR DOS 60.

Optimizing the hard drive

So, to work with a permanent swap file, set up a special area on the hard drive that's reserved for the entire time. This means that this area cannot be used for any other purpose. Unfortunately, this is the disadvantage of using this procedure. The advantage is that working with permanent swap files is much faster than working with temporary swap files. The permanent swap file is active until it's either deleted or modified.

Up to Windows 3.0

Up to Version 3.0, Windows had a special program for creating a permanent swap file, called SWAPFILE.EXE, which was located in the Windows directory. You could only make this setting if you started Windows in Real mode by entering WIN /R. You could call this program from the File Manager or by selecting the *Run* command in the *File* menu of the Program Manager.

Windows 3.1

Beginning with Windows 3.1, it's much easier to install and modify the permanent swap file. The additional memory that becomes available is also called Virtual memory in Windows 3.1.

Installing the swap file is easy and can be done at any time. However, before you install, save all data in any Windows applications that are running and then exit those applications.

To set up a swap file in Windows, open the Control Panel program in the main group to display the available setting options. Since a permanent swap file is important only in 386 Enhanced mode, the necessary option, *386 Enhanced*, is also available only in this mode. Double-click the option to select it. A window appears with a button called [Virtual Memory].

The valid settings are displayed under *Current Settings*. Select the [Change >>] button to add *New Settings* to the display. You can choose the desired *Drive*, *Type* (Permanent or Temporary) and determine the file size in kilobytes under *New Size*. You should use the *Recommended Size* and confirm by pressing Enter. A confirmation message appears, since you must restart Windows. After you select *Restart*, Windows automatically restarts; selecting *Continue* cancels the selected settings so you don't have to restart Windows.

How a permanent swap file works

Windows checks the current hard drive for free memory capacity and for the largest contiguous block that can be used for the swap file. Windows also sets the required file size in relation to the available memory. Windows then automatically calculates a recommendation from these values which refers to the permanent swap file being installed. Generally, you should accept this recommendation, since Windows always finds the optimum solution. If you prefer to install a smaller file to save memory, use the scroll bar to change the default.

Optimizing Windows in the network with temporary files

If there isn't enough memory for Windows and the applications currently running, Windows can relocate temporary data from memory, which isn't currently needed, to make new disk capacity available to applications.

For example, a temporary swap file contains all the information that Windows needs to correctly reconstruct the old status of an application when you switch back to it. The default drive is the hard drive and the directory into which Windows was copied during installation. In a network, the directory containing the user-specific data is automatically used. This directory is frequently on the hard drive of the file server.

Determining temporary swap files for Standard mode

To prevent swap files from burdening the network in Standard mode, you can use a local drive for them. For example, you could use a hard drive from one of the workstations. The easiest way to do this is to define the TEMP environment variable in the AUTOEXEC.BAT with the following line:

```
SET TEMP=C:\TEMP
```

As soon as this setting is in effect (the next time you start up your computer or run the AUTOEXEC.BAT), Windows will place temporary files in the C:\TEMP directory when running in Standard mode.

You could also use a different setting with the SYSTEM.INI system file. Simply specify the drive or subdirectory for the swap file with a line in the SYSTEM.INI file. Load this file in the Notepad and move the cursor to the end of the file. You'll see the [NonWindowsApp] entry there. Add the following line under this entry:

```
SWAPDISK=Path
```

You must specify both a drive and directory in this line. For example, you could enter the following:

```
SWAPDISK=C:\TEMP
```

Temporary swap files in 386 Enhanced mode

In 386 Enhanced mode, if there isn't enough disk space in RAM, a contiguous, unfragmented area on the hard drive is used as a swap file. Since this is an automatic process, it doesn't require any installation. The swap file is in the Windows directory under WIN386.SWP. Working with temporary swap files is usually slower than working with permanent swap files. However, the advantage is that the temporary swap file is created only when it's needed; otherwise it doesn't decrease the hard drive capacity.

In the SYSTEM.INI file you can control the arrangement of temporary swap files. For example, you can specify which hard drive to use for the swap files. This is useful if you have more than one hard drive or if you installed Windows on a network. So, you can prevent files from being automatically placed in the user directory on the file server, which would place a burden on the network.

Enter the following line in the [386enh] section:

```
PagingDrive=Drive letter
```

Under Drive letter, enter the drive letter of the local hard drive you want to use for the temporary swap file. This should be the fastest hard drive you have. It must also have enough space for all of the information. In most cases, the setting would look like this:

```
PagingDrive=C
```

Setting the maximum size of the swap file

By default, Windows uses 1024K for the swap file in 386 Enhanced mode and can expand this amount if necessary. This can lead to problems if Windows swaps a lot of information and uses the total hard drive capacity. In this case, you may no longer be able to start a particular application because there is no more disk space available. Also, you may not be able to create new files. In these instances, you can specify a maximum area to be used for temporary swap files.

To specify this maximum area, enter the following line in the SYSTEM.INI file under the [386enh] section:

```
MaxPagingFileSize=2048
```

Making this entry limits the size of the swap file to 2048K. This may be too small for some applications. You'll have to experiment to find the optimum setting. This setting actually depends on the programs you use and the size of your memory.

Setting minimum memory capacity of the hard drive

Another entry regulates the minimum size of hard drive memory that's available after you install the swap file. This is practical when you have only a limited amount of free disk space on the local hard drive, but still want to provide as much virtual memory as possible. Suppose that you still have 8 Meg free on the local hard drive and require at least 4 Meg for other (local) applications. You could enter the following line in the [386enh] section:

```
MinUserDiskSpace=4096
```

Swap file size in the network

If you don't have much conventional memory on the workstations in the network and there is enough space on the local hard drives, you should specify a larger value for the swap file. If there is enough capacity available, don't specify anything for *MaxPagingFileSize*, so Windows isn't limited by any restrictions. Otherwise, specify a small remainder under *MinUserDiskSpace*.

Remember that Windows can only use one contiguous area of the hard drive for WIN386.SWP and that the settings are only effective if you don't install a permanent swap file.

Setting the swap file from the Control Panel

Usually the swap file is set when you install Windows. Along with the option of using the entries the SYSTEM.INI, you can also set the values from the Control Panel.

First open Control Panel in the Main Group and then double-click the 386 Enhanced icon. Next, enable the Virtual Memory... button. You can monitor the current setting in a special window and select the Change >> button to enable another window, in which you can specify new settings.

How to start Windows in the network

If you installed Windows 3.1 correctly in the network and have made all the other arrangements as described, then starting Windows is very easy:

- First login as a user on the appropriate workstation. If you built the network as we described (so it's oriented to the user instead of the workstation), then you should also be able to start Windows from any workstation.

- Now ensure that a search path has been defined for the directory with the user-specific Windows files (\USER\MILLER). Also, a path to the directory of all Windows files can be helpful. You must install the user directory before the directory containing all the Windows files. You could specify such a complete search path from the login script for the user.

The following is an example of what this could look like:

```
PATH=F:\SYS\DOS;F:\SYS\BAT;F:\USER\MILLER;F:\PROG\WIN
```

We had some difficulty installing such a search path from the login script because the PATH command cannot be used directly in the script. So we start a batch file for each user with his or her name at the end of the login script. The last line in the login script could be something like:

```
EXIT "\F:\PUBLIC\MEYER.BAT"
```

In the batch file, it's easy to make the path specification with the following command line:

```
REM Batch file for MILLER
PATH F:\SYS\DOS;F:\SYS\BAT;F:\USER\MILLER;F:\PROG\WIN
CD \USER\MILLER
```

- Finally, start Windows by entering WIN. You could also add this call to the end of the batch file so Windows automatically starts up when you login with the right settings for each particular user.

Windows then uses the user-specific data from the \USER\MILLER directory. So, if the group and program files are modified, these changes only apply to this user. When the user exits Windows, only those files belonging to this user are changed; the files of other users aren't affected. However, the user MEYER must have the right to change files and create new ones in the \USER\MEYER directory.

31.6 Networks and Windows Applications

Working with applications in a network is the same as working on a stand-alone computer. The Windows Desktop hides most network details from the user on the workstation. The Program Manager is important to this process because it makes the icons for the applications available. Simply double-click an icon to start the desired application.

Using program groups

Programs that belong to the same topic are combined into a program group. The group also includes programs located in completely different directories on the hard drive. Actually groups can even include programs from different hard drives. This is an alternative to the current method, which involves placing programs that belong to the same topic in common subdirectories. Program groups are ideal for networks.

Installing applications in the network

When you install Windows, you'll be able to install existing applications on the hard drive on Windows. Obviously this makes sense only if there are programs on the disk. You don't have to perform a complete installation every time, because you can repeat this step at any time.

Installing existing applications

To install programs on the server's hard drive in Windows, follow the same procedure for installation on stand-alone computers. Start the Windows Setup program in the Main Group of Windows. Select *Options* and then *Set Up Applications....* You have the option of letting Windows search the complete hard drive for applications for you or entering your own application. The first option is ideal for use after installation or after you've made major changes to the programs in Windows; the second option is ideal for minor changes, or after you've installed a single program.

So, to install all or many applications on the file server for one user, select the first option and then choose the network drive from a list of drives. In our example, the network drive is F:SERVER_1/SYS:.

Next, SETUP searches all directories of the specified drive and displays the results of its search. In the left window you see a listing of all the programs that Windows has found on the hard drive. Select the button to transfer a selected program from the left window to the right window. You can also use the usual selection procedures to select more than one program. For example, you can select applications in sequence by holding down the Ctrl key and clicking the mouse at each application.

You could also select the Add All button so you don't have to search for the right applications. It's easy to remove individual applications later. After clicking the OK button to confirm your selections, the appropriate program groups are formed in Windows. All programs are represented by an icon in the *Applications* window.

Windows applications and their icons

Windows applications have their own descriptive icons. The non-Windows applications have simple icons, which you can easily change from the Program Manager in the *File/Properties...* command. The Program Manager of Windows 3.1 contains numerous icons.

When searching for applications, Windows usually finds only the popular ones, such as Word, Ventura Publisher, etc. There are also some smaller utilities that aren't displayed. You cannot add the unnamed applications using *Options/Set Up Applications....* In the following section, we'll explain some options for solving this problem.

Installing existing applications with the Program Manager

Installing existing applications in the Program Manager is entirely different. The Program Manager is much better suited for installing a single program. Essentially, an icon is created, for the application, in one of the groups of the Program Manager.

These icons contain information that makes it easy to call the programs. This is similar to calling a batch file in MS-DOS. As a batch file can change to a special directory and start the desired program, you can start an application from the Program Manager by clicking on the application's icon.

Steps for setting up programs in the Program Manager

To include a Windows application on the file server as an icon in a group, perform the following steps:

- Open the desired group or select it as an icon in the Program Manager.
- Use *New...* from the *File* menu of the Program Manager. Select the *Program Item* option button and press Enter.
- Enter a title for the application in the *Description:* text box. This title will appear under the icon later.
- Enter a command line for starting the program. If the program isn't in your current user directory (F:\USER\MILLER) and you don't enter the program directory as a start or work directory, then you must specify the complete path (here's an example of Word 5.5's path):

```
F:\PROG\WORD\WORD.EXE
```

Start directory and shortcut key

- Enter a default directory in the *Working Directory:* text box. This assigns the application a working directory. Don't use the current program directories on the file server for storing documents (and grant ReadOnly rights). Instead, use separate data directories. Windows 3.1 provides outstanding support for this separation by allowing you to enter a special data directory here, such as F:\USER\LETTERS. This directory would then automatically be used for storing Word data.
- The *Shortcut Key:* text box lets you specify a key combination for quickly changing to this running application.
- The *Run Minimized* check box gives you the option of starting the application in Minimized form.

Once you've entered the information, press Enter. A notice appears, informing you that the specified path is pointing to a file that may no longer be available at later Windows sessions, and asking whether you still want to create the icon. Click on Yes because if the application is no longer available, then Windows won't be available either, since essential parts of Windows are located on the file server.

However, the problem of the different drive letters with the server is more important. In a Novell network, you can assign different drive letters to different server paths. If these drive letter assignments change over the course of time, or even single letters are no longer available, you'll encounter problems when you start applications; Windows simply won't be able to find the programs or PIF files. The following example illustrates this problem:

Setting up a program

Drive	Allocation	Description
F:	SERVER_1/SYS	Root directory on the server
X:	SERVER_1/SYS:P ROG	Program directory
Y:	SERVER_1/SYS:P UBLIC	Directory of network commands on the server
Z:	SERVER_1/SYS	Root directory on the server

In Windows the program is defined with the following path using the letter X:

```
X:\WINWORD\WINWORD.EXE
```

After setting up the program:

Drive	Allocation	Description
F:	SERVER_1/SYS	Root directory on the server
Y:	SERVER_1/SYS: PUBLIC	Directory of network commands on the server
Z:	SERVER_1/SYS:	Root directory on the server

The path X:\WINWORD\WINWORD.EXE no longer exists and Windows can no longer start the program. If you used X: to define many programs, a change in allocation would lead to considerable problems.

When setting up the applications, first define a drive letter, whose allocation won't change. Doing this ensures that you can safely use this drive letter to define applications in the Program Manager.

We use F: as our allocation for the root directory of the server:

```
F:      SERVER_1/SYS:
```

Rules for Windows applications on the server

When you run Windows on a workstation in the network, there are several rules you should follow. Otherwise, you may encounter problems that could lead to data loss. The following rules also apply to stand-alone computers:

- Don't switch off the computer while running Windows.
- Don't exit DOS applications from the Control menu by selecting *Settings...* and clicking on the Terminate... button, or by pressing Ctrl+Alt+Del and then Enter. This may not properly save the files generated by the application. Instead, use the appropriate command or menu in the program.

Rules for network operation

There are some additional rules for the network:

- Don't log out while working on a version of Windows that was started from the server. Windows obtains all of its programs and most of its data from the file server and a log out immediately locks all access to any files still open. So, you can no longer save any data. Occasionally you can at least exit Windows, but in many cases the computer will crash when you try to exit. All unsaved data and all modified settings are lost.

  This is especially dangerous when you enter DOS from Windows (i.e., using the MS-DOS prompt). A solution to this problem is to call Windows from a batch file. First this batch file must set an environment variable WINDOWS=TRUE; only then can Windows be started. The Novell LOGOUT command would also have to be replaced by a batch file named LOGOUT.BAT. This batch file would only allow you to log out when a WINDOWS environment variable isn't set. We'll show you the exact procedure later in an example.

- When you log in again within the network, although you're still connected with the network, an automatic log out occurs. For example, if you're connected to the network as MILLER and start the LOGIN command again, a LOGOUT occurs with the consequences we described above. That's why you must prevent unintentional LOGINs from unintentionally logging out. You can use the same trick with the environment variable for a started version of Windows.

How to avoid unintentionally logging in or out:

The following is a very safe method:

1. Windows is started from the WIN.COM file in the user directory. You rename this file to WINCOM.DAT. Here's what it would look like for the user MILLER:

```
F:
CD \USER\MILLER
REN WIN.COM WINCOM.DAT
```

2. Now you cannot start Windows directly. The following batch file, called WIN.BAT in the \USER\MILLER directory, makes it possible to start Windows after setting an environment variable:

```
@ECHO OFF
REM WIN.BAT for starting Windows safely in the network
REM By Manfred Tornsdorf
IF NOT EXIST WIN_.COM GOTO OK
ECHO Warning, last Windows start not properly ended
ECHO There could be TMP files from Windows
ECHO Continue after pressing a key...
PAUSE >NUL
:OK
IF NOT EXIST WIN_.COM REN WINCOM.DAT WIN_.COM
SET WINDOWS=TRUE
WIN_ %1 %2 %3 %4 %5
REN WIN_.COM WINCOM.DAT
SET WINDOWS=
```

3. Rename the LOGOUT.EXE command in the F:\PUBLIC directory to LOGOUT_.EXE.

4. Create the following batch file in F:\PUBLIC:

```
@ECHO OFF
REM LOGOUT.BAT for safe LOGOUT
IF NOT "%WINDOWS%"=="TRUE" GOTO OK
ECHO ^G
ECHO Warning: Windows has not yet been exited
GOTO EXIT
:OK LOGOUT_.EXE
:EXIT
```

5. Rename LOGIN in the same way and create a similar batch file called LOGIN.BAT for safe LOGINs to the network.

Working with program files

A network provides excellent opportunities for protecting data and programs. Many of these options already exist under DOS, but there isn't an easy way to separate access rights by different users.

Protecting program files

Without going into detail about the specific access rights in your network, we can still make some suggestions for managing and protecting program files:

- All Windows users should have read and write access rights in the F:\PROG\WIN Windows directory, but shouldn't have the rights to create directories and delete attributes. You should define a group with the following access rights:

```
SYS:PROG/WIN   [RWOCD S ]
```

  Next, ensure that all Windows users are included in this group. Then set all the files in this directory to Shareable and ReadOnly. This allows several users to share the files, but not delete or modify them:

```
FLAG F:\PROG\WIN S RO
```

- You can also use this mechanism for other directories with other application programs. However, there are some programs that absolutely must change some INI files and either display error messages or even crash if they aren't allowed to change these files. With such programs, simply set all the INI files to changeable later. For all the INI files in the COREL directory, the command line would read:

```
FLAG F:\PROG\COREL\*.INI S RW
```

- Not every user should have access to every program or Windows application. Sometimes this is necessary because of copyright laws. For example, perhaps you haven't purchased a version of a program for every user. A relatively simple lock is to remove the program icon from the Program Manager. Simply delete it in the appropriate group.

  However, this protective measure isn't foolproof because the user can easily add the application again. In such a case, simply remove the program directory from the user's access rights.

  For example, if a user is allowed to work with Windows and Word for Windows, but not with Corel, you can use SYSCON to grant the following access rights to the user:

```
SYS:PROG/WIN   [RWOCD S ]
SYS:PROG/WINWORD       [R O   S ]
SYS:PROG\COREL         [        ]
```

Working with documents

You should also use access rights to documents in the network and for working with Windows. Dividing documents into several access groups and then distributing them to the corresponding directories is a popular method:

Access rights to documents

1. There are data to which only some users have access. For example, this could be the balance sheets of a company or the salaries of all its employees. You could create a directory called \DATA\SECRET for such data. Use the EVERYONE group to deny access to this directory by setting the following access rights for the group:

```
SYS:DATA\SECRET         [          ]
```

The network participants who must access these data obtain an explicit right to them via the appropriate allocation in SYSCON by *User Information* and *Trustee Directory Assignments*.

2. Some data are important to all network participants, but shouldn't be changed. You would keep them in a special directory or directory tree, such as F:\DATA\RESERVE. For example, you could store the originals of texts, as well as finished graphics, in this type of directory. All network participants obtain the right to open the files of this directory (as a group):

```
SYS:DATA/RESERVE        [R O   S ]
```

3. Then there are one or more data directories, in which common data are created and edited. Since several users can share access to the same files, this is where the effectiveness of the network is the highest. However, this is also where the data are in the greatest danger. While the network ensures that two users cannot edit the same text simultaneously, this only applies for programs, such as Word, which keep the text open the entire time as a file. However, even with Word, it would be disastrous if several users made contradictory changes one after the other.

If possible, use the available options in the application for monitoring the data. For example, in Word 5.5 and Word for Windows, you can use the integrated File Manager to determine who may currently edit the text, which version it is, and the author.

Regulating file sharing

If the application doesn't provide such options and you work as a group on documents, you can use a network-capable database such as Superbase. You can create a Superbase file and set up a data record for each document. When someone is editing a document, he/she records it in the Superbase file with information that's similar to the information found in the Word summary info sheet:

Title
: (40 characters) The title contains a short description of the document.

Author
: (40 characters) Information about the author.

Operator
: (20 characters) The persons editing this document.

Keywords
: (80 characters) Terms that identify the document more specifically so you can use the database prompt functions to search for documents that match.

Comment
: A comment on the document (220 characters) that records the special features or current results of the document.

Version number
: Numbering assigned to different versions of a text (10 characters).

4. Also, each network participant should have at least one directory, in which he/she can manage data exclusively. The user should have all the access rights to this directory, while all other users should have only read rights.

Exchanging data between users

5. There should also be a special directory for exchanging data that are only temporarily needed. Otherwise, only the work directory can be used to exchange data because it's the only place where all network users can read and write. Examples of such data are messages in the form of files, or data being copied from one local hard drive to another computer's hard drive using the file server. We use the F:\USER\TMP directory for exchanging files and the F:\USER\UMAIL directory for exchanging message files.

Every network participant receives the following group access rights:

```
SYS:USER/TMP          [RWOCDPSM]
SYS:USER/UMAIL        [RWOCDPSM]
```

Access protection and passwords

Now we'll briefly discuss the problems of access protection for the data of the server. Unfortunately, Windows 3.0 had almost no genuine access restriction. Unlike the DOS-Shell in MS-DOS 4.0, which could deny access to programs and menus, Windows is practically an open system. Anyone connected to the network who runs Windows can start almost any application.

Access protection through screen savers

In Windows 3.1 there is at least one option for restricting access via the supplied screen saver. Some screen savers can automatically protect the computer with a password. When the screen saver switches on, the only way to access the computer is by entering the password.

This form of protection is especially important when you temporarily leave a computer that's switched on and logged into the network. For example, suppose that you started several applications under Windows 3.1 and are currently working on a project that requires data exchange. If you must leave the computer unattended but don't use any protective measures, it would be possible to access the file server without the password. However, it's inconvenient to close all applications, save all unsaved data, exit Windows, log out, and then log back in a few minutes later.

Installing a screen saver with a password

To install a screen saver with password protection, start the Control Panel and double-click the *Desktop* icon. The *Screen Saver* option lists a display of all available screen savers, of which all but the first have a password option. The *Delay:* text box lets you set the time period that must elapse without mouse/keyboard activity before Windows enables the screen saver. To protect a network computer, you could set this delay to 5 minutes.

Click [Setup...] to make different changes to the screen saver. You can also select a password for the screen saver. To do this, check the *Password Protected* check box under *Password Options* and then select [Set Password...]. For security reasons, the characters of the password are displayed only as asterisks. So, you must enter the password twice to ensure there aren't any typing errors. If there is already a password, before setting a new one you must enter the old password in the *Old Password:* text box.

After confirming with the [OK] button you can test the screen saver by clicking [Test] in the *Desktop* window. You can cancel the screen saver by moving the mouse or pressing a key, but you must first specify the correct password.

Usually the screen saver switches on only when a DOS application isn't running in the foreground. If necessary, enable the Program Manager or some other Windows application.

Occasionally you can encounter problems when using passwords with the screen saver if a task is running in multitasking and the screen saver switches on after a while (while the task is running). We had problems copying files to a diskette and formatting a diskette when we set the screen saver with a very short delay (1 min).

31.7 The File Manager and the Network

Working with the File Manager in the network is the same as working with it on a stand-alone computer. The additional drive letters of the network appear in the drive line and are displayed differently than the disk drives or hard drives. However, you can use the network drives the same way as the other drives.

So, in this section we'll discuss only the File Manager's role in the network.

Special features of network drives

If you select a network drive in File Manager, the network name appears to the right of the drive icons in place of the disk name. This is especially useful when you use the Novell MAP command to assign a drive letter to a path to the file server. Then the File Manager shows the name, volume (partition), and the path along with the drive letter. The following is an example of what this looks like:

```
Z: SERVER_1/SYS:PUBLIC
```

In contrast to this, a disk name of a local drive appears in brackets:

```
C: [HARDDISK_C]
```

You cannot perform some operations with a network drive. For example, you cannot format or name disks. Of course, you cannot do these things from DOS either.

Connecting to a network

You can create new network drive letters with the File Manager. From DOS you would use the Novell MAP command to reproduce a new drive letter to a network path. In File Manager, you use the *Disk/Network Connections...* command.

This process is much more convenient with many networks than with MAP, because Windows can display the entire directory structure. So, it's easy to select the desired directory. Also,

Windows remembers the connections and automatically resets them the next time you start Windows. This means that you only need to use File Manager once to connect to a second server. As long as you don't break this connection in the File Manager, the second server will automatically be connected to the first file server each time you start Windows.

Problems changing to the next highest directory

If a network directory is selected, many programs have difficulty changing to the next highest directory when loading or saving files. This is because the two special entries "." and ".." are automatically included in all subdirectories on a local DOS disk. Since directory management on a network drive is completely different, these two special entries aren't located on a network drive.

You're probably wondering how to change to the next highest directory without "..". Fortunately, many new programs have a different way of displaying the directories that can be selected. All directories between the root directory and the current directory are individually listed and selectable. An example of this type of program is Microsoft Works for Windows.

If ".." is missing

To move to the next highest directory, simply double-click to enable the directory. If an application doesn't support this new technique, simply preset the file name in the root directory by specifying the drive, root directory, and wildcards:

```
F:\*.*
```

Then look for the proper subdirectory in the root directory you just enabled.

It's much easier to display the additional dots in a Novell network. The solution is provided by Novell and consists of writing the following to a configuration file called SHELL.CFG:

```
SHOW DOTS = ON
```

The network shell NET5.COM automatically runs the SHELL.CFG file every time you start the network if it's in the current directory. If the IPX and NET5 are processed in the root directory of the C: hard drive in an AUTOEXEC.BAT and this is the current directory, then the SHELL.CFG file must also be in the root directory.

As soon as the network shell starts with this configuration, it automatically inserts the two dots ".." for the next highest directory for the appropriate search instructions (Search First and Search Next).

Connecting to a network

You can use the File Manager to make a connection to a network. There are three very important applications:

1. You're working with a local version of Windows (i.e., you don't start Windows from the network, but from the local hard drive). To connect to the existing network, select the *Disk/Network Connections...* command in File Manager and set the desired connection. Windows automatically makes the connection the next time you start it. After selecting the Browse... button, a display of the logged in Server/Volumes appears. After clicking the desired volume, a list of the directories for that volume appears. If you still haven't logged in to the file server, then both split windows will be empty:

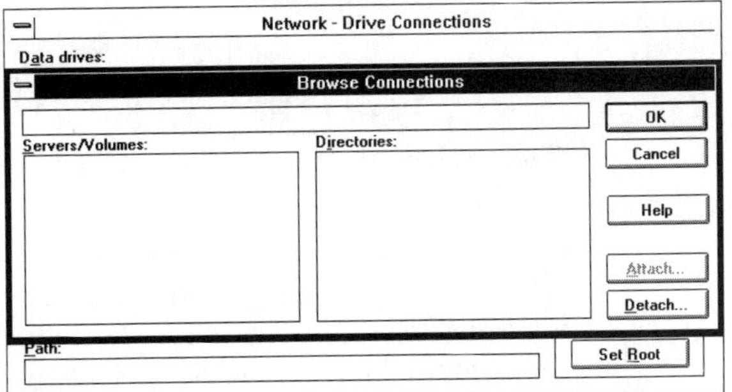

Still no connection to the file server

We'll explain this process in detail under item 3.

2. You're connected to the network and want to use another path under a new drive letter. Enable the *Disk/Network Connections...* command in the File Manager and click the Browse... button after clicking the desired drive letter. The *Browse Connections* window appears. You can set the file server in the left-hand box and the directory path in the right-hand box. After choosing OK, the path is entered after the previously selected drive letter, next to *Network Path*. You don't have to choose a password if there is already a valid connection to the file server.

3. To connect with a new file server, after selecting a drive letter from the list, click Browse..., and then click the Attach button in the *Browse Connections* dialog window. You can click Attach only if there are file servers connected to the network, to which you haven't yet logged in. Then a dialog box for logging in appears with the following three text boxes:

File server

You can specify the name of a file server here or choose one from the list.

User name:

Specify your valid user name for this file server here.

Password:

Enter the correct password here. The password is not displayed on the screen.

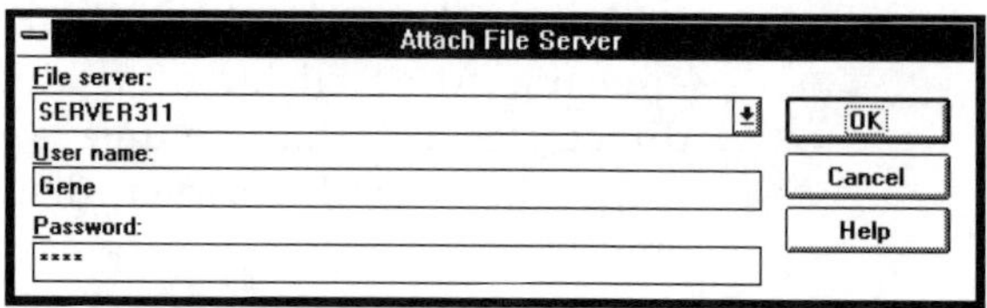

Logging in to the file server

Then select the OK button. The file server appears with the available volumes on the left side of the screen. The directories of the volume appear on the right side of the screen. Now you can select the directory, to which you want to assign a drive letter. Without assigning a drive letter, it's impossible to access the server. You may have already logged in to the server, but drive mapping hasn't assigned a drive letter to a path on the file server.

Assigning a drive letter

For example, select the root directory. Then choose the OK button and use the Map button to assign the drive letter to the set drive.

Although the connections to the network are immediately saved in the WIN.INI file in the [Network] section, the passwords you entered are not saved.

```
[Network]
X:=SERVER_1/SYS:PUBLIC
Y:=SERVER_1/SYS:MAIL
```

Disconnecting from a network

It's as easy to cancel an existing drive allocation with the File Manager. To do this, select *Disk/Network Connections...* in the File Manager and select the desired connection in the *Network - Drive Connections* window. Click on the Map Delete button to break the connection. This only cancels the assignment of a drive to a path on the server (Drivemapping). After that, the drive letter can no longer be used. However, you're still logged in to the network.

To end the entire connection to the file server (i.e., to log out), select *Disk/Network Connections...* and then click the Browse... button. Now select the Detach... button. A dialog box appears on the screen, informing you of the possible dangers. You can select the file server in the list and click the OK button to end the connection.

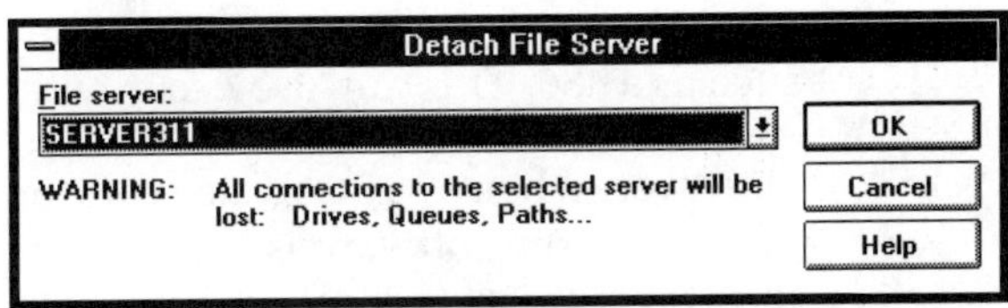

Breaking the connection to the file server

Be careful when detaching a network connection. Under certain circumstances, you could affect Windows' ability to run. If you end the connection to the file server, from which you started Windows, it will be impossible to do any more work. However, you can't do this with the Detach... button. Windows refuses to log off from the file server from which Windows was started. There are also other situations, in which detaching a connection can cause serious problems.

31.8 Networks and Printing

The Windows Print Manager provides several options for controlling document printouts. These options are also available in the network and the Print Manager even supports network-oriented printing options.

The advantages of a network printer

As we mentioned, it's also possible to print in Windows without special network options. However, now we'll discuss the special options for printing in the network.

The advantage of using a network printer is that all the workstations can print on it as if it were connected to their local computers. However, it would be too expensive to have a separate printer for each workstation instead of having one common network printer.

Also, a network printer automatically has the ability to manage print jobs in a waiting queue. While this is also possible with PRINT in MS-DOS or with Print Manager on local printers, the processing speed decreases significantly. However, when the file server receives print jobs, it's as though your workstation were connected to a super fast printer. The printing speed is influenced more by the speed of the printing software than it is by the network.

Also, the network barely loses any speed during printing. Anyone who has ever printed in Word 5.5 in the print queue will certainly remember how slow Word 5.5 becomes, even on very fast computers, such as a 486. This can also occur with PRINT under MS-DOS.

However, when you use a network printer, the printing process on the part of the software is very fast, and during the printout phase that follows on the network printer, you can continue working without any loss of speed.

☞ The Windows 3.1 Print Manager is much faster than it was in Windows 3.0. This is partially because Windows 3.1 can print directly to a port without accessing DOS interrupts. There are no compatibility problems because you can switch off this setting in the Print Manager.

Print Manager is now faster

Also, network print jobs from the File Manager can be transferred directly to the network print spooler, which can also contribute to increasing the speed.

In the following section, we use an HP LaserJet III, connected to the LPT3 port on the file server.

How to install a network printer

The following is an overview of the steps for installing a network printer:

- Connect the printer to the file server with a printer cable.
- If necessary, use the Novell PRINTCON command to set up the printer configuration.
- Redirect printer output to the workstations with the Novell CAPTURE command (for DOS and Windows) or with the Windows Control Panel (for Windows only).
- Set up the printer under Windows 3.1 if necessary.

We won't discuss the first two steps here. However, let's take a closer look at redirecting printer output.

Redirecting print jobs for DOS and Windows

To redirect print jobs under DOS and Windows to the network printer, select the Novell CAPTURE command. You can either do this in the workstation's AUTOEXEC.BAT file or add it to each user's login script.

As its name suggests, the CAPTURE command captures all sent data and passes the data to the file server for printing.

There are several setting options for CAPTURE that we won't discuss at this time. Use the following command line to print all output printer data on the workstation on LPT3: in the first queue (PRINTQ_0) on the network printer without automatic form feed and banner:

```
CAPTURE /NB /No FormFeed /L=3 /Queue=PRINTQ_0
```

We purposely selected the LPT3: (/L=3) printer port on the workstations, so we could continue operating existing local printers with LPT1: and reserve LPT2: for a label printer.

If you send data to the second parallel port in MS-DOS, they automatically go to the network printer.

This mechanism also works in Windows 3.1 if you select CAPTURE before starting Windows (in the AUTOEXEC.BAT file or from the login script).

Redirecting print in Windows

If you operate your workstation exclusively with Windows, you don't need to use CAPTURE. Instead, you can redirect print directly in Windows. Actually, this is no longer "redirecting" because in Windows you're free to send printed output to a port, a file, or a network printer. So, if possible, use the Windows Print Manager.

To print to a network printer from Windows, you should use the Control Panel in the Main group. Double-click the Printers icon to display the *Printers* dialog box. If necessary, you must set the desired printer type by clicking on Add>> and installing the printer (refer to Chapter 16 for more information).

After selecting the Connect... button, the *Connect* dialog box appears with a list of all available printer ports. Windows indicates whether a port is local and available in the computer or whether it is local and not present.

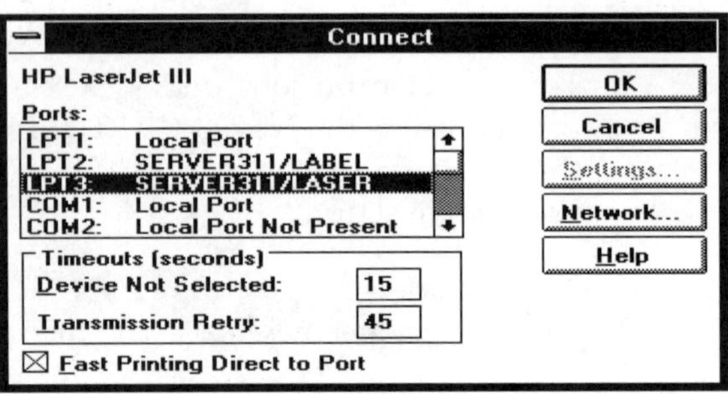

Local port display

Now you can connect a printer port directly to a network queue of the print server. To do this, enable the Network... button to display the available network connections. Select the desired printer port and select the desired print queue from the list of available queues. In our example, you would select LPT3: and SERVER311.

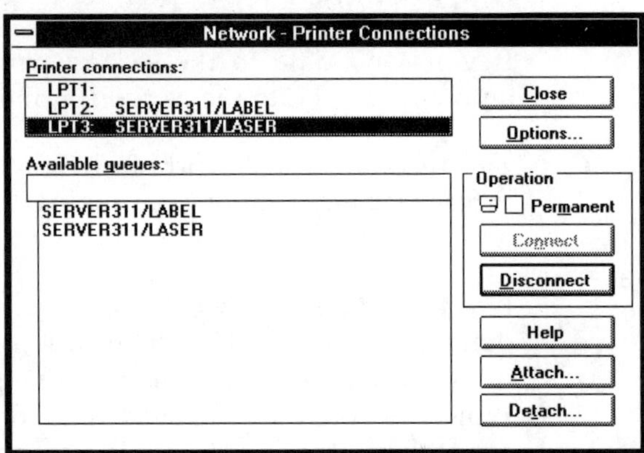

Connecting to the network printer queue

Then you can make the connection by clicking the Connect button and clicking Close to exit the dialog box. This connection is then listed under *Ports*. Click the OK button. Click on Close to close the *Printers* dialog box. Now you can use the network printer in all of your Windows applications.

Choosing local printers or network printers

To print from a program to a local printer connected to the workstation, you should select the print setup menu of the application and then make the local printer active.

Then, to print to the network printer again later, repeat the process with the set network printer. You should enable the Print

Manager so the Print Manager can control the printout. Use the print queue of the Print Manager to print to the local printer. For printing in the network, run the Print Manager and select *Options/Network Settings...* to enable the *Print Net Jobs Direct* check box. This is faster than the regular print queue, and relieves Windows of the task of printer management.

Managing the network printer and the print jobs

The Print Manager offers several options for managing the network printer and the print jobs:

- Connecting to, and disconnecting from, a network printer.
- Displaying all the print jobs of a print queue in the network.
- Managing print jobs in a separate queue before sending them to the print server. This lets Windows relieve the file server/print server.

Usually the available options mainly depend on the existing network operating system. The functions we describe are based on a Novell network, but other networks could vary in procedure and volume.

Connecting to, and disconnecting from, a network printer

We have already explained in detail how to connect to a network printer. To disconnect from a printer, run the Print Manager and select *Options/Network Connections....* The *Network - Printer Connections* dialog box appears. Select the appropriate network connection and click on the [Disconnect] button. Then click on [Close] to exit.

Network print settings

You can change two settings for printing in the network with the *Options/Network Settings...* command:

1. *Update Network Display*:
   If you enable this check box, the Print Manager will continuously display the current status of the print queue on the print server. Both the Print Manager and the server are involved in this process. If this check box is disabled, the Print Manager treats the display like a local printer.

2. *Print Net Jobs Direct*:
   If you enable this check box, the printout passes directly to the print server queue. This process is faster than having the Print Manager receive the data in its own queue. The print jobs in the print server queue can

still be displayed with Print Manager. If this check box is disabled, the Print Manager buffers the data. While this relieves the burden to the network, it could slow down printing and interaction with Windows.

Displaying a selected print queue

You can display the contents and status of the print queue at any time in Print Manager. To do this, select the desired print queue with the mouse and then choose the *Selected Net Queue...* command in the *View* menu.

Tips on printing in the network

Now we'll present some tips on printing in the network. Printing is a lot easier and faster if you use the options available in Windows 3.1.

Printing with Print Manager

You should use the Print Manager to print data in Windows. Perhaps you've never used the Print Manager and don't think you should change now. The print server may be sufficient for controlling print jobs.

However, accessing Print Manager on the server print queue is much easier from Windows than if you first started a DOS task by calling PCONSOLE. There's almost no loss in time or performance if you select *Print Net Jobs Direct* in the *Options Network Settings...* menu and check the *Fast Printing Direct to Port* box in the *Options/Printer Setup.../Connect* dialog box. Then the Print Manager doesn't buffer network print jobs, but routes them directly to the print server. Also, Windows bypasses the interrupts when printing and uses the network options directly.

Rerouting the printer port with Windows

Use the Windows options for setting up a printer port to the network printer. Using Windows is much more convenient than working with the Novell CAPTURE command. Also, you save the memory that CAPTURE would use in DOS as a TSR program.

The right setting for task switching

Determine your own optimum task division. For example, the burden on our network is no more than one third; usually it's only a few percentage points. You should relieve Windows from as many extra tasks as possible. For example, you could have the Print Manager print directly to the network queue. You could also eliminate the permanent update of the display of the queue in the printer server (*Options/Network Settings.../Update Network Display*), because it's time-consuming. Instead, select the queue and choose *Selected Net Queue...* from the *View* menu when you want to display the queue. You could also leave the option switched on, but minimize the Print Manager, since it doesn't have to update the display when it's minimized.

31.9 Exchanging Messages and Data

One of the advantages of using a network instead of a stand-alone computer is that the users can interact. For example, if a school has a network, both the teachers and administrative staff can access student data. So, any information, such as a student's address, can be automatically updated for all users.

Different departments in a company also have to access the same data. This prevents Meyer, in the Marketing Department, from promising 20 machines to a customer, if Miller already sold those 20 machines to another customer. All the network users must access the same inventory data.

The features mentioned in the above examples are automatically provided by a good network operating system. A database or an accounting program isn't a network-capable program unless it automatically handles such problems or provides some solutions.

Cooperation among network participants

However, problems can occur among network users while working on projects. Until recently, both Windows and Novell couldn't provide easy solutions to these problems. In this section, we'll present some practical examples of data exchange among several users. These examples and solutions can easily be adapted to your own situation.

How to organize data exchange among users

What do you do when user MEYER changes the CONFIG.SYS file on the local hard drive to get 50K more available memory, and SMITH wants to do the same? Or perhaps someone has created some nice looking icon files, and everyone else on the network wants to have those files. Both cases involve exchanging data among users.

Requirements for data exchange

The following are important factors:

- All participants must have unrestricted access to a common directory, so one person can place the data there and anyone else who is interested can retrieve the same data.
- The files in this directory should be automatically removed from the directory as quickly as possible, so data garbage doesn't consume valuable file server and backup capacities.
- A user must be able to inform all the other users that the data are now available. In other words, a user must be able to send messages to other users.

Practical directory structures and access rights are very important for smooth data exchange. Unfortunately, there is no network clipboard prepared for network users. Instead, you must make your own clipboard.

If you followed our suggestions on directory structures earlier, then you set up an F:\USER\TMP directory for exchanging files and an F:\USER\UMAIL directory for exchanging message files and assigned the following group rights to all the relevant users (e.g., by defining a network group):

```
F:\USER/TMP    [RWOCDPSM]
F:\USER/UMAIL  [RWOCDPSM]
```

Theoretically, you can already use F:\USER\TMP for data exchange. (\USER\UMAIL is for exchanging special messages.) However, there are a few things you should think about and discuss with all network participants:

- Files in F:\USER\TMP can be deleted at any time. This means that you can only keep copies or unimportant files in this directory. Delete all the files in this directory whenever they take up too much space on the file server or clutter up the directory.

- Do not use F:\USER\TMP as a temporary directory for DOS or Windows. In other words, you cannot set the TMP (SET TMP=) or TEMP (SET TEMP=) environment variable to this directory. Such a directory contains important temporary files. If you destroy these files, you could be losing data. Use a directory on your local hard drive (SET TEMP=C:\TEMP) or in your user directory (SET TEMP=F:\USER\MILLER\TEMP) for TEMP.

- If someone wants to send data to another user, he/she must copy it to F:\USER\TMP and sends the user a message. Of course, the receiver must copy the data to a "safe" directory as soon as possible, so they are not lost the next time the files in F:\USER\TMP are deleted. It's best to use the File Manager in Windows 3.1 and move the data with the mouse. This is not only quick and easy, but also the data disappear from the directory.

How to organize message exchange among users

A network provides an electronic way to exchange information an` make contacts. However, in Versions 2.15 and 3.11 of Novell NetWare you can only send messages to users who are connected to the network. If the user isn't currently logged in, you'll receive an error message, and must try again later.

In this section, we'll show you how to send "direct messages" and present a simple message system that notifies a user the next time he/she logs in to the network.

Direct messages with SEND and SESSION

Novell provides two options for sending messages to another user or all members of a group. These messages appear at the bottom line on a DOS screen and (if everything is properly set) in a separate window in Windows, and can be up to 45 characters long.

Sending messages with SEND

To send a message to a user with SEND, first ensure that the user is logged in to the network. To do this, go to DOS and enter the USERLIST command.

```
USERLIST
```

Next, a list of all users currently active in the network appears. The information about your own user ID has an asterisk next to the user name (in case you have forgotten your name or you have logged in to the network several times).

```
User Information for Server SERVER311
Connection  User Name        Login Time
----------  --------------   --------------------
     1        MILLER         6.12.1991    10:23
     2      * SUPERVISOR     6.12.1991    10:02
```

To send MILLER a message, enter the following command line:

```
SEND "Is the text finished?" TO MILLER
```

A message appears, indicating the file server and user to whom the message was sent, or else you see an error message if the user isn't connected to the network. In the DOS task of MILLER, the following message appears at the bottom line of the screen after a warning beep:

```
>> From SUPERVISOR[2]: Is the text finished? (CTRL-ENTER to
                                                 clear)
```

As soon as MILLER presses Ctrl + Enter, the message disappears, and he can respond to the message.

Receiving messages in Windows

To receive a message in Windows 3.0, you had to take a few precautions. For example, you had to start a special program called NWPOPUP.EXE with the following line in the WIN.INI file:

```
RUN=NWPOPUP.EXE
```

It's no longer necessary to do this in Windows 3.1. The existing network driver for Novell NetWare now handles this. However, you must be able to distinguish the various screen settings in Windows. As long as you're running a DOS task in Windows in text mode (such as the DOS prompt or a Word 5.5 screen), you'll also receive the same message at the bottom of the screen, as though Windows wasn't even present.

However, if the Windows Desktop is active, you'll see a separate window with the network message:

Getting a network message in Windows

The way you receive the message depends on which task is active and what the screen display of the active task looks like.

If you installed a screen saver, receiving a message on this computer ends screen blanking. If a password is still active, the dialog box for entering the password appears first. If you weren't even logged in when the message was sent, you won't receive a message; instead, the sender receives an error message.

Enabling and disabling messages

Use the Network icon in the Control Panel to enable message reception. You'll see a window containing the option for enabling and disabling messages. This window also used to have the options for logging in and logging out from a file server. Now these options are in File Manager in the *Disk* menu under *Network Connections...*.

To switch off network messages, select *Messages disabled*. After confirming your selection with the OK button, you'll no longer receive any direct messages. To switch network messages back on, select *Messages enabled*. Messages accumulated during the Windows session that haven't yet been displayed will then appear on the screen.

Sending messages without calling a DOS task

Always having to open a DOS prompt before sending a message can be annoying. The PIF Editor offers a simple solution:

Use the PIF Editor to create the following SEND.PIF file:

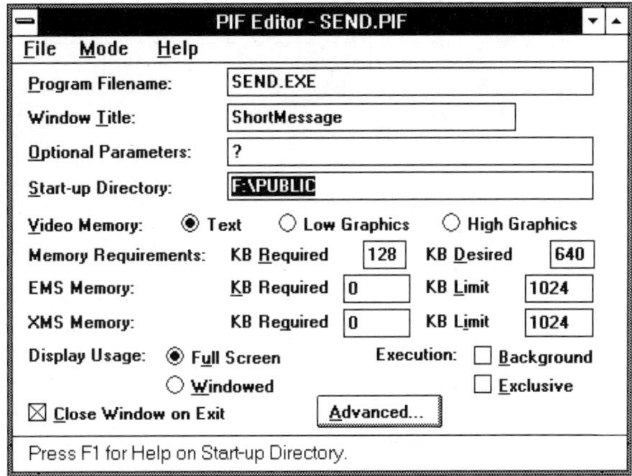

SEND.PIF—an easy way to send messages

Then use *New* from the *File* menu in the Program Manager to create a new icon called Send Message to start this PIF file.

When you start this application, a window appears with the title *Send Message* and the prompt: *Parameters*. Enter the message in the text box along with the recipient and press Enter:

```
"Is the text finished" To MILLER
```

This automatically starts the Novell SEND command with the correct parameters.

Sending messages with SESSION

A disadvantage of using SEND is that you must enter awkward parameter lines and can make mistakes in specifying the user name. The error message that Novell sends disappears with the message window. You can prevent this from happening by disabling the *Close Window on Exit* setting for SEND.PIF in the PIF Editor, but then you must close the DOS window on the desktop. This still doesn't make selecting users or groups any safer.

It's much safer to use the Novell SESSION command, which you can start in the F:\PUBLIC directory. This command has a menu item called *User List*. Select this, choose a name from the list, and then use *Send Message* to send the user a message.

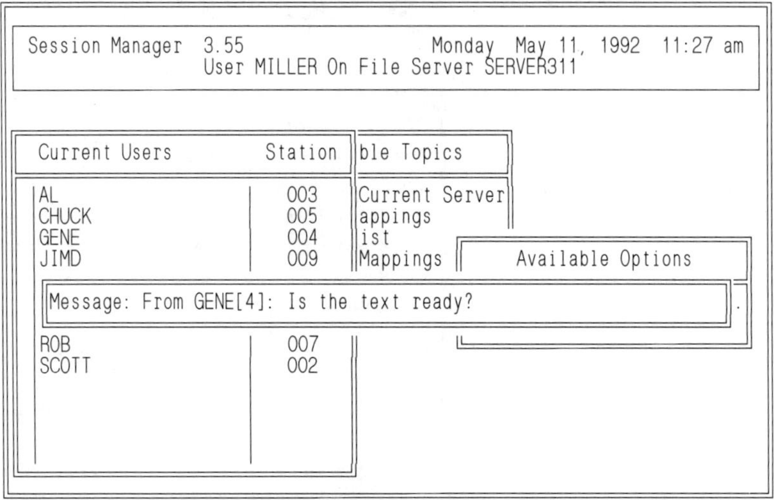

Sending messages with SESSION

The advantage of SESSION is not only that you can comfortably and easily select the name from a list, but you can also do the same for a group of users. This makes it very easy to exchange messages within a project group.

To exit SESSION, press Esc several times or press Alt + F10.

Delivering MAIL

One of the biggest disadvantages of SEND and SESSION is that you can send only relatively short messages. The message must fit in one screen line, including the sender's name and the note about clearing the message. Although this does save unnecessary typing, such short messages are usually insufficient. Therefore, you must either:

- Go to the other network participant and finish the message.

or

- Send off multiple messages.

Of course, neither of these solutions isn't really suitable. So we wrote our own application, called MAIL.EXE.

What MAIL does

To give you an idea of what our program can do, we've listed the options below:

- MAIL is a genuine Windows application.
- MAIL allows easy selection of a user name from a list.

- MAIL allows you to enter long messages within a window and then select a menu item to send the messages to selected receivers. The receiver receives a short message telling him that he can view the entire message with MAIL.
- MAIL also lets you read and edit a received message immediately. You can then send the modified message back to the sender.
- Also, MAIL lets you send short direct messages similar to SEND messages.
- The MAIL program manages message texts as .TXT files with user names, and places them in the G:\ directory. A message text sent to SUPERVISOR would be located on the file server under:

```
G:\SUPERVIS.TXT
```

If you receive a message and don't want to start MAIL immediately to read the message, you should at least copy it to your USER directory, since the file in the TMP directory could be deleted at any time.

The program supports the Clipboard, so you can copy messages to the Clipboard and paste them to the text window from the Clipboard.

How to use MAIL

After you start MAIL, you'll see the following screen:

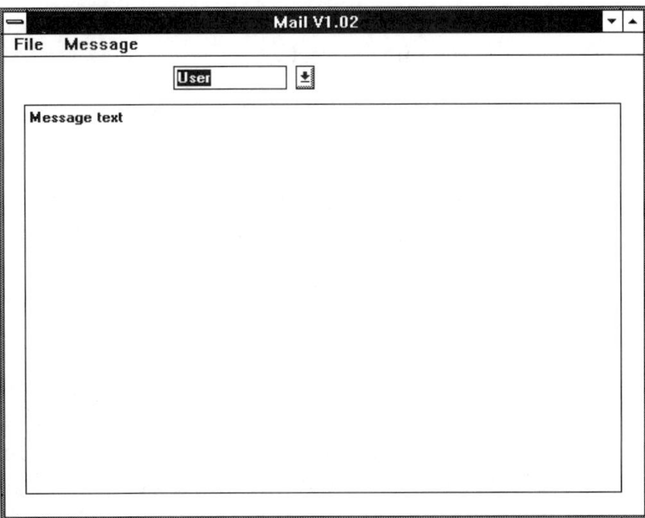

The MAIL application

At the top screen border you'll see the two menus, *File* and *Message*. Use the *File* menu to select *Exit*, returning you to Windows. The *Message* menu lets you send and receive messages. There is a text box for the user name, and you can select the name from drop-down list box connected to the text box. The majority of the screen contains the document window, in which you can enter your own messages or display messages from other users.

To send a message

- Type the message text in the document window.
- Select the name of the receiver from the drop-down list box, or type the name yourself.
- Select *Send* from the *Message* menu.

Then the message text is placed in the G:\ directory under the user name and SEND sends a message to the user, stating there is a MAIL message for him/her. The receiver can now start MAIL to read the message.

If you're writing a long message and want to save it during your work without sending it, enable *Message/Send* and click on [Cancel]. MAIL saves the text without sending it.

To read a message

Use the following procedure to read a message that you've just received:

- Start the MAIL program
- Select your user name from the drop-down list box, or type the name yourself.
- Select *Message/Read*. The message appears immediately in the document window.

Reading other messages

You can also use MAIL to read other messages. To do this, simply select the desired user name and then select *Message/Read*. You can also send such a message (e.g., after modifying the message) to any user by setting the user name and selecting *Message/Send* to send the message in the document window.

Sending a short message

You can also use MAIL to send short messages quickly and easily, similar to SEND. The advantage of this option is that the receiver doesn't have to start MAIL to read the message, but can read it directly from the screen.

To send a short message:

- Select the receiver's name from the drop-down list box, or type the name yourself.
- Select *Message/Quickmail*
- Type the text in the window that appears and click on OK to send the short message.

Short messages are sent only to users, not saved as files.

Providing a user with data using MAIL

MAIL supports clipping, copying, and pasting data from the Clipboard. This makes it easier to type long messages, by using your favorite editor, (such as Notepad) and then paste the text to the MAIL document window from the Clipboard.

Also, you can use the Clipboard to exchange data easily, without having to create a file in the G:\ directory first and then send a message.

For example, MEYER is writing a newspaper article and has inserted a risqué story at the beginning as an "attention grabber". Now he wants SMITH to browse through this passage. However, he doesn't want to exit the word processor so SMITH can access the file. MEYER also doesn't want to copy the passage from the text to a separate text file, give it a name, and store it in the G:\ directory.

With MAIL, the procedure would be as follows:

- MEYER selects the passage in the word processor and copies it to the Clipboard with Ctrl+ Ins.
- Then he starts MAIL (if he hasn't already done this) and pastes the text in the document window. He types a short sentence above it:

```
Please proofread the passage
```

and sends the message to SMITH.

- SMITH is working on a spreadsheet and receives the message that he's got a MAIL message. He starts MAIL, selects his own user name from the list, and selects *Message/Read* .
- MEYER's request appears on the screen, followed by the passage. SMITH reads the text and determines there are a few corrections needed.
- SMITH copies the text to his word processor from the Clipboard and makes the corrections. Then he copies the text

back to the MAIL program and changes the address at the beginning of the text.

- Finally he selects MEYER as the user, then selects *Message/Send*. After clicking on OK, the edited message with the corrections in the text returns to MEYER.

The Visual Basic MAIL program

When you use MAIL in your network, remember the following:

- Most likely you'll use other user names. Simply change the lines starting at Sub Form_Load.

- If you use a different temporary directory on the server, you'll have to make the corresponding changes to the path, G:\. Find the path specifications for "G:\" in the printed program and insert the correct path for your system.

```
Rem Mail - Messages within a network
Rem Copyright Manfred Tornsdorf

Sub Form_Load ()
Names.AddItem "Supervisor"
Names.AddItem "User"
Names.AddItem "Mike"
Names.AddItem "Gene"
Names.AddItem "George"
Names.AddItem "Everybody"
Names.ListIndex = 1
User$ = Names.Text
End Sub

Sub Names_Change ()
User$ = Names.Text
End Sub

Sub Names_LostFocus ()
User$ = Names.Text
End Sub

Sub MessageText_Change ()
MMessage$ = MessageText.Text
End Sub

Sub Message_Send_Click ()
NDir$ = "G:\"
NFile1$ = NDir$ + Left$(User$, 8) + ".TXT"
Open NFile1$ For Output As #1
Print #1, MMessage$
Close #1
I% = MsgBox("Send the message?", 1, "")

If I% = 1 Then
 Print "Sending message"
 MCmd$ = "Send " + Chr$(34) + "Message - MAIL V1.0 " +
Chr$(34) + " TO " + User$
```

```
I% = Shell(MCmd$)
End If
End Sub

Sub File_Exit_Click ()
Rem Print "End Program"
End
End Sub

Sub Message_Read_Click ()
NDir$ = "G:\"
NFile1$ = NDir$ + Left$(User$, 8) + ".TXT"
MMessage$ = ""
Open NFile1$ For Input As #1
While Not EOF(1)
   N$ = Input$(1, #1)
   MMessage$ = MMessage$ + N$
Wend
Close #1
MessageText.Text = MMessage$
End Sub

Sub Message_Quickmail_Click ()
MMessage$ = InputBox$("Please type the message:",
"QuickMail", "")
If Len(MMessage$) > 0 Then
   MCmd$ = "Send " + Chr$(34) + MMessage$ + Chr$(34) + " TO
" + User$
   I% = Shell(MCmd$, 4)
Else
   MsgBox "No message entered"
End If
End Sub
```

32. Windows Technology

No computer's an island

Early PC's suffered from a form of isolation. Until recently, a PC could run only one application at a time. As hardware became more sophisticated and powerful, the PC adopted methods that were available only to mainframes and minicomputer systems. In keeping with the hardware development, Windows offers many innovations to users, such as multitasking and other techniques.

No computer's an island

32.1 Data Exchange Between Programs: OLE and DDE

Programs work simultaneously

After working with Windows for awhile, you may find that accessing multiple applications becomes quite addicting. Since Windows allows you to execute several different tasks simultaneously, you must directly process the data created by these applications.

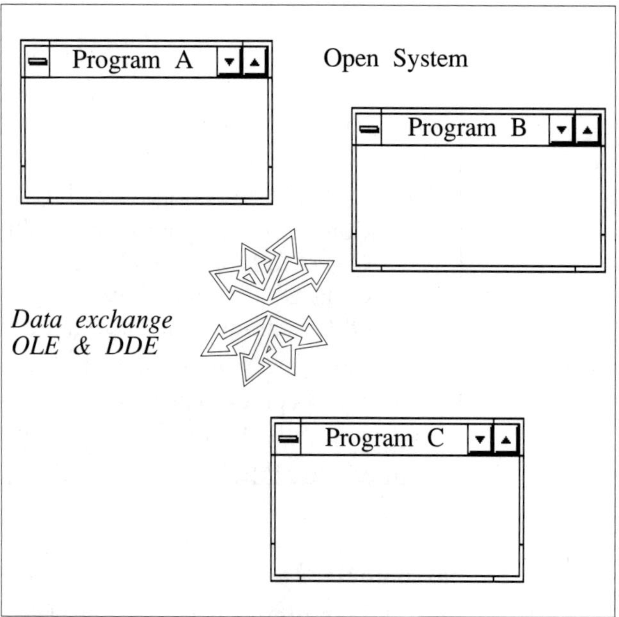

Open computer system

Open computer system

In commercial computer systems, often several different programs must be executed simultaneously to control an operation. A good example of this is an automobile. A car contains many different parts, each made or assembled by various people. These parts must fit together perfectly to create a fully functional automobile (something any consumer can appreciate).

A person who bought a subcompact car would be happy to find that an extremely powerful engine was accidentally installed in the car. However, a person who bought a sports car would be angry if he/she found a 75 horsepower compact car engine. This illustrates that when parallel processes are used to reach a goal, clear, detailed, and explicit communication is extremely important.

Communication problems

Windows features many different programs developed by many different companies. For these programs to communicate with each other, their developers must decide on a communication standard, which will be followed by these programs. Unfortunately, manufacturers don't like to work with their competitors. So, a third party sets a standard that all the other manufacturers can use.

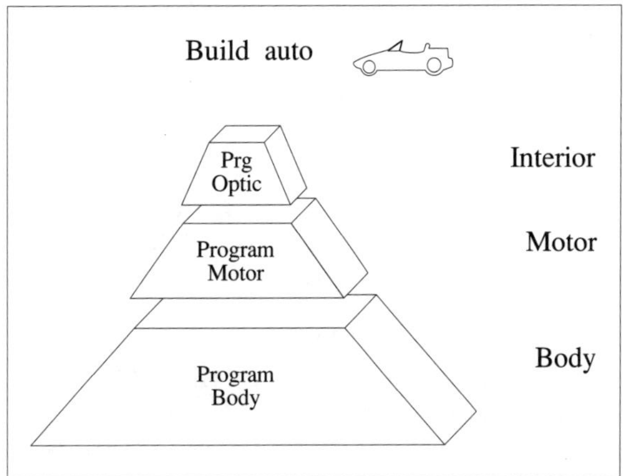

Sharing tasks

Standard protocol

You may think that shared files would be the most logical step. Although this would work, it would require large amounts of execution time and a standard protocol wouldn't be available.

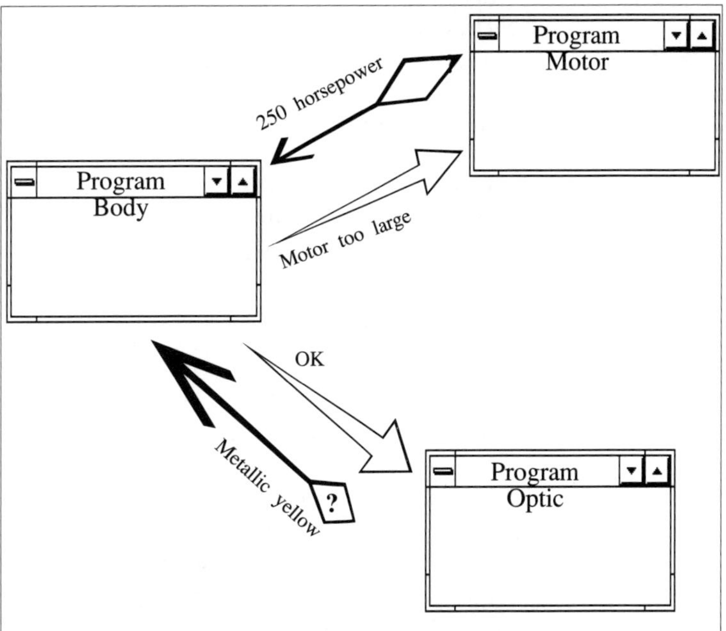

Program to program communication

A solution to this problem involves sharing information within the computer's memory. This solution is called Dynamic Data Exchange (DDE), which is exclusive to Microsoft Windows.

32.2 Communication Between Applications: DDE

DDE

First we'll explain some terms, such as DDE, OLE, protocol, and interface. As we mentioned, the goal is to facilitate communication between programs. This means that these programs will be exchanging data, which may consist of commands and, for example, spreadsheet data. So, the term Dynamic Data Exchange, or DDE is used.

The word "Dynamic" indicates that this exchange can be started and ended at any time. The applications using DDE have a *protocol* or common language. The point at which data passes from one application to another is called the *DDE interface*.

Communication

Under Windows, programs can be executed as part of a larger, intertwined system of loaded applications. Data from different programs can also be used as part of an application.

This cooperation and mutual support is made possible by various Windows components: the Clipboard, shared memory, DDE messages, and OLE. For example, by copying information from a particular program to the Clipboard, you can make this data available to all other active Windows applications. Generally, the Clipboard is used to store only information that's transferred manually and must therefore be temporarily stored.

Shared memory, however, provides a way to exchange data between programs that speak the same language. One technique under Windows uses dynamic link libraries (DLLs). Unfortunately, programs that use shared memory areas to communicate are limited to data exchange within a specific program segment, which is designed specifically for this purpose.

DDE sets standards

We mentioned that Windows DDE uses an official communication protocol based on message exchange. It consists of a collection of messages and data structures, developed specifically for inter-program communication. Since DDE forms a complete and uniform protocol, any program can participate in DDE communication if it adheres to DDE specifications. When this is achieved, DDE fulfills its ultimate purpose: allowing completely different applications to communicate with each other.

OLE simplifies communication

Now, we'll discuss Object Linking and Embedding (OLE). OLE is responsible for permanently linking and embedding objects (documents, files, etc.). To do this, a connection between the client and the server is re-established as soon as an embedded object is re-opened. DDE alone cannot perform this task, since either the user must establish a permanent link, or the application must establish a temporary link.

Use and scope of DDE

Use of DDE

DDE is especially useful when programs are given information independently, without any action from the user.

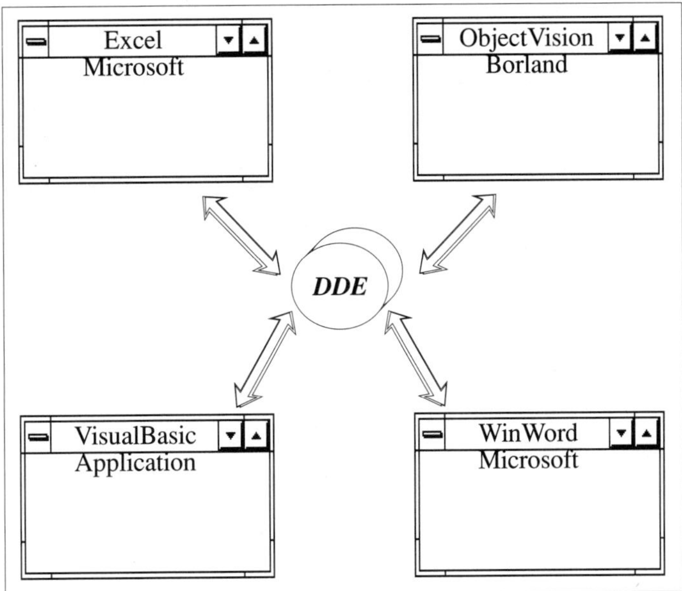

Possible uses of DDE

A few possible uses include:

- Data exchange with spreadsheets, such as Microsoft Excel.
- Data exchange with formula oriented programs, such as Borland Object Vision.
- Data exchange of graphics or text to word processors, such as Microsoft Word for Windows.
- Integrated applications that use standard programs as the basis for extensive calculations.
- Data exchange with different computers, such as SQL servers or mainframe emulators.

DDE access through macro

Most of the applications mentioned above use a macro language to access DDE. Microsoft Excel and Microsoft Word for Windows are two such applications. The following macros, for these two programs, illustrate how macros access DDE:

Establish communication link:

Word for Windows:

```
Channel=DDEInitiate( Application$, Topic$ )
```

Excel:

```
=INITIATE(application,document)
```

Transmit data:

Word for Windows:

```
DDEPoke(channel,itemtext,dataref)
```

Excel:

```
=POKE(channel,itemtext,dataref)
```

Read data:

Word for Windows:

```
Data=DDERequest$(channel,itemtext)
```

Excel:

```
REQUEST(channel,itemtext)
```

Execute commands:

Word for Windows:

```
DDEExecute(channel,command)
```

Excel:

```
EXEC(channel,command)
```

Terminate communication:

Word for Windows:

```
DDETerminate(channel)
```

Excel:

```
=TERMINATE(channel)
```

At the end of the chapter, you'll find an explanation of data exchange with other applications using ObjectVision as an example.

DDE is an abbreviation for Dynamic Data Exchange, which allows two applications to actively exchange data. Once you establish a link between applications, this transfer occurs automatically. You can transfer data continually between the two programs.

Consider this transfer as a conversation. The *client* initiates the conversation. Like a business client, the client application requests a particular service (the information) from the *server*. The server application tries to perform the service requested by the client.

A program can establish many such links simultaneously, and may be the client in one conversation, and the server in another. This simply means that, while an application has requested a service from another application, it has also been asked to perform a service for a different application.

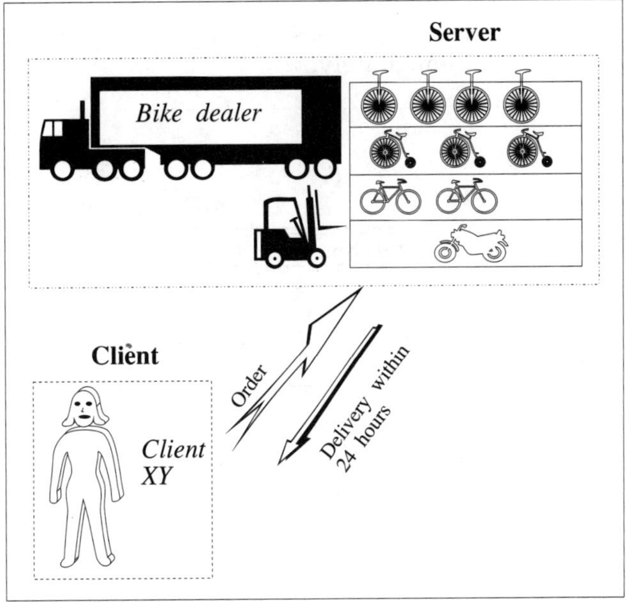

Client - server relationship

Usually, it's predetermined whether an application will act as client or server.

Creating a data link

For two participating applications to communicate, they must first establish a DDE link. The client application establishes this link, while the server application provides the requested information. Many applications establish this communication link for you.

However, the following must be specified before this can be done:

1. The server name (the name of the application with which the client wishes to communicate).
2. The topic of conversation.

When the server application receives a request for a DDE conversation, it examines the specified topic and data item. If the identities of these two elements are recognized, the server responds to the client, and the conversation is ready to begin.

Once a link has been established, the name of the server and the topic must remain unchanged during the conversation. The combination of server name and topic identify every specific conversation, and identify the conversation until the link terminates. If either the client or the server changes either of these elements during the conversation, the link terminates immediately.

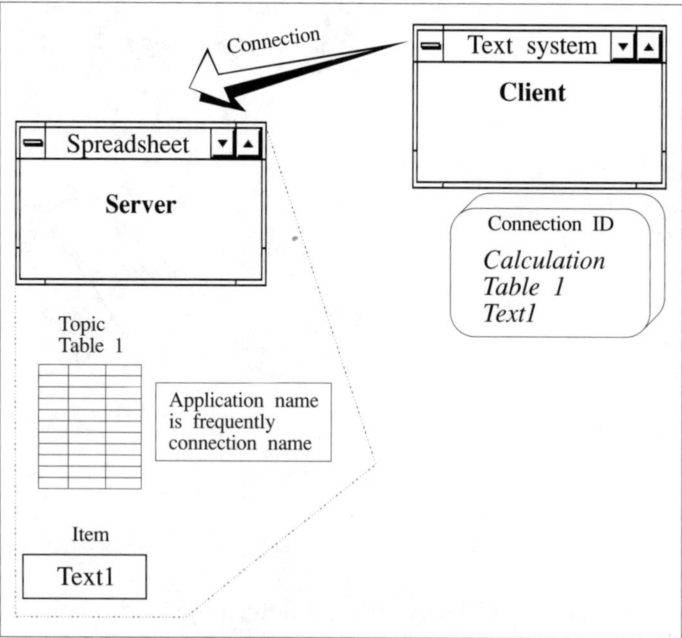

Creating a DDE link by defining the names

Dynamic data exchange (DDE) example

Example

In this section we'll present a group of examples that you'll find on the companion diskette. These examples, which are written in Visual Basic, establish a DDE link between three independent applications.

The first program is the server (the program that supplies information on request of the client). This server displays an icon in a picture box. The icon image changes about once a second, thanks to a timer. As soon as the server's picture box contains a new icon, DDE sends a message indicating the icon change to all clients, running under Windows, that contain valid links to this server. This results in the two client windows displaying the same icon that's currently in the server window.

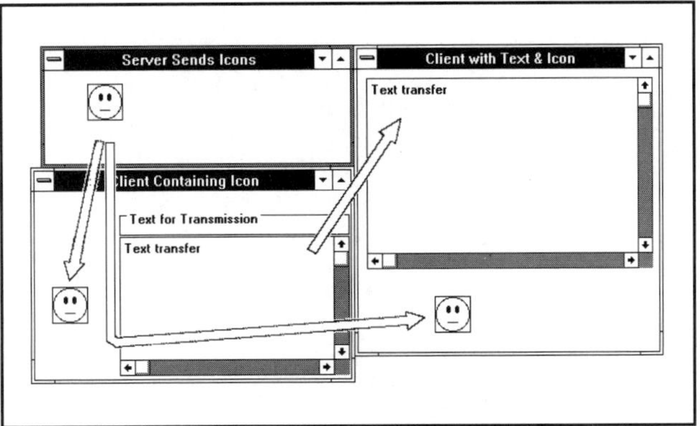

DDE example

Server and client

To try out the demonstration program group, run SERVPIC.EXE first. SERVPIC.EXE then runs the two client applications CL1PIC.EXE and CL2PIC.EXE. If you start either the CL1PIC.EXE or CL2PIC.EXE applications first, Windows will return a series of error messages.

The second client application (CL2PIC.EXE) is taking data from the text box of the CL1PIC.EXE application through DDE. So, CL1PIC.EXE acts as both client (displaying the icon) and server (passing data to CL2PIC.EXE).

Independent programs communicate

All three applications run in parallel. To verify this, open your Task Manager. You'll see SERVPIC.EXE, CL1PIC.EXE, and CL2PIC.EXE listed as independent programs. Two events then trigger a DDE request: an icon change in SERVPIC.EXE and the text box update in CL1PIC.EXE. This information may be transferred slowly if your PC is performing other tasks simultaneously.

For example, the DDE transfer will be noticeably slower if you're saving a document using a word processor. You'll see this delay in the changes between icons.

The following are the source listings for these Visual Basic programs. The companion diskette contains both source codes and .EXE files for these applications.

Server SERVPIC.EXE

```
SERVPIC.FRM

Declare Function WinExec Lib "KERNEL" (ByVal lpCmdLine As
String, ByVal nCmdShow As Integer) As Integer

Sub Stopwatch1_Timer ()
    Static nr%

    nr% = nr% + 1
    If nr% > 6 Then
        nr% = 0
    End If

    PictureName$ = CurDir$ + "\" + "DDEICON" +
LTrim$(Str$(nr%)) + ".ICO"
    Picture1.Picture = LoadPicture(PictureName$)
    Picture1.LinkSend
End Sub

Sub Form_Load ()
    PrgName$ = CurDir$ + "\" + "CL1PIC.EXE"
    i% = WinExec(PrgName$, 1)
    Stopwatch2.Enabled = 1

End Sub

Sub Stopwatch2_Timer ()
    PrgName$ = CurDir$ + "\" + "CL2PIC.EXE"
    i% = WinExec(PrgName$, 1)
    Stopwatch2.Enabled = 0
End Sub

Properties specified at design time:

Window:      Caption         = Server Sends Icons
             FormName        = Form1
Picture1:    CtlName         = Picture1
             AutoSize        = True
             Picture         = (Icon)
Timer:       CtlName         = Stopwatch1
             Enabled         = True
             Interval        = 1000
Timer:       CtlName         = Stopwatch2
             Enabled         = False
             Interval        = 2000
Project:     Project Name    = ServPic
```

Client CL1PIC.EXE

```
CL1PIC.FRM

Properties specified at design time:

Window:     Caption        = Client Containing Icon
            FormName       = Form1
Frame1:     Caption        = Text for Transmission
Text1:      Text           = Text transfer
            CtlName        = Text1
            Multiline      = True
            ScrollBars     = 3 - Both
Pict1:      LinkTopic      = ServPic|Form1
            LinkItem       = Picture1
            LinkMode       = 1 - Hot
            CtlName        = Picture1
            Picture        = (Icon)
Project:    Project name   = Cl1Pic
```

Client CL2PIC.EXE

```
CL2PIC.FRM

Properties specified at design time:

Window:      Caption        = Client with Text & Icon
             FormName       = Form1
Text1:       Text           =
             CtlName       = Text1
             LinkTopic      = Cl1Pic|Form1
             LinkItem       = Text1
             LinkMode       = 1 - Hot
Pict1:       LinkTopic      = ServPic|Form1
             LinkItem       = Picture1
             LinkMode       = 1 - Hot
             CtrlName       = Picture1
             Picture        = (Icon)
Project:     Project name = Cl2Pic
```

If the correct starting sequence is used, any entry in the server text box passes immediately to the client text box, in which the same entry is then displayed. It is quite interesting to see how it suddenly becomes possible to modify a foreign application.

Active and passive data links

Active links

As soon as a DDE conversation has been initialized, the client informs the server that a permanent data link should be created. This means that a certain piece of data must be continually updated. A link of this type results in a continual data flow, which remains intact until the conversation is closed.

This is also referred to as a Hot link, or an active link. The term "Hot" refers to the fact that any change of data immediately updates the client. You've already seen this type of link in the previous example. As soon as a server's icon or text box is updated, the client is informed of this change.

Passive links

Although a passive or cold link also establishes a connection, the server sends data to the client only when the latter specifically requests it.

Consider a passive link as a contract between a grocer (client) and a produce distributor (server), regulating the prices of produce. The contract states no specific delivery date, so new shipments of produce are sent only when the old shipment has been sold by the grocer. The client calls the server only when necessary.

An example of passive communication

In the next example, the client's text box remains unchanged until the client requests updated information. Once that request occurs, the text box's contents are updated. Clicking the Get Data button performs the update. Run the SERVPASS.EXE application. This automatically runs the CLPASSIV.EXE application.

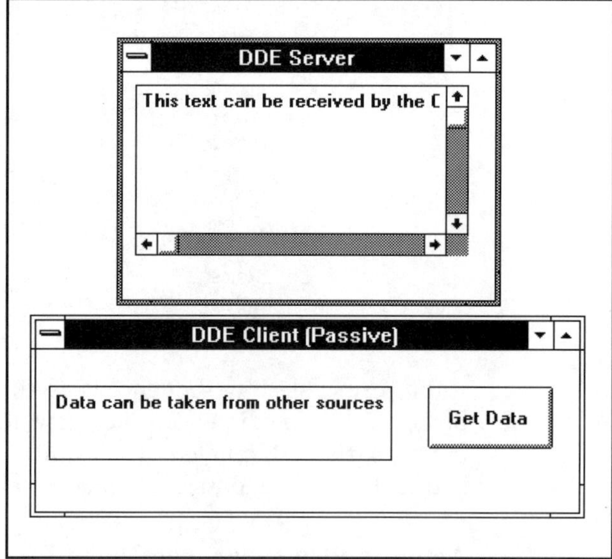

A client using a passive link

In a passive DDE link, data changes aren't automatically passed to the client by the server. So the client must specifically request the changes from the server.

The following are the source listings for these Visual Basic programs. The companion diskette contains both source codes and .EXE files for these applications.

Server ServPass.EXE

```
SERVPASS.FRM

Declare Function WinExec Lib "KERNEL" (ByVal lpCmdLine As
String, ByVal nCmdShow As Integer) As Integer

Sub Form_Load ()
    PrgName$ = CurDir$ + "\" + "CLPASSIV.EXE"
    i% = WinExec(PrgName$, 1)

End Sub

Properties specified at design time:

Window:     Caption        = DDE Server
            FormName       = ServerForm
            LinkTopic      = ServerForm
Text1:      Text           = This text can be received by the
                             Client
            CtlName        = ServerText
            ScrollBars     = 3 - Both
            Multiline      = True
Project:    Project name   = ServPass
```

Client CLPASSIV.EXE

```
CLPASSIV.FRM

Sub DDECmd1_Click ()
    ClientText.LinkRequest
End Sub

Properties specified at design time:

Window:      Caption        = DDE Client (Passive)
             FormName       = ClientForm
Text1:       Text           = Data can be taken from
                              other sources
             CtlName        = ClientText
             LinkTopic      = ServPass|ServerForm
             LinkItem       = ServerText
             LinkMode       = 2 - Cold
Command1:    Caption        = Get Data
Project:     Project name   = ClPassiv
```

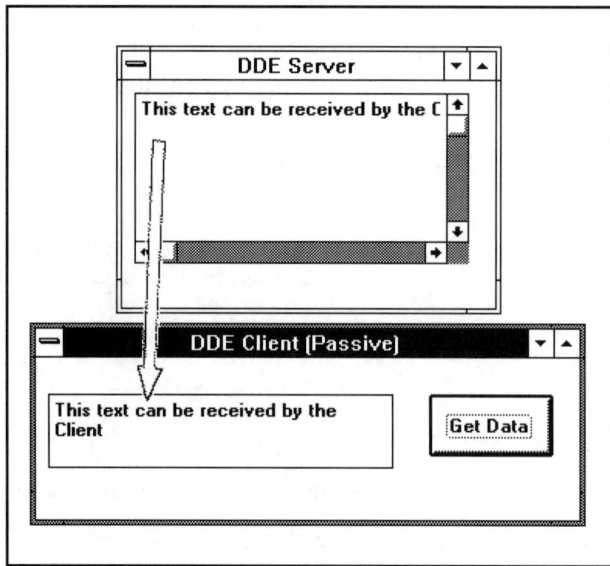

A mouse click updates data

DDE linking to Borland ObjectVision

DDE now offers the possibility of establishing communication between two completely different applications. A good example of this is the interaction between Microsoft Excel and Microsoft Word for Windows.

Since most users may be able to afford Excel <u>or</u> Word for Windows, but not both, we've found a less expensive way of demonstrating DDE access between different applications.

We've chosen Borland's ObjectVision as an example since it allows you to create a DDE link without requiring extensive knowledge of the application. On the companion diskette, you'll find an ObjectVision form. This form is structured quite simply and consists of only two fields, each of which receives data from a certain server.

From the Windows *File/Run...* command, run the SERVOBJ1.EXE and SERVOBJ2.EXE applications (these applications act as the server). Then run client application DDE.OVD (you'll need ObjectVision to run this application). Three windows appear.

Although you cannot edit the fields in the ObjectVision form, you can change the form's contents by editing the contents of the two server windows.

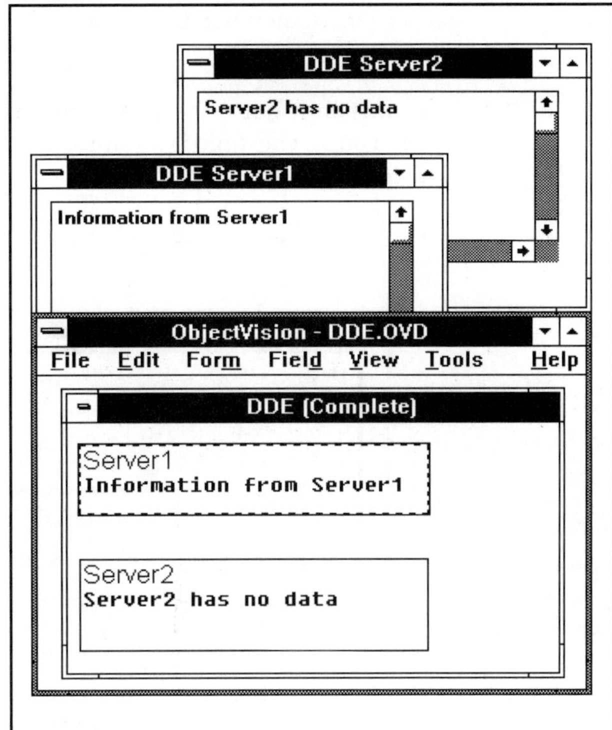

Server text box supplies an ObjectVision form with text using DDE

The first field of the form is the client of SERVOBJ1.EXE and the second field is the client of SERVOBJ2.EXE. Now, when you enter text in the *DDEServer1* window, the changes appear in the *DDE (Complete)* window's *Server1* field. Entering text in the *DDE Server2* window changes the text in the *DDE (Complete)* window's *Server2* field. Close the three applications.

Let's see how this link works. Using *File/Run...*, start the DDE.OVD application first. When the form appears, a dialog box informs you that SERVOBJ1.EXE isn't running. Click on Yes. A second dialog box informs you that SERVOBJ2.EXE isn't running. Click on Yes. All three applications are running, but a link doesn't exist because of the order in which you ran the applications. We'll need to re-establish the link information from the client application (DDE.OVD).

For the *Server1* field, this information consists of ServObj1, ServerForm, and ServerText. These three items of information identify the server's text box. For the *Server2* field, the identifying information consists of ServObj2, ServerForm, and

ServerText. Remember that these values or names were defined within both servers.

Using this link data, the DDE link must now be created within ObjectVision. The link is established individually for each field of the form.

From within ObjectVision, click on the *Server1* field. Select the *Tools/Links...* command.

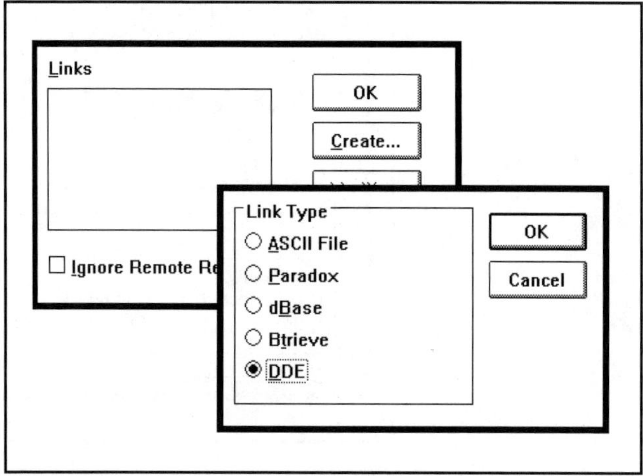

Establishing DDE links within Borland's ObjectVision

When the *Links* dialog box appears, click on the Create... button. Another dialog box appears. Select the *DDE* option button and click on OK. Another dialog box, into which you must enter the link information, appears. Type Server1 in the *Link Name* text box and press Tab. Type ServObj1 in the *Application* text box and press Tab. Type ServerForm in the *Document* text box and press Tab.

Click on the Connect button. Another dialog box appears. Enter ServerText in the *Remote Name* text box and click OK.

The *Field Name* dialog box appears. Click on <Add New Field> and click on OK. Type Server1 in the *Field Name* text box and click OK.

Click OK to establish the link.

The following illustration shows the completed information for Server1:

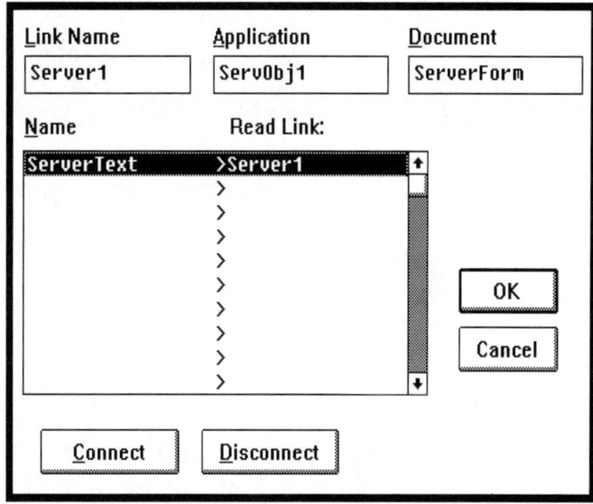

Establishing DDE links within Borland's ObjectVision

Using the same procedure, type the same information for Server2.

The following are the source listings for these Visual Basic programs. The companion diskette contains both source codes and .EXE files for these applications.

Server SERVOBJ1.EXE

SERVOBJ1.FRM

```
Properties specified at design time:

Window:        Caption          = DDE Server1
               FormName         = ServerForm
Text1:         Text             = Information from Server1
               CtlName          = ServerText
               Multiline        = True
               ScrollBars       = 3 - Both
Project:       Project name     = ServObj1
```

Server SERVOBJ2.EXE

SERVOBJ2.FRM

```
Properties specified at design time:

Window:        Caption          = DDE Server2
               FormName         = ServerForm
Text1:         Text             = Server2 has no data
               CtlName          = ServerText
               Multiline        = True
               ScrollBars       = 3 - Both
Project:       Project name     = ServObj2
```

These settings are particularly important, since the DDE partners will be unable to recognize one another if the settings are incorrect .

32.3 Object Linking and Embedding: OLE

You've seen the importance of program to program data exchange. As you'll remember, the original purpose was to exchange data between independent programs. The programs constituted the sources of data and DDE constituted the specific means of communication. It was particularly important to know precisely which data were to be exchanged. A second Windows tool allows you to embed information for updating (more on this later).

Data exchange and the Clipboard

You're probably already familiar with pasting information using your Clipboard. You can easily exchange data between drawing applications and word processors with the Clipboard. So you can insert a picture in a text, which results in a text file with an imported picture. Any errors in the picture must then be corrected with the original application, such as Paintbrush. Then the corrected picture must be re-pasted into the text document using the Clipboard.

The more errors that exist in such a file or perhaps the more errors are found in such a file, the more often the user must repeat the process. However, this procedure is impractical and actually outdated. You should be able to copy the picture to the text file using your Clipboard. Then perform any updates using DDE. This is exactly what OLE (Object Linking and Embedding) does.

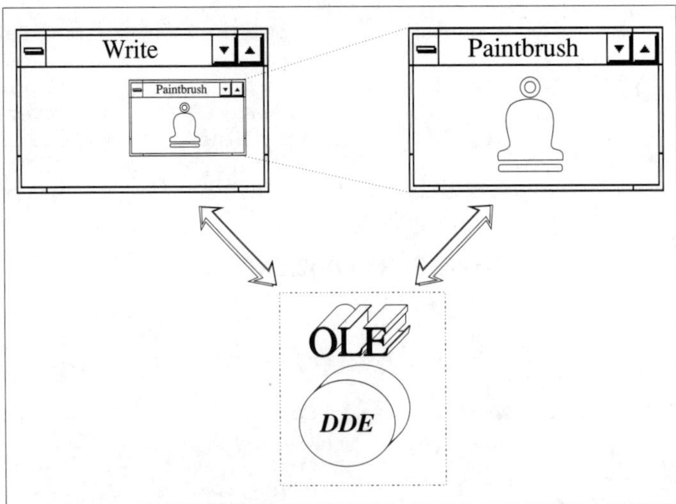

Possible uses of OLE

Eventually OLE will replace DDE

With few exceptions, OLE will eventually replace DDE. Some applications may require both DDE and OLE access:

- In cases where several links must be operating simultaneously.
- When these links require frequent updates.

Combining text and pictures: OLE

Embedding pictures

Here we'll deal with embedding pictures in a text file. Our example will use a bitmap graphic created with Paintbrush, which we'll embed in a Write or Cardfile document. The most practical and flexible way of doing this is through OLE.

The order in which you generate the document and picture is up to you. We'll follow two processes:

1. We'll generate the text document in Cardfile or Write, then call Paintbrush and create a picture for embedding.
2. We'll create a file in Paintbrush, then open Cardfile or Write and embed the Paintbrush picture.

Creating a document and embedding pictures

Insert object

Before you embed a picture in Write or Cardfile, you'll probably want to create the text in which the picture will be embedded. Suppose that you've reached the place in your text file where you want to insert the graphic.

First, you must select *Edit/Insert Object...*. If you're working with Cardfile, you must select *Edit/Picture*. A dialog box displays the settings for all permissible links. Since you'll create a Paintbrush graphic, select *Paintbrush Picture* and click [OK].

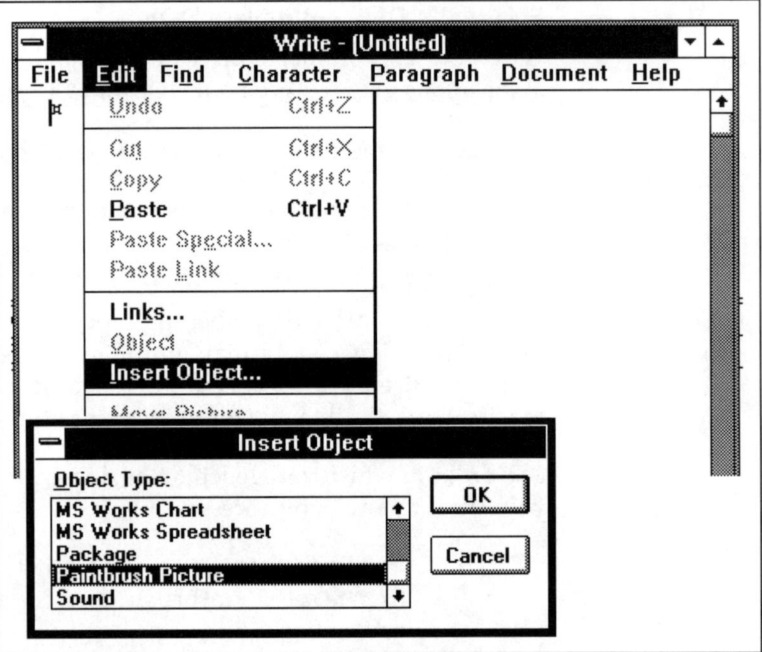

Embedding objects in Write

Embedding through Update

Paintbrush automatically starts and you can create your picture. When the picture is completed, you'll want to place it in the text document. By selecting *File/Update*, the picture data is transferred to Write or Cardfile, depending on which application you're using.

The *Update* command is available only when a picture must be embedded through OLE. This command usually doesn't appear in the Paintbrush *File* menu.

The process *Update* uses to transfer the picture to Write or Cardfile using OLE may seem confusing. However, the actual process is quite simple. Let's take a closer look at what happens during this process.

Write and OLE start Paintbrush

OLE technology

Let's return to the step where we selected *Edit/Insert Object....* When you select Paintbrush Picture from the *Insert Object* dialog box and click the OK button, an OLE link to Paintbrush occurs. Then Paintbrush automatically starts. Since Paintbrush is now aware that this picture is an embedded object, it replaces the *Save* command in the *File* menu with *Update*. When you select *Update*, the picture passes to Write or Cardfile through the OLE link.

Object consists of a display package and a special set of information

The actual bitmap picture isn't readable by Write in its original Paintbrush bitmap format. Because of this, Paintbrush uses OLE to supply Write with an object. This object consists of two information packages, one of which can be read and used by Write. The second information package consists of data that can be used only by Paintbrush. The picture that's visible within the Write window is therefore contained within the display package.

Graphics and text in one file

The old method of working separately with text and graphics required both sets of information to be stored in different files. However, you may be wondering where the drawing that you've created with Paintbrush is stored. Actually, the picture didn't receive its own file. So you won't be able to find it as a normal Paintbrush file. Instead, the picture has been stored as an object within Write or Cardfile.

Summary for Embedding New Graphics in a Body of Text

Text + Graphics

1. Create text file in Write or Cardfile.
2. Place insertion point at the desired location.

3. Select *Edit/Insert Object.....*

4. Select Paintbrush Picture in the *Insert Object* dialog box and click OK.

5. Paintbrush automatically starts. Create your picture.

6. Select *File/Update*.

7. Exit Paintbrush and continue your work with Write or Cardfile.

Creating a Paintbrush picture...

Embedding pictures with the Clipboard

If you have an existing Paintbrush picture that you want to embed in a Write or Cardfile document, your starting point will be Paintbrush, the graphics program containing your picture. Copy this picture to the Clipboard using *Edit/Copy*. Keep Paintbrush running and change to Write or Cardfile. If in Cardfile, select *Edit/Picture*. Now select *Edit/Paste* to paste the image into the text document at the current cursor position.

...and embedding it in Write or Cardfile

Until now you've seen little evidence of OLE. To change this, double-click the picture you just pasted into Write or Cardfile. A second copy of Paintbrush runs, this time including the OLE link. Notice the two title bars in the two versions of Paintbrush. The first version displays the file name (e.g., TESTPIC.PCX), while the second instance of Paintbrush lists *Paintbrush Picture in (file name)* (e.g., *Paintbrush Picture in (TEST.WRI)*). As seen earlier in this chapter, the *Save* command has been replaced by the *Update* command.

Proof of the OLE link

If you still aren't convinced that an OLE link has been established between Write (or Cardfile) and Paintbrush, try the following. Start Paintbrush with your File Manager or Program Manager and create a simple picture. Then select this picture and copy it to the Clipboard using *Edit/Copy*. Exit Paintbrush without saving the picture to disk.

The picture will remain in the Clipboard. Next, start Write or Cardfile from your File Manager or Program Manager. If in Cardfile, ensure that *Edit/Picture* is selected. Now select *Edit/Paste*. This pastes the picture into the text document. Double-click the picture to start Paintbrush and then minimize Paintbrush.

The title should read *Paintbrush - Paintbrush Picture in (Untitled)*. Then return to Write or Cardfile. The Paintbrush icon should remain visible on your screen for the purpose of this demonstration.

Now Write (or Cardfile) and Paintbrush will prove that they communicate through OLE. Save the text document as TEST.WRI. The Paintbrush icon changes to read *Paintbrush - Paintbrush Picture in TEST.WRI.*

Summary: Embedding existing pictures in a text document

1. Create picture in Paintbrush. Select the picture.
2. Select *Copy* from the *Edit* menu.
3. Save picture and exit Paintbrush.
4. Open Write and create document.
5. Place insertion point at the desired location.
6. If in Cardfile, make sure that *Edit/Picture* is selected. Select *Edit/Paste*.

Editing the picture

Summary: Editing an embedded picture

1. Double-click the picture within Write or Cardfile.
2. Paintbrush starts and automatically loads the picture.
3. Make all necessary changes to the picture.
4. Select *Edit/Update*.
5. Exit Paintbrush.

Object linking with OLE

Now, we'll introduce you to another feature of OLE. You'll need an existing graphic, such as a Paintbrush picture, and a text document created from within Write or Cardfile. You can link this picture to the document using OLE.

Linking: Text and graphic are separate

What's the difference between an embedded object and a linked object? When you embed an object, such as a picture, in a text document, the object is stored together with the text document. When objects are linked, they are stored in separate files. So, when you link a Paintbrush picture to a Write document, both files will be saved individually. In embedding, this would have resulted in only one file.

An object must exist as a file before linking. Once the link has been created, updates between the linked objects occur automatically. If you edit the Paintbrush picture, the contents of the Write file change accordingly.

Linking Graphics and Text

Let's examine a practical application. We want to link an existing Paintbrush picture with a Write or Cardfile document. First create and save a picture using Paintbrush, or open an existing picture. Select the picture using the Pick tool or Scissors tool, and select *Edit/Copy*. Exit Paintbrush and run Write or Cardfile.

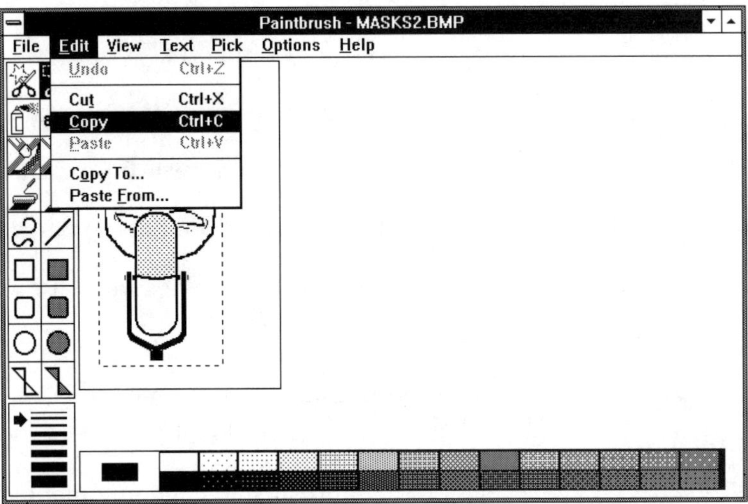

Linking a saved Paintbrush picture

If in Cardfile, select *Edit/Picture*. Now select *Edit/Paste Link*. This creates an OLE link between the Paintbrush picture and the Write or Cardfile document.

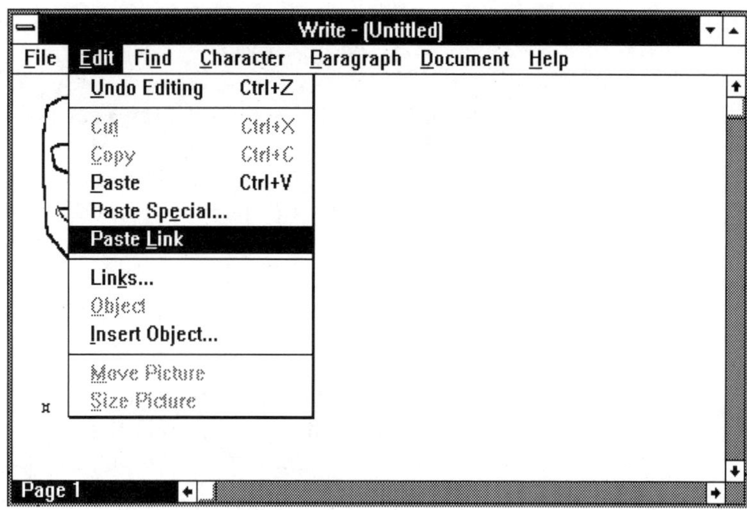

Linking a picture in Write

Verifying the link

This link now allows you to modify the Paintbrush graphic file, and OLE will automatically update the contents of the Write or Cardfile document file. You can verify a link by selecting *Edit/Link...* in Cardfile or *Edit/Links...* in Write. Either command opens a dialog box displaying existing links to the current file. The illustration below shows Write's *Links* dialog box, and its link to a file named MASKS2.BMP.

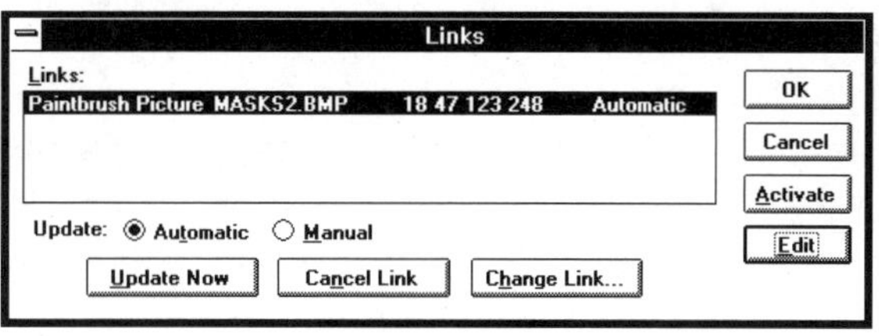

Link is verified

Summary: Linking Graphics and Text

Linking graphics + text

1. Create picture using Paintbrush.
2. Save and then select the picture.
3. Select *Edit/Copy*.
4. Create a text document in Write or Cardfile.
5. Place insertion point at the desired location.

6. If in Cardfile, make sure that *Edit/Picture* is selected. Select *Edit/Paste Link*.

Editing the picture

If you need to edit the picture, the process is the same as for an embedded object. Double-click the picture within the Write or Cardfile document. This runs Paintbrush and loads the linked picture. Since this object is linked instead of embedded, Paintbrush's title bar displays the name of the picture. Edit the file, select *Edit/Save*, and the link automatically updates the document file the next time you open the Write or Cardfile document.

Modifying OLE links

Once an OLE link has been created, you can modify this link. For example, you can specify whether a link should update automatically or manually. Select *Edit/Links...* in Write or *Edit/Link...* in Cardfile. The dialog box that opens lists all available links. To change the link for manual updating, select the link name from the list box and click the *Manual* option button.

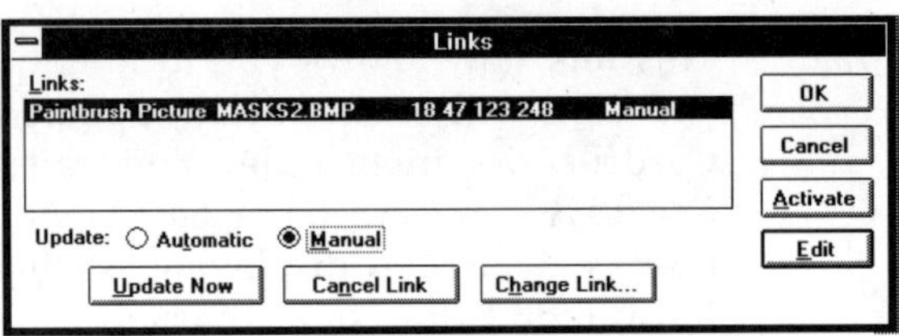

Manual link

Manual link

Once you've made this change, modifications to the picture with Paintbrush won't be passed to the text document. The update will only occur if you select *Edit/Link(s)...*, select the link, and click the Update Now button. This passes any changes in the picture to the document file.

Summary: Updating a manually linked object

Manual updates

1. Select *Edit/Link(s)...* in Write or Cardfile.
2. Select the correct object from the list of linked objects.
3. Click Update Now.

Breaking links

If you no longer need a link, click the Cancel Link button in the *Link(s)* dialog box. This breaks the link (removes the link from the list box) and makes the picture a static object. If you double-click the picture within the Write or Cardfile document, Paintbrush won't run. Instead, a dialog box states that you cannot activate this picture as a linked object.

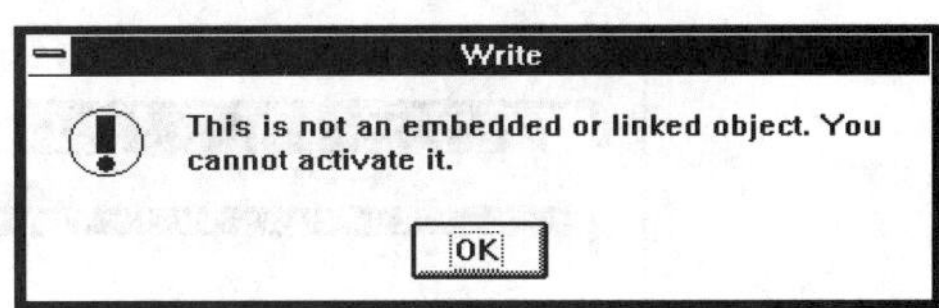

Broken link

You should break a link only if you're certain that it's no longer needed. There is no way of reversing this step, so if the link is needed again, you must re-link the object.

Fixing a broken OLE link

Link broken?

Links can occasionally be unintentionally broken by renaming files. For example, if we rename the MASKS2.BMP file to MASKS3.BMP, this action breaks the OLE link. If you select *Edit/Link(s)...* and click on the Update Now button, the following dialog box appears.

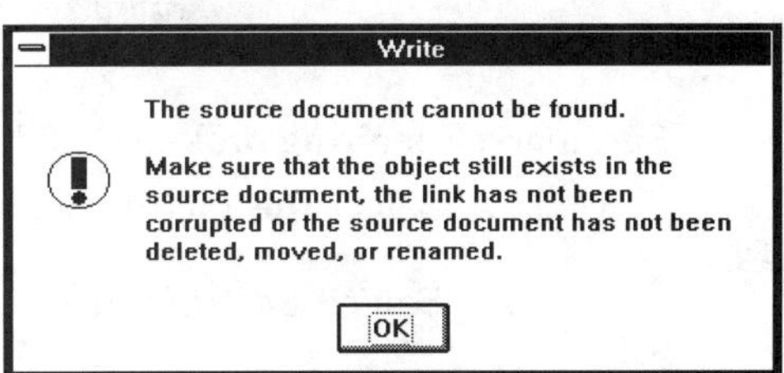

Write
The source document cannot be found.
Make sure that the object still exists in the source document, the link has not been corrupted or the source document has not been deleted, moved, or renamed.
OK

Broken OLE link

You can solve this problem by re-linking the picture file. From Write or Cardfile, select *Edit/Link(s)....* Next, click on the Change Link... button. A dialog box appears from which you can select the new linked picture.

Here we selected the renamed file (MASKS3.BMP). Select or type the new file name and click OK to restore the OLE link. To verify the fix, look in the *Link(s)* dialog box for the new entry (Paintbrush Picture MASKS3.BMP).

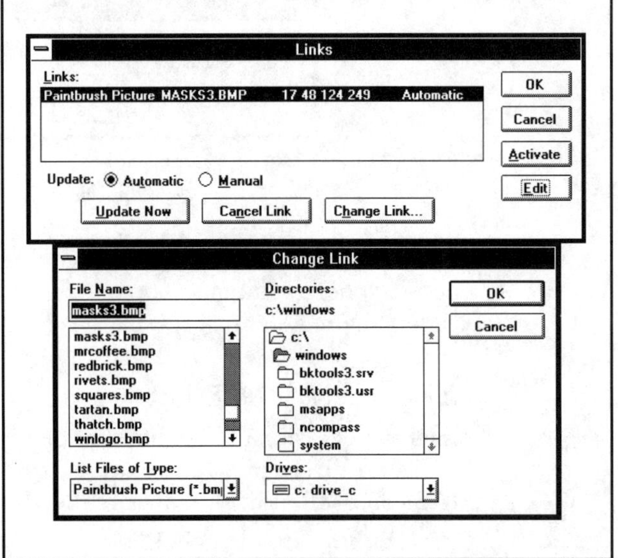

Repairing a broken link

Summary: Repairing broken OLE links

Repairing links

1. Select the picture within Write or Cardfile.
2. Select *Edit/Link(s)....*
3. Select the appropriate item from the list of linked objects.
4. Click Change Link... .
5. Select or type the new file name.
6. Click OK.

OLE Object Packager

Have you ever typed a letter knowing that some useful information that you could use is stored in some old document? Most likely you started a second word processor, opened that document, then copied the data to the file on which you were working. This is easy with one document, but multiple documents can make a search for the text time-consuming. A convenient solution is to select the documents from the File Manager and drag the documents to the current file.

Object package with drag and drop

Let's work through an example. Suppose that you stored an older document file named MYOLDDOC.WRI in your D:\LETTERS directory. This file contains important information that you need for a new document file named MYNEWDOC.WRI. Run Write and type the new document. Save it under the name MYNEWDOC.WRI and keep Write running. Run the File Manager and locate the D:\LETTERS directory.

Move the mouse pointer onto the MYOLDDOC.WRI icon. Press and hold the left mouse button and drag the MYOLDDOC.WRI icon into the *Write - MYNEWDOC.WRI* window. Release the left mouse button. This process is called *drag and drop*.

If you move the icon out of the File Manager window, its shape changes to a "No..." symbol. Moving the icon into the Write window changes it back to its "sheet of paper" icon.

The icon's shape shows whether the application, in which the icon is currently located, supports OLE. If the File Manager continues to display the icon as a "No..." symbol, then the application doesn't support OLE.

The icon of the MYOLDDOC.WRI document now appears in the *Write - MYNEWDOC.WRI* window.

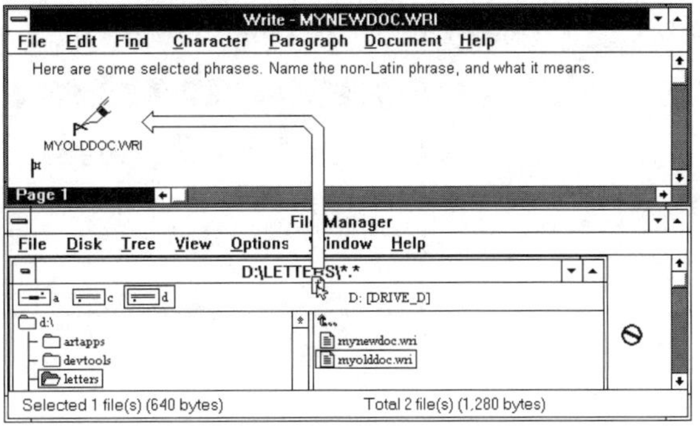

The File Manager supports OLE

Double-click the MYOLDDOC.WRI icon in Write to access this document. OLE starts another copy of Write, so the contents of the old file can be displayed. The MYOLDDOC.WRI icon is an object package.

Clipboard object package

Besides creating object packages by dragging File Manager icons with the drag and drop method, you can create object packages by copying files to the Clipboard. Select the file in the File Manager, then select *File/Copy* to copy the file to the Clipboard. Click on the *Copy to Clipboard* option button and click OK. This creates an object package on the Clipboard.

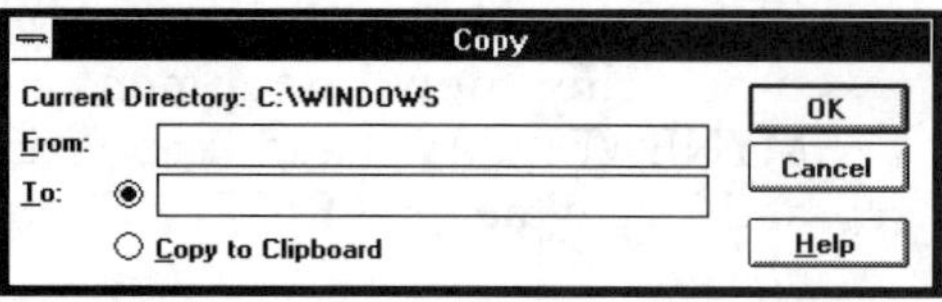

Copying an object package to the Clipboard

Select the destination document. Selecting *Edit/Paste* pastes the object package into the destination document.

Modifying object packages with the Object Packager

In addition to these File Manager techniques, Windows 3.1 provides a separate Object Packager. You can use the Object Packager to create, update, and transfer object packages.

Embedded document becomes an object package

An object package can consist of an embedded document or a linked document. The Object Packager allows you to interactively create an object package. When started, the Object Packager appears in a window that's divided into two different work windows.

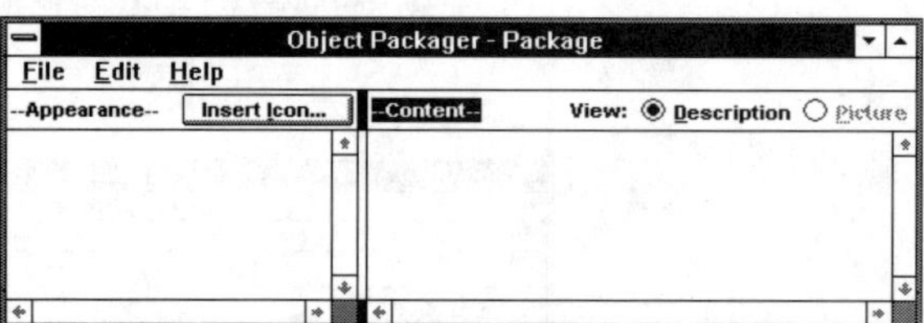

The Object Packager

The *--Appearance--* window displays the appearance of the object package (usually as an icon). The *--Content--* window displays the document's name and contents. In this case, the word *document* refers to the element acting as the source for the object package.

To create a new object package, click on the *--Content--* window, then select *File/Import....* The *Import* dialog box appears.

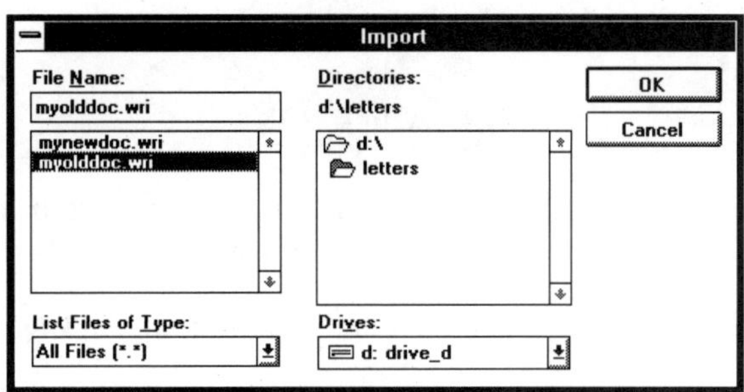

Importing to the Object Packager

From within the *Import* dialog box, select the MYOLDDOC.WRI file and click OK. The *--Appearance--* window displays the MYOLDDOC.WRI icon, while the *--Contents--* window lists a description named *Copy of MYOLDDOC.WRI.* When you selected *File/Import...,* the Object Packager recognized the specified file as a Write document, and thus displayed the Write icon. The object package can now be inserted in a destination document such as a Write or Cardfile document.

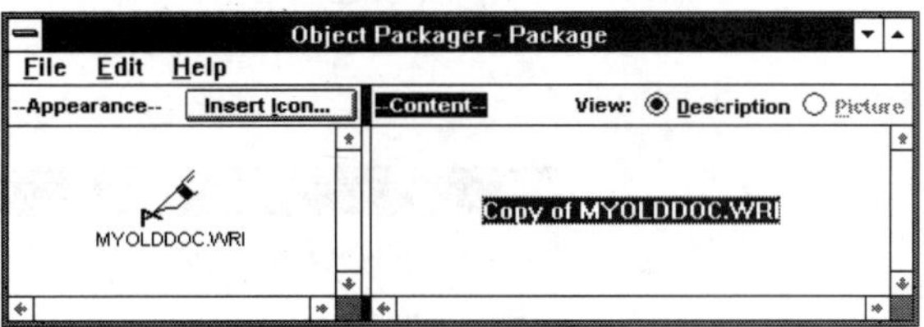

A new object package

The *Edit/Copy Package* command copies the object package to the Clipboard. It can then be inserted in a Write or Cardfile document by selecting *Edit/Paste* at the appropriate location. The object package created in this way produces the same result as the File Manager earlier in this section.

The object package is placed in the destination document. Double-click the icon to edit the object package. Although this procedure takes slightly longer than using the File Manager, The Object Packager is considerably friendlier toward the user than the File Manager.

Summary: Creating object packages with the Object Packager

Creating object packages

1. Run the Object Packager and select the *--Content--* window.

2. Select *Edit/Import....*

3. Select the source document.

4. Click OK .

5. The file name appears in the --*Content*-- window and the icon appears in the --*Appearance*-- window.

6. Select *Edit/Copy Package*.

7. Switch to the destination document.

8. Select *Edit/Paste* to copy the object package to the destination document.

Changing the object package icon

As soon as the Object Packager has been opened and an object package is loaded, an icon representing that object package appears in the --*Appearance*-- window. The default icon used by the Object Packager is the icon of the application used to create the document. You can change this icon by clicking the Insert Icon... button. You can select a default Windows icon, or select a user-defined icon. For a default Windows icon, search the *Current Icon:* list box.

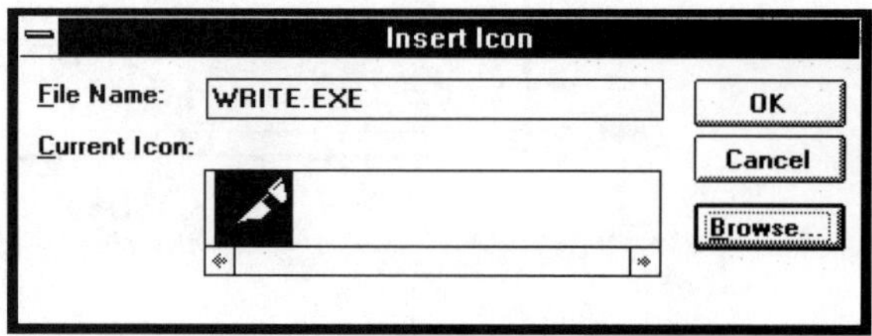

Using an icon of a standard Windows program

If you'd prefer another icon, click on the Browse... button. This opens a dialog box that allows you to select a specific application, from which you can select an icon.

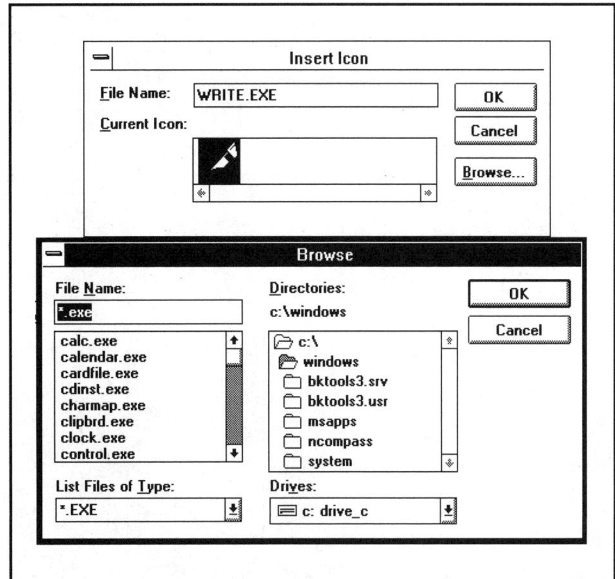

Getting an icon from a file

If you want to use your own icon, use Paintbrush to design your own and then copy it to the Clipboard. Then switch to the Object Packager and select the -- *Appearance* -- window. Select *Edit/Paste* to insert the new icon in the object package.

OLE technique

Like DDE, OLE forms a standard protocol for exchanging data and commands. The systems are realized exclusively through the exchange of Windows messages. Because of this, neither system requires the support of operating system calls.

OLE was based on existing DDE protocol, and operates through character string transfer using DDE. OLE and DDE applications are programmed using Windows API function calls. DLL's within Windows process these functions.

OLE uses the OLECLI.DLL dynamic link library for the client, and the OLESVR.DLL dynamic link library for the server. All DDE function calls are executed through DDEML.DLL.

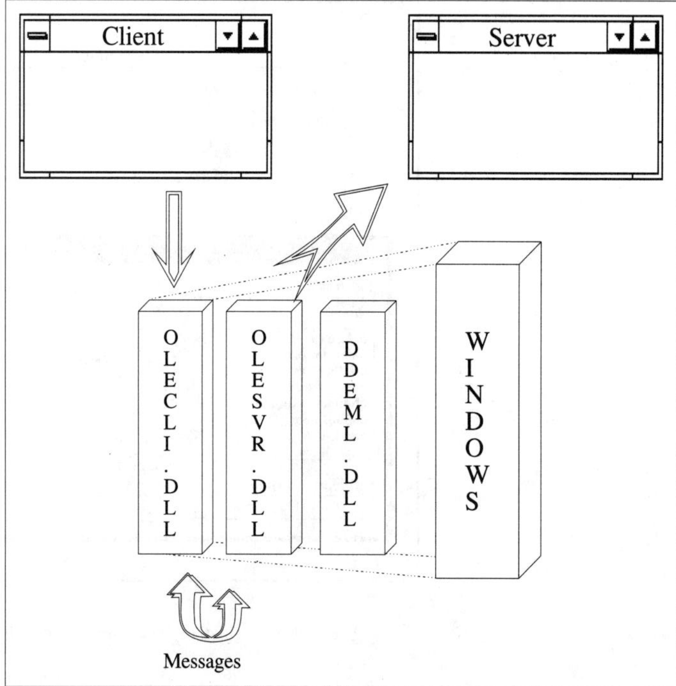

OLE and DDE technology

When is OLE used?

Permanent embedding of linked objects (documents)

OLE is mainly used for permanently linking and embedding objects (documents). This opens a connection between the client and server each time you open an embedded object. DDE cannot perform this operation, since the user must implement a permanent connection, and the application must implement a temporary connection.

Conversion of standard data formats

OLE performs data format conversions, such as bitmaps, device-independent bitmaps (DIB's), and metafiles.

The server converts special data formats

OLE API function calls allow the server to perform special data format conversions. After this, only a minimal amount of work is required from the client application to display this data.

OLE creates objects and links

OLE assumes most of the work required to copy or insert links using the Clipboard. In addition, objects can be exchanged directly over the Clipboard. DDE offers no functions that facilitate the exchange of data over the Clipboard.

Activating embedded and linked objects

OLE supports a server in modifying an embedded or linked object or in activating the object for the conversion of data.

When DDE properties are required, they can be accessed easily..

While DDE functions does OLE replace?

Since OLE is an extension of DDE, it can perform all DDE functions. So, a program that supports OLE can also can establish a link through a topic. Data will also be requested through a server item. The data is thus transferred in the previously defined format.

Data can be sent from the server to the client, and requested from the server by the client.

So instructions can be issued to the server, a command line can be sent from the client to the server in the form of a character string.

When is DDE used?

DDE is still used by applications that use a large number of simultaneous links, especially when many items are used, and when these are frequently updated. Applications, such as realtime information systems, are typical applications for DDE.

32.4 TrueType Fonts

The phrase "What you see is what you get" (WYSIWYG) is prominently displayed on many software packages. However, few of these packages actually live up to this promise.

The term WYSIWYG suggests that the output visible on your screen corresponds to the output you'll receive from your printer. For this to be completely true, the characters visible on your screen would have to look exactly like the ones on the printed page.

However, this only worked in theory until now. The reason is in the method by which characters are created and displayed on your screen.

TrueType vs raster fonts

Before discussing font conventions in more detail, examine the following illustration.

Raster versus TrueType

On the left you'll see a standard raster character; on the right you'll see a character from a TrueType font.

The demands and expectations of font and document display steadily increase, as does the number of available programs that use these. For example, CorelDraw provides complete control of font sizes and styles.

A single letter can be enlarged almost indefinitely, and appears on your screen as it will appear on your printer. You may wonder why CorelDraw is capable of displaying a character perfectly in any size while a word processor such as Write cannot.

CorelDraw uses its own fonts, while Write uses the fonts supplied by Windows. Windows versions through 3.1 displayed individual characters on the screen as raster fonts.

Consider a raster character as a picture created under Paintbrush, consisting of pixels. You cannot change a raster character's size without the character's quality deteriorating. This means that each font size would require a different group of rasters. Since such an approach would quickly consume all available memory, Windows cannot provide many font sizes.

Raster characters

Complications of raster fonts

Let's take a look at the word processor Write, which can display the Times Roman font in different sizes. However, Windows only supplies the font in 8 and 12 point sizes. When you use only these two sizes, the screen looks almost identical to the printed font. However, as soon as you enlarge the font size, the rasters of the font must be enlarged, but the number of pixels that make up each character remains the same. This results in characters that look like they were built out of dominos.

With TrueType fonts, the fonts appear distinct in any point size, corresponding to their printed counterparts.

However, the main question is what are the advantages of using a TrueType font.

Windows with raster characters

If our theory holds true, a text of identical contents created in Write would appear different on your screen depending on the font that's used. We experimented with the text "Truetype" in Write. First we assigned an old screen font named Times Roman, disabling the TrueType fonts from within the Control Panel. Then we started Write, typed the text, and set the characters to this Times Roman font at 110 points. The result looked like this:

Raster characters as they appear on your screen

Raster

You can see how rough the individual characters appear. The following illustration shows the TrueType Times New Roman font at 110 points, as it would appear on your screen in Write:

TrueType precision

TrueType font as it appears on your screen

Raster characters versus TrueType

If you compare the two illustrations closely, you'll notice that they have different print qualities and font sizes. However, both were created with the same version of Write under Windows 3.1 and with the same general font at a point size of 110.

Printed TrueType

Let's take this a step further. We took our screen fonts and placed them next to a PostScript® printout of the same text. Here's how the TrueType font compared:

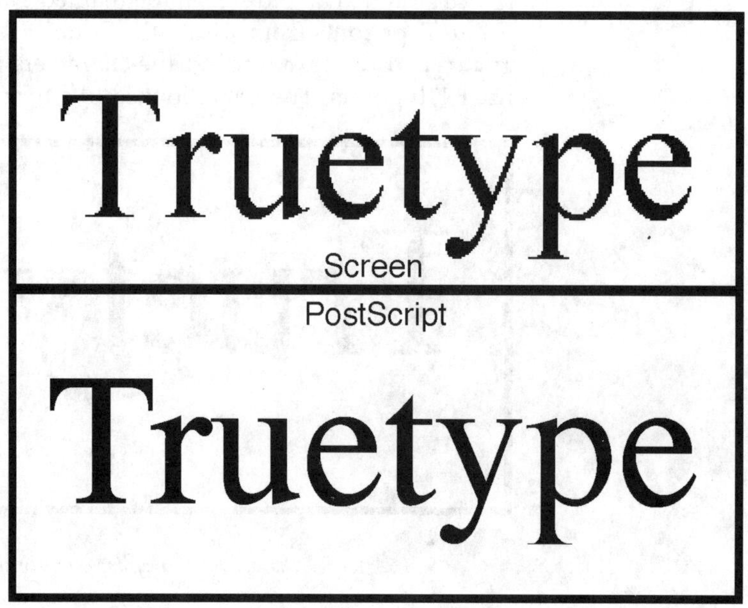

TrueType versus Postscript printer

TrueType = WYSIWYG

The fonts look almost the same, except that the TrueType text is slightly less smooth. This roughness is caused more by the video card resolution than TrueType itself.

Here's how the raster Times Roman font compared with PostScript:

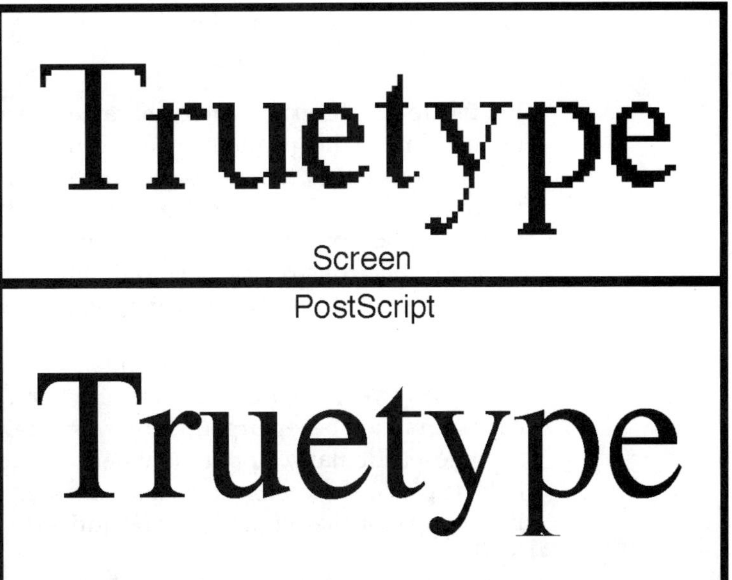

Raster font versus Postscript printer

The Development of TrueType

TrueType development

TrueType was developed by Apple and Microsoft for the Macintosh system. It was intended as competition for Adobe's PostScript. Microsoft and Apple's goal was to develop a font language that would be upwardly-compatible to PostScript, and would also permit fast display of high quality fonts on both screens and printers.

Computer font technology

The most commonly used output devices rely on raster images for displaying characters and graphics. Computers can process and display these rasters quickly and easily, since they don't require time-consuming calculations.

You've already learned that the quality display of characters in the form of rasters requires a separate raster for each typeface, size, and even for each output device. For simple word processing applications, the memory required for character rasters is quite manageable. However, more demanding graphics programs, such as CorelDraw, strain the capabilities offered by raster fonts.

Vector Fonts

Vector fonts

The preceding examples illustrate the drastic drops in quality that can occur with raster fonts. The more you enlarge a raster font, the grainier the characters appear, since the characters contain a limited amount of information. Vector fonts represent one solution to this problem.

Vector fonts describe each character through mathematically defined lines. This provides good results for characters composed of numerous edges, since these edges can be formed through a series of straight lines. However, P's and O's and other characters with round shapes present a definite problem for vector fonts. Each circle must be constructed of straight lines, so round edges can only be approximated and will never appear smooth.

Although they have been used under Windows for awhile, vector fonts aren't very popular because of several problems. Vector font characters can be enlarged, however, their inherent limitations become particularly apparent when characters are displayed in bold type. Since vector font characters are constructed of think lines, many of these lines must be added to one another to form a bold character.

PostScript, however, has been widely accepted by PC users, and can be described as a language that's a combination of raster and vector fonts.

Outline Fonts

Outline fonts

This combination of raster and vector fonts is known as an outline font. In this approach, characters are constructed as outlines, in a manner similar to vector fonts, then filled in with pixels. Bezier (pronounced "behz-ee-AY") curves added to the mathematical lines describe characters with round shapes, such as the "S" character.

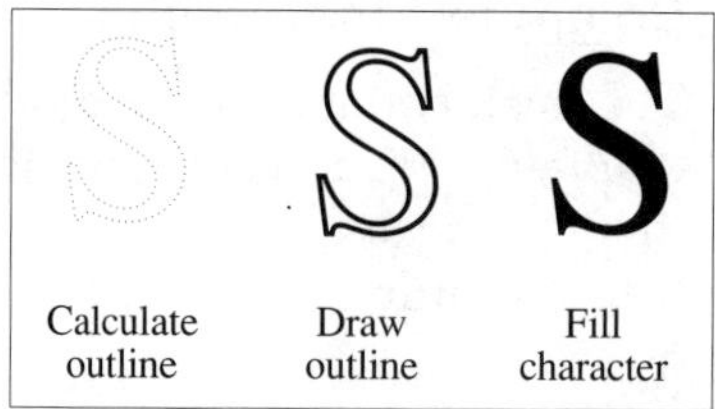

Creating an outline font character

The Adobe Type 1 system is an outline font system, used by Adobe for PostScript font display on computer screens.

TrueType Calculates Outlines in Points

TrueType outline

TrueType, however, uses an outline composed of individual pixels, instead of an outline defined by Bezier curves. This method defines the outline in a series of pixels that are calculated according to a process known as quadratic B splines.

Although Microsoft calls these character outlines *glyphs*, we'll continue to use the term outlines. Once this outline has been calculated, its area is filled by a simple algorithm.

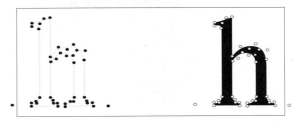

TrueType character outline

TrueType commands

TrueType uses a special language to display the characters, which allows the appearance of each individual character to be determined by specific commands. These commands strongly resemble assembly language instructions, although their meaning and function differ greatly from assembly language.

Using TrueType

New TrueType character set

In addition to its increased quality, TrueType includes a more extensive character set than previous Windows or DOS character sets. This character set consists of 332 characters.

This character set is almost identical to the Apple character set, except that it doesn't contain the character, which Microsoft wasn't allowed to use. This development may become quite helpful in future data exchange between Apples and PC's.

TrueType and Printers

TrueType printers

TrueType can be used on all printers, for which Windows possesses a driver. The Windows PostScript driver can convert TrueType to PostScript so Postscript printers can be used with TrueType.

Using Special Character in Applications

When you need to use special characters, which aren't included on your keyboard, in word processor documents, you'd usually press and hold the Alt key, then enter a number on the numeric keypad.

Instead of looking through manuals or memorizing key codes, you should use the Windows Character Map application. This program displays the available character set and allows you to select a character by simply clicking on it.

You can select several characters at once, and when you've created the desired character string, copy it to the Clipboard by clicking the Copy button. From there the characters can easily be copied to your document.

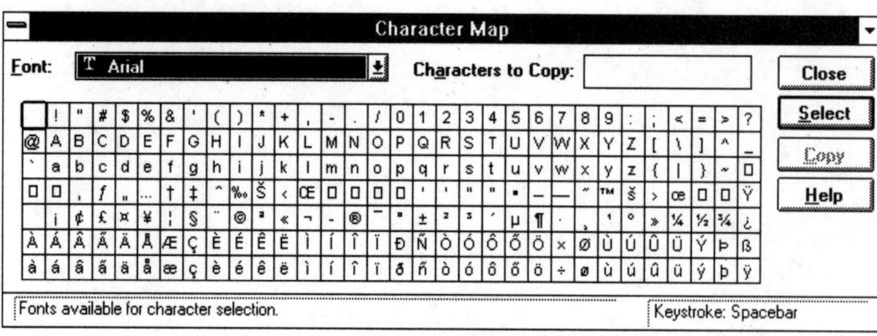

Character Map

33. Windows Programming

Programming Windows applications

In this chapter you'll begin programming Windows applications. We'll provide step-by-step instructions for developing a short Windows application in Microsoft QuickC for Windows, Borland's Turbo Pascal for Windows, and Microsoft Visual Basic.

By following the application's development in these different languages, you'll discover which language is best suited for you. Visual Basic is usually ideal for creating small and simple Windows applications in the shortest amount of time. Turbo Pascal is better for object-oriented programming. QuickC is probably the most versatile language of the three. There are also other ways to create Windows applications besides using these three languages.

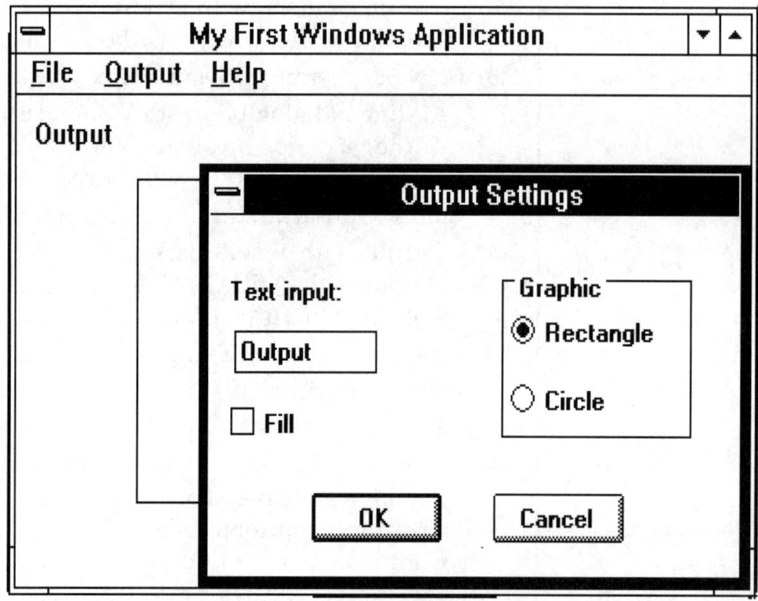

The finished sample application

The completed sample application will have a menu containing a command that allows the user to open a dialog box. The results of the settings in this dialog box are displayed in the window once they are verified by the user.

33.1 Step 1: Creating a Window

Display Window with Title

First you'll need to display a window on your screen. This window should have a system menu button, minimize and maximize buttons, a border, and a title bar containing a programmer-defined title.

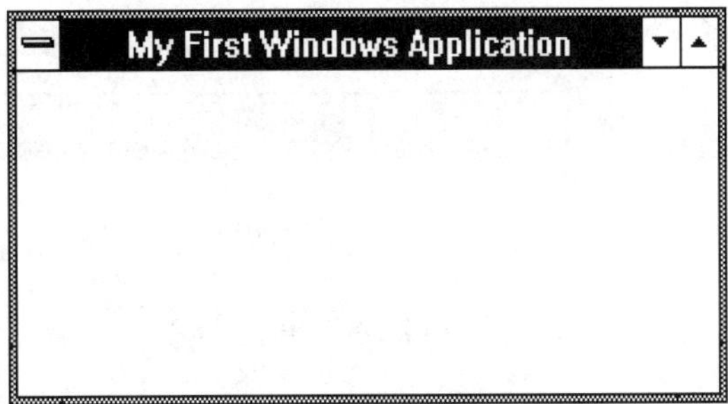

First step: Window with title

Creating a window with Visual Basic

Microsoft Visual Basic

After starting Visual Basic, several windows belonging to the Visual Basic environment normally appear on your screen.

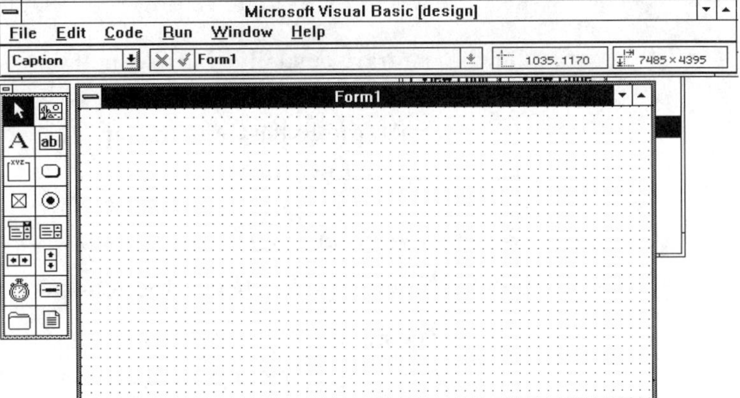

Starting Visual Basic

To create a new application in Visual Basic, you must start a new project by selecting *File/New Project*, because a project is always the basis for any Visual Basic application. Projects always consist of one window (form), as in this case, or of a combination of forms and modules. The first form (called Form1) appears on your screen automatically.

Properties Bar

By using the *Properties Bar*, you can view and modify the properties assigned to Form1. These properties settings define such things as the form's size and location, and are used as default values when the application is started.

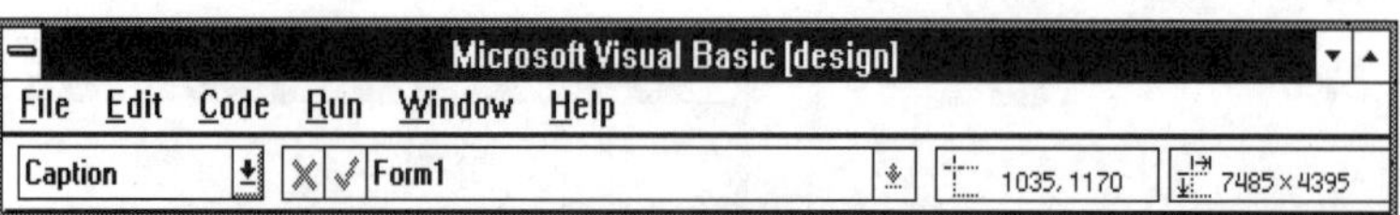

The Visual Basic Properties Bar

If you want to change a property's value, first you must select its name in the *Properties* list box. Click on the downward pointing arrow to the right of the *Properties* list box to drop down the list of properties available for the selected form.

Visual Basic automatically displays the setting of the currently selected property in the *Settings* box. The *Settings* box is a single-line list box, displaying all possible settings for the current property. When the down-arrow button to the right of the box is grayed and therefore doesn't open the settings list, this doesn't mean that only one single setting is available for that property.

On the contrary, usually this means that you're able to type the desired setting directly into the *Settings* box. As soon as you press Enter or click the Enter (√) button, the new value will replace the previous setting for that property.

Next to the Enter (√) button you'll also find the Cancel (X) button. If you haven't clicked the Enter (√) button and you don't want to change the text, you can press Esc or click the Cancel (X) button to restore the setting you've overwritten.

At this point you'll only want to specify the window's title. To do this, select the window Form1 by positioning your mouse pointer within this form and clicking your left mouse button. Then select the Caption property from the *Properties* drop-down list box. Visual Basic will then display the current Caption setting ("Form1" in this case) in the *Settings* text box, which you'll replace with "My First Windows Application". Then simply press Enter or click on the Enter (√) button.

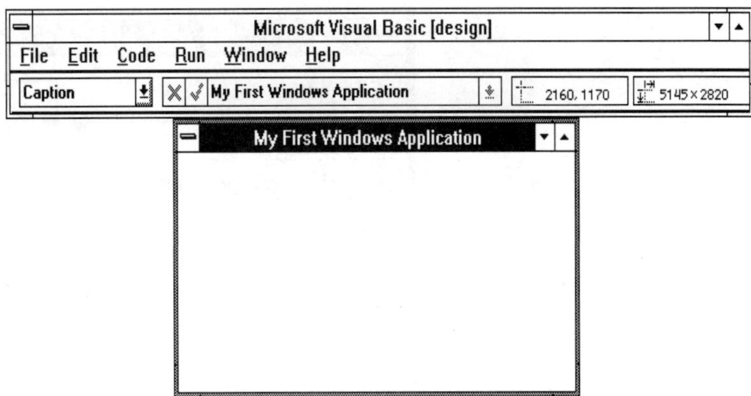

Setting the form title in Visual Basic

Saving the project

After this you'll want to save your mini-project. Select *File/Save Project As....* A dialog box appears, prompting you to save your Form1. After verifying your intention to save the form, another dialog box opens. Now you'll be able to specify a name for the form file. You can specify the directory in which the file is to be saved within the list box that's provided. We've used the file name VBSTEP1.FRM.

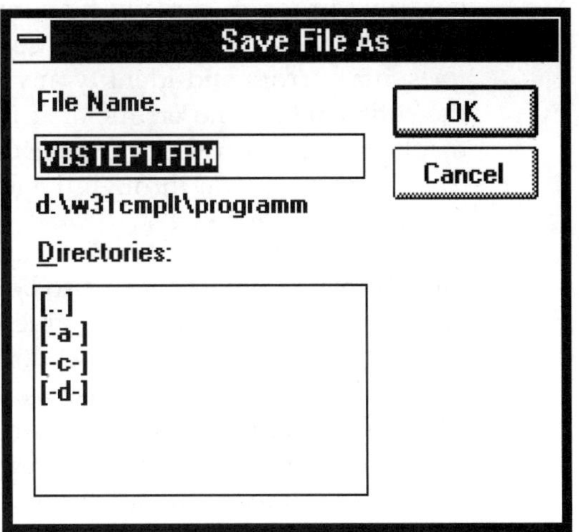

First dialog box for saving your project

Now you'll need to specify a name for the project as a whole, which will be used as the name for your .MAK file. To keep things as clear as possible, we've used the file name VBSTEP1.MAK for this file. Visual Basic stores all file names that belong to this project. At the beginning, you'll only be using a single form file. However, in the third step of developing this application, you'll be creating a second form file as well.

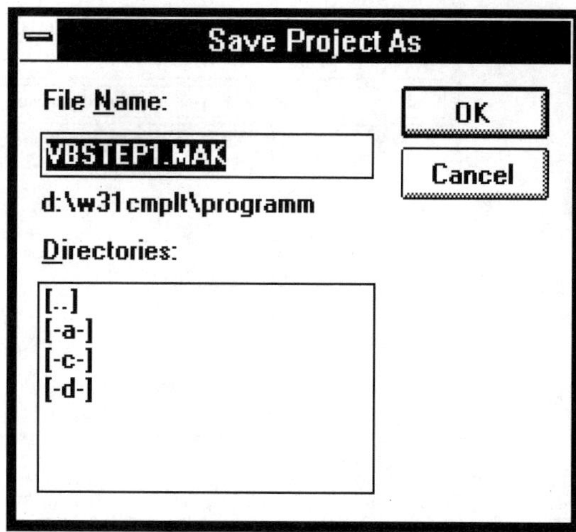

Second dialog box for saving your project

You'll now be able to use the *File/Save Project* command in order to save this project in the future.

Since Visual Basic acts as an interpreter, you won't need to create an executable .EXE file to test your program. Instead, you can try out your program directly by simply selecting *Run/Start*. If this sample program contained new code, Visual Basic would check it for syntax errors and identify any errors that were discovered. If the code contains no errors, or if no code is present, Visual Basic displays your form with the specified title in the foreground. You can end this test run through the form's System menu, or by your selecting *Run/End*.

Creating an EXE file

The completed program can also be converted in an executable and relatively small .EXE file, which will then run without the support of the Visual Basic environment. An executable Visual Basic file requires the presence of the dynamic link library VBRUN100.DLL. .EXE files are created by selecting the *File/Make EXE File...* command. Again, you'll be asked for a file name. This time the name is for the executable .EXE file, which we've called VBSTEP1.EXE.

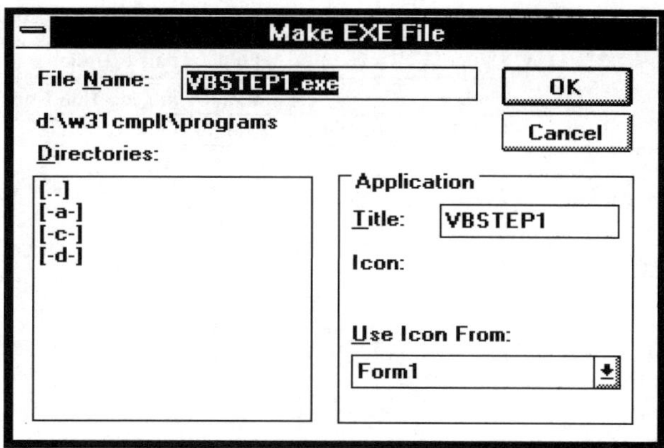

Dialog box for creating the EXE file

Upon completing the first project you should have three different files: VBSTEP1.EXE, VBSTEP1.FRM, and VBSTEP1.MAK.

Creating a window with QuickC

The C language presented the first opportunity for creating full-fledged Windows applications. Therefore, you'll find that most literature on Windows programming deals with this language. If you compare the source file listings of the different versions of the demonstration program, you'll find that the C version is the longest. However, much of this consists of the extensive comments that QuickCase:W inserts in the code. Of the three languages used here, C best illustrates Windows' inner workings, since the C version doesn't require a dynamic link library or an object library.

Before taking a closer look at how Windows works, let's look at a QuickC version of the same program we created using Visual Basic. Unlike other C language compilers, where you would type many lines of code, you can generate this C version using the QuickCase:W application. The QuickCase:W application creates a C source file for compilation based on your selections made in a prototype file.

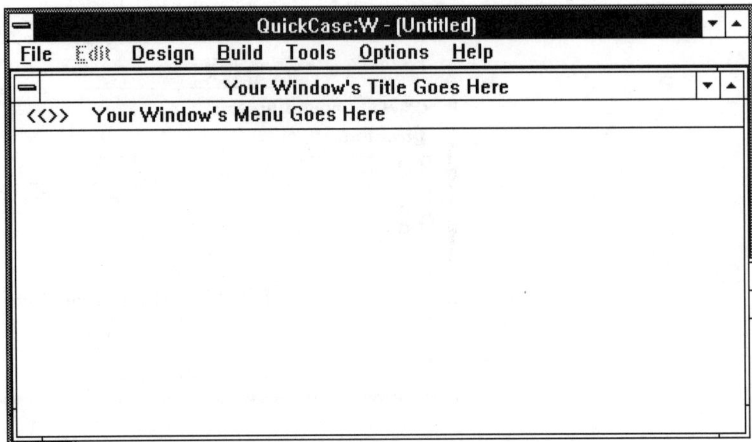

QuickCase: W

In QuickCase:W you can create your program window with a menu and, if you wish, link it to additional resources (more on this later). This prototype file you create from QuickCase:W determines how your application's operating environment will appear. The QuickCase:W interface is a window within a window. The outer window belongs to QuickCase:W, while the inner window comprises the prototype window that you're creating.

Entering the title

Double-click the QuickCase:W icon, or if you're already running QuickC for Windows, select *Tools/QuickCase:W*. The *Design* menu lets you configure your window's environment. Select the *Title...* command and type "My First Windows Application" in the *Window Title:* text box. Press Enter.

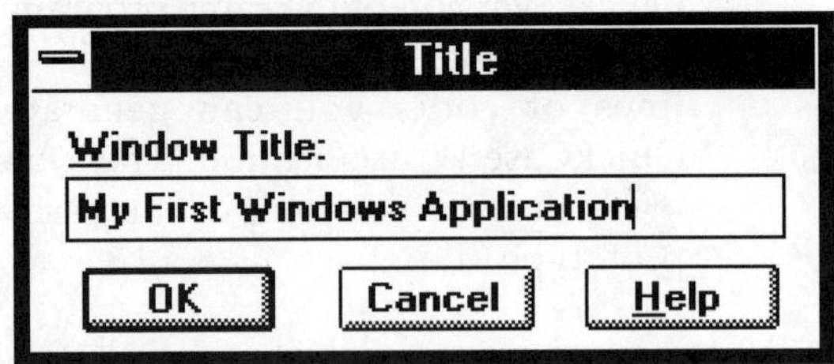

Entering the title in QuickCase:W

Window styles

Now let's ensure that your window will have a title bar. Select the *Style...* command from the *Design* menu. This opens a dialog box displaying all possible style parameters. Each check box determines whether a particular element appears in the window. When we first installed QuickC for Windows, all the check boxes in this dialog box were active except for the *Exclude Children when Painting* check box.

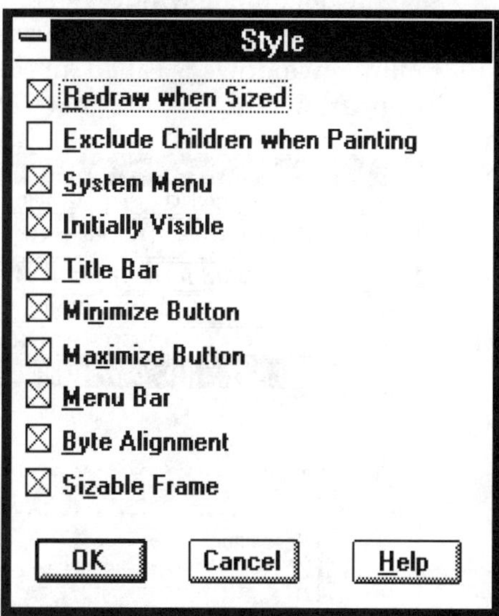

The Style dialog box in QuickCase:W

Since additional styles don't have to be added, click on Cancel to exit.

Generating code

Once you've drawn your window interface, save this prototype file by selecting *File/Save As....* Type the name QCSTEP1 in the *File Name:* text box and press Enter. QuickCase:W adds a .WIN extension to the file name and saves the prototype file.

The *Generate* command from the *Build* menu initiates the code generation. All files created in this process are assigned the same name used by the prototype (QCSTEP1 in this case). The Generate window appears as minimized while QuickCase:W generates a C source file, a makefile, and other files. The resulting files represent a project (more on this later).

If you want to see how the code generation is progressing, you can reopen the window by double-clicking the Generate icon. We suggest that you play Solitaire or Minesweeper while waiting for the code generation. When QuickCase:W has completed its task, it will beep and display a message box. This box may be hidden under other windows, especially if you're running another application while waiting for QuickCase:W to finish.

QuickC Text Editor

You can view the code generated by QuickCase:W by using the QuickC Text Editor. This application can display and manage several document windows simultaneously, and each document window can contain one C source file. An application that handles multiple windows is called an MDI (Multiple Document Interface) application.

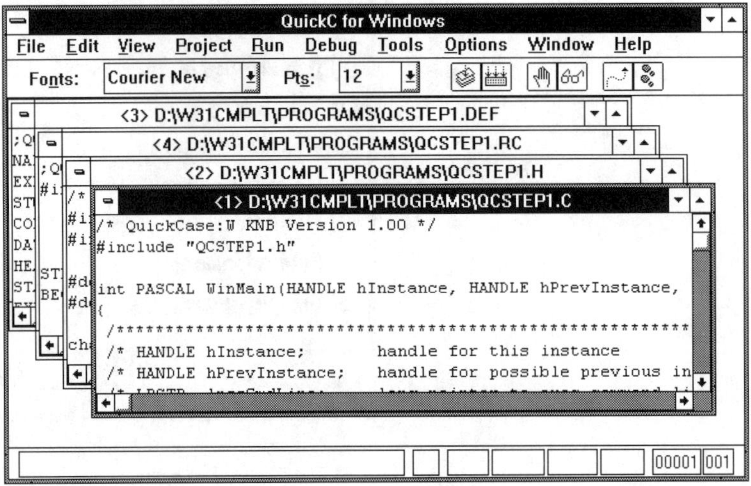

The QuickC development environment

This MDI capability lets you switch between document windows for editing. There are several different ways of switching from one document window to the next. You can either simply click the desired window, or press Ctrl + F6 or Ctrl + Tab to switch to the next window. You can also access the desired window by selecting the corresponding item from the *Window* menu. Other commands in this menu allow you to display the open document windows next to each other or overlapping one another, depending on which you prefer. If you've maximized the currently active document window by clicking its Maximize button, its title is displayed in the Text Editor's title bar.

A document window can be opened with either the *New* or *Open...* commands from the *File* menu. The *Open...* command lets you open an existing C source file. QuickC prompts you for a file name. Type the file name and press Enter.

You'll remember that we discussed projects earlier in this section. Visual Basic and QuickC both generate makefiles (files with .MAK extensions), but these files are incompatible with one another. While in the QuickC Text Editor, select *Project/Open...* to open the QCSTEP1.MAK file. Change to the correct directory, select QCSTEP1.MAK, and click OK.

Creating a Windows application in C requires many different files in addition to the source file. The C language itself accesses a compiler, linker, and resource compiler when creating an executable application, and these programs access different files in turn.

Files required for a Windows C application

- Source file (.C)
- Module definition file (.DEF)
- Header file (.H)
- Resource script (.RC)
- Project file (makefile) (.MAK)

The QuickCase:W application generates all five of these files when you select *Build/Generate*. When QuickC builds an executable Windows application, QuickC processes these files in the following order:

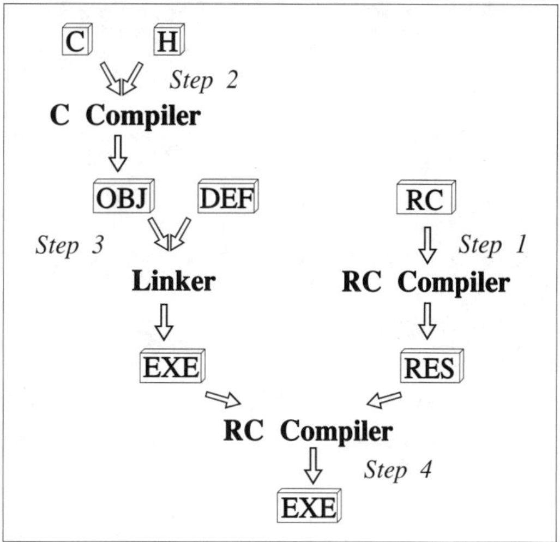

The sequence of creating an application

To help the programmer better understand the generated source file, QuickCase:W inserts comment lines. You can increase the level of commentary by selecting *Options/Comments....* When we first booted up QuickC, the system defaulted to the *Low* option button. The *Low* option yields low levels of commentary, while the *High* option goes into greater detail.

```
/* QCSTEP1.C                      */
/* QuickCase:W KNB Version 1.00 */
#include "QCSTEP1.h"

int PASCAL WinMain(HANDLE hInstance, HANDLE hPrevInstance, LPSTR lpszCmdLine, int nCmdShow)
```

```
{
/***********************************************************************/
/* HANDLE hInstance;       handle for this instance                   */
/* HANDLE hPrevInstance;   handle for possible previous instances     */
/* LPSTR  lpszCmdLine;     long pointer to exec command line          */
/* int    nCmdShow;        Show code for main window display          */
/***********************************************************************/

MSG        msg;          /* MSG structure to store your messages        */
int        nRc;          /* return value from Register Classes          */

strcpy(szAppName, "QCSTEP1");
hInst = hInstance;
if(!hPrevInstance)
  {
   /* register window classes if first instance of application        */
   if ((nRc = nCwRegisterClasses()) == -1)
     {
      /* registering one of the windows failed                        */
      LoadString(hInst, IDS_ERR_REGISTER_CLASS, szString, sizeof(szString));
      MessageBox(NULL, szString, NULL, MB_ICONEXCLAMATION);
      return nRc;
     }
  }

/* create application's Main window                                   */
hWndMain = CreateWindow(
            szAppName,                /* Window class name             */
            "My First Windows Application", /* Window's title          */
            WS_CAPTION       |        /* Title and Min/Max             */
            WS_SYSMENU       |        /* Add system menu box           */
            WS_MINIMIZEBOX   |        /* Add minimize box              */
            WS_MAXIMIZEBOX   |        /* Add maximize box              */
            WS_THICKFRAME    |        /* thick sizeable frame          */
            WS_CLIPCHILDREN  |         /* don't draw in child windows areas */
            WS_OVERLAPPED,
            CW_USEDEFAULT, 0,         /* Use default X, Y              */
            CW_USEDEFAULT, 0,         /* Use default X, Y              */
            NULL,                     /* Parent window's handle        */
            NULL,                     /* Default to Class Menu         */
            hInst,                    /* Instance of window            */
            NULL);                    /* Create struct for WM_CREATE */


if(hWndMain == NULL)
  {
   LoadString(hInst, IDS_ERR_CREATE_WINDOW, szString, sizeof(szString));
   MessageBox(NULL, szString, NULL, MB_ICONEXCLAMATION);
   return IDS_ERR_CREATE_WINDOW;
  }

ShowWindow(hWndMain, nCmdShow);           /* display main window        */

while(GetMessage(&msg, NULL, 0, 0))       /* Until WM_QUIT message      */
  {
   TranslateMessage(&msg);
   DispatchMessage(&msg);
  }

/* Do clean up before exiting from the application                    */
CwUnRegisterClasses();
return msg.wParam;
} /*  End of WinMain                                                   */
/***********************************************************************/
/*                                                                     */
/* Main Window Procedure                                               */
/*                                                                     */
/* This procedure provides service routines for the Windows events     */
/* (messages) that Windows sends to the window, as well as the user    */
/* initiated events (messages) that are generated when the user selects */
/* the action bar and pulldown menu controls or the corresponding      */
/* keyboard accelerators.                                              */
/*                                                                     */
/***********************************************************************/

LONG FAR PASCAL WndProc(HWND hWnd, WORD Message, WORD wParam, LONG lParam)
{
 HMENU       hMenu=0;            /* handle for the menu                 */
 HBITMAP     hBitmap=0;          /* handle for bitmaps                  */
 HDC         hDC;                /* handle for the display device       */
 PAINTSTRUCT ps;                 /* holds PAINT information             */
 int         nRc=0;              /* return code                         */
```

```
  switch (Message)
    {
     case WM_CREATE:

          break;        /*  End of WM_CREATE                                   */

     case WM_MOVE:      /*  code for moving the window                         */
          break;

     case WM_SIZE:      /*  code for sizing client area                        */
          break;        /* End of WM_SIZE                                      */

     case WM_PAINT:     /* code for the window's client area                   */
          /* Obtain a handle to the device context                             */
          /* BeginPaint will send WM_ERASEBKGND if appropriate                 */
          memset(&ps, 0x00, sizeof(PAINTSTRUCT));
          hDC = BeginPaint(hWnd, &ps);

          /* Included in case the background is not a pure color               */
          SetBkMode(hDC, TRANSPARENT);

          /* Inform Windows painting is complete                               */
          EndPaint(hWnd, &ps);
          break;        /*  End of WM_PAINT                                    */

     case WM_CLOSE:  /* close the window                                       */
          /* Destroy child windows, modeless dialogs, then, this window        */
          DestroyWindow(hWnd);
          if (hWnd == hWndMain)
            PostQuitMessage(0);  /* Quit the application                       */
         break;

     default:
          /* For any message for which you don't specifically provide a       */
          /* service routine, you should return the message to Windows        */
          /* for default message processing.                                   */
          return DefWindowProc(hWnd, Message, wParam, lParam);
    }
  return 0L;
}     /* End of WndProc                                                 */

/***************************************************************************/
/*                                                                         */
/* nCwRegisterClasses Function                                             */
/*                                                                         */
/* The following function registers all the classes of all the windows   */
/* associated with this application. The function returns an error code  */
/* if unsuccessful, otherwise it returns 0.                                */
/*                                                                         */
/***************************************************************************/

int nCwRegisterClasses(void)
{
 WNDCLASS   wndclass;    /* struct to define a window class                    */
 memset(&wndclass, 0x00, sizeof(WNDCLASS));


 /* load WNDCLASS with window's characteristics                                */
 wndclass.style = CS_HREDRAW | CS_VREDRAW | CS_BYTEALIGNWINDOW;
 wndclass.lpfnWndProc = WndProc;
 /* Extra storage for Class and Window objects                                 */
 wndclass.cbClsExtra = 0;
 wndclass.cbWndExtra = 0;
 wndclass.hInstance = hInst;
 wndclass.hIcon = LoadIcon(NULL, IDI_APPLICATION);
 wndclass.hCursor = LoadCursor(NULL, IDC_ARROW);
 /* Create brush for erasing background                                        */
 wndclass.hbrBackground = (HBRUSH)(COLOR_WINDOW+1);
 wndclass.lpszMenuName = szAppName;    /* Menu Name is App Name */
 wndclass.lpszClassName = szAppName; /* Class Name is App Name */
 if(!RegisterClass(&wndclass))
   return -1;


 return(0);
} /* End of nCwRegisterClasses                                                 */

/***************************************************************************/
/*  CwUnRegisterClasses Function                                           */
/*                                                                         */
/*  Deletes any references to windows resources created for this          */
/*  application, frees memory, deletes instance, handles and does         */
```

```
/*  clean up prior to exiting the window                                   */
/*                                                                         */
/**************************************************************************/

void CwUnRegisterClasses(void)
{
 WNDCLASS   wndclass;    /* struct to define a window class               */
 memset(&wndclass, 0x00, sizeof(WNDCLASS));

 UnregisterClass(szAppName, hInst);
}    /* End of CwUnRegisterClasses                                         */
;QCSTEP1.RC
#include "QCSTEP1.h"



STRINGTABLE
BEGIN
  IDS_ERR_CREATE_WINDOW,     "Window creation failed!"
  IDS_ERR_REGISTER_CLASS,    "Error registering window class"
END
/* QCSTEP1.H */
/* QuickCase:W KNB Version 1.00 */
#include <windows.h>
#include <string.h>

#define IDS_ERR_REGISTER_CLASS   1
#define IDS_ERR_CREATE_WINDOW    2

char szString[128];   /* variable to load resource strings          */

char szAppName[20];   /* class name for the window               */
HWND hInst;
HWND hWndMain;


LONG FAR PASCAL WndProc(HWND, WORD, WORD, LONG);
int nCwRegisterClasses(void);
void CwUnRegisterClasses(void);
;QCSTEP1.DEF
NAME            QCSTEP1
EXETYPE         WINDOWS
STUB            'WINSTUB.EXE'
CODE            PRELOAD MOVEABLE
DATA            PRELOAD MOVEABLE MULTIPLE
HEAPSIZE        4096
STACKSIZE       5110
EXPORTS         WndProc         @1
```

Source file

These files aren't as complicated as they may first appear. Let's examine the source file, so you can see what the code does.

QCSTEP1.C begins with an #include statement, which calls the QCSTEP1.H header file. Header files contain important information that can be included in the current file. QCSTEP1.H includes the WINDOWS.H header file in QCSTEP1.C. This header file contains the prototypes of all Windows functions, many file types, Windows messages, and many other frequently accessed constants.

QCSTEP1.C has two main components: the WinMain procedure and a window function.

WinMain

The main procedure WinMain always executes the following functions:

- Registering the classes

- Creating the main window
- Displaying the main window
- Message loop

The call for this procedure always looks as follows:

```
int PASCAL WinMain(HANDLE hInstance, HANDLE hPrevInstance, LPSTR lpszCmdLine, int nCmdShow)
```

hInstance

Windows provides all four parameters and passes them to the application. The first two parameters are the most important ones. Since you can have multiple instances of a Windows application (i.e., you can have one application running several times simultaneously), Windows must be able to differentiate between the different instances. If this wasn't true, two different instances of the same document could make unwanted changes to one of the instances.

To prevent this type of chaos, Windows assigns an explicit identification number to each application when it starts. This number is passed to the hInstance variable. This handle stored in hInstance refers to the corresponding object. The second value, hPrevInstance, refers to the previously started instance of the same application. When you start the first instance of an application, hPrevInstance contains a value of 0.

Registering the class

A class may only be registered in the first instance of the application. A class defines several basic window attributes such as background color, the appearance of the mouse pointer, and a pointer to the corresponding window function. This class then applies to all instances of the same program.

```
{
 WNDCLASS   wndclass;
 memset(&wndclass, 0x00, sizeof(WNDCLASS));
 wndclass.style = CS_HREDRAW |
                  CS_VREDRAW |
                  CS_BYTEALIGNWINDOW;
 wndclass.lpfnWndProc = WndProc;
 wndclass.cbClsExtra = 0;
 wndclass.cbWndExtra = 0;
 wndclass.hInstance = hInst;
 wndclass.hIcon = LoadIcon(NULL, IDI_APPLICATION);
 wndclass.hCursor = LoadCursor(NULL, IDC_ARROW);
 wndclass.hbrBackground = (HBRUSH)(COLOR_WINDOW+1);
 wndclass.lpszMenuName = szAppName;
 wndclass.lpszClassName = szAppName;
 if(!RegisterClass(&wndclass))
   return -1;

 return(0);
}
```

For the class registration, a variable of the WNDCLASS data structure must be filled with the desired variables, so that these can then be passed to Windows using the RegisterClass function.

Creating and displaying the window

Each window must have a reference to a registered class. In this example, the class, like the file name of our program, is called QCSTEP1, and is copied to the variable szarAppName. This parameter must therefore be used in the class registration as well as in the construction of the window. The WS constants passed to the CreateWindow function correspond to the enabled check boxes found in Quick Case:W's *Style* dialog box. The ShowWindow function displays the window on your monitor.

```
hWndMain = CreateWindow(szAppName,
        "My First Windows Application",
             WS_CAPTION       | WS_SYSMENU       |
             WS_MINIMIZEBOX   | WS_MAXIMIZEBOX   |
             WS_THICKFRAME    | WS_CLIPCHILDREN  |
             WS_OVERLAPPED,
             CW_USEDEFAULT, 0, CW_USEDEFAULT, 0,
             NULL, NULL,  hInst, NULL);
```

Message loop

Windows is a message-oriented system, which means that information is exchanged through sending messages and receiving messages. Information can originate from the user when he or she presses a key or moves the mouse. Windows also generates many messages independently (e.g., for window management). It's also responsible for receiving these messages and channeling them to the proper applications.

Capture and focus

For example, when you type text in a word processor, all messages generated by your keyboard input must be sent to the word processor, not some other program whose window might also be open on your screen. To ensure this, Windows notes which window should receive the entries from the keyboard, and which window should receive input from mouse movement and pressing mouse buttons. The terms "capture" and "focus" refer to this; focus refers to keyboard input and capture refers to mouse input.

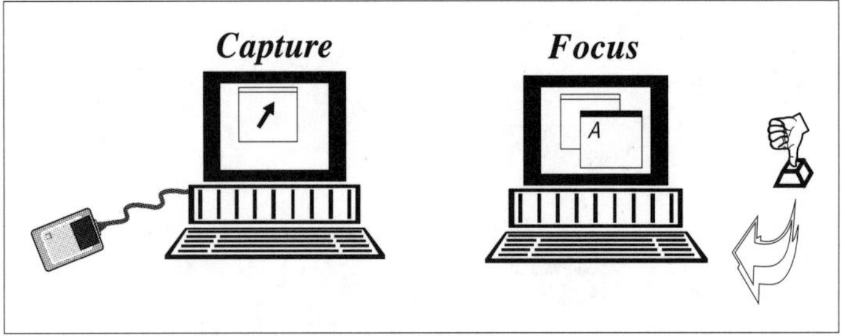

Capture and focus

Normally the active window has the focus, and the window over which the mouse pointer is currently positioned has the capture.

Message queue

Windows collects all window messages in a system message queue, which channels the messages to the correct application message queue. This means that one system message queue exists for the entire Windows system, and one application message queue exists for each active application.

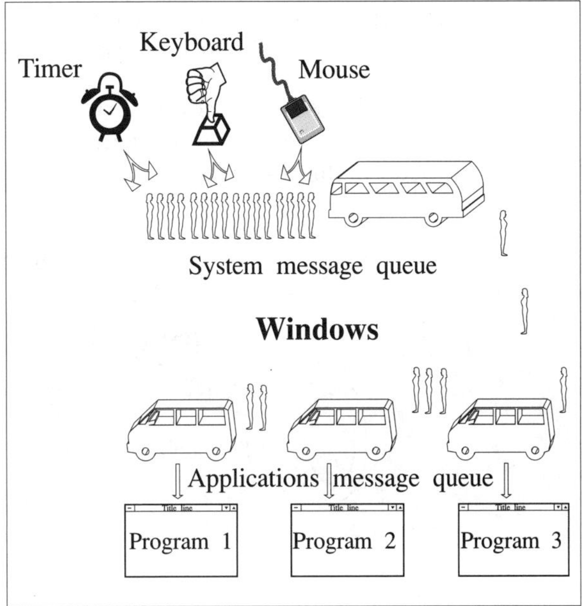

Message queues

Although it isn't possible to access the system message queue from your program, each GetMessage function call pulls one message from the application message queue for your application and places it in the variable msg within the MSG data structure. The MSG structure consists of six fields, the first four of which are the most important:

- hwnd Identifies the window to receive the message
- message The message to be processed
- wParam Varies with the message
- lParam Varies with the message

A message is basically a specific hexadecimal value that is specified by Windows. This value varies with the information that is being relayed. This information can originate either from a driver located within the system (i.e., the keyboard or mouse driver) or from Windows itself. The WINDOWS.H header file contains the names of these messages. Most messages begin with the two letters WM (Windows Messages).

The message WM_KEYDOWN in the msg variable indicates that the user pressed a key. The keycode is also included with this message, so the key that has been pressed can be identified. Pressing the left mouse button triggers a WM_LBUTTONDOWN message, which is accompanied by the current mouse pointer position as additional information.

The GetMessage function starts the message loop, which receives all messages and channels them to the corresponding window function. This is where the messages are processed.

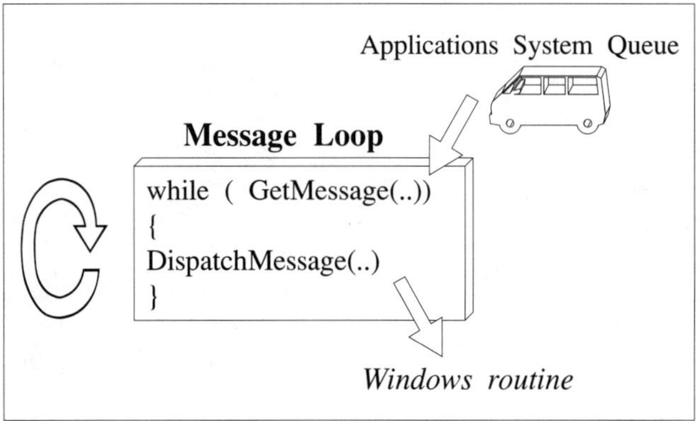

Message loop

The loop is formed within a While statement and always contains at least two functions: GetMessage and DispatchMessage.

```
while(GetMessage(&msg, NULL, 0, 0))
{
 TranslateMessage(&msg);
 DispatchMessage(&msg);
}
```

In addition to retrieving the next message from the application message queue, the GetMessage function is also important to the non-preemptive multitasking of Windows. If no more messages are waiting in the message queue, perhaps because the user hasn't made additional entries, the application pauses at this function and returns CPU control to Windows. Windows then delegates the CPU to the next application, which can then process its own application message queue. Once all other applications have accessed the CPU in this way, your application will again be able to use the CPU.

Instead of being processed by the WinMain main procedure, the messages are processed by the window function specified by the class. In our example this is named WndProc.

```
WNDCLASS   wndclass;
wndclass.lpfnWndProc = WndProc;
```

The DispatchMessage function passes the messages on to this window function.

The message loop must be interruptable when the user wants to end the application. Once GetMessage has pulled a message from the queue, it almost always returns the value TRUE. The value FALSE will be returned only at the WM_QUIT message, which is triggered when the user selects *Close* from the application's system menu or when Alt + F4 is pressed. The While loop terminates and the entire application ends.

Window function

We mentioned earlier that each Windows program requires at least one window function in addition to the main procedure WinMain. The size and extent of this window function depends on the tasks it must perform. The parameters passed to this function are identical to the first four fields of the MSG structure, so the messages can be processed together with their supplementary information.

```
LONG FAR PASCAL WndProc(HWND hWnd, WORD Message,
                        WORD wParam, LONG lParam)
```

In the window function a switch statement processes the individual messages. Only the messages, which are important to the application, are called. All other messages are passed on a default window function called DefWindowProc. This procedure reacts to several messages, ensuring that an application operates according to Windows standards, and ignores all other messages.

```
switch (Message)
  {
   case WM_CREATE:


        break;

   case WM_MOVE:
        break;

   case WM_SIZE:
        break;

   case WM_PAINT:
        memset(&ps, 0x00, sizeof(PAINTSTRUCT));
        hDC = BeginPaint(hWnd, &ps);

        SetBkMode(hDC, TRANSPARENT);

        EndPaint(hWnd, &ps);
        break;

   case WM_CLOSE:
        DestroyWindow(hWnd);
        if (hWnd == hWndMain)
          PostQuitMessage(0);
       break;

   default:
        return DefWindowProc(hWnd, Message,
                             wParam, lParam);
  }
```

Once a message has been processed, execution returns to the message queue, and the next message is then taken from the message queue.

A resource script has an .RC extension. Resource scripts contain resources used by their corresponding applications, such as menu and dialog box definitions. We'll examine resource scripts in more detail in Step 2 of this programming project.

The header file QCSTEP1.H contains global variables used in the WinMain procedure and the WndProc function.

```
HWND hInst;
HWND hWndMain;
```

When you run the program, the hInst variable receives the instance handle, while the hWndMain variable refers to the window. After a successful execution of the CreateWindow function, hWndMain is assigned a value.

Definition file

Module definition file

In addition to the source file, QuickCase:W generates a module definition file. The linker needs this file to make an executable Windows application.

```
;QCSTEP1.DEF
NAME            QCSTEP1
EXETYPE         WINDOWS
STUB            'WINSTUB.EXE'
CODE            PRELOAD MOVEABLE
DATA            PRELOAD MOVEABLE MULTIPLE
HEAPSIZE        4096
STACKSIZE       5110
EXPORTS         WndProc          @1
```

This file contains information about the use of code and data segments, the size of the local heap, and the stack, as well as other information. In addition to this, all functions that must be exported are specified at the EXPORTS statement. This is the case when a function is called by other programs or by Windows itself, such as the window function. The ordinal number at the end of the EXPORTS statement is optional.

Compiler and linker

Creating an executable program

You'll need to set the compiler, RC compiler, and linker options correctly, since QuickC can be used to create DOS applications, Windows applications, and other applications. By selecting *Options/Project...* you'll open a dialog box in which you can specify the type of program you want to create. Select the Windows EXE option button and the Debug option button (the latter will let you test your application). Separate dialog boxes are provided for setting the compiler and linker options. We used the following settings for our sample program:

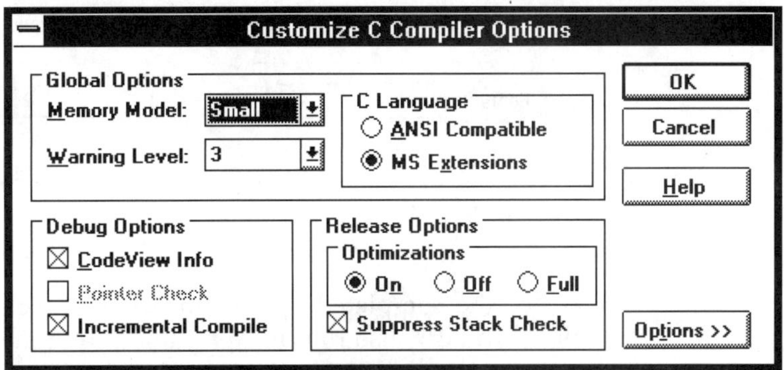

Settings for the compiler

The dialog box expands when you click the Options>> button, so you can set the compiler switches directly. All Windows applications require the /Gw and /Zp switches. So if you selected the *Windows EXE* option button, these switches are automatically added.

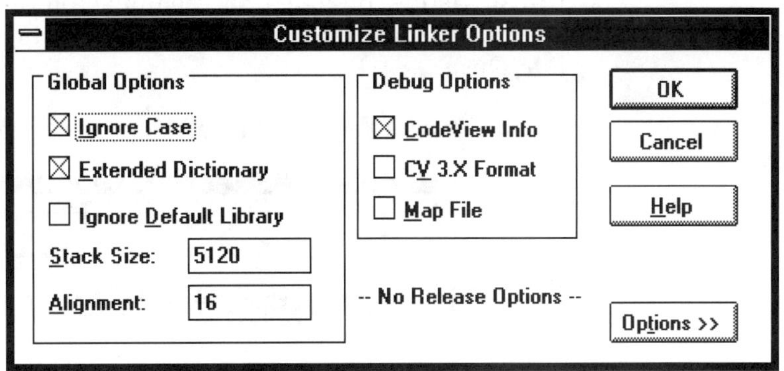

Settings for the linker

You must also enter the correct directories in the *Directories* dialog box, which lists the paths for include (header) files and library files.

Now you can convert your program to an executable file. Select *Build* or *Rebuild All* from the *Project* menu. If one or more errors were found during compilation or linking, QuickC interrupts the process, and the Errors window displays any error or warning messages. Buttons in the QuickC development environment's toolbar also let you compile and build (link) source files, mark breakpoints, watch for expressions, trace program execution, and step over program lines.

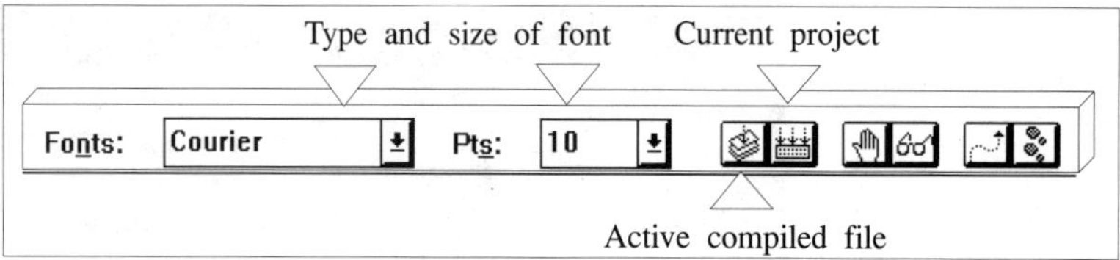

QuickC toolbar

Once the completed application is built, select *Run/Go* or press F5. You can also run the application from the File Manager, or by adding the application to a group and double-clicking its icon. The result should look just like the Visual Basic application VBSTEP1.

Creating a window with Turbo Pascal

Borland International's Turbo Pascal for Windows has an integrated development environment similar to Microsoft QuickC's environment.

The Turbo editor also allows you to edit multiple document files, with a window provided for each file. You can open a new file by selecting *File/New*, or open an existing file by selecting *File/Open....*

If you select the latter, a dialog box prompts you for the file name.

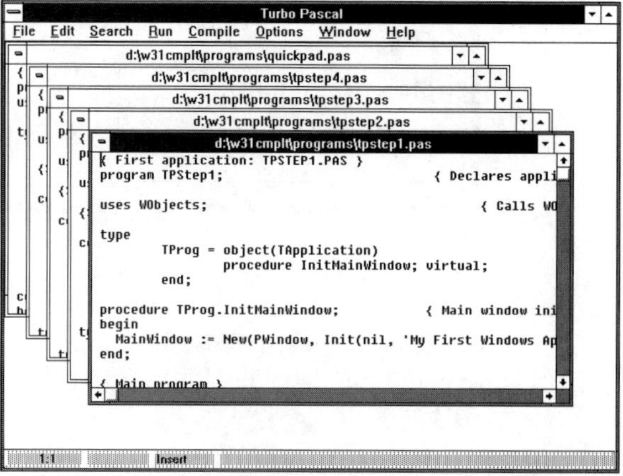

The integrated design environment of Turbo Pascal

The status bar (the bottom line of the Turbo window) contains four fields.

These fields indicate current cursor row and column, whether you've made changes to the source file, whether insert or overwrite mode is active, and any error messages.

To create a new application, you must open a new document window, in which the file will first receive the default name NONAME00.PAS. This name can be changed when you save this file. If you want to create your own first program in Turbo Pascal, you must type several lines of Pascal code:

```
{ First application: TPSTEP1.PAS }
program TPStep1;                          { Declares application name }

uses WObjects;                                  { Calls WObjects unit }

type
     TProg = object(TApplication)                         { Objects }
             procedure InitMainWindow; virtual;
     end;

procedure TProg.InitMainWindow;           { Main window initialization }
begin
  MainWindow := New(PWindow, Init(nil, 'My First Windows Application'));
end;

{ Main program }
var MyFirstApp: TProg;

begin
  MyFirstApp.Init('TPWin');
  MyFirstApp.Run;
  MyFirstApp.Done;
end.
```

Turbo Pascal for Windows is an object-oriented language. You'll find the "uses WObjects" statement in every Turbo Pascal program in this chapter.

The word *object* refers to any independent element or unit of Windows.

Defining an object

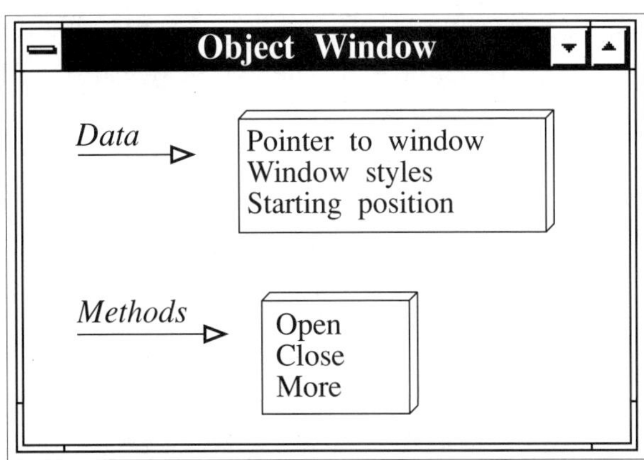

Object definition

Methods

The procedures and functions that are assigned to an object are called methods.

The TApplication object

The WObjects unit must be included in each Turbo Pascal program. Among other things, WObjects contains the standard types for window objects, such as TApplication. This is needed by every application because it's responsible for the basic operation of a program. However, TApplication creates children, rather than direct instances or variations of the TApplication object type.

This is the only way in which the application can receive its desired appearance, such as its own title and the necessary properties.

For this, inherited methods must be overwritten, which is only possible with newly defined object types, such as TProg. Object names usually begin with the letter "T" (for "Type").

Defining an object type

New object types are defined using the *object* keyword. The object on which this new type is based can be placed in parentheses following the keyword.

If the new object has no parent, this argument is simply omitted. The reserved word *End* completes the object declaration.

```
type
     TProg = object(TApplication)                          { Objects }
               procedure InitMainWindow; virtual;
     end;
```

In this example the TProg object type is defined as the child of the TApplication object type. The new object inherits all data fields and methods of the TApplication standard object.

Only those methods that must perform additional or new tasks need to be overwritten.

The InitMain-Window method

In your first program, the InitMainWindow method will be rewritten, so the window can display a programmer-defined caption in its title bar. If you were willing to omit the title, you could use the InitMainWindow method of the TApplication object. This method, in its default configuration, produces a standard window of type TWindow without a title. The InitMainWindow method must be appended with the word *virtual*, since it has been defined in the same way in the TApplication object. So, the method is virtual instead of static, and is central to the process of object-oriented programming. The actual declaration of this method occurs once the TProg object has been established.

```
procedure TProg.InitMainWindow;           { Main window initialization }
begin
  MainWindow := New(PWindow, Init(nil, 'My First Windows Application'));
end;
```

When declaring a method, the name of the object to which this method belongs must precede the name of the method, separated by a period. So the compiler can assign the method to the correct object.

This method calls the New function, which initiates an object of type TWindow. You can recognize this in the PWindow parameter, which functions as a predefined pointer to the TWindow object type.

Both the pointer PWindow and the object type TWindow were defined in the WObjects unit. The second parameter of the New function consists of an initialization routine that specifies a title.

The object-oriented main procedure

The main procedure of an object-oriented Turbo Pascal Windows application almost always looks the same:

```
{ Main program }
var MyFirstApp: TProg;

begin
  MyFirstApp.Init('TPWin');
  MyFirstApp.Run;
  MyFirstApp.Done;
end.
```

First a variable of the homemade object type TProg must be defined. This process is also known as *instancing*, or creating an instance of this particular object, TProg.

Then the three methods Init, Run, and Done are almost always called.

The TProg object type inherited these methods from the TApplication object. Init is responsible for the registration of the required class(es) and for constructing and showing windows. Run processes the message queue.

If specific cleanup chores must be performed before the program can be terminated, this is handled by the Done method. With this, the WinMain procedure of the C program has been realized in Turbo Pascal by simply using these three methods.

The next step consists of converting these lines to Pascal code to create an executable Windows application. Select *Compile* from the *Compile* menu. You can also start the compiler by pressing Alt + F9.

If you use Ctrl instead of Alt, the application will be started immediately upon the successful compilation of your code. This is the key combination for the *Run* command, found in the *Run* menu.

33.2 Step 2: Adding a Menu

Adding icon and menu

Now let's add two elements to our application: a menu set and an icon. The menu titles will allow access from both the keyboard and the mouse. The icon will allow us to minimize the application, and add the application to a group.

Menu

Almost all Windows applications have their own menu in addition to the System menu. This menu forms an important interface between the application and its user.

This increases the program's user-friendliness because the Windows commands are usually stored in program menus.

A menu consists of a series of elements, which are mainly commands that perform certain program tasks. These commands can be selected either through the keyboard or by using the mouse.

Such commands are also known as menu items. However, a menu can also contain the names of additional menus, called sub-menus.

These menus also contain their own menu items. Such sub-menus are identified by a triangle placed to the right of the command.

In this way, you can create a hierarchical menu structure consisting of up to six menu levels.

The menu bar should contain only menu names; otherwise, the user could easily select a certain command or function accidentally.

Accelerator key

Individual menu items in a menu often contain an underlined letter. The corresponding key is called an accelerator. By using this key, program functions can be selected quickly with the keyboard.

For example, menu items that have accelerators can be accessed by simply pressing Alt and the item's accelerator, instead of using the mouse or your cursor keys to first open the menu and then select the desired item.

Within a given sub-menu, you should never use the same letter as an accelerator for more than a one menu item because Windows wouldn't know which item should be activated when this accelerator is activated.

When creating your menus, you can define an accelerator for any given menu item by placing an ampersand (&) in front of the letter that you want to use as the accelerator key.

Keyboard shortcuts

A key combination, displayed to the right of a menu name or a menu item, indicates that you can access that menu or item by pressing that key combination, even without first opening the corresponding menu.

Since such key combinations provide shortcuts for accessing various functions and commands, they are called shortcut keys.

You must program the function of commands that the user can select from your program's menus. However, Windows handles the management of your menus and the display of individual menu items.

Icon

An icon is a small symbol or picture that graphically represents your application when it's minimized or reduced to its smallest on-screen size. The application can be minimized by simply clicking the Minimize button, or it can be minimized from within the actual application. The icons of all minimized applications are placed in the lower portion of the screen and can be moved around the desktop surface.

Each Windows application should have its own icon because this makes it easier for the user to find the correct program, especially when numerous applications have been minimized.

Resources

When you write a Windows program, in Turbo Pascal or QuickC, that contains a menu, a dialog box, or an icon, your application will include one or more code and data segments, as well as resource segments that are contained in the executable EXE file, just like the other segments.

There are several advantages to using separate resource segments. Instead of being loaded when the program starts, the resources are usually loaded as needed by the application. This saves memory. Such resource segments are also loaded into memory only once, so several instances of the same application can use the same resource segments.

The ease with which resource segments can be exchanged is another advantage. For example, when a QuickC application must be marketed in several different languages, storing the menus in resources allow easy upgrades to the other languages. If the menus are stored in the data segment, the entire application must be translated for each version. As long as the resource names remain unchanged, only the resource compiler must be run again.

Creating a menu with Visual Basic

Visual Basic includes its own IconWorks application for generating icons. To make this source file into an EXE file, load the project file of this program (ICONWRKS.MAK) into your Visual Basic environment and select the *Make EXE File...* command. After this you'll be able to use IconWorks outside of Visual Basic as well. The program consists of two different windows, the Editor and the Viewer. Upon starting IconWorks, the editor first appears, with which you can create new icons and modify existing ones.

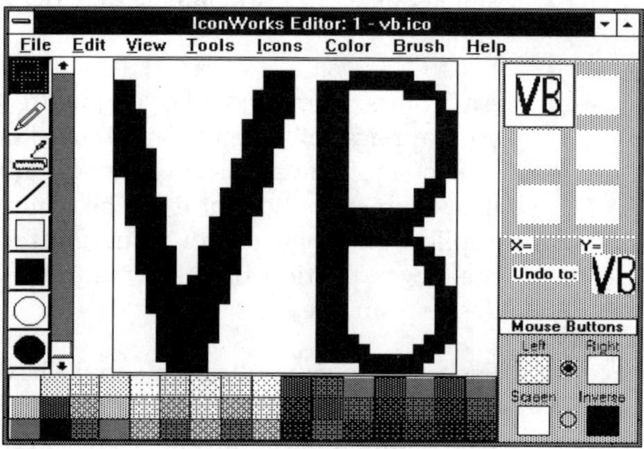

ICONWORKS

A rectangular box, in which the icon is constructed, appears. The right side of the IconWorks window displays the icon in almost its actual size.

Visual Basic's icon library contains hundreds of ready-made icons. However, we created our own. We've saved this icon under the name VB.ICO (you'll find this icon on the companion diskette for this book). The VB represents Visual Basic, while the .ICO extension indicates an icon.

The Icon property

In Visual Basic, the icon is usually set through a window property in the same way as the window's title. Open the VBSTEP1 project you created earlier in this chapter. To specify an icon for this Visual Basic program, select *Icon* in the *Properties* list box, upon which (none) should appear in the *Settings* box. If you now click the ... button to the right of the *Settings* box, a dialog box opens. Select the name of the icon (in our case, VB.ICO) and click OK.

Now (none) in the *Settings* box should have been replaced by (Icon).

Menus and shortcut keys

To equip your window with its own menu, select *Menu Design Window* from the *Window* menu.

Now, in the *Caption:* text box, enter the menu name that should appear in your window's menu bar. Each item also requires a name by which it can be referred to within the program code. This name is entered in the next text box, *CtlName:*. To move to the next property, click Next. The arrow buttons are used to switch to further menu levels; the right-arrow button will move you one menu level deeper, and the left-arrow button will move you one level closer to the top of the menu hierarchy.

You can also assign a shortcut key to each menu item by specifying a particular key in the *Accelerator:* list box. A shortcut key defined in this way will automatically appear to the right of the menu item in your finished application when the menu is pulled down. Once you've defined all menu titles and menu items in this way, click *Done* to validate your entries and to assign these settings to your Visual Basic form.

For our example, we've chosen the following menu Titles, CtlNames, and Shortcut keys. The dialog box defaults to the main menu level. To move the menu level to 2, click on the -> button:

Title	**CtlName**	**Menu level**	**Shortcut key**
&File	File	1	
&New	File_New	2	Ctrl+N
&Save	File_Save	2	Ctrl+S
&Output	File_Output	1	
&Settings	Output_In	2	F2
&Help	Help	1	
&Index	Help_Index	2	

Now you can perform your first test on the menu. You can do this without actually starting the program because it's possible to open your new menus directly within the interactive Visual Basic design environment.

However, at this point, selecting any one of the menu points doesn't trigger an action. This is the next step. When one of the three functions, *New*, *Save*, or *Index* is selected, a window containing the name of the selected menu item must appear on the screen.

The Visual Basic Code window

Unlike QuickC or Turbo Pascal, Visual Basic doesn't provide a text editor for editing your program code. Instead, Visual Basic is equipped with a *Code* window, which opens when you double-click your form.

However, the *Code* window can also be opened from the *Project* window by clicking the View Code button. The *Project* window can be brought to the foreground by selecting its name in the *Window* menu.

Visual Basic is also designed to be an object-oriented language. So both the window, or form, as well as each individual menu item is considered an individual object. All existing objects of the active form file are displayed in the left combo box, the *Object* box of the *Code* window. The Procedure box contains the events recognized by the object currently displayed in the *Object* box.

An event is simply a message, just as you encountered in the explanation of Windows operations in the previous step. As in QuickC or Turbo Pascal, you must deal only with those messages or events that are important to your application. Not all objects respond to the same events. For example, a double-click isn't used with a menu item but it is used with a list box. The *Code* window lists only those events which actually apply to the current object.

When the user clicks a menu item, a Click event is triggered, which relates specifically to that menu item. You'll write an event procedure which will respond specifically to that event. Since we intend to display message boxes for each of the three individual menu items, we'll need to write three different event procedures. Visual Basic provides us with a SUB for each one.

In your application, select the *File/New* command. A window opens, containing the following lines:

```
Sub File_New_Click ()

End Sub
```

In the blank line following the first line, type the following:

```
  MsgBox File_New.Caption, 48, "Menu item"
```

The code in this window should now look like this:

```
Sub File_New_Click ()
  MsgBox File_New.Caption, 48, "Menu item"
End Sub
```

Select the "MsgBox..." line and press Ctrl + Ins to copy it. Press Alt + F4 to close the window. Now select *File/Save* from the application. Another window appears. Move the insertion point to the second line of this window, and press Shift + Ins. Now edit the window so that it looks like this:

```
Sub File_Save_Click ()
  MsgBox File_Save.Caption, 48, "Menu item"
End Sub
```

Press Alt + F4 to close the window. Now select *Help/Index* from the application. Another window appears. Move the insertion point to the second line of this window, and press Shift + Ins. Now edit the window so that it looks like this:

```
Sub Help_Index_Click ()
  MsgBox Help_Index.Caption, 48, "Menu item"
End Sub
```

The Caption property

Each menu item is an independent object and is also equipped with specific properties. One of these is the Caption property, which you've already encountered in the Visual Basic form, and which contains the text that will appear within the menu.

Since we want to specify captions for each of the menu items, and not for the form as a whole, you must specify the name of the object in addition to the property (e.g., in addition to Help_Index.Caption).

To specify the object in this way, use the name that you've specified for that object in its CtlName property.

The MsgBox function

MsgBox produces a small window or box, in which you can display a title and any desired text. Through the second parameter of this function, you can specify whether to equip the message box with buttons and whether to display one of four default icons.

For example, the number 48 provides a message box containing an OK button and an exclamation point icon.

Once you've added the icon, the menu, the shortcut keys, and the three event procedures to your Visual Basic program, select *File/Save File As....*

Type the name VBSTEP2.FRM and click OK. Now select *File/Save Project As....* Type VBSTEP2.MAK and click OK. To create an .EXE file of this project, select *File/Make EXE File....* Make sure that the *File Name:* text box lists VBSTEP2.EXE and click OK.

Creating a menu with QuickC

The Image Editor graphics program provided with the QuickC software package lets you create your own icons, mouse pointers, and bitmaps. Upon starting this editor, you can either load an existing resource by selecting *File/Open...* or begin creating an entirely new picture by selecting *File/New*. When you select the latter, a dialog box prompts you for the type of resource you want to create. Bitmap is the default for this setting. Click on the Icon option button and click OK.

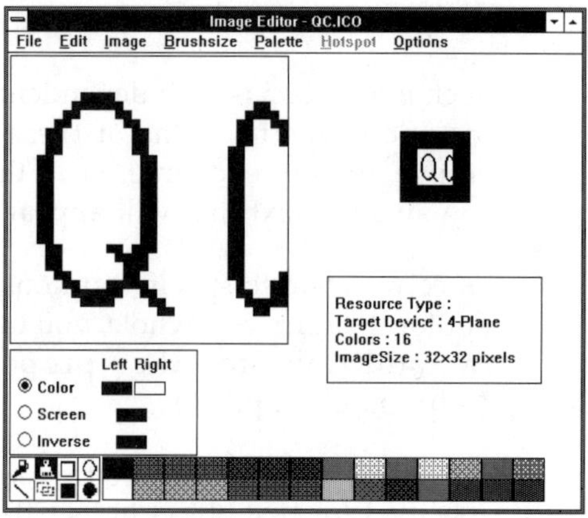

The graphics program IMAGEDIT

If you want to create a new icon with the Image Editor, you must specify the screen resolution. You'll be able to choose from several different options. After this, the Image Editor displays an empty box, in which you can draw your icon. As in IconWorks, the picture is also displayed to the right of this picture box, again in approximately the same size as the final icon. We saved the completed icon, using the name QC.ICO, by selecting *File/Save*. After you save the icon, select *File/Exit* to exit.

Adding an icon with QuickCase:W

Start QuickCase:W and open the QCSTEP1.WIN project you were working on earlier. You can attach your own icons using the *Icon...* command from the *Design* menu. This function opens a dialog box where you can specify a drive as well as a directory, and then select the icon file (.ICO) that you want to assign to your application and click OK.

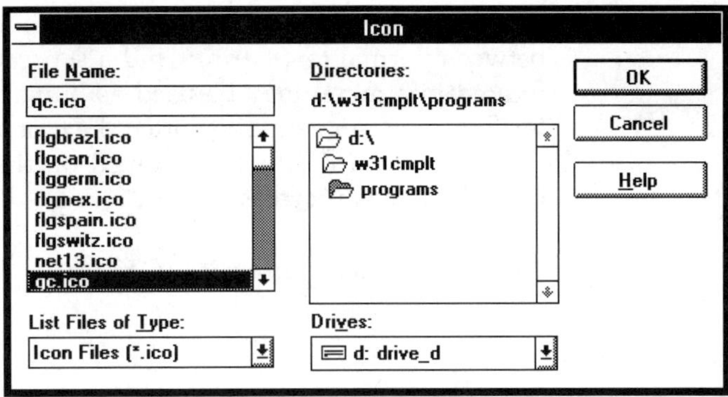

The Icon dialog box

Creating a menu with QuickCase:W

In QuickC, menus are also created by using QuickCase:W. Position your mouse pointer on the double-chevron marker (<<>>) and click on that marker. This will open a dialog box, in which you can enter a menu title or a menu item.

The *Link To* list box in the lower area of the dialog box lets you specify what type of menu element you want to create. From this list box you can assign one of four options to each string.

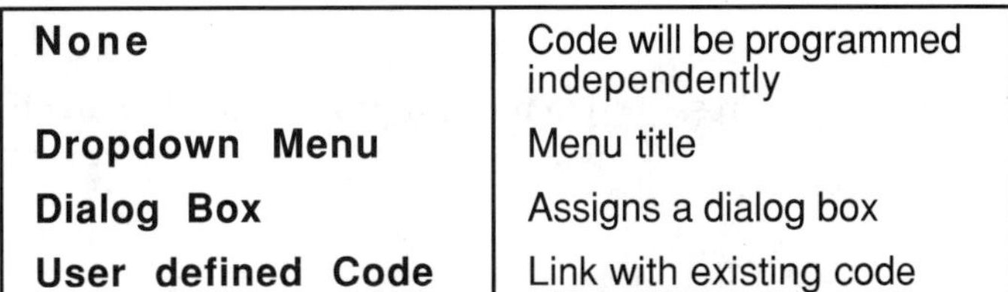

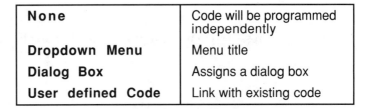

None	Code will be programmed independently
Dropdown Menu	Menu title
Dialog Box	Assigns a dialog box
User defined Code	Link with existing code

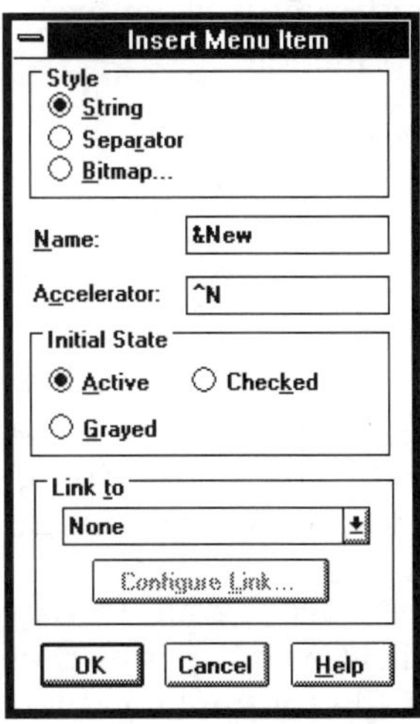

Dialog box for creating menus with QuickCase:W

When you want to add an entry to the menu bar, you can choose between normal text (string) and a separator. Menu items that are located in a menu may be used as bitmaps. Using the *Accelerator* text box, you can define a shortcut key for any given menu item. So, the Help menu title will be placed on the right end of the menu bar; its name is preceded by "\a".

Type the following and click OK:

```
&File
```

Click on the <<>> marker below the *File* menu title in your application window. Type the following in the *Name:* text box:

```
&New
```

Press Tab to move to the *Accelerator:* text box and type:

```
Ctrl+N
```

Click OK.

Click on the <<>> marker below the *New* menu item in your application window. Type the following in the *Name:* text box:

```
&Save
```

Press Tab to move to the *Accelerator:* text box and type:

```
Ctrl+S
```

Click OK.

Continue this process until you've entered the following information:

```
&File
  &New        Ctrl+N
  &Save       Ctrl+S
&Output
  &Settings   F2
&Help
  &Index
```

Once you've entered all menu titles and menu items, select *File/Save As...* and save the project as QCSTEP2. Select *Build/Generate* to generate three QCSTEP2 files. Exit QuickCase:W and run QuickC.

Menus and icons are resources

Since icons, as well as menus, are considered resources, QuickCase:W places their definitions in the .RC file. Until now, the file has contained a table containing two texts. These texts are displayed in case the class hasn't been registered, or if the window cannot be created. Each resource, except for this text table, has a name that can often be used either as an ASCII string or a number.

When resources are linked to the program with QuickCase:W, the name of the icon, the name of the menu, as well as the name of the table for the shortcut keys are always the same as the name of the entire project (QSTEP2).

```
;QCSTEP2.RC
#include "QCSTEP2.h"
QCSTEP2 ICON  QC.ICO


QCSTEP2 MENU
  BEGIN
    POPUP  "&File"
      BEGIN
        MENUITEM "&New\tCtrl+N", IDM_F_NEW
        MENUITEM "&Save\tCtrl+S", IDM_F_SAVE
      END
    POPUP  "&Output"
      BEGIN
        MENUITEM "&Settings\tF2", IDM_O_SETTINGS
      END
    POPUP  "&Help"
      BEGIN
        MENUITEM "&Index", IDM_H_INDEX
      END
  END


QCSTEP2 ACCELERATORS
  BEGIN
    "^N", IDM_F_NEW
    "^S", IDM_F_SAVE
    VK_F2, IDM_O_SETTINGS, VIRTKEY
  END

STRINGTABLE
BEGIN
  IDS_ERR_CREATE_WINDOW,      "Window creation failed!"
  IDS_ERR_REGISTER_CLASS,     "Error registering window class"
END
```

BEGIN and END statements precede and follow each menu title and menu item. The \t parameter within a menu item string assigns keyboard accelerators to the right of the respective items. Each menu item requires a unique ID value, which determines the action to be taken in the source file. This ID can consist of a number from 0 to 65535, or an icon name (which must be predefined in the QCSTEP2.H header file).

```
#define IDM_FILE                  1000
#define IDM_F_NEW                      1050
#define IDM_F_SAVE                     1100
#define IDM_OUTPUT                2000
#define IDM_O_SETTINGS                 2050
#define IDM_HELP                  3000
#define IDM_H_INDEX                    3050
```

QuickCase:W assigns these names according to a predetermined system. They always begin with the letters IDM, followed by an underscore character, followed by the first letter of the menu containing the item, followed by an underscore character. The name ends with the menu item caption (text). A sub-menu contains no ID value, since its selection only displays the menu items assigned to it. Windows automatically displays these menu items.

Linking resources to the source file

All resources defined in the .RC file must be loaded in the source file for access. The icon must be entered in the class, since it represents a separate class property. The *LoadIcon* function is responsible for loading the icon, using the instance handle as its first parameter and the icon name specified in the RC file as its second parameter.

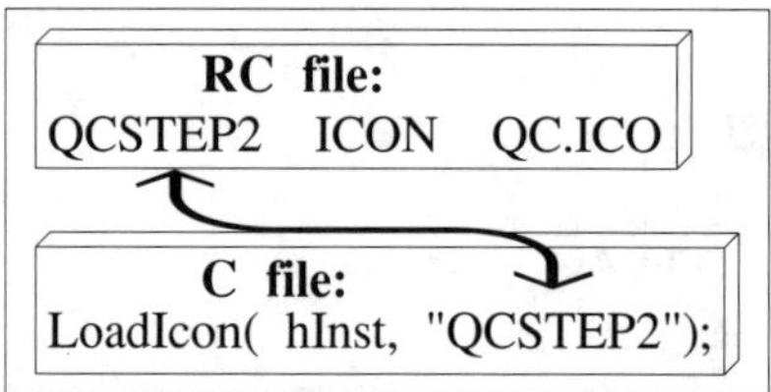

Specifying an icon in QuickC

The menu can also be assigned to the class, as in the use of QuickCase:W. However, the menu could also be declared when the window is created. If the menu is specified with the class, it doesn't need to be loaded using LoadMen. Instead, the menu name QCSTEP2 is written directly, being identical to the program name and contained in the variable szAppName.

```
int nCwRegisterClasses(void)
{
 WNDCLASS   wndclass;
 memset(&wndclass, 0x00, sizeof(WNDCLASS));

 wndclass.style = CS_HREDRAW |
                  CS_VREDRAW |
                  CS_BYTEALIGNWINDOW;
 wndclass.lpfnWndProc = WndProc;

 wndclass.cbClsExtra = 0;
 wndclass.cbWndExtra = 0;
 wndclass.hInstance = hInst;
 wndclass.hIcon = LoadIcon(hInst, "QCSTEP2");
 wndclass.hCursor = LoadCursor(NULL, IDC_ARROW);
 wndclass.hbrBackground = (HBRUSH)(COLOR_WINDOW+1);
 wndclass.lpszMenuName = szAppName;
 wndclass.lpszClassName = szAppName;

 if(!RegisterClass(&wndclass))
   return -1;

 return(0);
}
```

Even after the menu has been defined in the RC file and declared within the source file, selecting any one of the menu items still has no effect. Before the user can actually trigger an action by selecting a menu item, the corresponding code must be implemented. QuickCase:W automatically inserts the menu template into the window procedure, so you simply must complete it.

The WM_COMMAND message

Selecting a menu item triggers a WM_COMMAND message. This message processes the items individually because the accompanying parameter wParam contains the ID number of the menu item that has been selected.

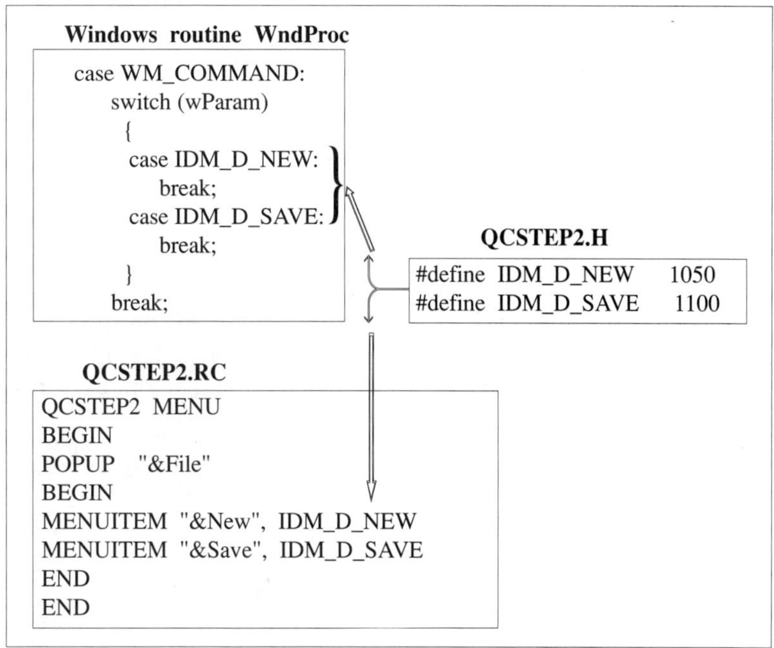

The connection between the WM_COMMAND message and a menu item

Now you must display a message box that contains the name of the menu item that has been selected. The GetMenuString function determines the current name, which is then passed to the *MessageBox* function. We added MessageBox functions to each menu item by using the QuickC Editor.

By doing this, the appearance of the message box is similar to the message box we created in Visual Basic using the MsgBox function. Add the commented data to your WndProc procedure so the code looks like:

```
LONG FAR PASCAL WndProc(HWND hWnd, WORD Message, WORD wParam, LONG lParam)
{
 HMENU       hMenu=0;
 HBITMAP     hBitmap=0;
 HDC         hDC;
 PAINTSTRUCT ps;
 int         nRc=0;

 switch (Message)
   {
    case WM_COMMAND:
         switch (wParam)
           {
            case IDM_F_NEW:
```

```
                                MessageBox(NULL,   "&New",   "Menu   Item",
                     MB_ICONEXCLAMATION);
          break;

     case IDM_F_SAVE:
                                MessageBox(NULL,   "&Save",   "Menu   Item",
                     MB_ICONEXCLAMATION);
          break;

     case IDM_O_SETTINGS:
          /* Place User Code to respond to the                   */
          /* Menu Item Named "&Settings" here.                   */
          break;

     case IDM_H_INDEX:
                                MessageBox(NULL,   "&Index",   "Menu   Item",
                     MB_ICONEXCLAMATION);
          break;

     default:
         return DefWindowProc(hWnd, Message, wParam, lParam);
   }
break;
```

Keyboard accelerator

Keyboard accelerators must be defined in the accelerator table within the .RC file. The shortcut key ID value must be identical to the ID number of the menu item about to be triggered.

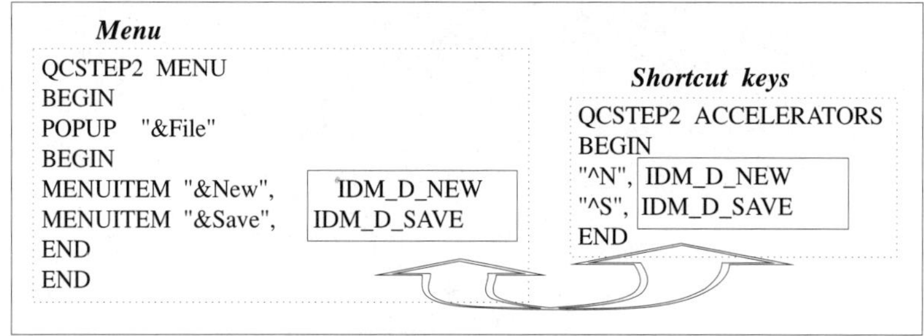

The connection between menus and shortcut keys

Within the table, the control character "^" represents the Ctrl key. This table is also inserted automatically into the .RC file by QuickCase:W if you've specified corresponding key combinations in the *Accelerator* text box when defining individual menu items. When you verify your settings, QuickCase:W checks whether the entry you've made is valid.

QuickCase:W must load the accelerator table into the source file using LoadAccelerators, so the shortcut keys can be recognized by Windows. The second parameter of LoadAccelerators contains the name of the table that was specified in the .RC file (QCSTEP2 in our example).

Also, the TranslateAccelerator function must be inserted in the message loop. This function checks each keyboard entry to determine whether a shortcut key has been pressed. If this is the case, the entry changes to a menu message, WM_COMMAND, which is then sent directly to the window procedure. So, the DispatchMessage function remains uncalled.

```
ShowWindow(hWndMain, nCmdShow);

hAccel = LoadAccelerators(hInst, szAppName);

while(GetMessage(&msg, NULL, 0, 0))
  {
   if(TranslateAccelerator(hWndMain, hAccel, &msg))
     continue;
   TranslateMessage(&msg);
   DispatchMessage(&msg);
  }
```

The QCSTEP2.H file defines hAccel handle as a global variable.

Since the complete listing would fill several pages, we've only listed the new lines. If you want to look at the code in greater detail, refer to the files stored on the companion diskette.

Creating a menu with Turbo Pascal

Use the Resource Workshop for creating resource files in Turbo Pascal. With its help you can create icons and menus, and define shortcut keys.

After starting the Resource Workshop, select *File/New Project...* and specify the file type of your project. With Turbo Pascal, you should save all your resources directly in a .RES file, since this file is later referenced in the source file TPSTEP2.PAS through the {$R} compiler directive, so it will be linked with the final compiled .EXE file.

Once you've clicked and verified the RES file type, a considerably larger number of menus will be displayed in the menu bar. We shall begin with creating a custom icon for the application. Select *Resource/New...* and select ICON in the dialog box for specifying the desired resource type.

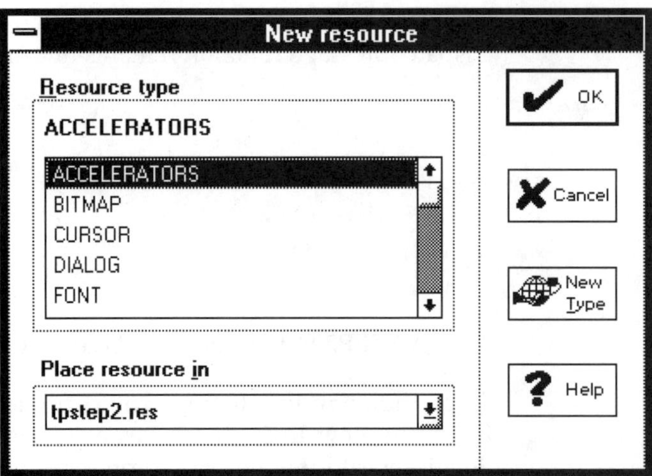

Deleting a new resource

The Resource Workshop Paint editor has more functions than Image Editor of QuickC, although many of these functions aren't normally used. Using its Tools palette, you can create spray effects, edit letters, enlarge portions of the picture, and create many other effects. The name of this icon, which must be specified later with the LoadIcon function, can be entered by selecting *Resource/Rename....* Name the icon TPSTEP2, since this is what the Pascal code refers to for an icon. You'll also need to rename the MENU and ACCELERATOR resources to TPSTEP2. Although you can change these names, use TPSTEP2 for now.

Drawing an icon with the Resource Workshop

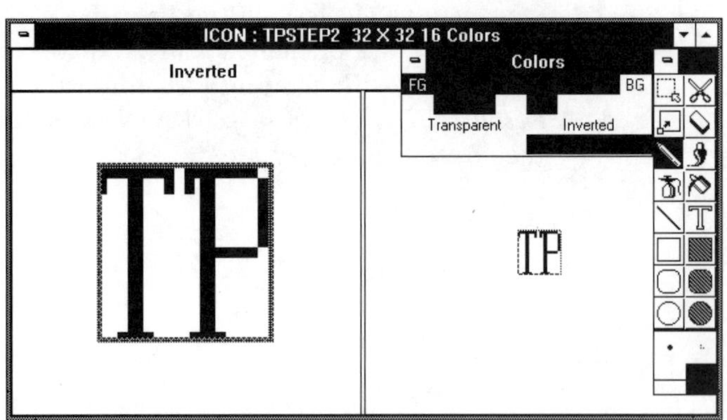

Drawing an icon with the Resource Workshop

Once you've completed the icon for your application, select *Save Project....* We've used the same name for our RES file as for the source file, TPSTEP2. If the ICO file type is currently selected, you must switch to type RES before saving the file.

Defining menus with the Resource Workshop

The menu is declared in basically the same way as the icon. First you must specify the MENU resource type upon selecting the *Resource/New...* menu item. Then the Resource Workshop will open several windows, not only allowing you to enter the individual menu items and their ID values, but also to view the resulting menus. Using the *Menu* menu, you can add any number of menu titles and menu items to your application menu. Remember to use *Resource/Rename...* to rename the MENU_1 resource type to TPSTEP2.

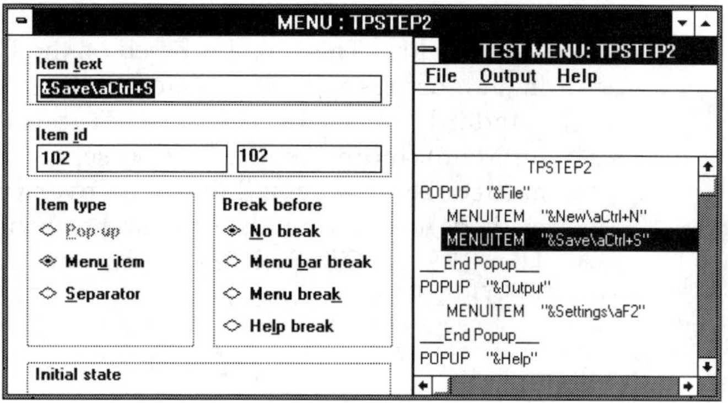

Defining menus with the Resource Workshop

Defining shortcut keys with the Resource Workshop

The third resource type that you'll need to define are the shortcut keys. Select *Resource/New...* again and specify the ACCELERATORS resource type. Remember that the ID values should be as follows:

```
New = 101      Save = 102      Settings = 103      Index = 104
```

If you don't remember the ID values of the corresponding menu items, you can simply display the menu definition window and the accelerator definition window simultaneously.

The key type can either be an ASCII or a virtual key. You must select the virtual key type if a key combination uses Ctrl, Shift or one of the function keys. So, you must specify the virtual key type for each of your shortcut keys *Accelerator/Key Value*. The Resource Workshop will then prompt you to enter the key; in our case this is the key combination Ctrl + N. After you've verified this entry, the characters "^N", which you've already encountered in QuickCase:W, will appear in the text box.

Alternately, you could click on the Ascii option button in the *Key type* option and enter an ASCII number in the *Key* text box. This will assign that number as the accelerator. Remember to rename the resource from ACCELERATORS_1 to TPSTEP2.

Select *File/Save Project* to compile the resource and save the TPSTEP2.RES file. Select *File/Exit* to return to Windows.

The WinProcs and WinTypes units

Start Turbo Pascal for Windows. Open the TPSTEP1.PAS source file. In subsequent programs, you'll need the *WinProcs* and *WinTypes* units in addition to the WObjects unit. WinProcs contains all Windows functions and WinTypes contains data type declarations, as well as numerous constants that QuickC stores in the WINDOWS.H header file.

You must also declare a second object, which we've named TMyWindow. This object is based on the TWindow standard object. In all other respects, it's created in the same way as the TWindow standard object of the first Turbo Pascal example in the InitMainWindow method. So, a separate window object will be needed because you'll have to overwrite or append specific methods to load your resources and respond to different menu items. The {R$ TPSTEP2.RES} compiler directive includes the TPSTEP2.RES resource file.

```
{ First application: TPSTEP2.PAS }
program TPStep2;                          { Declares application name }

uses WObjects, WinTypes, WinProcs;        { Calls WObjects, WinTypes, }
                                      {            WinProcs units }
{$R TPSTEP2.RES}                                { Calls resource file }

const                                      { Constants for menu items }
     IDM_NEW   = 101;
     IDM_SAVE  = 102;
     IDM_SET   = 103;
     IDM_INDEX = 104;

type
     TProg = object(TApplication)                          { Objects }
              procedure InitMainWindow; virtual;
     end;

type
  PMyWindow = ^TMyWindow;
  TMyWindow = object(TWindow)
     szItem: array[0..20] of Char;
     constructor Init(AParent : PWindowsObject; ATitle : PChar);
     procedure GetWindowClass (var AWndClass : TWndClass) ; virtual;
     procedure FNew(var Msg : TMessage); virtual cm_First + IDM_NEW;
     procedure Save(var Msg : TMessage); virtual cm_First + IDM_SAVE;
     procedure Index(var Msg: TMessage); virtual cm_First + IDM_INDEX;
  end;

procedure TProg.InitMainWindow;           { Main window initialization }
begin
  MainWindow := New(PMyWindow, Init(nil, 'My First Windows Application'));
  HAccTable :=LoadAccelerators(hInstance, 'TPSTEP2');{ Get accelerator }
end;                                                { info from the    }
                                                    { TPSTEP2.RES file}

constructor TMyWindow.Init(AParent: PWindowsObject; ATitle : PChar);
begin
  TWindow.Init(AParent, ATitle);
  Attr.Menu := LoadMenu(hInstance, 'TPSTEP2');     { Get menu info from }
end;                                               { TPSTEP2.RES file   }

procedure TMyWindow.GetWindowClass (var AWndClass:TWndClass);
begin
  TWindow.GetWindowClass(AWndClass);
  AWndClass.hIcon := LoadIcon(hInstance, 'TPSTEP2');    { Get icon info }
end;                                                    { TPSTEP2.RES   }

procedure TMyWindow.FNew(var Msg : TMessage);
```

```
begin
  GetMenuString(Attr.Menu, IDM_NEW, szItem, 15, MF_BYCOMMAND);
  MessageBox(hWindow, szItem, 'Menu Item', MB_ICONEXCLAMATION);
end;

procedure TMyWindow.Save(var Msg : TMessage);
begin
  GetMenuString(Attr.Menu, IDM_SAVE, szItem, 15, MF_BYCOMMAND);
  MessageBox(hWindow, szItem, 'Menu Item', MB_ICONEXCLAMATION);
end;
procedure TMyWindow.Index(var Msg: TMessage);

begin
  GetMenuString(Attr.Menu, IDM_INDEX, szItem, 15, MF_BYCOMMAND);
  MessageBox(hWindow, szItem, 'Menu Item', MB_ICONEXCLAMATION);
end;

{ Main program }

var MyFirstApp: TProg;

begin
  MyFirstApp.Init('TPWin');
  MyFirstApp.Run;
  MyFirstApp.Done;
end.
```

The GetWindowClass method

In object-oriented programming with Turbo Pascal, you can change a class attribute by overwriting the GetWindowClass method. This method specifies the icon you've created. When this method is defined for the child of a standard object, such as TWindow, it's often necessary to first call the existing method belonging to the parent and then execute additional separate functions.

The Standard call attributes are set with the TWindow.GetWindowClass(AWndClass) function call, in the same way the WNDCLASS structure is set in QuickC. After this, the AWndClass file can be overwritten with the handle of your custom icon. Just as in QuickC, this handle is determined with the LoadIcon API function. The HInstance parameter is a data field of the TWindow object and, by inheritance, also a data field of our TMyWindow object.

The Init method

We could declare the menu in this GetWindowClass method. However, we chose the second method, which involves loading the menu from within the Init method of our object. The inherited TWindow.Init method must first be called. The variable Attr is a data field of the TWindow object and is a record of type TWindowAttr. In addition to the menu handle, this field contains, among other information, the window's size and position, or, in effect, all the values that are passed to the CreateWindow function in QuickC.

The InitMainWindow method

The accelerator table addresses the application object TProg instead of our window. So, it loads from within the TProg.InitMainWindow method. In QuickC, the object was also loaded before the message loop in the WinMain main procedure, instead of in the WndProc window procedure. Because of the Run method, Turbo Pascal doesn't need to directly check whether a given keyboard input matches one of the accelerators because this method calls another method that automatically performs this check.

The methods for menu items

With ObjectWindows, the WM_COMMAND isn't used directly. Instead, a specific method is created for each individual menu item and is linked to that item by its ID value. Also, a special constant (cm_First) is added to the method, whose name can be freely selected, at its definition in the object type.

```
procedure FNew(var Msg : TMessage); virtual cm_First + IDM_NEW;
```

cm_First is defined in ObjectWindows and determines the range of constants for messages from menu items (WM_COMMAND). The ID values of the individual menu items have been defined as constants at the beginning of the program.

```
const
     IDM_NEW   = 101;
     IDM_SAVE  = 102;
     IDM_SET   = 103;
     IDM_INDEX = 104;
```

33.3 Step 3: Opening a Dialog Box

Adding a dialog box

The three STEP2 applications didn't react when you selected the *Output/Settings* menu item. Now we'll update the program to open a dialog box. This dialog box will provide several settings. When you select settings and exit the dialog box, the application stores this information so that it can be recalled later.

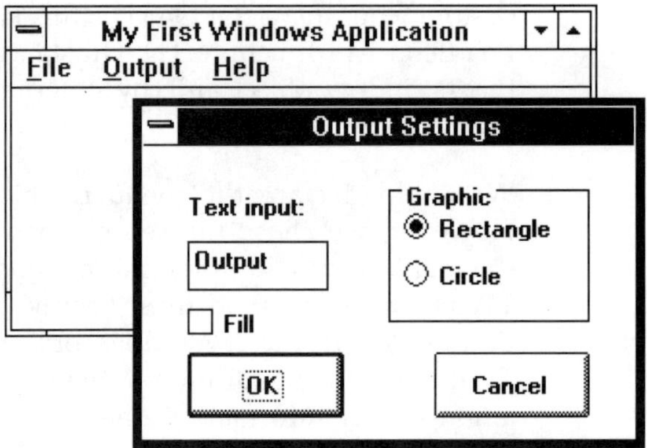

Third step: opening a dialog box

Dialog boxes are frequently used in Windows to exchange information between the user and the application. For example, when Windows requires specific information in order to execute a command that the user has selected, a dialog box prompts the user for this information.

A dialog box can contain several different controls, that enable the user to select different functions or options (more on this later). Dialog boxes usually contain a command button labeled OK, which allows the user to confirm his or her entries and instructs the application to accept these new settings. A second command button, usually labeled Cancel, closes the dialog box without changing the settings that were valid before the box was opened. System settings boxes, which are often used for controlling printer or mouse configuration, are common implementations of dialog boxes.

Any menu item name followed by three periods (...) indicates that this menu item will open a dialog box.

Modal and non-modal dialog boxes

There are two basic types of dialog boxes. The difference between them is based on how they relate to the window from which they were opened:

1. A non-modal dialog box can be opened at any time. This dialog box operates parallel to the parent window, without influencing the parent window's operation in any way.

2. A modal dialog box freezes the operation of its parent window. This means that until the user closes the dialog box, the parent window remains inaccessible. If the user tries to make entries into the main window, Windows emits a beep.

Adding a dialog box with Visual Basic

Visual Basic doesn't have an editor that's specifically designed for creating dialog boxes. Instead, the dialog boxes are created in exactly the same way as Visual Basic forms (program windows), in the Visual Basic design environment.

We'll use the first form for our third project. Simply save the VBSTEP2.MAK project as a new file named VBSTEP3.MAK. Then select the file VBSTEP2.FRM in your Project window and save it again under the name VBSTEP31.FRM.

Toolbox

Next you'll create the dialog box, including its controls. Select *File/New Form* to begin a new form that you can equip with different controls, which can be accessed through the toolbox. When you first start Visual Basic, the Toolbox is usually opened and visible on your screen. You can close and reopen the Toolbox at any time through the *Toolbox* function in your *Window* menu. The Toolbox consists of 16 buttons, each depicting a different control, except for the upper-left button, which represents the mouse pointer. The mouse pointer moves and sizes controls once you've placed them on your form.

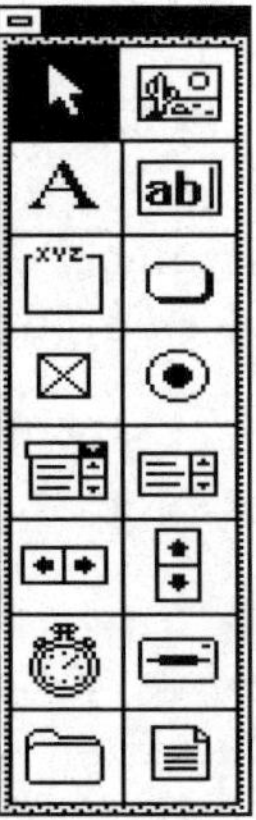

The Toolbox

Your dialog box will be equipped with eight objects: two command buttons, one frame, two option buttons, a label, a text box, and one check box. You draw these controls on your form one by one, in no particular order. We started with the label.

To place a control on your form, click the button in the Toolbox that represents the control you want to draw. Then position your mouse pointer on the location where you want to place the control. As you'll see, the mouse pointer changes to a cross once it's moved onto the surface of the form. Once this cross is at the desired position, press and hold the left mouse button. With the mouse button depressed, move the mouse pointer until the control has the desired shape and size. Then simply release the mouse button. If you want to delete a control that you've placed on your form, select that control and press Del.

You can use a grid to help you arrange the controls on your form. If a grid isn't visible on the form, select *Edit/Grid Settings...* and click the *Show Grid* check box to activate the grid.

Each option is a separate control

Once you've placed all eight controls on your form, as previously described, you must set the properties of each control. Like your form and the menu items it contains, these controls are also independent objects, which have their own properties, methods, and events. Each property consist of its predefined name and a certain value that can usually be changed.

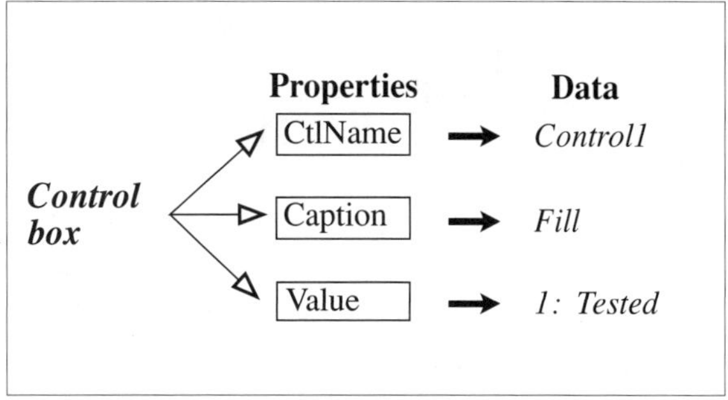

Properties of an object

The three properties shown above represent only some of the properties that apply to controls. A check box, for example, can use over twenty different properties.

The CtlName property contains the name that identifies the control within the program code. Visual Basic supplies default names for this property, depending on the type of control (command button, text box, etc.) and on the previous number of controls (Check1, Check2, etc.). However, this default name can also be changed. The control name forms the first portion of the name for the event procedure, which you'll remember from our work with menu items, with which they are associated.

```
Sub Check1_Click ()

End Sub
```

To keep things as clear as possible, we've simply used the default control names suggested by Visual Basic. In the caption property, you can specify a text that will appear as a label to the right of the check box. The setting of the Value property is automatically updated by Visual Basic as soon as the user clicks the check box.

To clearly show the user that this form is a modal dialog box, you can give it a thicker border and a fixed size. So, the user cannot change the window's size and shape. In Visual Basic this is determined through the BorderStyle property; you should specify the value 3 - Fixed Double.

The following table lists all properties whose default values have been changed at design time for this project. The individual controls are listed separately.

Object	Property	Value
Form1	Caption	My First Windows Application
Form2 (Dialog)	Caption	Output Settings
	BorderStyle	3: Fixed Double
Label	Caption	Text input:
Text1	Text	Output
Check1	Caption	Fill
Frame1	Caption	Graphic
Option1	Caption	Rectangle
	Value	True
Option2	Caption	Circle
Command 1	Caption	OK
	Default	True
Command 2	Caption	Cancel

When a project uses several forms, these forms must be able to access the same data. So, the global module VBSTEP3.BAS is included in this example. The variable values are stored when the dialog box is closed, so they can then be used in the main program form. The VBSTEP3.MAK project file therefore contains references to three different files: VBSTEP3.BAS, VBSTEP31.FRM for the main form, and VBSTEP32.FRM for the dialog box.

```
' VBSTEP3.BAS
Global Ok As Integer
Global bFill, bGraphic As Integer
Global szEditText As String

Global Const TRUE = -1
Global Const FALSE = 0

' VBSTEP31.FRM
Sub File_New_Click ()
  MsgBox File_New.Caption, 48, "Menu Item"
End Sub

Sub File_Save_Click ()
  MsgBox File_Save.Caption, 48, "Menu Item"
End Sub

Sub Help_Index_Click ()
  MsgBox Help_Index.Caption, 48, "Menu Item"
End Sub

Sub Output_In_Click ()
  Form2.Show 1
End Sub

Sub Form_Unload (Cancel As Integer)
  Unload Form2
End Sub
```

```
' VBSTEP32.FRM
'OK command button
Sub Command1_Click ()
  bFill = Check1.Value
  bGraphic = Option1.Value
  szEditText = Text1.Text
  Ok = TRUE
  Form2.Hide
End Sub
'Cancel command button
Sub Command2_Click ()
  Form2.Hide
  Ok = FALSE
  Option1.Value = bGraphic
  Option2.Value = Not bGraphic
  Check1.Value = bFill
  Text1.Text = szEditText
End Sub
'Load form
Sub Form_Load ()
  bGraphic = Option1.Value
  bFill = Check1.Value
  szEditText = Text1.Text
End Sub
```

The dialog box is opened by selecting the *Settings* menu item, which carries the control name Output_In, or by pressing F2. The Show method then displays the form or dialog box on the screen. The value 1 following this method call indicates that this form must be displayed as a modal dialog box. This event is the only new event, in the VBSTEP31.FRM form file, that you need to program for this step.

```
Sub Output_In_Click ()
  Form2.Show 1
End Sub
```

All further events occur when the program user interacts with the application's dialog boxes. The first time the dialog box is called, it must be loaded into memory. The three global variables are initialized in the Load event that's used for this purpose.

```
Sub Form_Load ()
  bGraphic = Option1.Value
  bFill = Check1.Value
  szEditText = Text1.Text
End Sub
```

When the user verifies the dialog box settings by clicking the OK button or by pressing Enter, the Command1_Click event is triggered. The value of the variable bFull indicates whether the Rectangle option button was clicked last. If this variable contains the value False, we can assume that the Circle option button is active, since only one option button can be active at any given time within a group of option buttons. The Ok variable isn't needed until the next evaluation step. Once the current settings have been stored, the dialog box is closed again using the Hide method.

```
Sub Command1_Click ()
  bFill = Check1.Value
  bGraphic = Option1.Value
  szEditText = Text1.Text
```

```
  Ok = TRUE
  Form2.Hide
End Sub
```

If the user clicks the Cancel button, the original settings of the Value property for the two option buttons and the check box, as well as of the Text property for the label, must be restored. The dialog box is removed from the screen just as when the user clicks the OK button.

```
Sub Command2_Click ()
  Form2.Hide
  Ok = FALSE
  Option1.Value = bGraphic
  Option2.Value = Not bGraphic
  Check1.Value = bFill
  Text1.Text = szEditText
End Sub
```

The Unload method

When the application must be exited, the *Unload* event Form_Unload is triggered. However, this event is generated only for the main form instead of for the dialog box. So, the Unload method must be called explicitly for the second form as well. So the Unload event is also triggered for the dialog box. Otherwise, the dialog box remains in memory and may subsequently lead to a system crash.

```
Sub Form_Unload (Cancel As Integer)
  Unload Form2
End Sub
```

Adding a dialog box with QuickC

Dialog boxes that are intended for QuickC are usually defined as resources. The QuickC software package includes a specific dialog box editor, DLGEDIT, which uses a Toolbox similar to the one found in Visual Basic. Using this editor, it's easy to select and position the individual controls that are needed in a dialog box.

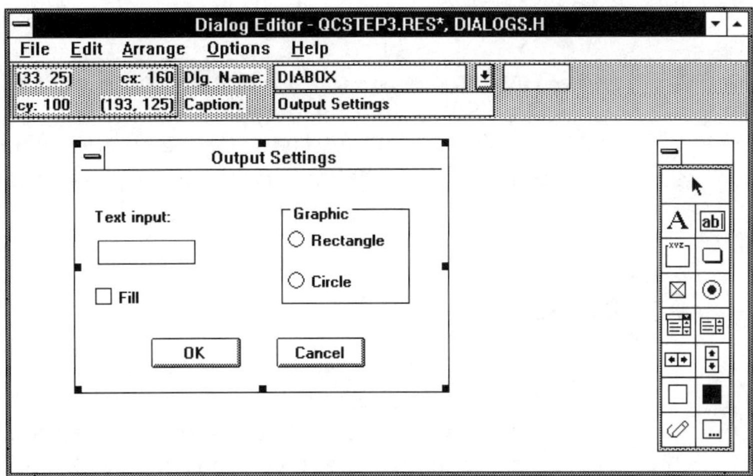

The dialog box editor DLGEDIT

Upon starting the editor, you'll see the editor window and the DLGEDIT Toolbox. Select *File New* to begin creating a new dialog box. DLGEDIT then opens a box that's automatically selected. This is indicated by the small black squares displayed in the corners of the box. When the mouse pointer is positioned over one of these small black squares, its shape changes to a double arrow, which allows you to change the shape and size of your new dialog box.

Within any application, each dialog box must possess a unique identification. This can be accomplished either through ID values, as in the case of individual menu items, or through the use of text strings, as in the case of the main menu and the icon. We've identified the dialog box, using the ASCII text DIABOX, by entering this name in the *Dlg. Sym.* field text box. Like Visual Basic, you can use the Toolbox to place the different controls in your dialog box. Each element must have an ID number. We created our elements in the following order (there's a reason for this, as you'll see later):

- Label (Text input:)
- Check box ([ ] Fill)
- Option button (Rectangle)
- Option button (Circle)
- Text box
- Command button (OK)

- Command button (Cancel)

You can also specify a name, in addition to this ID number, in the *Dlg. Sym.* field. A header file containing the corresponding definitions will automatically be created when you save this new dialog box. We've saved this file using the default name DIALOGS.H.

```
#define IDC_FILL        102
#define IDC_RECT        103
#define IDC_CIRCLE      104
#define IDC_EDIT        105
```

Several elements, such as labels and frames, don't require unique ID values because they usually aren't accessed within the program code. So, they are often assigned the value -1, which is usually entered in the right text box of the DLGEDIT properties bar. Otherwise, select (Unused) in the *Symbol* drop-down list box for that particular object.

To draw a control in your dialog box, click the button for the desired control in the Toolbox and move the mouse pointer to the correct location in the dialog box. Then press the left mouse button again and adjust the size of the control. Release the mouse button once the control is the correct shape and size.

To draw several identical controls without having to select the same control button in the Toolbox each time, press Ctrl while clicking that button the first time. After this, the cursor will remain active for this control instead of changing back to the standard mouse pointer once you've drawn the control. You can use one of the functions in the *Arrange* menu to help you arrange the dialog box if it contains several controls.

Besides defining the ID value, you can also specify several other settings for each object as well as for the dialog box itself. To do this, simply select the control you want to modify, and then choose *Edit/Styles...* or press Enter. An even faster method is to simply double-click the control. This will open a dialog box that varies with the type of control you've selected.

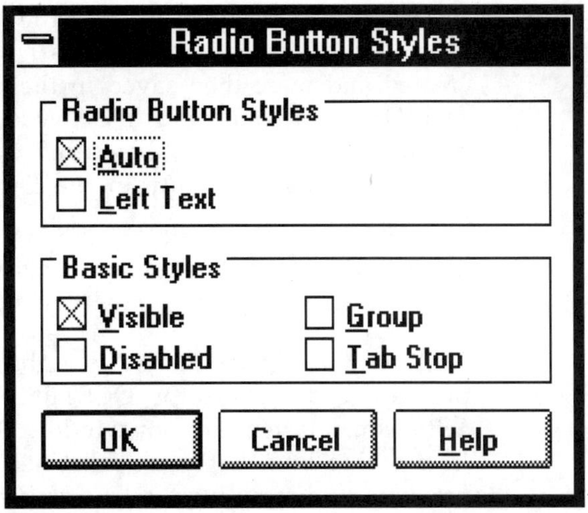

Radio Button Styles

Radio Button Styles

Auto

Left Text

Basic Styles

Visible

Group

Disabled

Tab Stop

OK

Cancel

Help

Dialog box for setting the style parameters of a control

Auto style

The *Auto* style de-selects the active option button in a group of option buttons when the user selects another option button. So, only one option button can be active at any one time. If this parameter isn't set, you must determine the on/off relationships between the option buttons independently.

When saving the completed dialog box, specify a file name without the file extension, since the Dialog Editor automatically saves two different files with the .RES and .DLG file extensions. We'll name our file DIALOGS. The RES file is used by the Dialog Editor to facilitate later changes to the dialog box. The DLG file contains the information that specifies your dialog box's appearance as well as its controls in a readable ASCII format. For our dialog box, this file looks as follows:

```
/*  DIALOGS.DLG  */
DLGINCLUDE RCDATA DISCARDABLE
BEGIN
    "DIALOGS.H\0"
END

DIABOX DIALOG 6, 18, 160, 100
STYLE DS_MODALFRAME | WS_POPUP | WS_VISIBLE | WS_CAPTION | WS_SYSMENU |
    WS_THICKFRAME
CAPTION "Output Settings"
FONT 8, "Helv"
BEGIN
    LTEXT           "Text input:", 101, 6, 18, 41, 8
    CONTROL         "Fill", IDC_FILL, "Button", BS_AUTOCHECKBOX | WS_TABSTOP,
                    7, 55, 40, 10
    CONTROL         "Rectangle", IDC_RECT, "Button", BS_AUTORADIOBUTTON, 93,
                    28, 52, 10
    CONTROL         "Circle", IDC_CIRCLE, "Button", BS_AUTORADIOBUTTON, 93,
                    48, 39, 10
    EDITTEXT        IDC_EDIT, 8, 33, 44, 12, ES_AUTOHSCROLL
    GROUPBOX        "Graphic", -1, 90, 15, 58, 49
    PUSHBUTTON      "OK", IDOK, 32, 80, 40, 14
    PUSHBUTTON      "Cancel", IDCANCEL, 88, 80, 40, 14
END
```

The IDOK and IDCANCEL ID values

The first four lines in the DLG file indicate that the individual controls were assigned ID values when the dialog box was first created and were then saved in the header file DIALOG.H. The two ID names IDOK and IDCANCEL aren't included in this file because they've already been defined in the WINDOWS.H file and can be used directly in the Dialog Editor. Whenever you include an OK button and/or a Cancel button in your dialog box, you should associate these controls with IDOK or IDCANCEL, since pressing Enter or Esc will also trigger these values.

Using QuickCase:W to link the dialog box

We'll now use QuickCase:W to embed the new dialog box in the program code. Open the QCSTEP2.WIN project and click the *Settings* menu item in your window. This opens the *Update Menu Item* dialog box that you've defined for this menu item in the previous programming step. Select *Dialog Box* in the *Link to* drop-down list box found in the lower area of this dialog box. Click the Configure Link... button, which is located just below this list box. QuickCase:W then opens another window, in which you can now select your new dialog box script.

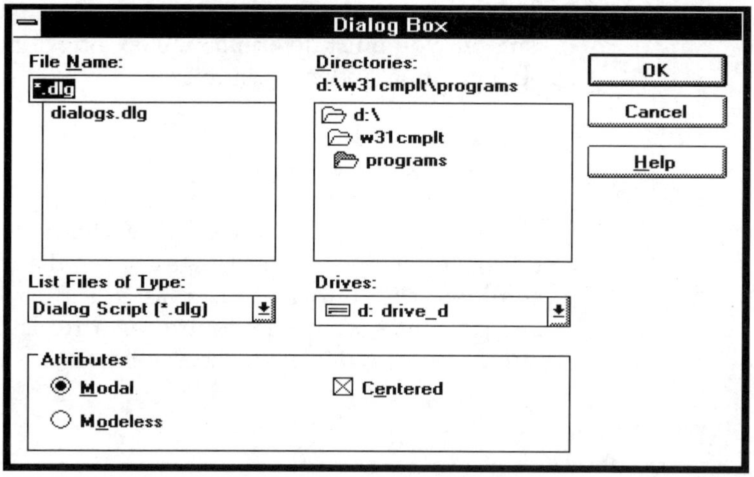

Linking a menu item with a dialog box

Select DIALOGS.DLG and click OK. Click OK again to return to the *QuickCase:W* window. Select *File/Save As...* and save the project under the name QCSTEP3.WIN. Now select *Build/Generate* to create the new code. A C #include statement includes the DIALOGS.H file in the resource script, since dialog boxes are also treated as resources.

```
/*  QCSTEP3.RC  */
#include "QCSTEP3.h"
QCSTEP3 ICON  QC.ICO
```

```
QCSTEP3 MENU
  BEGIN
    POPUP  "&File"
      BEGIN
        MENUITEM "&New\tCtrl+N", IDM_F_NEW
        MENUITEM "&Save\tCtrl+S", IDM_F_SAVE
      END
    POPUP  "&Output"
      BEGIN
        MENUITEM "&Settings\tF2", IDM_O_SETTINGS
      END
    POPUP  "&Help"
      BEGIN
        MENUITEM "&Index", IDM_H_INDEX
      END
  END

#include "DIALOGS.DLG"


QCSTEP3 ACCELERATORS
  BEGIN
    "^N", IDM_F_NEW
    "^S", IDM_F_SAVE
    VK_F2, IDM_O_SETTINGS, VIRTKEY
  END

STRINGTABLE
BEGIN
  IDS_ERR_CREATE_WINDOW,      "Window creation failed!"
  IDS_ERR_REGISTER_CLASS,     "Error registering window class"
END
```

The header file DIALOGS.H, which contains the ID values for the individual controls, is linked with the project header file QCSTEP3.H.

```
/* QCSTEP3.H */
/* QuickCase:W KNB Version 1.00 */
#include <windows.h>
#include <string.h>
#include "DIALOGS.h"
#define IDM_FILE                    1000
#define IDM_F_NEW                        1050
#define IDM_F_SAVE                       1100
#define IDM_OUTPUT                  2000
#define IDM_O_SETTINGS                   2050
#define IDM_HELP                    3000
#define IDM_H_INDEX                      3050

#define IDS_ERR_REGISTER_CLASS   1
#define IDS_ERR_CREATE_WINDOW    2

char szString[128];   /* variable to load resource strings         */

char szAppName[20];   /* class name for the window               */
HWND hInst;
HWND hWndMain;
HANDLE hAccel;

BOOL bFill, bGraphic;
char szEditText[20] = "Output";

LONG FAR PASCAL WndProc(HWND, WORD, WORD, LONG);
BOOL FAR PASCAL DIALOGSMsgProc(HWND, WORD, WORD, LONG);
int nCwRegisterClasses(void);
void CwUnRegisterClasses(void);
```

Once the code has been generated, you'll see the following lines in the QCSTEP3.C file at the WM_COMMAND message of the *Settings* menu item. They contain the ID value IDM_A_SETTINGS:

```
case IDM_O_SETTINGS:

     {
      FARPROC lpfnDIALOGSMsgProc;

      lpfnDIALOGSMsgProc = MakeProcInstance((FARPROC)DIALOGSMsgProc, hInst);
      nRc = DialogBox(hInst, (LPSTR)"DIABOX", hWnd, lpfnDIALOGSMsgProc);
      FreeProcInstance(lpfnDIALOGSMsgProc);
     }
     break;
```

The DialogBox function opens a modal dialog box. The remaining application pauses at this function call until the dialog box is closed by clicking the OK button or the Cancel button. The second parameter that is passed to the DialogBox function consists of the name of the dialog box, which you've already determined when you first drew the dialog box with the dialog box editor. In our case, this name is DIABOX.

Callback function

Every dialog box needs its own window procedure, which has a structure that's very similar to the window procedure of a main program window. The link between a dialog procedure and a dialog box is created by the DialogBox function. However, in this case, it isn't possible to use the fourth parameter to specify the function name (see also DIALOGSMsgProc) because the dialog procedure forms a callback function. These functions are called through Windows instead of the application itself. So, it's also necessary to declare the dialog procedure in the definition file (QCSTEP3.DEF) at the EXPORT statement just like any normal window procedure.

```
; QCSTEP3.DEF
NAME            QCSTEP3
EXETYPE         WINDOWS
STUB            'WINSTUB.EXE'
CODE            PRELOAD MOVEABLE
DATA            PRELOAD MOVEABLE MULTIPLE
HEAPSIZE        4096
STACKSIZE       5110
EXPORTS         WndProc         @1
                DIALOGSMsgProc          @2
```

All callback functions, except for normal window procedures, must first use a MakeProcInstance function to access a procedure instance address. This address must then be specified as the last parameter with the dialog box call. This ensures that the application data segment is used instead of a Windows data segment. Once the user has closed the dialog box, the FreeProcInstance function must be used to dissolve this link.

Dialog procedure

While generating the code, QuickCase:W also creates the additional window procedure required for the dialog box. The name of this procedure consists of the file name (DIALOGS.DLG) and the letters MsgProc.

Windows sends all the messages, which are generated when the user manipulates the dialog box controls, to the dialog procedure.

Then these messages can be processed, if necessary, or sent to a default procedure. However, unlike in the normal window procedure, in which the default function is called directly, the procedure that's called depends on the corresponding return value. If FALSE is returned, Windows internally calls a default routine; the message is processed independently when TRUE is returned.

The WM_INITDIALOG message

However, there are exceptions to every rule. In this case, the exception occurs with the WM_INITDIALOG message, which is received by the dialog procedure shortly before the dialog box is displayed on your screen. This message often triggers initializations (e.g., for assigning the focus to a specific control). So the value FALSE must be returned in these instances because Windows would otherwise pass the focus to yet another control.

```
/************************************************************************/
/*                                                                      */
/* Dialog Window Procedure                                              */
/*                                                                      */
/* This procedure is associated with the dialog box that is included in */
/* the function name of the procedure. It provides the service routines */
/* for the events (messages) that occur because the end user operates   */
/* one of the dialog box's buttons, entry fields, or controls.          */
/*                                                                      */
/************************************************************************/

BOOL FAR PASCAL DIALOGSMsgProc(HWND hWndDlg, WORD Message, WORD wParam, LONG lParam)
{
static HWND hButton;
static WORD idButton = IDC_RECT;
 switch(Message)
   {
    case WM_INITDIALOG:
         hButton = GetDlgItem(hWndDlg, idButton);
         SendMessage(hButton, BM_SETCHECK, TRUE, 0);
         SendDlgItemMessage(hWndDlg, IDC_FILL, BM_SETCHECK, (WORD)bFill, 0);
         SetDlgItemText(hWndDlg, IDC_EDIT, szEditText);
         SetFocus(GetDlgItem(hWndDlg, IDC_EDIT));
         /* initialize working variables                                */
         return (FALSE); /* End of WM_INITDIALOG                                  */

    case WM_CLOSE:
         /* Closing the Dialog behaves the same as Cancel               */
         PostMessage(hWndDlg, WM_COMMAND, IDCANCEL, 0L);
         break; /* End of WM_CLOSE                                      */

    case WM_COMMAND:
         switch(wParam)
           {
            case IDOK:
              bFill = (BOOL)SendDlgItemMessage(hWndDlg, IDC_FILL, BM_GETCHECK, 0, 0L);
              bGraphic = (BOOL)SendDlgItemMessage(hWndDlg, IDC_RECT, BM_GETCHECK, 0, 0L);
              if (bGraphic)
                idButton = IDC_RECT;
              else
                idButton = IDC_CIRCLE;
              GetWindowText(GetDlgItem(hWndDlg, IDC_EDIT), szEditText, 20);
              EndDialog(hWndDlg, TRUE);
              break;

            case IDCANCEL:
                 /* Ignore data values entered into the controls        */
                 /* and dismiss the dialog window returning FALSE       */
                 EndDialog(hWndDlg, FALSE);
                 break;
           }
         break;    /* End of WM_COMMAND                                 */

    default:
        return FALSE;
   }
 return TRUE;
} /* End of DIALOGSMsgProc                                   */
```

The WM_COMMAND message

Except for the WM_INITDIALOG message, the WM_COMMAND message is processed by almost every dialog procedure. This message is sent to the dialog box by a control when the user clicks or selects this control. The wParam parameter contains the ID value of the selected control, such as IDOK or IDCANCEL. As soon as the OK button or the Cancel button is clicked, the EndDialog function removes the dialog box from the screen.

The only difference between these two cases is that when the user clicks OK, the current settings within the dialog box are written to global variables. So they will be retained and, the next time the dialog box is opened, will be set at the WM_INITDIALOG message and displayed in the dialog box as the current settings. The variable bFull will contain TRUE if its check box is activated, and the variable bGraphic always contains the ID value of the option button that was most recently selected. The contents of the text box, which are accessed through its ID value IDC_EDIT, are written to the szEditText character string by the function GetWindowText.

The WM_CLOSE message

If your dialog box has a system menu, QuickCase:W will insert a third message into the dialog procedure. The WM_CLOSE message is generated when the dialog box is closed through its system menu. Since this action should have the same effect as clicking the Cancel button, the WM_COMMAND message is sent to the dialog routine along with the ID value of the Cancel button. This is done by the PostMessage function, which receives the same parameters as the dialog procedure.

All the files of the QCSTEP3 project are located on the companion diskette.

Adding a dialog box with Turbo Pascal

The Resource Workshop can also be used to create dialog boxes. Since we want to store the new dialog box in the RES file that contains the icon, the menu, and the shortcut keys, we'll select *File/Open project...* to open the TPSTEP2.RES project. Select an existing TPSTEP2 resource and select *Resource/Rename....* Rename this resource to TPSTEP3 and click OK. Do this to the remaining TPSTEP2 resources. Now select *File/Save file as...* and save the file as TPSTEP3.RES.

After saving TPSTEP3.RES, select *Resource/New...* and choose DIALOG from the list box. This will start the Dialog editor, which is specifically designed for creating dialog boxes.

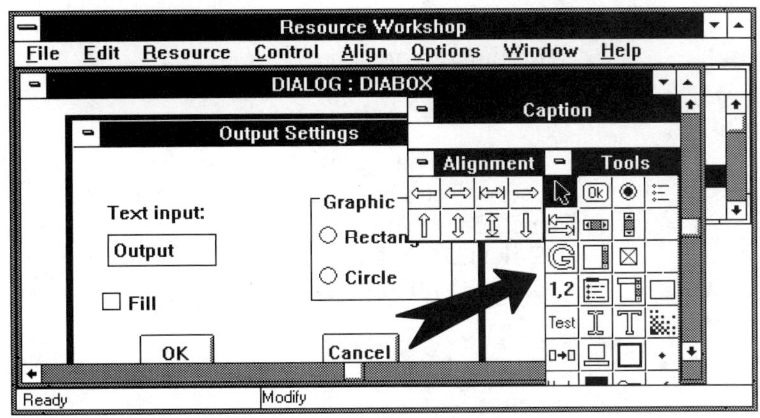

Drawing dialog boxes with the Resource Workshop

You can use either the Toolbox or the *Control* menu to create dialog box elements.

The title can be edited by selecting *Control/Style...*, or by double-clicking the title bar. In either case, the *Window style* dialog box opens, into which you can specify its settings. Type *Output Settings* into the *Caption* text box. Click OK.

Once you've placed the control, double-click it to open a dialog box for editing. Add the following controls, ensuring that the appropriate settings are active (we give you the *Control* menu commands):

Control/	Caption	Control	Attributes	Control type
Static text	Text input:	-1		Left text
Group box	Graphic	-1	Group	Group box
Radio button	Rectangle	102	Tab stop	Auto radio button
Radio button	Circle	103	Tab stop	Auto radio button
Edit text	Output	104	Tab stop/ Border/ Case insensitive/ Left justification/ Single line	
Check box	Fill	105	Tab stop	Auto check box
Push button	OK	1	Tab stop	Push button
Push button	Cancel	2	Tab stop	Push button

Close the *DIALOG* window. Ensure that the DIALOG_1 resource is still highlighted. Select *Resource/Rename...* and assign the name DIABOX to this resource. Click OK. Select *File/Save project*, then exit the Resource Workshop.

The TDialog object

The ObjectWindows library contains the TDialog object type, which supports the initialization and use of dialog boxes. Like normal windows, objects of this type are constructed and initialized with an init constructor. For this, the Init method receives a pointer to the window from which the dialog box has been called as well as the dialog box's name, as assigned by the Resource Workshop:

```
MyDlg := New(PMyDialog, Init(@Self,'DIABOX'));
```

The ExecDialog method activates a modal dialog box after the user selects the *Output/Settings* menu item, or when your Settings method of the TMyWindow window object is accessed. Like in QuickC, the Turbo Pascal application then pauses at the dialog box call until the user clicks on one of the two command buttons.

```
procedure TMyWindow.Settings(var Msg: TMessage);
begin
  Application^.ExecDialog(New(PMyDialog,
                       Init(@Self, 'DIABOX')))
end;
```

The Application variable is automatically set to $Self at the beginning of the TApplication method, and, therefore, points to the application throughout the program execution.

The TMyDialog dialog box object is a child of the TDialog standard type. Before control initialization, the inherited SetupWindow method is overwritten, instead of responding to the WM_INITDIALOG message. Clicking the OK button triggers the CanClose method. Since the current settings must be saved in this case, this method is also newly defined.

```
type                                        { Dialog box elements }
  PMyDialog= ^TMyDialog;
  TMyDialog = object(TDialog)
      hButton: hWnd;
      procedure SetUpWindow; virtual;
      function CanClose: Boolean; virtual;
end;
```

The Init method of the window object copies the text box's default string (Output) to the variable szEditText. Also, the variable idButton receives the value ID_RECT. So the Rectangle option button is selected when the dialog box is first opened.

```
constructor      TMyWindow.Init(AParent:      PWindowsObject;
                   ATitle : PChar);
begin
  TWindow.Init(AParent, ATitle);
  Attr.Menu := LoadMenu(hInstance, 'TPSTEP3');
                                  { Get menu info from }
  strCopy(MyFirstApp.szEditText,'Output');
                                  { TPSTEP3.RES file   }
  MyFirstApp.idButton := IDC_RECT;
end;
```

The szEditText, bFill, and bGraphic variables, which were defined in the header file QCSTEP3.H in the QuickC version, must be declared as data elements of the TProg application object here in Turbo Pascal. So the methods of all the other objects can access these variables. Their complete identification, consisting of the variable name of the object type (MyFirstApp) and the field name, such as bFull, must be specified. Like the menu item identifications, the object ID values are defined as constants at the beginning of the program.

```
procedure TMyDialog.SetupWindow; { Generate Output Settings dialog box }
begin
     hButton := GetDlgItem(HWindow, MyFirstApp.idButton);
     SendMessage(hButton, BM_SETCHECK, Word(TRUE), 0);
     SendDlgItemMessage(HWindow,IDC_FILL, BM_SETCHECK,
                              Word(MyFirstApp.bFill), 0);
     SetDlgItemText(HWindow, IDC_EDIT, MyFirstApp.szEditText);
end;
```

In addition to the tasks we performed in the QuickC version at the WM_COMMAND message with the value IDOK contained in wpParam, we must also call the CanClose method, inherited from the TDialog object. This is necessary because the inherited method is responsible for closing the dialog box controls correctly.

```
function TMyDialog.CanClose: Boolean;  { Can we close this dialog box? }
begin
     TDialog.CanClose;
     MyFirstApp.bFill := SendDlgItemMessage(HWindow, IDC_FILL,
                                        BM_GETCHECK, 0, 0);
     MyFirstApp.bGraphic := SendDlgItemMessage(HWindow,
                                        IDC_RECT, BM_GETCHECK,
                                        0, 0);
     if MyFirstApp.bGraphic = Word(TRUE) then
              MyFirstApp.idButton := IDC_RECT
     else
              MyFirstApp.idButton := IDC_CIRCLE;
     GetWindowText(GetDlgItem(HWindow, IDC_EDIT),
                    MyFirstApp.szEditText, 20);
end;
```

The complete listing of the TPSTEP3.PAS program is located on the companion diskette.

33.4 Step 4: Output

Adding output

In this fourth and final step we'll add output to our application by drawing graphics in our program window. The actual picture is determined by the user through activating the application's controls, and by editing or deleting a text within the dialog box.

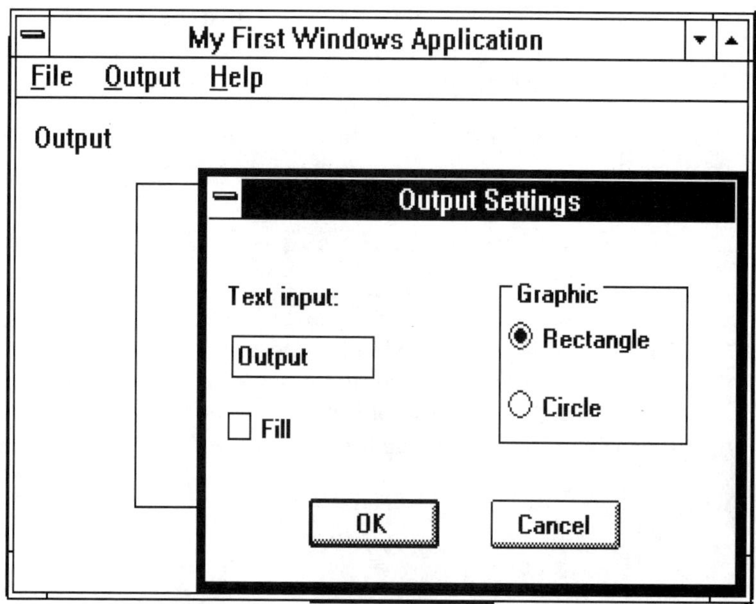

Fourth step: output

When you want to display output in any Windows application, you're automatically forced to work with Window's Graphics Device Interface (GDI). This interface is responsible for passing device-independent output function calls to the device driver. The driver, in turn, must then convert these GDI calls into device-dependent operations.

A painter needs a canvas or a piece of paper in order to create graphic images with brushes and pencils. This also applies to output programming under Windows, as you'll see later.

The device context

When you're programming with QuickC or Turbo Pascal, you must perform certain preparatory tasks for each output. This requires, among other things, a device context, which forms the link between a Windows application, a device driver, and an output device, such as a monitor or a printer. In Visual Basic this context is already implicitly included.

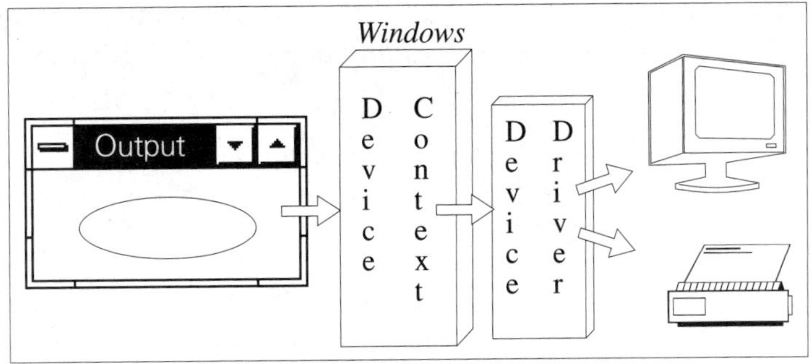

The device context

You could also picture a device context as a virtual surface that's associated with certain attributes and serves as a drawing surface. Each device context receives a certain data structure for these attributes. However, this data structure cannot be directly accessed. Instead, their individual values must be changed through specific functions, or, in Visual Basic, by setting properties.

When a new device context is created, it receives a data structure with default values that determine, for example, which colors are used to draw the border and fill the enclosed areas.

The WM_PAINT message

Output in Windows should, whenever possible, occur only at one location. In Visual Basic this is the Paint event, in QuickC the WM_PAINT message, and in Turbo Pascal the WMPaint or Paint method. The reason for this is that Windows immediately sends a WM_PAINT message to a window when it discovers that the window's contents are no longer up to date. This response can be triggered by various circumstances.

For instance, when several windows overlap each other on the screen and the user moves one of these to the foreground with a mouse click, the previously hidden portion of this window must be updated. A WM_PAINT message is also triggered as soon as the user changes a window's size. Only in a few instances will Windows retain the hidden portion of the screen and later restore it. For example, this occurs when the mouse pointer is moved across the surface of a window.

In this fourth step, we want to display a rectangle or a circle and a text, if the dialog box was closed by clicking OK. However, since the drawing must be displayed only under certain conditions, we need a method that creates these conditions.

In Visual Basic, the Refresh method serves this purpose, while the other two languages use the InvalidateRect function for this purpose.

Color settings

If the user activates the *Fill* check box in your dialog box, the figure (either a circle or rectangle), will be filled with the color cyan the next time it's displayed. This color is produced with the RGB function or statement, in which all three basic colors are each represented by a byte containing a value between 0 and 255.

The sequence of these three colors is red, green, blue (RGB). If all three values are 0, the result will be black. Cyan is created when the green and blue bytes are set to their maximum values, and when the red byte is set to 0.

```
FillColor = RGB( 0, 255, 255)
```

You can create an almost infinite number of colors with these three bytes. However, the actual colors and number of available colors depend on the capabilities of the device driver. So, many colors are interspersed with white or black dots instead of being pure.

Reference point

It's important to determine the reference point for each output (i.e., you must know how the coordinate system is situated). We'll use the default coordinate system for all output. With this system, the origin, or reference point, is located in the upper-left corner of our window's work area.

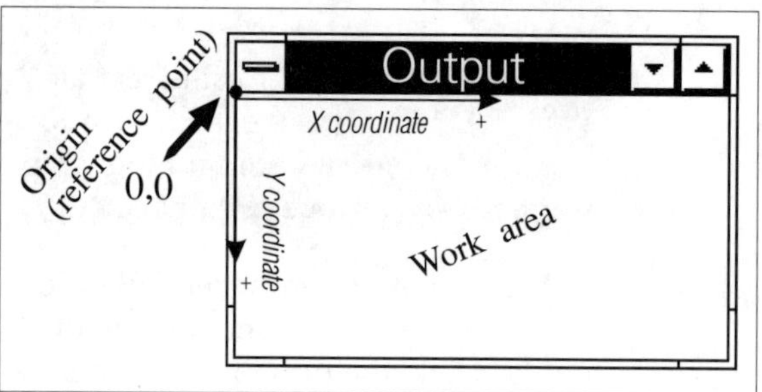

The output reference point

The horizontal values increase to the right while the vertical values increase from the top to the bottom.

Output with Visual Basic

Now that we've thoroughly discussed output, let's try to produce output in three different languages.

The Refresh method

The Command1_Click event that's triggered when the user closes your dialog box by clicking OK now also has the additional task of generating a Paint event for the main program form (Form1). For this we'll use the Refresh method. Since this function call occurs within the VBSTEP41.FRM and is triggered by the Command1 command button, the appropriate object name must be added to the name of the method.

```
' VBSTEP42.FRM
Sub Command1_Click ()
  bFill = Check1.Value
  bGraphic = Option1.Value
  szEditText = Text1.Text
  Ok = TRUE
  Form2.Hide
  Form1.Refresh
End Sub

Sub Command2_Click ()
  Form2.Hide
  Option1.Value = bGraphic
  Option2.Value = Not bGraphic
  Check1.Value = bFill
  Text1.Text = szEditText
End Sub

Sub Form_Load ()
  bGraphic = Option1.Value
  bFill = Check1.Value
  szEditText = Text1.Text
End Sub
```

The Paint event

Once the dialog box has been removed from the screen, all commands associated with the Paint event for Form1 are executed.

```
' VBSTEP41.FRM
Sub Form_Paint ()
    If (Ok = TRUE) Then
       Form1.Cls
       If (bFill = Checked) Then
         Form1.FillStyle = 0
         Form1.FillColor = RGB(0, 255, 255)
       Else
         Form1.FillStyle = 0
         Form1.FillColor = RGB(255, 255, 255)
       End If
       If (bGraphic = TRUE) Then
          x1 = Form1.ScaleWidth / 2 - Form1.ScaleWidth / 3
          y1 = Form1.ScaleHeight / 2 - Form1.ScaleHeight / 3
          x2 = Form1.ScaleWidth / 2 + Form1.ScaleWidth / 3
          y2 = Form1.ScaleHeight / 2 + Form1.ScaleHeight / 3
          Line (x1, y1)-(x2, y2), , B
       Else
          x1 = Form1.ScaleWidth / 2
          y1 = Form1.ScaleHeight / 2
          Radius = Form1.ScaleHeight / 3
          Circle (x1, y1), Radius
       End If
       Form1.CurrentX = 20
       Form1.CurrentY = 20
       Form1.Print Form2.Text1.Text
    End If

End Sub
```

At the start of the program, the OK switch is set to FALSE. This variable is set to TRUE only when the dialog box has been confirmed for the first time. This indicates that the new or old drawing must be displayed at each Paint event. First the work area is cleared, so the new image doesn't overlap the existing one.

If the user has selected the check box, the global variable bFull will contain the value 1, which has also been defined in the global module VBSTEP4.BAS as a constant named Checked.

```
Global Const Unchecked = 0
Global Const Checked = 1
```

In this case, the FillColor property is assigned the color cyan. Otherwise, white must be used to fill the shape to match the remaining background of the form.

The Line method

If the global variable bGraphic is set to TRUE, the Line method draws a rectangle. As this method name indicates, it's actually a function that draws lines. However, this function can also draw rectangles and boxes. To draw boxes with this method, you must include the letter B as the method's last parameter. The size, shape, and location of the rectangle or box are determined by two points, which are always at diagonally opposite corners of the box. We've used the size of our form's work area to determine the size of the rectangle, contained in the ScaleHeight and ScaleWidth properties.

If the Circle option has been selected in your dialog box, the Else portion of the "If (bGraphic = TRUE) Then..." statement is executed. Here the Circle method draws the desired picture in your form. This method requires two parameters specifying the center point as well as the radius of the circle that must be drawn.

The Print method

The Print method always displays text at the location currently specified by the CurrentX and CurrentY parameters. Since our text should always appear in the upper-left corner of the form, both of these properties are set to 20.

Once you've made these changes, your Visual Basic program is complete. You'll find the two form files VBSTEP41.FRM and VBSTEP42.FRM, the global module VBSTEP4.BAS, as well as the accompanying project file VBSTEP4.MAK on the companion diskette.

Output with QuickC

In QuickC, the first step in creating output always consists of obtaining a device context. A handle to this device is returned, which is then used as a parameter for virtually any output functions. Once that output has been completed, this connection must be deleted again, since only a limited number of device contexts may be used simultaneously. As with so many other tasks, QuickCase:W does this for you. If you take a close look at the code from the previous program step (QCSTEP3.C), you'll find the

WM_PAINT message, along with the following function calls, in the program's window procedure:

```
case WM_PAINT:     /* code for the window's client area                    */
     /* Obtain a handle to the device context                              */
     /* BeginPaint will send WM_ERASEBKGND if appropriate                  */
     memset(&ps, 0x00, sizeof(PAINTSTRUCT));
     hDC = BeginPaint(hWnd, &ps);

     /* Included in case the background is not a pure color                */
     SetBkMode(hDC, TRANSPARENT);
     /* Inform Windows painting is complete                                */
     EndPaint(hWnd, &ps);
```

BeginPaint obtains a device context, and the variable ps of the PAINTSTRUCT data structure is assigned values that are supplied by Windows. The variables then contain information indicating, for example, whether the entire work area must be recreated, and whether the old picture was deleted before the new one is to be drawn. EndPaint not only releases the device context handle, but also declares the entire work area as up-to-date, so Windows doesn't immediately trigger another WM_PAINT message.

The EndDialog function

In the last step, it didn't matter whether the user selected the OK or the Cancel button to close the dialog box. However, since a positive reply from the user must now trigger the program output, we must closely examine the EndDialog function, which is responsible for removing a modal dialog box from the screen. Because of this, the function can be found in the DialogsMsgProc dialog procedure. The second parameter of this function is an integer value that's passed as a return value (nRc) of the DialogBox function to indicate which of the two command buttons has been clicked.

```
case WM_COMMAND:
     switch(wParam)
       {
        case IDOK:
          bFill = (BOOL)SendDlgItemMessage(hWndDlg, IDC_FILL, BM_GETCHECK, 0, 0L);
          bGraphic = (BOOL)SendDlgItemMessage(hWndDlg, IDC_RECT, BM_GETCHECK, 0, 0L);
          if (bGraphic)
            idButton = IDC_RECT;
          else
            idButton = IDC_CIRCLE;
          GetWindowText(GetDlgItem(hWndDlg, IDC_EDIT), szEditText, 20);
          EndDialog(hWndDlg, TRUE);
          break;

        case IDCANCEL:
             /* Ignore data values entered into the controls         */
             /* and dismiss the dialog window returning FALSE        */
             EndDialog(hWndDlg, FALSE);
             break;
       }
     break;    /* End of WM_COMMAND                                      */
```

Now it's possible to check and respond to this value within the window procedure WndProc, from which the dialog box was first opened. The value TRUE is usually returned if the OK button has been clicked, which then causes the THEN portion of the IF THEN statement to be executed.

```
case IDM_O_SETTINGS:
     /* Place User Code to respond to the                  */
     /* Menu Item Named "&Settings" here.                  */


     {
      FARPROC lpfnDIALOGSMsgProc;

      lpfnDIALOGSMsgProc = MakeProcInstance((FARPROC)DIALOGSMsgProc, hInst);
      nRc = DialogBox(hInst, (LPSTR)"DIABOX", hWnd, lpfnDIALOGSMsgProc);
      FreeProcInstance(lpfnDIALOGSMsgProc);
     }
     if (nRc)
     {
        InvalidateRect(hWnd, NULL, TRUE);
        bOK = TRUE;
     }
     break;
```

The InvalidateRect function

When new output must occur, a WM_PAINT message must be added to the application message queue using the InvalidateRect function. The second parameter NULL indicates that the entire work area must be updated, and the value TRUE in the third parameter causes the existing picture to be deleted. (We mentioned this earlier when we discussed the PAINTSTRUCT data structure.)

The functions that QuickCase:W has inserted at the WM_PAINT message now form the framework for the code that will create the program output.

```
case WM_PAINT:    /* code for the window's client area              */
     /* Obtain a handle to the device context                       */
     /* BeginPaint will send WM_ERASEBKGND if appropriate           */
     memset(&ps, 0x00, sizeof(PAINTSTRUCT));
     hDC = BeginPaint(hWnd, &ps);

     /* Included in case the background is not a pure color         */
     SetBkMode(hDC, TRANSPARENT);

     if (bOK)
     {
     if (bFill)
     {
        hPntBrush = CreateSolidBrush(RGB(0,255,255));
        hOldPntBrush = SelectObject(hDC, hPntBrush);
     }
     GetClientRect(hWnd, &rct);
     if (bGraphic)
        Rectangle(hDC, rct.right/2-rct.right/3,
           rct.bottom/2-rct.bottom/3,
           rct.right/2+rct.right/3,
           rct.bottom/2+rct.bottom/3);
     else
        Ellipse(hDC,rct.right/2-rct.right/3,
           rct.bottom/2-rct.bottom/3,
           rct.right/2+rct.right/3,
           rct.bottom/2+rct.bottom/3);
     if (bFill)
     {
        SelectObject(hDC, hOldPntBrush);
        DeleteObject(hPntBrush);
     }
     TextOut(hDC, 10, 10, szEditText, strlen(szEditText));
    }
    /* Inform Windows painting is complete                          */
     EndPaint(hWnd, &ps);
     break;       /*  End of WM_PAINT                               */
```

The Brush attribute of the device context

The values of variables bOK, bFull, and bGraphic were discussed in the section on the Visual Basic program. In the Visual Basic application, the fill color has been determined by setting the FillColor property. However, this is a little more complicated with QuickC or Turbo Pascal.

First the CreateSolidBrush function must be used to create a brush with the color cyan; the function returns a reference to this brush. The brush is an attribute of the device context and must, therefore, be assigned to the latter by the SelectObject function. If the rectangle should have a red border instead of the standard black border, first you should create a red pen, which would then also be assigned to the context using the SelectObject function. Once SelectObject has been properly executed, all output functions that create closed shapes will recognize this newly defined brush.

Since the old attributes must be restored to the context before the device context is freed again, the reference to the previously selected brush or pen is always stored in a variable (hOldPntBrush). In addition to this, the self-defined attributes should be deleted, using the DeleteObject function, once these attributes are no longer needed.

The RECT data structure

So the size of the rectangle or circle can be matched to the size of the window's work area. Its current dimensions are determined using the GetClientRect function and are written to the variable rct or the RECT structure.

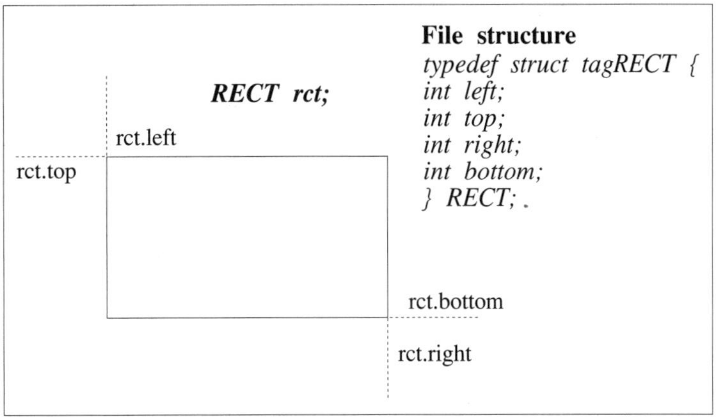

The RECT data structure

The five parameters used by the Rectangle and Ellipse functions are identical. First the device context must be specified, followed by the x and y coordinates of the upper-left and lower-right corners of the geometric figure. The text output is achieved through the TextOut function, and the starting position for the text output is passed directly to this function. The final parameter determines the length of the text, which is calculated with the strlen function.

This also concludes our example of the QuickC application. Refer to the listings for QCSTEP4 on your companion diskette.

Output with Turbo Pascal

In Turbo Pascal it's now also necessary to include an IF THEN statement at the dialog box call, so we can determine which of the two command buttons have been clicked. However, in Turbo Pascal, the direct ID values of the OK and Cancel buttons (IDOK and IDCANCEL) are returned instead of TRUE and FALSE.

```
procedure TMyWindow.Settings(var Msg: TMessage);
begin
     if Application^.ExecDialog(New(PMyDialog,
                                       Init(@Self, 'DIABOX')))
                                       = IDOK then
        begin
            InvalidateRect(HWindow, nil, TRUE);
            bOK := TRUE;

        end;
end;
```

The WMPaint and Paint methods

Since the goal in Turbo Pascal is object-oriented programming, we'll use either the WMPaint or Paint method instead of responding directly to the WM_PAINT message. The Paint procedure is, in turn, activated by the WMPaint method.

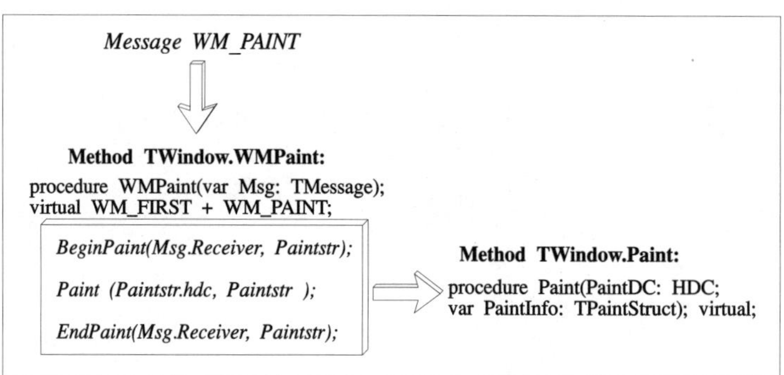

The Paint and WMPaint methods

The advantage of the Paint method is that its first parameter consists of a handle to the device context. So, it's no longer necessary to explicitly call the BeginPaint and EndPaint functions, since these are activated automatically at the correct points within the WMPaint method.

The actual execution of program output in Turbo Pascal is identical to the process described in QuickC. You only need to change the QuickC syntax to Turbo Pascal. The following procedure precedes the TMyWindow.SetupWindow procedure.

```
procedure TMyWindow.Paint(PaintDC: HDC; var PaintInfo: TPaintStruct);
var hPntBrush, hOldPntBrush: HBrush;
    Rect: TRect;
begin
   if (bOK = TRUE) then
   begin
     if MyFirstApp.bFill = Word(TRUE) then
     begin
         hPntBrush := CreateSolidBrush(RGB(0,255,255));
         hOldPntBrush := SelectObject(PaintDC,hPntBrush);
     end;
     GetClientRect(HWindow, Rect);
     if MyFirstApp.bGraphic = Word(TRUE) then
       Rectangle(PaintDC, Rect.right DIV 2-Rect.right DIV 3,
                 Rect.bottom DIV 2-Rect.bottom DIV 3,
                 Rect.right DIV 2+Rect.right DIV 3,
                 Rect.bottom DIV 2+Rect.bottom DIV 3)
     else
       Ellipse(PaintDc,Rect.right DIV 2-Rect.right DIV 3,
               Rect.bottom DIV 2-Rect.bottom DIV 3,
               Rect.right DIV 2+Rect.right DIV 3,
               Rect.bottom DIV 2+Rect.bottom DIV 3);
       if MyFirstApp.bFill = Word(TRUE) then
       begin
         SelectObject(PaintDC, hOldPntBrush);
         DeleteObject(hPntBrush);
       end;
       TextOut(PaintDC, 10, 10, MyFirstApp.szEditText,
               strlen(MyFirstApp.szEditText));
     end;
end;
```

This completes the last step of our Turbo Pascal application. All three of these completed applications (VBSTEP4.EXE, QCSTEP4.EXE, and TPSTEP4.EXE) should look and function identically after you start them.

33.5 Graphics

We hope that the previous sections provided a lot of helpful information about Windows programming. Finally, we'll present several short programs that are also included on the companion diskette.

Drag and drop in Windows 3.1

By using the drag and drop capability of Windows, the user can grab a file or group from the File Manager and drag the object(s) into another application. C provides four functions and the WM_DROPFILE message to implement drag and drop. However, we'll present a drag and drop application that was written with Visual Basic instead of C because this is much easier to implement than a C version.

Drag and drop

Drag and drop does just what it says. Dragging an object consists of placing your mouse pointer on that object, pressing and holding your mouse button, and then moving the mouse while keeping the button pressed. By releasing the mouse button, the object is dropped at the current location.

In the DRAGDROP application listed below, the six icons displayed in the program form can be dragged into a part of the form. For this, the user must position the mouse pointer on one of the icons and, while pressing the mouse button, drag that icon into the initially empty form. The appearance of the icon changes with its location in the form.

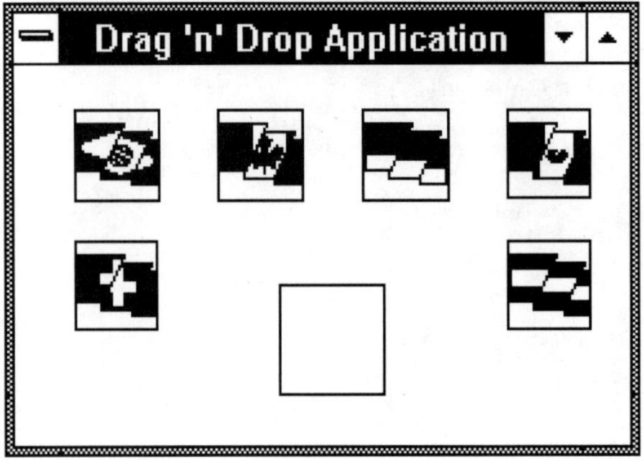

The DRAGDROP application

```
' DRAGDROP.FRM
Const ENTER = 0
Const LEAVE = 1

Sub DPict1_DragDrop (DSource As Control, X As Single, Y As Single)
    If TypeOf DSource Is PictureBox Then
        DPict1.Picture = DSource.Picture
        'NOTE: You may have to add path to the .ico file name
        DSource.DragIcon = LoadPicture("net13.ico")
    End If
End Sub

Sub DPict1_DragOver (DSource As Control, X As Single, Y As Single, State As Integer)
    If TypeOf DSource Is PictureBox Then
    Select Case State
     Case ENTER
        'NOTE: You may have to add a path to the .ico file name
        DSource.DragIcon = LoadPicture("trash01.ico")
     Case LEAVE
        'NOTE: You may have to add a path to the .ico file name
        DSource.DragIcon = LoadPicture("net13.ico")
    End Select
    End If
End Sub
```

This example uses the PictureBox object, found in the upper-right corner of your Visual Basic Toolbox. Six of these picture boxes are tied together as a control array, so they have the same CtlName and are differentiated by the contents of their Index properties.

The DragIcon and DragMode properties

In the DragIcon property, the NET13.ICO icon, which will represent the mouse pointer during drag and drop operations, is selected. This setting must be made for each of the six PictureBoxes. For the DragMode property, the automatic mode setting (1) is selected. This mode allows an object to automatically respond to a drag and drop operation at any time. All properties have been listed in the following table.

Object	Property	Setting
Form1	Caption	Drag 'n' Drop Application
Picture1	CtlName	Picture1
Picture2	CtlName	Flaggs
	Index	0
	DragIcon	
	DragMode	1
	Picture	flgbrazl.ico
	AutoSize	true
Picture3	CtlName	Flaggs
	Index	1
	DragIcon	net13.ico
	DragMode	1
	Picture	flgcan.ico
	AutoSize	true
Picture4	CtlName	Flaggs
	Index	2
	DragIcon	net13.ico
	DragMode	1
	Picture	flggerm.ico
	AutoSize	true
Picture5	CtlName	Flaggs
	Index	3
	DragIcon	net13.ico
	DragMode	1
	Picture	flgmex.ico
	AutoSize	true

Picture6	CtlName	Flaggs
	Index	4
	DragIcon	net13.ico
	DragMode	1
	Picture	flgswitz.ico
	AutoSize	true
Picture7	CtlName	Flaggs
	Index	5
	DragIcon	net13.ico
	DragMode	1
	Picture	flgspain.ico
	AutoSize	true

The DragOver and DragDrop events

The two drag events, DragOver and DragDrop, are closely related. Both use the Source parameter to indicate which object is being dragged. The target object is the picture with the CtlName Picture1.

The DragOver event is triggered when the mouse pointer, displaying the source's drag icon, is moved into or out of the target object. The State parameter distinguishes between these two situations.

State	Description
0	Source object entering target object area.
1	Source object leaving target object area.
2	Source object moving in target object area.

This event is particularly useful for setting a specific icon that indicates to the user that the object being dragged has reached its destination and can be dropped. Releasing the mouse button then triggers a DragDrop event for the target object.

Bitmaps as menu items

In our previous examples, we've implemented menu items as text strings. However, several Windows applications also offer the option of using bitmaps to depict menu items, which can often be much more descriptive than a short text. With QuickCase:W you can link a picture to a menu item. QuickCase:W also automatically inserts the required function calls while generating the source code.

The MENUBMP.C application is equipped with two menus, with three and four menu items, respectively. All seven menu items have been implemented as bitmaps.

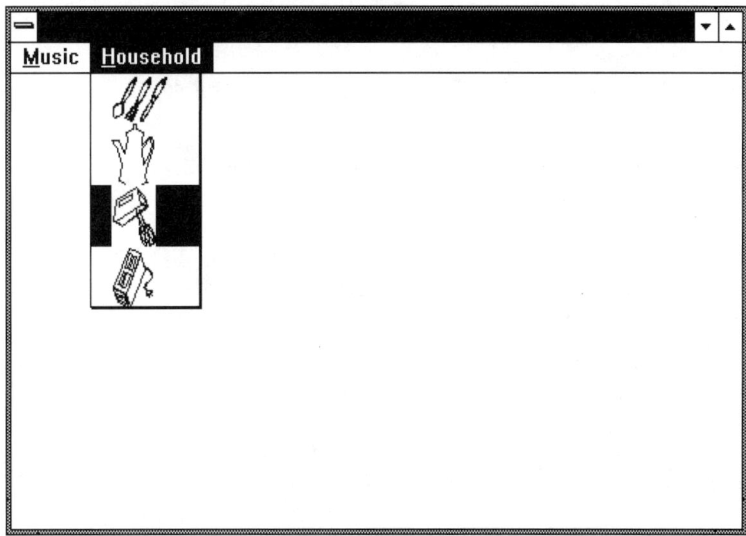

Sample program using bitmaps to represent menu items

To link a bitmap to a menu item using QuickCase:W, select the *Bitmap* option in the *Insert Menu Item* dialog box. This opens another dialog box, allowing you to set the desired bitmaps. When QuickCase:W generates the code, it then inserts the LoadBitmap and ModifyMenu functions at the WM_CREATE message for each bitmap item. QuickCase:W uses the file name as the resource names for the individual bitmaps.

```
;MENUBMP.RC
#include "MENUBMP.h"

TUBA BITMAP TUBA.BMP
GUITAR BITMAP GUITAR.BMP
PANFLUTE BITMAP PANFLUTE.BMP
FLATWARE BITMAP FLATWARE.BMP
C_POT BITMAP C_POT.BMP
MIXER BITMAP MIXER.BMP
TOASTER BITMAP TOASTER.BMP

MENUBMP MENU
  BEGIN
    POPUP  "&Music"
      BEGIN
        MENUITEM "TUBA", IDM_M_TUBA
        MENUITEM "GUITAR", IDM_M_GUITAR
        MENUITEM "PANFLUTE", IDM_M_PANFLUTE
      END
    POPUP  "&Household"
      BEGIN
        MENUITEM "FLATWARE", IDM_H_FLATWARE
        MENUITEM "C_POT", IDM_H_CPOT
        MENUITEM "MIXER", IDM_H_MIXER
        MENUITEM "TOASTER", IDM_H_TOASTER
      END
  END
```

```
STRINGTABLE
BEGIN
  IDS_ERR_CREATE_WINDOW,      "Window creation failed!"
  IDS_ERR_REGISTER_CLASS,     "Error registering window class"
END

/* MENUBMP.C: excerpts */
    case WM_CREATE:

         hMenu    = GetMenu(hWnd);
         hBitmap = LoadBitmap(hInst, "TUBA");
         ModifyMenu(hMenu, 1050, MF_BYCOMMAND | MF_BITMAP,
                          1050, (LPSTR)MAKELONG(hBitmap, 0));

         hBitmap = LoadBitmap(hInst, "GUITAR");
         ModifyMenu(hMenu, 1100, MF_BYCOMMAND | MF_BITMAP,
                          1100, (LPSTR)MAKELONG(hBitmap, 0));

         hBitmap = LoadBitmap(hInst, "PANFLUTE");
         ModifyMenu(hMenu, 1150, MF_BYCOMMAND | MF_BITMAP,
                          1150, (LPSTR)MAKELONG(hBitmap, 0));

         hBitmap = LoadBitmap(hInst, "FLATWARE");
         ModifyMenu(hMenu, 2050, MF_BYCOMMAND | MF_BITMAP,
                          2050, (LPSTR)MAKELONG(hBitmap, 0));

         hBitmap = LoadBitmap(hInst, "C_POT");
         ModifyMenu(hMenu, 2100, MF_BYCOMMAND | MF_BITMAP,
                          2100, (LPSTR)MAKELONG(hBitmap, 0));

         hBitmap = LoadBitmap(hInst, "MIXER");
         ModifyMenu(hMenu, 2150, MF_BYCOMMAND | MF_BITMAP,
                          2150, (LPSTR)MAKELONG(hBitmap, 0));

         hBitmap = LoadBitmap(hInst, "TOASTER");
         ModifyMenu(hMenu, 2200, MF_BYCOMMAND | MF_BITMAP,
                          2200, (LPSTR)MAKELONG(hBitmap, 0));


         break;        /*  End of WM_CREATE                           */
```

You'll find the complete code listing under the name MENUBMP on the companion diskette.

Text Editor

TPW

Anyone who's worked with Windows is probably familiar with the Windows Notepad (NOTEPAD.EXE). With object-oriented programming using Turbo Pascal, you can easily recreate this application yourself, since a specific window object, named TFileWindow, is provided specifically for this purpose. You'll find the source file for this object in the StdWnds unit, which is included with the Turbo Pascal for Windows software package.

The TFileWindow object type

The TFileWindow object type is basically a text box. Its methods allow you to open and save files, search for specific expressions, and access the Clipboard.

The StdWnds unit encompasses the resource file (STDWNDS.RES), which already contains the appropriate menus for the TFileWindow object, named FileCommands, as well as the corresponding keyboard accelerators. These simply need to be loaded using LoadMenu and LoadAccelerators. This menu, as well as the shortcut keys, meet the CUA guidelines and should therefore be used to offer the user a uniform user surface for all different types of Windows applications. Other resources, such as dialog boxes for opening and saving files, can be found in the STDDLGS.RES resource file in the STDDLGS.TPU unit which is, in turn, part of the StdWnds unit.

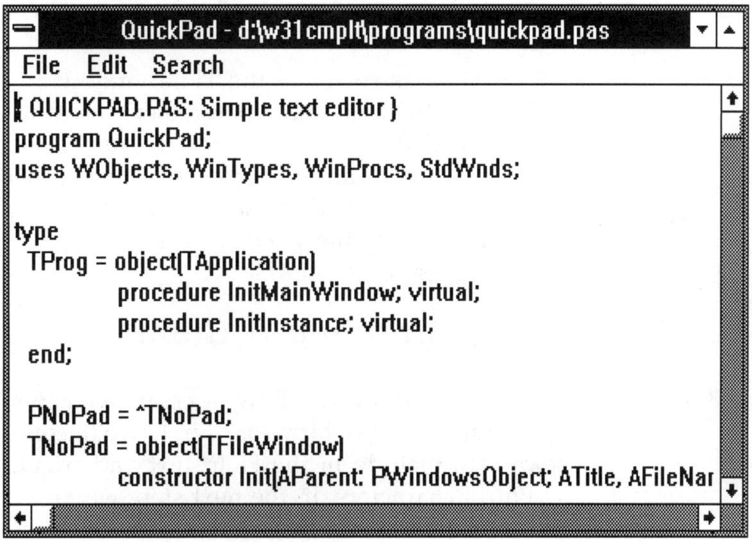

QUICKPAD application

```
{ QUICKPAD.PAS: Simple text editor }
program QuickPad;
uses WObjects, WinTypes, WinProcs, StdWnds;

type
  TProg = object(TApplication)
     procedure InitMainWindow; virtual;
     procedure InitInstance; virtual;
  end;

  PNoPad = ^TNoPad;
  TNoPad = object(TFileWindow)
     constructor Init(AParent: PWindowsObject; ATitle, AFileName: PChar);
  end;

constructor TNoPad.Init(AParent: PWindowsObject; ATitle, AFileName: PChar);
begin
  TFileWindow.Init(AParent, ATitle, AFileName);
  Attr.Menu := LoadMenu(HInstance, 'FileCommands');
end;

procedure TProg.InitMainWindow;
begin
  MainWindow := New(PNoPad, Init(nil, 'QuickPad',nil));
end;

procedure TProg.InitInstance;
begin
  TApplication.InitInstance;
  HAccTable := LoadAccelerators(HInstance, 'FileCommands');
end;

{ Main program }
var
  NoPad : TProg;

begin
  NoPad.Init('NoPad');
  NoPad.Run;
  NoPad.Done;
end.
```

The program remains quite manageable despite its wide array of capabilities. Dialog boxes belonging to specific methods are stored in the STDWNDS.RES or STDDLGS.RES resource file and are called automatically when their corresponding menu items are selected.

The Init constructor of the TFileWindow object (or actually of its child NoPad), has three parameters instead of the usual two. The additional third value represents the file name that appears in the title bar in addition to the application title. Since the value zero is passed as the last parameter when the InitMainWindow method creates the window, the word [Untitled] is displayed in the application's title bar.

33.6 Creating a Custom Help System

Now we'll show you how to create a custom Help system, which includes several bitmaps. First, we'll collect all the topics we want to include in the Help text and prepare them with special control characters. In the next step, we must create a Help project file containing the necessary instructions to the Help compiler. This lets us generate a Help file from our Help topic files. You'll find the complete source code on the companion diskette.

If you decide to create your own Help systems, you'll need the following for development (we'll discuss how these programs apply to development later in this section):

- A word processor that saves files in .RTF (Rich Text Format), and supports strikethrough and underline text. Microsoft Word for DOS (Versions 5.0 and 5.5) and Microsoft Word for Windows support these character formats.
- The Microsoft Windows Software Development Kit (SDK) Version 3.1. Specifically, you'll need the Help compiler files HC30.EXE, HC.BAT, HC31.EXE, and HC31.ERR to compile the RTF files you plan to use in the .HLP program.
- Microsoft QuickC for Windows to compile and link the HLPPROG C codes.

Planning a Help system

Planning

The first step in developing a custom Help system involves making a plan. This plan will list all the steps to be executed. Once we've laid out the basic steps, we can explore each step in detail.

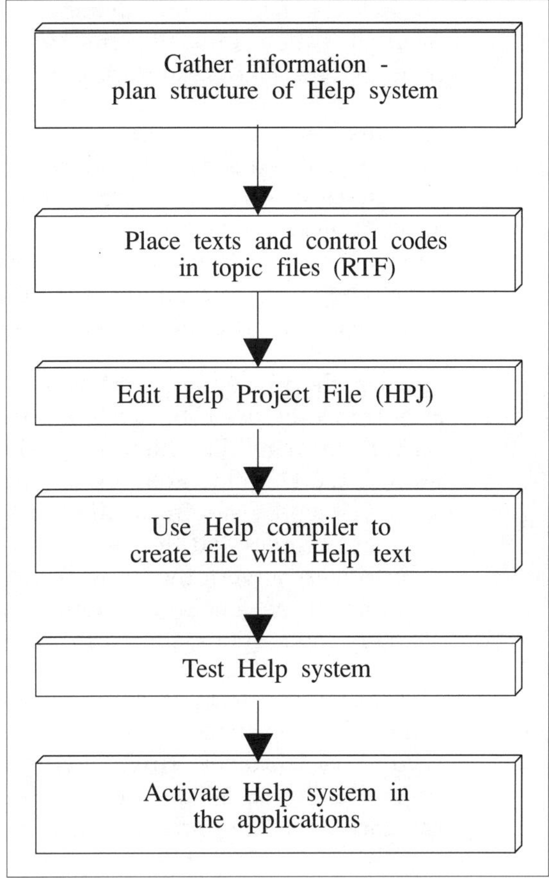

Creating a plan

The information presented by a Help system should be comprehensive, without being longwinded. The Help system should be aimed at one of four groups of users:

- Absolute beginners (new to PCs, new to Windows, and new to the application)
- Program beginners (new to the application or Windows)
- Intermediates (has some knowledge of Windows and the application)
- Experts (very familiar with the application)

Depending on the circumstances, the Help system must be oriented towards absolute beginners, who have no previous experience in computing. This requires clear, simple definitions of all technical terms. However, the application may be intended for experienced users. These users want advanced information, and they may be insulted if they think that the Help system is "talking down" to them. So, the Help system design will vary with the application.

Context-sensitive help

A context-sensitive Help system is best for beginning users. Through context-sensitivity, they can then call information about the currently selected menu command or other element of the application at any time by pressing F1 or Shift + F1. However, a context-sensitive Help system means more work for the software developer (you), and often the developer and author must decide which elements should receive context-sensitive Help.

Help hierarchy

After gathering enough information, then you must plan the appearance of the Help system structure. The individual topics must be arranged in a hierarchy, with the Index always at the top level of the Help hierarchy. Users must be given the opportunity to move step-by-step from the top level to the bottom level. The number of topics and the general size of the Help system (among other things) govern the number of hierarchy levels required. For example, these levels can stem from arranging the topics into chapters and sections, similar to a book.

The next illustration shows how we built our hierarchy in our sample Help system. Along with the main index, there are three secondary indexes (menu commands, window elements, programming languages), which list the topics of their particular categories and offer brief information.

It should be possible to go directly from one topic to the next (browse) with all the topics on the same level. Such logical sequences are important for users who want to read several related topics together (e.g., all the menu commands of the File Manager). There is a specific control code for this browsing option. The two browse buttons << and >> perform this task.

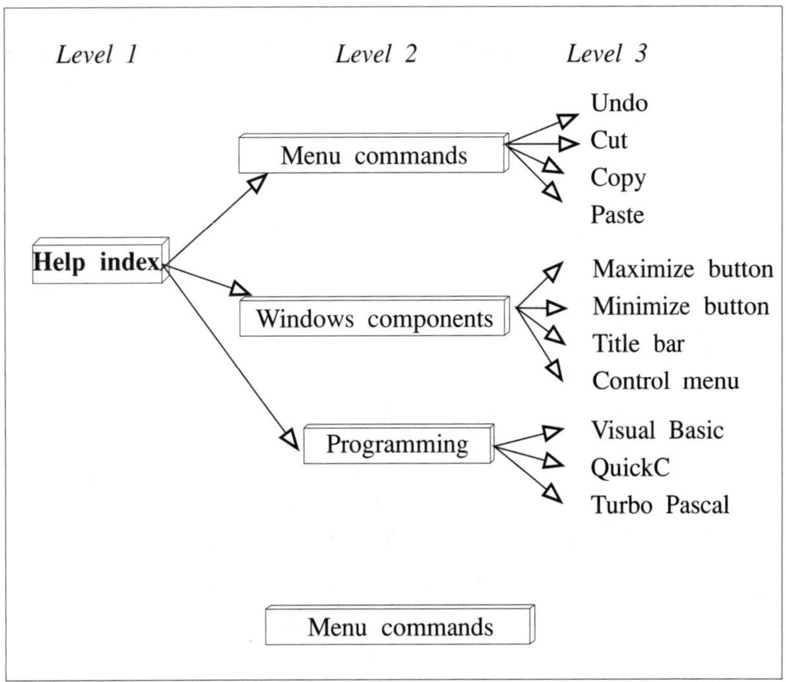

Hierarchy of the sample Help system

File structure

In the next step, the author must decide how to convert the Help hierarchy into files. Here, the amount of information is important.

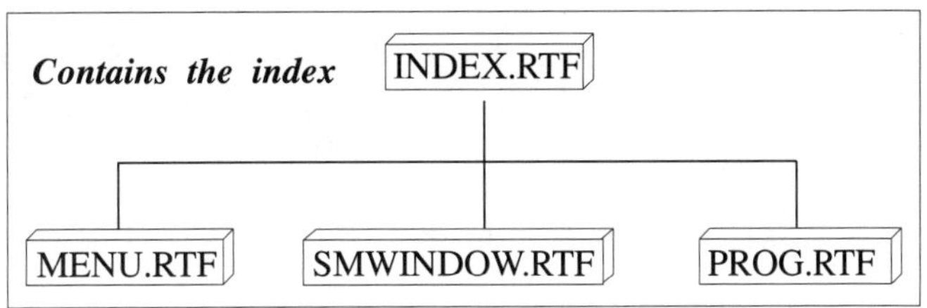

Structure of the files for the Help system

Each Help topic can be more than one page, describing a specific aspect of the application and can be in a separate file. However, it's also possible to combine all topics that belong to a secondary index into one file or to create a different file structure.

All files must be saved in .RTF format (Rich Text Format). In our example, the Help index is in a separate file. Also, each secondary index, along with its topics, is in a separate file. The file in which the topics of the menu commands are defined is called MENU.RTF. All the topics that describe window elements are in the SMWINDOW.RTF file, and the three topics related to programming languages are stored in the PROG.RTF file. If a file defines more than one topic, the topics must be separated by page breaks.

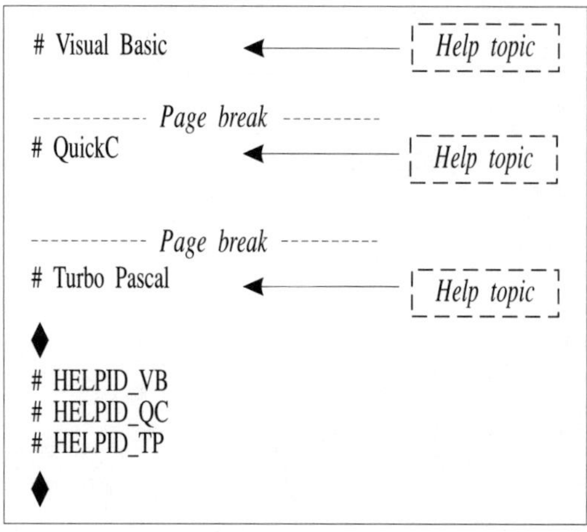

Combining several Help topics into one file

When you're planning the Help system, you should also pay attention to the layout of the Help texts. To make reading the information in Help as pleasant as possible for the user, you should follow the same guidelines used to create an instruction manual. Some software packages have comprehensive Help systems without any printed documentation.

Headers and important keywords stand out more when you make them bold or use a different font and font size. A topic shouldn't be too long. Also, it should be divided into paragraphs. There are certain topics that you can explain more quickly and easily with graphics than with text (more on this later).

Creating Help topic files

Topic files

When you're developing a Help system, you'll spend most of your time creating Help topic files. For example, you must edit or copy the text to the file structure you created in the planning stages. Also, you must set control codes which determine how the user can move around in the Help system. You can insert these control characters while you're editing the text, or add them to the existing text later.

To create topic files, you'll need an editor that can save files in .RTF (Rich Text Format), can work with footnotes, and is able to underline and strike through words, since these are the characteristics used to make the control codes. For example, the text editor of Microsoft Word for Windows or Microsoft Word 5.0, which was used to create this example, fulfill these requirements.

Control characters

There are eight different control characters produced by footnote characters or formatted text. In part, it's the combination of two control characters that results in a control code.

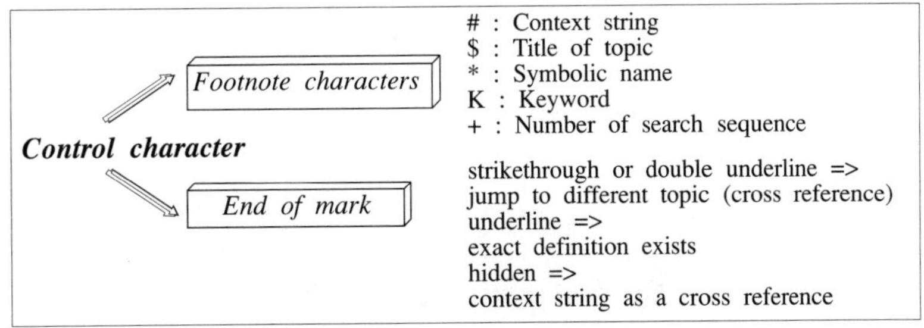

Control characters

The following lists the characteristics that can be linked to a topic by these control codes. After this list, the characteristics are described in the same sequence.

- Context string
- Title
- Keyword
- Browse sequence number
- Cross reference
- Definition of terms
- Symbolic name
- Control code for a context string

Context string

Every topic in the Help system needs its own context string for identification. A valid context string can be up to 255 letters, numbers, and underscores (_). Letters can be uppercase or lowercase. The strings are used for jumping between topics (see the Cross reference heading in this chapter). Only the index, which displays the topic at the top level, doesn't need the context string.

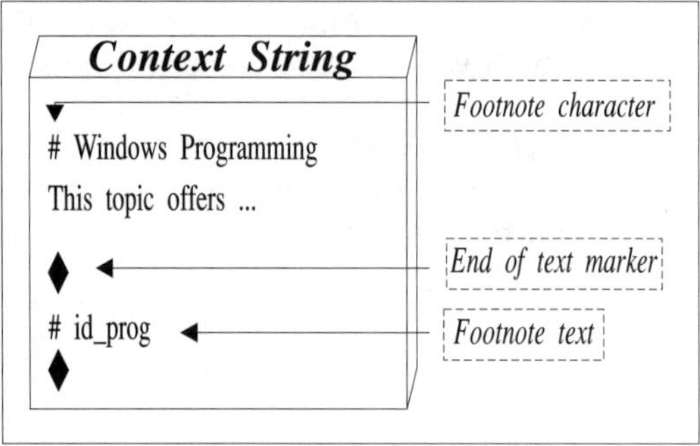

Context string

Control code for a title

Title

Most Help topics have a title. In this case, we're referring to a title used in the Help system, instead of the title usually found in the first line of the Help text.

For example, this title is presented to the user as a model when a bookmark is defined. It also appears in the *Go To* list in the *Search* dialog box when a search for a keyword is successful.

To define a title, enter the $ footnote character at the beginning of the text for the appropriate topic. The title is then written as the topic's footnote text, which cannot be formatted.

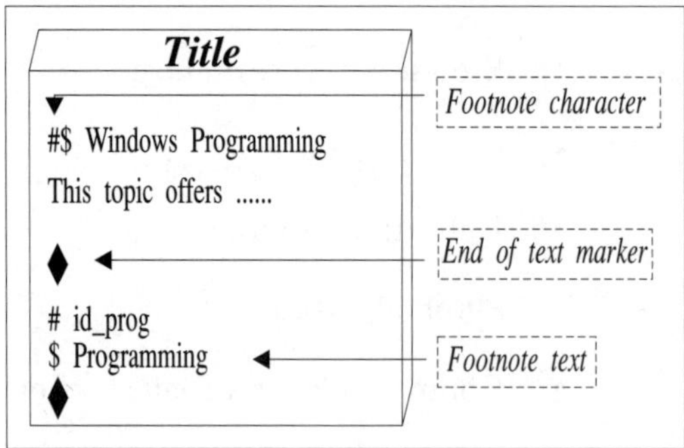

Definition of a title

Control code for a keyword

Keyword

One of the best ways to use a Help system is to search for certain terms and then jump directly to the passage containing the term. Keywords make this process possible. You can compare these keywords with the index of a book. Most likely you've searched an index for a specific term but couldn't find it. This will also happen to users of your Help system if you don't insert enough keywords in the topic. However, specifying as many keywords as possible is only part of the job. You must also use the keywords in the right place.

You can define any number of keywords for a topic in a Help system. The keywords then appear in a list box when you select the Search button. Again, the application doesn't distinguish between uppercase and lowercase letters. If several topics have the same keyword, the *Go to* list box alphabetically displays the titles of all relevant topics. The user can then select the desired topic by double-clicking it or clicking the Go To button.

The footnote character for the keywords is the uppercase or lowercase 'K'. Enter all the keywords, separated by hyphens, as the footnote text for the topic. This text can also be several lines long.

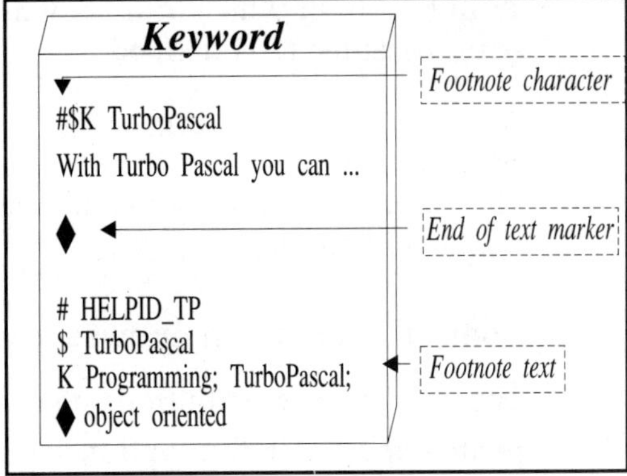

Definition of keywords

Keyword table

All keywords created with the letter 'K' are in a common table. You can also create additional keyword tables. For example, you could do this so that the user must first enter a password before he/she can use a hidden table to search for more information. The program, instead of the Search button, would perform the search.

The keywords for the new keyword table must be marked by a letter other than 'K', and the program is case-sensitive. A word can be part of both the default table and an additional table. A Help system can have a total of five keyword tables at the same time.

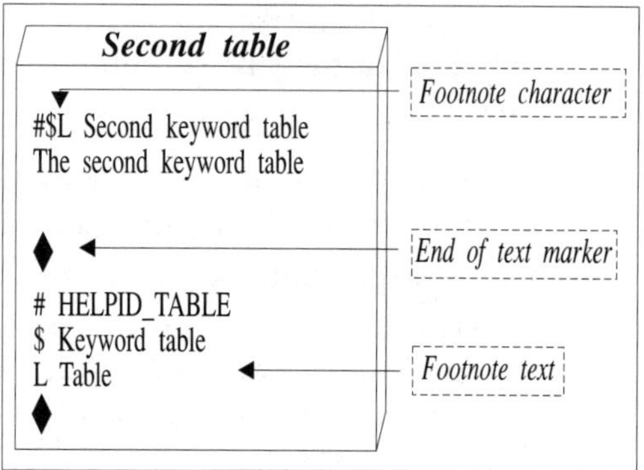

Definition of an additional keyword table

Topics with keywords in a different file than the standard keyword table can be saved in the same file as the other topics or in a separate file, as in our example. There is a file called TABLE.RTF, in which a topic, which accesses an additional table with the letter L, is defined.

Along with the definition of the table in the topic file, the additional option, MULTIKEY, must be linked to the project file. This option is necessary to announce the letter of the new table to the Help compiler.

Control code for a browse sequence number

Browse sequence number

The [<<] and [>>] buttons enable the user to move among the related topics. If this option isn't implemented in a particular program, as is the case in the Help system of the Program Manager, then the two buttons disappear. The sequence in which the topics are presented is called the browse sequence. The author of the Help system determines the browse sequence with sequence numbers.

The '+' footnote character is used for the browse sequences. The sequence number usually consists of a sequence name and a number, separated by a colon.

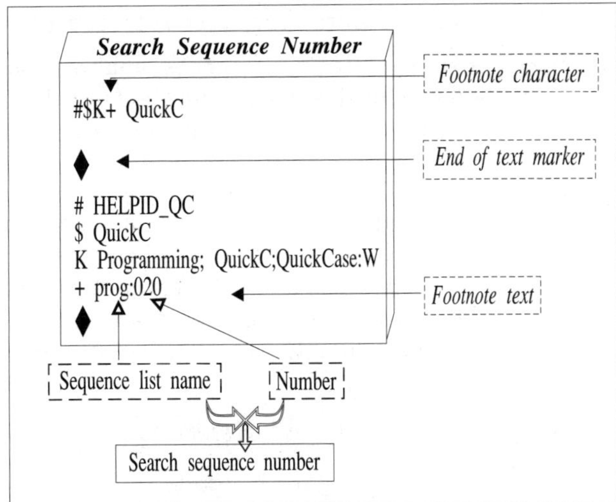

Sequence number

All sequence numbers with the same name belong to a browse sequence. If you don't specify a name, the topic is noted in a null list. The number determines the sequence within the browse sequence. Often numbers aren't assigned sequentially in order to leave room for additions. These numbers must have the same number of digits because the Help compiler handles them alphanumerically, instead of numerically. This means that topic number 100 would precede topic number 99, since the Help compiler only compares the first two digits.

Since the three topics have the same sequence name, 'prog', you can jump from one topic to the next. You can determine whether you have this option by clicking the Search and Glossary buttons. As soon as you reach the beginning or end of the sequence, the relevant button is dimmed automatically so you can no longer use it.

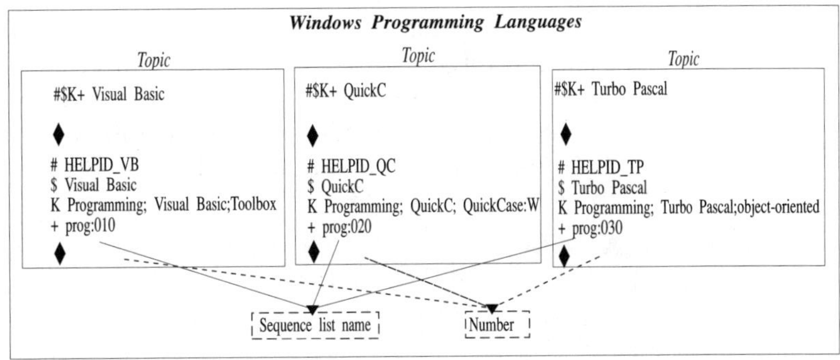

Browse sequence of Windows programming

Control code for a cross reference

Cross reference

Existing cross references enable you to go from the highest hierarchical level to the next until you reach the lowest level. Context strings of separate topics are needed to jump from one level to the next.

First you must determine a passage from which you want to jump. This text must be formatted in strikethrough or double underline character format. Then enter the context string of the topic as hidden text to which you want to jump. The hidden text must be attached directly to the strikethrough or double underlined text.

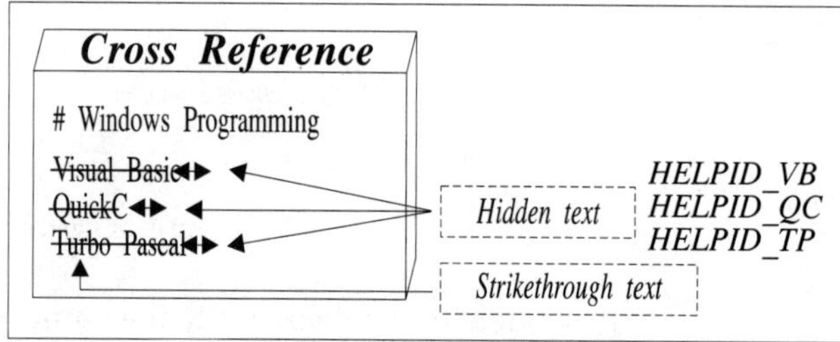

Cross references

This illustration demonstrates how to jump by displaying the passage as underlined. The Help compiler converts the strikethrough or double underlined character format to underline.

Windows Programming Languages
This topic offers a brief overview. . . .

<u>Visual Basic</u>
<u>QuickC</u>
<u>Turbo Pascal</u>

Control code for defining terms

Definition of terms

Topic files often contain words or expressions that must be defined (e.g., foreign words). To avoid cluttering the text with these definitions, the Help system enables the user to display the definitions only when needed. A dotted line appears under the expressions that contain definitions.

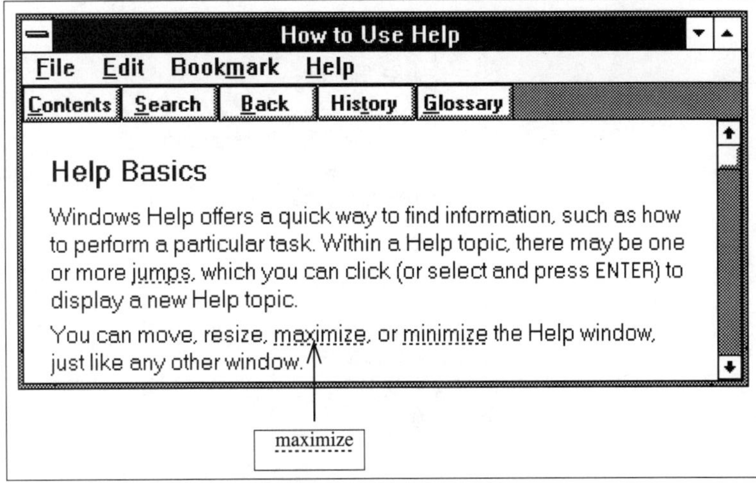

It's possible to display additional information

When the user selects text that's underlined in this way, a secondary window appears with additional information, as described earlier. The additional text disappears when you release the left mouse button or press a key.

According to the Help compiler, these additional definitions are independent topics. So they also require a context string. These definitions can be either combined into one separate file (the same file as the topic to which they refer) or separate files for each definition.

Expressions that have definitions appear in underlined character format. Then the context string of the topic, which provides the definition, is written as hidden text.

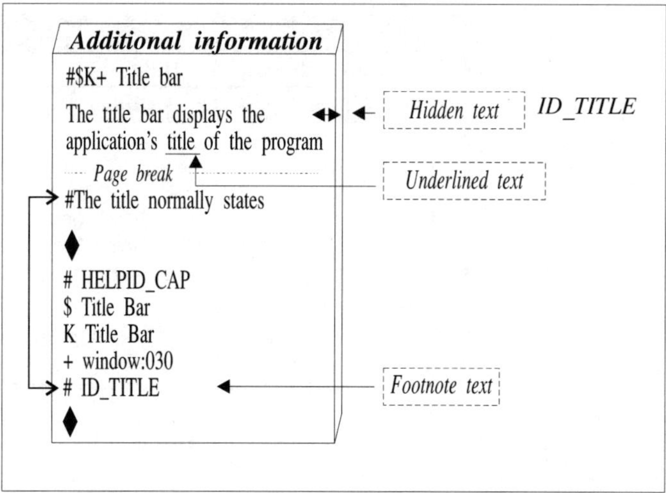

Definition of terms

Our sample Help system contains two terms with definitions. The two words are *Title* and *Minimize*, and can be found in the SMWINDOW.RTF file with additional information.

Control code for a symbolic name

Symbolic name

"Build Tags" are switches with names that can be inserted into a topic. This is done so the Help compiler can build the topic into the Help file. This option is useful if you've created Help files for different versions of an application and one version has more attributes than the others. For example, this could be the case with a demo version which wouldn't actually need a Help system.

The '*' footnote character, which was described earlier, is used for these symbolic switches. The Help compiler will work more efficiently if you insert this character in front of all other footnote characters. Enter the name of the switch as the footnote text.

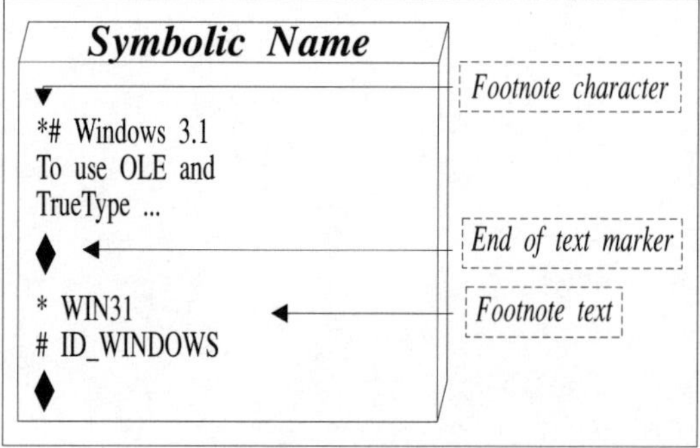

Symbolic name

When you insert the build tag footnote, the switch is set to TRUE if it matches the name in the BUILDTAGS; section in the project file. With the help of the BUILD option in the *Options* section, you can change the status of these switches (see next paragraph). Only topics with switches whose symbolic names are set to TRUE are accepted into the Help file by the Help compiler.

All topics without switches are automatically written to the Help file. So, switches are mainly used to exclude certain topics from the Help file. To exclude a topic, set the switch to FALSE.

Control code for importing bitmaps

Bitmaps

There are two ways to add pictures stored as bitmaps to the Help system. If you own a word processor, such as Word for Windows, which supports directly importing graphics, you can easily place the bitmaps in the Help file. For example, you could obtain the picture from the Clipboard and paste it in the correct location in the text. When saving the file, the imported bitmap is also converted to .RTF file format and linked to the Help file.

The second option for displaying bitmaps in the Help system is to specify a reference to a .BMP file. You can place the picture to the right or left of the text.

```
{bml arrow.bmp}        left
{bmc qc.bmp}           character
{bmr prog.bmp}         right
```

For example, here's a portion of the SMWINDOW.RTF topic file:

```
{bml arrow.bmp}id_smwindow #$K+Maximize Box
{bml Maximize.bmp} Clicking the Maximize box displays the
current window in Maximized form (encompassing the entire
screen when possible).
```

You can reach this topic by pressing Shift + F1 and then clicking the Maximize box with the mouse pointer. The contents of the Help system window should look like the following:

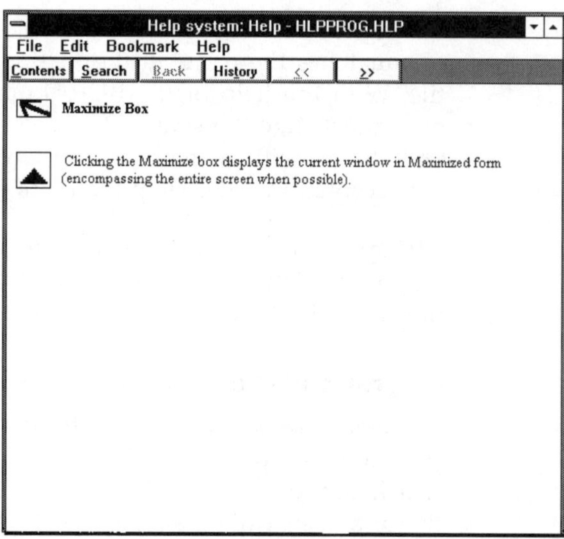

Linking a bitmap

In specifying bmc (bitmap character), the bitmap is treated like a character so text can appear in the same line before and after the picture. The line spacing is automatically determined by the height of the characters and bitmap.

QuickC Help system

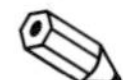

If you worked through the earlier sections of this chapter, you probably frequently called the Help system for information on a function or a message in the QuickC Help system. You probably also noticed several bitmaps, which aren't only static elements, but also frequently can be clicked to go to a different topic or for additional information. For example, the Index topic is made up of many bitmaps, which you click to go to the desired topic area.

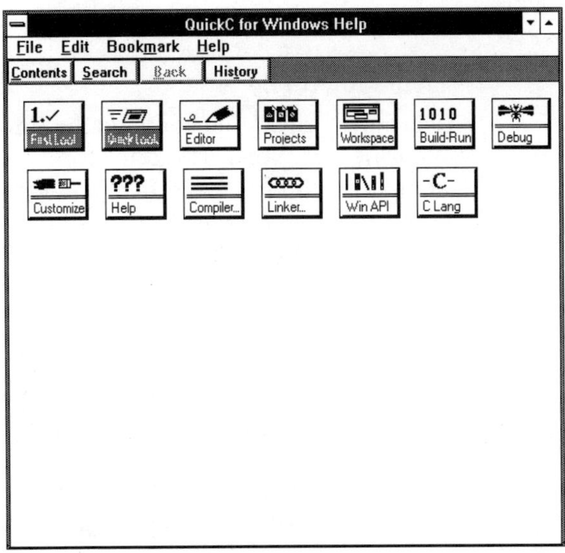

Bitmaps in the QuickC Help system

Our Help system also contains several bitmaps that trigger specific actions when selected with the mouse pointer, just like the underlined terms. This can be done in the same way as previously described, for example, the braces plus contents, such as {bml arrow.bmp} can also be provided with format characters such as strikethrough, underscore, etc. Then you also add the context string of the Help topic as hidden text.

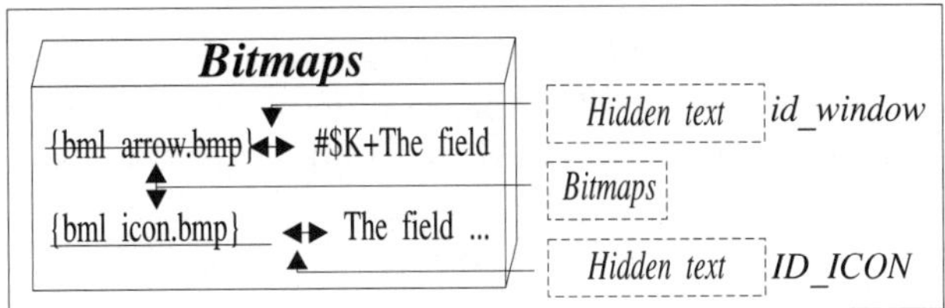

Linking control codes to bitmaps

Also, all bitmaps used must be listed in the BITMAPS section in the project file. You can also specify the complete path name in case the bitmaps aren't in the current directory.

If a bitmap must be displayed several times in a Help file, then all the references refer to the same graphic (i.e., the bitmap only has to be imported once). This prevents the Help file from becoming too large.

Creating a Help file (HLP)

Help Project File

Project file

The Help project file contains the information needed by the Help compiler to convert Help topic files into a WINHELP.EXE compatible binary Help file. You can use any ASCII text editor to write this file, which consists of a maximum of six sections. The file extension is HPJ.

Section	Function
[FILES]	Contains all topic files
[OPTIONS]	Contains different formats
[BUILDTAGS]	Specifies the valid symbolic names
[MAP]	Links context strings with context numbers
[ALIAS]	Assigns same context string to several topics
[BITMAPS]	Specifies bitmaps to be linked

Sections of the Help project file

Although the section order is usually arbitrary, in a few instances the [ALIAS] section must precede the [MAP] section. A semicolon must precede any comments that are added. When the Help compiler encounters a semicolon, it ignores any text following that character in the current line.

Section: [FILES]

[FILES] Lists all topic files

Every Help project file needs this section. The [FILES] section lists the topic files that will be used to make the binary Help file. The Help compiler searches the current directory and the path specified by the Root option for these files. If it cannot find a file, the compiler displays an error message.

```
[FILES]
index.rtf ; Contains the Index
menu.rtf  ; Contains menu item information
smwindow.rtf; Contains window element information
prog.rtf ; Contains programming language information
table.rtf
```

The larger the Help system, the more topic files it will contain. Often the names of these files are placed into a separate header file for clarity. You can use an #include statement to link this file to the [FILES] section.

```
[FILES]
#include <hlpprog.h>
```

Assuming the same example, the contents of the HLPPROG.H file are identical to the previous five lines:

```
index.rtf
menu.rtf
smwindow.rtf
prog.rtf
table.rtf
```

Section: OPTIONS]

[OPTIONS] Options

The OPTIONS section can contain up to nine different options.

[OPTIONS]
BUILD
COMPRESS
FORCEFONT
INDEX
MAPFONTSIZE
MULTIKEY
ROOT
TITLE
WARNING

The [OPTIONS] section

OPTIONS: BUILD

If symbolic names (Build Tags) have been defined in the Help topic files, use the Build option to link the desired topics. Otherwise, this option isn't useful. Build expressions can be a maximum of 255 characters and must be single spaced.

You can link all the switches together by using the logical operators OR (|), AND (&), and NOT (~). When creating the Help file, the Help compiler only considers topics whose switches have been set to TRUE.

```
[OPTIONS]
BUILD = ~WIN31
```

The switch instructs the Help compiler to consider all topics that aren't named WIN31. This makes it possible to create a Help system that's suitable for Windows Version 3.0 and the new version Windows 3.1. Topics, such as OLE and TrueType, which didn't exist in the previous version, are provided the WIN31 switch. This switch is set to TRUE or FALSE, depending on the Help system you're creating.

OPTIONS: COMPRESS

Use the Compress option to reduce the size of the Help file that results from compiling the topic files.

```
[OPTIONS]
COMPRESS = TRUE
```

Since a compressed Help file is smaller and can be loaded more quickly by the Help system, use this option as often as possible. Compression occurs with the help of a phrase table (a file containing the .PH extension). The Help compiler either creates a new phrase table, or uses the existing one. You get the greatest possible compression when the compiler doesn't find any old phrase tables. So, always delete the old .PH file before compiling.

OPTIONS: FORCEFONT

In normal cases, a Help system consists of a collection of texts that resulted over the course of a project. Frequently, the contents of the individual text files are formatted with different fonts.

However, when you display the finished Help text, different fonts should be used only to make specific details stand out from the rest of the text. Otherwise, the user will be confused by the different fonts. You can use the *Forcefont* option to force one specific font for all topics.

```
[OPTIONS]
FORCEFONT = Times
```

This option sets any Windows font, provided there are no spaces in the font name. For example, you cannot use Tms Rmn. If you pass a font name, which the compiler doesn't recognize, to this option, an error message appears. The text will then appear in the default font, Helvetica (Helv).

OPTIONS: INDEX

If the project file consists of only the FILES section, the Help compiler enters the topic of the file, which is named there first as the top hierarchy level. In this case, the index doesn't need a context string. However, you can also specify the index from the *Index* option. When you choose this option, the Help compiler must enter the context string of the desired topic. This prevents another Help index from suddenly appearing later when you're adding new Help topic files because someone placed the new files at the beginning of the FILES section.

```
[OPTIONS]
INDEX=index_info
```

You can display the Index topic in the Help window at any time by clicking the Contents button.

OPTIONS: MAPFONT-SIZE

You can use the MAPFONTSIZE option to define the font and font size in this section or change the sizes of fonts. This is helpful when you also want to publish the help text as a manual, using a different font than the one used in the screen display.

```
[OPTIONS]
MAPFONTSIZE=10-12:20
```

This line causes the source font, which can be between 10 and 12 units in size, to be displayed in a new size of 25 units. Also, you don't always have to change an entire range; it's possible to reset only one size.

```
[OPTIONS]
MAPFONTSIZE=15:10
```

OPTIONS: MULTIKEY

If you've created extra keyword tables in the topic files, you must use the MULTIKEY option to announce them in the project file.

```
[OPTIONS]
MULTIKEY=L
```

In the example, the letter L was defined in the TABLE.RTF topic file as a flag for an additional keyword table. You can use any letter except K, which is used for the default table. Remember that the program is case-sensitive. Although you can create up to five keyword tables, usually you won't need more than two or three.

OPTIONS: ROOT

Use the ROOT option to set the root directory of the Help project. This is where the Help compiler looks for Help topic files. If you don't set a root directory, the compiler will search the current directory.

```
[OPTIONS]
ROOT=d:\w31cmplt\help
```

OPTIONS: TITLE

Use the TITLE option to assign a title to your Help system. This title then appears in the title bar of the Help function. A title can have a maximum of 32 characters.

```
[OPTIONS]
TITLE=Help system:
```

OPTIONS: WARNING

Use the WARNING option to specify the kinds of error messages the Help compiler outputs. There are three error message categories (1,2,3), with level 3 set as the default. If you set the error level to 1, only serious error messages are output. If you select level 3, all other error messages are displayed.

```
[OPTIONS]
WARNING=3
```

The errors are usually displayed on the screen. You could also redirect them to a file, called ERROR.TXT, for example. To do this, call the Help compiler as follows:

```
HC FILENAME.HPJ > ERROR.TXT
```

Section: [BUILDTAGS]

[BUILDTAGS] Symbolic names

If you want to work with symbolic names, the Help project file must include the BUILDTAGS option as well as the Build option. The names of valid switches are listed in this option; a maximum of 30 switches are available.

```
[BUILDTAGS]
WIN31 ; for Windows 3.1 Topics
```

Section: [MAP]

[MAP] Context-sensitive Help

If you want your Help system to support context-sensitive Help, the MAP section must be included in the Help project file. Context-sensitive Help provides help text for topics outside the workspace of the application window and about menu commands in an opened menu. You must call Help within the program that's working with the corresponding Help file. To obtain information about an element, you usually press F1 or the Shift + F1 key combination.

If the user selects context-sensitive Help with the key combination mentioned in the last paragraph, usually the mouse pointer changes to a different shape, turning from an arrow into a question mark. This lets the user know that he/she is in Help mode. Then the user can click the element he/she wants defined. To find out more about a menu command, the user simply must highlight the menu command (don't click it) and press F1.

Context number

In the MAP section, context strings are combined with context numbers. However, to display a certain topic, the context numbers must match the ones that the application sends at runtime. Numbers can be written either in decimal or hexadecimal notation. You can also use a #define statement which, in turn, is in a separate header file that you can link by using an #include statement.

```
[MAP]
HELPID_Undo    100
HELPID_Cut     101
HELPID_Cop     102
HELPID_Pas     103
HELPID_MIN     200
HELPID_MAX     201
HELPID_CAP     202
HELPID_CTL     203
```

or

```
[MAP]
#include <hlpprog.h>
```

or

```
[MAP]
HELPID_Undo    0x064
HELPID_Out     0x065
```

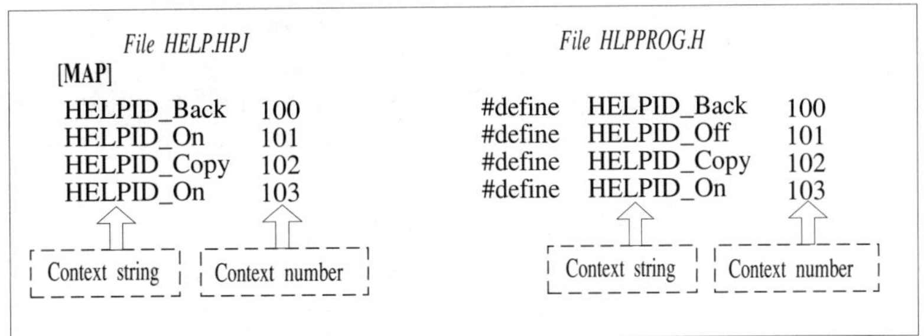

Map section in the project file

The header file, HLPPROG.H is required for programming the HLPPROG.EXE application, which provides context-sensitive Help.

Section: [ALIAS]

[ALIAS] Exchanging topics

The ALIAS section is needed when the same context string is assigned to more than one topic. For example, this is useful when you want to replace two old topics with a new topic. If you want to delete old topics but didn't use the ALIAS section, you must search all other topics for invalid cross references. If the Help system is very large, searching through all the topic files can be lengthy and prone to error. To avoid this, use ALIAS. The context string of the deleted topic is overwritten by the string of the new topic. The new context string can also occur more than once.

We didn't use ALIAS in our system. However, we could have expanded the SMWINDOW.RTF file with the Minimize and Maximize box topics. The HELPID_MAX and HELPID_MIN context strings identified the topics. We could have replaced the entries in the SMWINDOW.RTF file with two new topics, which have the ID-BIG and ID_SMALL context strings.

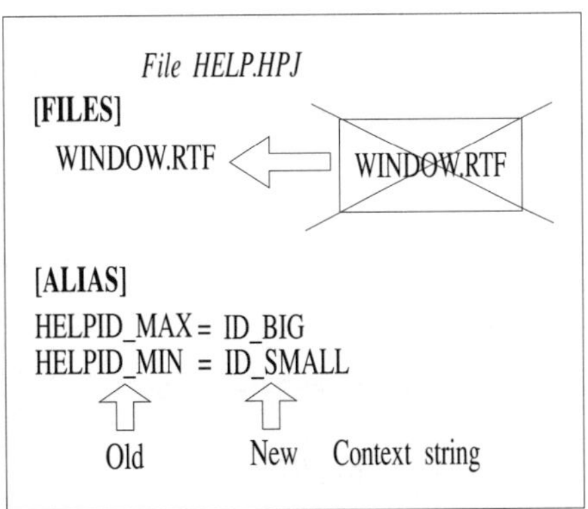

Alias section in the project file

So the only file we must change is the Help project file, instead of the files of the other topics. If you use Alias names in the MAP section, the ALIAS section must precede the MAP section in the Help project file so the link to the context numbers occurs properly.

Section: [BITMAPS]

[BITMAPS]

If the Help system accesses bitmaps that aren't imported, but included in the text from a reference, then you must list the file name and any path specification in this section.

```
[BITMAPS]
qc.bmp
tp.bmp
vb.bmp
minimize.bmp
maximize.bmp
title.bmp
ctlmenu.bmp
arrow.bmp
menu.bmp
smwindow.bmp
prog.bmp
```

This completes our discussion of the project file. The entire HELP.HPJ file looks as follows:

```
[OPTIONS]
INDEX=index_info
TITLE=Help system:
FORCEFONT=Times
MAPFONTSIZE=10-12:20
MULTIKEY=L
COMPRESS=TRUE
WARNING=3

[FILES]
index.rtf ; Contains the Index
menu.rtf  ; Contains menu item information
smwindow.rtf; Contains window element information
prog.rtf   ; Contains programming language information
table.rtf

[BITMAPS]
qc.bmp
tp.bmp
vb.bmp
minimize.bmp
maximize.bmp
title.bmp
ctlmenu.bmp
arrow.bmp
menu.bmp
smwindow.bmp
prog.bmp

[MAP]
HELPID_Undo     100
HELPID_Cut      101
HELPID_Cop      102
HELPID_Pas      103
HELPID_MIN      200
HELPID_MAX      201
HELPID_CAP      202
HELPID_CTL      203.i).Help project file ;
```

Help compiler

Help file

After creating the Help project file, you can call the Help compiler from the DOS environment by using the name of the project file as a parameter. In our example, we called the file HLPPROG.HPJ.

```
HC HLPPROG.HPJ
```

If the project file isn't located in the current directory, you must include the entire path.

```
HC D:\W31CMPLT\HELP\HLPPROG.HPJ
```

During compilation, dots appear on the screen to document the process. A message appears when an error or warning is detected. For example, warnings could happen in the test phase if all the topics haven't been implemented and references aren't found to existing context strings. However, you can still test the existing links.

The Help file that results from the compilation has the same name as the project file and is created in the current directory. The Help file receives the .HLP extension. WINHELP.EXE can now load and read this new file.

Our sample Help system has a total of five Help topic files (INDEX.RTF, MENU.RTF, PROG.RTF, SMWINDOW.RTF, TABLE. RTF). These files were created with Word 5.0 and converted to .RTF format. All the topics have titles; most of them can also be addressed with one or more keywords. We documented how the topics are related to each other in the section on planning. The TABLE.RTF file contains the topic with the additional keyword table. Here are the listings of all the Help topic files used in the HLPPROG.EXE application:

Topic file: INDEX.RTF

```
#$+ Indexindex_info

This Help file implements three major topics:
     Summary of menu items
     Summary of window elements
     Summary of programming languages
You can add new topics, delete old ones, and more.

Help file contents:
     {bmc menu.bmp}id_menu {bmc smwindow.bmp}id_smwindow
{bmc prog.bmp}id_prog
.........................................................

◆
# index_info
$ Help Index
+                                  i  n  d  e  x  :  0  0  0  5
◆
```

Topic file: MENU.RTF

```
#$K+Summary of Menu Items

The Edit menu contains four items intended for use with the Clipboard.

Select the item name listed below for more information.
```

~~Undo~~HELPID_Undo Undoes the last operation.
~~Cut~~HELPID_Cut Cuts text and places it in the Clipboard.
~~Copy~~HELPID_Cop Copies text to the Clipboard.
~~Paste~~HELPID_Pas Pastes text from the Clipboard.

....

~~{bml arrow.bmp}~~id_menu #$K+**Edit: Undo**

This menu item undoes the last command performed.

1) Select Edit/Undo.

....

~~{bml arrow.bmp}~~id_menu #$K+**Edit: Cut**

This menu item copies text to the Clipboard, cutting the text from the current window.

1) Mark the text you want cut.
2) Select Edit/Cut.

....

~~{bml arrow.bmp}~~id_menu #$K+**Edit: Copy**

This menu item copies the marked text to the Clipboard. The original text remains intact in the current window.

1) Mark the text you want copied.
2) Select Edit/Copy.

....

~~{bml arrow.bmp}~~id_menu #$K+**Edit: Paste**

This menu item pastes text stored in the Clipboard at the current insertion point position, in the current window.

1) Move the insertion point to the position at which you want the text pasted.
2) Select Edit/Paste.

....

◆
id_menu
$ Menu
K Menu
+ commands:010
# HELPID_Undo
$ Undo
K Undo; Undo
+ menu:010
# HELPID_Cut
$ Cut
K Cut; Cut
+ menu:020
# HELPID_Cop
$ Copy
K Copy; Copy
+ menu:030
# HELPID_Pas
$ Paste
K Paste; Paste
+ menu:040
◆

Topic file: PROG.RTF

#$K+**Windows Programming Languages**

This topic offers a brief overview of the three programming languages found in Chapter 33 of this book.

Visual BasicHELPID_VB
QuickCHELPID_QC
Turbo PascalHELPID_TP

....

~~{bml arrow.bmp}~~id_prog #$K+**Visual Basic**

{bml vb.bmp} Visual Basic provides a quick method of writing short Windows applications. Double-clicking the Visual Basic icon opens a number of windows, all applying to the Visual Basic environment.

....

~~{bml arrow.bmp}~~id_prog #$K+**QuickC**

```
{bml qc.bmp} Microsoft QuickC for Windows permits almost unlimited capabilities for program
development in Windows.
The QuickCase:W environment allows fast and easy window, menu and resource design. You can
then generate code for compiling and linking.
.........................................................
{bml arrow.bmp}id_prog #$K+Turbo Pascal

{bml tp.bmp} Turbo Pascal for Windows offers the most practical concept of object-oriented
programming.
Turbo Pascal's development environment includes a text editor running under Windows, similar
to the QuickC editor. Resources can be generated using the Borland Resource Workshop.
.........................................................
◆
# id_prog
$ Programming
K Programming; Visual Basic; QuickC; Turbo Pascal
+ commands:030
# HELPID_VB
$ Visual Basic
K Programming; Visual Basic; Toolbox
+ prog:010
# HELPID_QC
$ QuickC
K Programming; QuickC; QuickCase:W
+ prog:020
# HELPID_TP
$ Turbo Pascal
K Programming; Turbo Pascal; object-oriented
+ prog:030
◆
```

Topic file: SMWINDOW.RTF

```
#$K+Summary of Window Elements

A typical window consists of a title bar, which contains the application name, the Control
menu, the Maximize box and the Minimize box.

For more information, select the corresponding name listed below.

Maximize boxHELPID_MAX          The window appears in Maximized
     form.
Minimize boxHELPID_MIN          The window appears in Minimized
     form.
Title barHELPID_CAP     Application title.
Control menuHELPID_CTL  Appears in upper-left corner.
.........................................................
{bml arrow.bmp}id_smwindow #$K+Maximize Box

{bml Maximize.bmp} Clicking the Maximize box displays the current window in Maximized form
(encompassing the entire screen when possible).

.........................................................
{bml arrow.bmp}id_smwindow #$K +Minimize Box

{bml Minimize.bmp}ID_MINIMIZE Clicking the Minimize box displays the current window in
Minimized form (as an icon). This is similar to selecting MinimizeID_MINIMIZE from the
Control menu.

.........................................................
{bml arrow.bmp}id_smwindow #$K +Title Bar

{bml title.bmp}ID_TITLE The title bar displays the application's titleID_TITLE (name). The
current window's title bar appears in a different color from the other windows (this
coloration can be changed using the Control Panel).

.........................................................
{bml arrow.bmp}id_smwindow #$K +Control Menu

{bml ctlmenu.bmp} The Control menu box appears in the upper-left corner of most windows.
Clicking on this box displays a number of menu items, from which you can Restore, Move, Size,
Close, Minimize or Maximize a window.
.........................................................
#The title normally states the name of the application. If the current window contains a
document, this title may include the document name, with or without path. Multiple document
window numbers may also appear, when multiple instances of the same document occur.

.........................................................
```

#The Minimize box can be drawn using different paint programs. All three programming languages have their own paint applications: Visual Basic includes ICONWORKS, Microsoft QuickC for Windows has the Image Editor, and Turbo Pascal for Windows has the Resource Workshop.

....

```
◆
# id_smwindow
$ Window
K Window; Maximize; Minimize; Title Bar
+ commands:020
# HELPID_MAX
$ Maximize Box
K Maximize
+ window:010
# HELPID_MIN
$ Minimize Box
K Minimize
+ window:020
# HELPID_CAP
$ Title Bar
K Title Bar
+ window:030
# HELPID_CTL
$ Control Menu
K Control Menu
+ window:040
# ID_TITLE
# ID_MINIMIZE
◆
```

Topic file: TABLE.RTF

#$L**Second keyword table**

The second keyword table contains other topics. This current table can be implemented later.

....

```
◆
# HELPID_TABLE
$ Keyword table
L                                  T   a   b   l   e
◆
```

33.7 Applications with Help Support

The application that belongs with the topic files previously listed is called HLPPROG.EXE and was created using Microsoft QuickC. The program has two menus named *Edit* and *Help*. You can enable the Help system from the *Help* menu, or use context-sensitive Help. Context-sensitive Help is available for the first four of the five commands in the *Edit* menu, for the Minimize box, Maximize box, Control menu, and the title bar.

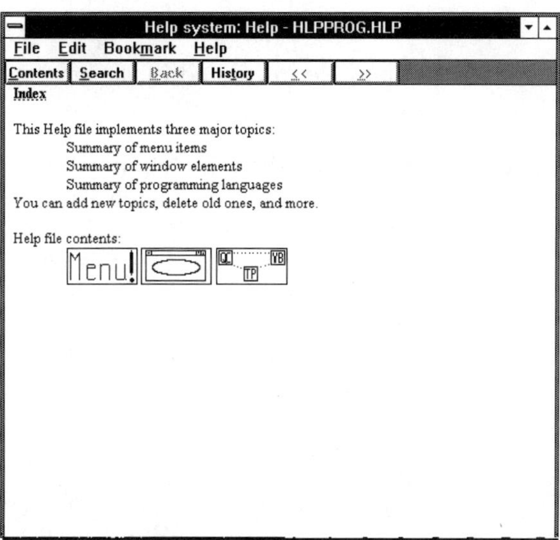

The HLPPROG.EXE application in action

Using the HLPPROG.EXE application

Operation

Selecting the *Index* command starts Help and fills its window with the Index topic of our Help system, as you can see from the previous illustration. You can now select a secondary topic by clicking on one of the three bitmaps. Some topics have an arrow bitmap in the upper-left corner that you can click to move up one level in the Help system. The two topics, Icon and Title bar, can be used to call additional information about either the underlined word or the corresponding bitmap.

To jump directly to the Windows Programming secondary index, simply select the *Programming* command. The topic, which is entered in a second keyword table, can be reached from the *2nd Key Table* command. Select the *Help on Help* menu command to load the Windows Help system's Help file.

For example, to obtain information about the *Edit/Copy* command, you could also select the term *Edit* in the menu bar, to open up the menu. Then move the selection cursor to the desired command with the ↓ key and press F1. The Help system then starts and displays the Copy topic.

Another way to get context-sensitive Help is to ask for information about window components. To do this, first press Shift + F1. The normal shape of the pointer changes to a question mark, indicating Help mode. If you then clicked the "Full-screen" button", the window isn't maximized. Instead, the Help function starts with the text about the Maximize button.

Overview of programming Help

Programming

You may be interested in the process of programming for a Help system.

The WinHelp function

You must use the WinHelp function to enable the Help system from an application. It doesn't matter whether you're working with Visual Basic, Turbo Pascal, or QuickC. Since HLPPROG was written in C, you'll also see this language in the following excerpts from the listing.

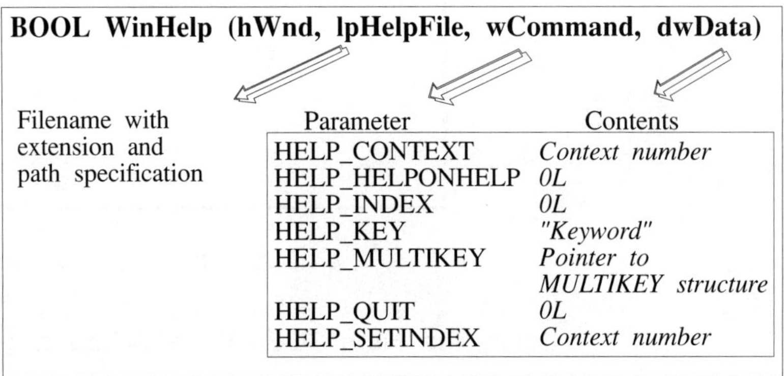

The WinHelp function

The *Index* command serves as an example of how you can use this function. When you click this command, the Index topic appears in the Help window. To make this happen, the HELP_INDEX value is passed to WinHelp as the third parameter. The dwData is set to 0L. The name of our Help file was placed in the szHelpFileName variable beforehand.

```
ccase WM_COMMAND:
  switch (wParam)
  {
    case IDM_H_INDEX:
      WinHelp(hWnd,szHelpFileName,
        HELP_INDEX,0L);
      break;
  }
```

Additional keyword table

To call a topic about a keyword that's in a different keyword table than the default, the value HELP_MULTIKEY must be passed to the wCommand parameter. A variable in the MULTIKEYHELP structure defines the table and keyword. The pointer of the structure is the last parameter of the WinHelp function.

```
BYTE szKeyName1[10];   /* place holder for the keyword */
MULTIKEYHELP mk;
BYTE szKeyName[]="Table";

case IDM_H_KEYTABLE:
  mk.mkSize = sizeof(MULTIKEYHELP)+(WORD)lstrlen(szKeyName);
  mk.mkKeylist = 'L';
  strcpy(mk.szKeyphrase, "Table");
```

```
WinHelp(hWnd,szHelpFileName,HELP_MULTIKEY,
        (LONG)(LPSTR)&mk);
break;
```

Since the szKeyphrase field is only defined as a 1 byte field, a corresponding amount of space must be kept free on the stack so another variable on the stack isn't overwritten when the keyword is copied. That's why the szKeyName variable is defined before the mk variable. You could also use the GlobalAlloc function to allocate dynamic disk space for this. Calling the WinHelp function takes the topic with the keyword table title from the additional table and displays it in the Help window.

Context-sensitive help

Implementing context-sensitive Help is time-consuming and no longer so easy to understand. The support of the F1 key is a result of the two messages, WM_COMMAND and WM_ENTERIDLE. If you want to provide Help for elements outside of the workspace by pressing Shift + F1, you must also respond to the WM_NCLBUTTONDOWN, WM_KEYDOWN, and WM_SETCURSOR messages in the program. In the two messages, WM_COMMAND and WM_NCLBUTTONDOWN, the context numbers, which are assigned to the context strings of the appropriate topics in the MAP section, are accessed. These numbers must then also be defined in the program's HLPPROG.H header file.

Setting the cursor

The mouse pointer, which is represented by an arrow with a question mark in Help mode, is loaded at the beginning in the WM_CREATE message. If necessary, the mouse pointer is set by the SetCursor function, as is the case in the WM_SETCURSOR message.

```
case WM_SETCURSOR:
   if (bHelp)
      SetCursor(hHelpCur);
   else
      return (DefWindowProc(hWnd, Message, wParam, lParam));
break;
```

Here's the complete C source code used in creating HLPPROG.EXE:

```
/* HLPPROG.H */
#include <windows.h>
#include <string.h>

#define IDS_ERR_REGISTER_CLASS   1
#define IDS_ERR_CREATE_WINDOW    2

char szString[128];  /* variable to load resource strings */
char szAppName[20];  /* class name for the window         */
HWND hInst;
HWND hWndMain;

LONG FAR PASCAL WndProc(HWND, WORD, WORD, LONG);
int nCwRegisterClasses(void);
void CwUnRegisterClasses(void);

#define IDM_EDIT                   2000
#define IDM_E_EDITUNDO                  2050
#define IDM_E_EDITCUT                   2150
#define IDM_E_EDITCOPY                  2200
#define IDM_E_EDITPASTE                 2250
```

```
#define IDM_E_EDITCLEAR                2300
#define IDM_H_INDEX                3000
#define IDM_H_PROG                     3050
#define IDM_H_KEYTABLE                 3100
#define IDM_H_HELP                     3150

#define  HELPID_Undo  100
#define  HELPID_Cut   101
#define  HELPID_Cop   102
#define  HELPID_Pas   103

#define  HELPID_MIN   200
#define  HELPID_MAX   201
#define  HELPID_CAP   202
#define  HELPID_CTL   203

;HLPPROG.DEF
NAME            HLPPROG
EXETYPE         WINDOWS
STUB            'WINSTUB.EXE'
CODE            PRELOAD MOVEABLE
DATA            PRELOAD MOVEABLE MULTIPLE
HEAPSIZE        4096
STACKSIZE       5110
EXPORTS         WndProc          @1

/* HLPPROG.C */
/* Microsoft QuickC for Windows */
#include "HLPPROG.h"

int PASCAL WinMain(HANDLE hInstance, HANDLE hPrevInstance, LPSTR lpszCmdLine, int nCmdShow)
{
/*****************************************************************/
/* HANDLE hInstance;       handle for this instance              */
/* HANDLE hPrevInstance;   handle for possible previous instances */
/* LPSTR  lpszCmdLine;     long pointer to exec command line     */
/* int    nCmdShow;        Show code for main window display     */
/*****************************************************************/

MSG  msg;           /* MSG structure to store your messages       */
int  nRc;           /* return value from Register Classes         */

 strcpy(szAppName, "HLPPROG");
 hInst = hInstance;
 if(!hPrevInstance)
      {
       /* register window classes if first instance of application */
       if ((nRc = nCwRegisterClasses()) == -1)
             {
              /* registering one of the windows failed         */
              LoadString(hInst, IDS_ERR_REGISTER_CLASS, szString,
                                            sizeof(szString));
              MessageBox(NULL,szString, NULL,MB_ICONEXCLAMATION);
              return nRc;
             }
      }
 /* create application's Main window                              */
 hWndMain = CreateWindow(szAppName, /* Window class name           */
        "HLPPROG Demo",              /* Window's title             */
        WS_CAPTION      |            /* Title and Min/Max          */
        WS_SYSMENU      |            /* add Control menu box       */
        WS_MINIMIZEBOX  |            /* Add minimize box           */
        WS_MAXIMIZEBOX  |            /* Add maximize box           */
        WS_THICKFRAME   |            /* thick sizeable frame       */
        WS_CLIPCHILDREN |     /* don't draw in child window areas  */
        WS_OVERLAPPED,
        CW_USEDEFAULT, 0,     /* Use default X, Y                  */
        CW_USEDEFAULT, 0,     /* Use default X, Y                  */
        NULL,                        /* Parent window's handle     */
        NULL,                        /* Default to Class Menu      */
        hInst,                       /* Instance of window         */
        NULL);                       /* Create struct for WM_CREATE */

 if(hWndMain == NULL)
       {
        LoadString(hInst, IDS_ERR_CREATE_WINDOW, szString,
                                     sizeof(szString));
        MessageBox(NULL, szString, NULL, MB_ICONEXCLAMATION);
        return IDS_ERR_CREATE_WINDOW;
       }
 ShowWindow(hWndMain, nCmdShow);    /* display main window */

 while(GetMessage(&msg, NULL, 0, 0))     /* Until WM_QUIT message  */
```

```
        {
         TranslateMessage(&msg);
         DispatchMessage(&msg);
        }

 /* Do clean up before exiting from the application                    */
  CwUnRegisterClasses();
  return msg.wParam;
 } /*  End of WinMain                                                  */

/*********************************************************************/
/*                                                                   */
/* Main Window Procedure                                             */
/*                                                                   */
/* This procedure provides service routines for the Windows events   */
/* (messages) that Windows sends to the window, as well as the user  */
/* initiated events (messages) that are generated when the user selects */
/* the action bar and pulldown menu controls or the corresponding    */
/* keyboard accelerators.                                            */
/*                                                                   */
/*********************************************************************/

LONG FAR PASCAL WndProc(HWND hWnd, WORD Message, WORD wParam, LONG lParam)
{
 HMENU        hMenu=0;             /* handle for the menu             */
 HBITMAP      hBitmap=0;           /* handle for bitmaps              */
 HDC          hDC;                 /* handle for the display device   */
 PAINTSTRUCT ps;                   /* holds PAINT information         */
 int          nRc=0;               /* return code                     */
 static BOOL bHelp;
 char szHelpFileName[] = "hlpprog.hlp";
 DWORD dwHelpContextId;
 static HCURSOR hHelpCur;
 BYTE szKeyName1[10];    /* place holder for the keyword */
 MULTIKEYHELP mk;
 BYTE szKeyName[]="Table";

 switch (Message)
        {
         case WM_ENTERIDLE:
                if ((wParam == MSGF_MENU) && (GetKeyState(VK_F1) & 0x8000))
                {
                        bHelp = TRUE;
                        PostMessage(hWnd, WM_KEYDOWN, VK_RETURN, 0L);
                }
                break;

         case WM_COMMAND:
                /* Are we in help mode (SHIFT+F1), or did the user       */
                /* press F1 while selecting a menu item?                 */
                if (bHelp)
                {
                  dwHelpContextId =
                        (wParam == IDM_E_EDITUNDO) ? (DWORD)HELPID_Undo:
                        (wParam == IDM_E_EDITCUT) ? (DWORD)HELPID_Cut:
                        (wParam == IDM_E_EDITCOPY) ? (DWORD)HELPID_Cop:
                        (wParam == IDM_E_EDITPASTE) ? (DWORD)HELPID_Pas:
                        (DWORD) 0L;

                  if (!dwHelpContextId)
                  {
                         MessageBox(hWnd, "No Help available for this item.",
                                "HLPPROG Demo", MB_OK);
                         bHelp = FALSE;
                         return (DefWindowProc(hWnd, Message, wParam, lParam));
                  }
                  bHelp = FALSE;
                  WinHelp(hWnd, szHelpFileName, HELP_CONTEXT, dwHelpContextId);
                }
                else
                {
                        switch (wParam)
                        {
                                case IDM_H_INDEX:
                                        WinHelp(hWnd,szHelpFileName,HELP_INDEX,0L);
                                        break;
                                case IDM_H_PROG:
WinHelp(hWnd,szHelpFileName,HELP_KEY,(LONG)(LPSTR)"Programming");
                                        break;
                                case IDM_H_KEYTABLE:
                                        mk.mkSize = sizeof(MULTIKEYHELP)+(WORD)lstrlen(szKeyName);
                                        mk.mkKeylist = 'L';
```

```
                        strcpy(mk.szKeyphrase, "Table");
                        WinHelp(hWnd,szHelpFileName,HELP_MULTIKEY,
(LONG)(LPSTR)&mk);
                        break;
                  case IDM_H_HELP:
                        WinHelp(hWnd,szHelpFileName,HELP_HELPONHELP,0L);
                        break;
                  default:
                        MessageBox(hWnd, "This menu item serves no purpose.",
                          "HLPPROG Demo", MB_OK);
                        break;
                  }
            }
            break;      /* End of WM_COMMAND                    */

      case WM_CREATE:
            hHelpCur = LoadCursor(hInst, "QUESTIONMARK");
            break;        /*  End of WM_CREATE                    */

      case WM_KEYDOWN:
            if (wParam == VK_F1)
            {
                  if (GetKeyState(VK_SHIFT))
                  {
                        bHelp = TRUE;
                        SetCursor(hHelpCur);
                        return (DefWindowProc(hWnd, Message, wParam, lParam));
                  }
                  else
                        WinHelp(hWnd, szHelpFileName, HELP_INDEX, 0L);
            }
            else if (wParam == VK_ESCAPE && bHelp)
            {
                  bHelp = FALSE;
                  SetCursor((HCURSOR)GetClassWord(hWnd, GCW_HCURSOR));
            }
            break;

      case WM_SETCURSOR:
            if (bHelp)
                  SetCursor(hHelpCur);
            else
                  return (DefWindowProc(hWnd, Message, wParam, lParam));
            break;

      case WM_NCLBUTTONDOWN:
            if (bHelp)
            {
              dwHelpContextId =
                  (wParam == HTREDUCE)  ? (DWORD)HELPID_MIN:
                  (wParam == HTZOOM)    ? (DWORD)HELPID_MAX:
                  (wParam == HTCAPTION) ? (DWORD)HELPID_CAP:
                  (wParam == HTSYSMENU) ? (DWORD)HELPID_CTL:
                  (DWORD) 0L;
              if (!dwHelpContextId)
                    return (DefWindowProc(hWnd, Message, wParam, lParam));
              bHelp = FALSE;
              WinHelp(hWnd, szHelpFileName, HELP_CONTEXT, dwHelpContextId);
            }
            else
                  return (DefWindowProc(hWnd, Message, wParam, lParam));
            break;

      case WM_MOVE:     /*  code for moving the window          */
            break;

      case WM_SIZE:     /*  code for sizing client area         */
            break;      /*  End of WM_SIZE                      */

      case WM_PAINT:    /*  code for the window's client area      */
            /* Obtain a handle to the device context            */
            /* BeginPaint will send WM_ERASEBKGND if appropriate  */
            memset(&ps, 0x00, sizeof(PAINTSTRUCT));
            hDC = BeginPaint(hWnd, &ps);
            /* Included in case the background is not a pure color */
            SetBkMode(hDC, TRANSPARENT);

            /* Inform Windows painting is complete              */
            EndPaint(hWnd, &ps);
            break;        /*  End of WM_PAINT                   */

      case WM_CLOSE:  /*  close the window                      */
            /* Destroy child windows, modeless dialogs, then,   */
```

```
              /* Destroy this window                                    */
                     WinHelp(hWnd, szHelpFileName, HELP_QUIT, 0L);
                     DestroyWindow(hWnd);
                     if (hWnd == hWndMain)
                     {
                       PostQuitMessage(0); // Quit the application
                     }
              break;


        default:
/* For any message for which you don't specifically provide a     */
/* service routine, you should return the message to Windows      */
/* for default message processing                                  */
              return DefWindowProc(hWnd, Message, wParam, lParam);
        }
 return 0L;
}     /* End of WndProc                                             */

/******************************************************************/
/*                                                                */
/* nCwRegisterClasses Function                                    */
/*                                                                */
/* The following function registers all the classes of all the   */
/* windows associated with this application. The function returns */
/* an error code if unsuccessful, otherwise it returns 0.         */
/*                                                                */
/******************************************************************/

int nCwRegisterClasses(void)
{
 WNDCLASS   wndclass;   /* struct to define a window class        */
 memset(&wndclass, 0x00, sizeof(WNDCLASS));
 /* load WNDCLASS with window's characteristics                   */
 wndclass.style = CS_HREDRAW | CS_VREDRAW | CS_BYTEALIGNWINDOW;
 wndclass.lpfnWndProc = WndProc;
 /* Extra storage for Class and Window objects                    */
 wndclass.cbClsExtra = 0;
 wndclass.cbWndExtra = 0;
 wndclass.hInstance = hInst;
 wndclass.hIcon = LoadIcon(NULL, IDI_APPLICATION);
 wndclass.hCursor = LoadCursor(NULL, IDC_ARROW);
 /* Create brush for erasing background                           */
 wndclass.hbrBackground = (HBRUSH)(COLOR_WINDOW+1);
 wndclass.lpszMenuName = szAppName;  /* Menu Name is App Name   */
 wndclass.lpszClassName = szAppName; /* Class Name is App Name  */
 if(!RegisterClass(&wndclass))
        return -1;

 return(0);
} /* End of nCwRegisterClasses                                    */

/******************************************************************/
/*  CwUnRegisterClasses Function                                  */
/*                                                                */
/*  Deletes any references to windows resources created for this  */
/*  application, frees memory, deletes instance, handles and does */
/*  clean up prior to exiting the window                          */
/*                                                                */
/******************************************************************/

void CwUnRegisterClasses(void)
{
 WNDCLASS   wndclass;   /* struct to define a window class        */
 memset(&wndclass, 0x00, sizeof(WNDCLASS));
 UnregisterClass(szAppName, hInst);
}     /* End of CwUnRegisterClasses                                */

;HLPPROG.RC
#include "HLPPROG.h"

QUESTIONMARK CURSOR Helpc.cur

HLPPROG MENU
  BEGIN
        POPUP  "&Edit"
               BEGIN
                 MENUITEM "&Undo", IDM_E_EDITUNDO
                 MENUITEM SEPARATOR
                 MENUITEM "Cu&t", IDM_E_EDITCUT
                 MENUITEM "&Copy", IDM_E_EDITCOPY
                 MENUITEM "&Paste", IDM_E_EDITPASTE
                 MENUITEM "C&lear", IDM_E_EDITCLEAR
```

```
            END
        POPUP   "\a&Help"
            BEGIN
              MENUITEM "&Index", IDM_H_INDEX
              MENUITEM "&Programming", IDM_H_PROG
              MENUITEM "&2nd Key Table" IDM_H_KEYTABLE
              MENUITEM "&Help on Help", IDM_H_HELP
            END
  END


STRINGTABLE
BEGIN
  IDS_ERR_CREATE_WINDOW,     "Window creation failed!"
  IDS_ERR_REGISTER_CLASS,    "Error registering window class"
END
```

Appendix A: Character Sets

ANSI Character Set

Dec	Hex	Char	Dec	Hex	Char	Dec	Hex	Char
0	00		43	2B	+	86	56	V
1	01		44	2C	,	87	57	W
2	02		45	2D	-	88	58	X
3	03		46	2E	.	89	59	Y
4	04		47	2F	/	90	5A	Z
5	05		48	30	0	91	5B	[
6	06		49	31	1	92	5C	\
7	07		50	32	2	93	5D	]
8	08		51	33	3	94	5E	^
9	09		52	34	4	95	5F	_
10	0A		53	35	5	96	60	`
11	0B		54	36	6	97	61	a
12	0C		55	37	7	98	62	b
13	0D		56	38	8	99	63	c
14	0E		57	39	9	100	64	d
15	0F		58	3A	:	101	65	e
16	10		59	3B	;	102	66	f
17	11		60	3C	<	103	67	g
18	12		61	3D	=	104	68	h
19	13		62	3E	>	105	69	i
20	14		63	3F	?	106	6A	j
21	15		64	40	@	107	6B	k
22	16		65	41	A	108	6C	l
23	17		66	42	B	109	6D	m
24	18		67	43	C	110	6E	n
25	19		68	44	D	111	6F	o
26	1A		69	45	E	112	70	p
27	1B		70	46	F	113	71	q
28	1C		71	47	G	114	72	r
29	1D		72	48	H	115	73	s
30	1E		73	49	I	116	74	t
31	1F		74	4A	J	117	75	u
32	20		75	4B	K	118	76	v
33	21	!	76	4C	L	119	77	w
34	22	"	77	4D	M	120	78	x
35	23	#	78	4E	N	121	79	y
36	24	$	79	4F	O	122	7A	z
37	25	%	80	50	P	123	7B	{
38	26	&	81	51	Q	124	7C	|
39	27	'	82	52	R	125	7D	}
40	28	(	83	53	S	126	7E	~
41	29	)	84	54	T	127	7F	
42	2A	*	85	55	U	128	80	

Dec	Hex	Char
129	81	
130	82	
131	83	
132	84	
133	85	
134	86	
135	87	
136	88	
137	89	
138	8A	
139	8B	
140	8C	
141	8D	
142	8E	
143	8F	
144	90	
145	91	‘
146	92	’
147	93	“
148	94	”
149	95	•
150	96	–
151	97	—
152	98	
153	99	
154	9A	
155	9B	
156	9C	
157	9D	
158	9E	
159	9F	
160	A0	
161	A1	¡
162	A2	¢
163	A3	£
164	A4	¤
165	A5	¥
166	A6	¦
167	A7	§
168	A8	¨
169	A9	©
170	AA	ª
171	AB	«
172	AC	¬
173	AD	-
174	AE	®
175	AF	¯
176	B0	°
177	B1	±
178	B2	²

Dec	Hex	Char
179	B3	³
180	B4	´
181	B5	µ
182	B6	¶
183	B7	·
184	B8	¸
185	B9	¹
186	BA	º
187	BB	»
188	BC	¼
189	BD	½
190	BE	¾
191	BF	¿
192	C0	À
193	C1	Á
194	C2	Â
195	C3	Ã
196	C4	Ä
197	C5	Å
198	C6	Æ
199	C7	Ç
200	C8	È
201	C9	É
202	CA	Ê
203	CB	Ë
204	CC	Ì
205	CD	Í
206	CE	Î
207	CF	Î
208	D0	Ð
209	D1	Ñ
210	D2	Ò
211	D3	Ó
212	D4	Ô
213	D5	Õ
214	D6	Ö
215	D7	×
216	D8	Ø
217	D9	Ù
218	DA	Ú
219	DB	Û
220	DC	Ü
221	DD	Ý
222	DE	Þ
223	DF	ß
224	E0	à
225	E1	á
226	E2	â
227	E3	ã
228	E4	ä
229	E5	å

Dec	Hex	Char
230	E6	æ
231	E7	ç
232	E8	è
233	E9	é
234	EA	ê
235	EB	ë
236	EC	ì
237	ED	í
238	EE	î
239	EF	ï
240	F0	∂
241	F1	ñ
242	F2	ò
243	F3	ó
244	F4	ô
245	F5	õ
246	F6	ö
247	F7	÷
248	F8	ø
249	F9	ù
250	FA	ú
251	FB	û
252	FC	ü
253	FD	ý
254	FE	þ
255	FF	ÿ

Sorting Characters Tables

Dec	Hex	Char
32	20	
160	A0	
0	00	
1	01	
2	02	
3	03	
4	04	
5	05	
6	06	
7	07	
8	08	
9	09	
10	0A	
11	0B	
12	0C	
13	0D	
14	0E	
15	0F	
16	10	
17	11	
18	12	
19	13	
20	14	
21	15	
22	16	
23	17	
24	18	
25	19	
26	1A	
27	1B	
28	1C	
29	1D	
30	1E	
31	1F	
33	21	!
34	22	"
35	23	#
36	24	$
37	25	%
38	26	&
39	27	'
40	28	(
41	29	)
42	2A	*
43	2B	+
44	2C	,
45	2D	-
46	2E	.
47	2F	/

Dec	Hex	Char
58	3A	:
59	3B	;
60	3C	<
61	3D	=
62	3E	>
63	3F	?
64	40	@
91	5B	[
92	5C	\
93	5D	]
94	5E	^
95	5F	_
96	60	`
123	7B	{
124	7C	|
125	7D	}
126	7E	~
127	7F	
128	80	
129	81	
130	82	
131	83	
132	84	
133	85	
134	86	
135	87	
136	88	
137	89	
138	8A	
139	8B	
140	8C	
141	8D	
142	8E	
143	8F	
144	90	
145	91	‘
146	92	’
147	93	“
148	94	”
149	95	•
150	96	–
151	97	—
152	98	
153	99	
154	9A	
155	9B	
156	9C	
157	9D	

Dec	Hex	Char
158	9E	
159	9F	
161	A1	¡
162	A2	¢
163	A3	£
164	A4	¤
165	A5	¥
166	A6	¦
167	A7	§
168	A8	¨
169	A9	©
170	AA	ª
171	AB	«
172	AC	¬
173	AD	-
174	AE	®
175	AF	¯
176	B0	°
177	B1	±
178	B2	²
179	B3	³
180	B4	´
181	B5	µ
182	B6	¶
183	B7	·
184	B8	¸
185	B9	¹
186	BA	º
187	BB	»
188	BC	¼
189	BD	½
190	BE	¾
191	BF	¿
48	30	0
49	31	1
50	32	2
51	33	3
52	34	4
53	35	5
54	36	6
55	37	7
56	38	8
57	39	9
65	41	A
192	C0	À
193	C1	Á
194	C2	Â
195	C3	Ã

Dec	Hex	Char
196	C4	Ä
197	C5	Å
198	C6	Æ
97	61	a
224	E0	à
225	E1	á
226	E2	â
227	E3	ä
228	E4	ã
229	E5	å
230	E6	æ
66	42	B
98	62	b
67	43	C
199	C7	Ç
99	63	c
231	E7	ç
68	44	D
208	D0	Ð
100	64	d
240	F0	∂
69	45	E
200	C8	È
201	C9	É
202	CA	Ê
203	CB	Ë
101	65	e
232	E8	è
233	E9	é
234	EA	ê
235	EB	ë
70	46	F
102	66	f
71	47	G
103	67	g
72	48	H
104	68	h
73	49	I
204	CC	Ì
205	CD	Í
206	CE	Î
207	CF	Î
105	69	i
236	EC	ì
237	ED	í
238	EE	î
239	EF	Ï
74	4A	J
106	6A	j
75	4B	K
107	6B	k
76	4C	L
108	6C	l
77	4D	M
109	6D	m
78	4E	N
110	6E	n
209	D1	Ñ
241	F1	ñ
79	4F	O
210	D2	Ò
211	D3	Ó
212	D4	Ô
213	D5	Õ
214	D6	Ö
215	D7	×
216	D8	Ø
111	6F	o
242	F2	ò
243	F3	ó
244	F4	ô
245	F5	õ
246	F6	ö
247	F7	÷
248	F8	ø
80	50	P
112	70	p
81	51	Q
113	71	q
82	52	R
114	72	r
83	53	S
115	73	s
223	DF	ß
84	54	T
116	74	t
85	55	U
217	D9	Ù
218	DA	Ú
219	DB	Û
220	DC	Ü
117	75	u
249	F9	ù
250	FA	ú
251	FB	û
252	FC	ü
86	56	V
118	76	v
87	57	W
119	77	w
88	58	X
20	78	x
89	59	Y
221	DD	Ý
121	79	y
253	FD	ý
255	FF	ÿ
90	5A	Z
122	7A	z
254	FE	Þ

Symbol Fonts

Dec	Hex	Char
0	00	
1	01	
2	02	
3	03	
4	04	
5	05	
6	06	
7	07	
8	08	
9	09	
10	0A	
11	0B	
12	0C	
13	0D	
14	0E	
15	0F	
16	10	
17	11	
18	12	
19	13	
20	14	
21	15	
22	16	
23	17	
24	18	
25	19	
26	1A	
27	1B	
28	1C	
29	1D	
30	1E	
31	1F	
32	20	
33	21	!
34	22	∀
35	23	#
36	24	∃
37	25	%
38	26	&
39	27	∋
40	28	(
41	29	)
42	2A	*
43	2B	+
44	2C	,
45	2D	−
46	2E	.
47	2F	/
48	30	0
49	31	1
50	32	2
51	33	3
52	34	4
53	35	5
54	36	6
55	37	7
56	38	8
57	39	9
58	3A	:
59	3B	;
60	3C	<
61	3D	=
62	3E	>
63	3F	?
64	40	≅
65	41	Α
66	42	Β
67	43	Χ
68	44	Δ
69	45	Ε
70	46	Φ
71	47	Γ
72	48	Η
73	49	Ι
74	4A	ϑ
75	4B	Κ
76	4C	Λ
77	4D	Μ
78	4E	Ν
79	4F	Ο
80	50	Π
81	51	Θ
82	52	Ρ
83	53	Σ
84	54	Τ
85	55	Ψ
86	56	ς
87	57	Ω
88	58	Ξ
89	59	ψ
90	5A	Ζ
91	5B	[
92	5C	∴
93	5D	]
94	5E	⊥
95	5F	_
96	60	
97	61	α
98	62	β
99	63	χ
100	64	δ
101	65	ε
102	66	ϕ
103	67	γ
104	68	η
105	69	ι
106	6A	φ
107	6B	κ
108	6C	λ
109	6D	μ
110	6E	ν
111	6F	ο
112	70	π
113	71	θ
114	72	ρ
115	73	σ
116	74	τ
117	75	υ
118	76	ϖ
119	77	ω
120	78	ξ
121	79	ψ
122	7A	ζ
123	7B	{
124	7C	|
125	7D	}
126	7E	~
127	7F	
128	80	
129	81	
130	82	
131	83	
132	84	
133	85	
134	86	
135	87	
136	88	
137	89	
138	8A	
139	8B	
140	8C	
141	8D	
142	8E	
143	8F	
144	90	
145	91	
146	92	

Dec	Hex	Char	Dec	Hex	Char	Dec	Hex	Char
147	93		198	C6	∅	249	F9	⎤
148	94		199	C7	∩	250	FA	⎥
149	95		200	C8	∪	251	FB	⎦
150	96		201	C9	⊃	252	FC	⎫
151	97		202	CA	⊇	253	FD	⎬
152	98		203	CB	⊄	254	FE	⎭
153	99		204	CC	⊂	255	FF	
154	9A		205	CD	⊆			
155	9B		206	CE	∈			
156	9C		207	CF	∉			
157	9D		208	D0	∠			
158	9E		209	D1	∇			
159	9F		210	D2	®			
160	A0		211	D3	©			
161	A1	ϒ	212	D4	™			
162	A2	′	213	D5	∏			
163	A3	≤	214	D6	√			
164	A4	⁄	215	D7	⋅			
165	A5	∞	216	D8	¬			
166	A6	ƒ	217	D9	∧			
167	A7	♣	218	DA	∨			
168	A8	♦	219	DB	⇔			
169	A9	♥	220	DC	⇐			
170	AA	♠	221	DD	⇑			
171	AB	↔	222	DE	⇒			
172	AC	←	223	DF	⇓			
173	AD	↑	224	E0	◊			
174	AE	→	225	E1	〈			
175	AF	↓	226	E2	®			
176	B0	°	227	E3	©			
177	B1	±	228	E4	™			
178	B2	″	229	E5	∑			
179	B3	≥	230	E6	⎛			
180	B4	×	231	E7	⎜			
181	B5	∝	232	E8	⎝			
182	B6	∂	233	E9	⎡			
183	B7	•	234	EA	⎢			
184	B8	÷	235	EB	⎣			
185	B9	≠	236	EC	⎧			
186	BA	≡	237	ED	⎨			
187	BB	≈	238	EE	⎩			
188	BC	…	239	EF	⎪			
189	BD	⏐	240	F0	ν			
190	BE	⎯	241	F1	〉			
191	BF	↵	242	F2	∫			
192	C0	ℵ	243	F3	⌠			
193	C1	ℑ	244	F4	⎮			
194	C2	ℜ	245	F5	⌡			
195	C3	℘	246	F6	⎞			
196	C4	⊗	247	F7	⎟			
197	C5	⊕	248	F8	⎠			

Zapf Dingbats Fonts

Dec	Hex	Char	Dec	Hex	Char	Dec	Hex	Char
0	00		49	31	✑	98	62	❂
1	01		50	32	✒	99	63	❃
2	02		51	33	✓	100	64	❄
3	03		52	34	✔	101	65	❅
4	04		53	35	✕	102	66	❆
5	05		54	36	✖	103	67	❇
6	06		55	37	✗	104	68	❈
7	07		56	38	✘	105	69	❉
8	08		57	39	✙	106	6A	❊
9	09		58	3A	✚	107	6B	❋
10	0A		59	3B	✛	108	6C	●
11	0B		60	3C	✜	109	6D	❍
12	0C		61	3D	✝	110	6E	■
13	0D		62	3E	✞	111	6F	❏
14	0E		63	3F	✟	112	70	❐
15	0F		64	40	✠	113	71	❑
16	10		65	41	✡	114	72	❒
17	11		66	42	✢	115	73	▲
18	12		67	43	✣	116	74	▼
19	13		68	44	✤	117	75	◆
20	14		69	45	✥	118	76	❖
21	15		70	46	✦	119	77	◗
22	16		71	47	✧	120	78	❘
23	17		72	48	★	121	79	❙
24	18		73	49	✩	122	7A	❚
25	19		74	4A	✪	123	7B	❛
26	1A		75	4B	✫	124	7C	❜
27	1B		76	4C	✬	125	7D	❝
28	1C		77	4D	✭	126	7E	❞
29	1D		78	4E	✮	127	7F	
30	1E		79	4F	✯	128	80	
31	1F		80	50	Π	129	81	
32	20		81	51	✱	130	82	
33	21	✁	82	52	✲	131	83	
34	22	✂	83	53	✳	132	84	
35	23	✃	84	54	✴	133	85	
36	24	✄	85	55	✵	134	86	
37	25	☎	86	56	Ç	135	87	
38	26	✆	87	57	Ω	136	88	
39	27	✇	88	58	✸	137	89	
40	28	✈	89	59	❙	138	8A	
41	29	✉	90	5A	✺	139	8B	
42	2A	☛	91	5B	✻	140	8C	
43	2B	☞	92	5C	✼	141	8D	
44	2C	✌	93	5D	✽	142	8E	
45	2D	✍	94	5E	✾	143	8F	
46	2E	✎	95	5F	✿	144	90	
47	2F	✏	96	60	❀	145	91	
48	30	✐	97	61	❁	146	92	

Dec	Hex	Char
147	93	
148	94	
149	95	
150	96	
151	97	
152	98	
153	99	
154	9A	
155	9B	
156	9C	
157	9D	
158	9E	
159	9F	
160	A0	
161	A1	❡
162	A2	❢
163	A3	❣
164	A4	❤
165	A5	❥
166	A6	❦
167	A7	❧
168	A8	♣
169	A9	♦
170	AA	♥
171	AB	♠
172	AC	①
173	AD	②
174	AE	③
175	AF	④
176	B0	⑤
177	B1	⑥
178	B2	⑦
179	B3	⑧
180	B4	⑨
181	B5	⑩
182	B6	❶
183	B7	❷
184	B8	❸
185	B9	❹
186	BA	❺
187	BB	❻
188	BC	❼
189	BD	❽
190	BE	❾
191	BF	❿
192	C0	➀
193	C1	➁
194	C2	➂
195	C3	➃
196	C4	➄
197	C5	➅
198	C6	➆
199	C7	➇
200	C8	➈
201	C9	➉
202	CA	➊
203	CB	➋
204	CC	➌
205	CD	➍
206	CE	➎
207	CF	➏
208	D0	➐
209	D1	➑
210	D2	➒
211	D3	➓
212	D4	➔
213	D5	→
214	D6	↔
215	D7	↕
216	D8	➘
217	D9	➙
218	DA	➚
219	DB	➛
220	DC	➜
221	DD	➝
222	DE	➞
223	DF	➟
224	E0	➠
225	E1	➡
226	E2	➢
227	E3	➣
228	E4	➤
229	E5	➥
230	E6	➦
231	E7	➧
232	E8	➨
233	E9	➩
234	EA	➪
235	EB	➫
236	EC	➬
237	ED	➭
238	EE	➮
239	EF	➯
240	F0	■
241	F1	➱
242	F2	➲
243	F3	➳
244	F4	➴
245	F5	➵
246	F6	➶
247	F7	➷
248	F8	➸
249	F9	➹
250	FA	➺
251	FB	➻
252	FC	➼
253	FD	➽
254	FE	➾
255	FF	

Appendix B: The Companion Diskette

The companion diskette contains the examples mentioned in the chapters on programming along with the Backup and Snapshot programs for Windows.

Before using these programs, you must install the programs from the diskette.

First make a backup copy of the diskette. You can copy the diskette using Windows or under DOS. We'll discuss the DOS method of copying here. To use the File Manager, read the chapter on the File Manager.

Check whether the original diskette is write-protected and then place the original diskette in the appropriate drive. Make sure you have a double sided, 3.5" double density diskette available for the backup. Now type the DOS command:

```
DISKCOPY A: A:
```

and press Enter. Follow the instructions on the screen.

Diskette Installation

We've included a SETUP program on the companion diskette for easy installation. Insert the companion diskette in a disk drive.

To start the SETUP program from DOS, type one of the following and press Enter:

```
WIN A:SETUP
WIN B:SETUP
```

To start the SETUP program from Windows, run Windows. Select the *File/Run...* command and type one of the following in the *Command Line:* text box and press Enter:

```
A:SETUP
B:SETUP
```

Once installed, the executable files can be started in various ways. You can start them from the *Win 3.1 Complete* group (generated during installation), use the *Run...* command in the *File* menu of the Program Manager, use *File/New...* to set up the programs, or start the program from the File Manager. For more information on these options, refer to the appropriate chapters.

Remember that the executable files created with Visual Basic need the VBRUN100.DLL file in order to run. You may want to copy this DLL to your System directory, or to the directories containing the Visual Basic programs.

The Backup Program

The Backup program provides a complete and easy-to-use Windows-based utility for making backup copies of data on your hard drive. With Backup you can easily backup your important files to floppy diskettes. With the backup copies and Backup's Restore operation, you can restore the data on your hard drive or another hard drive.

Backing up data on hard drives is important for maintaining the integrity of your data. Don't underestimate the importance of backing up your hard drive. Hard drive failure can happen at any time, even after years of trouble-free use. So, when you least expect hard drive failure, expect it. Remember that your hard drive is a precision mechanical device that operates under very low tolerance. A small disturbance could render all or part of the data on the disk unreadable.

This could happen during a head crash, when the read/write head actually comes in contact with the magnetic surface of the disk and damages it. A head crash can be caused by something bumping your computer or by dust and dirt in the mechanism. Accidental errors such as reformatting may also make data unreadable.

We should also mention the danger from computer viruses. Most viruses send only harmless messages to your screen or crash your system at inconvenient times. However, some of the more malicious viruses could reformat the hard drive, destroying all the data it contains.

In addition to protecting yourself from these kinds of disasters, backing up your hard drive also has some other practical uses. For example, you may want to temporarily transfer all or some of your programs and data to another computer. Or, if you purchase a new computer, you may need an easy and efficient way to transfer all the data from the old system to the new one.

You may be wondering why you need a special program to perform a backup. It's possible to simply copy all the data, file by file, from the hard drive to floppy diskettes. However, if you consider the amount of work involved in this process, you would realize that a specialized backup program saves you time and diskettes.

Backup programs are faster because you don't have to enter all the file or directory names individually. These programs also save disk space because each floppy diskette is completely filled with data.

Usually, it isn't possible to fill a disk completely by manually selecting and copying files. A backup program also stores all the information on directory structures. So, when you use the Restore routine to return the data to your hard drive, all the files will be in their proper directories.

As we mentioned, you can return the backed up data to your hard drive with the Restore routine. Backup and Restore are similar to the DOS commands BACKUP and RESTORE, but they are much faster.

Backup runs under Windows 3.1. In addition to a hard drive or a network drive, you'll also need one or more floppy disk drives.

Points to remember:

1. Backup isn't compatible with other backup programs, including the DOS BACKUP and RESTORE programs. To avoid any confusion, keep any copies of old backups with the software that was used to create them.

2. If your hard drive is divided into partitions, you should work with each partition separately.

3. Don't use Backup for drives that have been renamed with the DOS ASSIGN command, or with drives or search paths created with JOIN or SUBST. Backup cannot work with virtual drives, but you can still back up your entire hard drive even if it has been configured to contain virtual drives.

We provide specific instructions on operating Backup. It's important that you read these instructions carefully before using the program. Doing this will help prevent accidental data loss.

Backup/Restore basics

The purpose of the backup procedure is to back up data using the least possible amount of time and diskettes. You back up data to protect yourself from data loss, which results from hard drive defects as well as accidental deletion of data. You should back up your data at regular intervals.

Since most of your work is done on the hard drive, you usually back up data from the hard drive to diskettes. However, you can also back up diskettes to a hard drive.

With important data, it's a good idea to perform a complete backup daily. Use different diskettes for each day of the week so that the backup is always current. By doing this, you'll have multiple copies of the data. So if the most recent backup is bad, you'll only lose one days worth of data.

Technically, a backup is a copy of files that you want to secure. A backup differs from a normal copy because the target diskette will be filled to its capacity, down to the last byte. A file that is larger than the capacity of the diskette will be saved on more than one diskette. A backup program saves as much as it can on the first diskette and writes the rest of the data on the next diskette. If you have more than one target diskette, it's important to note the sequence of the backup diskettes. You must use the same sequence when restoring the data. Be sure to label your backup diskettes correctly.

Backup uses the .BB extension to identify the backup files it creates. It also indicates the number of the diskette in the backup file name (e.g., DISK0001, DISK0002, etc.). So you know which backup diskette in the series you're using.

The opposite of backing up data is restoring the backup data to the original directory. In this procedure, the data is in the same condition that it was in before the backup. Backup also provides many options for the Restore operation.

Restored files will be written to their original directory. This can overwrite files in the target directory that are more current than the files contained in the backup. When you use Backup to perform a backup, it's impossible to overwrite files that are more current. When a file is in danger of being overwritten, Restore will display a dialog box warning you.

Using Backup

You'll find the Backup program stored in the W31CMPLT\BACKUP directory. If you've added Backup to a program group, start the Backup program by double-clicking its icon. You can also start Backup from the File Manager, or using the *File/Run...* command in the Program Manager, running the BTBACKUP.EXE file.

Backup work window

When Backup is started, a large work window appears containing a menu bar:

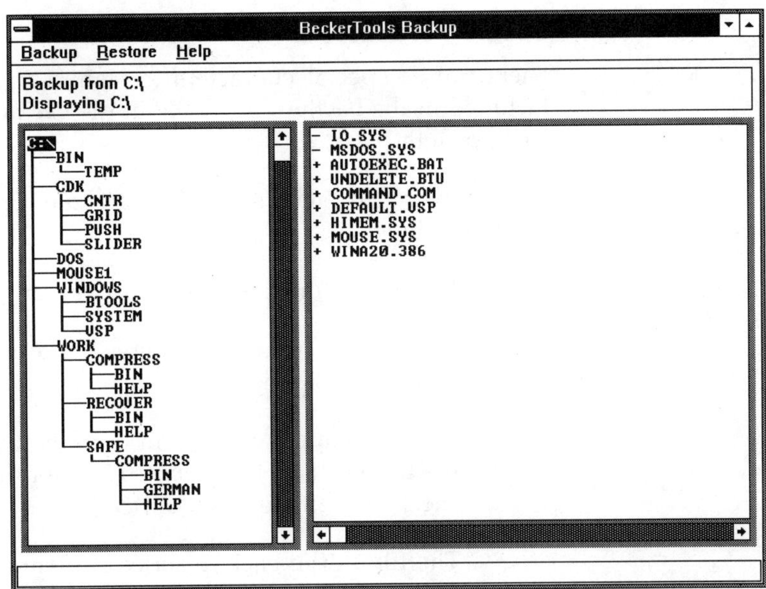

Backup work window is divided into two sections

In the left half of the work window you'll see a directory tree. You can use the mouse or the direction keys to move within the directory tree. A selection cursor makes it easy for you to select a particular directory.

The contents of the selected directory are displayed in the right half of the window. Use Tab to change to this window so you can select individual file entries. The entries in the right display window are preceded by a character, which changes depending on whether the files are set for a data backup.

A "+/-" sign indicates whether the file will be backed up. A file selected for backup is preceded by the "+" sign. A minus (-) sign indicates that the file isn't included in the backup. You can change the backup status of the file names with the space bar or a mouse click.

Press Alt and an underlined letter in the menu line to open a menu. If you're using a mouse, click the appropriate menu. Here you'll find the important commands that help you control the backup and restoration procedures.

When a menu item is selected, a dialog box opens containing the necessary information about the menu. Often, the instructions are self-explanatory, so you can operate Backup automatically.

Special characters

Backup uses special characters to signify whether a file will be included in the backup, if the file in the backup is the same as the backup on the disk, etc.

The following list shows all the characters that Backup uses and their meanings:

Characters signifying the file's status

+ File will be included in the backup or restore operation.

- File will not be included in the backup or restore operation; it will be skipped.

? The file name is present in both the backup series and on the target disk. The *Compare...* menu item can be used to check if the files are identical.

= The file in the backup series is identical to the file on the target disk.

* The file in the backup series is not present on the target disk.

► The file in the backup series is newer than the file on the target disk.

◄ The file in the backup series is older than the file on the target disk.

→ The file in the backup series is newer than the file on the target disk and contains different data.

← The file in the backup series is older than the file on the target disk and contains different data.

◄► Same creation date, different data.

Backup examples

In this section we'll present some examples that demonstrate how to use Backup. You can practice using the individual commands. Frequently used tasks are discussed in detail so that you'll become familiar with them.

Complete hard drive backup

After starting the program, open the *Backup* menu. The first menu item is *Backup from....* Select this menu item. A dialog box appears in which you can select the drive to be backed up.

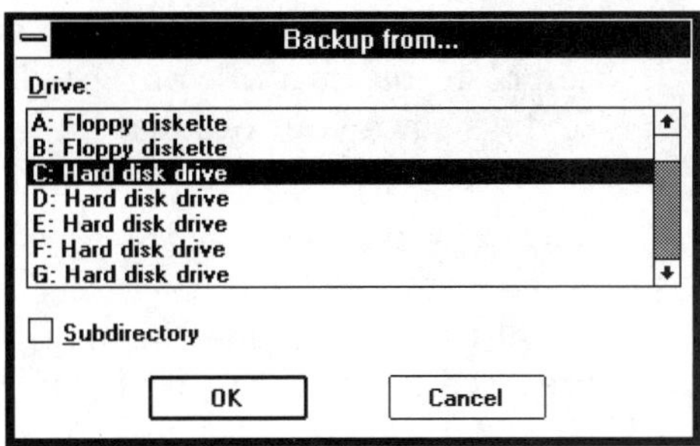

Backup from... dialog box

Use the direction keys to select the drive to be backed up. This can be a floppy diskette, a hard drive, or a network drive. The *Subdirectory* check box lets you select a single subdirectory to back up. The default selection is the root directory. Since you want to keep this directory, close the dialog box by clicking OK.

Choose the *Backup* menu again. To back up all the files, select the *All Files* menu item. To back up only files that changed since the last backup, choose the *Changed Files* menu item. A check mark appears beside these items when they are active. If *All Files* is active, press Esc to leave the menu.

Next select the *Backup* menu and then the *Exclude/Include Files...* menu item. A dialog box is displayed that lets you exclude or include specified files from the backup.

Exclude/Include dialog box

The *Exclude system files* and *Exclude Windows directory* check boxes let you easily exclude DOS system files and the files contained in your Windows directory. The first check box omits system files from the backup and the second check box omits the files of the Windows directories.

Disable these check boxes to ensure that you're performing a complete backup of your hard drive. Both options are default settings since your original DOS and Windows diskettes can serve as backups. This dialog box will be discussed in more detail in a later example. Select OK to exit this dialog box.

All of the entry names in the right work window should now be preceded by the "+" sign. If you excluded unchanged files from the backup using the *Changed Files* menu item, then some files will have a "-" sign.

You can also use the *Exclude/Include Files* menu item to select the files that should be backed up. If you see files that are selected or unselected and you don't know why, check the *Exclude/Include Files* menu item for discrepancies. The last example explains this function in more detail.

Now open the *Backup* menu again and select the *Start Backup...* menu item. The *Create backup* dialog box opens. The number of files and directories to be backed up along with the number of diskettes you'll need for the backup is displayed in this dialog box. Make sure you have the required number of diskettes. These diskettes, which will make up the backup series, should be clearly labeled and numbered.

Select the drive you wish to use for the backup. Backup can determine which kind of drive is installed in your computer and its capacity. Use the direction keys or the mouse to select the desired drive.

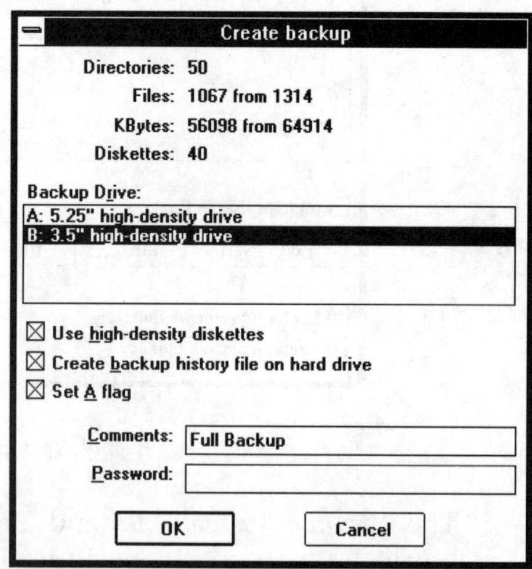

Create backup dialog box

Two option buttons allow you to select high density diskettes and determine whether to set the archive flag. Use the mouse to make your selections or use Tab to move to the buttons and press the Spacebar to make the selections. You should always use high density diskettes when backing up large amounts of data.

Ensure that the *Create backup history file on hard drive* check box is active. This option creates a file on the hard drive that can be used to restore the backup if the first backup diskette in the series is damaged.

You can add a comment to the backup. In the comment text box, enter any text about the contents of the files to be backed up. You can also protect the backup with a password. In the password text box, enter a password. You must confirm the password after leaving the dialog box. When you restore the files, Backup will ask for this password. If the password isn't given correctly, the files cannot be restored. So, you should write down the password so that you don't forget it.

Clicking OK confirms these settings, and the backup procedure begins. A dialog box, containing four bar charts, opens. The bar charts show the progress of the backup. The diskette number is also displayed. Then a dialog box opens with a message that prompts you to insert the first backup diskette in the selected drive.

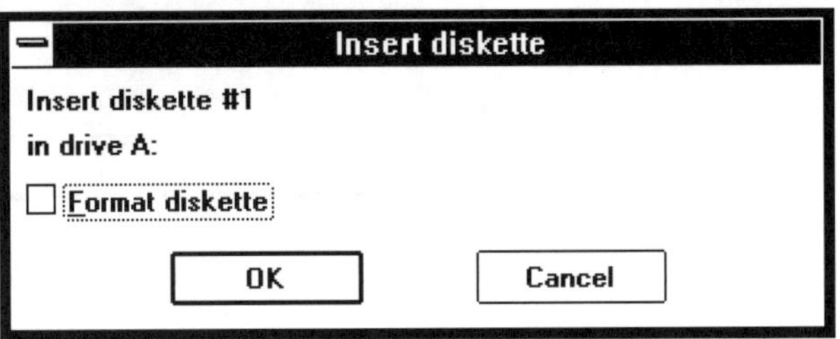

Insert diskette

Click on the *Format diskette* option button if you want to format the diskette. You don't have to do this if the diskette is formatted. In that case, you should turn off the option button. The default for this option can be set in the *Options* dialog box.

Click the OK button to start the backup. The first backup diskette (numbered and labeled) should be in the selected drive. If the diskette contains data, a message will inform you of this:

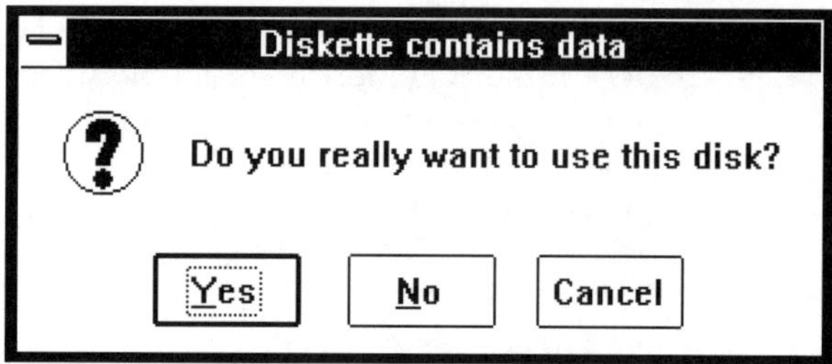

Diskette contains data

You can remove this diskette and replace it with a different one. If you don't, the contents of the diskette will be overwritten. Click OK and start the backup process. The bar charts show the progress of the backup procedure. The dialog box also displays the current file and directory being backed up.

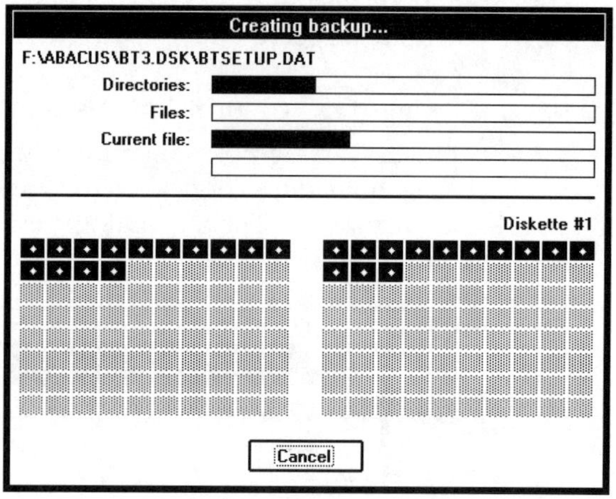

Creating backup...
F:\ABACUS\BT3.DSK\BTSETUP.DAT
Directories:
Files:
Current file:
Diskette #1
Cancel

Create Backup

Insert the numbered diskettes that make up the backup series when requested by Backup. You must complete the backup process (i.e., don't cancel or interrupt it). Otherwise, the entire backup could be useless. In this case, you'll receive an error message if you try to restore the backup.

When the backup is complete, you'll be asked to enter a name for the backup history file. Type the name into the file selection dialog box.

Create Backup History file

The history file will be created only if the *Create history file* check box is active.

Finally, a message informs you of the successful backup. After clicking OK, you automatically return to the work window displaying the directory tree and the files.

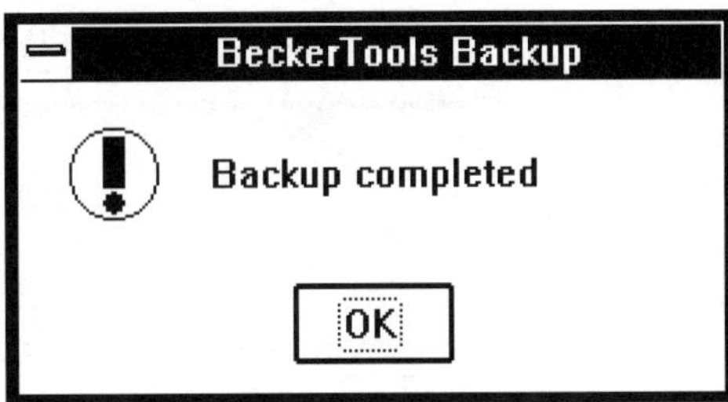

Backup finished

Store the backup series diskettes in a safe place. Your hard drive is now completely backed up. The next time you run Backup, select *Changed Files* from the *Backup* menu. Only the files that have changed will be backed up. This will usually fill only one or two disks.

See the *Backup* menu reference section for more information on backing up files.

Backing up a single directory

Backing up a single directory follows the same basic procedure as a complete backup. Backup offers two ways to select a single directory.

One method involves selecting one subdirectory for a backup using the menus, so you don't have to back up your entire hard drive or diskette.

The other method involves deselecting all files and then selecting a single directory with the mouse.

Menu method

Select the *Backup from...* menu item from the *Backup* menu, activate the "Subdirectory" option button, and then activate the OK button. The file selection dialog box opens.

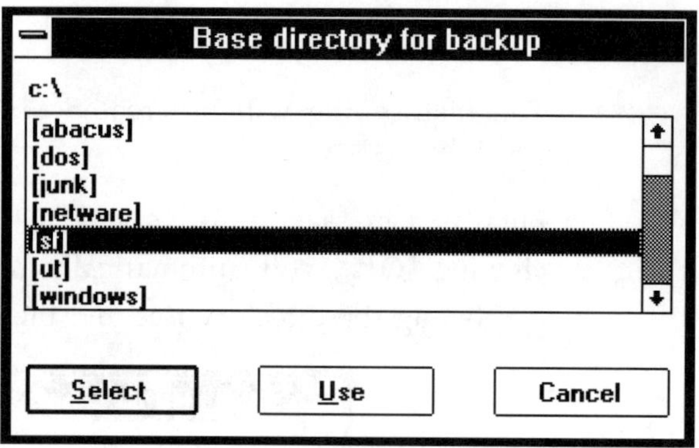

Base directory for backup

Now use either the direction keys or the mouse to choose the directory that you want to use as the starting point of your backup. Use the Select button to open the selected directory. The name of the selected directory will be displayed in the top line.

If you decide to use this directory, select Use. You'll return to the Backup work window and only the selected directory will be displayed in the work window.

You can select single files with either the Spacebar or a mouse click. If a file is already selected, pressing the Spacebar or clicking the mouse removes the selection. That's why you should be careful when you select files. If you go too fast, you could deselect files that have already been selected.

Mouse method

To select files for a backup using the mouse, you must first unselect all selected files. Double-click on the root directory (C:\). A dialog box is displayed which lets you unselect all files:

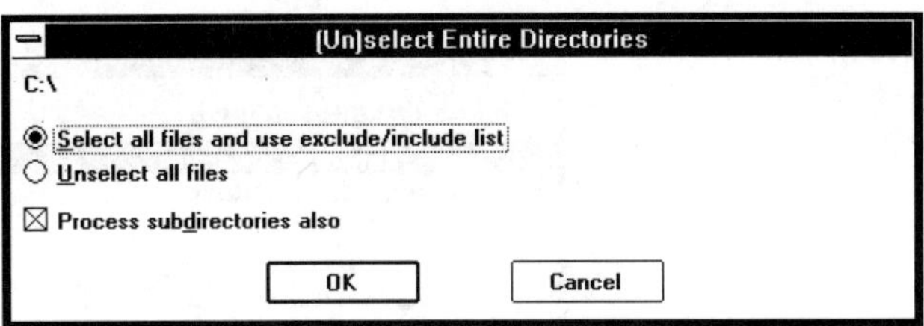

Unselecting files

Ensure that the *Unselect all files* option button is activated. Select the OK button to unselect all files. Now you can select a single directory. In the left half of the work window, double-click on the directory name that you want to back up. The same dialog box lets you select all the files contained in the directory.

Ensure that the *Select all files and use exclude/include list* option button is active. If you want all the subdirectories in the directory to be selected, the *Process subdirectories also* check box must be active. Click OK to exit the dialog box. The files in the selected subdirectory will be included in the backup. Empty directories will also be created for all the other directories.

The Exclude/Include file list will also affect the files that are selected for backup. After you've selected the directory, start the backup by selecting *Start Backup...* from the *Backup* menu.

Backing up multiple directories

Multiple directories can be selected the same way as a single directory. After the first directory has been selected, simply select the other directories. You can backup multiple directories on a single drive using this method.

Restoring your data

If you want to restore the backup data to the hard drive at a later time, you'll need the diskette series containing the backup data. Keep these diskettes in the same order so that you don't waste any time during the restoration process.

First select the *Open...* menu item in the *Restore* menu. The other items are ghosted so that you can't select them. Select *Open...* to prepare the backup data for the actual process. In the dialog box that opens, you can make the following settings:

Open Backup for Restore

Backup diskettes in drive:

A: 5.25" high-density drive

B: 3.5" high-density drive

Target directory is:

A: Floppy diskette

B: Floppy diskette

C: Hard disk drive

D: Hard disk drive

E: Hard disk drive

Subdirectory

OK Cancel

Open created backup for restore

In the drive list box, select the drive for the backup diskettes by using the cursor or the mouse. The available drives, along with the corresponding types (normal/high density), are displayed here. The target directory list box lets you specify the drive to which the data in the backup files should be copied.

The *Subdirectory* check box lets you choose a different directory as the target. You should always do this when the target directory isn't the root directory. Select the desired directory in the file selection dialog box. This process is described in the example on backing up a single directory.

After you confirm these settings by clicking OK, a dialog box prompts you to insert the first backup diskette in the specified drive.

Insert diskette

After you click OK, the program reads the first and last diskettes in the backup series. If the program determines that the files in the backup and the target directory are identical, the *Quick Compare* dialog box opens.

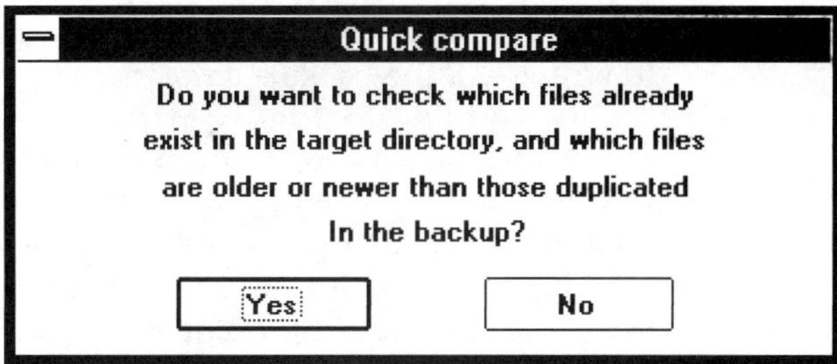

Quick Compare dialog box

This dialog box lets you perform a quick comparison of the backup files and the files on the target directory. You can check which files are in the target directory as well as which of these files are older or newer than the matching entries in the backup.

Select Yes to use this option; otherwise select No. The files are compared by their creation date. The file names of the backup files are displayed in the right work window.

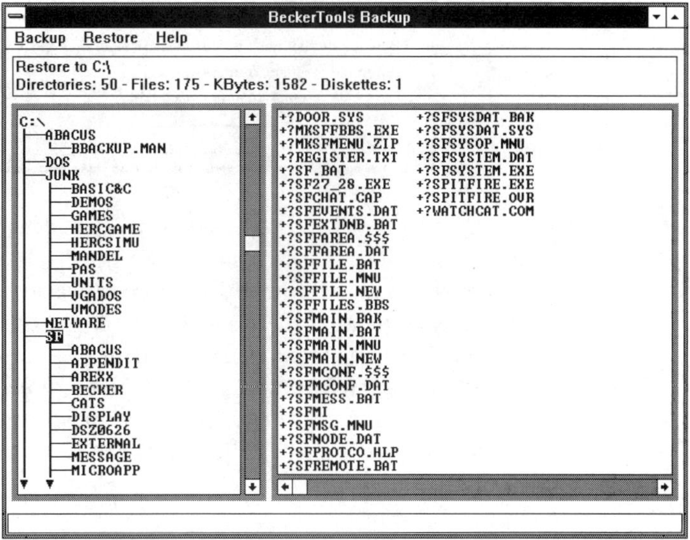

Restore files

If you selected No in the *Quick Compare* dialog box, files that have the same name but different dates are preceded by a question mark.

The *Compare...* menu item can also be selected from the *Restore* menu. This option lets you determine whether you should perform a restore. If the file creation dates are the same, the question marks in front of the name disappear. In this case, you don't need to write back the backup data.

File names marked with an asterisk after the Quick compare are files which don't exist in the target directory. So, you must write them back to the target directory. If the file names don't have any markings, it's not necessary to perform a restore because these files exist in an unchanged form on the target drive.

An arrow in front of the file name indicates that the file in the target directory has been changed. This file is either newer or older than the file in the backup series. You must decide whether it makes sense to restore the file to the target directory. If you do, the existing file will be overwritten and the changes will be lost. You should exclude such files from the writing back process.

To select files to restore, use the *Select...* menu item in the *Restore* menu. The *Auto-select* dialog box opens:

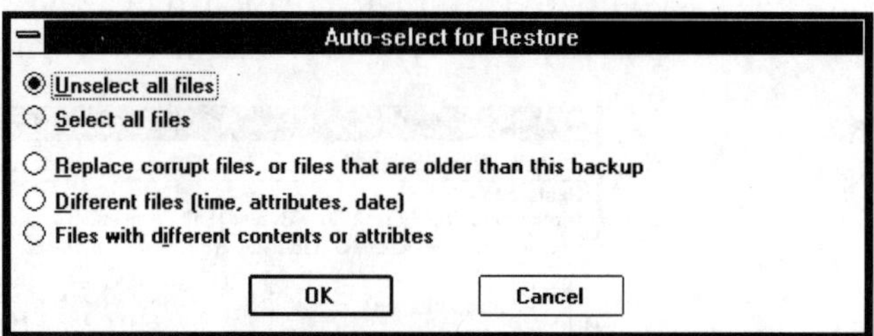

Auto-select for restore

The default option button is *Unselect all files*. This button indicates that all the files are excluded from the restore operation. The next option button, *Select all files*, will restore all files in the backup series. To replace older files and corrupt files, select the *Replace corrupt files* option button. Use the mouse or the Alt key and the underlined character to select the correct option button.

After confirming the settings with OK, the character preceding the file name indicates whether the file will be included in the restoration process. A plus (+) sign indicates the file will be restored from the backup series to the hard drive.

To start the restoration process, select the *Start Restore...* menu item in the *Restore* menu. The Restore backup dialog box opens.

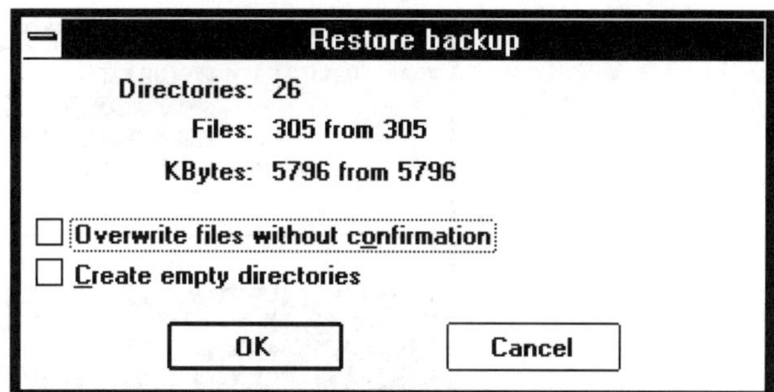

Restore backup

If you are absolutely certain that the files in the target directory are no longer current, activate the *Overwrite file without confirmation* check box. Select the *Create empty directories* check box to create the directories in the target directory that don't contain any files from the backup. Start the restoration process by clicking OK.

If you don't activate the *Overwrite file without confirmation* check box and one of the files exists in the target directory, another dialog box is displayed before the file is restored. Neither of these options are set by default.

File exists
C:\AUTOEXEC.BAT
Name: Extension
New name Overwrite Cancel

File exists

You have the option of renaming the file contained in the backup series; using the New name button. The target directory will contain two different files after the restoration process. You could also overwrite the file in the target directory by selecting the Overwrite button. Click Cancel to cancel the process.

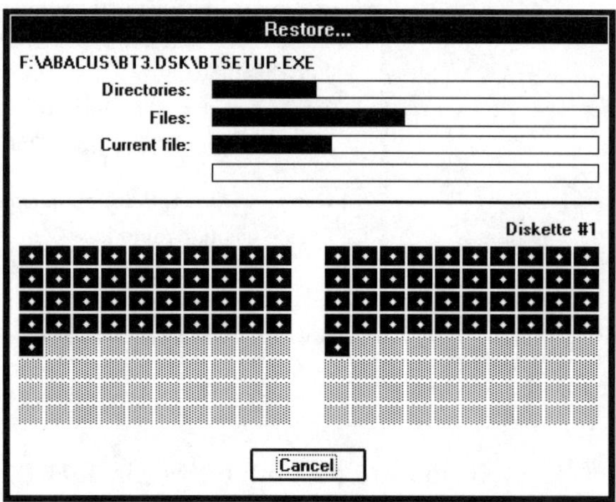

Restoration progress

This dialog box contains bar charts that show the progress of the restoration process. You can determine the speed of the process from the bar chart. To cancel this process at any time, select the Cancel button.

However, you must manually check which files have been restored, and a final completion message won't appear at the end of the process. If you don't cancel the restoration, this message will appear on the screen when the process is complete.

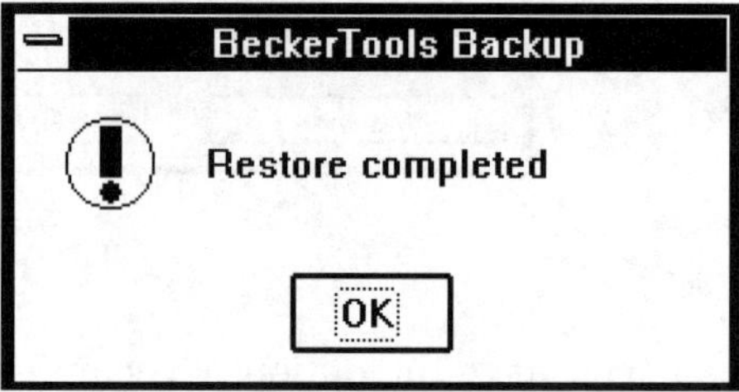

Restore complete

Working with Exclude/Include lists

Excluding files

There are two ways to exclude certain files from being selected for backup. One method is to use the keyboard or the mouse to unselect all the files that you don't want to back up.

To do this, use the mouse or the Tab key to select the work window and then use the Spacebar to unselect the appropriate files. A minus sign (-) will appear in front of the unselected files. Once you've done this, you can perform the backup as previously described.

Another method is to create an exclusion or inclusion list. This can be done with the *Exclude/Include Files...* menu item in the *Backup* menu.

When you select this option, the *Backup Exclude/Include* dialog box is displayed. This dialog box lets you build exclusion or inclusion lists. These can be based on file names and extension or dates.

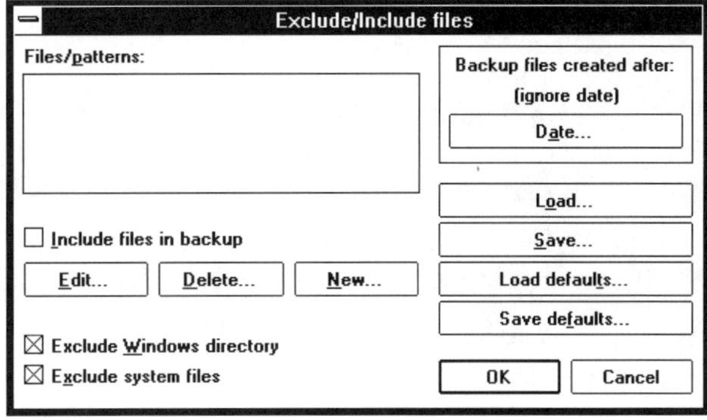

Exclude/Include dialog box

At first, you won't see any entries in the "Exclude/Include" window. To place an entry in this window, select the New... button. The *Exclude/Include entry* dialog box will appear. Now you can enter a file name or extension. Wildcards can also be used.

If you enter "*.*" in the Exclude/Include list, there won't be any selected files in the work window. So you can select the files you want to back up in the right work window by using the Spacebar or the mouse. Then perform the backup as previously described.

All the files described by this list are excluded from the backup. You can create different exclusion lists that contain different file names and extensions. Just select the appropriate list and perform the backup as described. You can always check the directories in the right work window to ensure that unselected files are displayed in white and have a "-" character in front of their names.

To create a list of files to be excluded from the backup, select the New... button. A dialog box is displayed in which you can enter the names of files to be excluded from the backup.

For example, you can exclude all files with the .BAK extension by entering "*" for the file name and ".BAK" for the extension.

Including files

If you activate the *Include files in backup* check box, the files described by the File/patterns list will be selected for the backup.

Exclude System and Windows directory files

With the *Exclude system files* and *Exclude Windows directory* check boxes, you can easily exclude system files and the files contained in your Windows directory.

The first option omits system files from the backup and the second option omits the files of the Windows directories. Both options are default settings. You may want to switch off these options when performing a complete backup of your hard drive.

Saving and Loading Exclude/Include lists

You can save the Files/patterns lists with the Save... button. Simply enter a file name in the file selector dialog box. Backup uses the .BBS extension for saved lists. Use Load... to load a saved list.

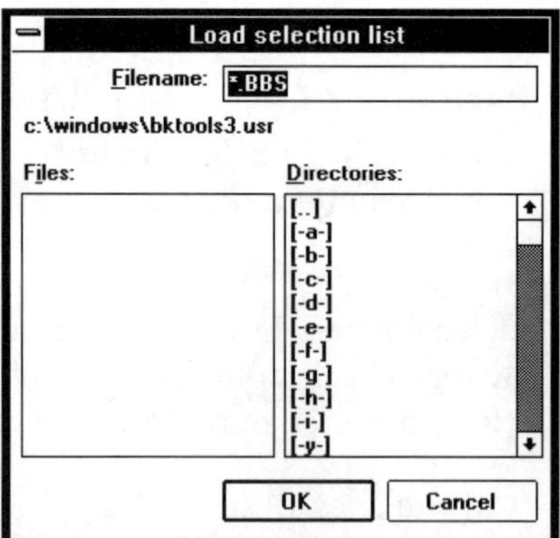

Load dialog box

When you select OK, the file names or extensions that were included or excluded from the backup are displayed in the Files/patterns list window.

However, if you select Save defaults..., the file names and extensions become the new default setting.

Since this overwrites the previous default setting, you must confirm it with OK. To load the defaults, select Load defaults....

Specifying files by date

You can also specify files by date. When the Date button is selected, the *File select: By date/time...* dialog box opens. A table displaying the year, month, and day (as well as the hours, minutes, and seconds) appears in the dialog box.

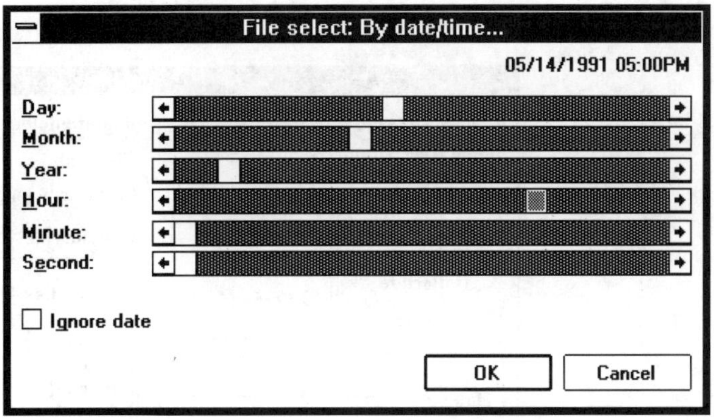

File select: By date/time...

05/14/1991 05:00PM

Day:
Month:
Year:
Hour:
Minute:
Second:

Ignore date

OK Cancel

Date selection

The *Ignore date* check box controls whether the date is considered a backup option. If you want to use the date, first you must deactivate this option button.

When the *Ignore date* check box is inactive, you can use the scroll bars to select the date of the files you want to back up. Any files created after the selected date will be included in the backup.

Backup Help Files

The Backup Help files give a complete online manual for the Backup program. To access the help file, select the *Help* menu and then the *Index* menu item. Simply click on the menu item to display the online documentation.

The SnapShot Program

With the Snapshot program you can easily capture Windows screens, windows, and selected areas of the screen. They can be captured in PCX or BMP format for editing in PaintBrush.

Using SnapShot

You'll find the SnapShot program stored in the W31CMPLT\SNAPSHOT directory. If you've added SnapShot to a program group, start the Snapshot program by double-clicking the icon labeled "SNAPSHOT." You can also start SnapShot from the File Manager, or using the *File/Run...* command in the Program Manager, running the SNAPSHOT.EXE file.

SnapShot Dialog Box

When SnapShot is started, a large dialog box containing the SnapShot options appears. You can set all the options of SnapShot in this dialog box.

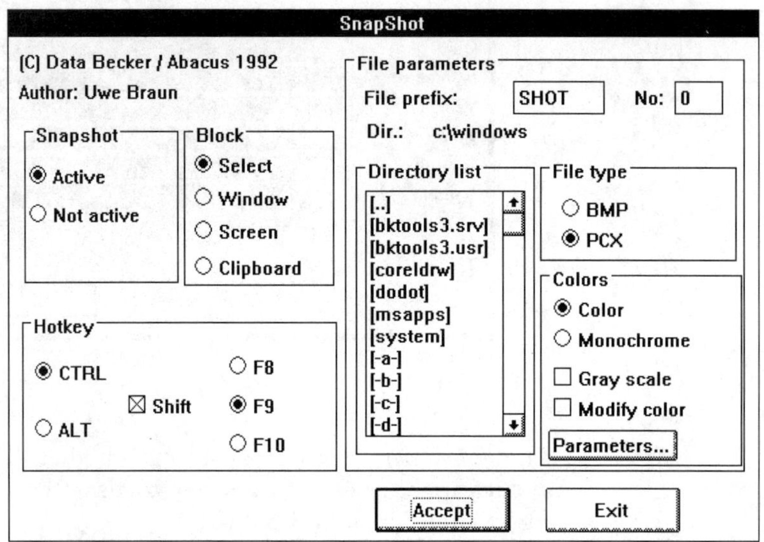

SnapShot dialog box

SnapShot can be "Active" or "Not Active". You can capture a selected portion of a screen, a windows, the complete screen, or the clipboard. The "Hotkey" can be defined using a combination of the Ctrl, Alt, Shift, F8, F9, or F10 keys.

In the File parameters section you specify the "File prefix" and the series number. The "File prefix" can be four characters and the series number can go to 1000. The extension will be determined by the "File Type", either BMP or PCX.

The "Directory list" allows you to specify the directory where the files will be stored. The Colors section allows you to select either Color or Monochrome.

You can also save the image in "Gray Scale" or you can select "Modify color" to change the colors of the image. The *Parameters* dialog box allows you to specify the colors to be changed.

To exit this dialog box with the selected SnapShot settings, select the Accept command button. When the SnapShot hotkeys are pressed you can select the area, window, or screen to be captured, depending on the settings made in the SnapShot dialog box.

Once the area is selected the SnapShot Parameters dialog box is displayed.

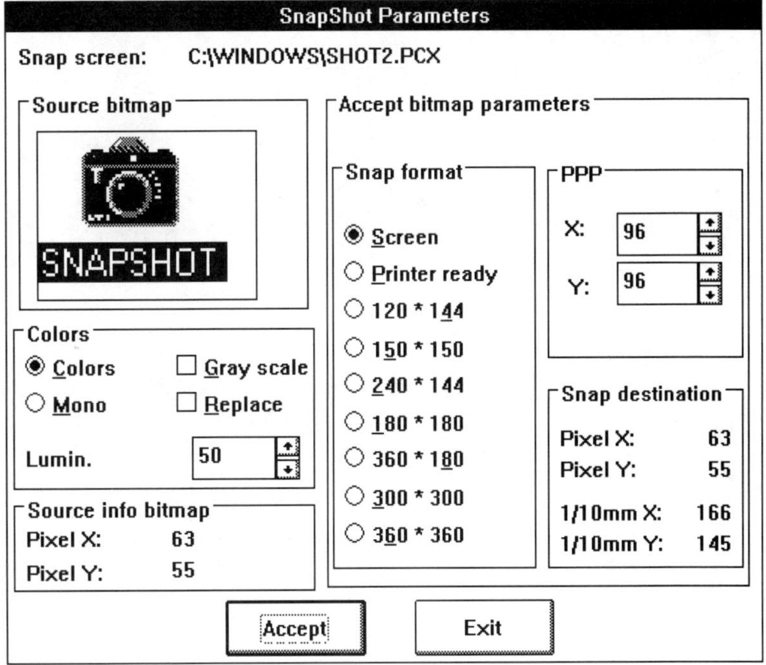

SnapShot Parameters dialog box

This dialog box displays the bitmap image of the selected area and allows you to make any final adjustments to the parameters of the saved image.

You can select whether the image should be saved in Color, Mono, or Gray Scale or if the Colors should be replaced. The colors will be replaced using the setting specified in the *SnapShot* dialog box. You can also specify the luminosity, between 50 and 150. The "Source info bitmap" displays the size of the image in pixels.

The "Snap format" area allows you to specify the bitmap parameters to be saved. This is used to format the image for printed output. Select the resolution that best matches your printer. The PPP (Printed Pixel Parameter) shows the resolution of the saved image. This can also be changed to match your printer.

Once you're satisfied with your choices, select the Accept command button to save the image. A dialog box that displays the progress in bar chart form is displayed. The saved image can be edited with Paintbrush or linked to your documents for printing.

Appendix C: Glossary

Alt

This key is used to create characters that aren't usually available on the PC keyboard. These characters include graphic characters. Also, this key activates the menu bar in Windows.

Enter

Pressing Enter instructs the computer to execute the MS-DOS command currently entered at the DOS prompt line. This key is also called Return.

3.5" disk drive

The smaller format disk drive. 3.5" diskettes are more rugged and hold more data than 5.25" diskettes. See also *Diskettes.*

5.25" disk drive

The larger format disk drive. This type of diskette can store up to 1.2 Meg of data (approximately 1,200,000 characters).

Access rights

Rights of a user to use programs or data. The supervisor uses SYSCON to install and change access rights. In Novell NetWare, access rights for each user and directory can be individually determined. Along with attributes familiar from DOS such as "Hidden", there are also special rights for opening or closing files and creating subdirectories.

Active

When you want to work with an object (window, icon, entry), first you must select it to make it active. All other objects aren't active.

Active printer

The active printer is the default printer which can be selected in the Control Panel using the Printers icon.

ANSI character set

Windows uses the ANSI (American National Standards Institute) character set and DOS uses the OEM character set. The ANSI character set allows easy access to foreign language characters.

Application
A Windows program designed for a specific purpose. Word processors, worksheets, and databases are applications.

Application Icon
The icon representing an application in Windows. When an application is minimized, its icon is displayed on the desktop.

Application Window
The main window of an application. It contains the menu and work areas of the windows.

Archive attribute
When this attribute is set, the file is included in the next backup.

ASCII
Acronym for American Standard Code for Information Interchange. ASCII is the standard for keyboard character codes, which apply, to some extent, to keyboards and printers. The ASCII standard covers key codes 0 to 127; individual computer manufacturers assign their own characters to codes 128 to 255. See also *Byte*.

ASCII text files
These files are saved without formatting or graphic commands so that they can be used by other DOS applications, or transferred to another type of computer.

Attribute
See *File attributes*.

Backup copy
Duplicate of an original diskette or file. Making backup copies is a good habit to develop. Data on a diskette can easily and accidentally be destroyed.

Bank switching
A method of expanding memory beyond the normal memory limits by quickly switching between two banks of memory chips.

Base memory
The first, or lower, 640K of the first megabyte of memory.

Basic Input/Output System
See *BIOS*.

Baud rate
The unit used to measure the rate of data transmission, for

example when communicating with another computer by telephone. A baud equals approximately 1 bit per second. The term comes from J.M.E. Baudot, the inventor of the Baudot telegraph code, and was originally designed to describe the transmission capabilities of telegraph facilities.

Today, the baud rate is the number of signal events (the signal for a 1 bit and the signal for a 0 bit are both "events") that take place on a communications line each second. Standard baud rates include 300 baud, 1200 baud, and 2400 baud.

Bernoulli box

A type of mass storage device featuring removable cartridges that contain a rapidly spinning diskette similar to a floppy diskette. The high rotation speed and the small distance between the head and the diskette make a high recording density possible, and give the Bernoulli diskette a memory capacity comparable to a hard drive.

Binary

A number system consisting of only two numbers (0,1), sometimes called bits. Unlike the decimal number system with its 10 numbers (0-9), the binary number system is better suited to the internal structure of a computer. Just as larger numbers can be composed in the decimal system, larger binary system numbers are constructed from several digits. Both number systems rely on the positional value of numbers. The numbers 0 - 9 in the 10 to the 0 power column have the value 0 - 9. The same numbers in the next column (10 to the 1 power) refer to 10 - 90, etc. In the binary system the column value increases as follows: 0, 2, 4, 8, 16, 32, etc.

BIOS

Acronym for Basic Input Output System. BIOS is a program permanently stored in the memory of the computer and is available without an operating system diskette. For example, it performs the internal self test of the computer (counting up the memory available, and testing for connected peripherals such as disk drives). It also triggers the search for the operating system (MS-DOS) on the diskette in the drive.

Bit

The smallest unit in the binary number system. It can only assume two states (0,1) and therefore store only two different pieces of information. To store a character, several bits must be combined into a byte.

Bitmap

A graphic file that contains individual pixels.

Boot
The loading process that places the operating system in memory. A diskette used for booting a PC must have two "hidden" files available for telling the PC to boot, as well as the COMMAND.COM file.

Bootable
A diskette that can be used for booting. See also *Boot*.

Byte
A group of eight bits. While a bit can only assume two states, 0 and 1, a byte can store from 0 to 255 conditions. Usually a character is stored in a byte. So a byte can store up to 255 different characters. The standard ASCII character set consists of 128 characters; the additional characters generally used in PC software bring the total number of characters up to 255.

Cache
A special area of RAM, in which the most frequently accessed information is stored. You can significantly improve the speed of your system by using cache memory because it "optimizes" the cooperation among the different components of your system.

Cartridge system
A removable module, or cartridge, containing a magnetic tape or diskette. It's used as a storage device.

CD-ROM drive
A storage device that uses compact discs (CDs) to store data. Although a large amount of data can be stored on these disks, they're "Read Only Memory" drives.

The advantage of using a CD-ROM include extremely high data density, storage capacity of approximately 680Mb per diskette, and its excellence in multimedia applications.

CD-WORM disk drive
A storage device based on further development of CD-ROM disk drives. It's an acronym for "Write Once Read Many". These disk drives can write on the CD only once but read it as often as required.

The advantages of these disk drives include data security, acceptable access times (50-80 ms), and the fact that it's impossible to overwrite or accidentally delete data since the data cannot be removed from the diskette.

Centronics

Standard connection between the PC and a printer. The connection of other devices to the PC occurs through interfaces. These interfaces use standardized connectors. There are serial interfaces, in which data is sent as individual bits, and parallel interfaces, in which a byte can be transmitted simultaneously. Both interfaces have their own standards: Centronics interfaces for parallel; RS-232 interfaces for serial. Most printers are attached through the parallel Centronics interface. It has the device designation LPT1: (Line Printer 1).

Check box

These are used to select one or more options from a list that appears in a dialog box. A selected check box is contains an 'X,' while an unselected check box remains blank. You can select multiple check boxes in a dialog box.

Click

To press and quickly release a mouse button (usually the left mouse button). To "click" a button, menu, or other object refers to moving the mouse pointer to that object and selecting it by pressing a mouse button (usually the left mouse button).

Clipboard

A temporary storage space that contains the most recent text or graphics that were cut or copied. You can then copy or paste the item into other documents.

CMOS

A Complementary Metal-Oxide Semiconductor that pretends to duplicate the functions of memory chips or other processors. CMOS chips are used primarily in portable PCs, which receive their power from batteries.

Cold start

Switching the computer off and on. Unlike the warm start, the cold start is the complete turning off and turning back on of the computer. The cold start is the last chance to have the computer start completely new. Since switching the computer off and on puts much stress on the electronic components, use the warm start (Ctrl + Alt + Del) whenever possible.

Co-processor

Name for electronic components that relieve the microprocessor of some important tasks. Increased performance can often be achieved through the use of co-processors. For example, a math co-processor often performs many of the math functions that can slow down the microprocessor during complicated graphic calculations.

Current directory
: To access a file or a directory, use the current directory. This is the directory with which you're currently working.

Current drive
: The standard drive or current drive is the drive to which all diskette commands of the computer apply.

Cursor
: A small, rectangular, blinking spot of light on the screen which marks the spot where a character can be placed from the keyboard. The direction keys (also called cursor keys) move the cursor back and forth.

Databases
: Applications that allow fast access to data. Many database programs allow different sets of data to be combined into one package, permitting access to the different data sets simultaneously.

Data transfer rate
: The rate that data is transferred from a computer to a disk drive or from one computer to another computer.

DDE
: Dynamic Data Exchange. DDE transfers data between applications.

Dedicated
: Opposite of non-dedicated. A file server is dedicated if it cannot be used as a workstation. The entire performance of the computer is available for network management.

Device driver
: A subprogram to control communications between the computer and a peripheral.

Dialog box
: Many menu options, commands, or other items require additional information to complete a task. You confirm information or answer prompts by responding with some type of input in a dialog box. You cannot move or enlarge dialog boxes.

Digital-Analog-Converter (DAC):
: A device used to convert digital numbers to continuous analog signals.

Digitizing tablets
An input device that converts graphic and pictorial data into binary data.

Dimmed
Refers to the menu items and buttons that cannot be selected. The names of these menu items or buttons appear dimmed and fuzzy. Some menu items and buttons remain dimmed until you select another item or button.

DIP switch
A series of small switches used by computers and peripherals to configure the equipment.

Directory
Part of a storage medium. Before the hard drive was commonly used, all files were stored in one directory, the root directory. Because of the large capacity of the hard drive, a separation into various directories became necessary. These directories are arranged in a tree structure, in which the root directory can contain files and subdirectories. Every subdirectory in turn can contain files and subdirectories. Most commands act only on the current directory, which can be indicated with CD.

Disk drive
Disk drives are devices that permit the PC to work on the data stored on the diskette. Depending on the size and type of the disks, there are drives for 5.25" disks and for 3.5" disks. The PC must have at least one disk drive built in. The usual configuration is two disk drives. Between the two disk drives that may be present, there are differences of rank. If the PC wants to read in the MS-DOS operating system, it accesses first the upper or left drive, depending on the construction of the PC. This can be seen by observing the LED on the disk drive. This is the main drive. Its designation is A:. The other drive is then drive B:. If there is a hard drive, it has the designation drive C:. If the PC has only one drive, that drive has the drive A: designation. This designation is important because with it commands and files can be assigned. Only one drive can be current. Its letter appears in front of the system prompt on the screen and is constantly displayed to the user.

Diskettes
Removable data storage media. PC systems use two sizes. When purchasing new disks, make sure they are double sided and double density. Double sided means that the PC can write on both sides. Double density refers to the density of the magnetic material coating.

DOS
See *MS-DOS.*

Dot-matrix printer
Printer that produces characters on paper by driving a set of pins onto a ribbon, which leaves an impression of a character on paper.

Double-click
Refers to pressing the mouse button twice in rapid succession. You can open a file or directory and start applications by double-clicking.

Double density
Double density means that this type of diskette has twice as much magnetic material for recording as a single density diskette. Use double density disks only for PCs.

Double sided
A diskette that is double sided can record on both sides. This is the usual case for a PC and should be remembered when buying disks.

Dragging
Refers to moving an object or selecting a group of objects. To drag an object, you must select the object, hold down the left mouse button, move the mouse so that the object is at the proper location, and then release the mouse button.

Dynamic RAM chips (DRAM)
A RAM chip that must be continuously refreshed. These chips vary in their access time, which is measured in nanoseconds.

Editing
Editing is the process of changing text or program code within the computer.

Enhanced Graphics Adapter (EGA)
A high resolution graphics card with superior resolution compared to the CGA. The EGA combined the operating modes of the MDA and the CGA. This type of graphics adapter is capable of displaying all 16 colors in text mode with a resolution of 640 x 350 pixels.

EPROM
Acronym for Erasable Programmable Read Only Memory. It's a ROM chip that can be erased and reprogrammed any number of times. These chips are erased by ultraviolet light and shouldn't be exposed to direct sunlight.

ESDI

An acronym for Enhanced System Device Interface. Hard drives that use this standard transfer data 2.5 times faster than the earlier ST506 standard.

Expanded memory

Memory above the 640K limit for DOS Version 3.3 (and earlier versions) that can be used for programs requiring large amounts of memory. Note that this area of memory requires special drivers and works only with software written for it.

Expanded Memory Specification (EMS)

A section of RAM above the 1 Meg limit set by PCs and XTs. Software and applications cannot work with EMS unless specifically written for EMS. See also the *LIM/EMS Standard.*

Expansion card

A printed circuit card that you can install to add new features and expand the current capabilities of your system.

Expansion slots

Slots or spaces inside the case for connecting cards to the motherboard. Most PCs contain these slots so it is easy to upgrade the system.

External hard drive

A hard drive that isn't located inside the case of the PC. Instead it's outside the case and connected by cables.

Extended DOS partition

These are nonbootable partitions that define other logical drives in your system.

Extended memory

Area of memory above 1 Meg that a computer using a 286, 386, or 486 processor can access.

File

Data stored under a name assigned by the user or manufacturer. Data files (e.g., programs, text, graphics, etc.) appear in the directory of a diskette or hard drive as an entry containing the name, extension, size, and date of storage.

File Allocation Table (FAT)

A portion of all DOS formatted diskettes containing information on the number and location of files and available storage space.

File attributes

Refers to a characteristic of a file. You can change or view the four types of file attributes in File Manager. See also *Archive attribute, Hidden attribute, System attribute.*

File management

Working with data. Related information is stored in a data set and these are presented in sorted format. An address file is a simple form of file management.

File server

Also called the server; highest computer in the network, the data which all the users access are stored on this computer. Usually file servers are 386s or even 486s with large hard drives and at least 4 Megs of RAM so they can manage the central tasks of the network. However, the actual work takes place on the workstations.

File structures

The type and method of storing files on a medium. The root directory can contain both files and subdirectories, and any subdirectory can also contain files and subdirectories.

File name

A group of letters and numbers indicating a specific file stored in a directory. A file name consists of the file name itself, which can be up to eight characters long; and the extension, which can have no more than three characters. It's important to note that spaces are prohibited and result in error messages.

Floppy diskette

Popular designation of the disk drive, mainly in the personal computer field. The term is derived from the flexible property of the medium. Early disks were 8 inches square and inflexible. When the first 5.25" diskettes appeared on the market, people referred to them as "floppy disks."

Floppy diskette controller

The card or chip that controls the floppy disk drive.

FORMAT

Formatting a diskette (preparing a diskette to store data). Before the command can be used, the diskette must be inserted into the drive.

Formatted capacity

The amount of available storage space remaining on the diskette after formatting. It's always less than the capacity before formatting.

Gigabyte

A unit of measurement equal to 1024 Meg.

Group

One or more users with (at least partially) the same rights. Within a network, you can refer to a group instead of a user to call the several users in the network - just like using wildcards in MS-DOS. This is especially practical for sending messages.

Hard drive

A hermetically sealed disk drive that usually cannot be removed from the PC (a few newer models are removable). Hard drives have much higher storage capacity than floppy disks.

Hardware

Hardware consists of the computer itself and usually everything connected to it (processor, keyboard, monitor, disk drives, hard drive). The opposite of hardware is software.

Head crash

Damage of the hard drive and possible loss of data through the contact between the medium and the read/write head on the hard drive. This can be caused by dropping or moving your computer while the hard drive is operating. You should always use the SHIP or PARK command to place the read/write head in an area where a head crash cannot occur.

Hercules Graphics Card

Also known by its acronym HGC. It features a text mode of MDA and graphics mode with a resolution of 720 x 348 one color (monochrome) pixels. Since 1982 the Hercules card (and compatibles) have been the most commonly used PC monitor adapter.

Hertz (Hz)

A unit of measure that equals a frequency of one cycle per second.

Hidden attribute

When the Hidden attribute is set, the file isn't displayed in the directory window. You cannot display, erase, or copy files set with the hidden attribute.

High density diskette

Refers to a floppy diskette (both 3.5" and 5.25") that can hold more information than low density diskettes, such as double density diskettes. A 5.25" high density diskette can store up to

1.2 Meg of information and a 3.5" high density diskette can store up to 1.44 Meg of information.

Hotkey combination
A selected key or key combination you can use to choose a specific menu item or command. If a keyboard accelerator is available, it will appear at the right edge of the menu. Also called *Shortcut Keys* or *Keyboard Accelerator.*

Hourglass pointer
The mouse pointer will change its appearance after you select certain options or commands. The pointer appears as an hourglass when you're waiting for the computer to complete an operation.

Icon
Graphical representation of a object, including files, drives, directories, applications, etc.

Impact printer
See *Dot-matrix printer.*

Insertion point
The appearance of the mouse pointer when in an application that requires text or number handling.

Interface
Connection between a PC and various peripherals. Allows data to be exchanged between the PC and peripherals, such as printers. Two interfaces of different design are used: Parallel interfaces (see *Centronics*) and serial interfaces (see *RS-232 interface*). If a device should be attached to the PC and a suitable interface isn't available, circuit boards, which contain an interface, can be obtained. Also called a port.

Initialization
Another term for the process of formatting a diskette or hard drive so it's available for use.

Integrated circuit (IC)
A single, small electronic component containing multiple transistors and other electrical circuitry.

Interleave ratio
Also called interleave setting. This is the ratio between the physical sectors of a hard drive that are skipped for every sector used. If the hard drive has an interleave ratio of 3:1, the diskette writes to one sector, skips three sectors, writes to one sector, etc.

Jumper

Electrical connectors that allow you to customize a circuit board. It's a small piece of rectangular plastic with up to three receptacles.

K

See *Kilobyte.*

Keyboard accelerator

A selected key or key combination you can use to choose a specific menu item or command. If a keyboard accelerator is available, it will appear at the right edge of the menu. Also called *Shortcut Keys* or *Hotkey combination.*

Kilobyte (K)

1,024 bytes and usually abbreviated simply as K, for example, 512K.

LAN

Abbreviation for Local Area Network or a local network. Unlike "global networks", a local network can also share available hardware resources.

LPT port

The parallel interface of the computer.

Laser printer

Printer that creates characters on paper with a special printing process involving an industrial laser. Laser printers are still expensive. However, they're extremely quiet and create very good print quality.

LIM/EMS standard

A standard, introduced by Lotus, Intel, and Microsoft, to allow software to work with expanded memory above the normal 640K of RAM. Note that software must be designed to run under the LIM/EMS standard to work with expanded memory.

Local network

A network that is only available at a local place. In a local network, it is possible to use hardware components such as printers, modems and fax machines from different computers in the network. This kind of network is also called a LAN (local area network) in contrast to "global networks".

Logging in

Access to a network by a user (usually at a workstation). Ordinarily, the user must also specify a password. Logging in gets the user a valid drive letter for the file server.

Logging out
Opposite of logging in. After logging out, it is no longer possible to access the data and programs of the file server.

LOGIN
Command for logging in to a file server.

Login script
A command file for each user similar to the AUTOEXEC.BAT file on a PC with MS-DOS. If a login script for a user is present, it is automatically processed when the user logs in on the file server. One especially practical option of a login script is to have it start a special shell for a user to make accessing the applications easier. Of course, you could also use Windows for this purpose.

LOGOUT
Command for logging out of a network.

Low density diskette
Refers to the storage capacity of a floppy diskette. A 5.25" low density diskette can store 360K of data and a 3.5" diskette can store 720K of data.

Low-level format
Also called physical format. This is the physical pattern of tracks and sectors created on a diskette during formatting.

Math co-processor
A microprocessor that increases the speed of the main processor by performing mathematical operations.

Meg
Abbreviation for megabyte. See *Megabyte*.

Megabyte (Meg)
1,024K and usually abbreviated simply as Meg, for example, 20 Meg.

Megahertz (MHz)
A unit of measurement that equals a frequency of 1 million cycles per second.

Microprocessor
Another word for chip. When used in computer science, the term chip usually refers to the main microprocessor of the computer, which controls the basic functions.

Microsoft LAN Manager

A network operating system from Microsoft. Novell NetWare is the competitor's product.

Maximize

Expand the active window to full size. See also *Minimize.*

Menu

A list of items, options, and commands under one name.

Menu bar

A horizontal bar appearing across the top of the active window. It displays the menu names of the application (such as *File, Edit, Options,* etc.).

Minimize

Reduce the active window's size.

Modem

Abbreviation for MODulator/DEModulator. This device converts the digital signals of your computer into electrical impulses (modulates) and transmits these impulses over telephone lines. Another modem then converts received impulses back into signals (demodulates) that another computer can understand.

Mouse

An alternate means of cursor control. The mouse is a small box with two or three buttons on top and a ball poking out the bottom. Moving the mouse on a table moves the cursor in the same direction on the screen. The mouse is most important for painting programs and graphical user interfaces.

MS-DOS

The standard operating system developed by Microsoft Corporation for IBM compatible PCs. Your PC only becomes usable after the MS-DOS operating system has been loaded. It consists generally of a catalog of resident and transient commands that can be accessed when needed.

Multitasking

This is the process of running multiple programs or tasks on the same computer at the same time. So, you don't need to exit one application before starting a different application.

The number of programs you can have open simultaneously depends on the operating system, amount of available memory, CPU speed, capacity, and peripheral speed.

Network

Connecting several computers (file server and workstations) to a network, allowing data and programs to be exchanged and hardware to be shared.

Network card

Network cards provide data transfer from the connection cable. Along with the performance of the file server (memory capacity, processor and storage medium), network cards are an essential criterion for total performance in the network. Typical network cards can transfer data at 10 megabits per second, that is, more than 1 Meg per second. A serial cable is ordinarily capable of a maximum of 115200 baud (or 14K per second). Also, with a serial cable, the computer would be so intensively involved with data transfer that it would hardly have time for other tasks. In contrast, with a network card, data transfer places much less of a burden on the computer.

Network drive

A driver letter assigned by MAP or the *Network Connections* command in File Manager. This drive letter is only available when the file server is available in the network and the user has logged in on the network with a valid user ID. The File Manager can store connections to the file server and automatically sets them up the next time you start Windows.

Network driver

A special device driver for the network card, which also determines the transmission protocol, that is, the language for communication. In Novell the network driver is called IPX.COM.

Network path

A directory path on the file server which has been assigned a drive letter. For example, if a user gets access to the network path, SERVER_1/SYS:PROG from the drive letter D:, then he or she can only move within the \PROG directory path.

Network printer

A printer available to all users in the network. Usually this printer is connected to the server.

Network shell

After the network driver for the special network card has been started, the network or the redirector can make the connection to the file server. Until the user logs into the file server, he/she only has access to the \LOGIN directory with the data and programs for logging in to the network. In Novell

NetWare, the redirectors are called NET3.COM to NET5.COM for MS-DOS 3.X to MS-DOS 5.0.

NLQ
Acronym for Near Letter Quality: Higher print quality offered by dot-matrix printers. The printer prints a line, then reprints the same line after shifting the position of the print head slightly. NLQ mode reduces print speed considerably.

Non-dedicated
Opposite of dedicated. A file server is termed non-dedicated, when it can also be used as a workstation. It can then be operated in operating system mode as well as console mode (network operation). However, a program failure in operating system mode can have serious effects on network operation, so that beginning with Novell NetWare 3.0, a file server can only be used as a dedicated server.

Novell network
A Novell NetWare local network. Novell offers a standard for local PC networks and is supported by all common network programs.

OEM character set
The normal DOS character set used by DOS programs. Windows uses the ANSI character set.

Option button
A mutually exclusive round button displayed in a dialog box. This button is used to select one item from a list of options.

Parallel interface
Centronics interface, usually leading to a printer (see also *Centronics*). Parallel interfaces exchange data 8 bits at a time. LPT1: is the device designation for the first parallel interface. Additional parallel interfaces (if present) are accessed as LPT2: and LPT3:.

Password
A password that, along with a user ID, regulates access to a file server.

PATH
The PATH command indicates the directory where DOS should search for the resident DOS commands. Without such a path, the search is limited to the current directory. PATH without a parameter displays the path that has been set.

Path name
Indicates the location of a file or a directory on a volume. It

consists of the drive specifier and subdirectories separated by a backslash. For example, a valid path name for a file named TEXT.TXT could be:

```
A:\TEXT\PRIVATE\TEXT.TXT
```

PCX file format
: The file format used by PC Paintbrush images.

Peripheral
: A device connected to the computer but outside the computer's CPU. These devices include printers and disk drives.

PIF file
: Abbreviation for Program Information File, which contains important system information for running non-Windows applications in Windows. The PIF Editor is used to alter the setting of a PIF file.

Pixels
: An abbreviation of picture elements. These are the individual dots on your screen. The more pixels a computer can display, the better the *resolution*. The resolution defines the maximum number of dots into which a screen is divided. The picture quality improves and becomes more reliable with higher resolutions.

Pointer
: The small image (hourglass, I-beam, or crosshair) on the screen that moves as you move your mouse.

Press
: Refers to holding down one of the buttons on the mouse usually when dragging or selecting objects.

Print server
: A computer which processes the print jobs of the individual workstations. Usually a file server also performs the task of a print server. You use the special CAPTURE command to intercept printer output and route it to a print server queue.

Proportional character set
: A character set in which the width of the characters are proportional to the character shape.

Protected mode
: Advanced feature of the 80286 and 80386 processors where memory is protected and allocated for specific programs and extended memory.

Radio button
These buttons let you choose from several options. Only one option in a group can be selected at one time. You can determine if a radio button option is selected when it's darker than the other options.

RAM
Abbreviation for Random Access Memory. This is memory in which data can be stored temporarily. Unlike ROM, RAM can be written to and read from. The contents of RAM vanish when the computer is switched off. See also *ROM*.

RAM disk
Pseudo disk drive created in the computer's RAM with the help of a program on the DOS diskette. Because it isn't a mechanical device, the RAM diskette allows very fast file access, but loses all data when the computer is switched off. PC users with only one disk drive will find the RAM disk extremely important. Anything can be kept in a RAM disk, if the files don't exceed the memory limits set for the RAM disk.

Read
The process of retrieving data, usually from a hard drive or floppy disk drive.

Real mode
An operating mode where specific memory locations are given to programs and peripherals.

Redirector
Another name for the Network shell.

Removable storage systems
A secondary, usually high capacity, storage device. The diskette or tape is inside a cartridge or cassette which can be removed from the drive for safekeeping. Examples include Bernoulli boxes.

Resolution
A measurement expressed in horizontal and vertical dots for printers and pixels for monitors. The larger the resolution, the sharper and better the image.

ROM
Abbreviation for Read Only Memory. ROM consists of information permanently stored on a chip, which remains intact after the computer is switched off. When the user switches on the computer, the computer reads the information

from this ROM as needed. Unlike RAM, the user cannot write to ROM (hence the name).

ROM BIOS

The two ROM chips that contain BIOS (Basic Input Output System) code and system configuration information. See also *BIOS*.

Root directory

The main directory or first level directory of either a floppy diskette or a hard drive.

RS-232 interface

Standard serial interface. Serial transfer involves the transfer of data one bit at a time.

Select

To highlight or choose objects, text, menu items, buttons, etc. An object is usually selected by clicking it with the mouse.

Serial interface

See *RS-232 interface*.

Server

Abbreviation for file server.

Shareable

File attribute in a network. Labels data and programs that can be used by several users at the same time.

Shortcut keys

A selected key or key combination you can use to choose a specific menu item or command. If a keyboard accelerator is available, it will appear at the right edge of the menu. Also called *Hotkey combination* or *Keyboard Accelerator*.

SIMM

Acronym for Single In-Line Memory Module. These are memory modules plugged into the motherboard or memory expansion boards. They usually store data 9-bits wide and add 256K to 1 Meg of RAM.

Slot

Name for a connector inside the PC where additional circuit cards can be inserted to enhance the capabilities of the computer. Lately some PCs on the market don't have these slots. So, it's difficult to enhance them.

Small Computer System Interface (SCSI)

An interface standard for hard drives and other peripherals.

Software
: Computer programs, including the operating system, utility programs, and application programs written in a language that the computer can understand.

Software Cache
: See *Cache*.

Spreadsheet
: Also called worksheet. Application often used for accounting, calculations, data tracking, business, and financial "what-if" situations. As its name implies, a spreadsheet displays a set of cells into which numeric data and characters may be entered, similar to a printed accounting spreadsheet.

Startup
: See *Cold start* and *Warm start.*

Storage capacity
: The quantity of data the computer can store and access internally. The PC generally has from about 256,000 (256K) to 1,000,000 characters (1 Meg=1000 kilobytes) of memory capacity.

Storage media
: The various devices used to store the contents of the PC's memory outside the computer. Generally these include disk drives, hard drives, and tape drives.

Streamer
: A streamer is a tape drive on which data are recorded. A streamer is a good alternative to the usual diskettes for backing up, since you can back up your hard drive to a single cassette instead of 20 diskettes. Data exchange is also relatively easy with a streamer, because you simply play back the data of the cassette. Streamers allow you to copy files of up to 50 Meg and more from cassettes.

Subdirectory
: Refers to a relative directory stored within another directory. For example, the following path refers to drive A:, the TEXT directory, the PRIVATE subdirectory contained within the TEXT directory and the GIFTS subdirectory contained within the PRIVATE subdirectory:

```
A:\TEXT\PRIVATE\GIFTS
```

Supervisor
: User who has the supervisor user ID. The supervisor has unrestricted rights in the network and is responsible for

administrative tasks. Only the supervisor can set up and remove new user IDs or grant or revoke access rights.

SYSCON
: Novell program for managing users, groups and access rights. SYSCON lets you handle these tasks conveniently from menus.

System attribute
: Since only system files are protected with this attribute, you don't need to change this attribute. The System attribute doesn't affect your everyday work.

System prompt
: Characters displayed on the screen, indicating readiness for user input.

Target diskette
: Also called the destination diskette. It's the diskette that will receive data during the backup procedure. When copying data from one diskette to another, the diskette being copied is the source diskette and the target diskette is the diskette receiving data.

TIFF
: An acronym for Tagged Image File Format. Standard file format used to capture graphic images. These images are stored in a bit-mapped format.

Title bar
: Displays the name of the active window in a horizontal bar across the top of the window.

VGA
: Acronym for Video Graphics Adapter. It's a video display standard that offers a maximum of 256 simultaneous colors, and offers better resolution than previous standards.

User
: A person who has direct access to the data of the file server and can log in on a workstation with a user ID (and usually a password). The supervisor is a special user who has unlimited rights in the network and manages the users and access rights.

User ID
: Name by which a user is known in the network. Usually this name is linked to a password and one user can work on several file servers with different user IDs. The supervisor installs user IDs with SYSCON.

User interface
The communication point between the user and the computer.

Utilities
Programs that either help the programmer program more efficiently, or act as tools for helping the user in diskette and file management. Some utilities optimize the performance of a hard drive, others help the user recover deleted or destroyed files.

Warm start
The simplest method of returning the PC to its original condition is to switch off the electric power (see *Cold start*). However, the warm start deletes the contents of memory and restarts the system without reloading the BIOS. This means that the computer doesn't count up its memory capacity, test peripherals, etc. Pressing Ctrl + Alt + Del warm starts the computer.

Word processor
An application for creating and editing text files. Most of word processors on the market today allow you to include graphics, text formatting, etc.

Workstation
A PC in a network, on which the actual work takes place. In contrast to workstations, the file server is only concerned with managing users and saving data. A workstation requires a cable connection, a network card and a special software program (network driver and network shell) in order to access the data of the file server.

Write
The process of storing data, usually onto a hard drive or floppy disk drive.

Write-protect
Protects disks from accidental formatting or file deletion. Disks can be write protected by covering the square notch on the side with a write-protect tab (5.25" diskettes) or by moving the write-protect slider (3.5" diskettes).

X-axis
The horizontal line in a graph. It normally displays the categories of the graph, such as month, year, etc.

Y-axis
The vertical line in a graph. It normally displays the values of the graph, such as dollar amount, etc.

Index

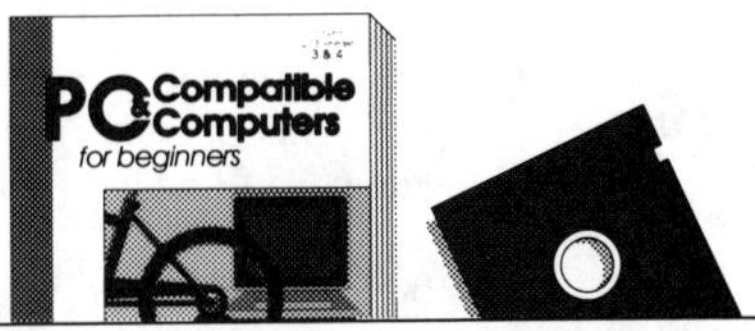

Abacus pc catalog

Order Toll Free 1-800-451-4319

5370 52nd Street SE • Grand Rapids, MI 49512
Phone: (616) 698-0330 • Fax: (616) 698-0325

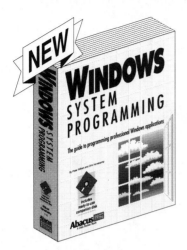

Productivity Series books are for users who want to become more productive with their PC

Turbo Pascal for Windows

is the complete 'Window' to using Turbo Pascal under Windows. **Turbo Pascal for Windows** will show you how to program Turbo Pascal from Borland with professional results.

Turbo Pascal for Windows includes an extensive introduction to the integrated Turbo Pascal environment. This guide includes a practical overview of the fundamentals and special features of Pascal programming under Windows. **Turbo Pascal for Windows** also includes an introduction to the Unit Concept that's vital to understanding object oriented programming.

Turbo Pascal for Windows. ISBN 1-55755-141-3.
Authors: Gunther Faeber and Martin Pauly.
Suggested retail price $39.95 with companion disk.
Available May

To order direct call Toll Free 1-800-451-4319

In US and Canada add $5.00 shipping and handling. Foreign orders add $13.00 per item. Michigan residents add 4% sales tax.

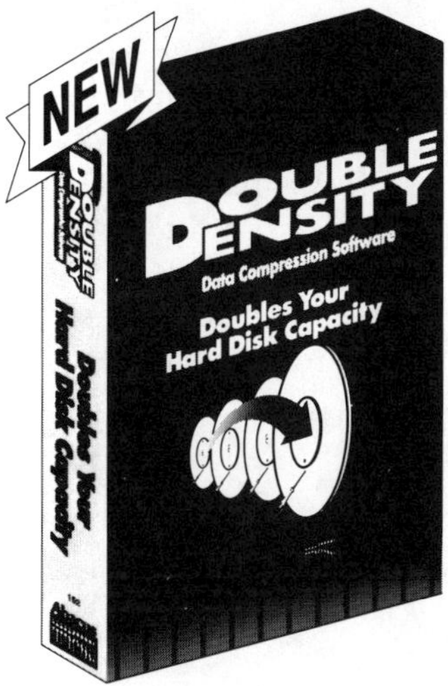

DoubleDensity

Double your disk storage space!

DoubleDensity is a hard disk doubler for DOS. **Double Density** increases the storage capacity of any hard drive. For example increasing a 40 meg hard drive to 80 meg, or a 200 meg hard drive to a 400 meg hard drive. At the same time, **DoubleDensity** increases the speed of read accesses on faster computers.

DoubleDensity does not require any additional hardware purchases. Thanks to the fully automatic installation program anyone can install Double Density quickly and easily. You don't need to open the PC.

DoubleDensity:

- Increases the memory capacity of your hard drive up to twice its original capacity.
- Increases the speed of read accesses of 386s and higher.
- Is easy to install because installation is fully automatic.
- Offers continued availability of all DOS commands such as DIR or UNDELETE.
- Works with system programs such as SpeedDisk, Compress, DiskDoctor and many cache programs.
- Is fully compatible with Windows 3.0.
- Takes up no space in the main memory with DOS 5.0.
- Provides you with the option of protecting your data with passwords.
- Uses approximately 47K and can be loaded in high memory.

System requirements:
IBM 100% compatible XT, AT, 386 or 486 (recommend minimum AT 12 MHZ). Microsoft DOS 3.1 or higher.

Order Item #S152. ISBN 1-55755-152-0. Suggested retail price $79.95.

To order direct call Toll Free 1-800-451-4319

In US and Canada add $5.00 shipping and handling. Foreign orders add $13.00 per item.
California and Michigan residents add appropriate sales tax.

The Companion Diskette

This book is a complete reference and practical guide to using Microsoft Windows 3.1. ***Windows 3.1 Complete*** contains numerous sample applications to show you how to get the most out of Windows 3.1. This companion diskette features executable applications created using Microsoft Visual Basic (VBRUN100.DLL included), Microsoft QuickC for Windows, and Borland Turbo Pascal for Windows, and their respective source codes. You'll also find two very useful Windows applications: SnapShot (for snapping Windows screens and screen areas in .PCX and .BMP formats) and Backup (for backing up and restoring hard drive contents).

See Appendix B for installation instructions.

The companion diskette included with this book saves you time because you don't have to type in the program listings presented in the book.

W31CMPLT directory

- The W31CMPLT directory contains all the subdirectories in which the applications and data are stored.

BACKUP directory

- This directory contains the BTBACKUP.EXE application, for easy disk backup and restoration from within Windows. See Appendix B of this book for detailed information on operating the Backup application.

DDE directory

- This directory contains a series of Windows applications demonstrating Dynamic Data Exchange (DDE) as described in Chapter 32 of ***Windows 3.1 Complete***. These applications feature both client and server applications. The DDE directory entries include demo source codes written in Microsoft Visual Basic. You'll also find executable codes in ready to run form under Microsoft Visual Basic (Visual Basic executable files require VBRUN100.DLL, included with this companion diskette in the MAIL directory) and Borland ObjectVision (not included with this companion diskette).

HELP directory

- This directory contains a stand-alone Help system application, written using Microsoft QuickC for Windows, Microsoft Word 5.5. (IBM) and the HC Help compiler programs packaged with the Microsoft Windows Software Development Kit (SDK) Version 3.1 (not included with this companion diskette).

MAIL directory

- This directory contains sample applications as described in Chapter 31 of ***Windows 3.1 Complete***. These feature two examples of network communication between users: SEND.PIF for SENDing single line messages to another user in the network, and MAIL.EXE, for sending and receiving both single line messages and longer messages as text files.

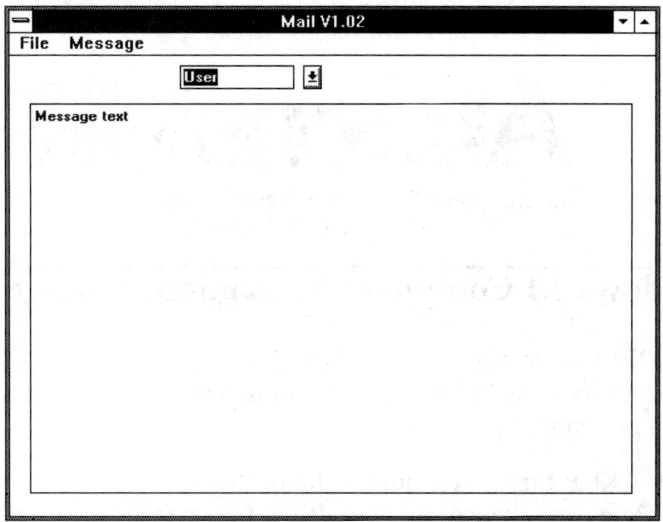

SEND.PIF was written using the Microsoft Windows PIF Editor. You'll find executable code for MAIL.EXE (Visual Basic programs require VBRUN100.DLL, included with this companion diskette) and Visual Basic source code for MAIL.EXE.

PROGRAMS directory

- This directory contains sample applications as listed in Chapter 33 of ***Windows 3.1 Complete***. These applications include parallel demo program source codes, developed using Microsoft Visual Basic, Microsoft QuickC for Windows and Borland Turbo Pascal for Windows. You'll also find executable codes in ready to run form (Visual Basic executable files require VBRUN100.DLL, included with this companion diskette in the MAIL directory).

SNAPSHOT directory

- This directory contains the SNAPSHOT.EXE application for snapping Windows screens and areas as .BMP and .PCX files. See Appendix B of this book for detailed information on operating the Backup application.

Windows 3.1 Complete Companion Diskette

W31CMPLT directory

This directory contains the six directories with the applications and program listings presented in the book:

- The BACKUP directory contains the BTBACKUP.EXE application for backing up diskettes and hard drives under Microsoft Windows, as described in Appendix B.
- The DDE directory contains applications which demonstrate Dynamic Data Exchange (DDE) as described in Chapter 32.
- The HELP directory contains a stand-alone Help application and source codes, as described in Chapter 33.
- The MAIL directory contains a Windows PIF file for SENDing messages over a network and a stand-alone network mail application, as described in Chapter 31.
- The PROGRAMS directory contains a series of Windows applications written in Visual Basic, QuickC for Windows and Turbo Pascal for Windows.
- The SNAPSHOT directory contains the SNAPSHOT.EXE application for capturing Windows screens and graphics as .BMP and .PCX files, as described in Appendix B.

Turn back: for information on Companion Diskette